I0823030

Fine Specimens

A showcase of contemporary **type design**

Edited by
Elliot Jay Stocks

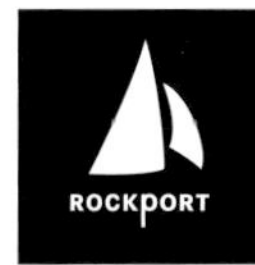

Contents

Serif

Sans Serif

Sans Serif (Cont.)

Blackletter, Script, Calligraphic, Handwritten

Classification-Defying

INTRODUCTION TO

Back in 2010, while working as a web designer, I'd grown frustrated with how ephemeral my work had become and set out to make something that would last—an artefact that I could put on my shelf and still expect to find there several years later. This desire, coupled with a sort of coming-of-age for web design at that very particular moment in time, resulted in *8 Faces:* a magazine where I interviewed eight type designers, graphic designers, web designers, lettering artists, illustrators, educators, and so on about their life and work, and asked them to choose their eight favorite typefaces, which we then set in an elaborate specimen spread for each interviewee. *8 Faces* ran for eight issues, expanded to include a series of limited-edition artwork prints, and also existed as a popular Tumblr blog. Its final form was a 540-page book that collected all of that and was funded by a successful Kickstarter campaign in 2018.

The physical manifestation of *8 Faces*—which also, accidentally, sent me hurtling head-first into the world of type, serving as a huge educational experience for my naive designer's brain—managed to scratch that itch: It countered the fleeting existence of my digital work with something very, very real. And yet that frustration has never subsided; in fact, it's stronger today than ever before. But this time it's not a frustration with my own work—it's a reaction to the transitory nature of internet culture at large.

Whenever a type foundry releases a new font, they make specimen graphics to showcase the type. These specimens may take the form of printed books, graphics for font retailers, or social media posts. But all too often, they're lost in the continual flood of information we encounter on a daily basis. And this is *crazy,* because the specimen graphics can sometimes be as beautiful as the typefaces themselves.

If an image was made to be viewed on a social network, is it any less worthy than one intended for a printed poster? Of course not. But one thing for sure is that that social graphic is going to be scrolled past and forgotten about—if it's even seen at all, such is the state of algorithmic recommendations—and I'd rather counter that with a way of preserving that imagery. Once again, I think it should live on a bookshelf.

But for all the criticism of the internet, its ability to level the playing field can often be a very good thing. Ultimately, it's never been easier to start a type foundry and release your fonts to the world. A typeface created by a young (or often career-switching) designer can and should sit alongside those created by respected industry veterans, whether that's on a font distributor's website, in a design-focused newsletter, or—yes—on a user's social feed. And this level playing field is something I've sought to replicate throughout the pages that follow, in which you'll find type designed by some of the biggest names in the type industry, yes, but you'll also discover names of emerging designers you might not have heard of until now.

An interesting thing emerges when you combine the output of the veterans and the rookies: The graphics produced by the household-name foundries aren't necessarily better than the one-person, bedroom-based type nerds. In fact, a beautifully designed, well-made typeface isn't necessarily represented by a beautifully designed, well-made specimen graphic—and, of course, the inverse is true. So in this book you'll find imagery that was chosen on its own merit—stronger even, perhaps, than the typeface it advertises. You'll also find imagery that doesn't necessarily push the boundaries of design but was chosen for the sheer quality of the type it serves to promote. Perhaps this is controversial,

The title on this spread is set in Ty Finck's ***Anybody*** *typeface, using its weight and width variable axes to fill the space as required.*

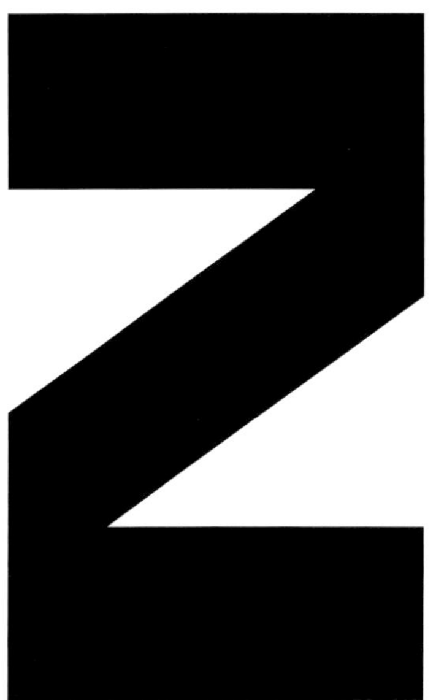
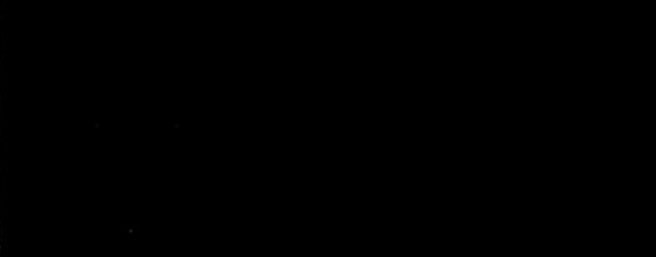
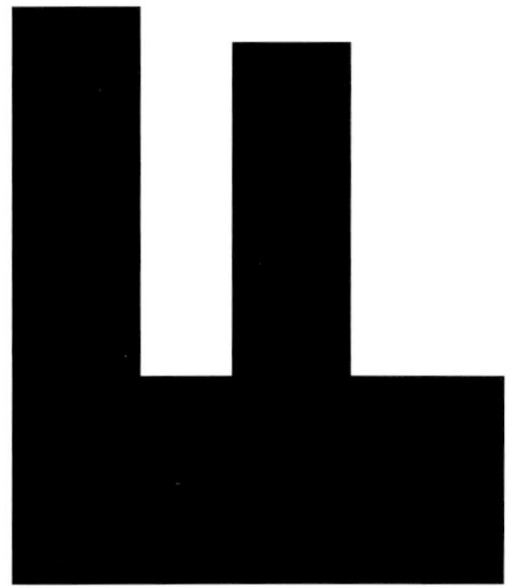

SPECIMENS

but I've approached it in an attempt to capture the zeitgeist of the type industry: the spirit of contemporary type design, yes, but also the state of the graphic design being created and commissioned by type foundries.

In order to accurately represent *contemporary* type, some ground rules had to be set: namely, that the book would include only typefaces that were released from 2023 onward. This ensures that when browsing through the pages that follow, in search of inspiration, you can assume that you'll be greeted by type designs that are trying to do something new rather than the ubiquitous "classics" that have done the rounds in so many publications already. I made an exception to the 2023 rule for any designs that had been released earlier but have been significantly updated from 2023 onward, adding features such as new weights and styles, or improved language support.

On the subject of language support, I felt from very early on in the process that *Fine Specimens* should do a decent job of representing multiple writing systems. While the book certainly leans heavily toward Latin type, you'll also find families that cover Arabic, Cyrillic, Devanagari, Greek, Hangeul, Hebrew, Japanese, Thai, and many other writing systems. And these are presented "inline"—in other words, not separated out into a non-Latin section of the book, as so often can be the case. When creating for global brands, limited language support in fonts continues to hamper designers worldwide.

The book *has* been divided, however, into four different sections: Serif; Sans Serif; Blackletter, Script, Calligraphic, Handwritten, and Classification-Defying. Type classification is a difficult and often-criticized practice—especially when using some of the more traditional categories—but ultimately I felt like it'd be helpful for the reader to navigate using these four rather loose divisions. The arrangement might not be perfect, but hopefully it provides a little structure while searching for typographic inspiration.

It's important to note that not a single foundry paid to have their work included in this book. They were either personally invited by me or came by way of a recommendation. Not that there's nothing wrong with foundries paying to appear in publications—in fact, it's a great way to get such publications funded—but for me, it was important to represent contemporary type designs and their graphics as fairly as possible, and this meant removing any temptation to be swayed by a financial incentive.

Whether you're searching for a very particular kind of typeface for your current project or simply soaking up the talent on display, ready to add a font or two to your library—who doesn't love inventing a reason to use some beautiful new type?—I hope you'll enjoy the variety on display on the pages that follow. Thank you for picking up this book and helping these type specimens live on beyond the scroll.

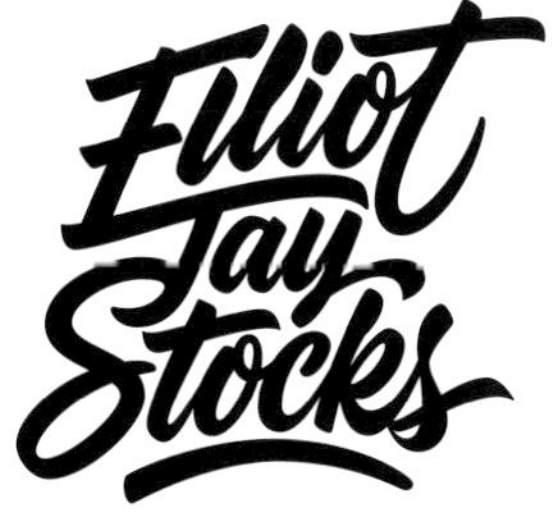

SERIF

Where better to start than with the serif? Often the initial choice in a font filter menu, it's the first part of this book, too. Here you'll find elegant revivals that reference the pens, brushes, or chisels that influenced the construction of their letterforms to ultracontemporary designs that push the definition of what we call a serif. (That said, a few typefaces that sit on the edge—somewhat serif-like, but ultimately not technically with actual serifs present—you'll find in the final *Classification-Defying* part of the book.) From the most neutral of forms intended for long-form reading, to high-contrast, ultracondensed expressive designs intended for display settings, all appear here as equals.

And, as in the other parts of this book, you'll find single-style fonts sitting alongside giant families with multiple weights, widths, styles, and optical sizes—and everything in between. The goal with this collection has been to level the playing field; to paint an accurate picture of contemporary type design rather than get lost in the details of classifications and arbitrary groupings. My hope is that you'll enjoy the typefaces and the graphics for what they are rather than get bogged down in how they've been cataloged.

A note on slab serifs: While it might be fair to say that many slabs bear a closer relationship to their sans cousins (strip the actual slabs off and you'll often find yourself with something quite close to a sans), when we're searching for a typeface to use in a project, the suitability of a serif or slab serif is often interchangeable. So, in an attempt to simplify the organization of this book, slabs have been bundled here along with regular serifs. I'm sure you'll spot them.

Typeface: IvyBodoni, designed by Jan Maack (page 18)

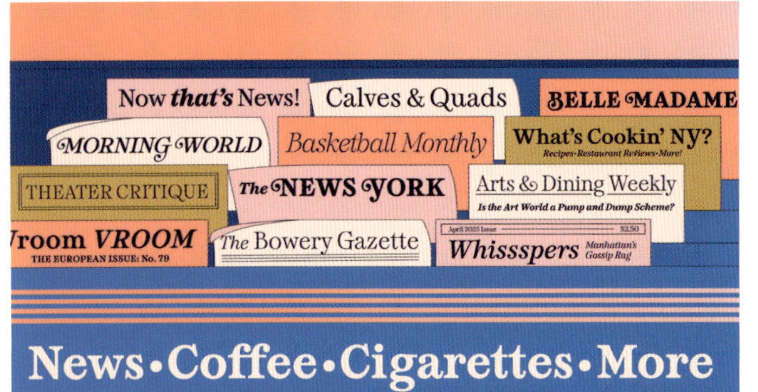

Tickets *on Sale* Friday *1979* April Residency @CBGB's / *The Velvet Underground* & Nico Max Capacity *N.Y.C.*

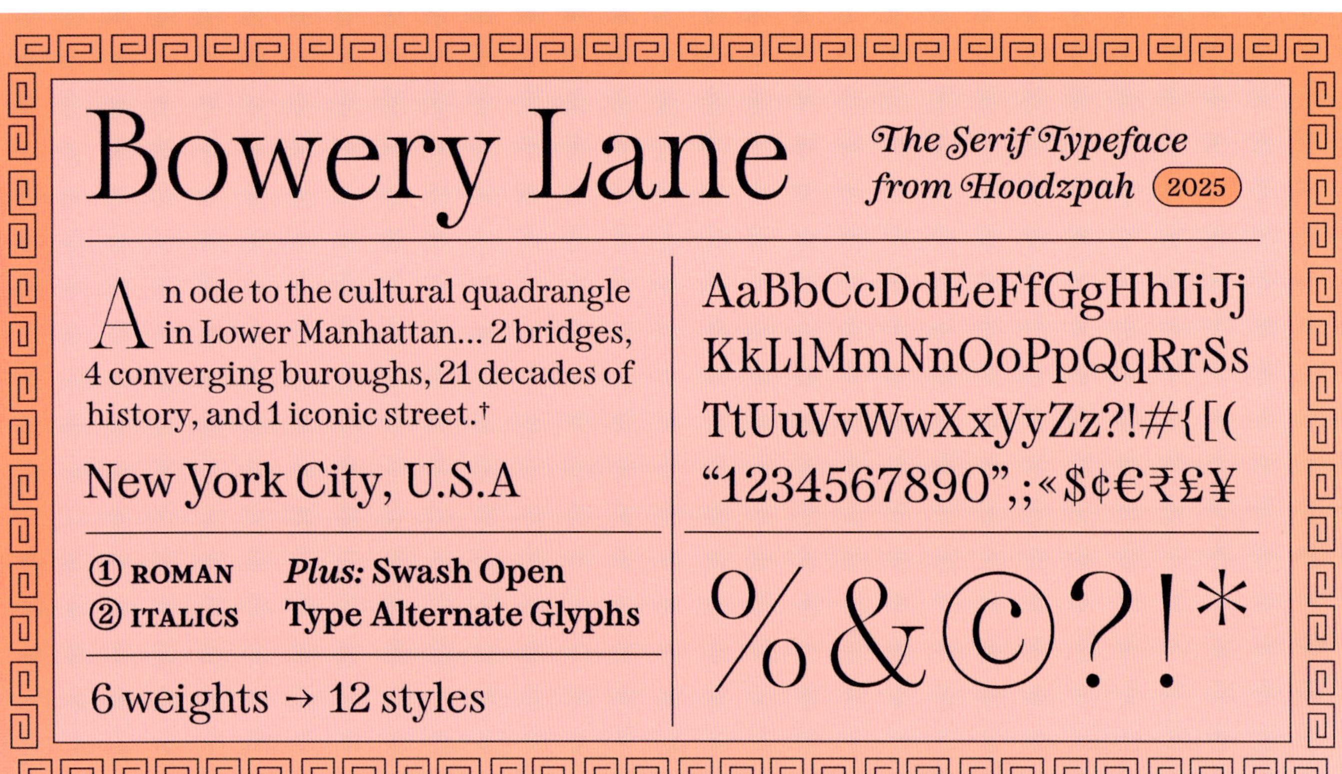

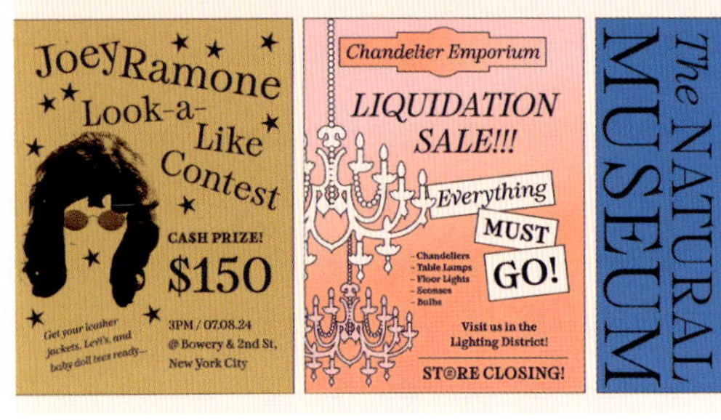

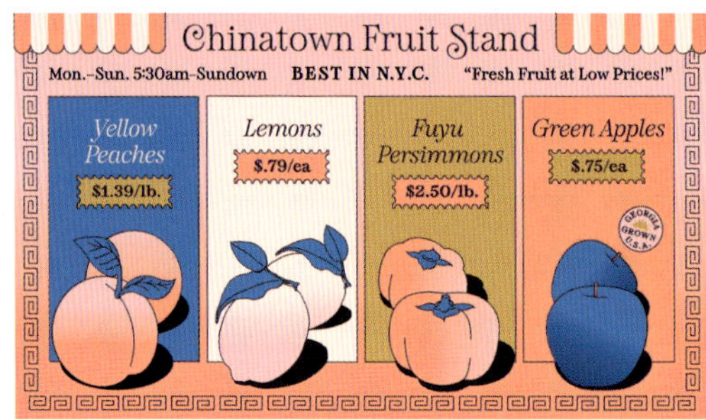

Bowery Lane

hoodzpahdesign.com

Designed by *Amy Hood*
Published by *Hoodzpah*

Bowery Lane

Roman	Italic
Elizabeth →	*Elizabeth*
Mulberry →	*Mulberry*
Chrystie →	*Chrystie*
Bleecker →	*Bleecker*
Allen →	*Allen*
Ludlow →	*Ludlow*
Great Jones →	*Great Jones*
Houston →	*Houston*
LaGuardia →	*LaGuardia*
Spring →	*Spring*

Bowery Lane Swash

Roman	Italic
Elizabeth →	*Elizabeth*
Mulberry →	*Mulberry*
Chrystie →	*Chrystie*
Bleecker →	*Bleecker*
Allen →	*Allen*
Ludlow →	*Ludlow*
Great Jones →	*Great Jones*
Houston →	*Houston*
LaGuardia →	*LaGuardia*
Spring →	*Spring*

Bowery Lane

	Roman	Italic
①	Thin Roman	*Thin Italic*
②	Light Roman	*Light Italic*
③	Regular Roman	*Regular Italic*
④	Medium Roman	*Medium Italic*
⑤	**Bold Roman**	***Bold Italic***
⑥	**Black Roman**	***Black Italic***

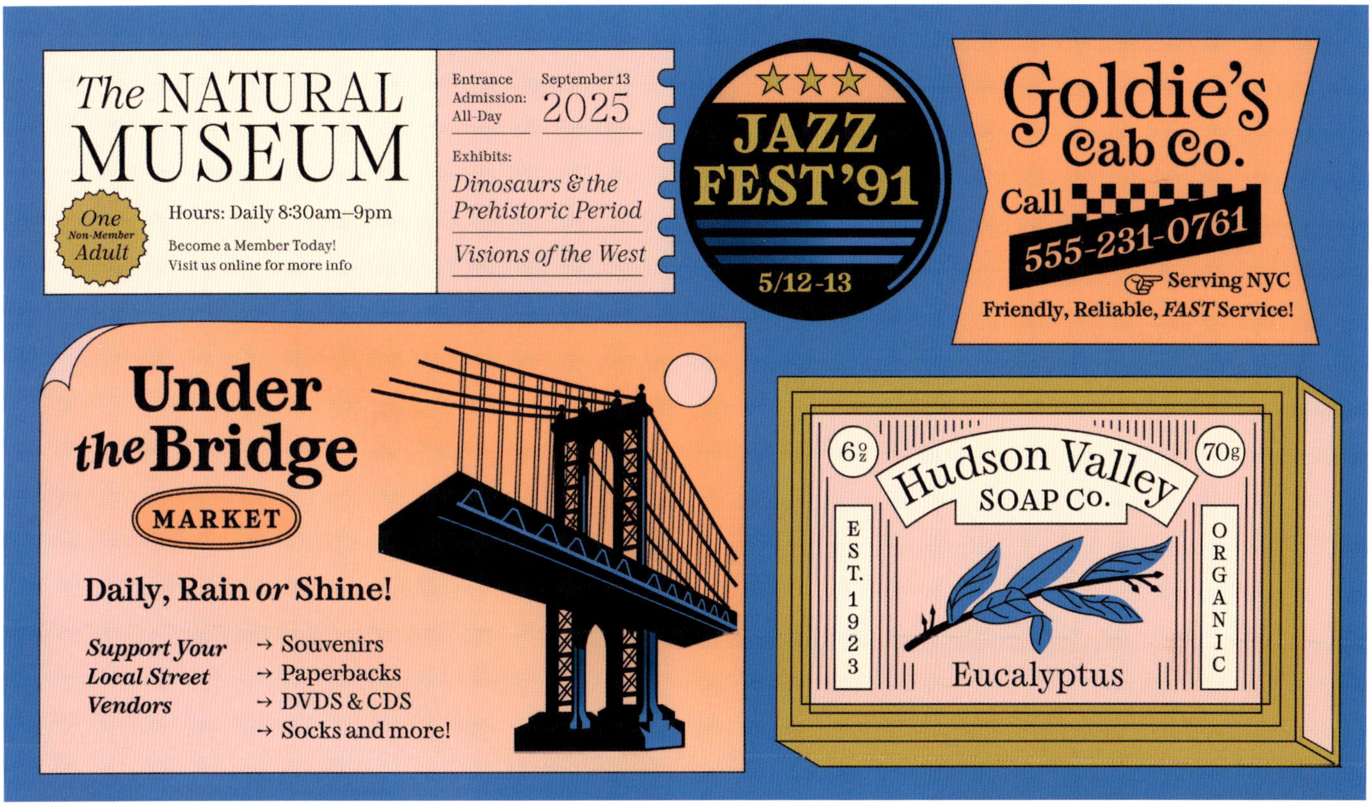

The NATURAL MUSEUM

One Non-Member *Adult*

Hours: Daily 8:30am–9pm

Become a Member Today!
Visit us online for more info

Entrance Admission: All-Day

September 13 2025

Exhibits:
Dinosaurs & the Prehistoric Period
Visions of the West

JAZZ FEST'91

5/12-13

Goldie's Cab Co.

Call 555-231-0761

Serving NYC

Friendly, Reliable, *FAST* Service!

Under *the* Bridge

MARKET

Daily, Rain *or* Shine!

Support Your Local Street Vendors

→ Souvenirs
→ Paperbacks
→ DVDS & CDS
→ Socks and more!

6oz

Hudson Valley SOAP Co.

70g

EST. 1923

ORGANIC

Eucalyptus

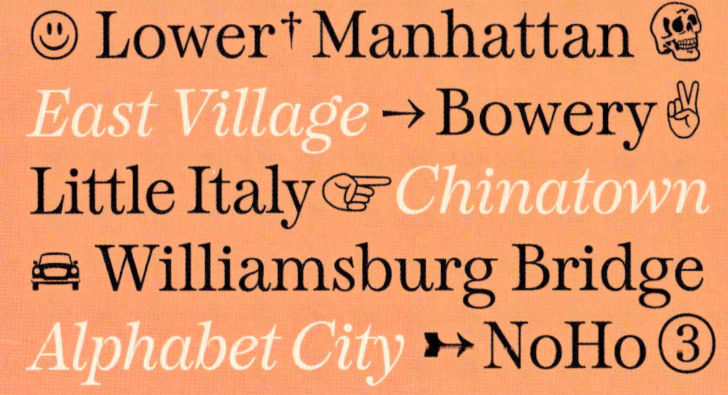

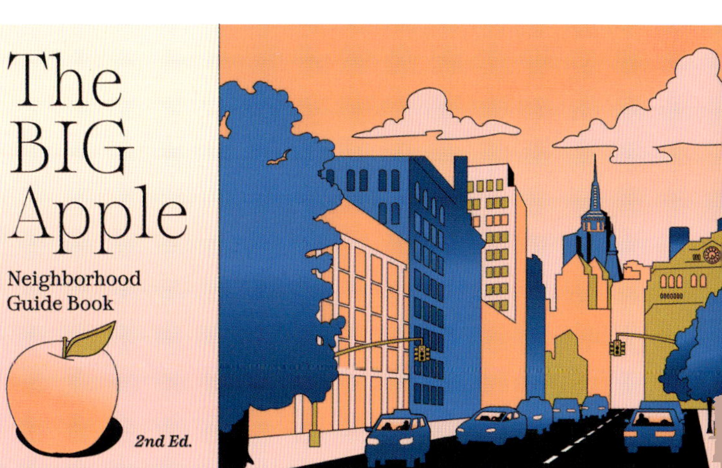

Something unique but highly usable—somewhere between a Scotch Modern, transitional, and slab serif, like if Clarendon and Georgia had a love child.

Just like Windsor, only half the charm. A modern interpretation of the classic Windsor typeface, offering a condensed design that fits effortlessly into space-conscious layouts.

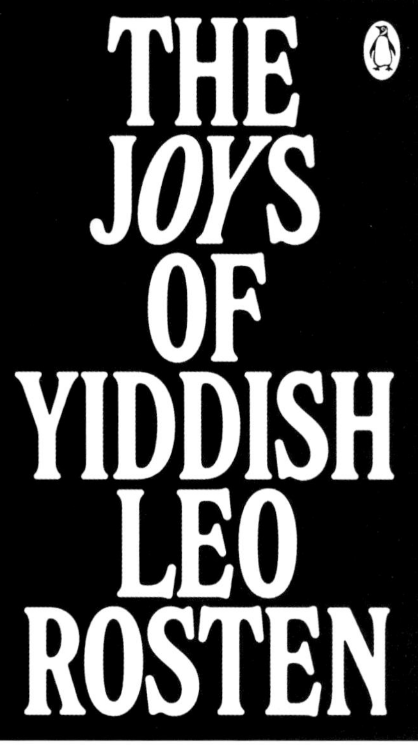

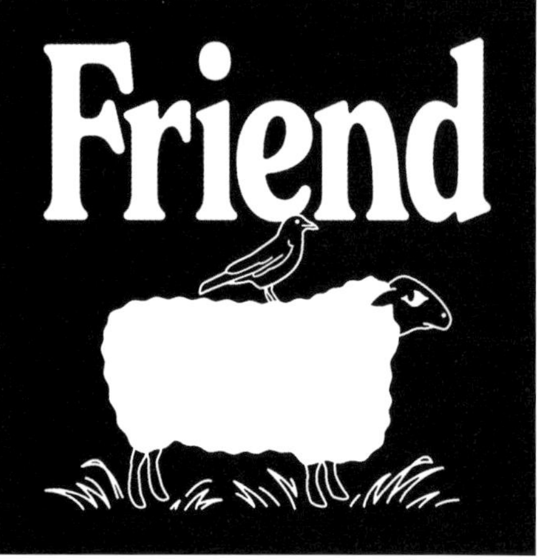

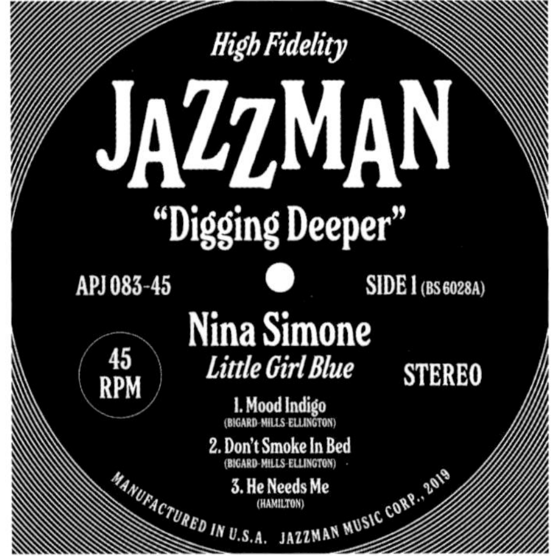

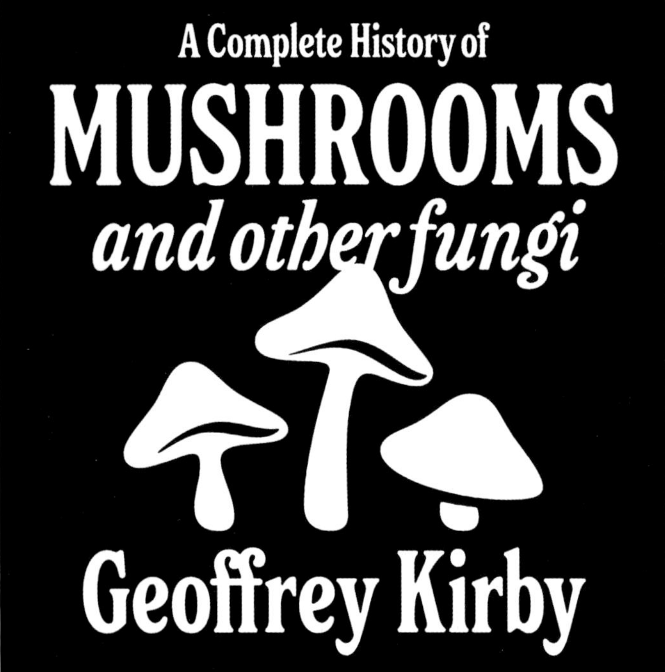

Oficina Creativa
MONUMENT CO.
RIO MOSELA
No.222
SAN PEDRO, G.G.
CP.66220/MÉXICO
Lun-Vie 9-13/15-18:30
office@monumento.co
2025

Friend

beastsofengland.co

Designed by *Simon Walker*
Published by *Beasts of England*

Neil Simon's masterpiece → comes to life this *January

Rauchburg Ioots*
Amorize & Cope
Zeotroper Größeren
Quizshard £1.99

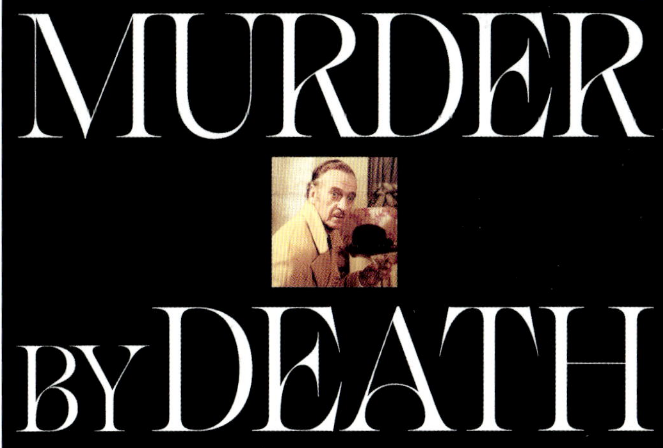

A display serif inspired by the movies of David Niven. Answers the question "what if a typeface was gushingly flamboyant but self-effacingly so?"

beastsofengland.co

Niven

Designed by *Simon Walker*
Published by *Beasts of England*

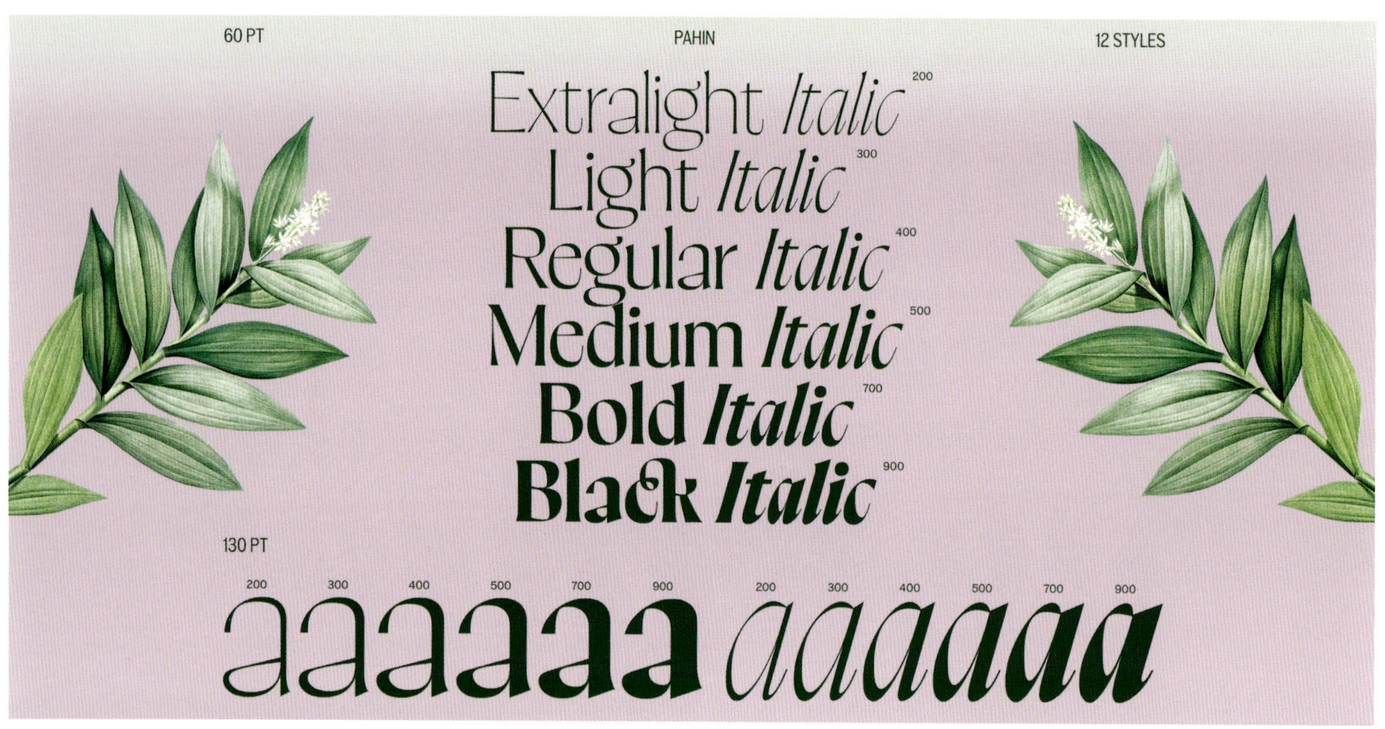

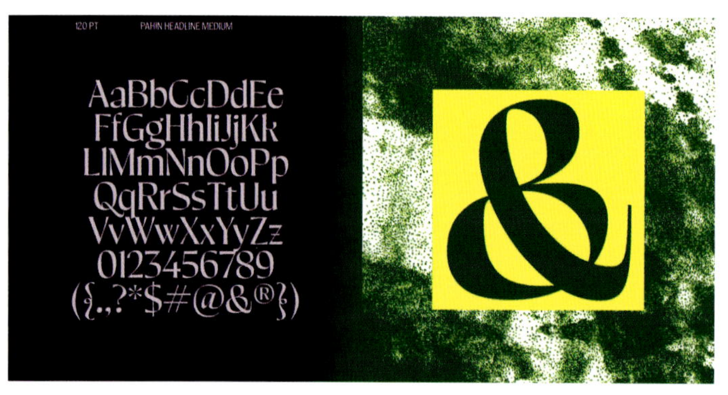

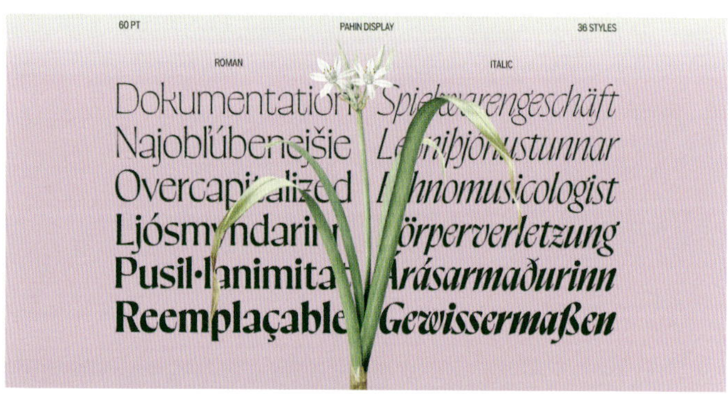

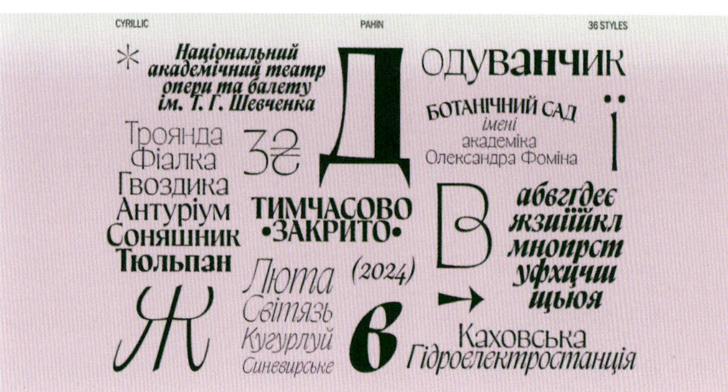

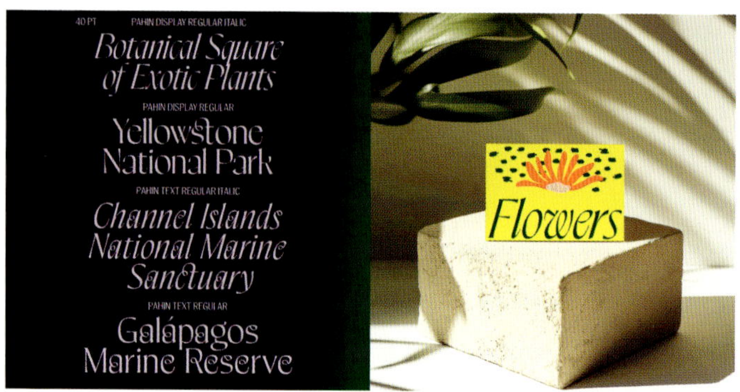

Pahin

blazetype.eu

Designed by *Maksym Kobuzan*
Published by *Blaze Type*

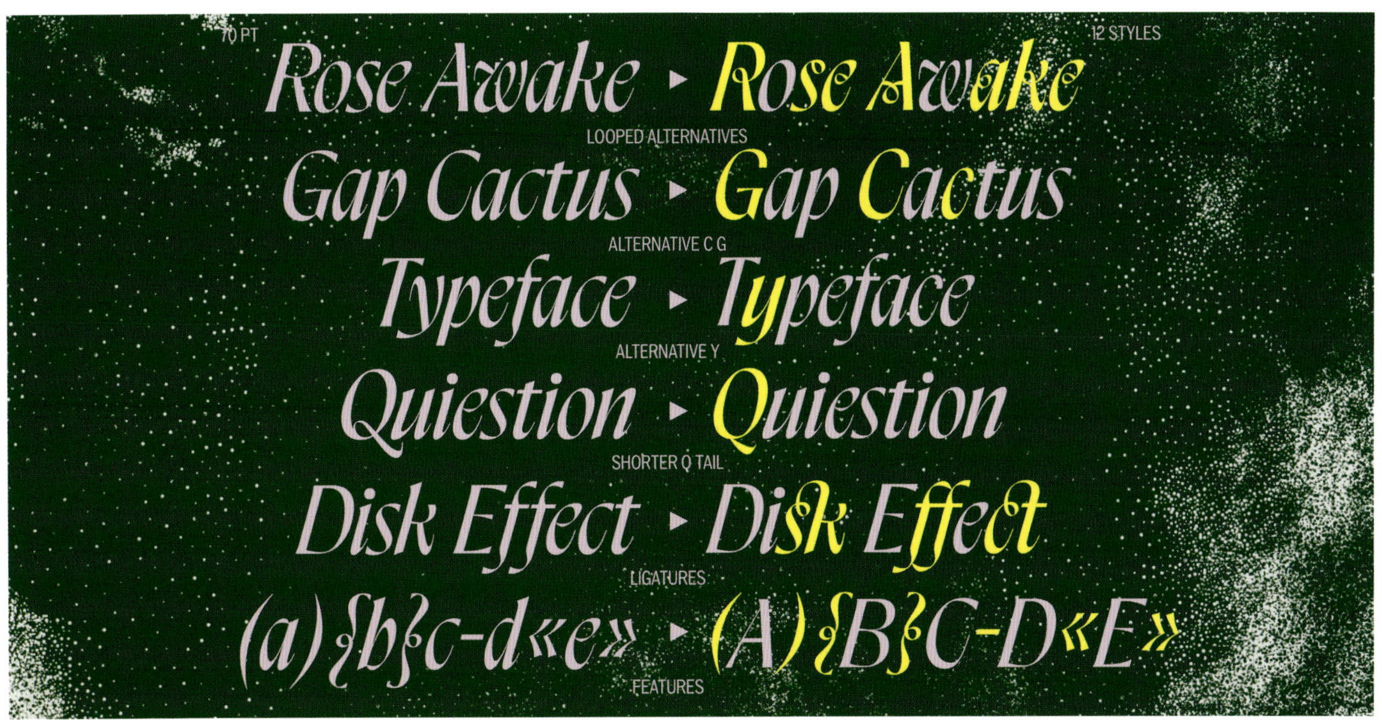

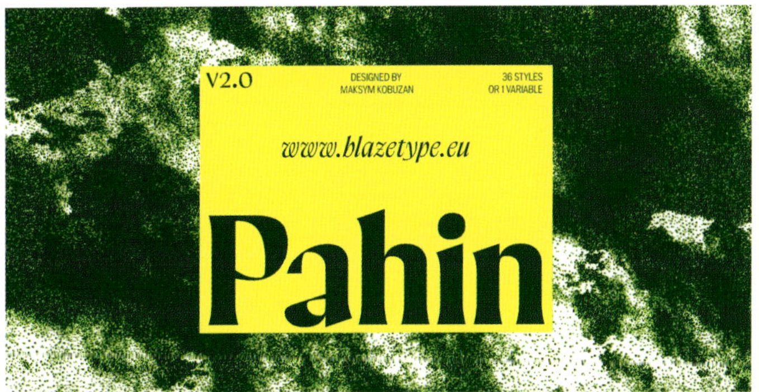

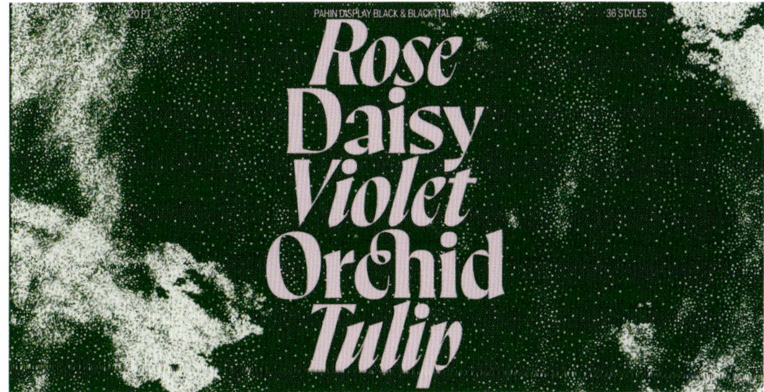

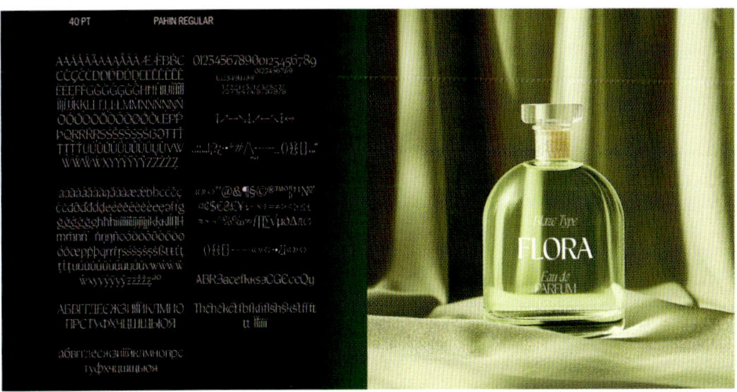

85 PT PAHIN DISPLAY BLACK ITALIC & EXTRALIGHT ITALIC 36 STYLES

®Sunflower∅Magnolia
Plant@Iris£8,12/sweet
stem¤earth©Delicate¶
%Flowers№563{a}Great
Kiwi{a}7₴&By‡Marine

Pahin is an expressive flared serif that combines sharp forms with intricate contours. Its plasticity is inspired by the graceful curves of stems and flowers, creating vibrant and organic forms. Sharp elements contrast with soft and flowing lines, reminiscent of thorns protecting delicate flowers or fruits. At the same time, Pahin inherits and is based on the tradition of calligraphy, distinguished by an abundance of loops, especially in the alternative set, which resemble a grapevine. These elements give the typeface freshness, flexibility, and naturalness, making it ideal for use in large sizes, where its expressiveness is fully revealed.

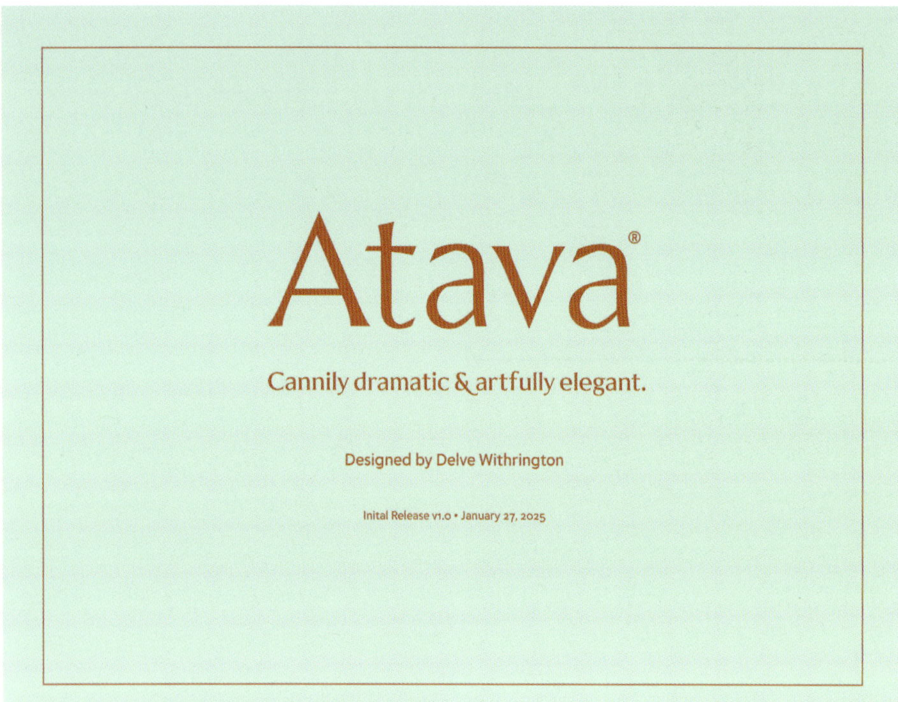

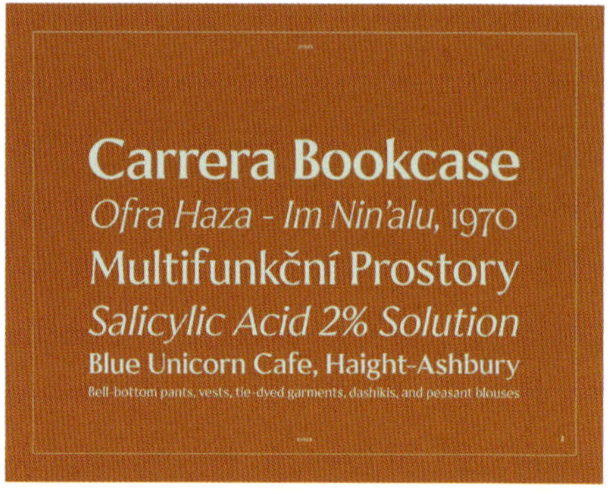

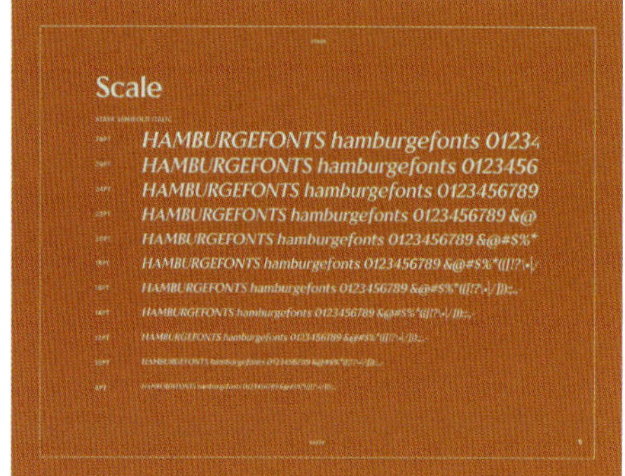

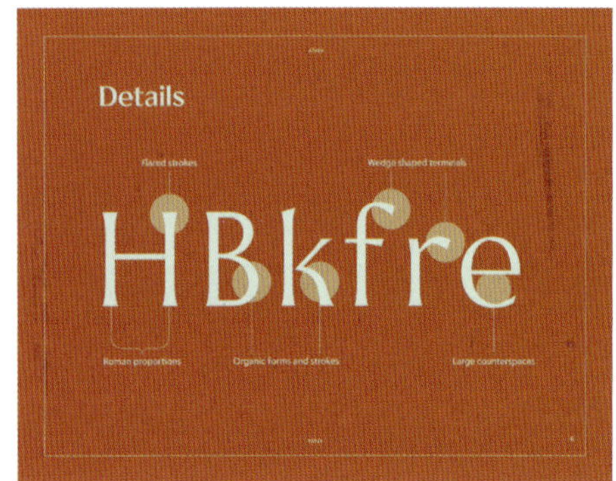

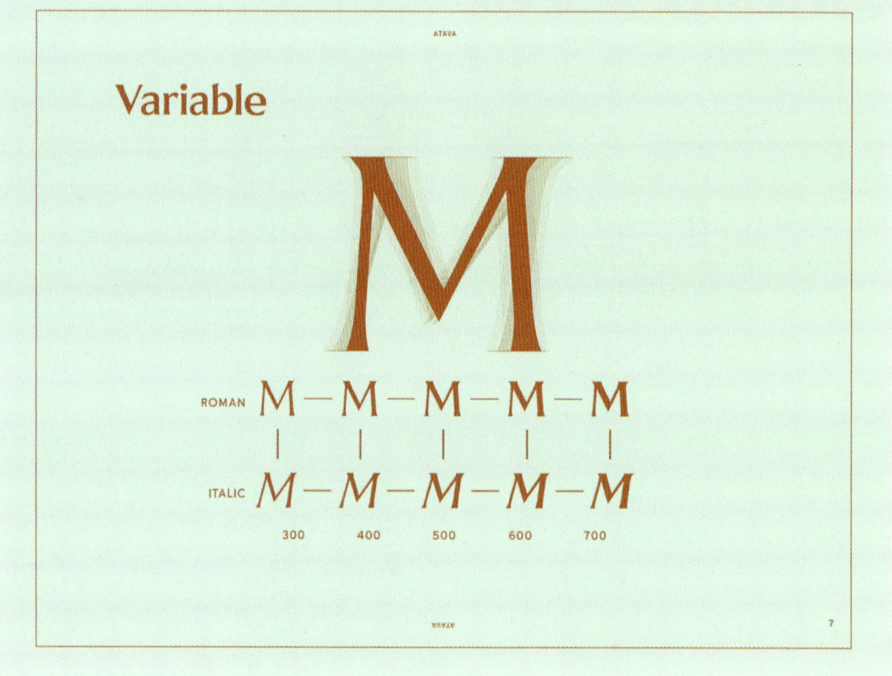

Roman inscriptional letterforms served as the basis of Atava, and that foundational origin point is most evident in the classic proportions of the capitals, flared stroke ends, and wedge-shaped terminals and exit strokes echoing the use of a chisel or brush. At text sizes, Atava's ample x-height and familiar proportions provide a comfortable reading experience. Atava has five upright weights plus companion italics, with a large complement of glyphs for advanced typography and broad language support.

Atava

delvefonts.com

Designed by *Delve Withrington*
Published by *Delve Fonts*

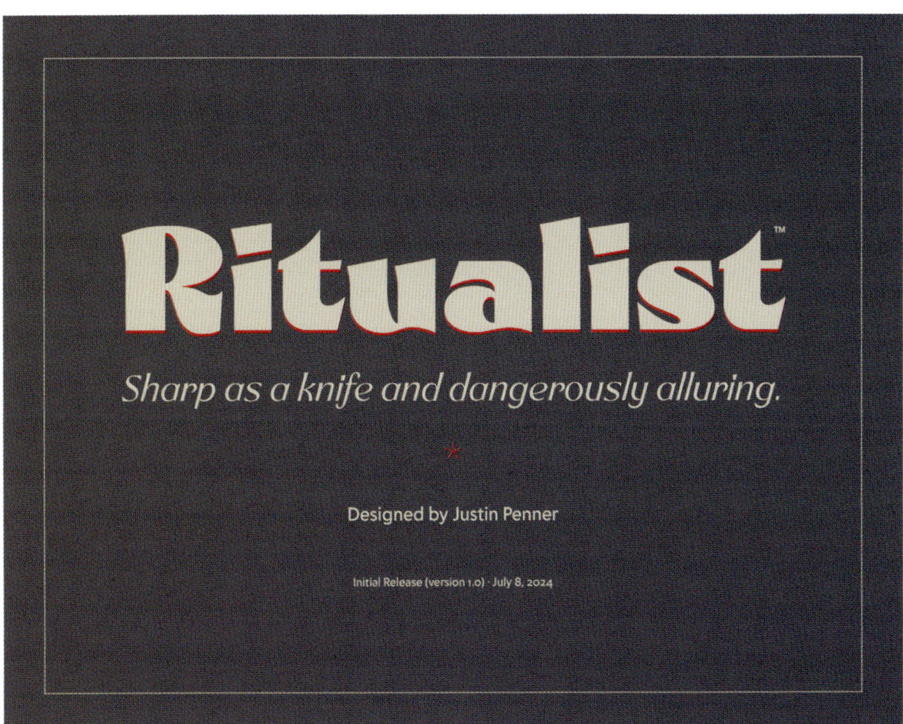

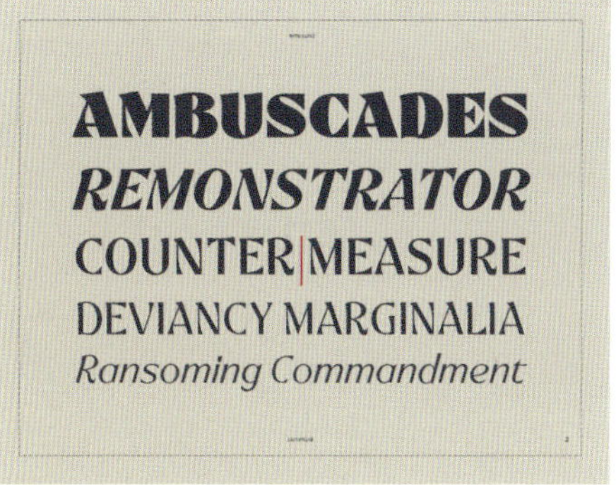

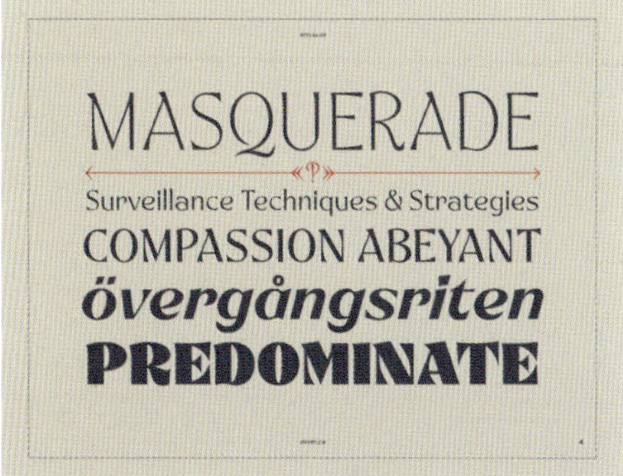

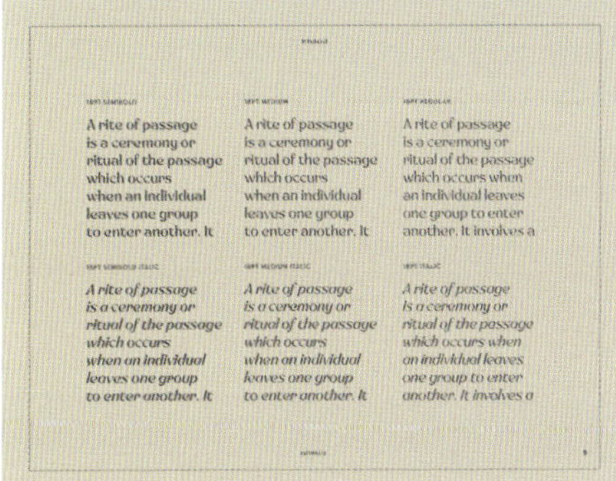

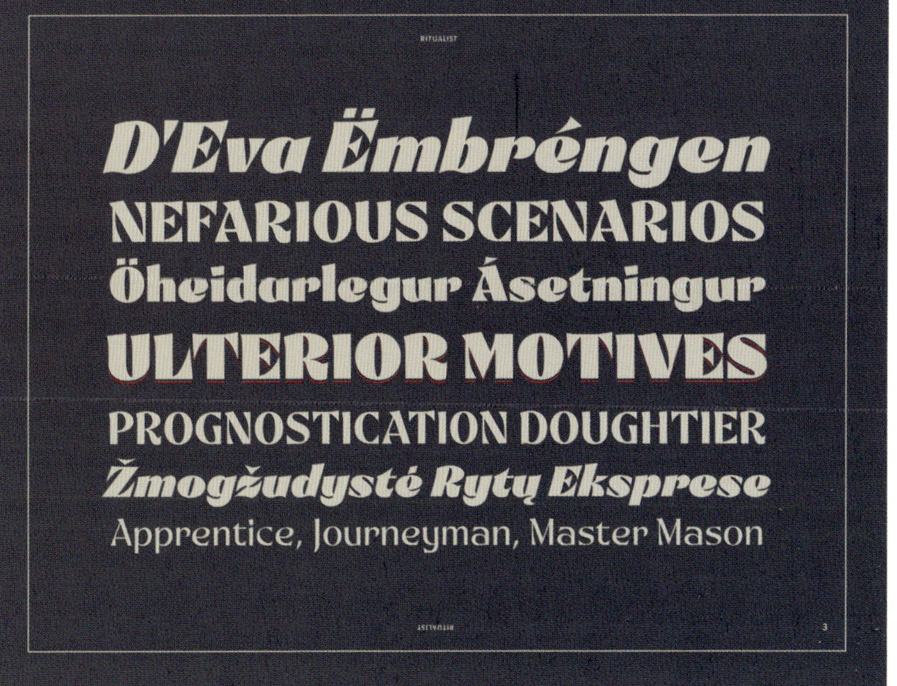

Ritualist is inspired by high-contrast wedge serif designs, like De Vinne, but viewed through a macabre lens. Defined by its sharp points and dangerous, bladelike curves, this beguiling display face occupies a space between beauty and darkness. Ritualist has eighteen styles, a variable version, and a 1,000+ glyph set supporting 259 languages.

delvefonts.com

Ritualist

Designed by *Justin Penner*
Published by *Delve Fonts*

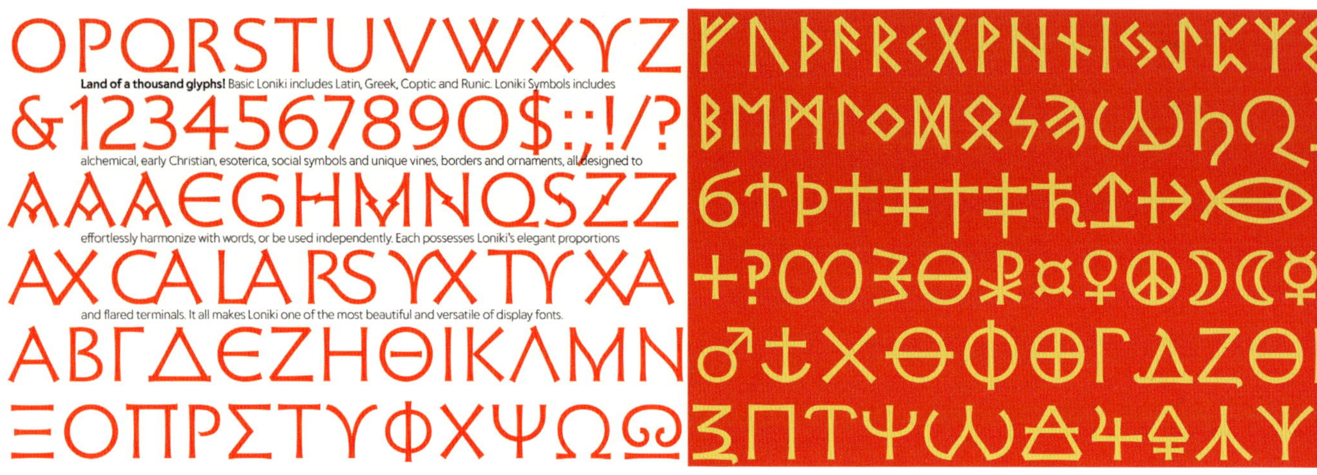

Land of a thousand glyphs! Basic Loniki includes Latin, Greek, Coptic and Runic. Loniki Symbols includes alchemical, early Christian, esoterica, social symbols and unique vines, borders and ornaments, all designed to effortlessly harmonize with words, or be used independently. Each possesses Loniki's elegant proportions and flared terminals. It all makes Loniki one of the most beautiful and versatile of display fonts.

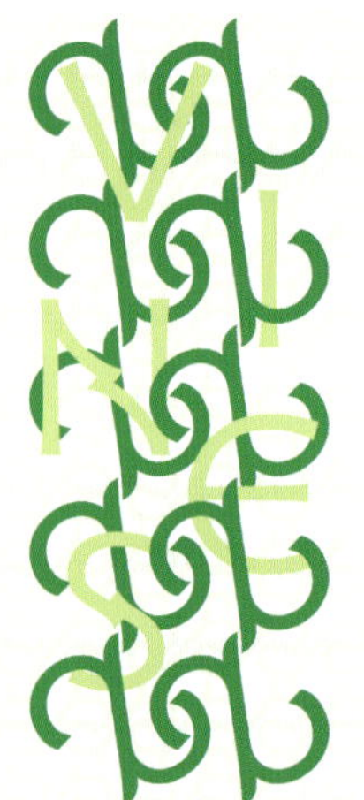

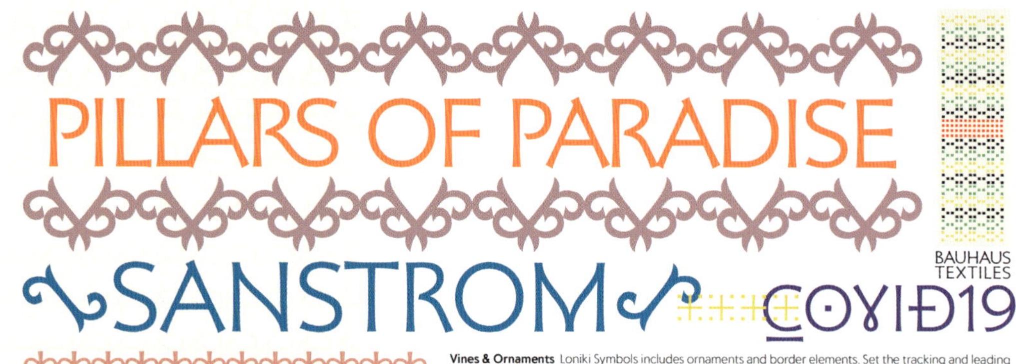

Vines & Ornaments Loniki Symbols includes ornaments and border elements. Set the tracking and leading values to have them interlock in fascinating ways. The vines stylistically match all of the other letters and glyphs; use them as individual ornaments or combine them into intricate patterns.

THE GOOD LIFE
IS A LIFE ROOTED
IN KINDNESS

"JUSTQ+"

·Q·V·

MARGINALIA
A NOVEL
REGINA COX

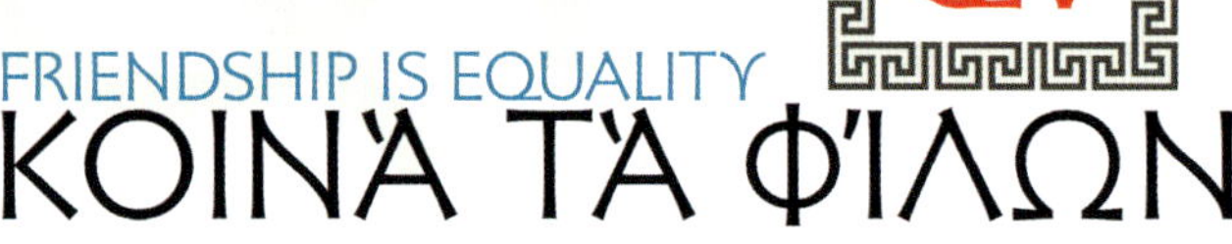

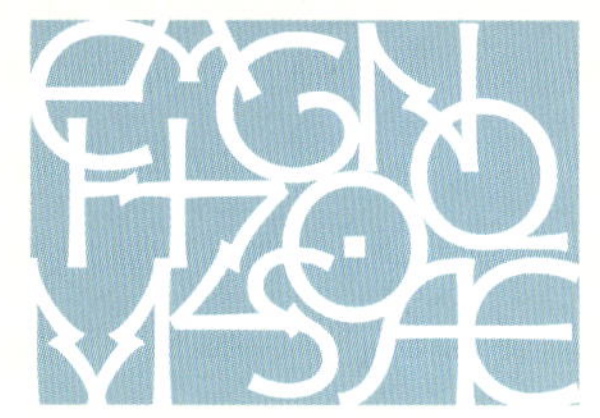

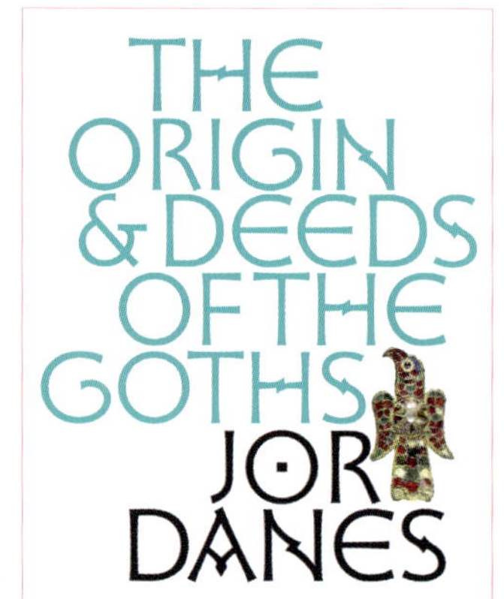

Based on a fifth-century inscription, Loniki's rational geometry and sinuous curves embody the blend of cultures prevalent in the Thessaloniki region at the time. This admixture is emblematic not only of late antiquity but of our own time as well. Loniki is a distinctive, beautiful display font, available in two styles (Regular and Symbols).

Loniki

delvefonts.com

Designed by *Steven Skaggs*
Published by *Delve Fonts*

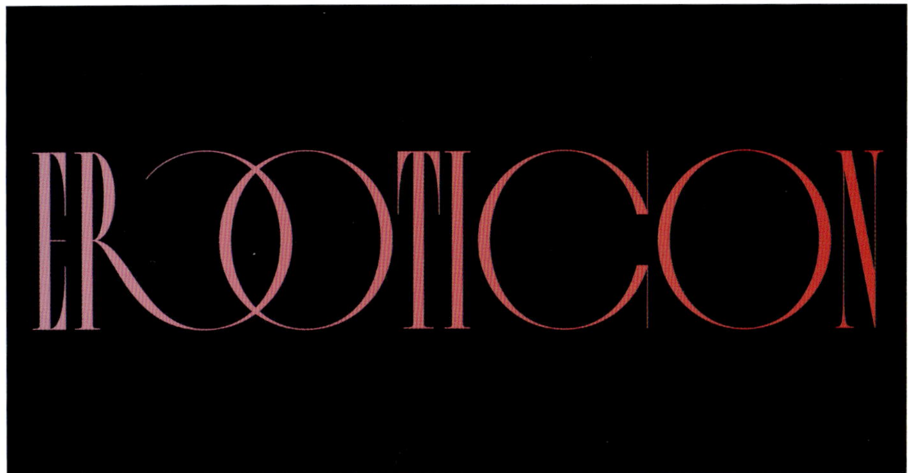

MISFORTUNE

NIGHT MUSIC ON KIEFERSTADTEL STEPHANIE WURMBRAND-STUPPACH
SERGEI RACHMANINOFF CAPRICE BOHÉMIEN
HOLLANDSCHE OVERTURE DINA APPELDOORN
HANS BRONSART VON SCHELLENDORFF STRING SEXTET
SYMPHONY NO. 8 IN G MAJOR ANTONÍN DVOŘÁK
AGATHE BACKER GRØNDAHL 3 KLAVERSTYKKER, OP. 35

LATIN ABCDEFGHIJKLMNOPQRSTUVWX
КИРИЛЛИЦА АБВГДЕЁЖЗИЙКЛМНОПР
ΕΛΛΗΝΙΚΑ ΑΒΓΔΕΖΗΘΙΚΛΜΝΞΟΠΡΣΤΥΦ

MONOCHROMATIC
ΕΝΑΠΟΘΕΣΗ
— PETER HUJAR
EYES OPEN IN THE DARK —

ABSTRACTOR SPERMATOID GRASSWORM
STORMINESS CONFRONTER SQUARSONRY
CLOCKHOUSE MICROCOLON CIRCUMFLEX

ARCHISWINDLER
СЕКСУАЛЬНІСТЬ ЦЕ ПРО КОНТАКТ ЗІ СВОЇМ ЗАДОВОЛЕННЯМ

Eroticon is a high-contrast serif typeface with a distinctly narrow shape. Wide alternations of rounded characters and swash variations give the typeface an unmistakable character and dynamic nature. The character set, in addition to the extended Latin alphabet, includes Cyrillic and Greek alphabets.

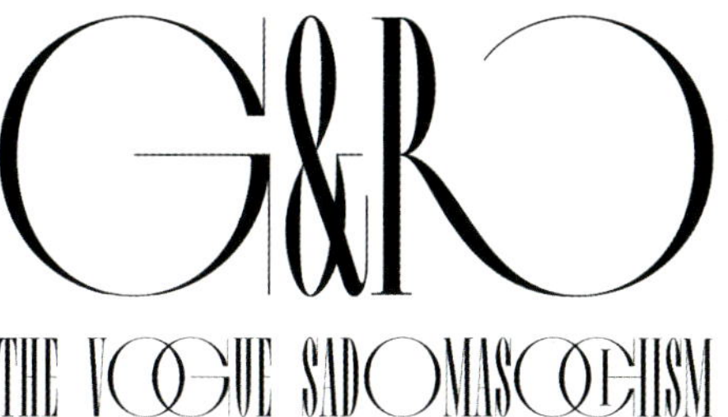

THE VOGUE SADOMASOCHISM

suitcasetype.com

Eroticon

Designed by *Tomáš Brousil*
Published by *Suitcase Type*

The New York 1970s style

MESSAGE

Le Monde d'Hermès

SH&L

IVY BODONI FONT

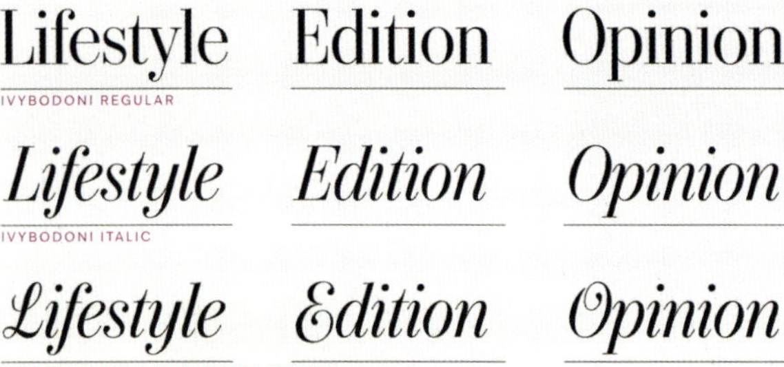

CRISP DETAILS, FINE *STROKES*

IvyBodoni *Display Font*

IvyBodoni is an homage to the modern serif designs of the '60s and '70s with crisp hairlines, distinct ball terminals, and precise curves. This twenty-first-century Bodoni was made for fashion and editorial design.

IvyBodoni

ivyfoundry.com

Designed by *Jan Maack*
Published by *Ivy Foundry*

FIELDS DISPLAY 100 PT

REGULAR Barley
MEDIUM Rågbröd
SEMI BOLD Kvieši
BOLD Oats
EXTRA BOLD Rīsi
BLACK Maísól

FIELDS 80 PT

EXTRA LIGHT Millet
LIGHT Ječmen
REGULAR Rapšu
MEDIUM Saulespuķe
SEMI BOLD Buckwheat
BOLD Rugbrød
EXTRA BOLD Zirņi
BLACK Bean

FIELDS BIG 80 PT

ULTRA Wheat

VARIABLE 80 PT

OPTICAL Spelt
WEIGHT Corn

Fields

adam ladd design

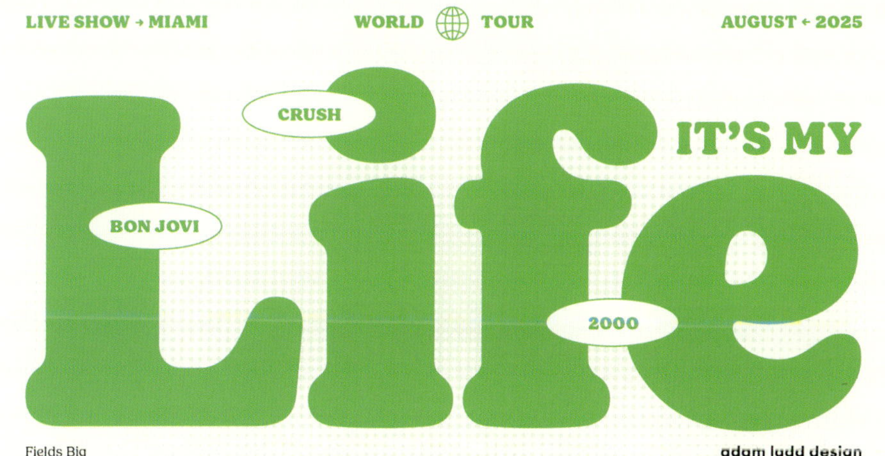

Fields, Fields Display, and Fields Big form a versatile family with three optical sizes blending casual, retro tones with modern touches. The details like rounded serifs, teardrop terminals, and subtle tails make this typeface friendly and approachable. Whether you want that vintage 1970s vinyl record vibe or on-trend packaging with a nod to the handmade, Fields Variable can precisely fine-tune the tone of voice and meet your typographic goals and needs.

A soft serif typeface

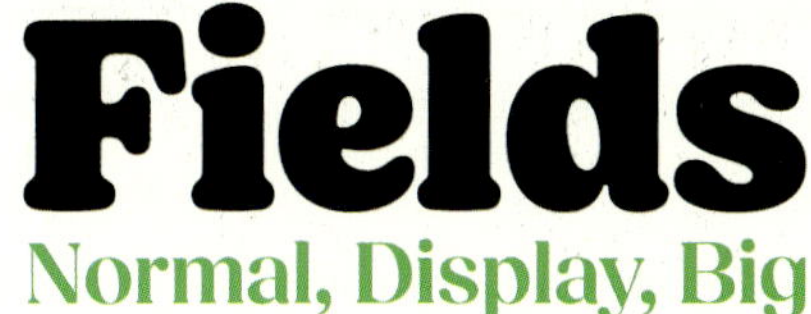

3 subfamilies 15 fonts Variable support adam ladd design

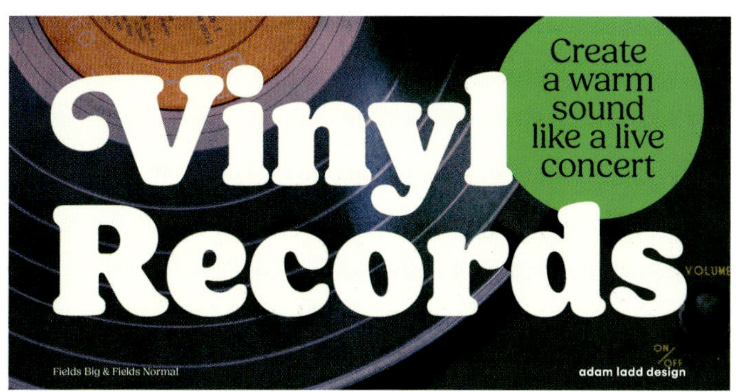

ladd-design.com

Fields

Designed by *Adam Ladd*
Published by *Adam Ladd Design*

The First Type Specimens
An Essay by John Boardley

↓ *Erhard Ratdolt's broadside type specimen, dated April 1, 1486.*

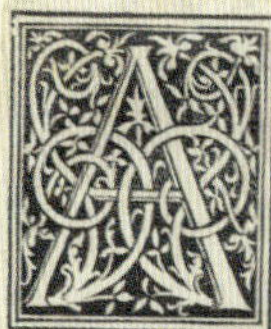

Out walking among the dunes, a father, hoping to both amuse and instruct his children, picked up a piece of bark and carved a letter in it. When it fell from his hands and he leaned over to retrieve it, he saw that it had left an impression of the letter in the sand. In this happy accident and epiphany, the Dutchman Laurens Coster saw the entire typographic process unfold before him. This tale, although apocryphal and only first recorded in the sixteenth century, does, however, highlight the simple principle behind printing with movable type.

Bi Sheng (畢昇) independently invented movable type in China in the mid-eleventh century. Four hundred years later, sometime in the late 1440s, Johannes Gutenberg in Germany, entirely ignorant of the Chinese invention, was trying to figure out a way to mass-produce books. We don't know if he had a eureka moment like the legendary Laurens Coster, but we do know that he succeeded in inventing a brilliant solution comprising metal movable type, a printing press, and specialized ink with a varnish-like viscosity. But Gutenberg still had to figure out a way to cast and manufacture tens of thousands of pieces of metal type quickly and efficiently. He appears to have invented a handheld mold, into which was poured a molten alloy of tin, lead, and antimony. The latter ingredient, although only added in small proportions, was crucial to the type's hardness and durability—that ultimately meant more and crisper printed impressions.

At first, Gutenberg printed small schoolbooks for teaching Latin grammar and single-sheet Indulgences, sold by the church and what we might crudely describe as a kind of get-out-of-jail-free card when it came to accounting for one's sins in the afterlife. Around 1454, Gutenberg completed the magnificent book he is best known for, a large-format Latin Bible. Keen

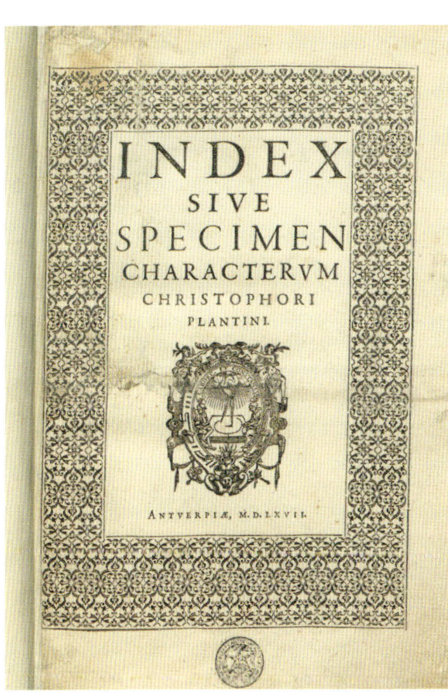

↑ *Title page of Christophe Plantin's type specimen pamphlet of 1567.*

to keep this new technology to himself (one he'd invested vast sums in), Gutenberg wasn't interested in selling his fonts, and so he had no need to produce type specimens. Gutenberg was in the bookselling business, not in the font-selling business.

As word of Gutenberg's breakthrough new technology spread, along with his new printed books, it wasn't long before others had discovered how to make metal type and print from them. From his hometown of Mainz in Germany, printing spread rapidly so that by the end of the century every major city in Europe had established a printshop. In less than fifty years, from Gutenberg's debut until 1500, more than ten million books were printed—not to mention the millions of pamphlets and printed ephemera that rolled off Europe's printing presses.

But who made the type? Gutenberg was familiar with punchcutting and various other metalworking and casting techniques. Most of those early printers were entrepreneurs or sometimes monied scholars, who typically turned to local goldsmiths to produce their punches. These hard steel punches were then struck into a softer metal, like brass, to make matrices, from which a lead alloy piece of type was cast. As early as the 1470s, there are records of goldsmiths cutting punches and matrices for a printshop in a convent in Ripoli, Northern Italy. In 1472, a seal engraver is recorded as making letters (punches) for Bernhard Richel, a printer setting up shop in Basel.[1]

Cutting a tiny letter, just millimeters tall, on the end of a piece of steel is highly specialized work. A survey of very early typefaces reveals mixed results in both their design and execution. Some early fifteenth-century typefaces, despite their novelty, are beautifully conceived and expertly made—like those by Nicolas Jenson, for example—while others are typographic train wrecks, some with bouncy baselines and clumsily cut letters, and are examples of someone thinking, *How hard can this be?*

Although not as familiar a name as Johannes Gutenberg, Nicolas Jenson, or Aldus Manutius, Erhard Ratdolt from Augsburg in Southern Germany was one of the fifteenth century's most innovative printers. Ratdolt was the first to print a decorated title page, played a key role in early polychromatic printing and printing in gold, and pioneered new techniques for printing complex diagrams. Adding to Ratdolt's many typographic firsts is a trimmed broadside measuring approximately 34 × 22 cm. Dated April 1, 1486, Ratdolt's *Index characterum diversarum* is the first known type specimen. Featured is a large woodcut initial (in the southern or classical style) and specimens of fourteen fonts, including ten rotunda in various sizes, three Roman, and one Greek.[2]

The specimen was discovered by chance in the late nineteenth century, hidden away in the binding of another book. This sole surviving copy is now in the Bavarian State Library in Munich. Ratdolt's type specimen is almost certainly not an advertisement for the sale of types but rather one for the printshop that he was relocating from Venice to his hometown of Augsburg. At the end of the type specimen, in the bottom-right corner, Ratdolt signs off—and I paraphrase—that the illustrious and celebrated Ratdolt, famed in Venice for his exemplary skill in printing, is now ready to begin publishing books of exemplary quality in Augsburg.[3]

The earliest known type specimen from an actual typefounder, rather than a printer or publisher, is from François Guyot in Antwerp and dated to about 1565. The specimen includes handwritten marginalia recording the cost of matrices.[4]

One of the most interesting and extensive type specimens of the sixteenth century is Christophe Plantin's *Index characterum* of 1567. Plantin was not a type designer or punchcutter, but a printer and publisher of some renown in Antwerp. He had an excellent eye for fine typography and quality type, and commissioned typefaces from the leading type designers and punchcutters of his day. Plantin's type specimen pamphlet includes forty-five typefaces in Hebrew, Greek, and Latin, including types by Claude Garamond, Robert Granjon, and Guillaume Le Bé. Unfortunately, very few type specimens have survived from the early centuries of printing. Like many other loose-leaf or single-sheet printed items, specimens, advertisements, notices, and other similarly ephemeral printed matter ended up in the bin or as binders' waste or were used to start fires—saddening present-day typophiles but warming the cockles of early printers.

1 *Harry Carter,* A view of early typography up to about 1600, *p. 103*

2 *For details on the typefaces in Ratdolt's specimen, see Riccardo Olocco's superb essay, "Ratdolt's Index characterum, the earliest known type specimen."* poem-editions.com/products/ratdolt

3 *Bettina Wagner, "Als die Lettern laufen lernten. Medienwandel im 15." Jahrhundert, 2009, no. 40*

4 *Harry Carter,* A view of early typography up to about 1600, *p. 96 & fig. 67*

Mother

Αστέρια έλαμπαν, νύχτα σιγή

Gertakariak

Hearts raced, passions ignited

Reconhecimento

Любов цвіте, серця віддаються

Diário

Misunderstood

Stelle brillavano, notte calma

Предпочитам

Реки течут, время бежит

Επικοινωνία

wer of

oception

'sixth sense' – and become healthier

ere we are in space and is essential to our
are simple, everyday ways to test and train it.

ardes.
ves to
' to keep
onal." Or,
ng clear,
mproves,
uing our
y to our

ve've
in
udies, and
leeply
of it are
ptive
ise phys-
ll. *"Re-*
fic neural

How to check and improve your proprioception

Want to see what you can already do? Try these simple tests.

HEEL-TOE WALKING

It's like tightrope walking, but without the risk. Find a straight line on the ground – or mark one out with tape – and walk along it, touching your front heel to your rear toe at each step. Try not to wobble, or step off to the side.

WALL BOUNCES

This one's about hand-eye coordination. Grab a small, bouncy ball – a tennis ball will do – and throw it underhand into a wall, then catch it with the other hand as it bounces. Repeat as many times as you can.

says McDowell – but als
the weight of objects yo
interacting with, or pick
changes in the surface y
walking on.

Some people seem to
more finely tuned propr
tors than others, but it c
depend on the task. It's
for instance, to be rock-
a yoga pose but have bel
erage hand-eye coordin
or vice versa. It's also so
that can be affected by h
issues including stroke,
ical disorders or even di

It also worsens wher
older. *"As we age, propr*

Pulso was designed to withstand various printing conditions. Developed to provide durability and consistency, Pulso excels in intensive text settings, even under the most challenging circumstances. With its three grades and two sets of italics, Pulso ensures flawless performance, thanks to its generous x-height and open shapes.

Pulso

dstype.com

Designed by *Pedro Leal, Dino dos Santos*
Published by *DSType*

Pro
Latin Extended
Greek
Extended Cyrillic
1410 — 1638 Glyphs

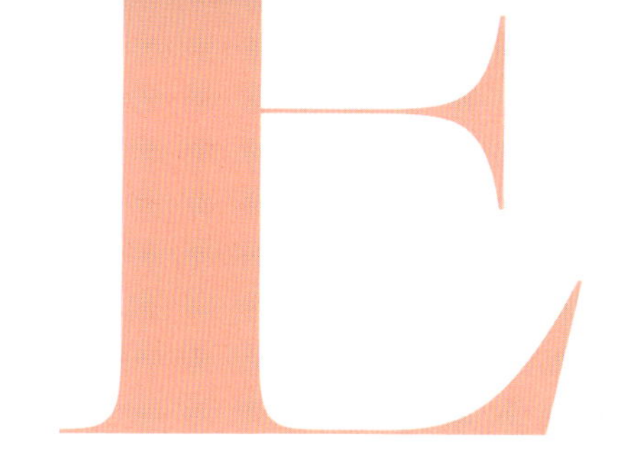

ΕΠΙΧΕΙΡΗΣΗ ΑΓΟΡΑ

ΣΗΜΕΙΩΣΕΙΣ ΚΑΙ ΟΜΟΛΟΓΑ

Οικονομία καλύτερη από τ αναμενόμενη.

Η οικονομία του Ηνωμένου Βασιλείου αναπτύχθηκε ταχύτερα από το αναμενόμενο τον Μάιο, βοηθούμενη από τις ισχυρές επιδόσεις των λιανοπωλητών και του κατασκευαστικού κλάδου.

Η οικονομία επεκτάθηκε κατά 0,4%, ανακάμπτοντας από τη μηδενική ανάπτυξη τον Απρίλιο, όταν ο βροχερός καιρός απέτρεψε τους αγοραστές και επιβράδυνε τα οικοδομικά έργα.

Οι κατασκευές αναπτύχθηκαν με τον ταχύτερο ρυθμό σε σχεδόν ένα χρόνο τον Μάιο, με την ανέγερση κατοικιών και τα έργα υποδομής να ενισχύουν τη βιομηχανία, δήλωσε η Εθνική Στατιστική Υπηρεσία (ONS).

Οι αναλυτές δήλωσαν ότι τα νέα στοιχεία, μαζί με τα πρόσφατα σχόλια από τους υπεύθυνους χάραξης πολιτικής της Τράπεζας της Αγγλίας, σήμαιναν ότι η απόφαση για το εάν τα επιτόκια θα μειωθούν τον επόμενο μήνα ήταν σε «κόψη μαχαιριού».

Το ποσοστό ανάπτυξης του Μαΐου ήταν διπλάσιο από το αναμενόμενο. Η Liz McKeown, της ONS, είπε ότι πολλοί έμποροι λιανικής και χονδρέμποροι «πέρασαν έναν καλό μήνα, με τους δύο να ανακάμπτουν από τον αδύναμο Απρίλιο».

Ο τομέας των υπηρεσιών, που κυριαρχεί στην οικονομία του Ηνωμένου Βασιλείου και

όπως ο καιρός. Το τρί
2024, η οικονομία αν
σε σύγκριση με τους
μήνες, που σύμφωνα
χύτερος ρυθμός για
χρόνια.

Οι αναλυτές είπα
ισχυρά μεγέθη ανάπτ
μειώσουν τις πιθανότ
γλίας να μειώσει τα ε
16 ετών του 5,25% ότ
Αυγούστου.

Τα επιτόκια αυξήθ
προκειμένου να επιβρ
πληθωρισμού - ο ρυθ
βαίνουν οι τιμές. Ωστό
χεία για τον πληθωρι
σοστό είχε υποχωρήσ
Τράπεζας του 2%.

Παρά το γεγονός
Επιτροπής Νομισματι
της Τράπεζας, η οποία
δο των επιτοκίων, δή
μάδα ότι εξακολουθοί
πληθωριστικές πιέσει

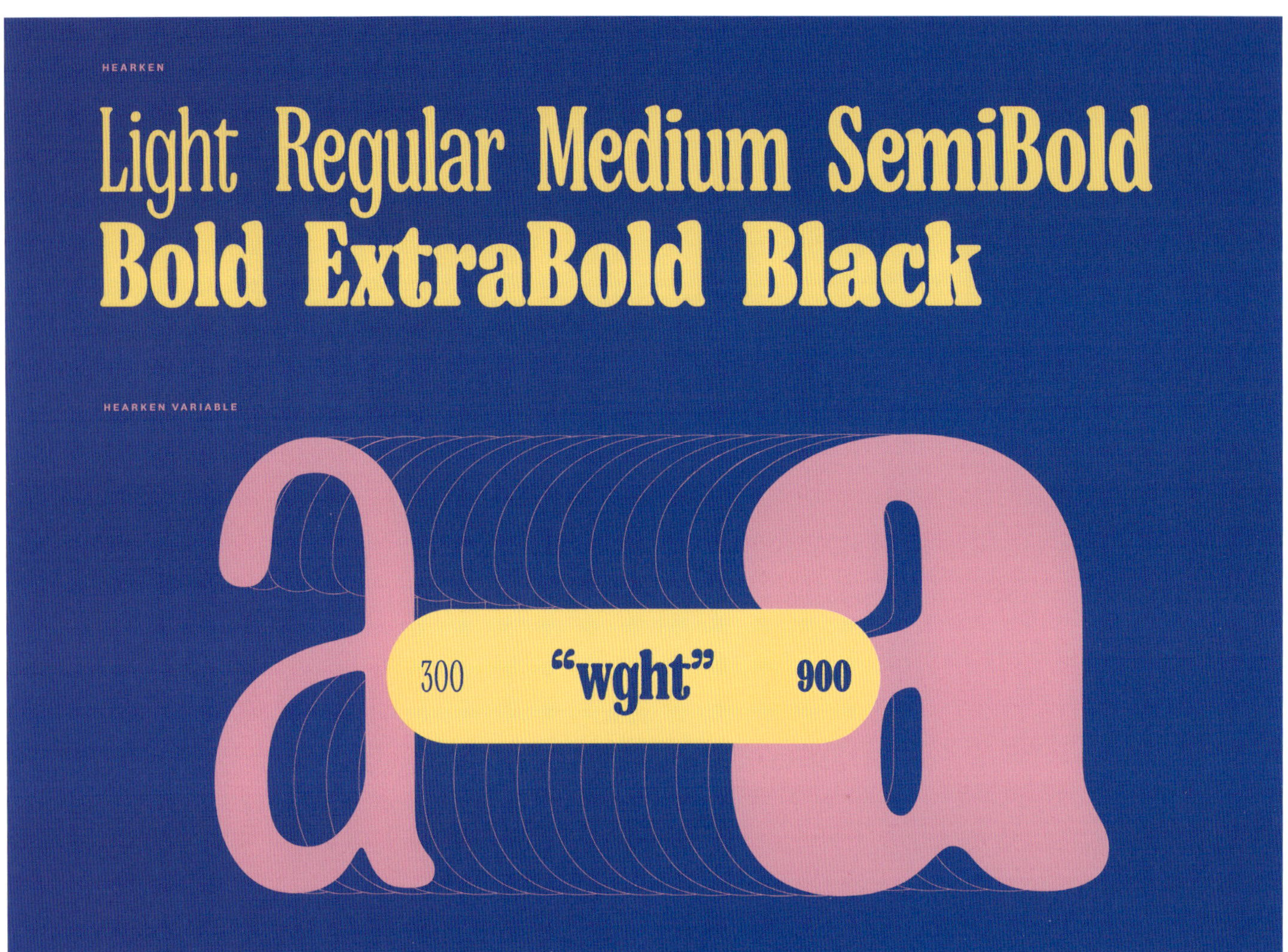

pachyderm strategy quickens lunchtimes
pachyderm strategy quickens lunchtimes
pachyderm strategy quickens lunchtimes
pachyderm strategy quickens lunchtimes
pachyderm strategy quickens lunchtimes
pachyderm strategy quickens lunchtimes
pachyderm strategy quickens lunchtimes

California
arbitrary
freshest
collegiate
idioteque
filmy

California
arbitrary
freshest
collegiate
idioteque
filmy

The friendliest condensed typeface you've ever seen. Bold claim, maybe. At least, that's the goal. Hearken was made as an alternative to the much wider Cooper Black. Other than being quite narrow, it contains a variable weight axis.

Hearken

etceteratype.co

Designed by *Ty Finck*
Published by *Etcetera Type Company*

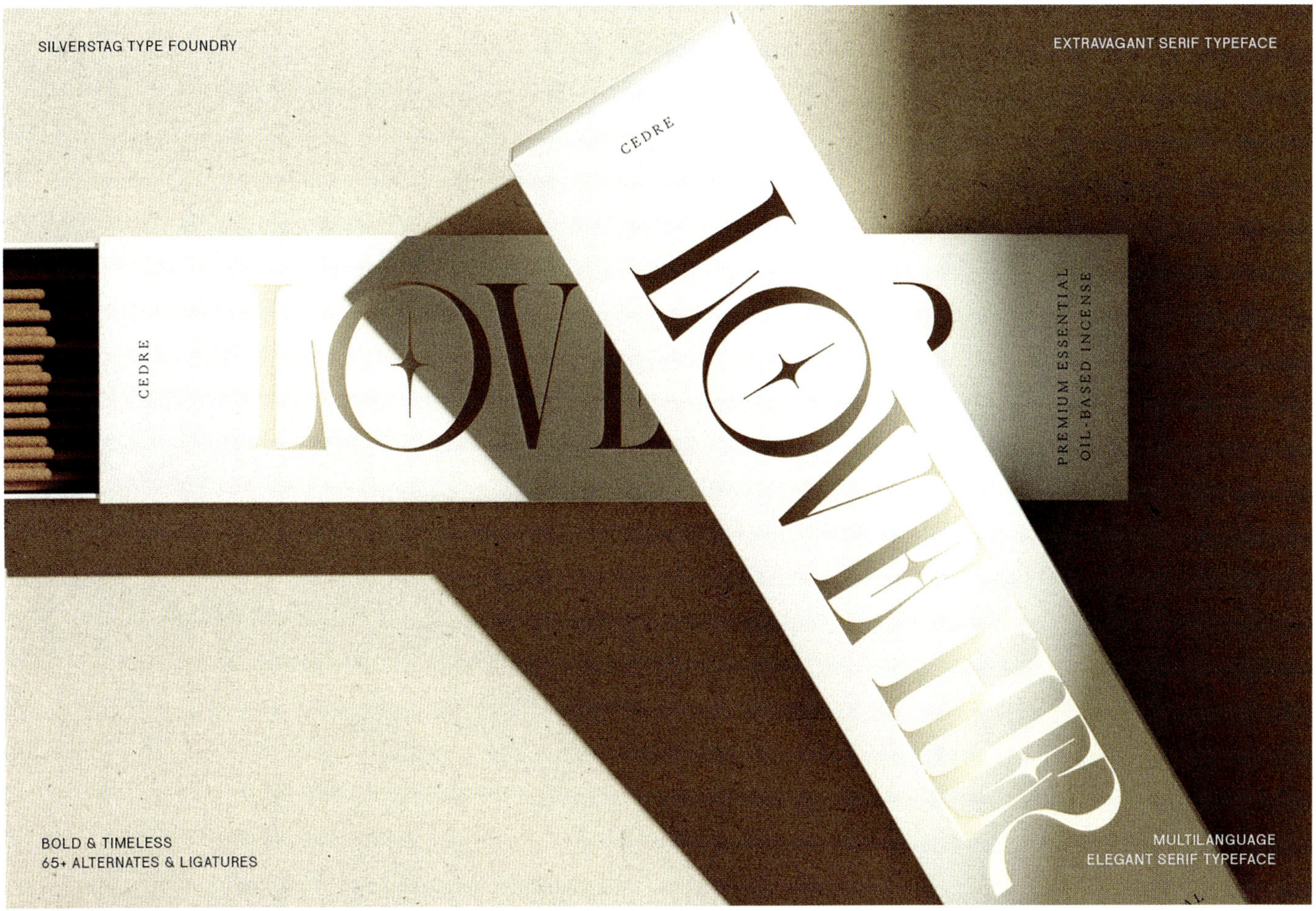

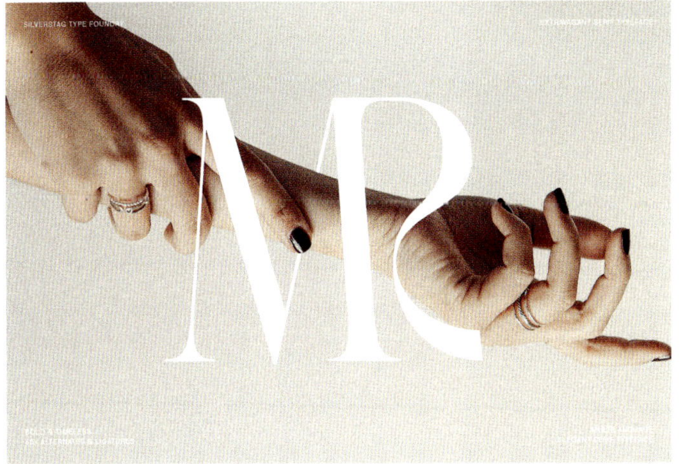

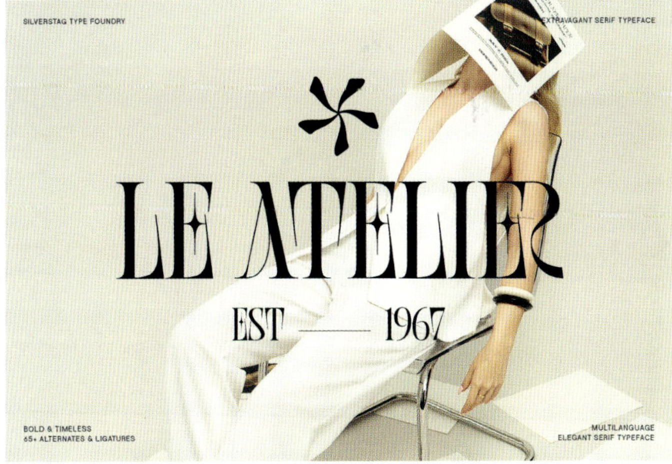

SLTF Boxroom is a bold, modern, serif typeface that merges vintage elegance with expressive, contemporary character. Featuring sharp, extended serifs and unexpected decorative touches on letters like O, Q, E, and F, Boxroom adds a dash of sophistication and surprise to every layout.

silverstag.design

SLTF Boxroom

Designed by *Alen Kapetanovic*
Published by *SilverStag Type Foundry*

Icona™ is a fixed system of alphanumeric characters with specific characteristics to be used repetitively.

Latin

Acapul

Cyrillic

Юбилé

Greek

Υπόλοι

The Riddles of the Sphinx

*

Inheriting the Feminist History of the Crossword Puzzle

*

Anna Shechtman

Thin ***Bold***

Light ***Semibold***

Regular *Medium*

Medium *Regular*

Semibold *Light*

Bold *Thin*

Jacknapes

Some types look larger, size for size, than others, because they have unusually short descenders and ascenders. This allows more room for the "x" or middle part of the lower-case. A good newspaper type is one in which seven-point manages to achieve almost as much legibility as a normal ten-point book face. Hence every modern news text-face has a "large x" and short ascenders and descenders.

Burgundy Crush/Baltic Blue

ORGANISATION *of* EVERYTHING

Завершающий

The word typography in English comes from the Greek roots τύπος [*typos* ('type')] and -γραφία [-*graphia* ('writing')].

Sparkle

Brings Updated Design and Performance

Differences between the two versions

This innovation seems to require a fuller justification than has so far been forthcoming, for, while it cannot be doubted that the average reader is glad to be provided with a full-coloured text type, it does not follow that this is the only important factor in readability.

General

Although it was popular in the metal type period for book printing, it was apparently never digitised.

Everything

A gold standard is a monetary system in which the standard economic unit of account is based on a fixed quantity of gold. The gold standard was the basis for the international monetary system from the 1870s to the early 1920s, and from the late 1920s to 1932 as well as from 1944 until 1971 when the United States unilaterally terminated convertibility of the US dollar to gold, effectively ending the Bretton Woods system. Many states nonetheless hold substantial gold reserves. Historically, the silver standard and bimetallism have been more common than the gold standard. The shift to an international monetary system based on a gold standard reflected accident, network externalities, and path dependence. Great Britain accidentally adopted a de facto gold standard in 1717 when Isaac Newton, then-master of the Royal Mint, set the exchange rate of silver to gold too low, thus causing silver coins to go out of circulation. As Great Britain became the world's leading financial and commercial power in the 19th century, other states increasingly adopted Britain's monetary system. The gold standard was largely abandoned during the Great Depression before being re-instated in a limited form as part of the post-World War II Bretton Woods system. The gold standard was abandoned due to its propensity for volatility, as well as the constraints it imposed on governments: by retaining a fixed exchange rate, governments were hamstrung in engaging

Στίξης @ Συμβόλων

Жаңа қаріппен терілген Таймстың жаңа саны 1932 жылы 3 қазанда жарық көрді.

Icona Serif

suitcasetype.com

Designed by *Tomáš Brousil*
Published by *Suitcase Type*

Located at the corner of Madison Avenue and 75th Street, the structure is well known for its inverted ziggurat shape.

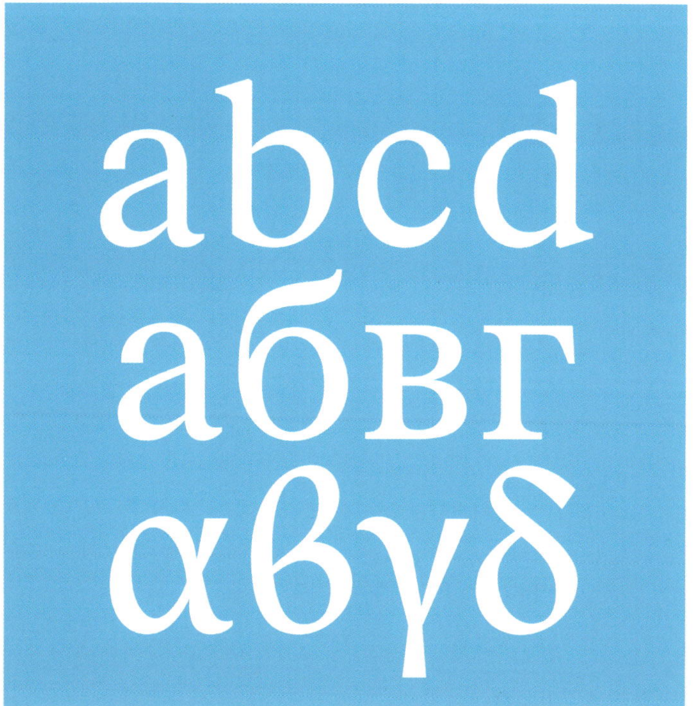

Icona™ Serif Latin

ABCDEFGGHIJKLMNOPQRRSTUVWXYZ
aabcdefgghiijjklmnopqrstuvwxyyz

Икона™ Сериф Кириллица

АБВГДДЕЁЁЖЗИЙКЛЛМНОПРСТУФХЧЦШЩЬЫЪЭЮЯ
аабвгддеёёжзийкллмнопрстуфхчцшщьыъэюя

Ικονα™ Σερíφ Ελληνικό

ΑΒΓΔΕΖΗΘΙΚΛΜΝΞΟΠΡΣΤΥΥΦΧΨΩ
αββγδεζζηηθικλμνξξοπρςστυφχχψω

On the imaginary line graph of the excitement of creation, work on neutral typefaces lies somewhere close to the horizontal axis. Creating a new typeface, which most users perceive unapologetically as any standard, notorious system font, can seem foolish and a waste of time. Yet a well-crafted neutral font has values not found in fonts that try to draw attention to every single glyph. Icona Serif is a neutral typeface with a high x-height, a wide range of weights with adequate italics, and an extensive character set covering Latin, Cyrillic, and Greek. Many alternative characters find use in changes of typesetting character, but they stand out especially in display sizes, where they can attract attention even in a seemingly serious presentation.

Aman Display Thin & *Italic*
Aman Display ExtraLight & *Italic*
Aman Display Light & *Italic*
Aman Display Regular & *Italic*
Aman Display Medium & *Italic*
Aman Display SemiBold & *Italic*
Aman Display Bold & *Italic*
Aman Display ExtraBold & *Italic*
Aman Display Black & *Italic*

Aman Headline Thin & *Italic*
Aman Headline ExtraLight & *Italic*
Aman Headline Light & *Italic*
Aman Headline Regular & *Italic*
Aman Headline Medium & *Italic*
Aman Headline SemiBold & *Italic*
Aman Headline Bold & *Italic*
Aman Headline ExtraBold & *Italic*
Aman Headline Black & *Italic*

Aman Text Thin & *Italic*
Aman Text ExtraLight & *Italic*
Aman Text Light & *Italic*
Aman Text Regular & *Italic*
Aman Text Medium & *Italic*
Aman Text SemiBold & *Italic*
Aman Text Bold & *Italic*
Aman Text ExtraBold & *Italic*
Aman Text Black & *Italic*

Aman Caption Thin & *Italic*
Aman Caption ExtraLight & *Italic*
Aman Caption Light & *Italic*
Aman Caption Regular & *Italic*
Aman Caption Medium & *Italic*
Aman Caption SemiBold & *Italic*
Aman Caption Bold & *Italic*
Aman Caption ExtraBold & *Italic*
Aman Caption Black & *Italic*

Aman family ***72 styles***

Art **TROÏENNE** Épopée **Fauna's lies**
Labyrinthe *$ 9,21;* krieg ***dialogues***
Nymphs | **Péloponnèse** ↓ **(ghosts)**
Zeus ↔ MYRMIDONS ***sirènes**** 2012
Achilleus [folies] **Griechischer Wein** chaos
Méditerranéen : & Humanistisches © £7
Télamonides sacrifice ! ***Polyxène* FLOOD**
@Olymp 34 % ***ÉPIQUE,*** Apollon² ***folk*** &c.

Aman Headline ***18 styles***

BIBLIOGRAPHIE : **Hésiode** Les Travaux et les Jours [VIIIe siècle av. J-C] **Hérodote** L'Enquête [-440] **Sophocle** Œdipe roi [-425] **Platon** Le Banquet [-380] **Aristote** De la poétique [-335 ap. J-C] **Plutarque** Vies des hommes illustres [-120] **Lucrèce** De la nature des choses [Ie siècle av. J-C] **Tite-Live** L'Histoire de Rome depuis sa fondation [-31] **Ovide** L'Art d'aimer [1] **Ovide** Les Métamorphoses [1] **Sénèque** Transformation de l'empereur Claude en citrouille [54] **Sénèque** De la vie heureuse [58] **Apulée** L'Âne d'or [IIe siècle] **Épictète** Manuel [125] **Lucien de Samosate** Dialogues des morts [160] **Lucien de Samosate** Histoires vraies [166] **Suétone** Vie des douze Césars [IIe siècle]

Aman Text ***Bold & Regular***

Superscripts

XIIe M^{r}

Subscripts

C_2H_5O

Fractions

1/2 56/83

Case sensitive form

{@H-O}

Old style figures

312,85

Lining figures

312,85

Aman family ***Features***

→ ANDROMAQUE ∞ *FINALE* 201,89 €
«PÉNÉLOPE», *GRENADIERS** TALES
'TROJAN WAR' LOVE DEATH *ROMA*
CASSANDRE? (TRISTESSES) & KING.
***SICK* DÉMOKOS 4,17° *HISTORIANS* THÉSÉE**
GODDESS,* PLAYWRIGHTS PRIAM *LEGEND
CROWS ‡ PALM TREES 7/54 TROÏLUS. £85,3
[632 GOLDEN APPLES] *PURPOSES* TIMES
NOVEL *1 MYRRHE* "MONSTERS SWARM"

Aman Display ***18 styles***

Aman

blazetype.eu

Designed by *Matthieu Salvaggio, Ferdinand Del Fabbro*
Published by *Blaze Type*

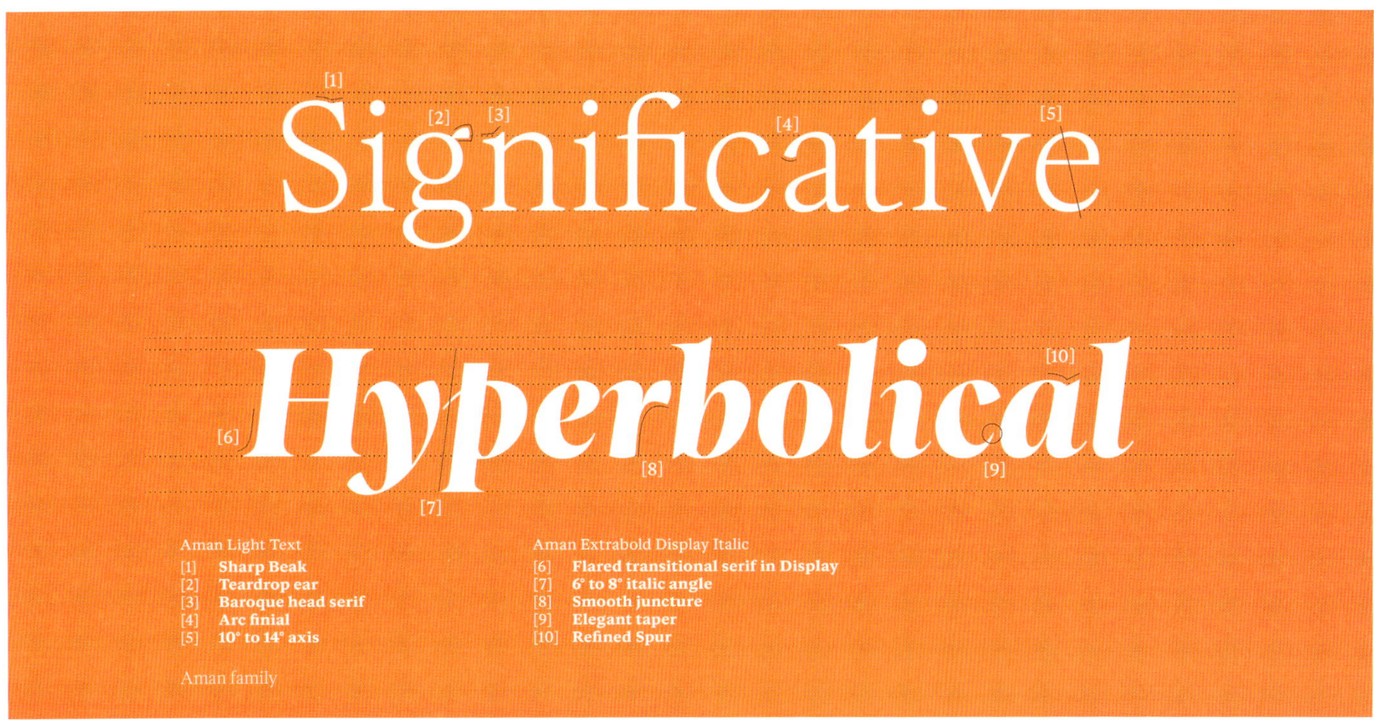

Aman family

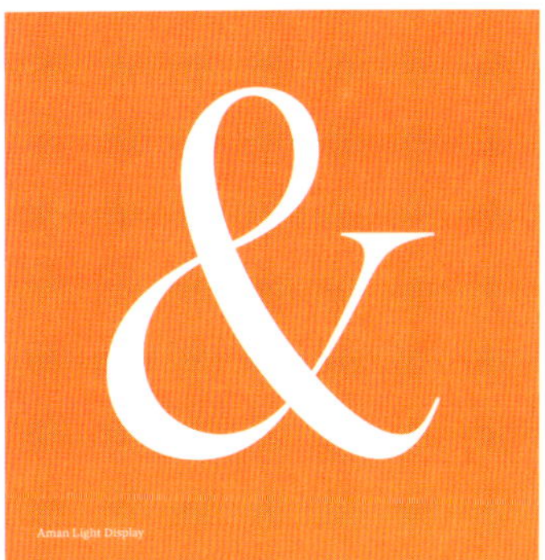

Aman Light Display

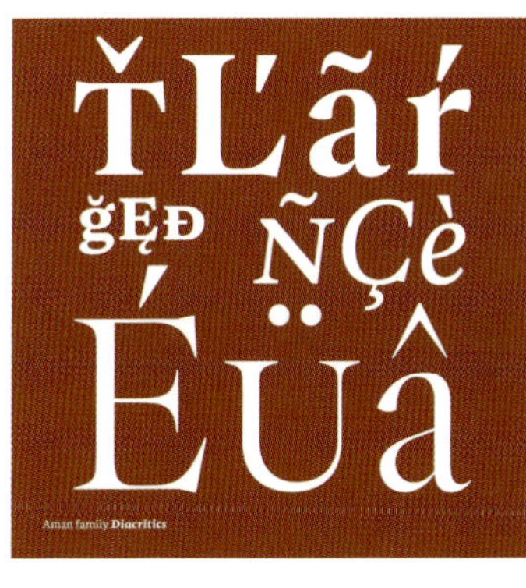
Batrakhomyomakhia

YOUR AID[1], ye Heav'n-born Muses[2], hither bring,
Who sung the wandring *Greek* and *Ilium's* Wars,
Hard Argument for mortal Bard I sing
The Sport tumultuous of Revenger *Mars*.[3]
How Mice renown'd with Frogs a War maintain'd
For Fame, for Vengeance, and for Empire strove
While each side sternly sought, yet neither gain'd
The hard-fought field; Mean-time sky-ruling *Jove*[4]
In equal Ballance[5] pois'd their Fortunes long;
Dire Arms, and Wounds, and Deaths shall fill th'
advent'rous Song.

Aman family

Aman family Diacritics

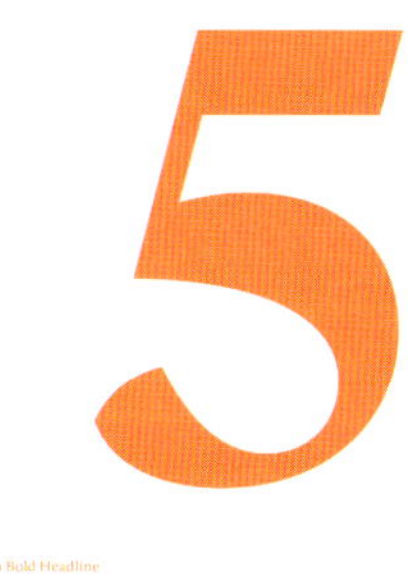

Aman Bold Headline

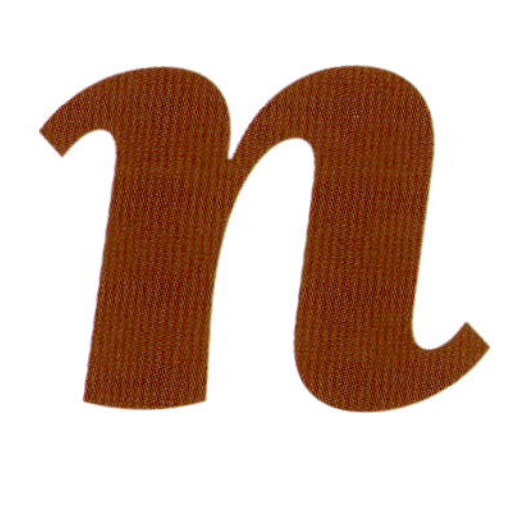

Aman Extrabold Text Italic

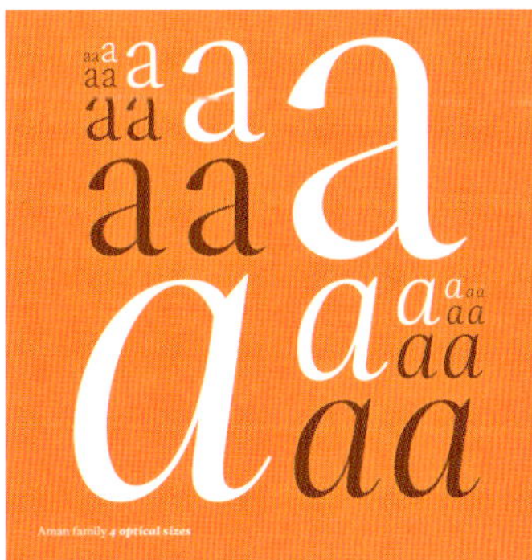

Aman family 4 optical sizes

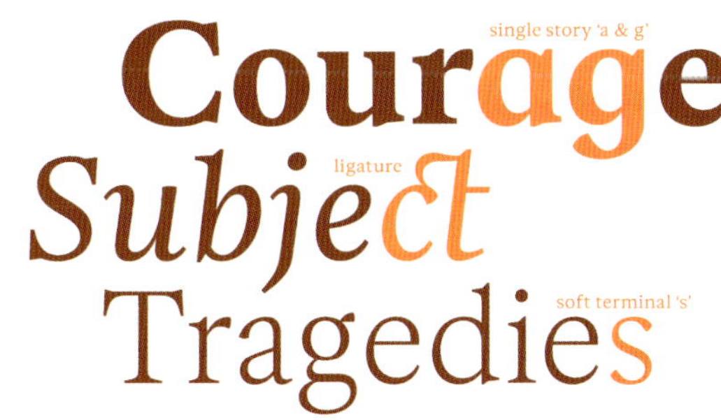

Aman family Features

Aman is a versatile serif typeface family, crafted to perform seamlessly across a wide range of sizes—from striking display headlines to fine, legible captions. Inspired by the lettering from the book Aman, *this typeface brings together the timeless elegance of old-style designs like Plantin with the refined sophistication of transitional styles such as Times New Roman. Its most distinctive features are the baroque flourishes seen in the beaks and head serifs, while its gracefully arcing terminals lend a subtle, refined touch to the letterforms. Carefully tuned for different optical sizes, Aman's counter shapes, proportions, and contrast ensure optimal performance in every instance, whether used for bold, attention-grabbing titles or comfortably readable body text. This balance of style and functionality makes Aman an exceptional choice for editorial design, offering a wide array of styles and weights to cater to the needs of any project while maintaining visual coherence and harmony.*

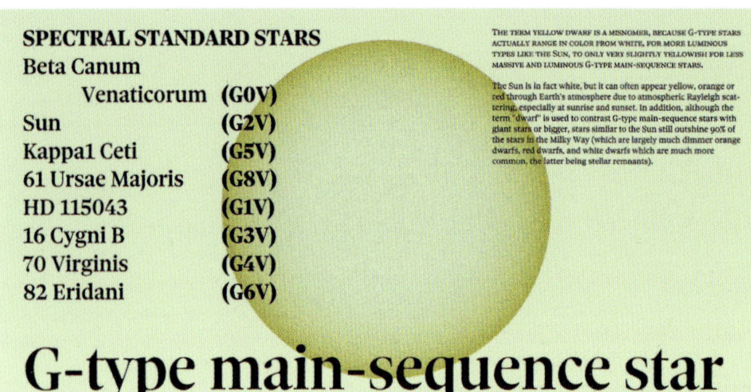

4 optical size / 6 weights for each style!

Subhead	Headline	Display	Big Display
Light	Light	Light	Light
Regular	Regular	Regular	Regular
Medium	Medium	Medium	Medium
Bold	Bold	Bold	Bold
ExtraBold	ExtraBold	ExtraBold	ExtraBold
Black	Black	Black	Black

You spin me round (Like a typeface)

The new display version of our masterpiece, Sole Serif Rounded is now available!

Mean distance from Earth

1 AU

149,600,000 KM

92,000,000 MI

8 MIN 19 S,

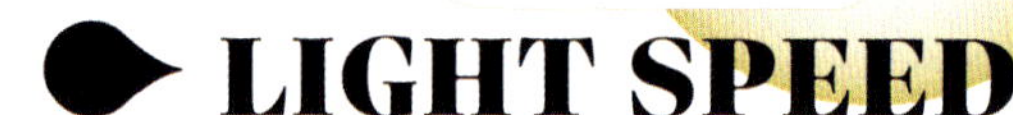

MURKINESS

Miscalculating

Leonard de Vinci

INSTITUTIONALIZE

duomo di cologna veneta

BATMAN: ARKHAM ORIGINS

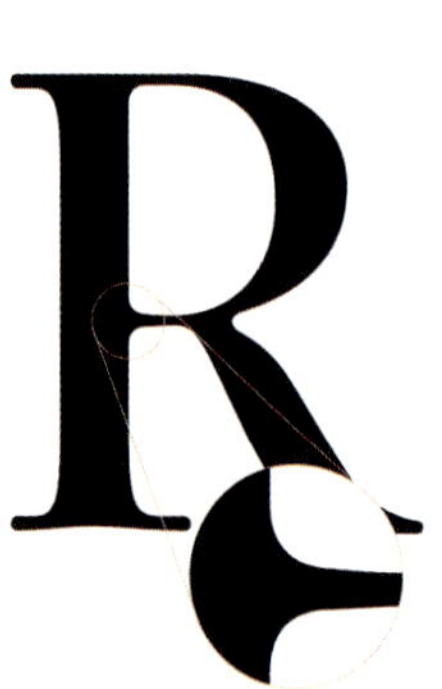

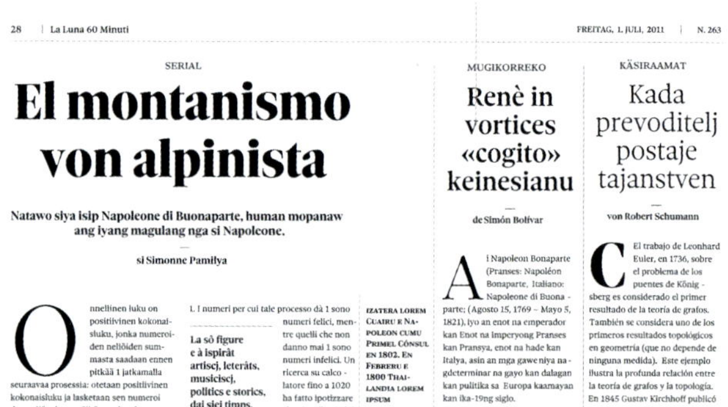

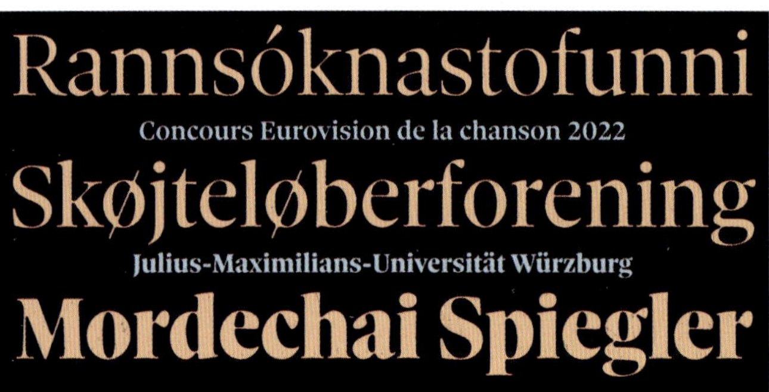

Sole Serif Rounded is the new cut of CAST*'s most successful typeface for newspapers. Compared with its closest competitor Sole Serif Display, it features rounded edges, lighter joints, shorter bracketed serifs. With its peculiar design it works specifically as a display face, providing users with the best results on magazine and newspaper headlines, and on packaging, posters, and other similar applications. Sole Serif Rounded is available in six weights and four optical sizes: Subhead, Headline, Display, and BigDisplay.*

Sole Serif Rounded

c-a-s-t.com

Designed by *Luciano Perondi*
Published by *CAST—Cooperativa Anonima Servizi Tipografici*

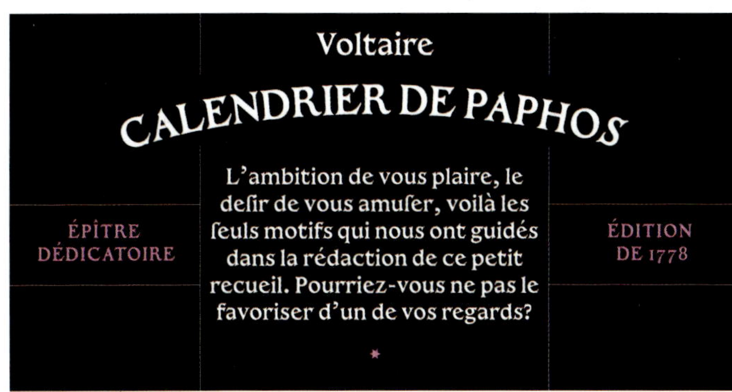

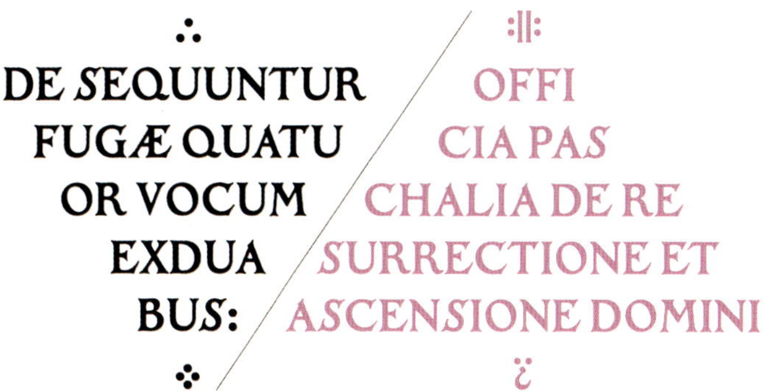

With its peculiar and rough stylistic features, Rhau is a type revival based on four woodcuts used on four title pages of the Officia Paschalia, *a collection of masses and choral compositions printed by Georg Rhau in Wittenberg in 1539. Originally intended for a selected audience of composers, this digital revival is an inspiration for display work.*

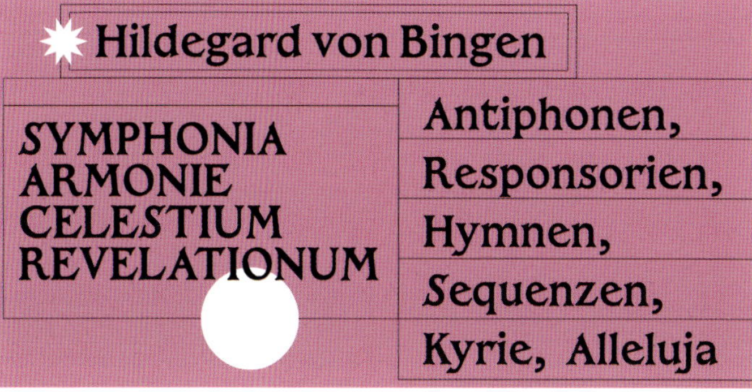

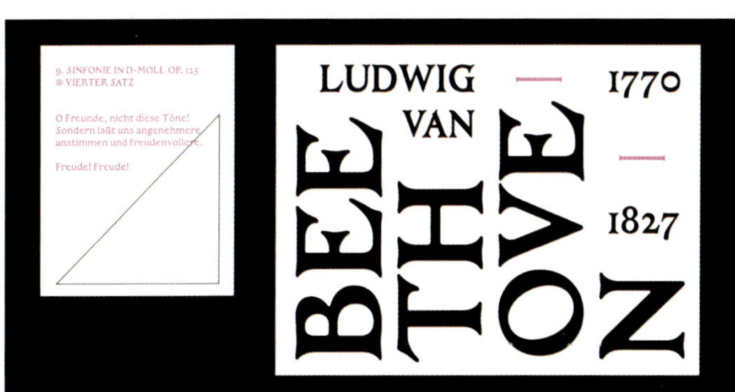

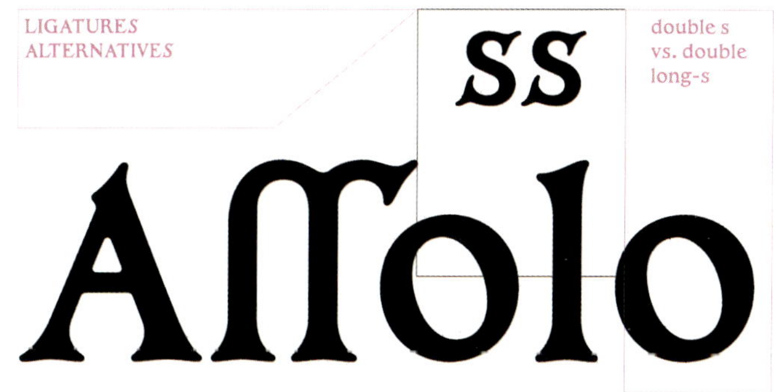

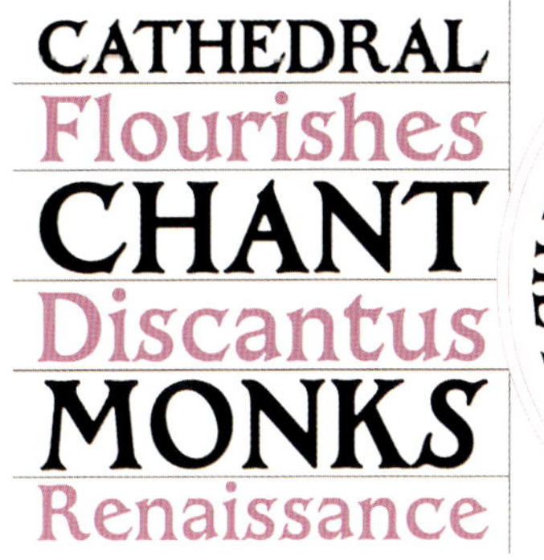

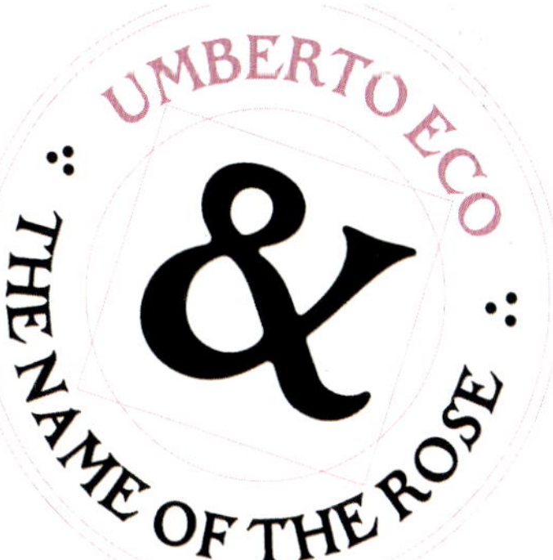

Contrapunt of polyfonie is de techniek waarbij twee of meer
kelijke gelijkwaardige stemmen gelijktijdig klinken. Vanwe
meer horizontale verloop van deze stemcombinaties word
ste onderwerp apart van de harmonieleer bestudeerd. Bij
nieleer ligt het accent op de verticale verbinding van de ak
(homofonie). Toch is de hantering van de stemvoering var
met name bij het schrijven van de stempartijen voor een v
a-capellakoor. Met andere woorden, de akkoordenverbin
dienen zodanig geschreven te zijn, dat een goedlopende st
vanwege de zingbaarheid, noodzakelijk is.
De hantering van de stemvoering bij de traditionele harmon

c-a-s-t.com

Rhau

Designed by *Giulio Galli*

Published by *CAST—Cooperativa Anonima Servizi Tipografici*

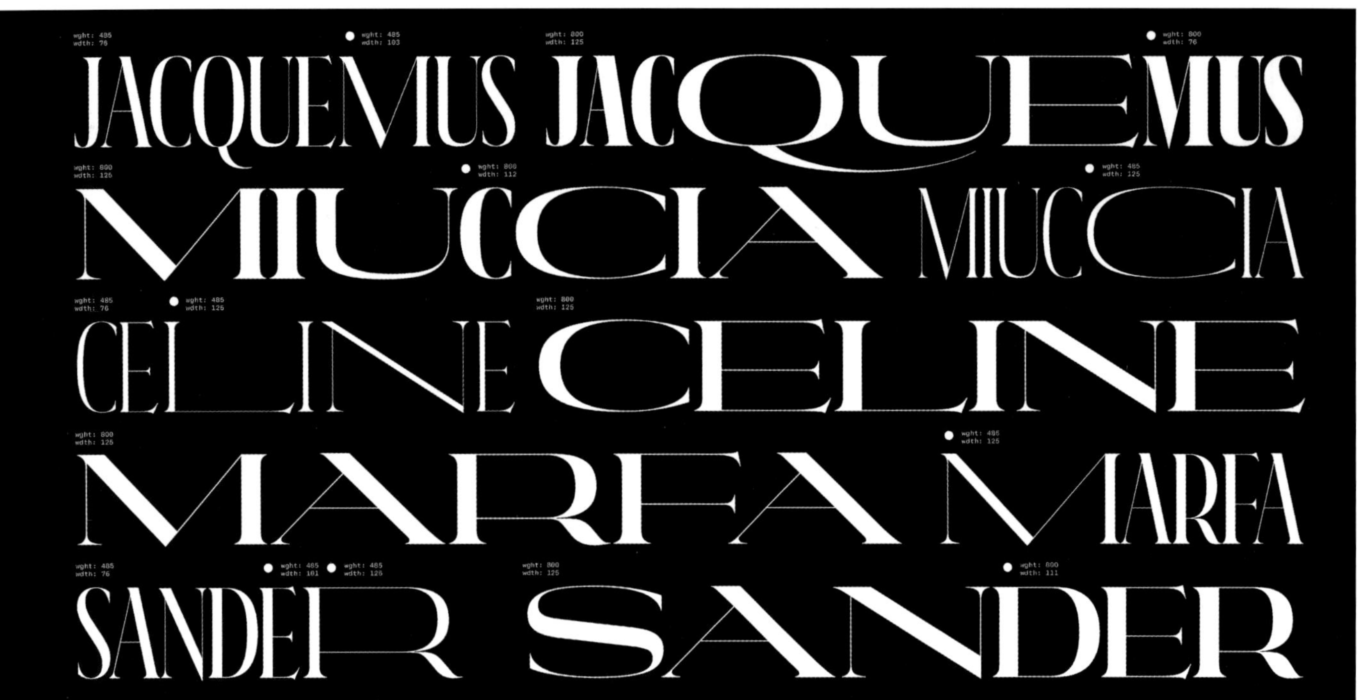

stylistic sets

DIE GLUCKS

ss01: very small caps ss06: open nested ligatures ss02: swash alternates

VALENTINO

ss07: contraction ligatures ss06: open nested ligatures ss06: open nested ligatures

SAGITTARIUS

wght: 100
wdth: 80

ss07: contraction ligatures ss06: open nested ligatures

Nova Caps is a striking and globe-trotting editorial typeface that steals inspiration from Roman inscriptions and Art Deco architectural lettering.

Nova Caps

rosettatype.com

Designed by *Tania Chacana*
Published by *Rosetta*

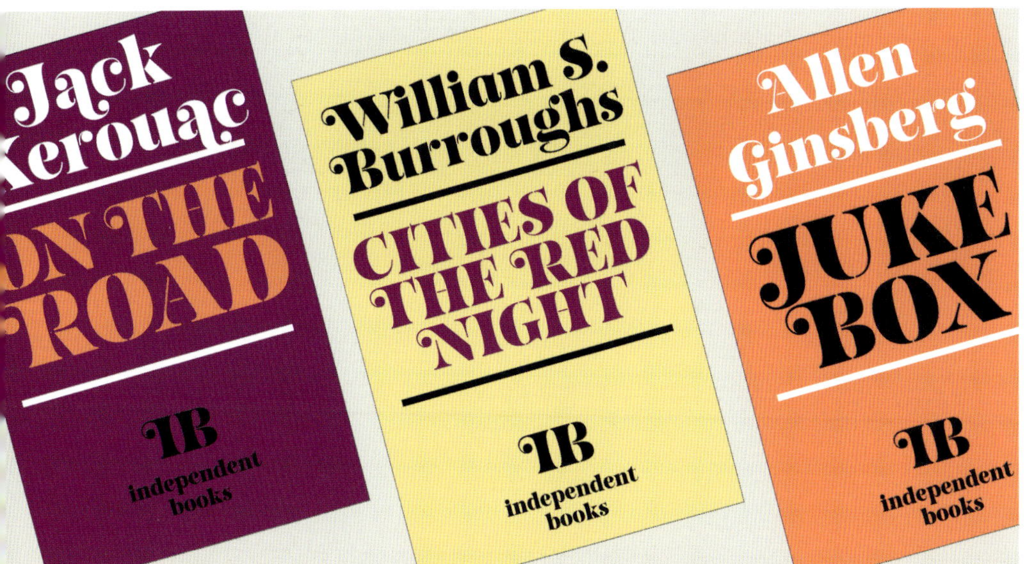

Fabulosa merges the bold contrasts of the nineteenth-century "fat face" style, pioneered by Robert Thorne, with the ornate swashes of Ed Benguiat's Caslon Black Swash, blending historical influences with mid-twentieth-century flair. Designed by Laura Meseguer, it is a glamorous, retro-fantastical typeface that makes a bold visual statement, ideal for everything from high-fashion editorials to indie film posters.

The Leftovers Cookbook

By Lyota Wooding

A cookbook for money-saving yummy meals

Fabulosa

Designed by *Laura Meseguer*
Published by *Type-Ø-Tones*

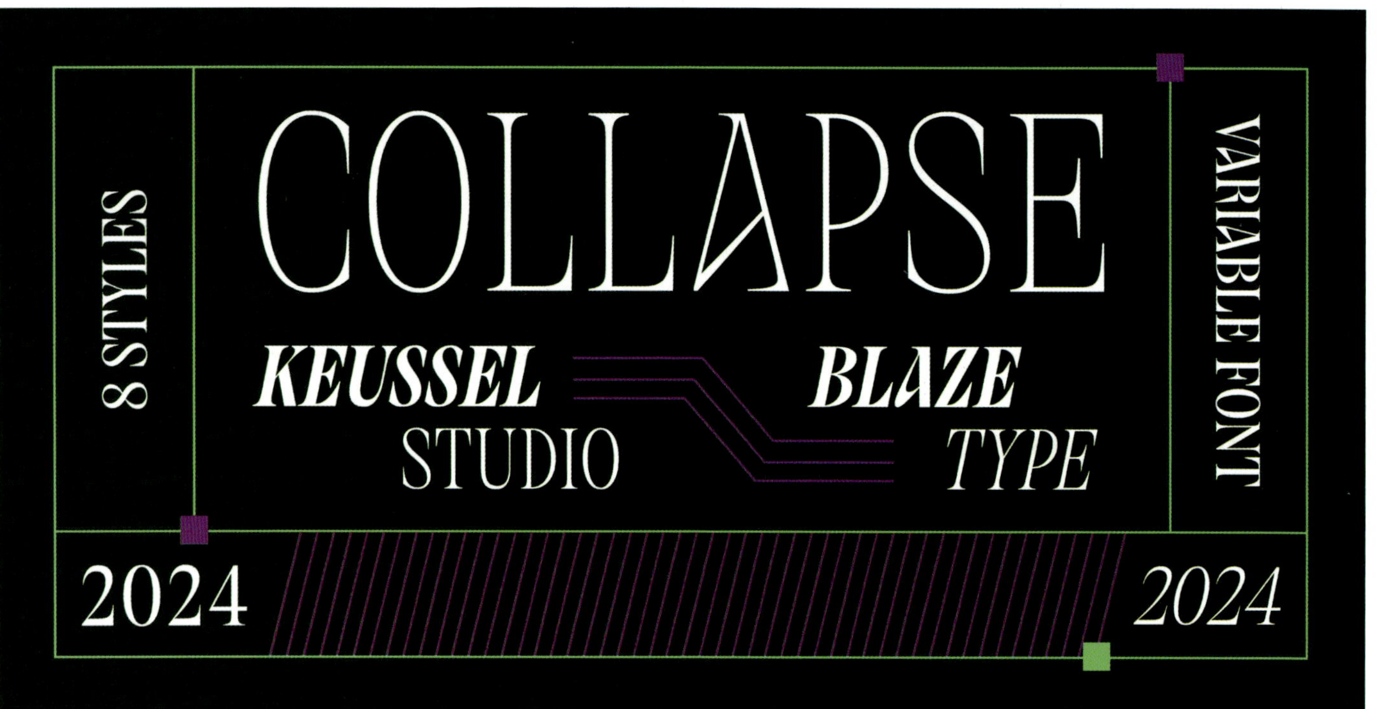

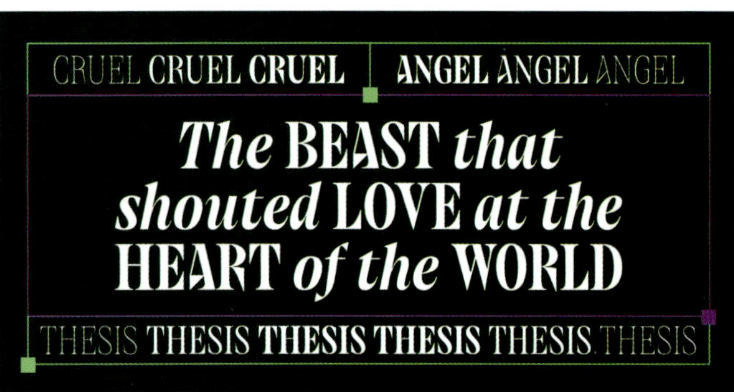

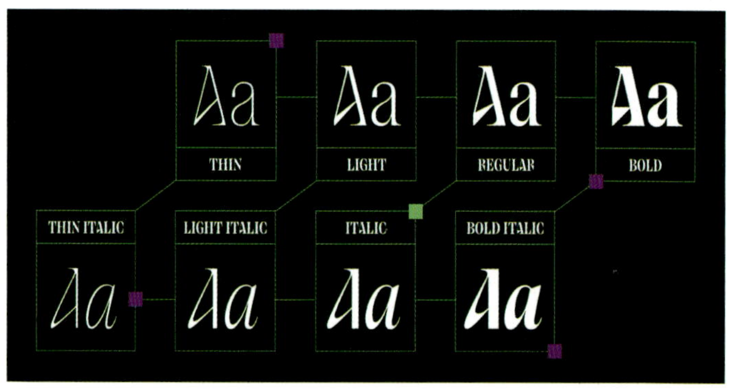

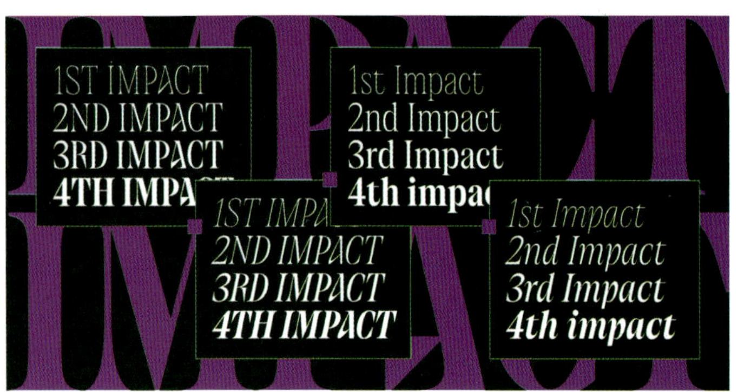

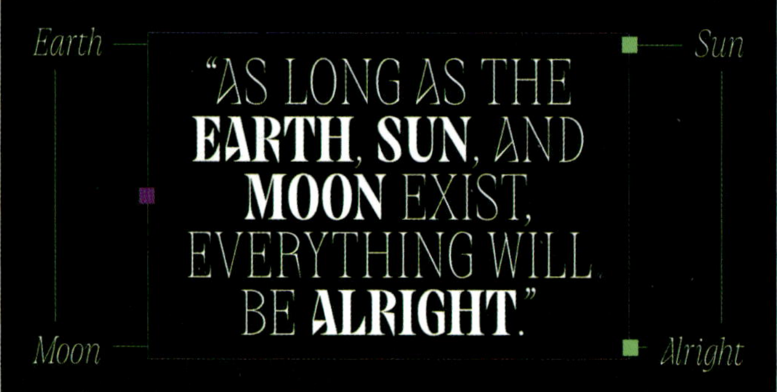

Collapse

blazetype.eu

Designed by *Axel Keussel Andre*
Published by *Blaze Type*

AAAA aaaa BBBB bbbb CCCC cccc DDDD dddd EEEE eeee FFFF ffff GGGG gggg HHHH hhhh IIII iiii JJJJ jjjj KKKK kkkk
LLLL llll MMMM mmmm NNNN nnnn OOOO oooo PPPP pppp QQQQ qqqq RRRR rrrr SSSS ssss TTTT tttt UUUU uuuu
VVVV vvvv WWWW wwww XXXX xxxx YYYY yyyy ZZZZ zzzz ZZZZ zzzz YYYY yyyy XXXX xxxx WWWW wwww VVVV vvvv
UUUU uuuu TTTT tttt SSSS ssss RRRR rrrr QQQQ qqqq PPPP pppp OOOO oooo NNNN nnnn MMMM mmmm LLLL llll
KKKK kkkk JJJJ jjjj IIII iiii HHHH hhhh GGGG gggg FFFF ffff EEEE eeee DDDD dddd CCCC cccc BBBB bbbb AAAA aaaa

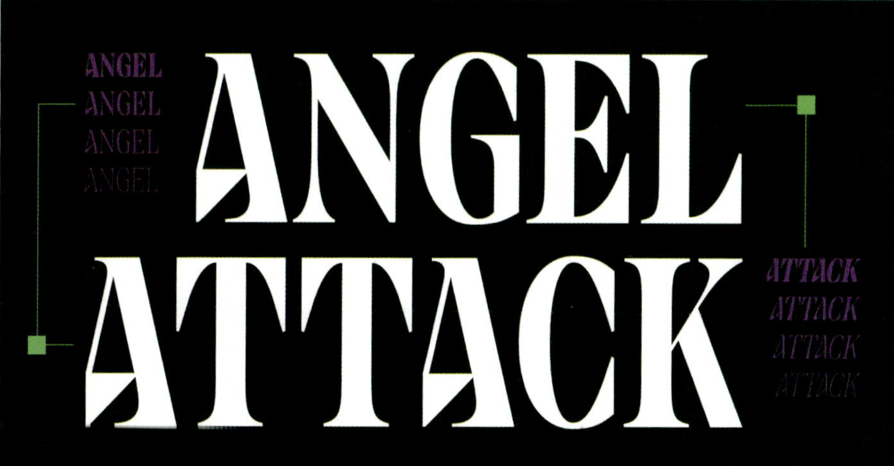

Collapse is an austere and melancholic condensed serif, crafted with an air of stark pessimism. Loosely inspired by the iconic serif typeface seen in the opening titles of Neon Genesis Evangelion, *it draws upon the haunting atmosphere of that series while quickly diverging into something more expressive, more severe. This typeface embodies a tension between restraint and rebellion, its sharp edges and compressed form evoking an unsettling beauty. Collapse plays with the contrast between elegance and intensity, making it ideal for projects that demand both sophistication and a sense of underlying urgency.*

Absolute Terror Field / Additional Impact / Angels / Ark / Artificial Evolution Laboratory / Beast Mode /Berserk Mode / Bethany Base / Black Moon / Blood Type / Book of Life / Calvary

Base / Central Dogma / Contact Experiment / Core / Dead Sea Scrolls / Dummy Plug Plant / Earth Defense Band / Euro-NERV / Eva Pseudo-Evolution / Evangelions / First Ancestral Race / First

ABCDEFGHIJK
LMNOPQRSTU
VWXYZabcdef
ghijklmnopqr
stuvwxyz.,:;
!?1234567890
&ß"@$£€()[]{}

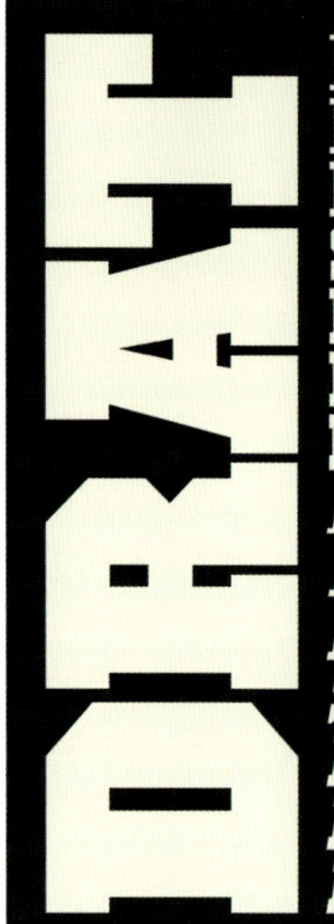

Light
Regular
Medium
Semibold
Bold
Extra Bold
Black
Light Italic
Italic
Medium Italic
Semibold Italic
Bold Italic
Extra Bold Italic
Black Italic

SPECIALS
RAILROAD
BOMBARD
CHARMER
WEDLOCK
HANDSAW

The Clash
Buzzcocks
Undertones
Sex Pistols
The Damned
The Adverts
Stranglers
X-Ray Spex

Dug is a bottom-heavy, ultra-bold display family that evokes the personality and warmth of the best fonts of the psychedelic era. Drawn with large round shapes and sturdy geometric sans construction, Dug is big, loud, and friendly.

Dug

centraltype.com

Designed by *Mark Butchko*
Published by *Central Type*

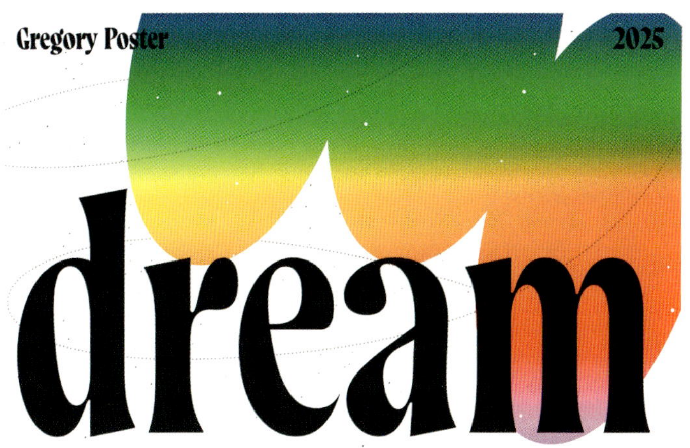

Imagine reality an
Уявіть реальність
Hãy tưởng tượng t
Φαντάσου την πρα
Представи си реа

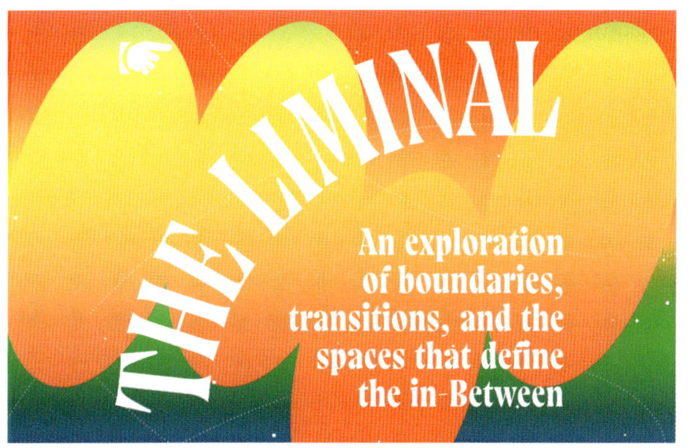

Giấc mơ làm mờ ranh
Les rêves brouillent les f
Мрії розмивають
Мечтите размиват границ
Dreams blur the line

Recent findings in **Dream Pat**
reveal an unexpected correlatio
tional **narrative structures**
dream sequences. When mappi
section points between consciou
and REM - **state dream arch**

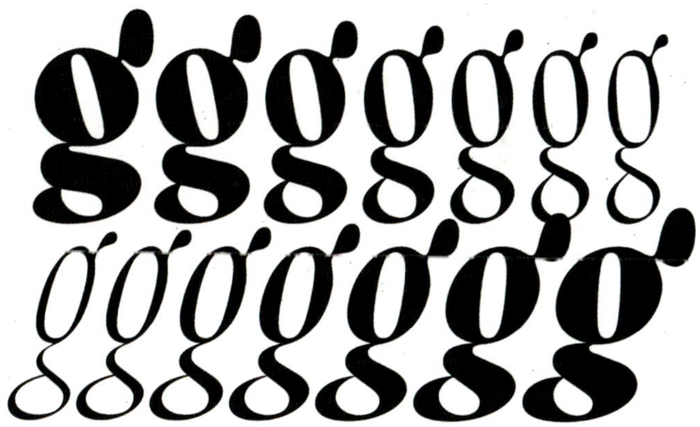

A weird and wonderful flared serif with a dazzling smile, Gregory Poster is suitable for evocative art, genuine beauty, and otherworldly storytelling. Surprising in its bold detail and nostalgic romance, it embraces an enticing mix of spiky and soft sentiment.

---

typemates.com

Gregory Poster

Designed by *Jakob Runge, George Triantafyllakos, Seryozha Rasskazov*
Published by *TypeMates*

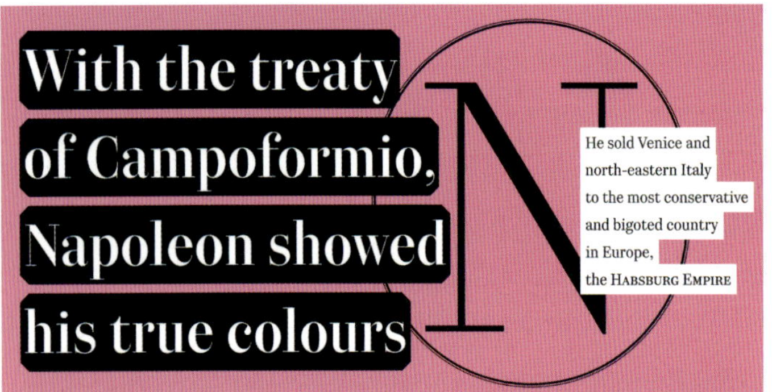

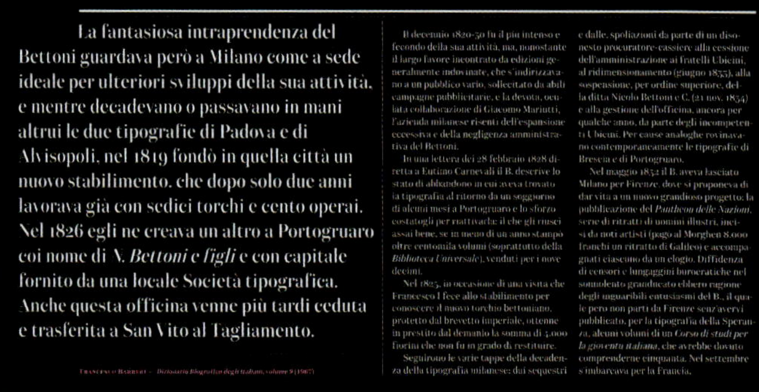

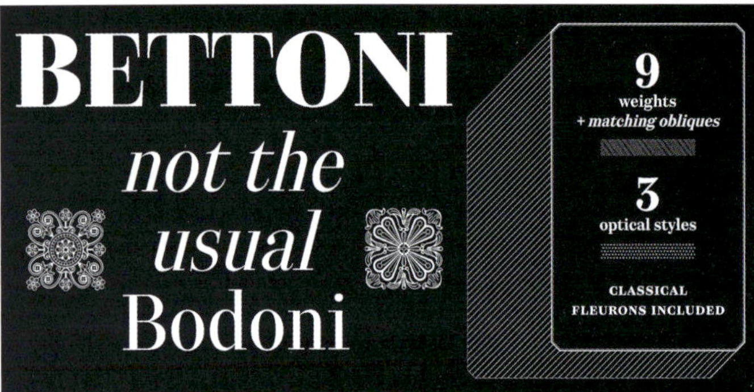

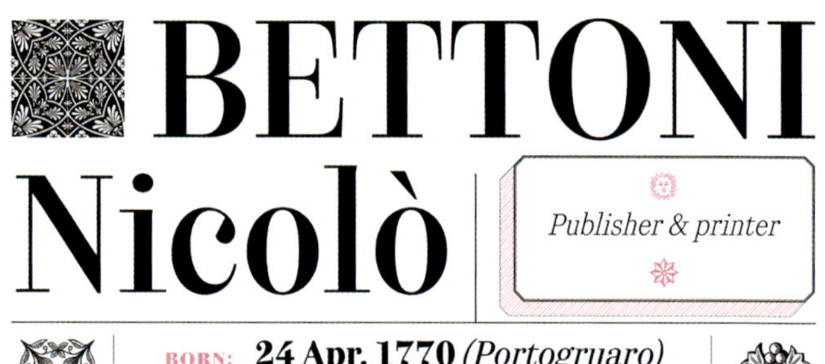

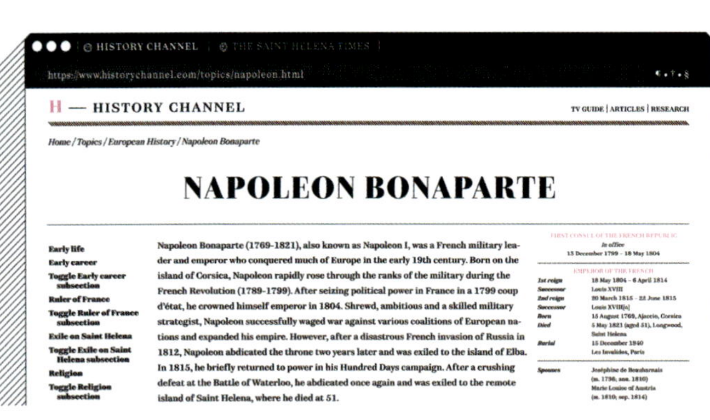

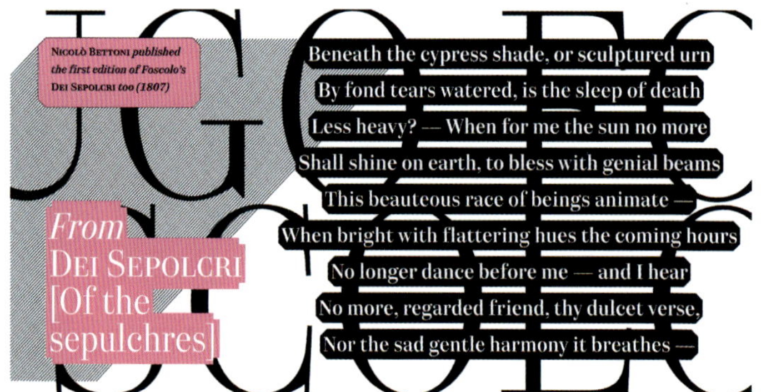

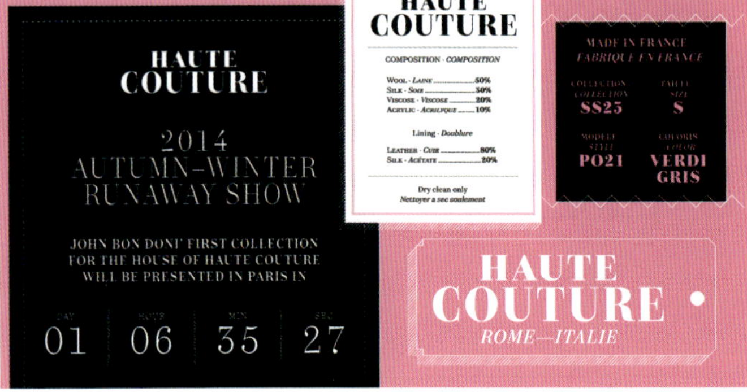

Bettoni is an extensive typeface family in the Bodonian style. Three optical sizes—Text, Subhead, and Display—make it outstandingly valuable for publishing, from books to magazines and newspapers, both in print and on screen.

Bettoni

c-a-s-t.com

Designed by *Riccardo Olocco*
Published by *CAST—Cooperativa Anonima Servizi Tipografici*

Federico Martín Aramburú
CANDY MONTGOMERY
Otton Ier du Saint-Empire
RIANE MNOUCHKINE
sport Layer Security
NT CAPELLUTO
giment de zouaves
MY DEAR F***ING
Armée républicaine irla
CHARLOTTE DI CALYPS
Brightburn : L'Enfant du mal
ÉCONOMIE DU MEXIQUE
Affaire Stéphane Moitoiret
JOHANNES GUTENBERG

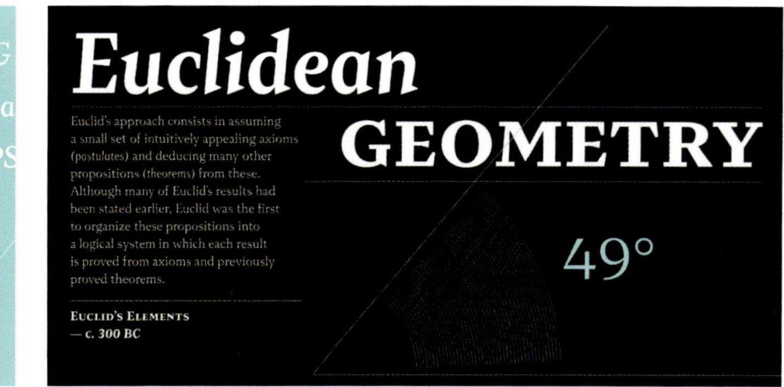

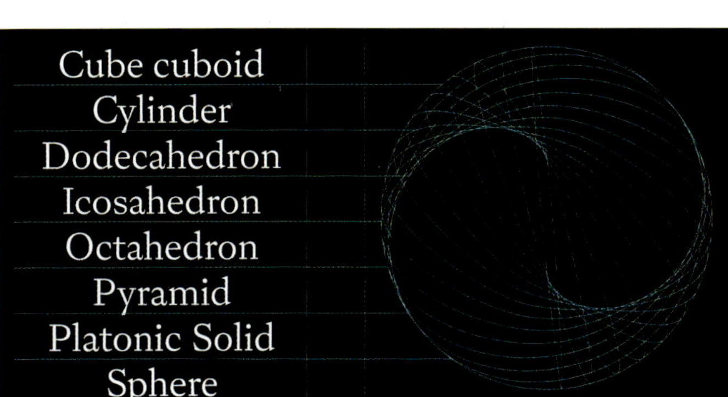

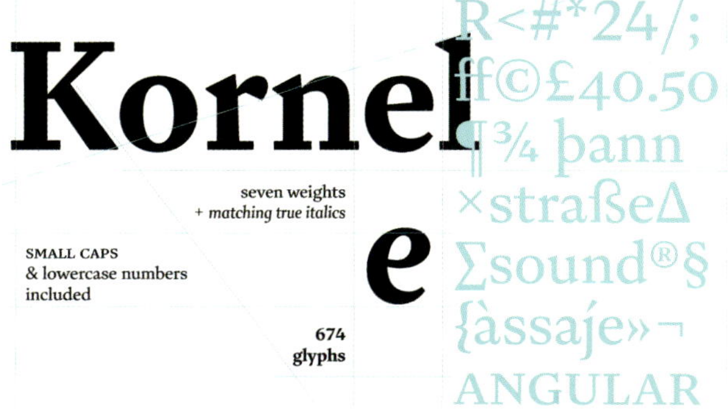

Kornel is a serif type family designed for long texts. Its confident appearance derives from classic proportions and sharp details, both of which allow excellent performances for print and web. With the design priority of producing texts with a harmonious rhythm, inspiration for Kornel came from Renaissance typography in general, rather than any specific typeface. Treatment of terminals and diagonal strokes produce a distinguished contemporary twist, and the gently slanted italics are the perfect complement to the roman. Sharp entry and exit strokes and oblique strokes of the Italics make for the simplified shapes of letters such as R, K, k, v, x, y, and w. With its seven weights—Book, Regular, Regular-Dark, Medium, Bold, ExtraBold, and Black—and related Italics, Kornel meets the most demanding of text compositions.

Maria Wisława Anna Szymborska

Wisława Szymborska was born on 2 July 1923 in Prowent, the second daughter of Wincenty Szymborski and Anna (née Rottermund) Szymborska. Her father was, at that time, the steward of Count Władysław Zamoyski, a Polish patriot and charitable patron. After Zamoyski's death in 1924, her family moved to Toruń, and in 1931 to Kraków, where she lived and worked until her death in early 2012.

When World War II broke out in 1939, she continued her education in underground classes. From 1943, she worked as a railroad employee and managed to avoid being deported to Germany as a forced labourer.During this time, her career as an artist began, with illustrations for an English-language textbook. She also began writing stories and occasional poems. In 1945, she began studying Polish literature before switching to sociology at Jagiellonian University in Kraków.There, she became involved in the local writing scene, and met and was influenced by Czesław Miłosz. In March 1945, she published her first poem, "Szukam słowa" ("Looking for words"), in the daily newspaper Dziennik Polski.

Her poems continued to be published in various newspapers and periodicals for a number of years. In 1948, she quit her studies without a degree, due to poor financial circumstances; the same year, she married poet Adam Włodek, whom she divorced in 1954. They remained close until Włodek's death in 1986. Their union was childless. Around the time of her marriage, she was working as a secretary for an educational biweekly magazine as well as an illustrator. Her first book was to be published in 1949, but did not pass censorship as it "did not meet socialist requirements".

Szymborska adhered to the People's Republic of Poland's (PRL) official ideology early in her career. For example, during the Polish anti-religious campaign, she signed an infamous 1953 political petition condemning Polish priests accused of treason in a Kraków show trial.[13] Her early work supported socialist themes, as seen in her debut collection Dlatego żyjemy (That is what we are living for), containing the poems "Lenin" and "Młodzieży budującej Nową Hutę" ("For the Youth who are building Nowa Huta"), about the construction of a Stalinist industrial town near Kraków. She became a member of the ruling Polish United Workers' Party.

Although initially close to the official party line, as the Polish Communist Party shifted from the Stalinist communists to "national" communists, Szymborska grew estranged from socialist ideology and renounced her earlier political work. Although she did not officially leave the Communist party until 1966, she began to establish contacts with dissident intellectuals. As early as 1957, she befriended Jerzy Giedroyc, the editor of the influential Paris-based émigré journal Kultura, to which she contributed. In 1964, she opposed a Communist-backed protest to The Times against independent intellectuals, demanding freedom of speech instead.

Kobieta leżąca, **1946** *Relief II,* **1946** *Postać,* **1947** *Rybaczka II,* **1947** *Akt z jabłkiem,* **1948** *Autoportret,* **1948** *Portret kobiety,* **1949** *Studium głowy kobiety w chuście,* **1949** *Akt Kobiecy,* **1949–1950** *Kobieta z dzieckiem (Pokój, Nadzieja matki),* **1949–1950** *Nu (Grande Figure, Anita),* **1949–1950** *Głowa Chopina,* **1950** *Macierzyństwo III,* **1950** *Medalion, ok.* **1950** *Portret matki,* **1950** *Głowa dziewczynki,* **1951**

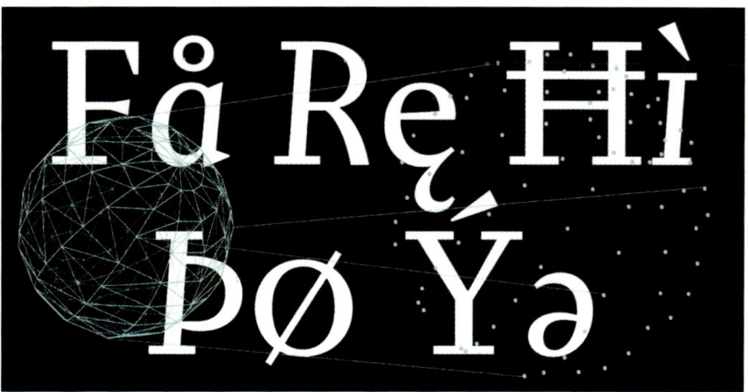

c-a-s-t.com

Kornel

Designed by *Radek Łukasiewicz*
Published by *CAST—Cooperativa Anonima Servizi Tipografici*

fi fj fl ft
fk fh fb
ffk ffh fft
ffi ffj ffl

Elfjähriger
Magnificent
Cauliflower
Aufklärerin
Reshuffling
Semiofficial
Riffkoralle

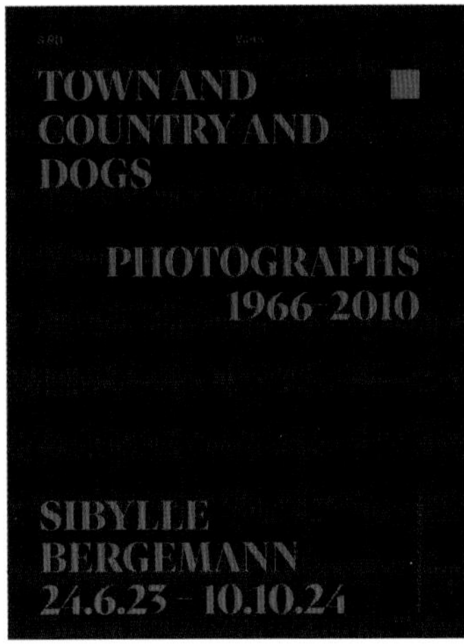

Layouts

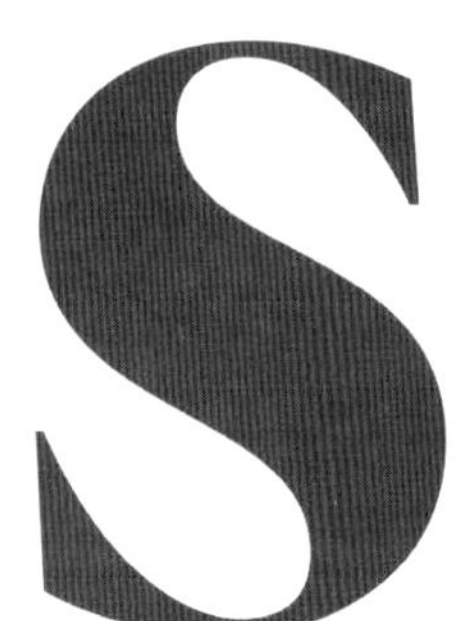

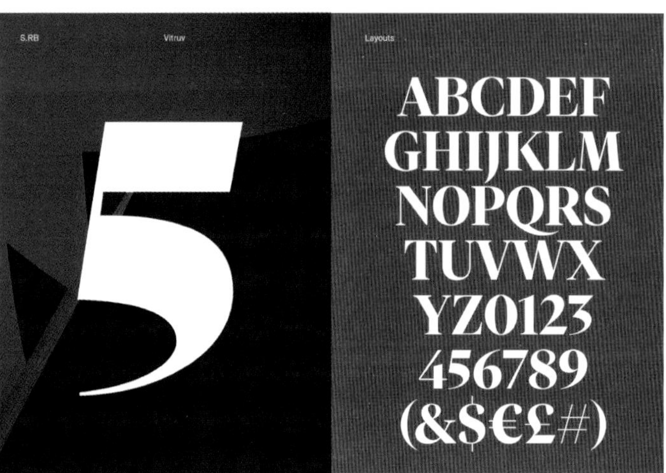

The Vitruv typeface collection is a modern interpretation of French Renaissance Antiquas with their masterpieces of the fifteenth and sixteenth centuries. The family combines the elegance and timelessness of Garamond and Plantijn with the robustness and versatility required by contemporary graphic design.

Vitruv

renebieder.com

Designed by *René Bieder*
Published by *Studio René Bieder*

LDN FARRINGDON

ABC
1234

London Farringdon

LDN FARRINGDON

ABCDEFGHIJKLMN
OPQRSTUVWXYZ&
abcdefghijklmnopqr
stuvwxyz&ABCDE
FGHIJKLMNOP
QRSTUVWXYZ
0123456789€£$¥!

In LDN Farringdon, designer Paul Hickson was influenced by the clean sharp lines of Bodoni and Walbaum, but also wanted to introduce a degree of softness into the letterforms, eventually achieved with the addition of rounded serifs, ball terminals, and smoother final strokes on some of the lowercase characters. The end result is an elegant type family in two weights with matching italics, a distinctive hybrid style that merges contemporary and classical features to stunning effect. Paul also decided to create a set of initial swash caps echoing the steel-cut engraving of the eighteenth and nineteenth centuries.

In the London Borough of Islington

FARRINGDON

Southern Clerkenwell and the small parish of St Sepulchre Middlesex

SMITHFIELD

Farringdon coordinates: 51.520905°N 0.103675°W

Market

CHARTERHOUSE

There are numerous places in England called Farringdon; all meaning *fern covered hill*

The Barbican

In 1394 the ward was split into Farringdon Within & Without

GLASSHOUSE

Turk's Head or Fox & Knot?

londontype.co.uk

LDN Farringdon

Designed by *Paul Hickson*
Published by *The London Type Foundry*

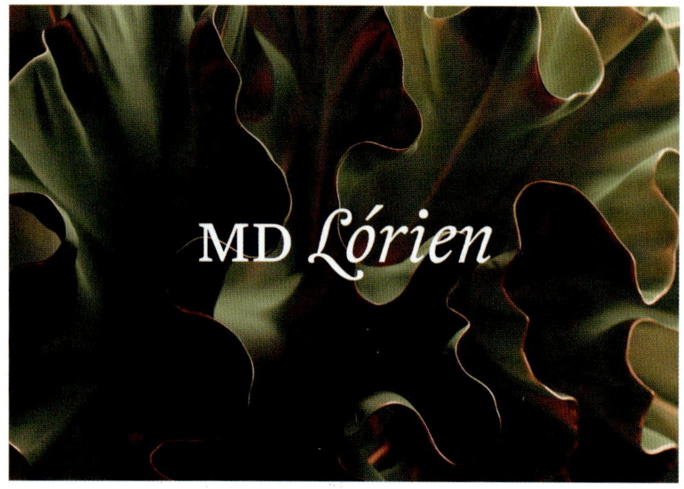

Regular, *Italic,* Book, *Book Italic,* **Semibold,** ***Semibold Italic,*** **Bold,** ***Bold Italic,*** **Black,** ***Black Italic.***

613 Antwerp,
Den Haag 47
Rotterdam,
'Amsterdam'
Haarlem 395
280 LONDON

Ascender Baroque Caslon Designers Elzevir Fleischmann Granjon Haarlem Imprimerie Jenson Kis Leiden Manutius Netherlands Optically Punch Quote Roman Spaces Type Uytwerf Voskens Wetstein Xylograph Yearling Zeitgeist

Los Angeles
November, 2019

A quarter of a millennium after William Caslon's eponymous classic, MD Lórien is a new English interpretation of the Dutch Baroque. Based on a careful selection of late-seventeenth to mid-eighteenth-century typefaces from the Low Countries, it gently adapts the ornate, decorative Baroque designs into a practical contemporary family.

MD Lórien

mass-driver.com

Designed by *Rutherford Craze*
Published by *Mass-Driver*

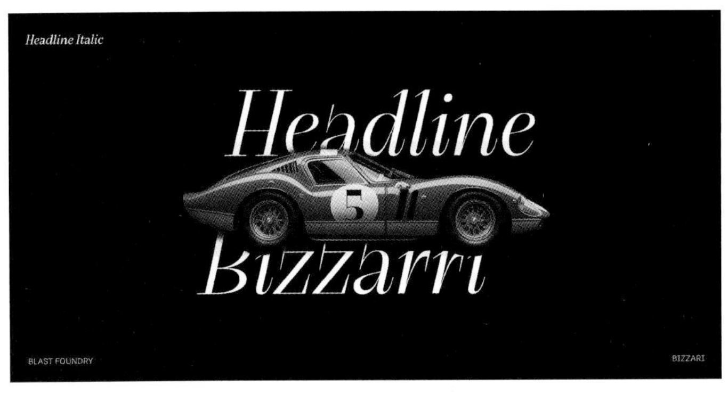

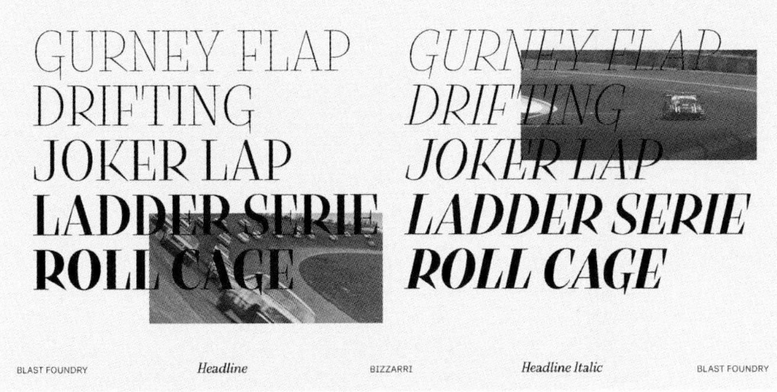

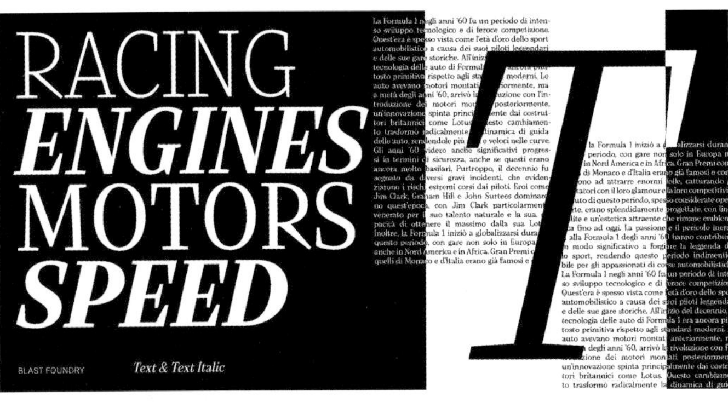

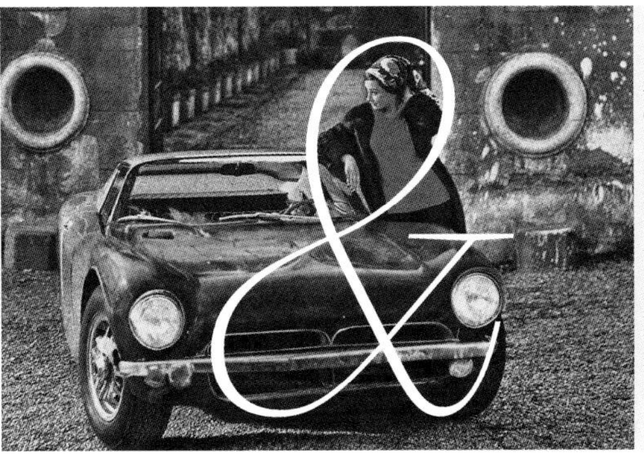

PNEUMATICO & VELOCE

Inoltre, la Formula 1 iniziò a globalizzarsi durante questo periodo, con gare non solo in Europa ma anche in Nord America e in Africa. Gran Premi come quelli di Monaco e d'Italia erano già famosi e continuarono ad attrarre enormi folle, catturando gli spettatori con il loro glamour e la loro competitività. Le auto di questo periodo, spesso considerate opere d'arte, erano splendidamente progettate, con linee pulite e un'estetica attraente che rimane emblematica fino ad oggi.

La passione e il pericolo inerenti alla Formula 1 degli anni '60 hanno contribuito in modo significativo a forgiare la leggenda dello sport, rendendo questo periodo indimenticabile per gli appassionati di corse automobilistiche. Le auto avevano motori montati anteriormente, ma a metà degli anni '60, arrivò la rivoluzione con l'introduzione dei motori montati posteriormente, un'innovazione spinta principalmente dai costruttori britannici come Lotus. Questo cambiamento trasformò radicalmente la dinamica di guida delle auto, rendendole più agili e veloci nelle curve.

Headline Black BIZZARRI BLAST FOUNDRY

Asfaltato
Qualifica

Bizzarri is a dynamic type family drawing inspiration from the sleek lines of racing cars. With two distinct subfamilies—Bizzarri Headline and Bizzarri Text—this versatile typeface bridges the gap between impactful display work and legible body text. Tall ascenders, high contrast, and angular serifs give Bizzarri Headline a sophisticated and bold presence in large formats, while the Bizzarri Text subfamily softens these features, providing clarity and comfort for extended reading without sacrificing personality. The italics strike a unique balance between elegance and sharpness, enhancing the family's versatility.

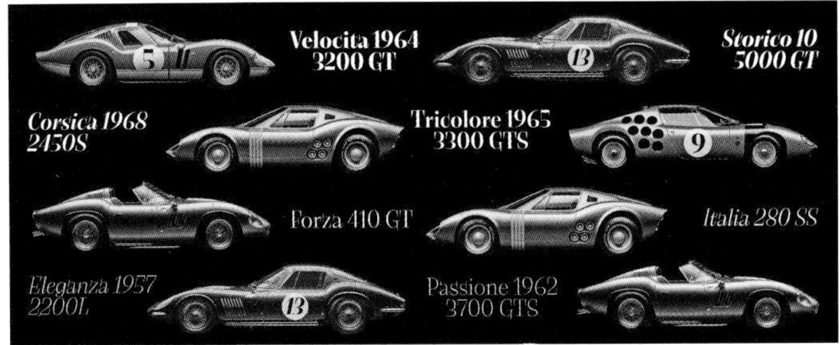

blast-foundry.com

Bizzarri

Designed by *Diana Ovezea*
Published by *Blast Foundry*

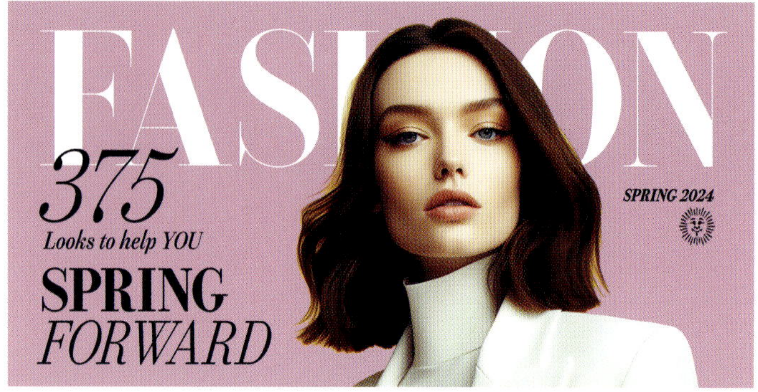

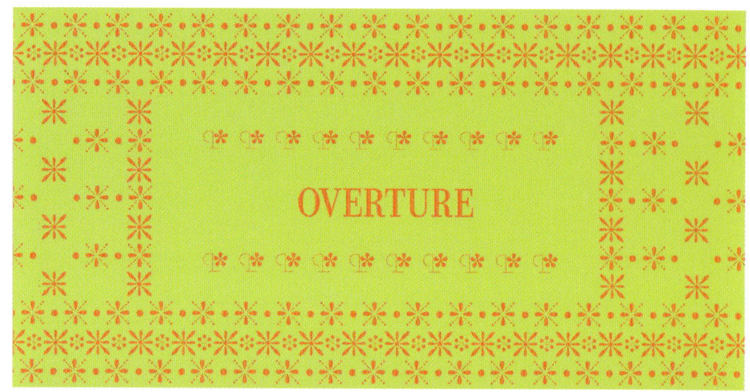

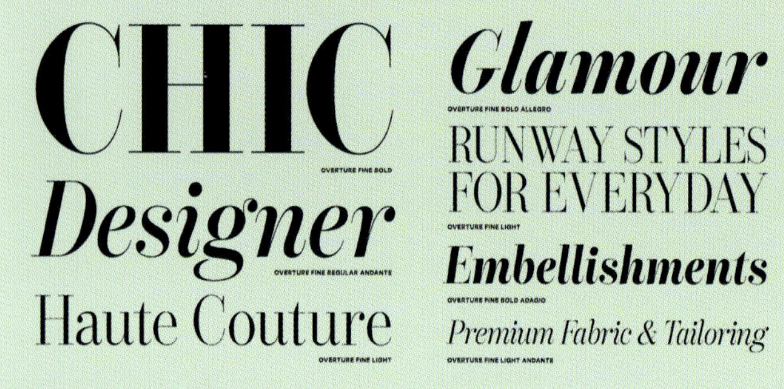

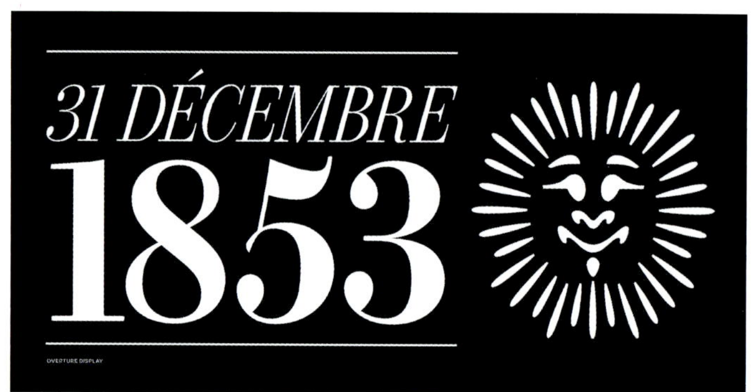

"BUY *LESS*, CHOOSE *WELL*, MAKE IT *LAST*." – *Vivienne Westwood*

Overture is a modern homage to Bodoni, decades in the making. Designed with three italic speeds—Adagio, Andante, and Allegro—it brings classical nuance and expressive motion to a high-contrast serif family. Rooted in personal history and shaped by reverence for typographic tradition, it's both redemption and reinvention.

Overture

positype.com

Designed by *Neil Summerour*
Published by *Positype*

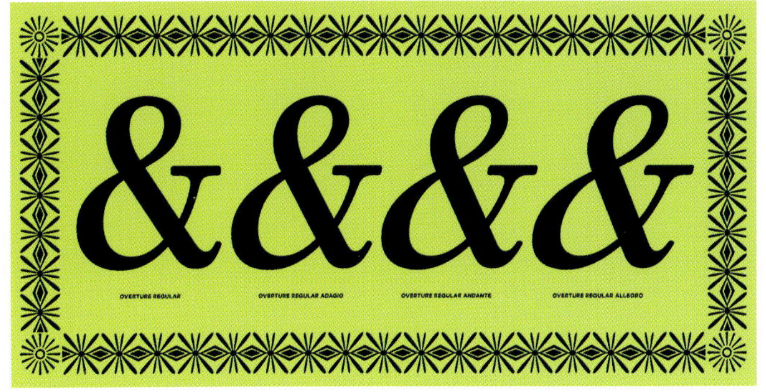

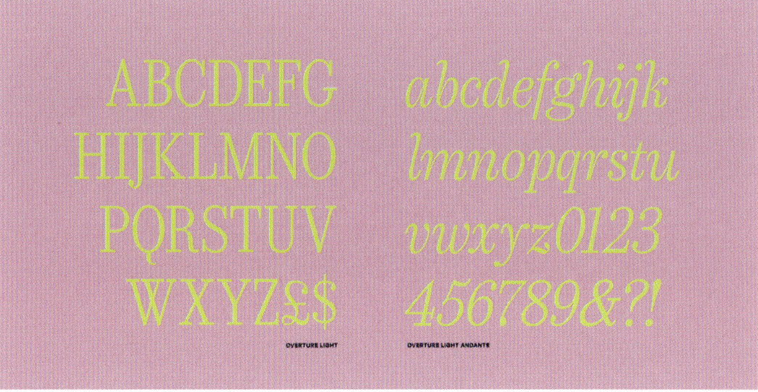

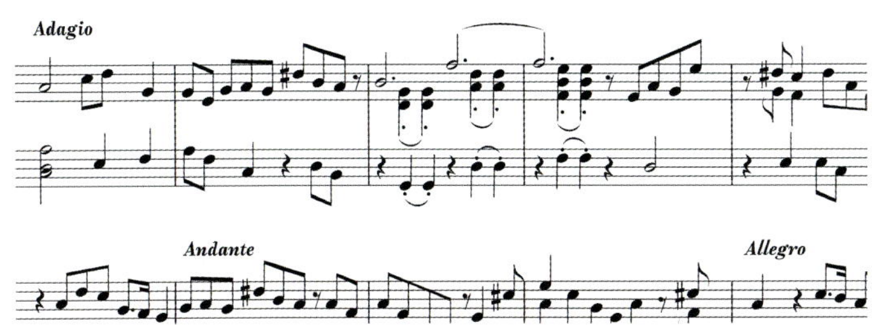

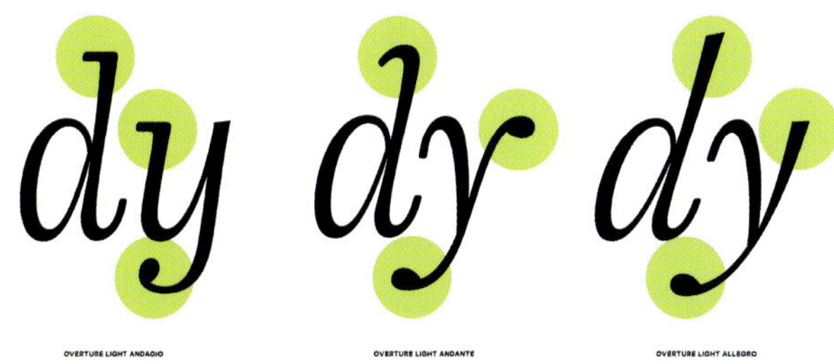

SARTORIALISM

OVERTURE FINE LIGHT SMALL CAPS

Haberdashery

OVERTURE FINE LIGHT ANDANTE

SPREZZATURA

OVERTURE FINE LIGHT

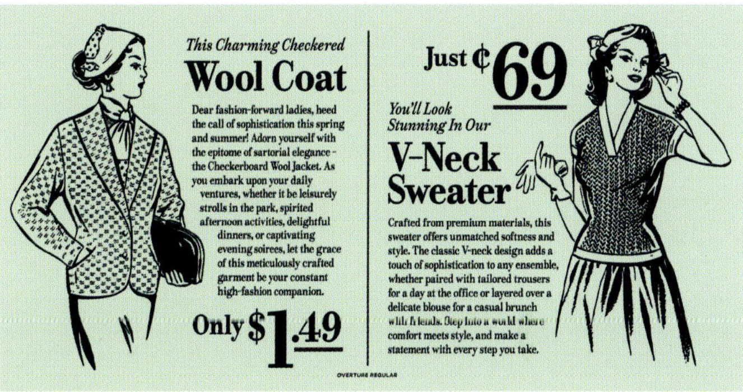

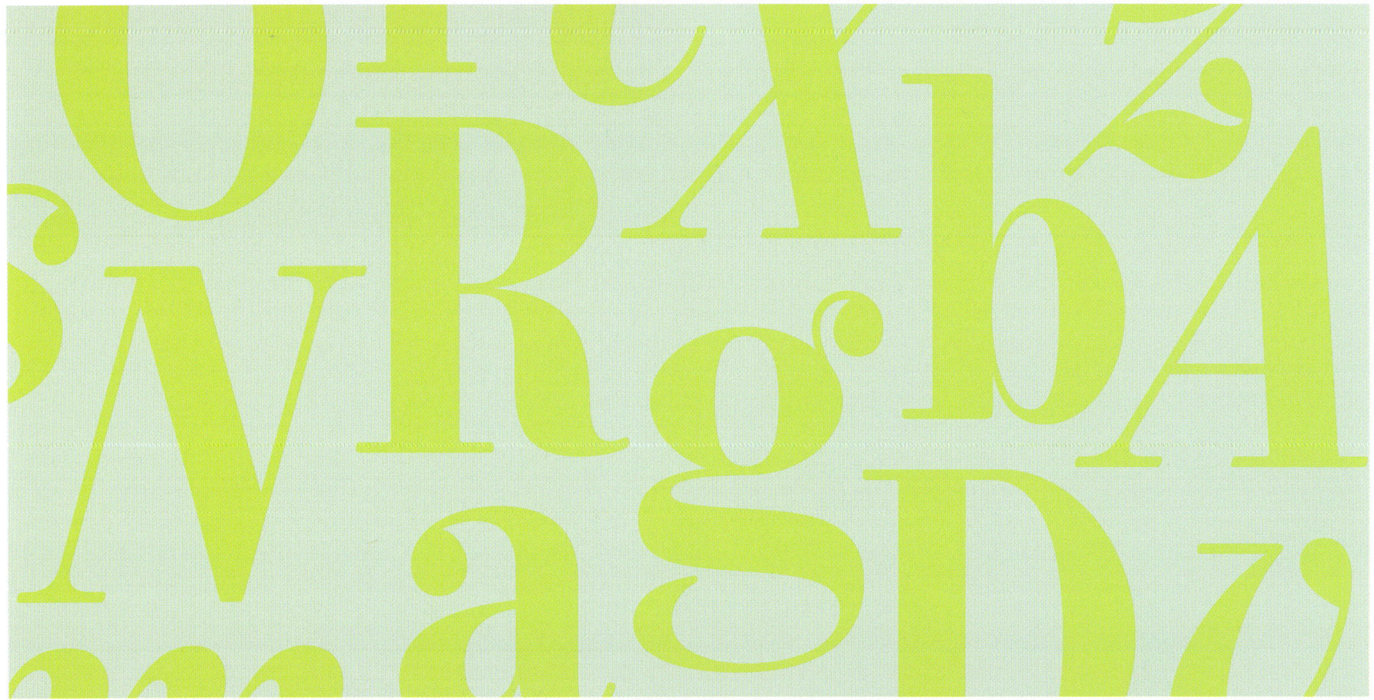

MAGNIFICENCE
HELIOTROPISM
QUARTERFINAL
PROBLEMAKER
KENOPHOBIAS
POSTMODERN

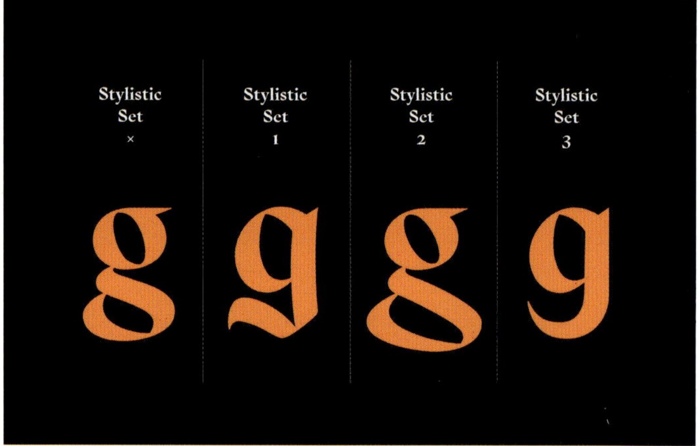

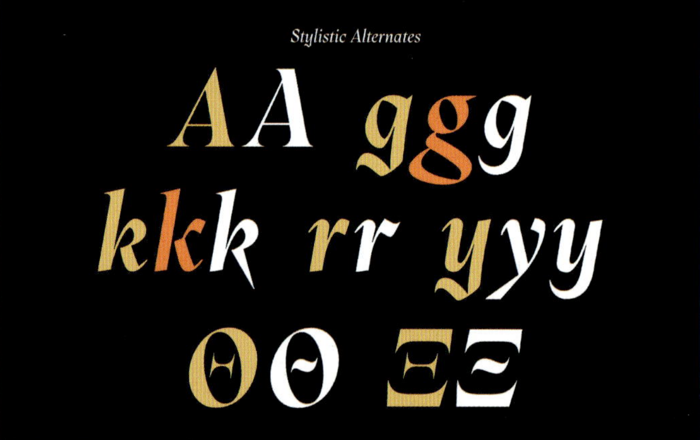

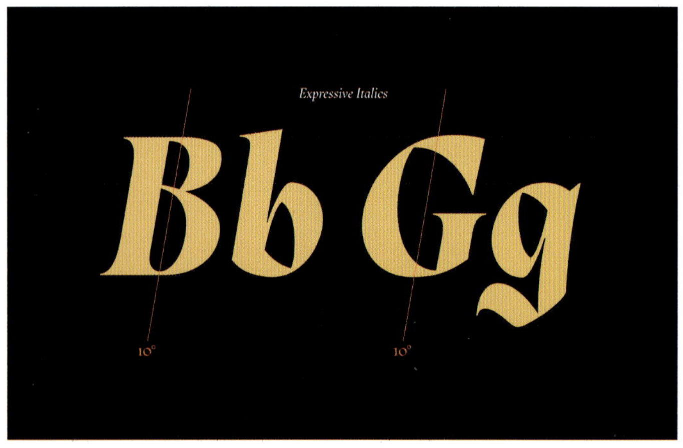

Ξηρολιθοδομή Γεωδιαμόρφωση
Αλατωρυχείον Καμηλοπάρδαλη
Μενεξεδένιος Θηριοδαμαστής
Ηδονοθηρικά Αστεροσκοπείο
Εσωστρέφεια Λαθρεπιβάτιδα
Κυματοειδής Διαγαλαξιακός

PF Grecia seamlessly combines the sharpness of blackletter with roman elegance, creating a truly distinctive serif typeface. Inspired by Darley, the 1930s typeface designed by National Geographic *cartographer Charles E. Riddiford, it offers variable flexibility across Text and Display styles, with extravagant details that stand out in larger sizes and heavier weights.*

PF Grecia

parachutefonts.com

Designed by *Panos Vassiliou*
Published by *Parachute*

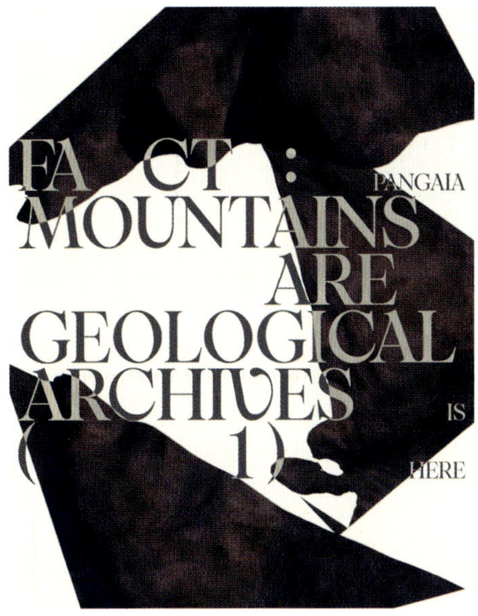

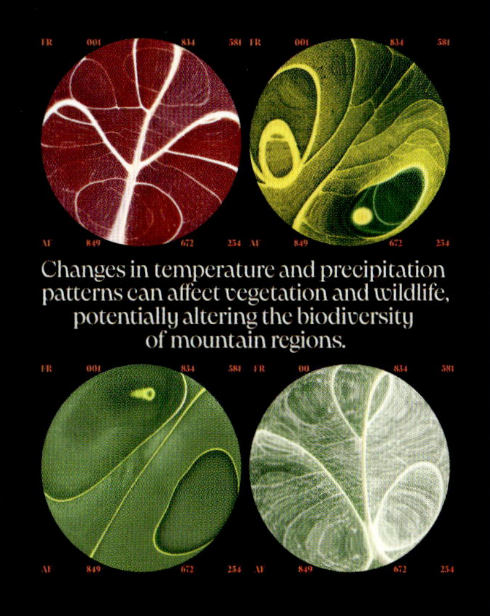

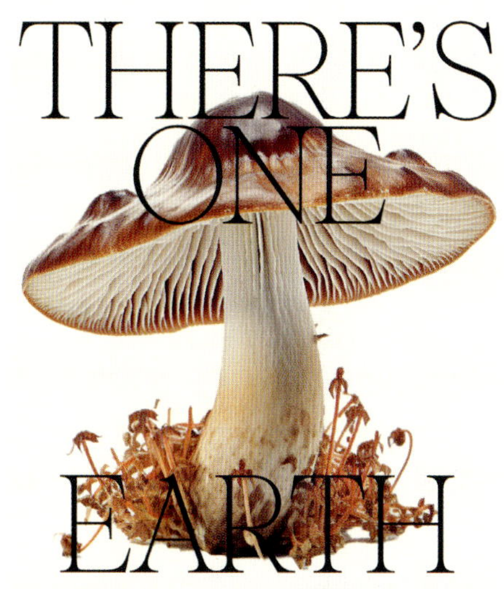

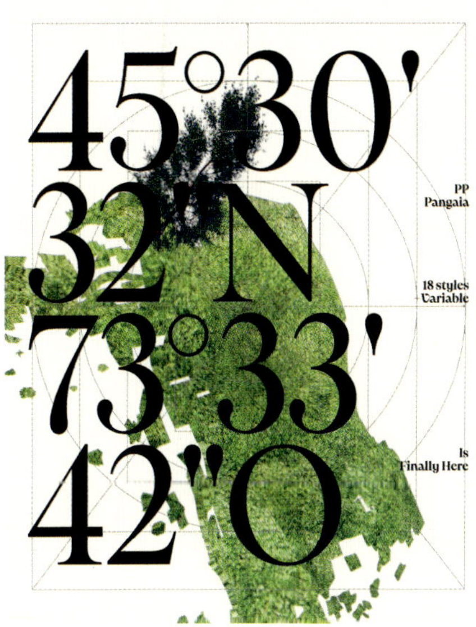

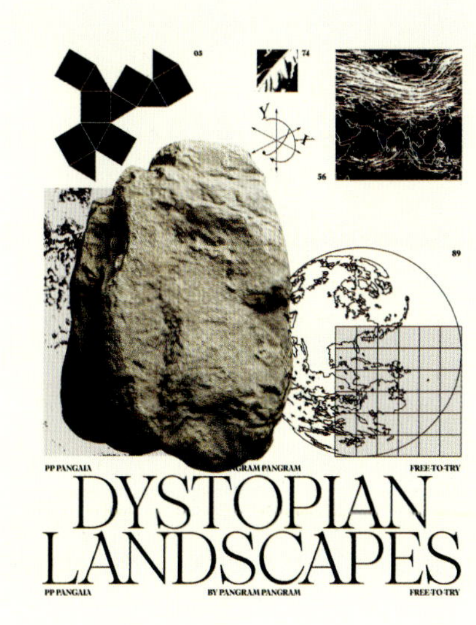

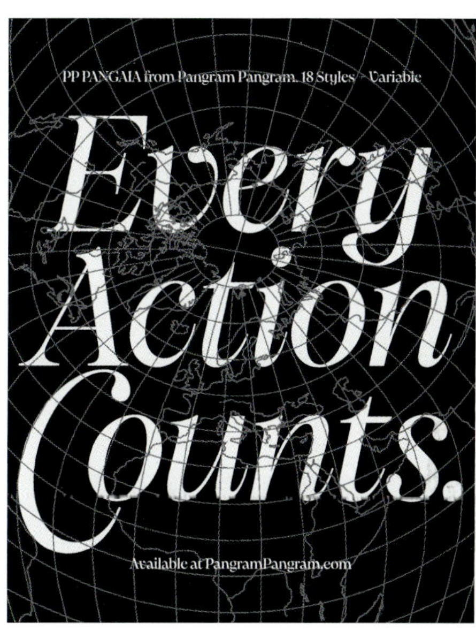

Pangaia is a typeface seamlessly blending the splendor of traditional serif fonts with the rough, raw, organic beauty of Mother Nature. Pangaia inhabits and enlivens our unity with the Earth, both celebrating and making aware of the delicate balance shared between us and the wider world, from its plunging, striking swashes to its powerful italic cuts across eighteen total styles. No matter the application, be it brand, book, and anything in between, Pangaia is more than just a typeface. Pangaia is a proud, earnest embodiment of nature's uncorrupted grandeur—offering a sense of connection and respect for our planet through each and every structural form.

pangrampangram.com

Pangaia

Designed by *Samuel Salminen, Mat Desjardins, Francesca Bolognini*
Published by *Pangram Pangram*

SILVERSTAG TYPE FOUNDRY

EDITORIAL SERIF FONT

INTRODUCING
A BRAND NEW SERIF TYPEFACE

the Silver
EDITORIAL

A MULTILINGUAL EDITORIAL SERIF FONT
BY SILVERSTAG FONT FOUNDRY

ELEGANT & CHIC
REGULAR & ITALIC SERIF

MULTILANGUAGE
EDITORIAL TYPEFACE

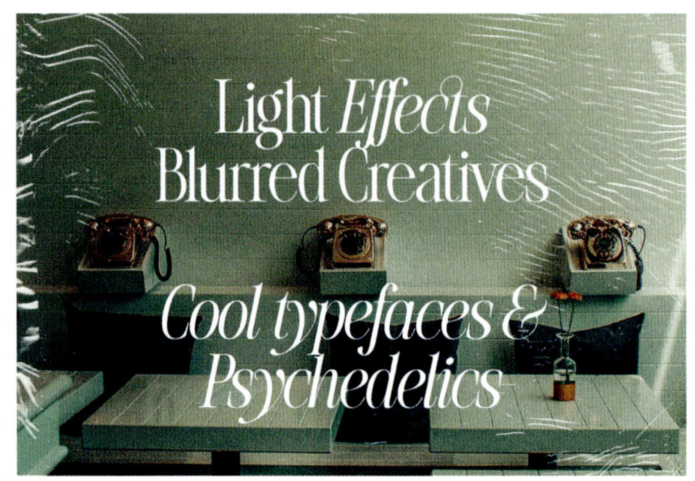

SILVERSTAG TYPE FOUNDRY

EDITORIAL SERIF FONT

"Believe you can, and you're halfway there."

THEODORE ROOSEVELT

ELEGANT & CHIC
REGULAR & ITALIC SERIF

MULTILANGUAGE
EDITORIAL TYPEFACE

Remember the bold, expressive serifs that graced the pages of high-fashion magazines and cutting-edge publications in the '80s? The Silver Editorial channels that vintage charm while pushing the boundaries of contemporary design.

The Silver Editorial

silverstag.design

Designed by *Alen Kapetanovic*
Published by *SilverStag Type Foundry*

FLOW

A Journey Below the Surface THE SPECIAL EDITION

DELLE MEANDRI FLUVIALI, LANCHE & CANALI INTRECCIATI

THE UPSTREAM!

“Ríos desempeñan un papel clave en el ciclo del agua.”

¶ La Merwede [1] (1500 m³/s & max. NAP [2] de –7 m à –3.6 m) [3] est une rivière néerlandaise faisant partie du delta de la *Meuse* et du Rhin. Il s’agit du COURS INFÉRIEUR du Waal. [4]

The flow of a STREAM is controlled by three inputs; surface runoff (from precipitation or *meltwater*), daylighted subterranean water, and surfaced groundwater (spring water). The *surface and subterranean water* are highly variable between periods of RAINFALL. Groundwater, on the other hand, has a constant input and is also *controlled by long-term precipitation patterns*.

Eaux de Surface

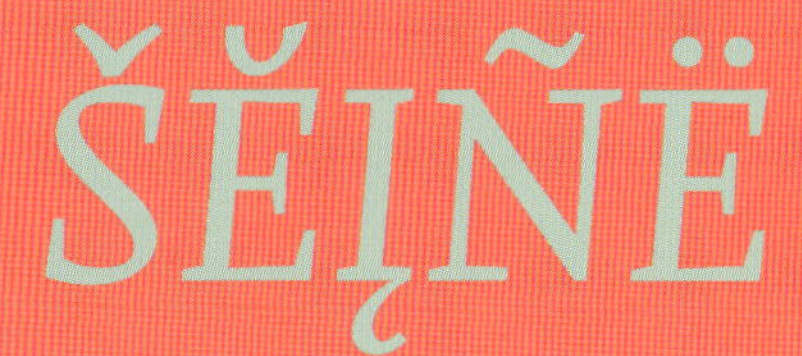

1.243.892.076,85 km³

THE #125 *WILDEST RIVERS* @STROOMRICHTINGEN[34]

Donau

§1.4 ***Vltava*** (německy **MOLDAU**) je s délkou 430,2 km nejdelší řekou na území Česka (Německo: *0,43%*). →

By definition, a TIDAL RIVER will be affected[2] by tides, surges, and *sea level variation*. This section[3] of river can be known as a *“tidal freshwater river”* or *“river reach”*. In terms of tides, tidal rivers are classified as *microtidal* (<2 m), *mesotidal* (2–4 m), *and macrotidal* (>4 m). The *higher tides* could be noticed as far as 100 kilometres (*62 mi*) upstream. The areas of *tidal rivers* can be difficult to define, as the term tidal river generally encompasses *the area upriver* of the maximum limit of salinity intrusion and downriver of tidal water level *fluctuations*. This classification is based on both tidal trends and salinity. — *wikipedia.com*

ÜÇ ANA YÜZEY SUYU TÜRÜ VARDIR.

Macroinvertebrates, Macrophytes & Fish

↗ Ein Märchen aus alten Zeiten, das kommt mir nicht aus dem Sinn.[78] Die Luft ist kühl und es dunkelt, und ruhig fließt der Rhein. Der Gipfel des Berges funkelt im Abendsonnenschein. [*HEINRICH HEINE, 1824, P. 90*]

THE LIFE AQUATIC

»Gamle Kongeåen«

Realtime Water Levels Rivieren in Nederland

RIVIER	VERWACHT	ASTRONOMISCH
Beneden Merwede	101 cm	94 cm
Afgedamde Maas	97 cm	86 cm
Bijlands Kanaal	79 cm	77 cm

{THE TIME HAS COME TO SHINE, LIKE A BRIDGE OVER TROUBLED WATER © NYC IN 1970}

† De **Merwede** is een getijrivier in de *Nederlandse* provincies *Zuid-Holland* en *Noord-Brabant*. Van 1273 tot 1904 was de rivier de BELANGRIJKSTE BENEDENLOOP van rivier de Maas (bron 1).*

¶ Die **Merwede** (manchmal auch *Mervede*) ist der heutige Unterlauf der Waal, des südlichen Rheinarms im Rhein-Maas-Delta in den Niederlanden. Der Fluss bildet die Grenze der Provinzen Zuid-Holland und Noord-Brabant.

¶ At first, a disconnected branch of the **Meuse** joins the Waal at Woudrichem to form the Boven Merwede (*Upper Merwede*). A few kilometers downstream it splits into the Beneden Merwede (*Lower Merwede*) and the Nieuwe Merwede (*New Merwede*).

¶ **Novi Merwede** se združi z BERGSE MAAS blizu Lage Zwaluwe, in tvori estuar Holandskega Diepa, ter ločuje otok Dordrecht od narodnega parka Biesbosch. Spodnji Merwede se pri Papendrechtu razcepi na reko Noord in STARI MAAS.

¶ Tanto el **Merwede** actual como todos sus tramos más bajos (ahora llamados río NOORD, OUDE MAAS y NIEUWE MAAS) ahora son alimentados casi exclusivamente por el Rin, mientras que en el Mosa se ha construido una desembocadura artificial, Bergse Maas, y los dos ríos.

¶ La Merwede commence près du château de Loevestein (à l’est de Woudrichem), à l’ancien confluent du Waal et de la Meuse. La frontière historique entre les comtés de Hollande et du Gueldre se trouve à cet endroit. De nos jours, la première partie de la Merwede, la Merwede supérieure ou Boven-Merwede, forme la frontière entre les provinces du Brabant-Septentrional

The names of s
stretches of the
RIVERS were th
changed to refle
FOR EXAMPLE t
Oude Maas an
Nieuwe Maas.

Actuele Waterhoogte
Beneden Merwege

DORDRECHT

GRAFIEK

DATUM	TIJD	VERWACHT	ASTRONOMISCH
17–10–2024	02:30	101 cm	94 cm
17–10–2024	02:00	97 cm	86 cm
17–10–2024	01:30	79 cm	77 cm
17–10–2024	01:00	61 cm	59 cm
17–10–2024	00:30	37 cm	38 cm
17–10–2024	00:00	24 cm	32 cm
16–10–2024	23:30	13 cm	28 cm
16–10–2024	23:00	4 cm	24 cm
16–10–2024	22:30	–1 cm	22 cm
16–10–2024	22:00	–5 cm	20 cm
16–10–2024	21:30	–8 cm	19 cm
←→ 16–10–2024	21:00	–9 cm	17 cm

Merwede is an extensive text typeface with a pleasant rhythm that allows readers to effortlessly immerse themselves in any given text. References and inspiration were early Renaissance typefaces, and the work of typographers and type designers such as Pierre Simon Fournier, Eric Gill, Jan van Krimpen, Helmut Salden, and Martin Majoor, without following any particular model.

boldmonday.com

Merwede

Designed by *Titus Schulz*
Published by *Bold Monday*

Modern
Neoclassical
Scotch

g

Take Only
what is in
Box 2

Montris is a refined, digitally authentic neoclassical typeface, balancing Modern and Scotch Roman styles. Designed for books and magazines, it includes three optical sizes: S for body text, M for medium headlines, and L for large titles.

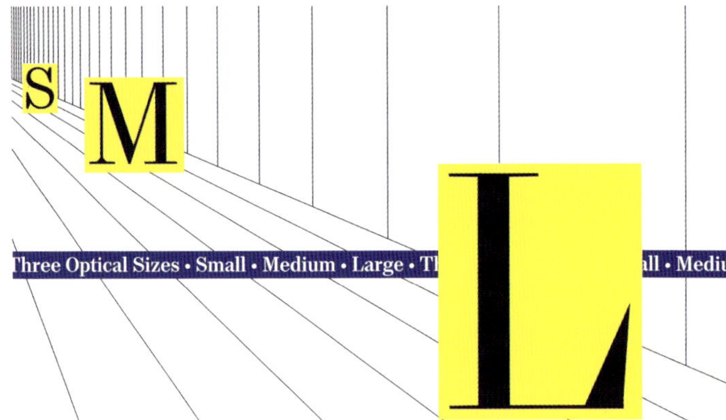

Neue
Sachlichkeit

Montris

r-typography.com

Designed by *Rui Abreu*
Published by *R-Typography*

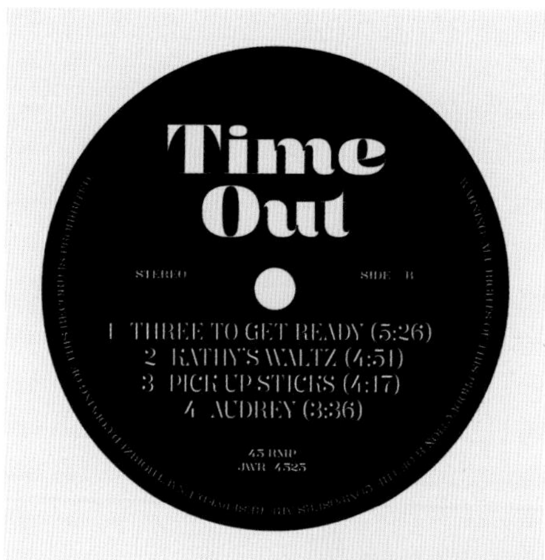

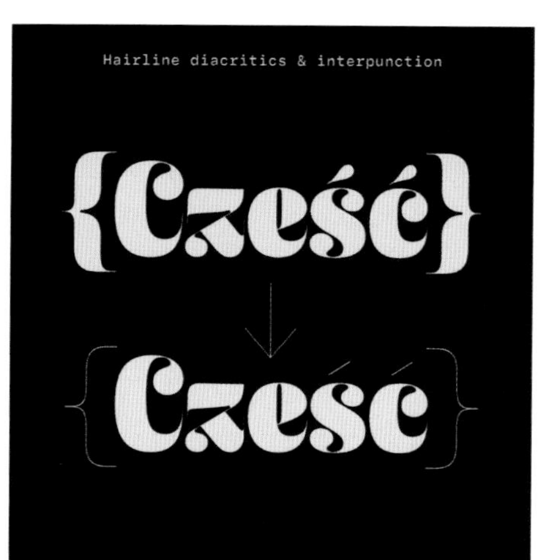

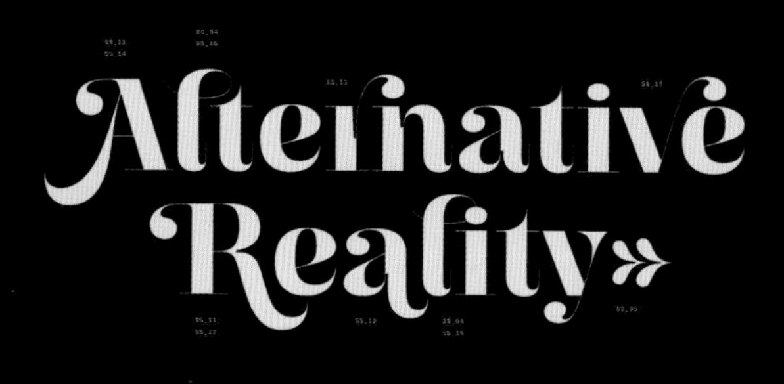

Butik is a buoyant Didonesque display typeface with a full palette of weights and widths and an ensemble of lively alternates, swashes, and expressive ball terminals.

rosettatype.com

Butik

Designed by *Anna Štěpanovská*
Published by *Rosetta*

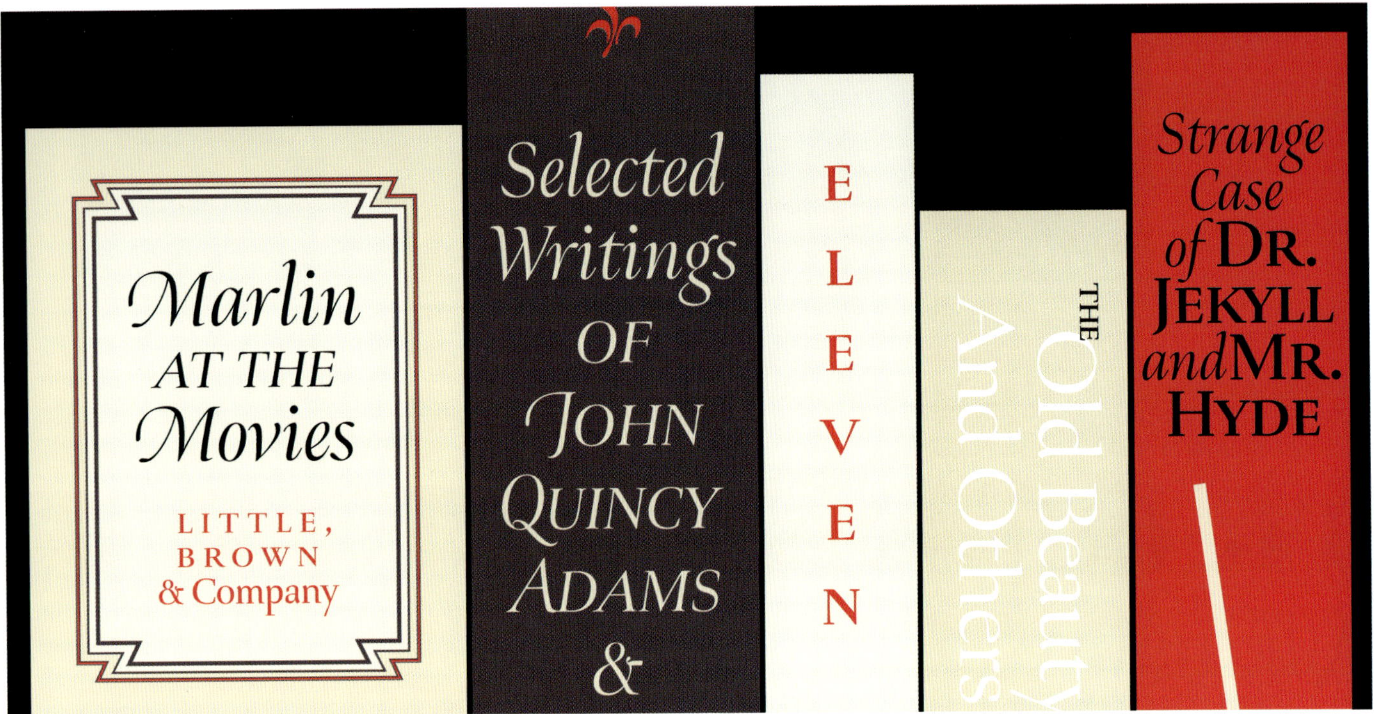

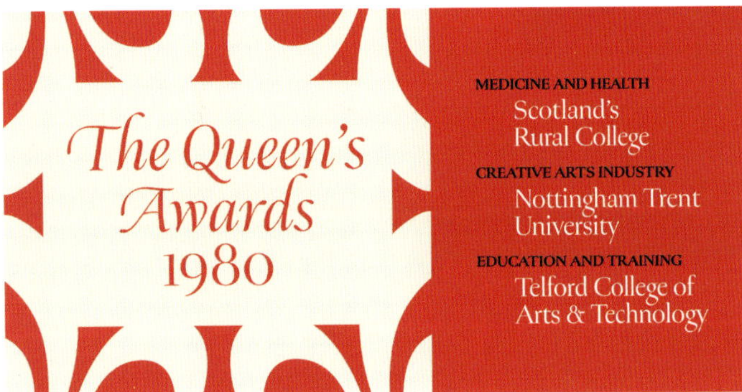

38 · THE CHRONICLES OF THE OLD MOAT HOUSE ·

Yet his tastes were singular, and not usually such as obtained sympathy from the Squire, though Mr. Elliot Herbert's report of him as a student was thoroughly satisfactory. He would spend hours watching the clouds; would steal among the cattle, and coax them into picturesque groups; tether a sheep or a goat, and take its naked portrait; study every variety of foliage that adorned the changing seasons; and within the cover of his little despised portfolio, treasured art-secrets that should be revealed some future

Ellery is an elegant display typeface inspired by Oscar Ogg's calligraphed book jackets from the 1940s for Atlantic/Little-Brown & Company. This delicate and warm family has a suggested size range of 14 point and higher. The flowing italic pairs well with the roman, yet is also truly expressive on its own in large display settings. Richard Lipton's Ellery is ideal for any typography needing distinction and grace. Available in Regular, Medium, Bold, and Extra Bold, with italics, or as variable fonts.

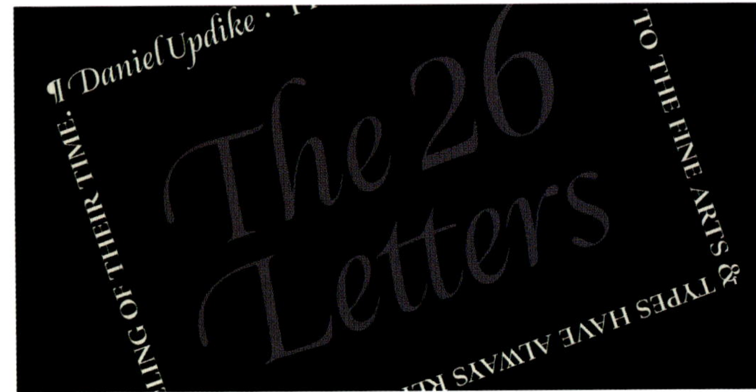

Ellery

liptonletterdesign.com

Designed by *Richard Lipton*
Published by *Lipton Letter Design*

DREAM OF THE RAREBIT FIEND

4TH OF JULY

YPSILANTI

“INVENTOR OF ANIMATED DRAWING”

WILLIAM RANDOLPH HEARST

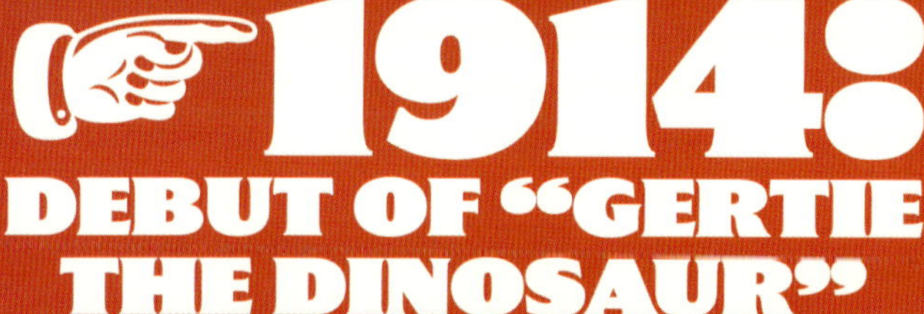

HE JUST SIMPLY COULDN’T STOP IT

LITTLE SAMMY SNEEZE

HE NEVER KNEW WHEN IT WAS COMING

FLO & EDDIE

Gertie was inspired by the lettering of comic artist and animation pioneer Winsor McCay—specifically the title lettering in his Little Nemo *comic strip, which ran in Sunday newspapers from 1905 to 1927. The name comes from his 1914 animated short, "Gertie the Dinosaur." Gertie (the typeface) is an ultra-bold all-caps spur-serif design for display use with an early twentieth-century feel, and includes a set of matching dingbats.*

---

marksimonson.com

Gertie

Designed by *Mark Simonson*
Published by *Mark Simonson Studio*

What Are Serifs For?
An Essay by Ellen Lupton

How did serifs come to be? Are they essential bits or quirky historical leftovers? Basic type courses teach us to divide the world of Latin typefaces between "serif" and "sans." Designers grow up accepting this binary distinction as fact. But where do serifs come from? Why do they still exist? What function do they serve?

Serifs are a Roman thing. When the ancient Romans started writing their alphabet with squared-off reed pens on leaves, linen, or papyrus, they used small gestures to begin and finish their strokes. These gestures got the ink flowing at the top of the stroke and stopped it from blobbing up the bottom. Today, we call these marks serifs, and the Romans were the first to make them. Greek, Phoenician, and Egyptian scribes, who wrote their monoline characters with a blunt stylus, didn't bother.

As the Romans built towns, cities, and a vast empire, they used big letters to mark their territory.

They painted signs on the walls of Pompeii (buried in 79 BCE), and they carved inscriptions on monuments of war and conquest, such as Trajan's Column (113 BCE). Large-scale letters acquired new terminating strokes—refined, delicate, and suited to the anatomy of each character. Roman conquerors spread carved capitals wherever they went, from Britannia to Mesopotamia. Marching across the empire, Roman capitals established the supremacy of the Latin writing system. For over two thousand years, Trajan's letters have been touchpoints for countless typefaces and lettering designs.

The definitive work on this subject is *The Origin of the Serif,* published in 1968 by Father Edward Catich. I have long heard about Catich's lifelong study of Trajan's Column. Like many typographic pilgrims, he journeyed to the Roman Forum to measure, trace, and revere those iconic letterforms. Students and designers who couldn't get to Rome could visit a plaster cast in London's Victoria and Albert Museum, seeking solace and certainty in these canonical models of the Latin alphabet.

I recently purchased a 1985 reprint of Catich's legendary book. This big, creamy volume is over three hundred pages long. I knew the book would be impressive, but I didn't expect it to be mesmerizing. Combining hands-on scholarship with gorgeous diagrams and cheeky class warfare, Catich thumbs his nose at the standard wisdom of how Trajan's serifs came to be.

Although it is not a type specimen per se, this glorious compendium celebrates the life of letters through extraordinary drawings, including large-scale capitals standing over 4½ inches (11 cm) tall. Before Catich, typographic experts believed that the serifs inscribed on Trajan's Column resulted from the stone-carving process. According to this theory, chiseled serifs helped carvers end their letters with clean and decisive strokes. The process of working the chisel determined the shape of serifs. Experts repeated the chisel theory again and again. True believers included Eric Gill, an outstanding stone carver and devoted fan of Trajan's Column, and Frederic Goudy, who designed his own homage to Trajan in 1930.

Catich rebelled against history and told a different story. Sign painting, not carving, is the model for Imperial capitals. It all comes down to how the body moves. A deftly handled square brush loaded with liquid paint produces the distinctive brackets, curves, and dents of Trajan's serifs—and yields the subtle curves that modulate the seemingly straight lines in letters such as V and M. All the stone carver had to do was capture the push and pull of the brush with his slow-going chisel.

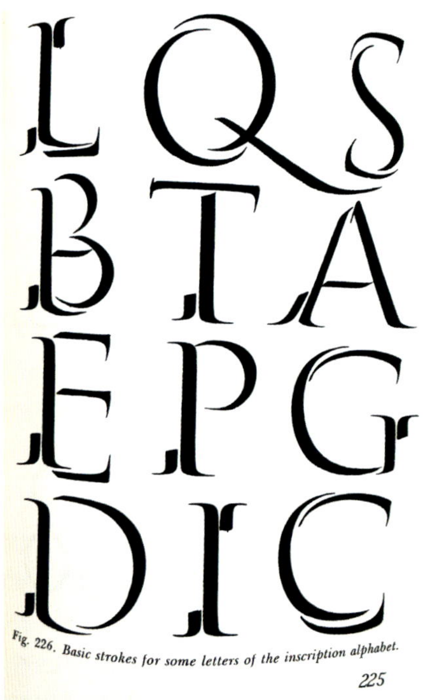

↑ Basic brushstrokes

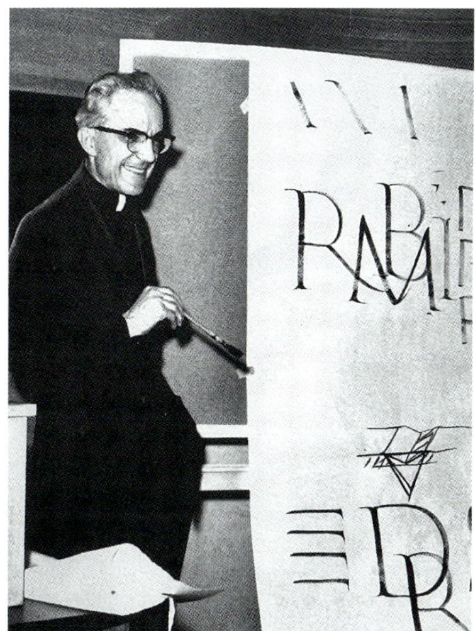

↑ *Father Edward Catich making Imperial capitals at the Rockefeller Institute, New York City, 1960*

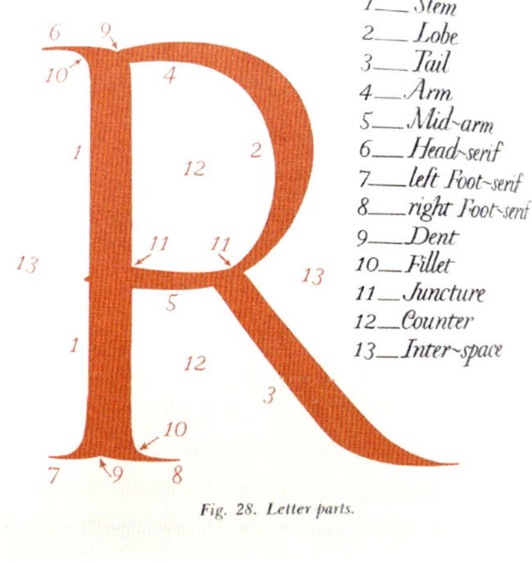

↑ *Letter parts*

Sources: *Beier, Sofie.* Reading Letters: Designing for Legibility *(BIS Publishers, 2012)* ◆ *Bigelow, Charles.* "Typeface features and legibility research" *(Vision Research 165, 2019)* ◆ *Catich, Edward M.* The Origin of the Serif: Brush Writing & Roman Letters, Second Edition *(Catich Gallery, St. Ambrose University, 1985)* ◆ *Coles, Stephen.* "Chocolate Chunk Serifs: Stephen Coles's List" *(luc.devroye.org/fonts-55911.html)* ◆ *Kelly, Rob Roy.* American Wood Type, 1828-1900 : Notes on the Evolution of Decorated and Large Types and Comments on Related Trades of the Period *(Van Nostrand Reinhold Co., 1969)* ◆ *Lund, Ole.* "Why Serifs Are (Still) Important" *(Typography Papers 2, 1997)* ◆ *Shaw, Paul.* The Eternal Letter: Two Millennia of the Classical Roman Capital *(The MIT Press, 2015)*

Catich, born in 1906, lost his parents as a young boy. He grew up in an Illinois orphanage, where he worked as a sign painter's apprentice. As a young man, he became a union sign writer and attended the School of the Art Institute of Chicago. He spent four years in Rome (1935–1939) studying to become a Catholic priest while exploring Roman capitals. To improve his calligraphy, he befriended William A. Dwiggins as a mentor in the 1940s and '50s. Catich returned many times to Rome to see and touch Trajan's Column. This lover of letterforms came to know in his bones—from scholarly research and tactile experience—that sign writing was the guiding spirit of those canonical letters. Catich, who died in 1979, changed the way type designers think about carved inscriptions in general (and serifs in particular). He argued that Trajan's capitals were made in three stages.

First, they were painted on stone. Next, they were carved. Finally, the incised letters were filled in with paint (usually orange red) to make them more visible. (The sign painter strikes twice.)

Since the Renaissance, artists and archaeologists believed that classical buildings and sculptures were stark white, but modern research proved they were polychrome instead—including the carved inscriptions. The monochrome myth of antiquity, by idolizing light, shadow, and naked stone, helped carve the chisel theory into stone.

Revived in the Renaissance, classical letterforms became the basis of Roman typefaces. Nicolas Jenson emulated Roman forms in his fifteenth-century typefaces. Jenson's serifs took their cues from the broad-nibbed pen. Later, the serifs of Caslon, Baskerville, and Bodoni drew inspiration from the delicate work of copperplate engraving and the improved ability of ink, paper, and presses to hold fine details. When eye-catching advertising fonts exploded in the nineteenth century, serifs abandoned calligraphic references and became creatures of the mind, unleashing the serif. Wood type letters featured wedge serifs, slab serifs, and serifs adorned with lavish bumps, bulges, curves, and curlicues.

Now that serifs were free to be anything, they were also free to disappear. Early sans serif typefaces were called grotesque because they seemed rather ugly, cut loose from any ties to Roman glory. By the early twentieth century, having a serif or not became a marker of a Latin typeface's basic identity, much like race had joined gender as a binary marker of human identity.

A person was White, or they weren't. A person was a man, or they weren't. A Latin typeface had serifs, or it didn't. In the 1920s, Jan Tschichold proclaimed serifs obsolete. In the 1930s, Beatrice Warde defended them as protectors of readability. Her classic essay "The Crystal Goblet" condemned sans serif fonts as merely "legible" (easily discerned by the eye), while promoting serif typefaces as bastions of readability (supporting comfort and comprehension).

Today, typefaces can have serifs, no serifs, or something in between. Yet the binary category of serif / sans has lasting currency. Nearly every client knows about the "little feet" on letters, even if they know nothing else about fonts. Furthermore, many clients think they know which one is more functional. Sofie Beier's work on legibility explores the many interlocking factors that contribute to reading, from the features of letterforms (weight, width, contrast, size, x-height, serifs, and so on) to aspects of layout (line length, line spacing, background contrast, and more). Charles Bigelow has surveyed the scientific literature devoted to proving whether typefaces with or without serifs are more or less legible; most studies have "found little or no significant difference." Bigelow reminds us, however, that reader preferences and cultural norms are powerful and abundant. Centuries of habit dictate that most print books are rendered with serifs; mere decades of habit dictate that most web content is set in sans serif. Custom, not science, controls this print / web divide.

The Roman Empire rose and fell, but serifs lived on and on. One theory about the function of serifs is that they guide the horizontal movement of the eye. Research studies have failed to prove this theory, but that doesn't mean that serifs have no purpose at all. Serifs convey a link to tradition. These juicy wedges of DNA reach back to ancient Rome. They also provoke playful expression, creating opportunities for humor, charm, shock, beauty, and taste. Serifs help make a typeface warm or cool, sharp or cuddly. Stephen Coles's list of "Chocolate Chunk Serifs" includes Cooper Black, Goudy Heavyface, and Paddington—each one a recipe for delight. The histories of fashion and architecture glitter with fancy finials and decorative doodads. Shoes and furniture legs may support the body or protect the floor, but their sheer variety far exceeds the demands of function. Hairstyles and moustaches contribute to human hygiene, but—like serifs—their main purpose is announcing who we are.

Swedish Modern Set

30th ANNIVERSARY COLLECTION

AUKIO PLAZA

Berlingska Stilgjuteri, 1951

Aurore boréale

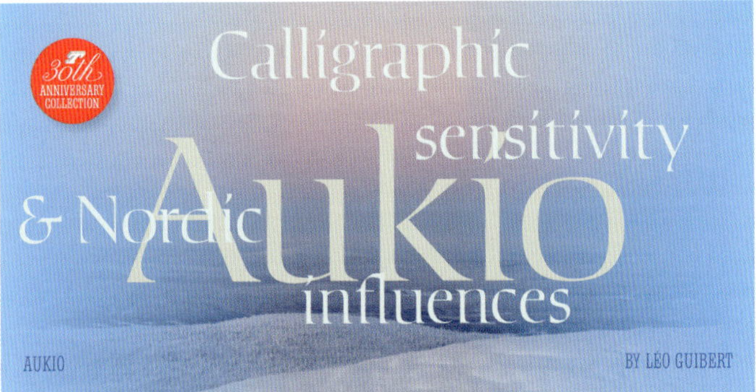

Roman Uncial
GÖTEBORG
Finnish Design
Ex Libris
NORTH POLE

a

ded to today's taste. Thus we have created it, a modern
gant typeface, both practical & robust. In recent years, a
tendency has become manifest in the decorative arts. W
simplicity of the lines has been preserved, the straightne
ding & a distinguished elegance is coming into its own a
Typography has not been neglected in these developme
which have been expressed by an obvious reversion to c
styles. However, most of the existing types were old-fash

types were old-fashioned & r
adapted to today's working
thods, owing their fragility. A
new typeface had to be foun

Aukio (meaning "square, angular" in Finnish) is a high-contrast display typeface with details inspired by the calligraphic practice of the Nordic countries. Its large, squarish structure and angular inner shapes are a direct reference to this crafty and artistic world. Its digital drawing approach combined with its high contrast give it a contemporary dimension—especially for sensitive yet striking titles.

Aukio

typofonderie.com

Designed by *Léo Guibert*
Published by *Typofonderie*

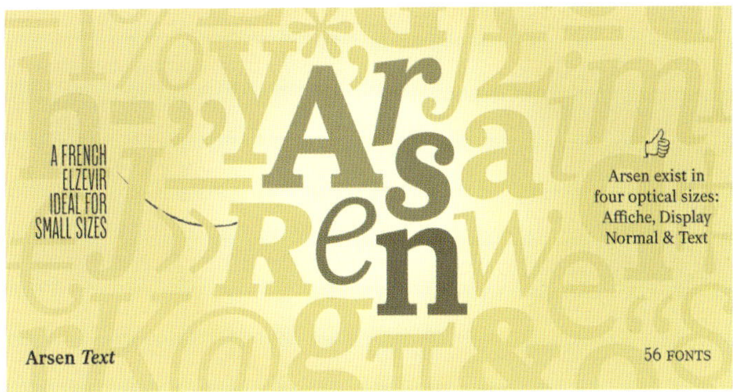

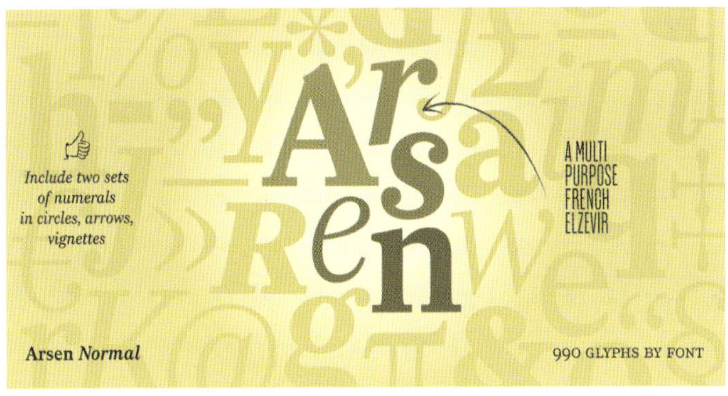

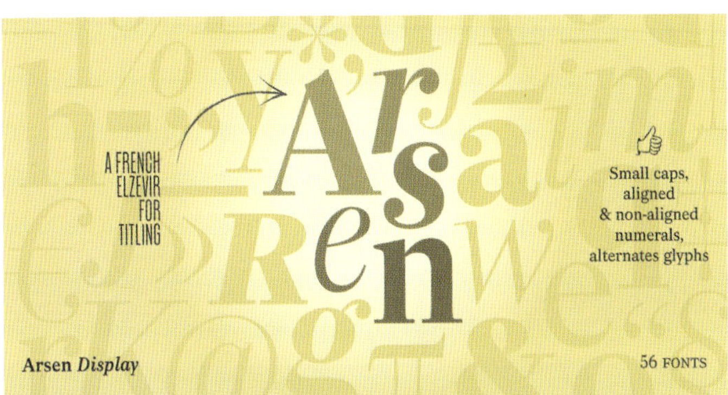

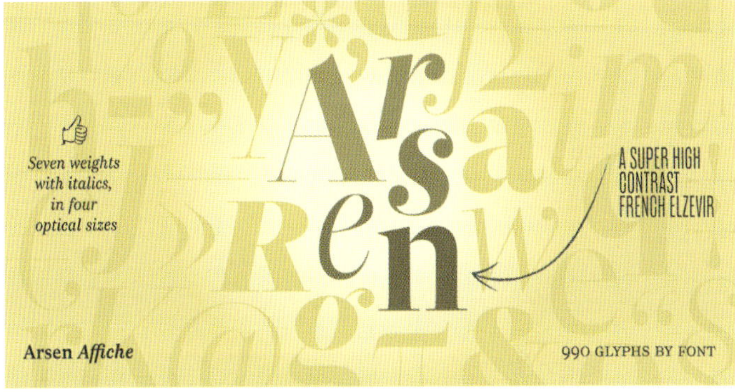

Le Bouchon de Crystal
BOULEVARD
Revue des Nouvellles Sciences Naturelles
The Market

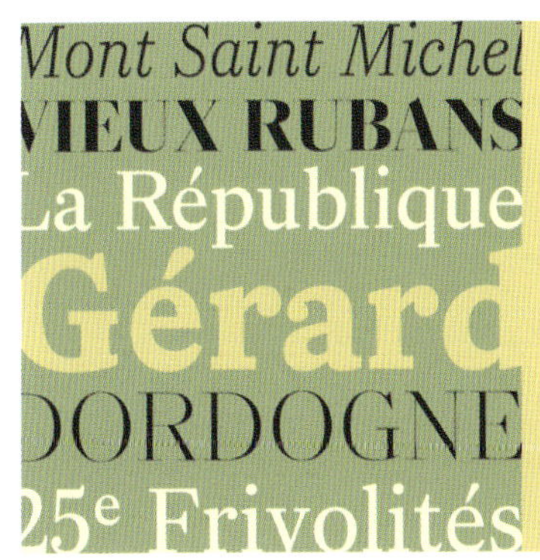

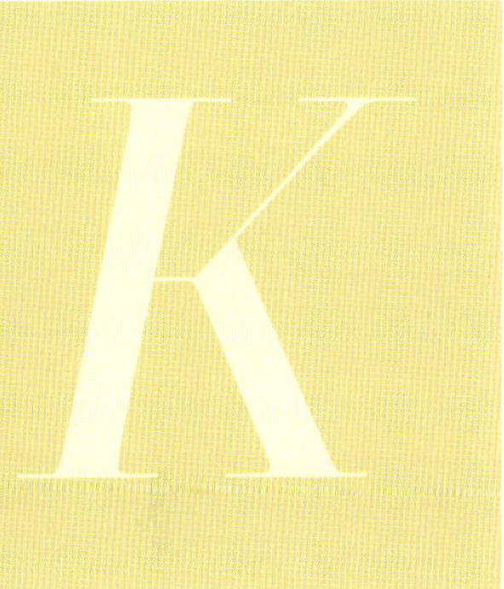

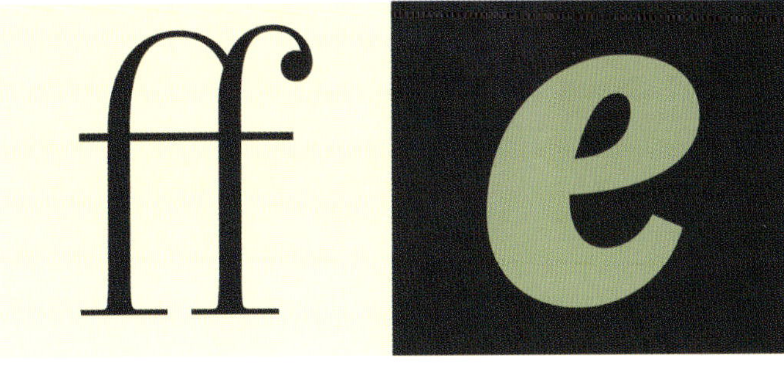

ponded to today's taste. Thus we have created it, a n & elegant typeface, both practical & robust. In recen a new tendency has become manifest in the decorat While the simplicity of the lines has been preservec straightness is yielding & a distinguished elegance i coming into its own again. Typography has not been glected in these developments, which have been exp by an obvious reversion to certain styles. However, n

Arsen is a "French Elzevir" that brings a distinctive touch to your projects while ensuring excellent readability, thanks to its four optical sizes. Arsen, influenced by typefaces from the Parisian foundry Turlot, published around 1895, is neither a Didot, nor a genre of Garamond, nor Caslon, nor Baskerville, nor even Fournier. This is why it will bring the unique style to your design that you're looking for.

typofonderie.com

Arsen

Designed by *Joachim Vu*
Published by *Typofonderie*

	Micro		Text		Display	
Light	Aa	*Aa*	Aa	*Aa*	Aa	*Aa*
Regular	Bb	*Bb*	Bb	*Bb*	Bb	*Bb*
Medium	Cc	*Cc*	Cc	*Cc*	Cc	*Cc*
Bold	**Ee**	***Ee***	**Ee**	***Ee***	**Ee**	***Ee***
Black	**Dd**	***Dd***	**Dd**	***Dd***	**Dd**	***Dd***

Variable Font
Weight & Optical Size Axes

GT Pantheon is an interpretation of historic shapes in a contemporary manner. It exhibits an expressive and dynamic character, visible in every stroke. At its core is the conception of three optically adjusted faces, each designed to best represent the same type at different sizes: Display, Text, and Micro. Within this spectrum, the family moves between elegance, sharpness, warmth, and robustness—matching expression with functionality.

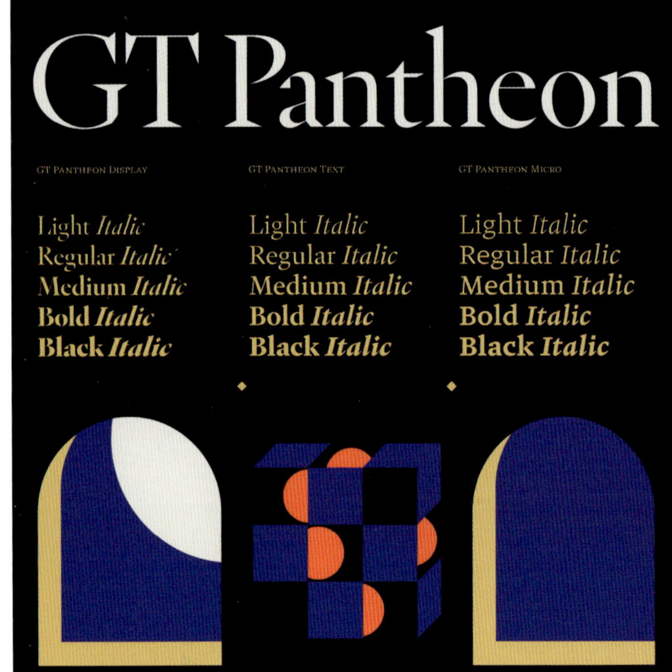

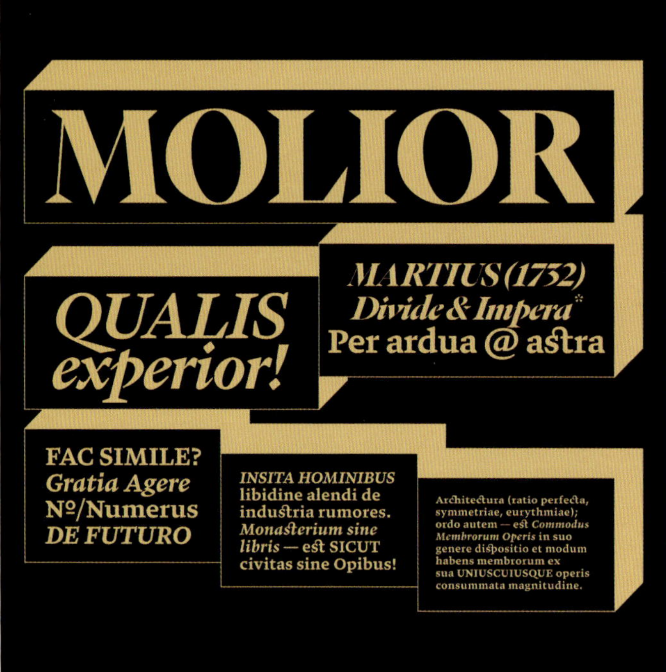

GT Pantheon

grillitype.com

Designed by *Tobias Rechsteiner, Noël Leu*
Published by *Grilli Type*

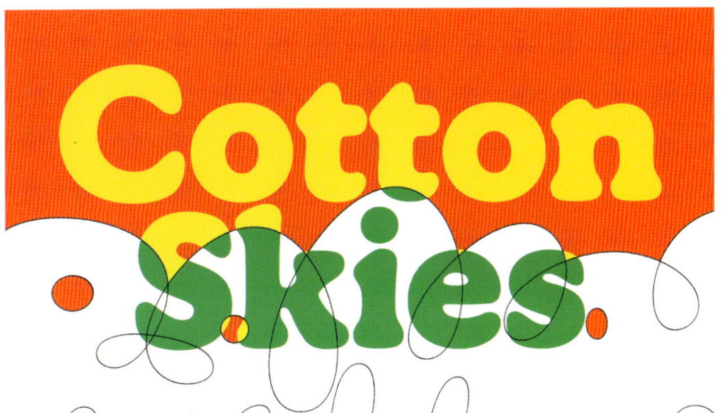

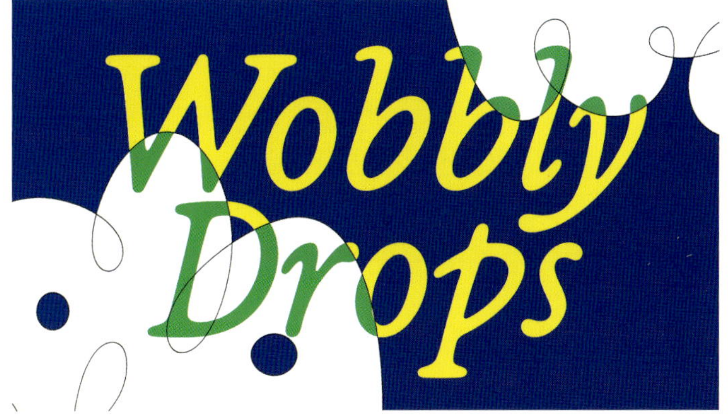

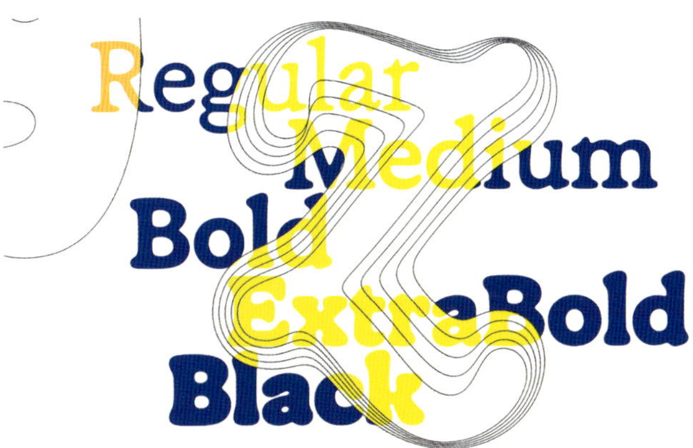

Once upon a time, in ancient Greece, deep in the woods, **Roman** there lived a young woman. Atlanta was *her name & was as swift as the wind. She grew up in* ***Italic*** *the wilderness, raised first by a kind she-bear and later by hunters…*

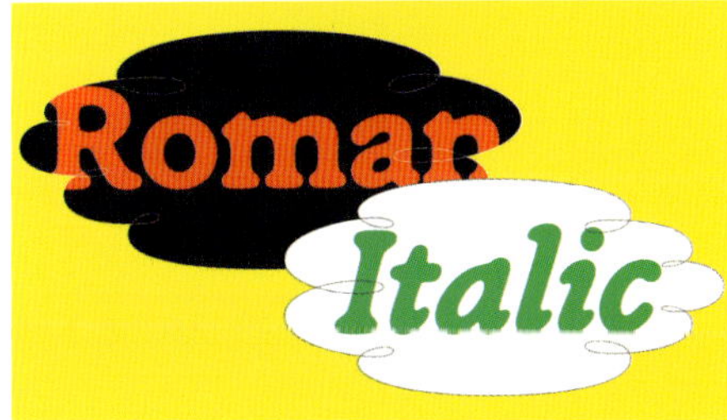

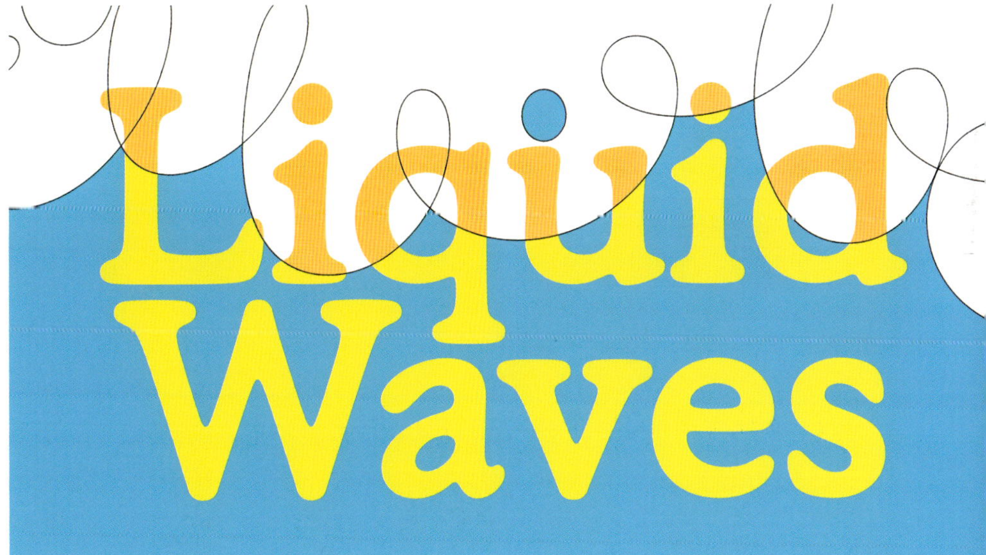

Ramboia is a playful reinterpretation of the French Old-Style tradition, crafted from loose, flowing curves, free of angles for a soft, fluid feel.

r-typography.com

Ramboia

Designed by *Rui Abreu*
Published by *R-Typography*

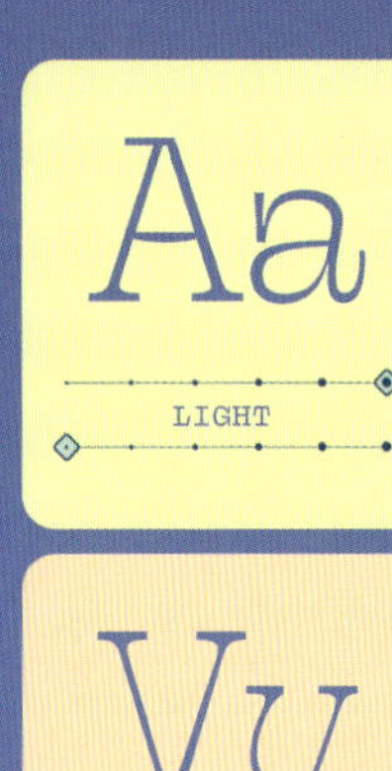

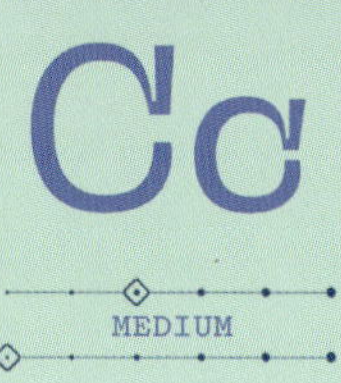

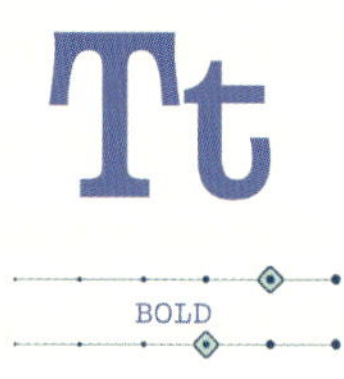

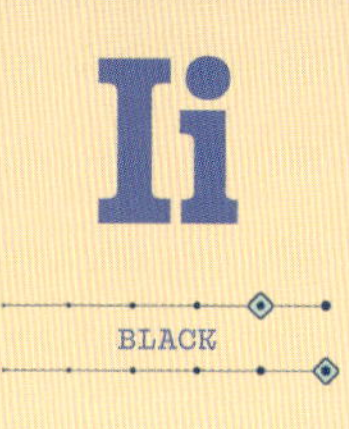

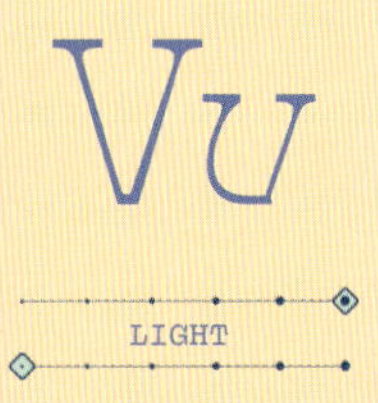

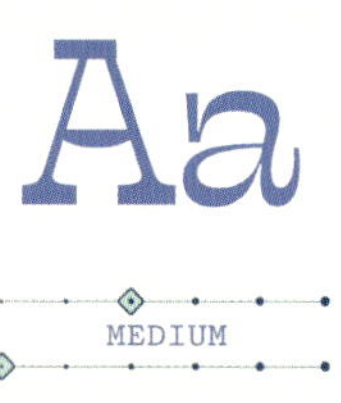

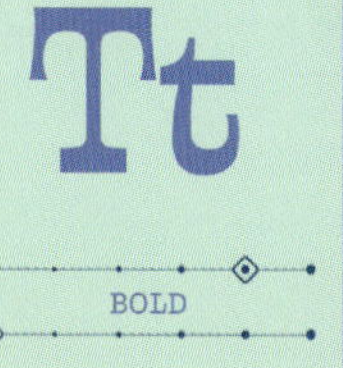

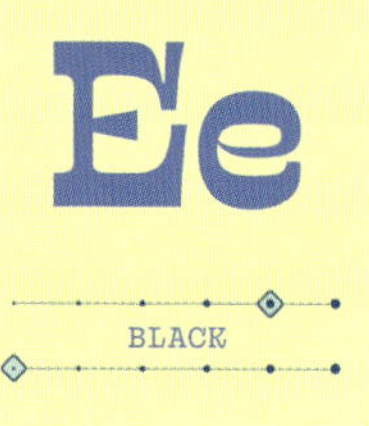

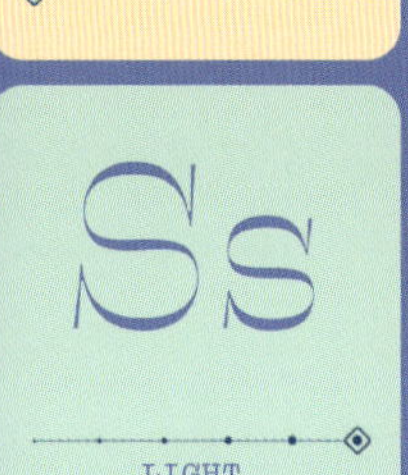

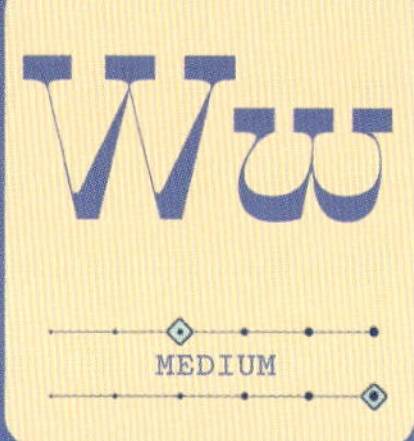

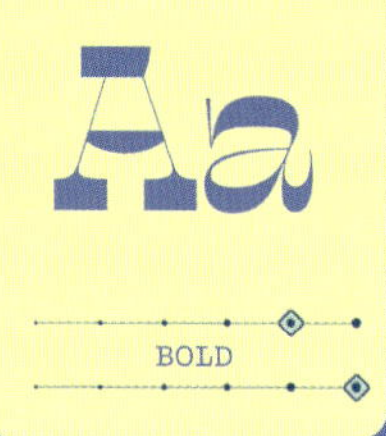

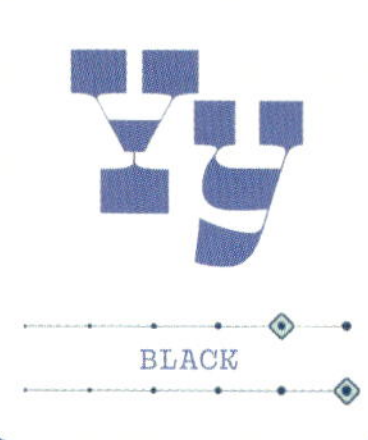

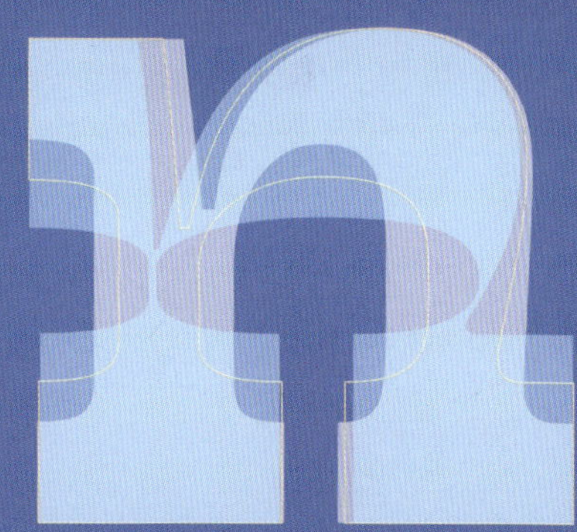
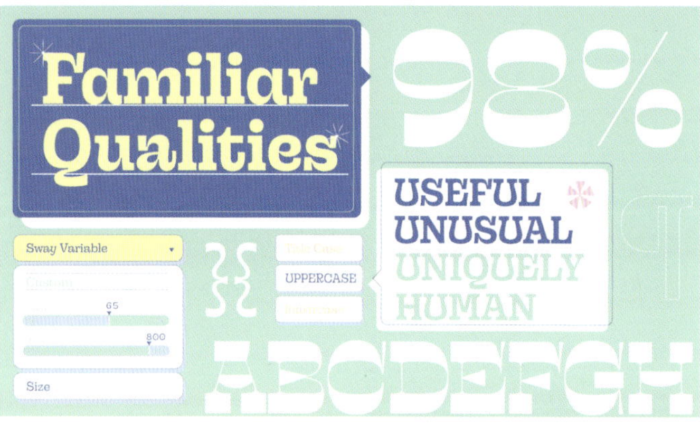

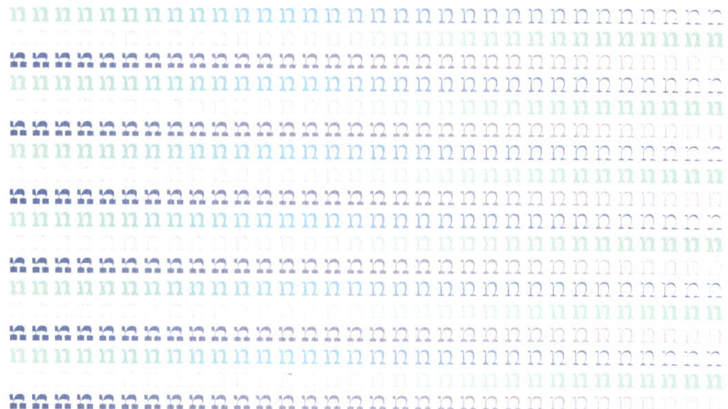
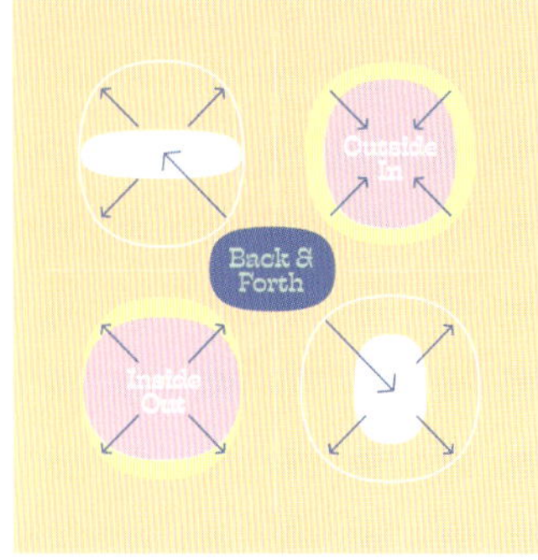

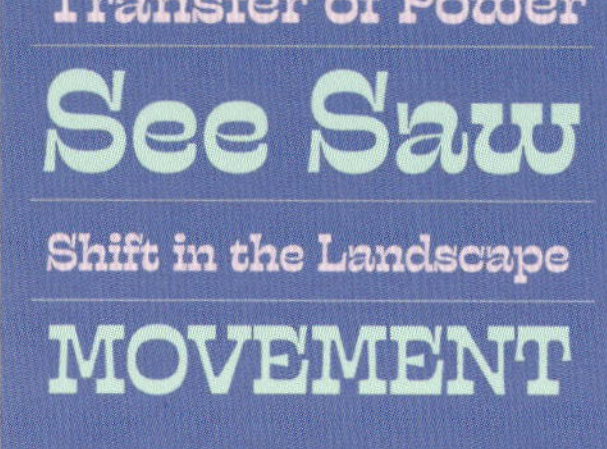

Sway is a variable font that explores the attributes of a family with extremely contrasting opinions. Seamlessly shifting from Horizontal to Vertical stress, this double-axis variable font lets you dial in your desired level of funk.

Sway

pstypelab.com

Designed by *Mark Caneso*
Published by *PSTL*

Jan Ingenhousz

The Dutchman Jan Ingenhousz (1730–99) studied phy
medicine. He was one of the first people to study phot
the discovery by Joseph Priestley (1733–1804) that pla
later published a work that the green part of plants tak

1857–65

Coral islands

ASSEMBLY ROOMS · EDINBURGH NEW TOWN

The Pacific Ocean

10 March, 6.30–8.30pm

ice as large as its nearest rival, the Atlantic, the Pacific is the world
gest ocean, and covers one-third of the Earth's surface. It stretches

elindine · Mountain · Leek · Blackish · Verdigri
· Apple · Bluish · Emerald · Grass · Duck · Sap ·
· Pistachio · Asparagus · Olive · Oil · Siskin ·

Liberation

PART ONE

The Setting of Text Matter

By far the greater volume of type composition today is of a matter for continuous reading, i.e. text. And so it has been since the day when printing from movable types was invented. For this reason the first part of this book has been devoted to an explanation of some of the fundamentals involved in the proper setting of body matter, viz. spacing between the words, the determination of the measure, or length of line, and the leading or spacing between the lines. Indications are then given showing how the principles which govern these vital factors are translated into day to day practice.

In beginning with text settings we are simply putting first things first.

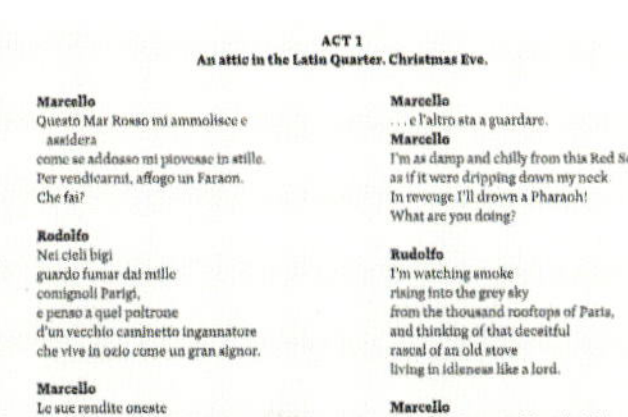

ACT 1

An attic in the Latin Quarter. Christmas Eve.

Marcello
Questo Mar Rosso mi ammolisce e assidera
come se addosso mi piovesse in stille.
Per vendicarmi, affogo un Faraon.
Che fai?

Rodolfo
Nei cieli bigi
guardo fumar dai mille
comignoli Parigi,
e penso a quel poltrone
d'un vecchio caminetto ingannatore
che vive in ozio come un gran signor.

Marcello
Le sue rendite oneste
da un pezzo non riceve.

Rodolfo
Quelle sciocche foreste

Marcello
. . . e l'altro sta a guardare.

Marcello
I'm as damp and chilly from this Red Sea
as if it were dripping down my neck
In revenge I'll drown a Pharaoh!
What are you doing?

Rudolfo
I'm watching smoke
rising into the grey sky
from the thousand rooftops of Paris,
and thinking of that deceitful
rascal of an old stove
living in idleness like a lord.

Marcello
But he hasn't received his rightful dues
for some time

Rudolfo

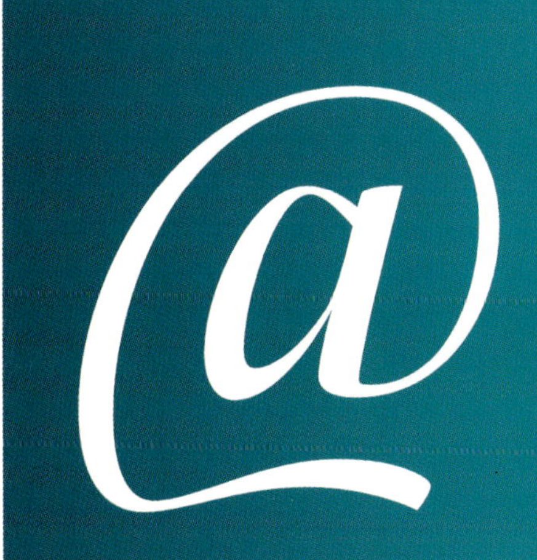

a meeting was called at Tw
eaceful Breckland village o
ully the villagers assemble
workers, trades people, sc
bers of the Home Guard. C
ers in the area, Lord Walsi
everal men the villagers di
g to address them stood a v
nneth Anderson, General C

Wood anemones

SCENTED WHITE FLOWERS

Native woodlander *Anemone nemorosa* flourishes under deciduous trees and shrubs, producing drifts of scented white flowers just before the canopy comes into leaf. Cultivated forms include double-flowered 'vestal' (pictured).

Flowers: March to April
H × S: 15cm × 15cm

An old face slab serif principally designed for typographers to craft extended text, the design of books, and detail in publishing. There are four optical sizes: Text, Large Text, Display, and Fine. The Text fonts are low in contrast while the Display variants show a higher degree of stroke difference. This increases in the Fine fonts, which owe more to mannered lettering, with tighter proportions and sharper detailing, designed for short text at large sizes.

typography.net

Ravenscar

Designed by *Jeremy Tankard*
Published by *Jeremy Tankard Typography*

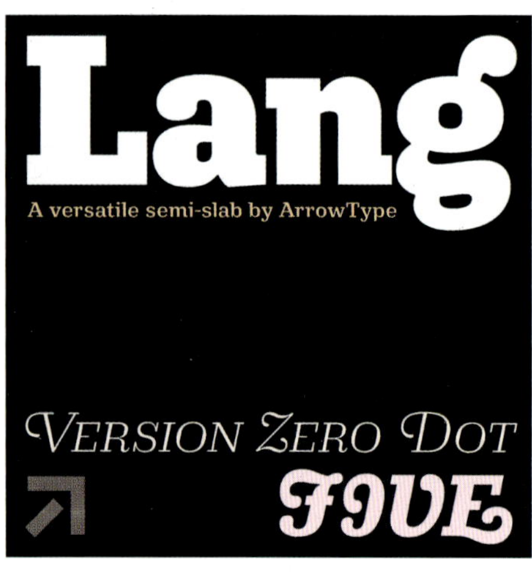

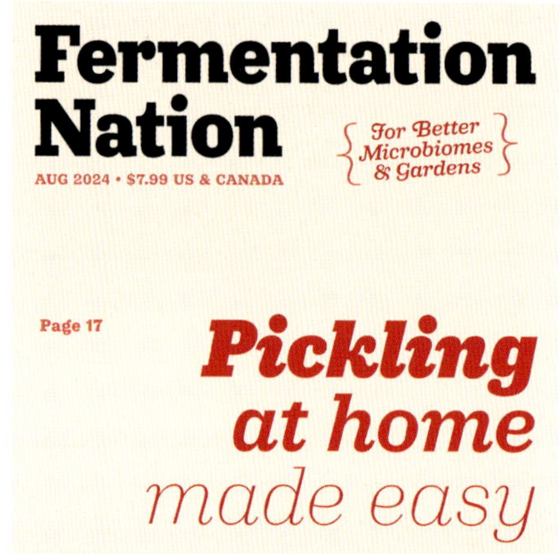

SWASH SUPPORT FOR ACCENTED CAPS:

A À Á Â Ã Ä Å Ā Ă Æ Ǻ

Ạ Ằ Ẳ Ẵ Ấ Ậ Ầ Ẩ Ẫ Ạ Ȧ Ą

A À Á Â Ã Ä Å Ā Ă Æ Ǻ

Ặ Ằ Ẳ Ẵ Ấ Ậ Ầ Ẩ Ẫ Ạ Ȧ Ą

A À Á Â Ã Ä Å Ā Ă Æ Ǻ Ặ

Ằ Ẳ Ẵ Ấ Ậ Ầ Ẩ Ẫ Ạ Ȧ Ą

ETCETERA

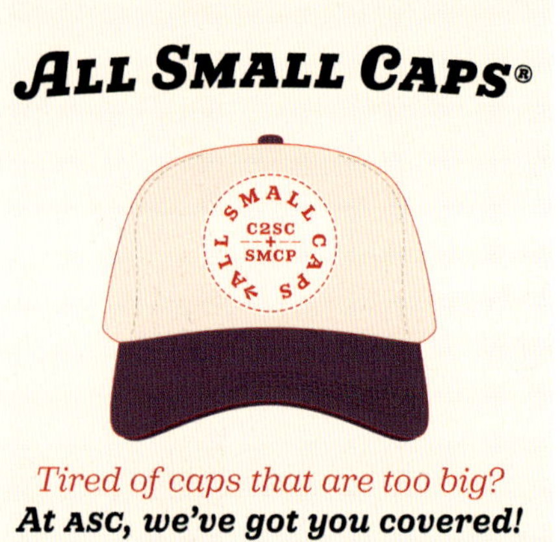

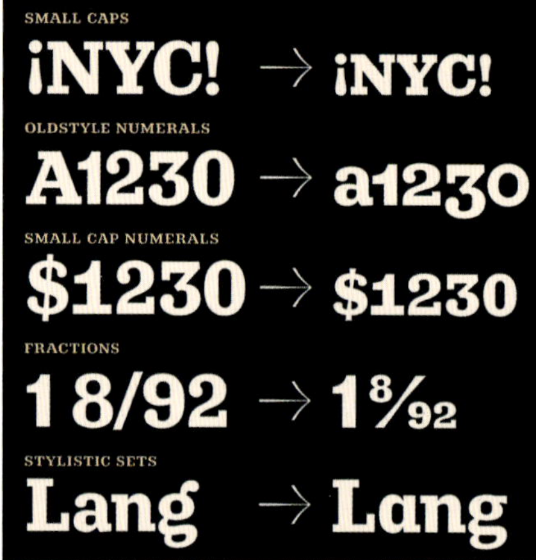

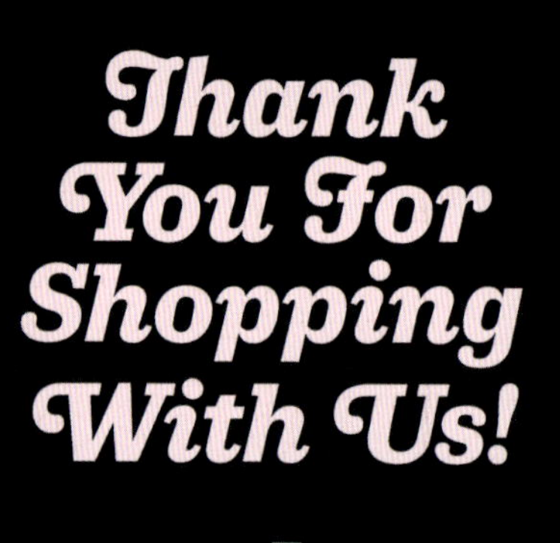

GEOGRAPHY & HISTORY • SIXTEEN MONTHS AT THE GOL

CALIFORNIA extends from Oregon to Sonoma a
from the Rocky Mountains to the Pacific. It show
ten degrees of latitude, from the thirty-second to the
the voyager it presents only high and forbidding head
es which step down from the broad *table-lands* in the
foot far out into the waters of the ocean.

This country possesses *423,970 square kilometer*
its lofty ranges of mountains, among which lie intersp
tiful valleys and more extensive plains. Its diversity o
great as the varieties of its surface.

The channel which forms the entrance into this sin
Pacific is *two miles* in width and three in length, and i
same parallel of latitude, to the Straits of Gibraltar.

After passing through this channel, the lowest of th
San Francisco, opens broadly before you, dotted with

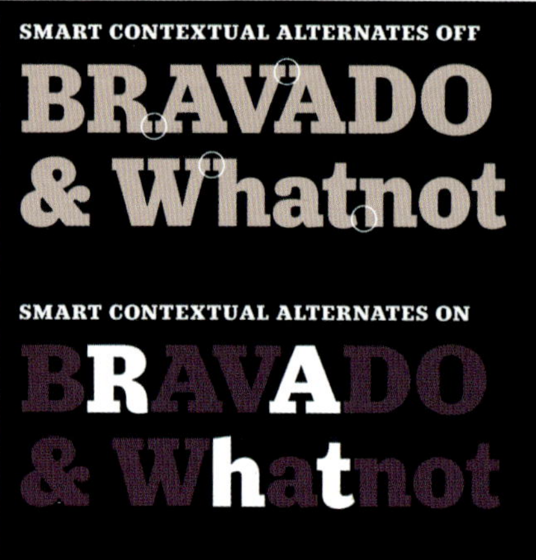

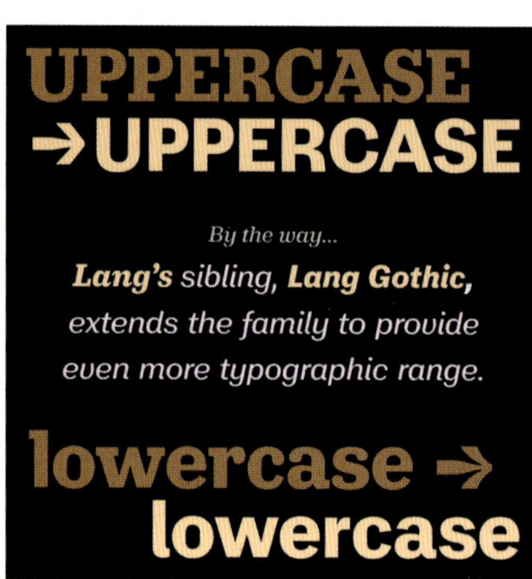

Lang

arrowtype.com

Designed by *Stephen Nixon*
Published by *Arrow Type*

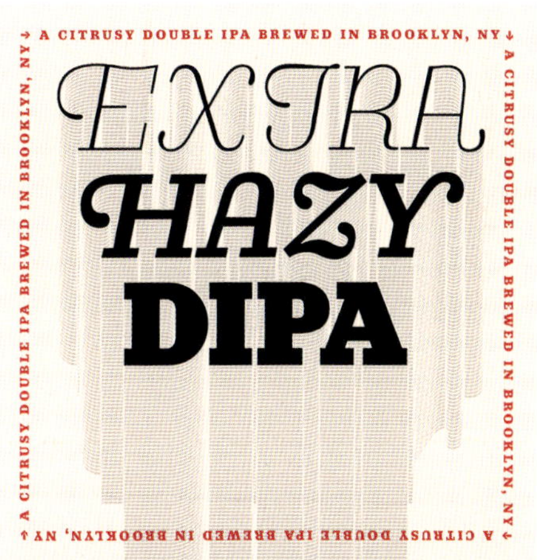

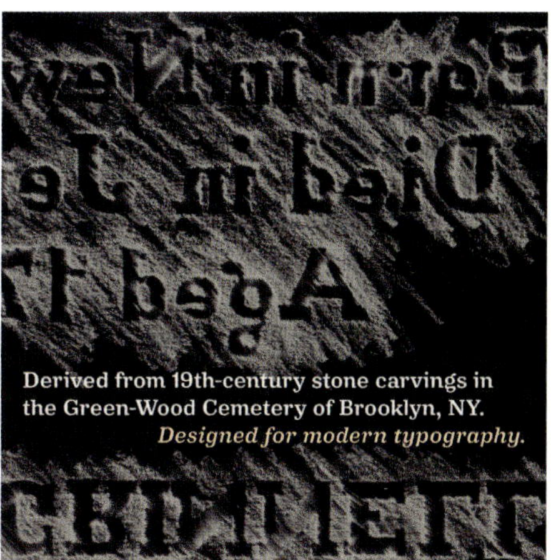

AT LANG

Black *Italic*
ExtraBold *Italic*
Bold *Italic*
SemiBold *Italic*
Medium *Italic*
Regular *Italic*
Light *Italic*
ExtraLight *Italic*
Thin *Italic*

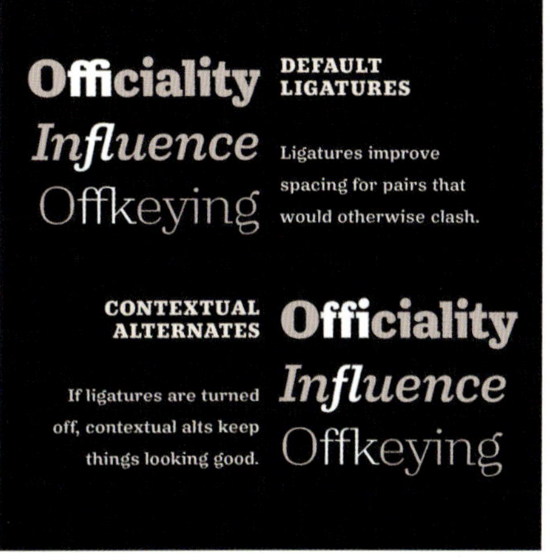

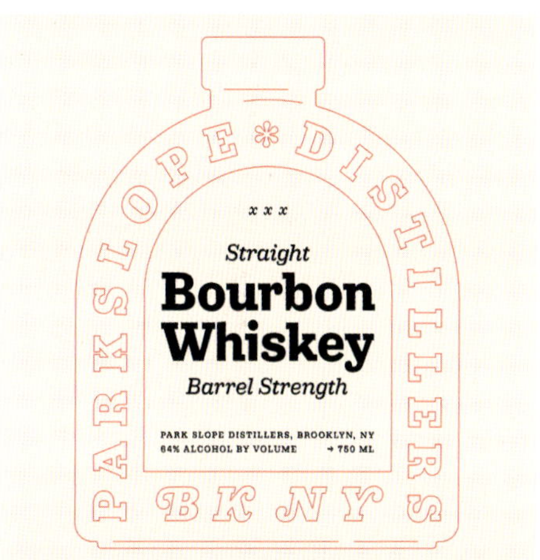

WHEREAS UNDER AND BY VIRT
ACT OF THE LEGISLATION OF TH
YORK, ENTITLED AN ACT TO AL
AN ACT TO INCORPORATE THE
CEMETERY PASSED APRIL 11TH, 1
(AMONG OTHER THINGS) GRANTE
SHALL BE LAWFUL FOR THE STO
THE SAID GREENWOOD CEMETERY
EXTINGUISH THEIR STOCK IN SU
THE BOARD OF DIRECTORS SHALL
WHEREAS THE SAID BOARD OF DI
PRESCRIBED AND DIRECTED THA
MONEYS HERETOFORE PAID BY T
STOCKHOLDERS FOR AND IN CONS
HELD BY THEM RESPECTIVELY BE
THAT THE SAID STOCKHOLDERS R
EXECUTE A SURRENDER OF THE S

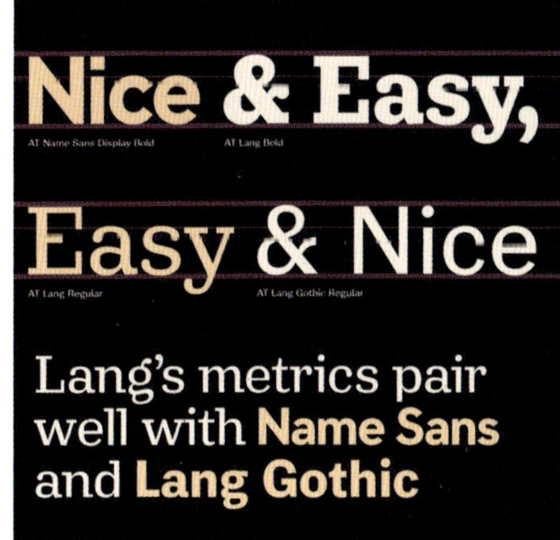

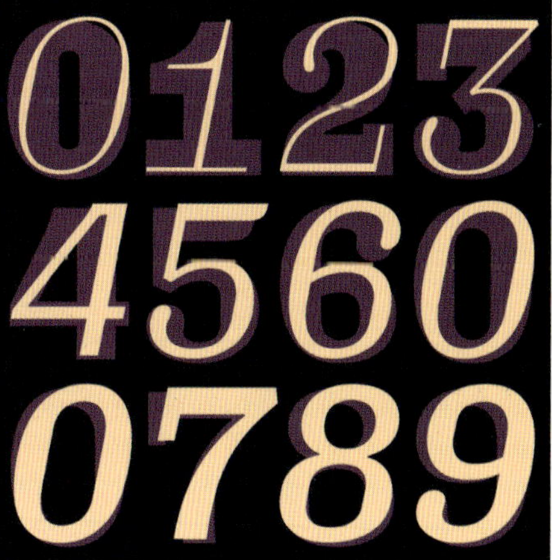

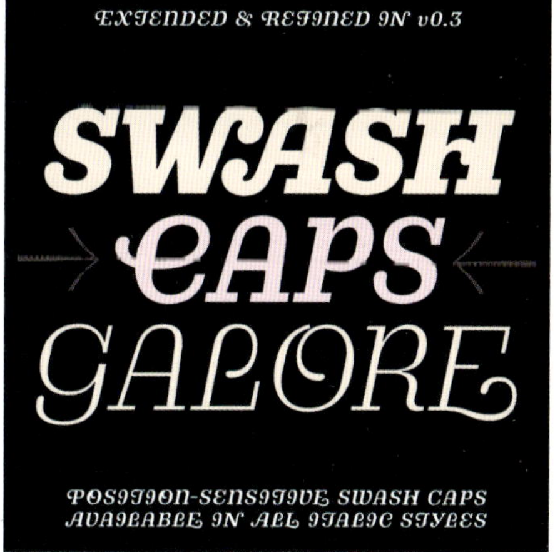

Lang is a type family derived from a recurrent (surprisingly friendly) semi-slab serif style of lettering in nineteenth-century grave carvings within the Green-Wood Cemetery of Brooklyn, New York. Lang is an exploration of dualities: life and death, past and present, self and family, nature and design, tradition and progress.

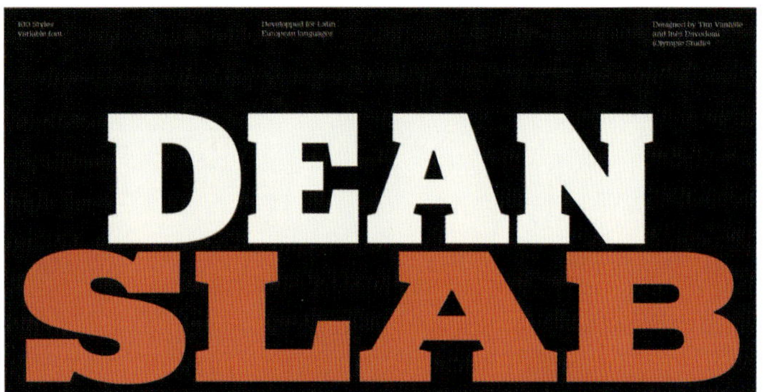

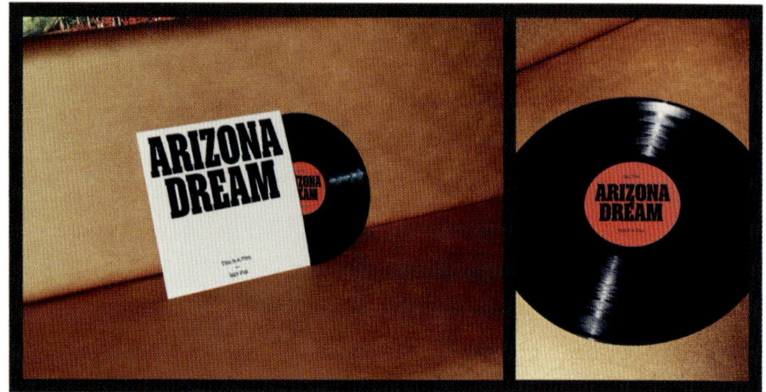

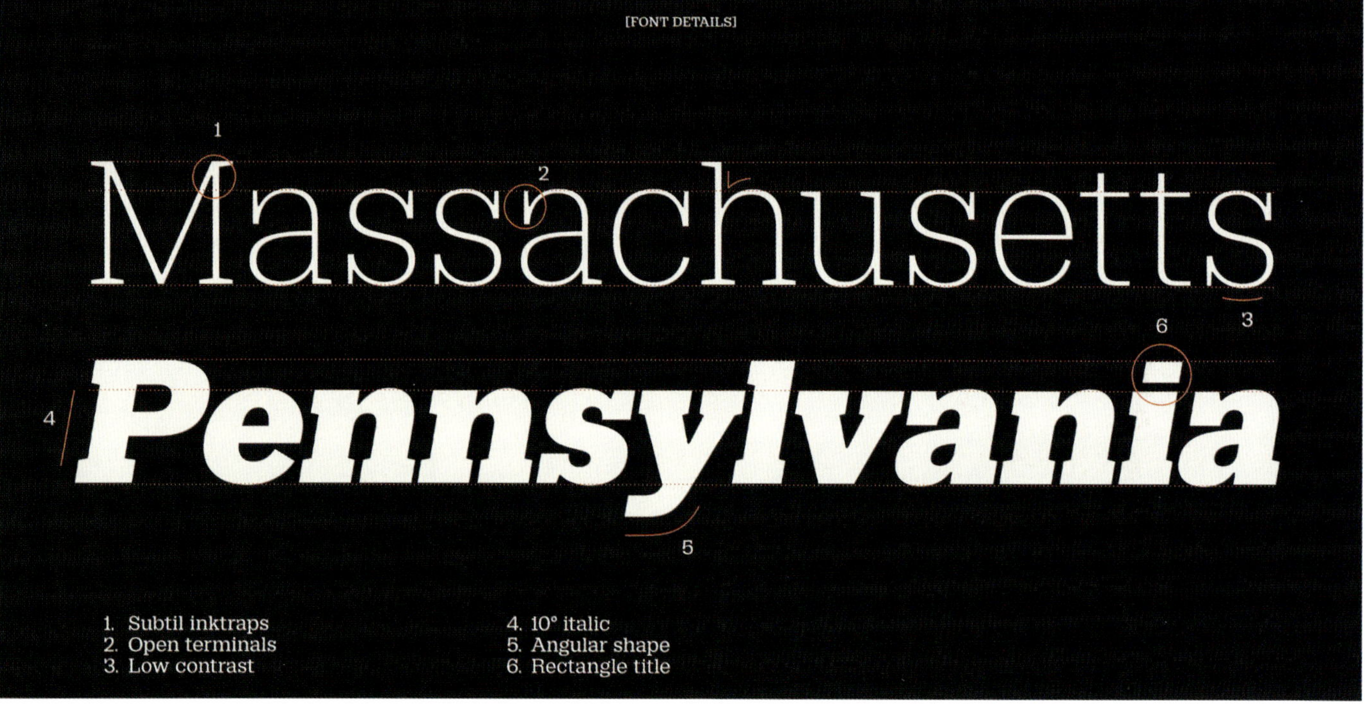

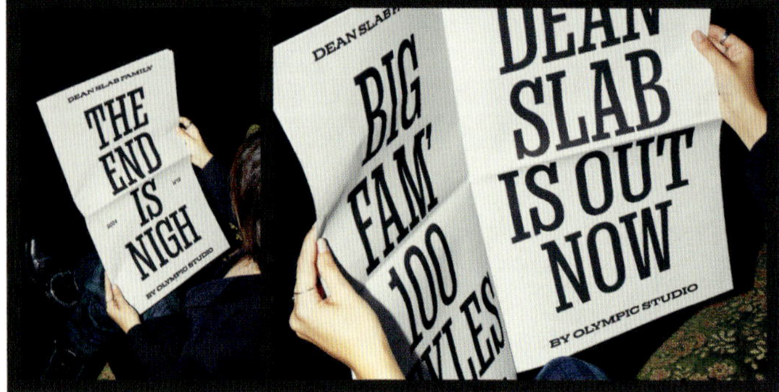

Dean Slab is a vibrant tribute to the musical and cinematic culture of mid-twentieth-century America. Together with Dean Gothic, its design is rooted in the legacy of wood types and period posters, reflecting an era of intense creativity when design served as the voice of a culture in full swing. Dean Slab preserves the authenticity of historical forms while introducing a contemporary touch. Its bold serifs and commanding proportions honor the raw energy of posters and advertisements from that era. It's a typeface that embodies the strength and singularity of the American heritage, while being perfectly attuned to modern sensibilities.

Dean Slab

blazetype.eu

Designed by *Tim Vanhille, Ines Davodeau*
Published by *Blaze Type*

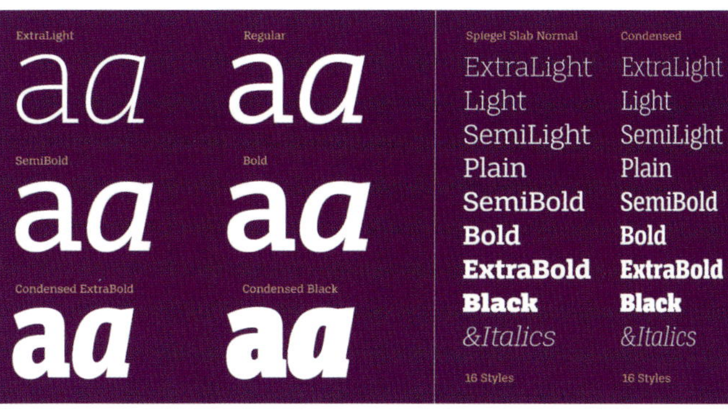

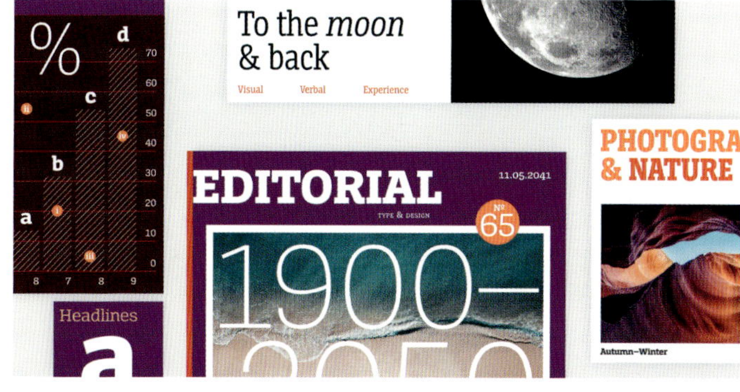

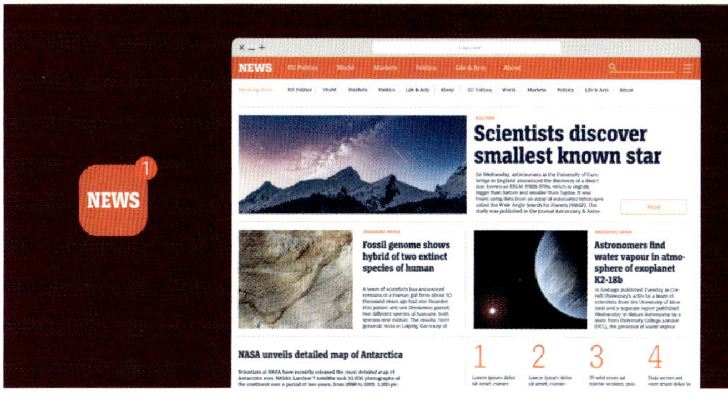

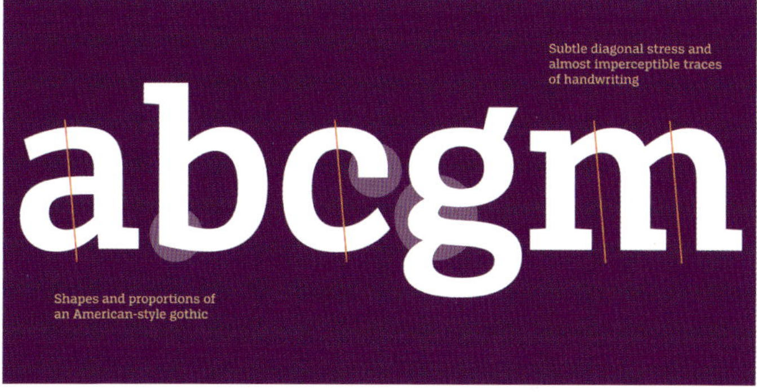

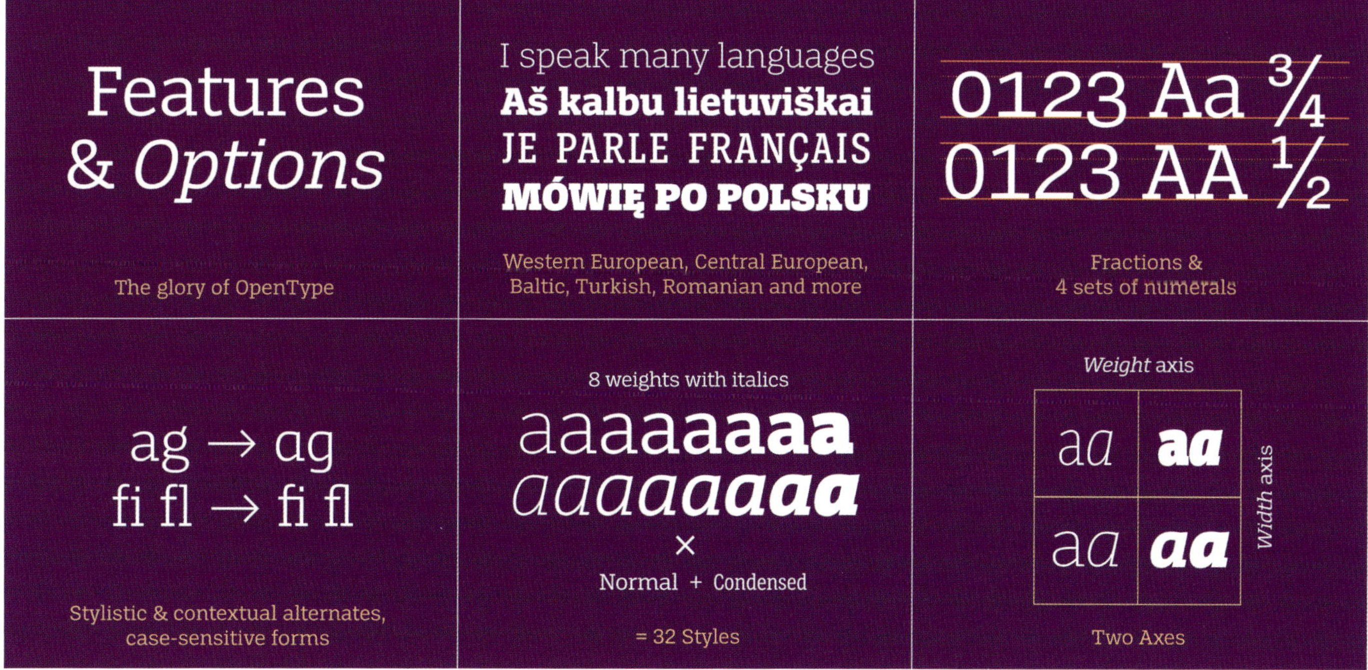

Spiegel Slab shares the features of its sibling, Spiegel Sans, including the shapes and proportions of an industrial-style gothic, combined with subtle diagonal stress and almost imperceptible traces of handwriting. Low contrast and robust serifs help Spiegel Slab confidently hold its ground on the page for subheads in the lighter weights, as well as being extremely striking in the heavier weights.

lucasfonts.com

Spiegel Slab

Designed by *Luc(as) de Groot*
Published by *LucasFonts*

SANS SERIF

You could be forgiven for assuming that the humble sans serif—and the seemingly ever-popular desire to seek out a sans that's "serious but friendly" (sigh) or one that "walks the line between geometric and humanist" (double sigh)—would result in a collection of contemporary typefaces that are essentially all variations on the same theme. Thankfully, this isn't the case. In the pages that follow, you'll find an almost mind-boggling variation in sans serif designs: Sharp and rounded. Monospaced and proportional. True italics and obliques. Monolinear and contrasting. Compressed and wide. And, of course, everything in between.

As with the other parts of this book, the order in which these families are presented doesn't attempt to play favorites or to impose any sort of hierarchy in the presentation. But I will say this: The sans section is *big.* A testament to the current popularity of this genre, surely.

Typeface: Kensington, designed by Jennifer Hood (page 90)

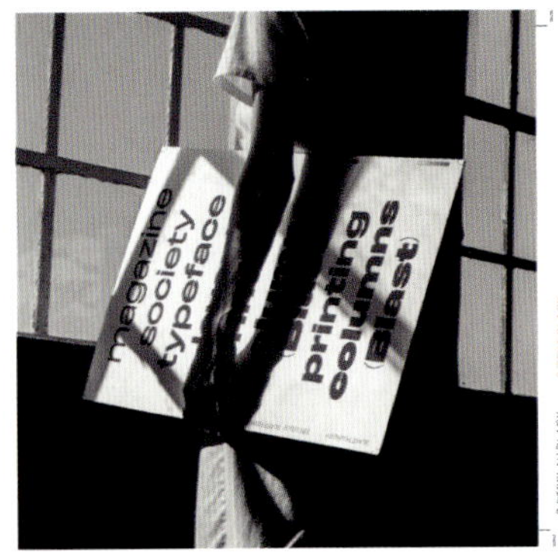

S DISPLAY BLACK

S

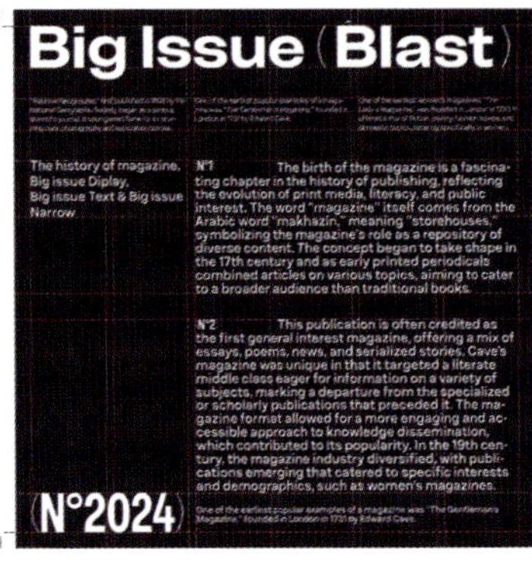

Big Issue (Blast)

The history of magazine,
Big issue Diplay,
Big issue Text & Big issue
Narrow

N°1 The birth of the magazine is a fascinating chapter in the history of publishing, reflecting the evolution of print media, literacy, and public interest. The word "magazine" itself comes from the Arabic word "makhazin," meaning "storehouses," symbolizing the magazine's role as a repository of diverse content. The concept began to take shape in the 17th century and as early printed periodicals combined articles on various topics, aiming to cater to a broader audience than traditional books.

N°2 This publication is often credited as the first general interest magazine, offering a mix of essays, poems, news, and serialized stories. Cave's magazine was unique in that it targeted a literate middle class eager for information on a variety of subjects, marking a departure from the specialized or scholarly publications that preceded it. The magazine format allowed for a more engaging and accessible approach to knowledge dissemination, which contributed to its popularity. In the 19th century, the magazine industry diversified, with publications emerging that catered to specific interests and demographics, such as women's magazines.

(N°2024)

One of the earliest popular examples of a magazine was "The Gentleman's Magazine," founded in London in 1731 by Edward Cave.

Publication	Publication	**Publication**
Issue	Issue	**Issue**
Article	Article	**Article**
Editor	Editor	**Editor**
Photography	Photography	**Photography**
Layout	Layout	**Layout**
Cover	Cover	**Cover**
Feature	Feature	**Feature**
Illustration	Illustration	**Illustration**
Editorial	Editorial	**Editorial**
Content	Content	**Content**
Column	Column	**Column**
Subscription	Subscription	**Subscription**
Print	Print	**Print**
Circulation	Circulation	**Circulation**
Publisher	Publisher	**Publisher**
Headline	Headline	**Headline**
Advertising	Advertising	**Advertising**
Design	Design	**Design**
NARROW REGULAR	TEXT MEDIUM	DISPLAY WIDE BOLD

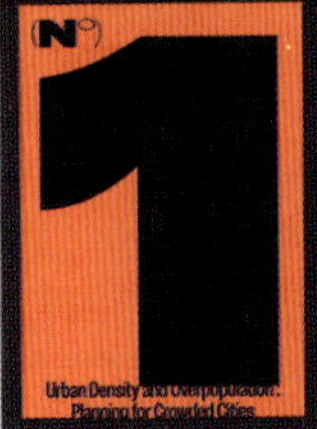

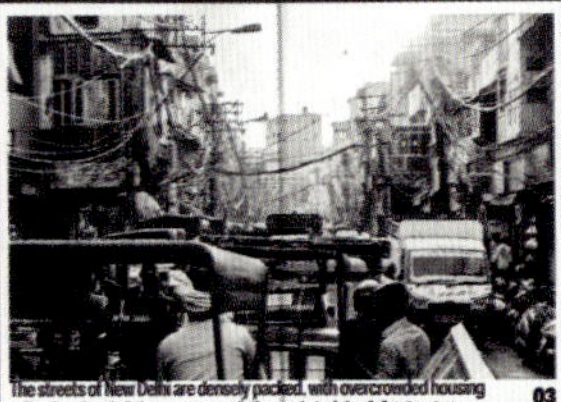

VERTICAL URBANISM: HIGH-RISE BUILDINGS ARE A SOLUTION TO OVER POPULATION, ALLOWING FOR MORE PEOPLE TO LIVE IN SMALLER FOOTPRINT.

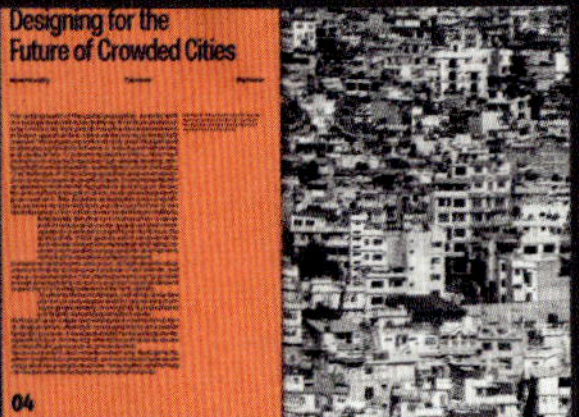

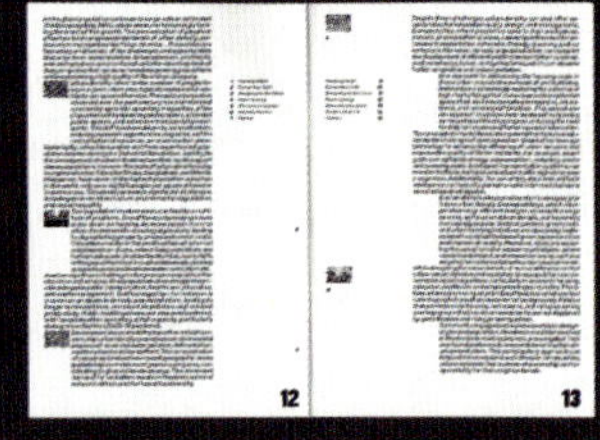

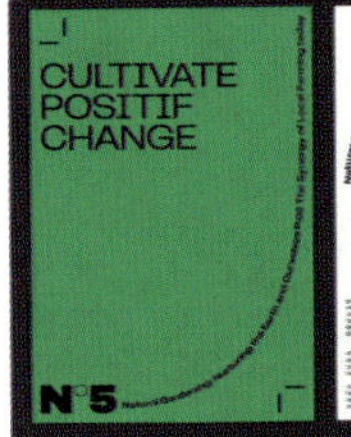

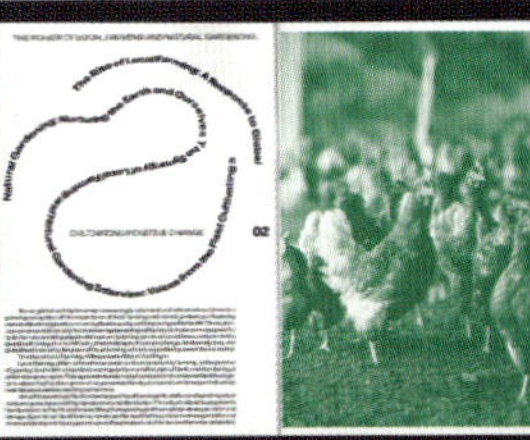

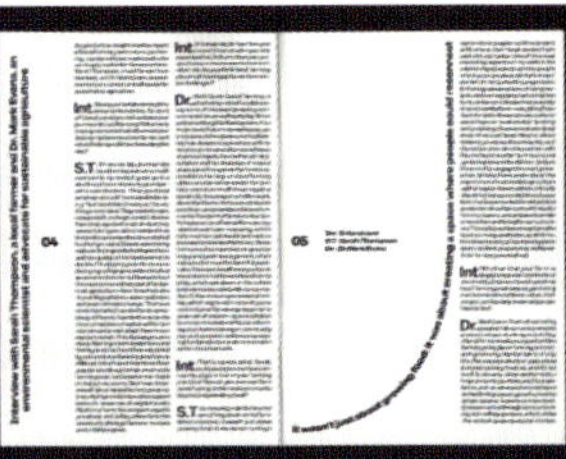

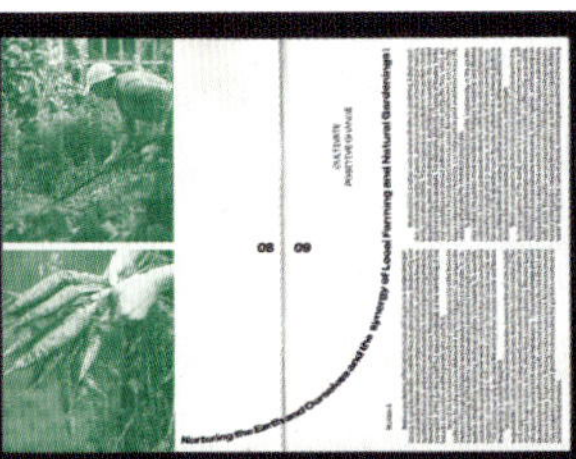

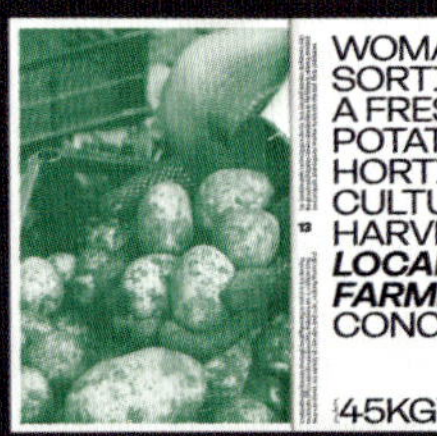

DISPLAY LIGHT	DISPLAY REGULAR	DISPLAY WIDE MEDIUM	DISPLAY WIDE BOLD	DISPLAY XW
B	B	B	B	B

BIG ISSUE

BLAST FOUNDRY

Big Issue

blast-foundry.com

Designed by *Barbara Bigosińska, Diana Ovezea*
Published by *Blast Foundry*

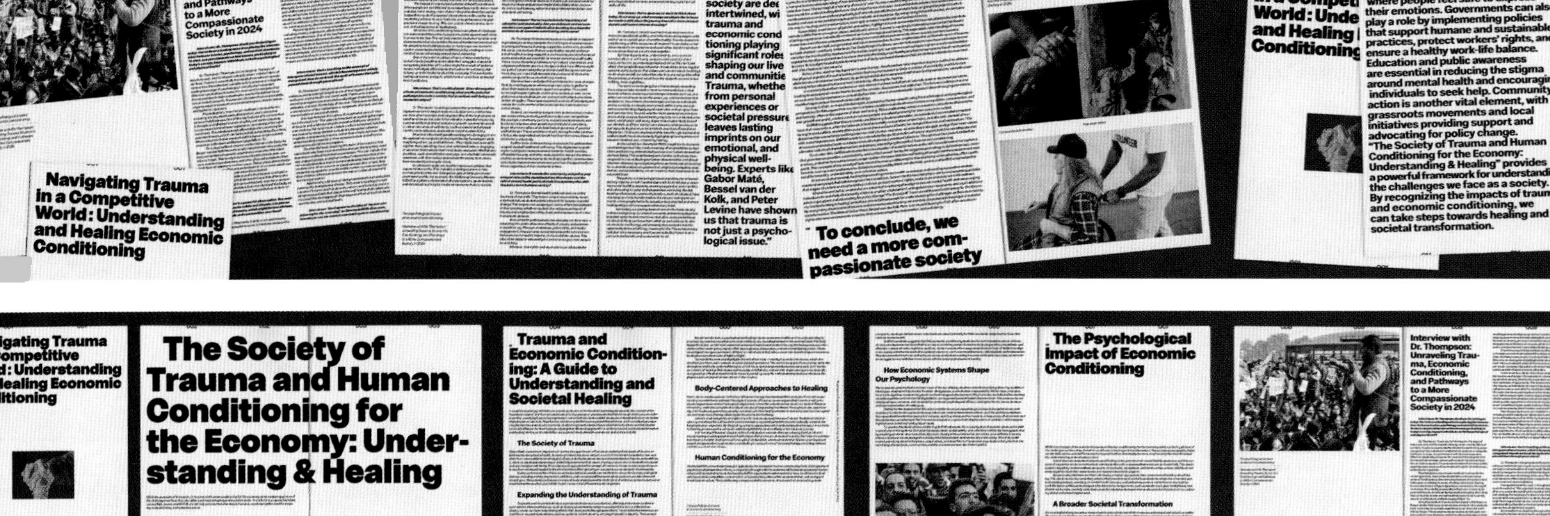

Narrow *weight*

NARROW BLACK	NARROW EXTRA BOLD	NARROW BOLD	NARROW MEDIUM	NARROW REGULAR	NARROW LIGHT	*LIGHT ITALIC*	*REGULAR ITALIC*	*MEDIUM ITALIC*	*BOLD ITALIC*	*EXTRA BOLD ITALIC*	*BLACK ITALIC*	*BIG ISSUE NARROW*
ABCDEFGHIJKLMN	ABCDEFGHIJKLMN	ABCDEFGHIJKLMN	ABCDEFGHIJKLMN	ABCDEFGHIJKLMN	ABCDEFGHIJKLMN	*ABCDEFGHIJKLMN*	*ABCDEFGHIJKLMN*	*ABCDEFGHIJKLMN*	*ABCDEFGHIJKLMN*	*ABCDEFGHIJKLMN*	*ABCDEFGHIJKLMN*	*TYPEFACE*
OPQRSTUVWXYZ	OPQRSTUVWXYZ	OPQRSTUVWXYZ	OPQRSTUVWXYZ	OPQRSTUVWXYZ	OPQRSTUVWXYZ	*OPQRSTUVWXYZ*	*OPQRSTUVWXYZ*	*OPQRSTUVWXYZ*	*OPQRSTUVWXYZ*	*OPQRSTUVWXYZ*	*OPQRSTUVWXYZ*	*BLAST FOUNDRY*
1234567890@£&	1234567890@£&	1234567890@£&	1234567890@£&	1234567890@£&	1234567890@£&	*1234567890@£&*	*1234567890@£&*	*1234567890@£&*	*1234567890@£&*	*1234567890@£&*	*1234567890@£&*	*12 WEIGHT*

DISPLAY XWIDE EXTRA BLACK

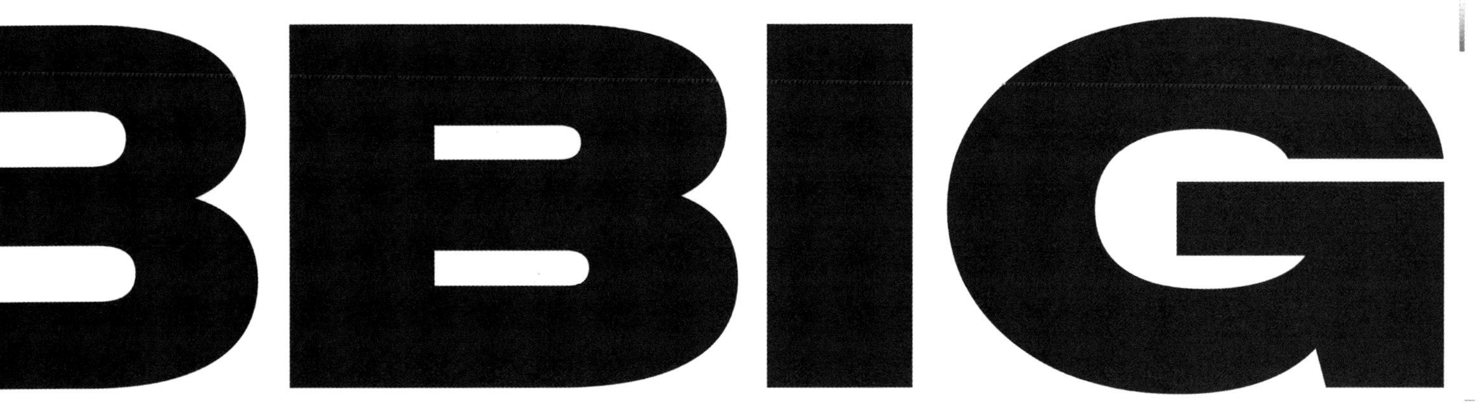

The Big Issue superfamily is a modern grotesque sans developed with The Big Issue *magazine. It started with a bold, single-weight typeface for the thirtieth-anniversary cover, created in collaboration with Pentagram. Since then, Blast Foundry has expanded it into a flexible family featuring Narrow, Standard, Wide, and XWide widths. Big Issue's design is rooted in historical British grotesque typography, blending classic typographic influences with modern-day functionality. Ten percent of all proceeds from the superfamily are donated to the Big Issue Foundation, extending the type family's impact beyond design.*

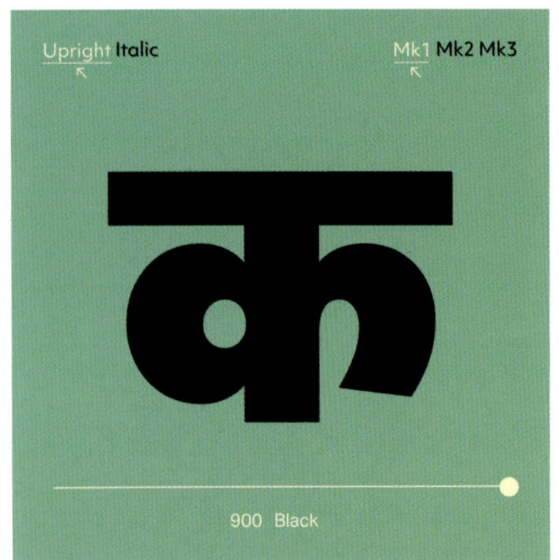

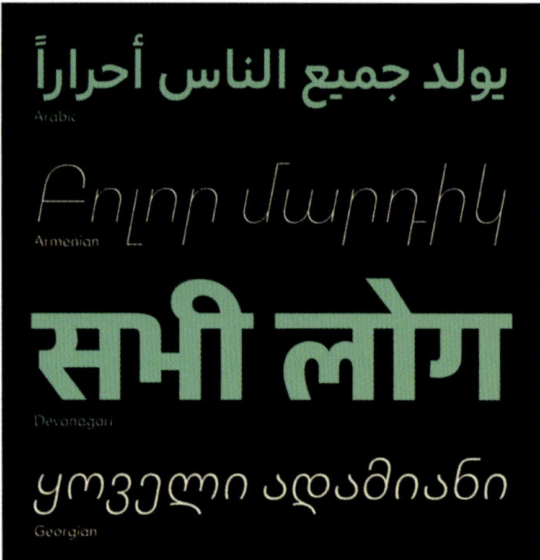

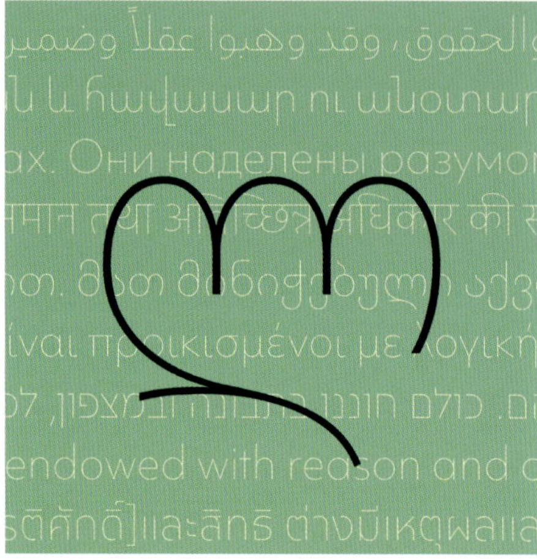

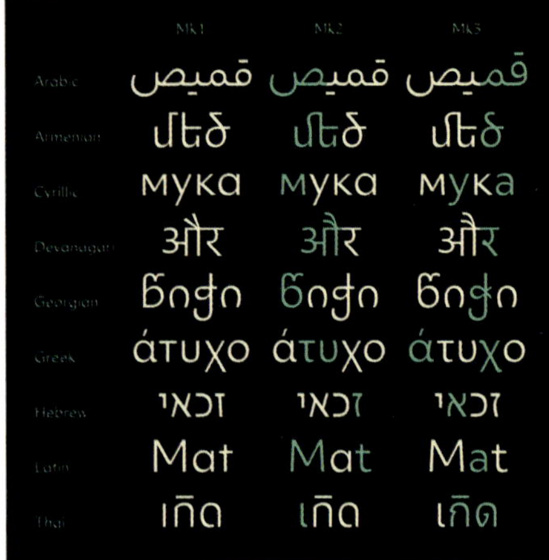

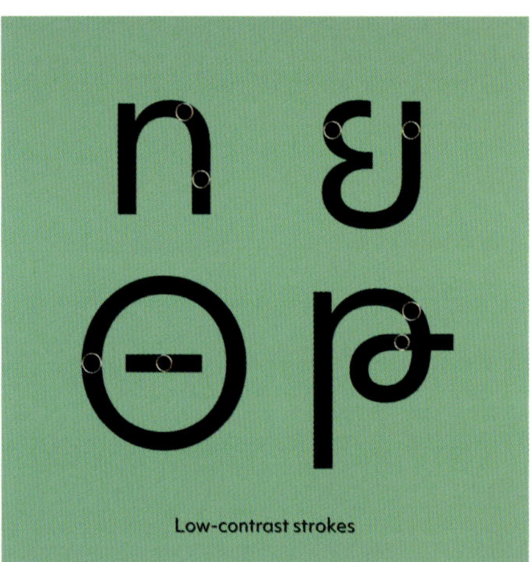

Objektiv Multiscript is a clean, geometric sans typeface with unique human appeal. Its extensive weight and italic variable font axes, support for nine global writing systems, and three stylistic variants provide flexibility and adaptability across diverse applications and media.

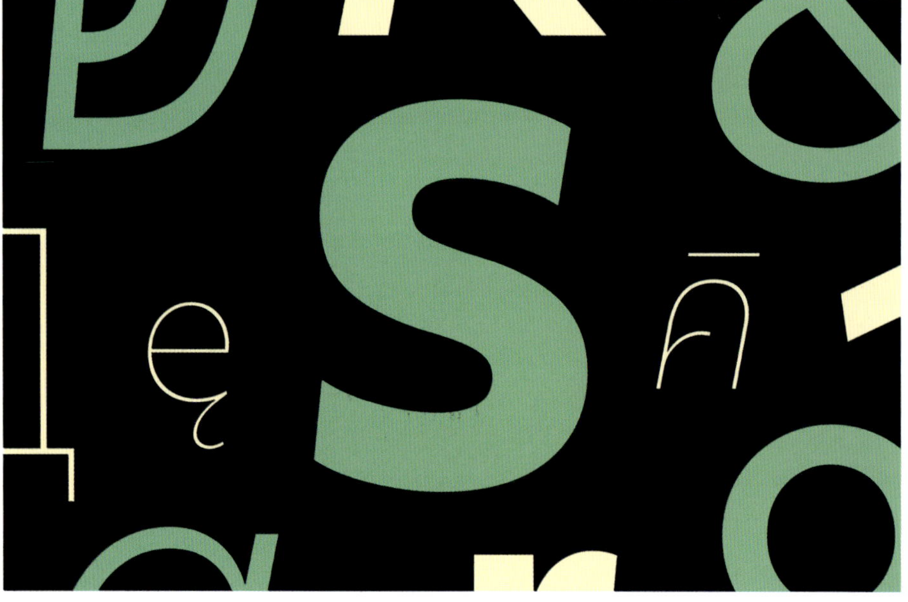

Objektiv Multiscript

daltonmaag.com

Designed by *Bruno Mello, Sahar Afshar, Carlos De Toro, Hanna Donker, Maria Fontenelle, Pablo Gámez, Ben Jones, Jonny Pinhorn*
Published by *Dalton Maag*

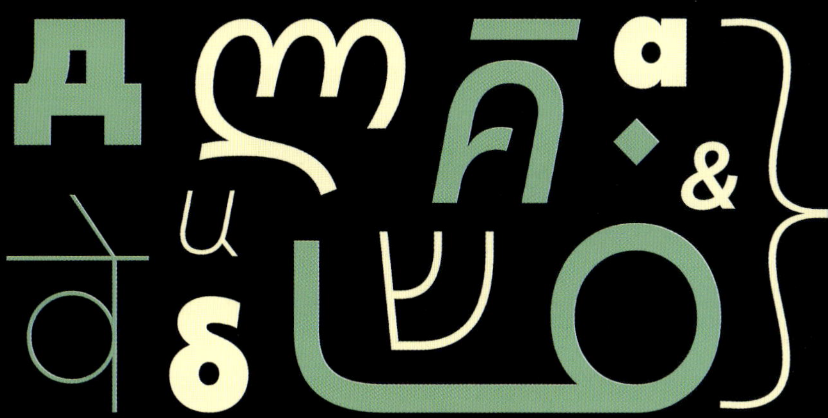

والحقوق. وقد وهبوا عقلاً وضميرًا
جنس أو اللغة أو الدين أو الرأي الس
الحق في الحياة والحرية وسلامة
أي شخص. ويحظر الإسترقاق وتج
للعقوبات أو المعاملات القاسية
ما وجد الحق في أن يعترف بشخ
تفرقة، كما أن لهم جميعاً الحق
ية لإنصافه عن أعمال فيها اعتدا
ض على أي إنسان أو حجزه أو

ու իրավունքներով: Նրանք ո
ռի, լեզվի, կրոնի, քաղաքակ
յու, ազատության ու անձի ա
վում. պետք է արգելվեն ստր
ւժան, անմարդկային կամ ս
իրավունք ունի ճանաչվել ո
ր պաշտպանության իրավ
կանգնման իրավունք, եթե
մայական կալանքի, քանն

вах. Они наделены разумом
отношении расы, цвета кожи
на жизнь, на свободу и на л
невольном состоянии; рабст
м, бесчеловечным или униж
ходился, имеет право на пр
защиту от какой бы то ни б
национальными судами в
нут произвольному арест

मानता प्राप्त है। उन्हें बुद्धि और अन्तरा
धर्म, राजनीति या अन्य विचार - प्रणाल
जीवन, स्वाधीनता और वैयक्तिक सुरक्ष
या जाएगा, ग़ुलामी - प्रथा और ग़ुलामों
ी और न किसी के भी प्रति निर्दय, अम
न की निगाह में व्यक्ति के रूप में स्वीकृ
मण करके कोई भी भेद-भाव किया
तिक्रमण करने वाले कार्यों के विरु
से गिरफ़्तार, नज़रबन्द या देश-नि

ბით. მათ მინიჭებული აქვთ
აბელდობრ, რასის, კანის ფ
ს, თავისუფლებისა და პირ
მორჩილების მდგომარე
სტიკი, არაადამიანური, ო
ს იგი, უფლება აქვს, რომ
ყველა ადამიანს აქვს უფლ
ნდა ჰქონდეს სამართლე
რომ თვითნებურ დაკავებ

Είναι προικισμένοι με λογική κ
προς τη φυλή, το χρώμα, το φ
στη ζωή, την ελευθερία και την
κής ή μερικής. Η δουλεία και
ανιστήρια ούτε σε ποινή ή με
ει δικαίωμα στην αναγνώριση
χουν δικαίωμα σε ίση προστ
ια κατά των πράξεων που π
λαμβάνεται, να κρατείται ή

יהם. כולם חוננו בתבונה ובמצפון, לפי
גזע, צבע, מין, לשון, דת, דעה פוליטית
ם יש לו הזכות לחיים, לחרות ולבטחון
או משועבד; עבדות וסחר עבדים יאס
ים, ולא ליחס או לעונש אכזריים, בלו
אי להיות מוכר בכל מקום כאשיות ב
הכל זכאים להגנה שווה מפני כל הפ
ים המוסמכים נגד מעשים המפירים
אדם, לא ייעצר ולא יוגלה באופן

e endowed with reason and co
y kind, such as race, colour, se
right to life, liberty and the se
hall be prohibited in all their f
re or to cruel, inhuman or deg
o recognition everywhere as
entitled to equal protection
onal tribunals for acts violat
bjected to arbitrary arrest,

ยรติศักดิ์]และสิทธิ ต่างมีเหตุผลและ
ดังเช่น เชื้อชาติ ผิว เพศ ภาษา ศาส
นการดำรงชีวิต เสรีภาพ และความ
้องภาระจำยอมไม่ได้ความเป็นทาส
บผลปฏิบัติ หรือการลงโทษที่โหดร้
การยอมรับนับถือว่า เป็นบุคคลตา
ทุกคนมีสิทธิที่จะได้รับความคุ้ม
นาจแห่งชาติต่อการกระทำอันล
กุม กักขัง หรือเนรเทศไปต่างถิ่น

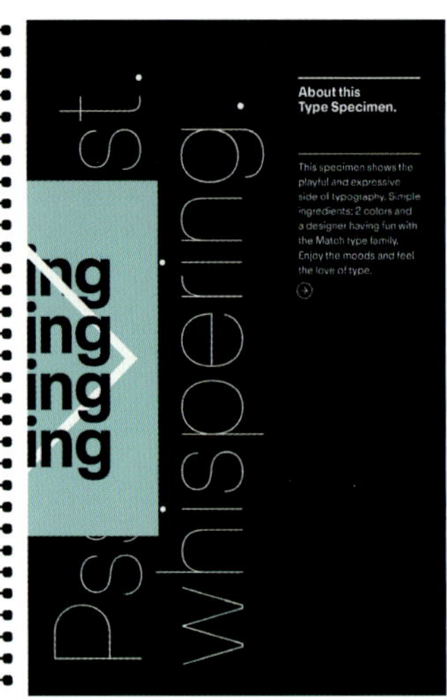

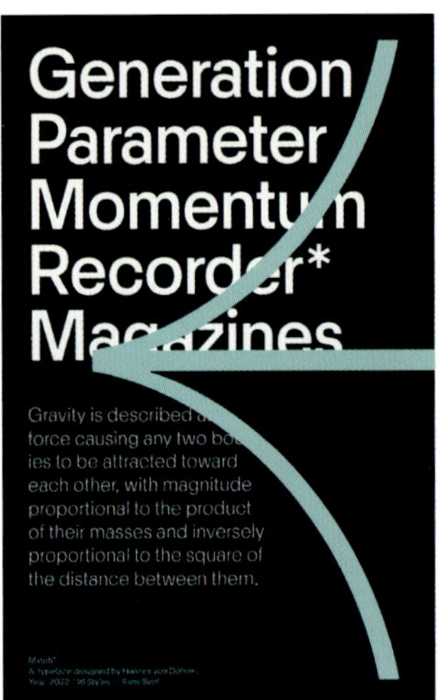

Self-confidence is an attitude about your skills and abilities. It is something that can be found in both typography and design. A self-confident designer is willing to take risks and to go the extra mile in order to achieve the best possible solution. Starting with the initial sketches in 2017, Hannes von Döhren wanted to create a typeface that starts with a simple idea: appearing compact with certainty and sticking to its principles—not leaving any doubt in its message.

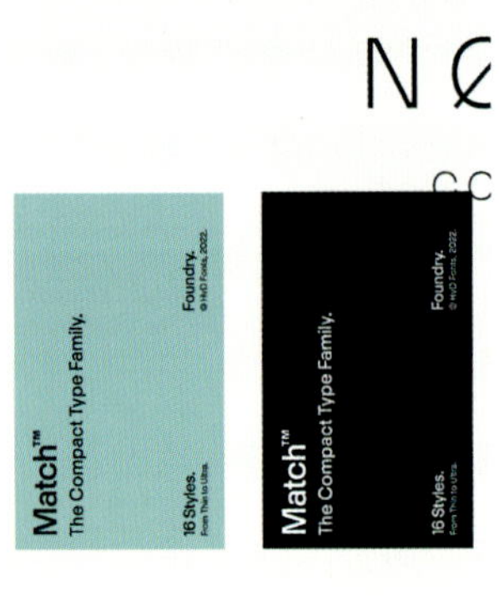

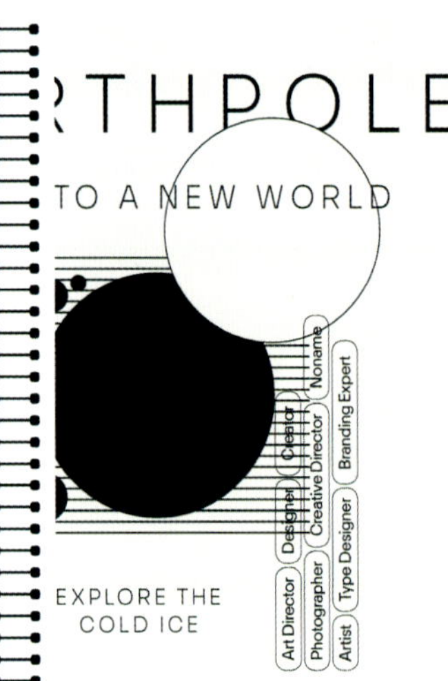

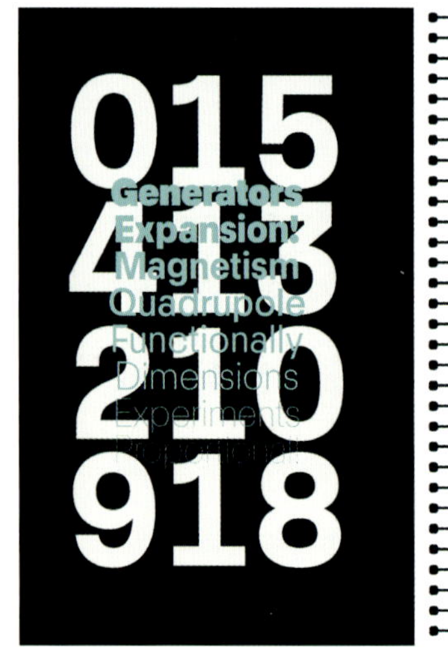

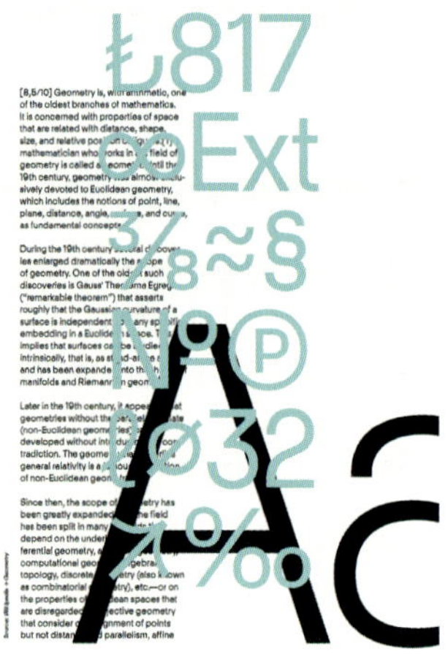

Match

hvdfonts.com

Designed by *Hannes von Döhren*
Published by *HvD Fonts*

Disconnnect Power Supply Before Changing Fuse
INTENTIONAL USE OF TRANSIENT LIMITS IS PROHIBITED
Modulation Of The Voltage Controlled Filter
ATTENTION, RISQUE DE CHOC, NE PAS ENLEVER
KSY34 High-Frequency NPN Transistor
PARASITIC-CAPACITANCE PREAMPLIFIER
Device must have a volume control
ENSEMBLE DE LANCEMENT ARIANE-ELA4

JTD Type Foundry — Enfilade Display

The subthreshold I-V curve depends exponentially upon threshold voltage
COOLING AIR ENTERS FROM REAR OF MACHINE OR THROUGH FILTER IN BOTTOM
Performance assessments for LEO orbits between 5° and 85
THIS PUBLICATION REPLACES MSFC-MAN-507 FOR VEHICLE SA-507
To prevent electrical shock do not remove top cover
THE CABLE CAN NOT BE CHANNELED WITH POWER CABLES
Metal Oxide Semiconductor Field-Effect Transistor
TEST OPERATOR & TEST CONDUCTOR CONTROL CONSOLES

JTD Type Foundry — Enfilade Headline

Magneto-Resistive Stationary Heads
DIELECTRIC WITHSTAND VOLTAGE TEST
Heterojunction Bipolar Transistor
THIS APPLIANCE MUST BE EARTHED
Mikroelektronikai Vállalat / MEV
DIRECT DRIVE TURNTABLE SYSTEM
Less Than 30 Amperes Per Leg
BIPOLAR JUNCTION TRANSISTOR

JTD Type Foundry — Enfilade Small

Hybrid Photovoltaic System
REFERENCE LEVEL 260 NWB/M
Auxiliary Power Distributor
CAPSTAN SIGNAL GENERATOR
Ground Support Interface
ALPHA CUT-OFF FREQUENCY
Joule Magnetostriction
RELAY K3-28 IS ENERGIZED

JTD Type Foundry — Enfilade Tiny

Enfilade is a condensed Grotesk with four optical variations. Each optical variant is optimized to work at half the point size of the previous variant to make establishing hierarchy a breeze.

jtdtype.com

Enfilade

Designed by *James Hultquist-Todd*
Published by *JTD Type*

СМАК

СПОЖИВАЮТЬ ЇХ БЕРУЧИ ПО ОДНІЙ, ТРИМАЮТЬ У РУЦІ Й ВІДКУШУЮТЬ ПО КУСОЧКУ, ЗАПИВАЮЧИ ПРИ ЦЬОМУ

Готові вироби посипають

За необхідності до тістечок можна подати чайну ложку, щоби гості могли вибрати

Торт «Павлова» — це повітряний десерт з безе з ніжною хрусткою скоринкою і м'якою серединкою, яка нагадує зефір. Його зазвичай

ЗА НЕОБХІДНОСТІ до тістечок можна подати чайну ложку

Oh! あら!

Bagels are also sold (fresh or frozen) in many SUPERMARKETS. ベーグルの起源ははっきりしておらず、17世紀に東ヨーロッパのユダヤ人コミュニティーで食べられていたとされる。

コンフォート・フード COMFORT FOOD

最古のケーキはスイスの新石器時代の村落跡から見つかっている。Cake is often served as a celebratory dish

Doughnut holes are small, bite-sized doughnuts made from the dough taken from the center of the doughnuts. リングドーナツの成形には、硬めの生地をドーナツ型でリン

Let's go out and grab a bite. 夕食（ゆうしょく）とは、夕刻や晩に取る食事のこと。

Đường

ĐÂY LÀ HIỆN TƯỢNG giao lưu và tiếp biến văn hóa trong nghệ thuật ẩm thực rất sáng tạo để đáp ứng sở thích của nhiều đối tượng

Nước cốt có độ ngọt thanh

Muốn làm kẹo ngon, khâu chọn nguyên liệu rất quan trọng. Thóc nếp nấu mạch nha phải là nếp tốt

Kẹo dừa là một loại đặc sản có nguồn gốc từ tỉnh Bến Tre, Việt Nam. Kẹo được chế biến từ nguyên liệu chính là cơm dừa, đường và mạch nha. Đây là loại kẹo đặc sản

Theo truyền thống xưa nay các cơ sở sản xuất kẹo dừa luôn xem trọng

ζάχαρη

Για την παραγωγή της αμυγδαλόπιτας, τα ξηρά συστατικά της αμυγδαλόπιτας διπλώνονται αργά σε κρεμώδες βούτυρο και ζάχαρη.

ΣΥΝΑΝΤΆΤΑΙ και σε άλλες

Στη Βόρεια Ελλάδα παραγγέλνεται συνήθως απλά σαν «μια με τυρί» ή «μια με κρέμα», μια και

Μπουγάτσα Θεσσαλονίκης, μήκους 2,5 μέτρων, με γέμιση τυρί και ρύζι, κέρδισε τις εντυπώσεις στο Παρίσι, στη διεθνή έκθεση Γεωργίας, στα τέλη Φεβρουαρίου του

Η ζύμη διπλώνεται σε διάφορα σχήματα, τηγανίζεται σε καυτό

사탕이다

퓨전 음식의 또 다른 형태는 한 문화의 재료와 풍미를 활용하여 다른 문화의 요리에 독특한 트위스트를 만들어 낼 수 있습니다. 예를 들어 타코 피자는 타코 재료를 사용하여

컴포트 푸드는 음식을 만들지 않는 편리

음식 자체는 실제보다 더 큰 것을 상징할 수 있습니다. 미국에서 패스트푸드는 빠른 저녁 식사가 필요한 바쁜 가족

음식 자체는 실제보다 더 큰 것을 상징할 수 있습니다. 미국에서 패스트푸드는 빠른 저녁 식사가 필요한 바쁜 가족을 나타낼 수 있습니다. 음식의 사회학이 어떻게 상징화될 수 있는지

많은 문화권에서 음식은 사람들을 하나로 모으는 역할을 합니다. 함께 어울려 먹는 문화!

मूंगफली

गुलाब जामुन एक प्रकार का पकवान है जो मैदे, खोये तथा चीनी से बनाया जाता है। गुलाब जामुन नामक एक फल भी होता है, जिसके बारे में बहुत कम लोग जानते हैं। गुलाब जामुन एक फ़ारसी भाषा का शब्द है।

चिक्की सामान्य रूप से मूँगफली और गुड़

एक चौड़े और बड़े बर्तन में मावा, पनीर और मैदा डालकर नरम व चिकना आटा गूथ लें। गुलाब जामुन बनाने के लिये मावा तैयार रखें। अब इसमें

खीर एक प्रकार का मिष्टान्न है जिसे चावल को दूध में पका कर बनाया जाता है। खीर को पायस भी कहा जाता है। 'खीर' शब्द, 'क्षीर' (= दूध) का अपभ्रंश रूप है। जो इसकी एक अलग मिठास देता है। इसकी खुशबू

चांदी का वरक़ या सिर्फ़ वरक़, (अन्य नाम: वरक या वरख या वर्क), चांदी अथवा शयोजकमांसर्क से

GT America International connects two centuries of typographic genres, combining nineteenth-century American Gothic and twentieth-century European Grotesk styles. The result is one cohesive typeface family unified under the best design features from both traditions. Originally released in 2016, the 2024 update implements the typographic system in variable font format and adds five new scripts.

GT America International

grillitype.com

Designed by *various type designers**
Published by *Grilli Type*

ขนม

ส่วนผสมของขนมส่วนใหญ่จะมีพื้นฐานเป็น กะทิน้ำตาล และแป้ง ๓ ถึง ๔ ชนิด แล้วแต่ สูตร และความชอบเนื้อขนมในแต่ละแบบ นอกจากนี้แป้งแต่ละอย่างก็จะมีคุณสมบัติ ทำให้ขนมมีเนื้อที่

ขนมบ้าบิ่น ขนมไทยทำจากแป้ง

ลอดช่อง คือ ขนมพื้นบ้านที่ใช้แป้งข้าวเจ้าเป็นวัตถุดิบ เป็นที่นิยมแพร่หลายในไทยชนิดหนึ่ง มีจุดกำเนิดร่วมในทั่วทั้ง

البقلاوة

تعتبر الحلويات الشامية من أشهر أنواع الحلويات وخاصة في الوطن العربي إذ تشتهر بطعمها اللذيذ وطريقة صنعها المتقنة، واعتمادها على تنوع المكونات الداخلة.

حلويات المشرق والمغرب العربي

لطالما امتازت دول الوطن العربي وتحديداً بلاد الشام بالحلويات الشرقية.

גלידה

בייגלה (בעברית: שלובית) הוא חטיף אפוי, אשר משוזר לתוך צורה של לולאה. הבייגלה עשוי מקמח חיטה ומשמרים, לרוב בתוספת מלח או שומשום.

לרוב בתוספת מלח או שומשום

שֶׁלְגּוֹן או שַׁלְגּוֹן (הידוע גם בשמו העממי אַרְטִיק) הוא מעדן גלידה על מקל. בדומה

卡拉OK

兩個最常見的貝果種類是滿地可 Montreal風格與紐約New York風格。 THE TWO COMMON BAGEL STYLES ARE: MONTREAL AND NEW YORK.

Is my comfort food 這是我的安慰食物

English speakers call this drink BUBBLE TEA or BOBA. 現時非台裔居民依然說BOBA或Bubble。

現代速食的起源通常與Burgers連上關聯，因為最早的速食店是以漢堡為主要產品。 The fastest form of "FAST FOOD" consists of pre-cooked meals which reduce waiting periods to mere seconds.

食物可以將不同背景和經歷的人們連結起來。 Come join this POTLUCK!

Aperture — Stroke endings in characters like S become more angled the heavier the weight. This helps to prevent closed, dark counters.

Ultra Light

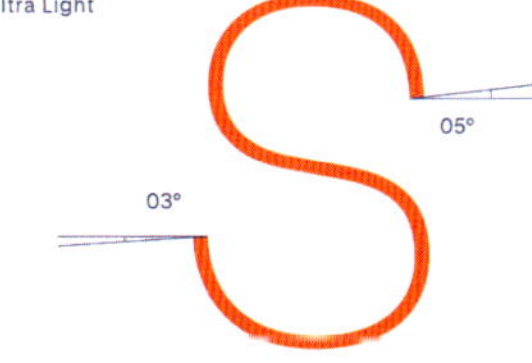

Regular

Black

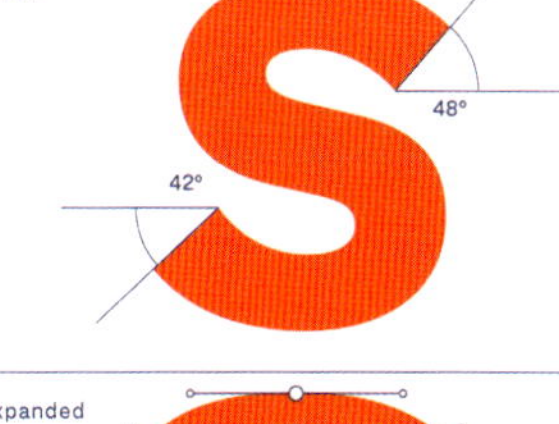

Pathing — Characters like C, O, e, s were drawn to allow for both straight and curved vertical sides, depending on the subfamily.

Compressed

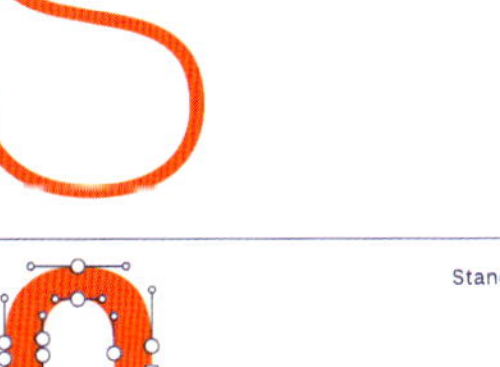

Standard

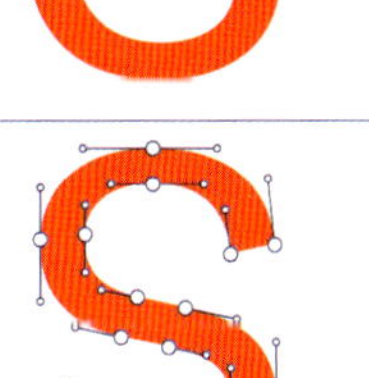

Expanded

Italic — GT America's Italics are manually corrected to make sure they fit with Roman styles in both construction and text color.

Roman

Before Correction

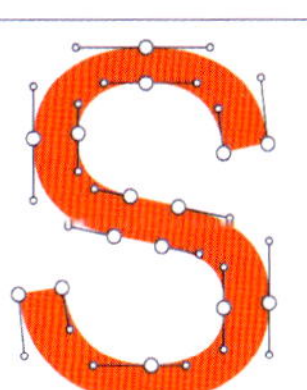

Italic

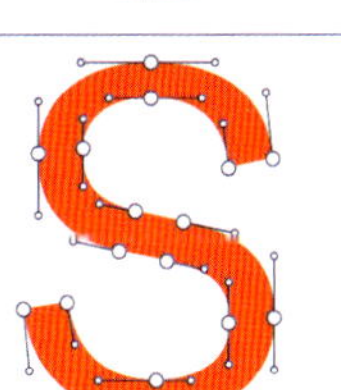

* GT America International designed by Noël Leu. Arabic script extension designed by Wael Morcos and Khajag Apelian. Hangeul script extension designed by Minjoo Ham. Devanagari script extension designed by Hitesh Malaviya. Cyrillic, Greek, and Vietnamese script extensions designed by Grilli Type with consulting by Maria Doreuli (Cyrillics), Vassilis Georgiou (Greek), and Donny Trương (Vietnamese). Hebrew script extension designed by Yanek Iontef and Daniel Grumer. Thai script extension designed by Knaz Uiyamathiti and Smich Smanloh from Cadson Demak.

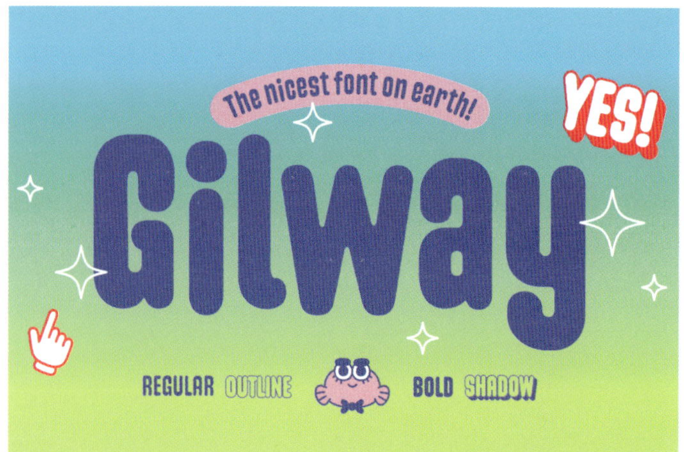

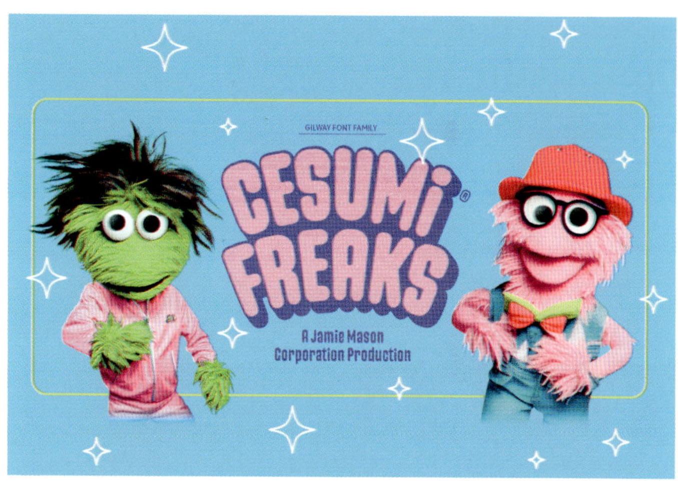

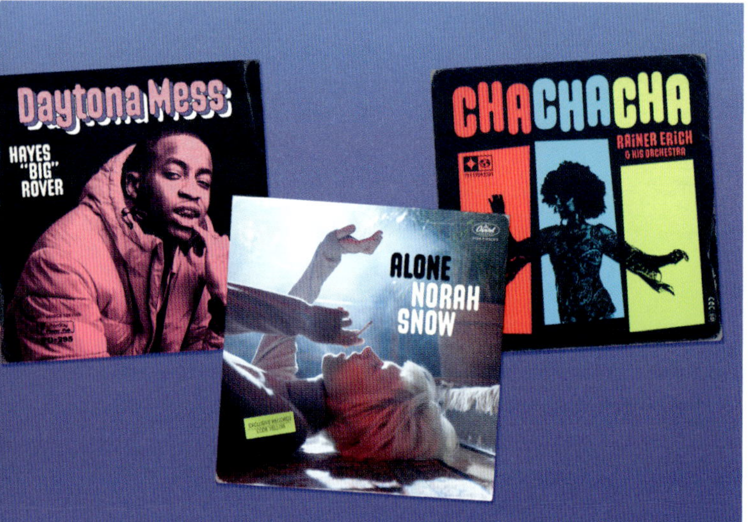

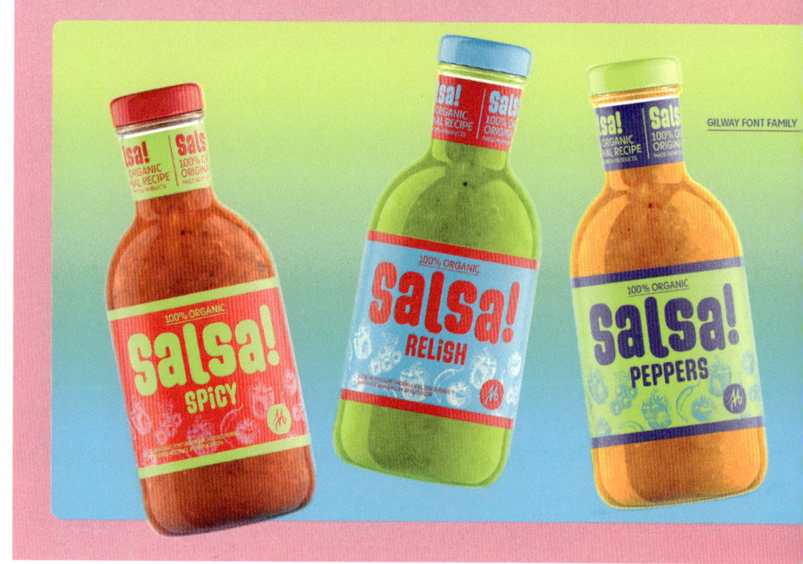

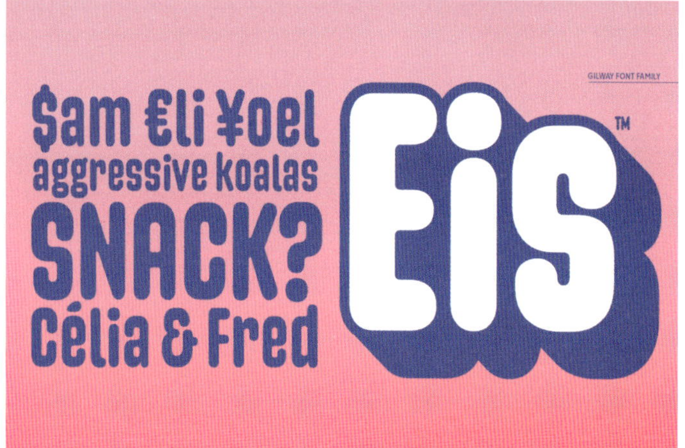

Gilway is a playful, rounded display with tremendous personality. Inspired by rounded types from the nineteenth century, Gilway has a distinctive hand-lettered feel because of its subtle variances. Layered options allow you to combine the various styles, and a unique Opentype feature makes your letters dance.

Gilway

grootfontein.net

Designed by *Stéphane Mattern*
Published by *Art Grootfontein*

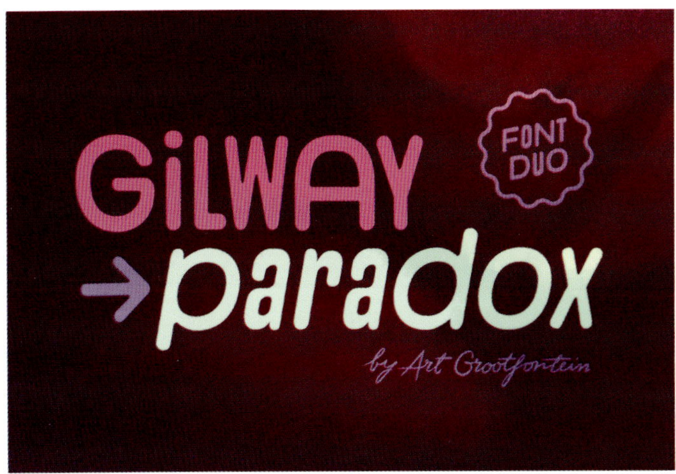

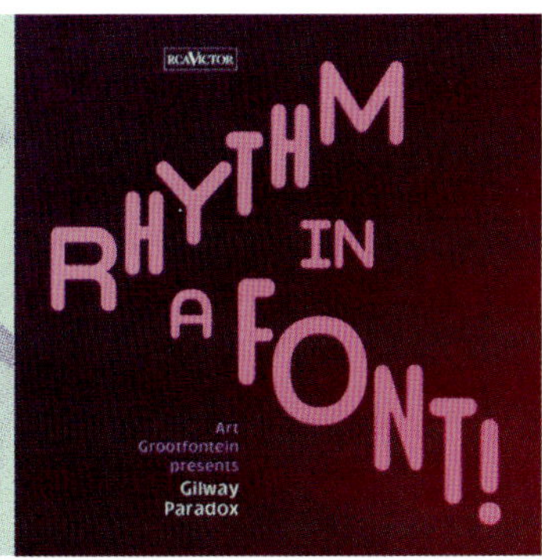

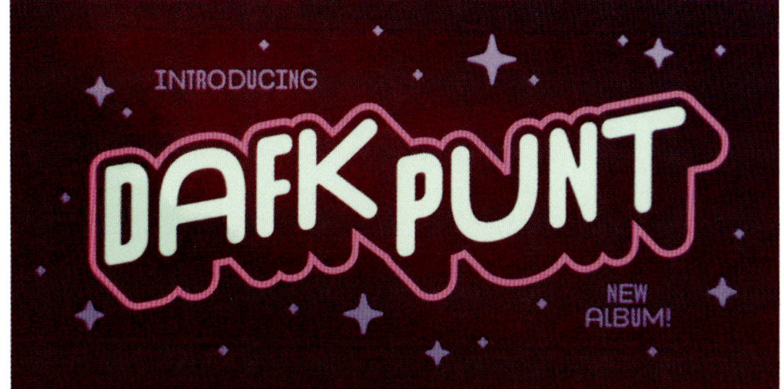

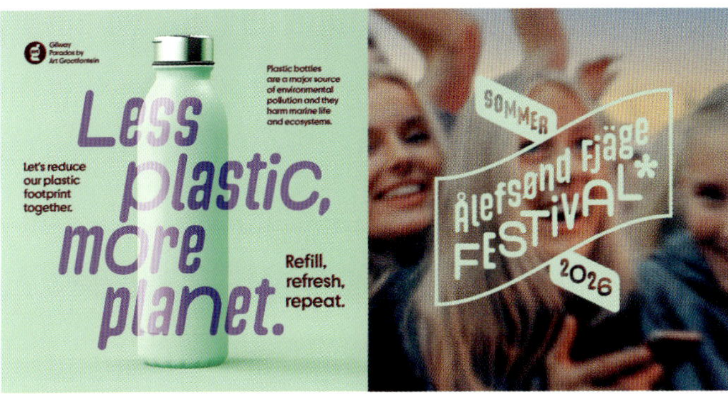

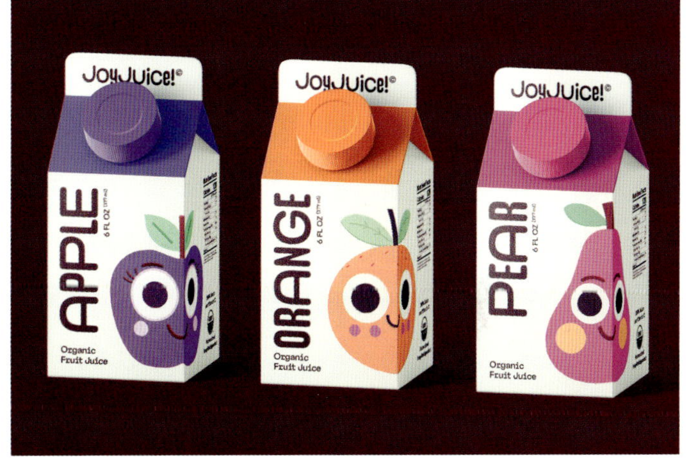

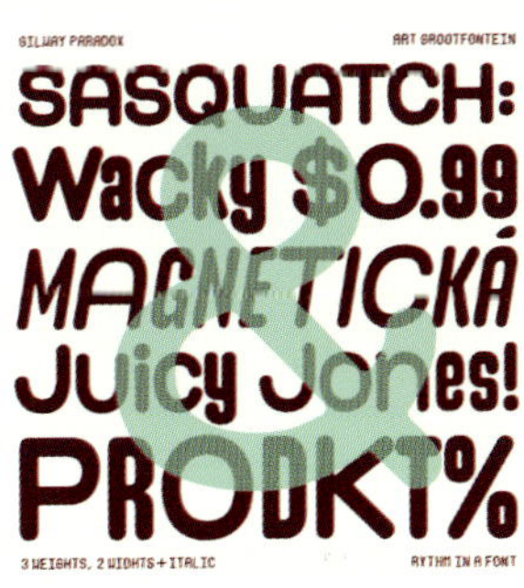

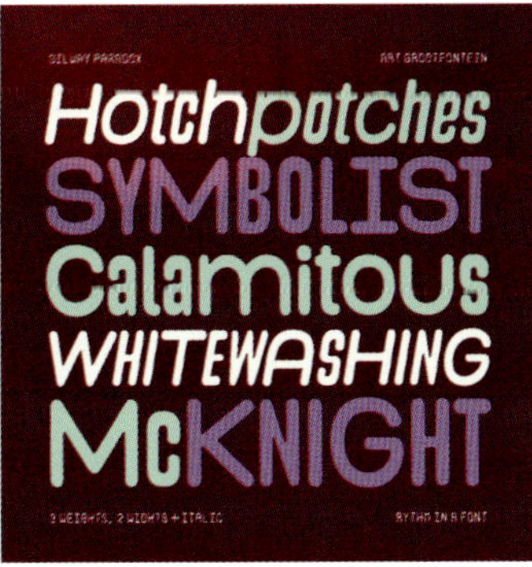

Experience the rhythm of a unique, dual-width font—Gilway Paradox is a versatile, rounded typeface, where warmth meets motion. With its striking dual-width characters, this font creates an irresistible visual rhythm, adding dynamic energy to any design. Seamlessly toggle between widths with a single click using OpenType, unlocking endless creative possibilities.

grootfontein.net

Gilway Paradox

Designed by *Stéphane Mattern*
Published by *Art Grootfontein*

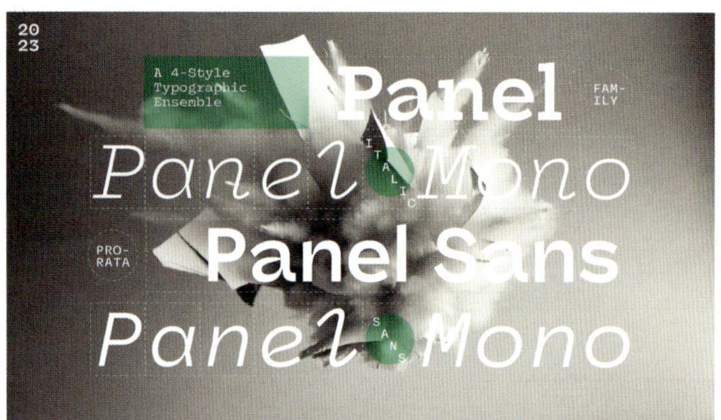

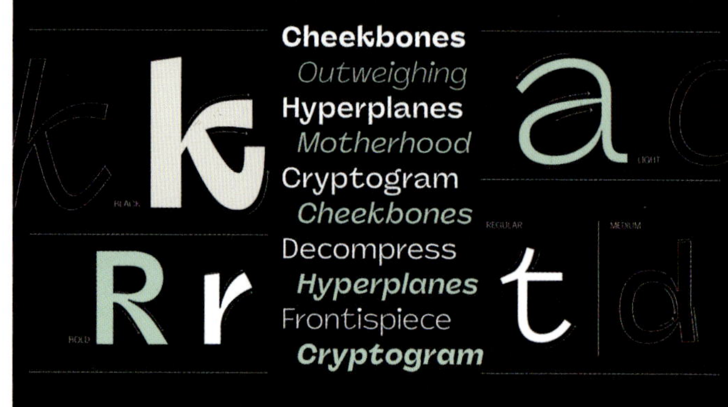

_→AaBbCcDdEeFfGg
HhIiJjKkLlMmNnOo
Sans_Mono*PpQqRr
SsTtUuVvWwXxYyZz
([{0123456789}])

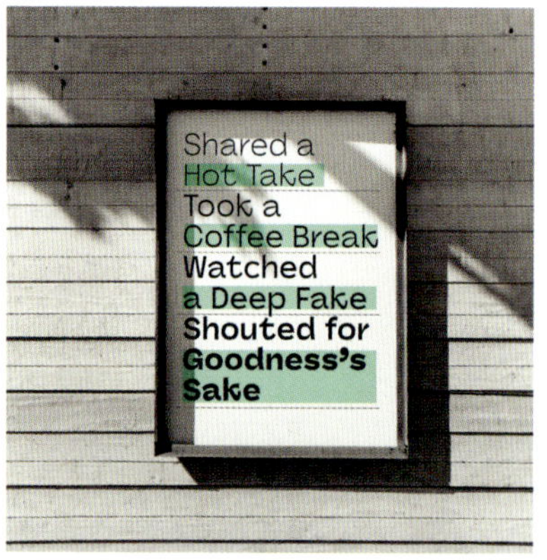

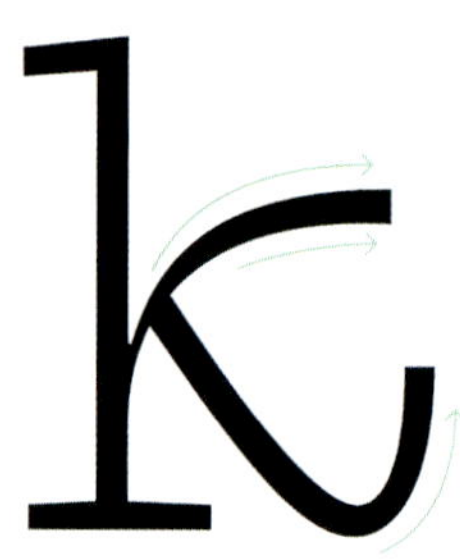

→AaBbCcDdEeFfGg
HhIiJjKkLlMmNnOo
PpQqRrSans*
TtUuVvWwXxYyZz
([{0123456789}])

Those asteroids are about ⅜ the size of Earth
Gochujang Paste
Things can get out of hand quickly
BLAME THE UMPIRE
when do you think this will all begin to feel normal again?
WELCOME TO THE MOTHERSHIP

Panel Sans is part of the Panel family—a four-style font ensemble originally conceived as a monospaced design. The initial concept for the monospace was to juggle the idea of "constraint versus restraint" and explore the concept of a typeface with lively personality in a fixed-width design space.

Panel Sans

pstypelab.com

Designed by *Mark Caneso*
Published by *PSTL*

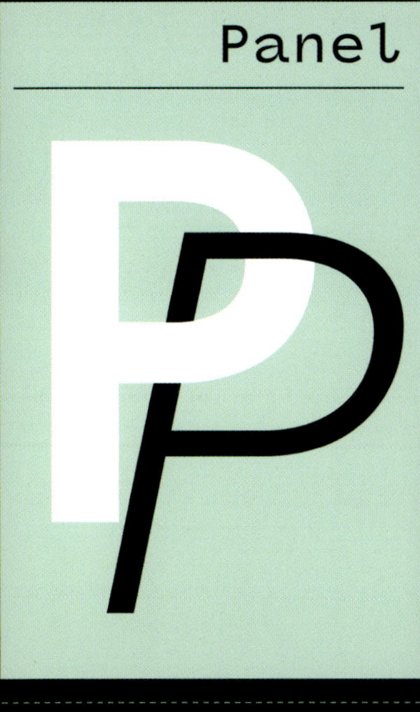

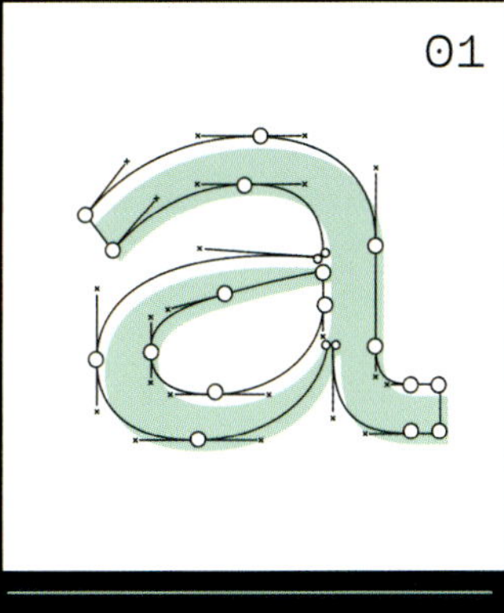

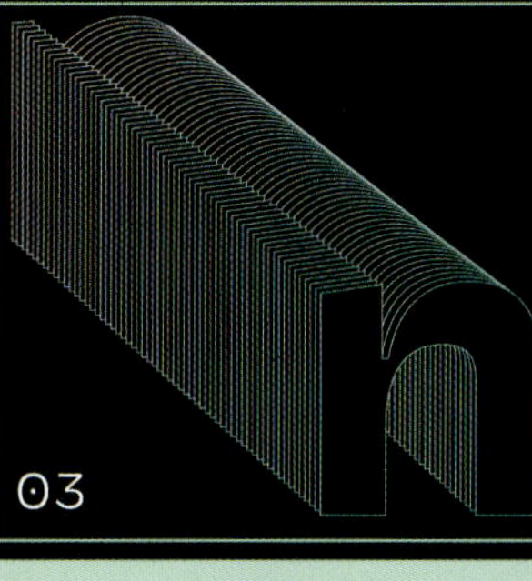

02

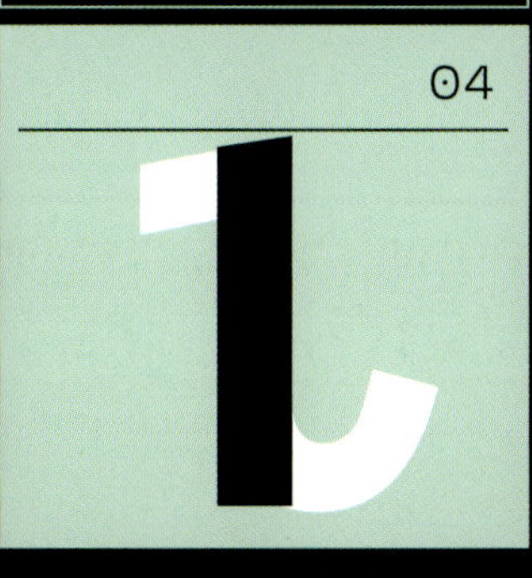

A Sophisticated Typographic Ensemble

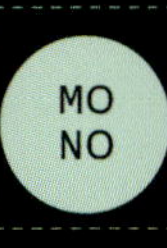

ITA LIC

S A N S

ITA LIC

PRO-RATA

05 DEFINED INSTANCES

❶****Light Intertidal Handmaiden Fancifully Mousetraps Undismayed

Submersion ❷**Regular Promulgate Sonorously Worryingly Overprints

Variable

WEIGHT AXIS | CUSTOM

300 420 900

Modularize Toxicology ❸***Medium Attendants Critically Metastable

Quadrilles Antitheses Ecumenical ❹*****Bold Uncritical Conditions

Mechanical Iconoclast Retraction Scarifying ❺****Black Compressed

"LET TER" HEAD

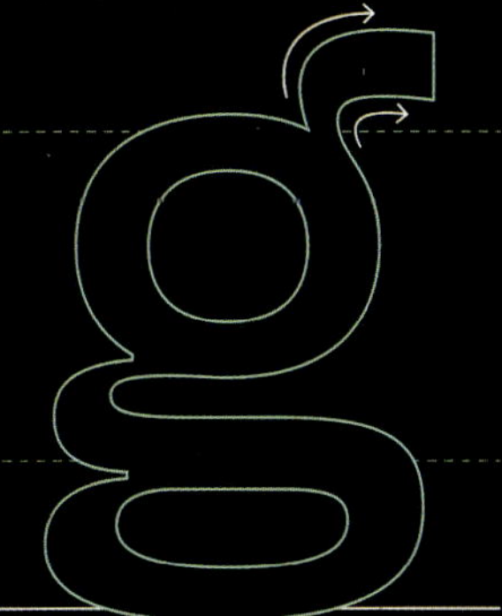

Outweighing
Motherhood
Cheekbones
Hyperplanes
Cryptogram

Once upon a time, in a small circus on the outskirts of a bustling city, lived a clown named Ziggy. Ziggy wa your or … as known boundl … atiable cu His red … ored wig, sized s … o everyor watche … under the One bri … ing, as Zig prepar … utine, a co spread … s grounds fire. A g … had arriv Dr. Astrid Stern, a renowned astrop They had come to the circus to rec clown for a unique and top-secret to outer space.

Ziggy's heart raced with excitemer watched Dr. Stern approach him. Sh plained that they needed someone spirit as lively as the stars themse

Rr

{12345
TINDERBOX
JOYRIDING
ASTROLABE
STRANGELY
BRICKLESS
CHAMPAGNE
67890}

pstypelab.com

Compressed 0001 Extra Condensed 0125
Condensed 0250 Semi Condensed 0375
Lipo™ 0500 Semi Expanded
0625 Expanded 0750
Extra Expanded 0875
Extended 1000

Αποτελεσματικούς

Music based on a single theme is called 'monothematic', while music based on several themes is called 'polythematic'.

Майбутність

I don't want to be the palate cleanser anymore.

RECHARGEABLE

Since Zen is a form of Mahayana Buddhism, it is grounded on the schema of the bodhisattva path, which is based on the practice of the "transcendent virtues" or "perfections" (Skt. pāramitā, Ch. bōluómì, Jp. baramitsu) as well as the taking of the bodhisattva vows.

WHEN YOU NEED TO EXPRESS YOUR IMPORTANT MESSAGE TO THE WORLD.

WHEN YOU'RE … FOR YOUR PROJECT. AND YOU'RE DE

MATERIALS

The first meeting of the World Health Assembly finished on 24 July 1948, having secured a budget of US$5 million(then £1,250,000) for the 1949 year.

International conference

SMOG

У виді порошку, змішаного з водою, наноситься на керамічний виріб і згодом обпалюється при значній температурі. Полива може бути прозорою (безбарвною і кольоровою) і непрозорою.

Demonstrate

Most transistors are made from very pure silicon, and some from germanium, but certain other semiconductor materials are sometimes used.

ABCDEFGHIJKLMNOPQRSTU
abcdefghijklmnopqrstuvwxy
АБВГДЕЖЗИЙКЛМНОПРСТУ
абвгдежзийклмнопрстуфхчц
ΑΒΓΔΕΖΗΘΙΚΛΜΝΞΟΠΡΣΤΥΦΧ
αβγδεζηθικλμνξοπρςστυφχψω

Stripper

Men gốm là một lớp thủy tinh có chiều dày từ 0,15-0,4 mm phủ lên bề mặt xương gốm. Lớp thủy tinh này hình thành trong quá trình nung và có tác dụng làm cho bề mặt sản phẩm trở nên sít đặc, nhẵn, bóng.

Technique

AN ORIGINAL IDEA IS ONE NOT THOUGHT UP BY ANOTHER PERSON BEFOREHAND.

Ceramic glaze

Температура її плавлення 1125—1360 °C.

Brain Illness

Lipo

suitcasetype.com

Designed by *Tomáš Brousil*
Published by *Suitcase Type*

Electroencephalogram Lipo Compressed Thin	Hermaphrodites Lipo Extra Condensed Thin	Employment Lipo Condensed Thin	Protesters Lipo Semi Condensed Thin	Rebound Lipo Thin	Unpack Lipo Semi Expanded Thin	Inborn Lipo Expanded Thin	Slings Lipo Extra Expanded Thin	Days Lipo Extended Thin
Immunocompromised Lipo Compressed Light	Musculoskeletal Lipo Extra Condensed Light	Recapitulate Lipo Condensed Light	Herbicides Lipo Semi Condensed Light	Carcases Lipo Light	Reefing Lipo Semi Expanded Light	Delete Lipo Expanded Light	Called Lipo Extra Expanded Light	Fiord Lipo Extended Light
Greatgranddaughter Lipo Compressed Regular	Revolutionising Lipo Extra Condensed Regular	Unbreakable Lipo Condensed Regular	Quadruple Lipo Semi Condensed Regular	Spinners Lipo Regular	Quotas Lipo Semi Expanded Regular	Result Lipo Expanded Regular	Digits Lipo Extra Expanded Regular	Irons Lipo Extended Regular
Hypersensitiveness Lipo Compressed Medium	Communicants Lipo Extra Condensed Medium	Predestined Lipo Condensed Medium	Wineglass Lipo Semi Condensed Medium	Fuchsias Lipo Medium	Looked Lipo Semi Expanded Medium	Flours Lipo Expanded Medium	Ballet Lipo Extra Expanded Medium	Quiff Lipo Extended Medium
Electromagnetism Lipo Compressed Demibold	Renegotiation Lipo Extra Condensed Demibold	Gymnasium Lipo Condensed Demibold	Gradation Lipo Semi Condensed Demibold	Ugandan Lipo Demibold	Display Lipo Semi Expanded Demibold	Ghana Lipo Expanded Demibold	Pump Lipo Extra Expanded Demibold	Allies Lipo Extended Demibold
Unceremoniously Lipo Compressed Semibold	Operationally Lipo Extra Condensed Semibold	Wellspoken Lipo Condensed Semibold	Censoring Lipo Semi Condensed Semibold	Oscillate Lipo Semibold	Ironical Lipo Semi Expanded Semibold	Bright Lipo Expanded Semibold	Frigid Lipo Extra Expanded Semibold	Caps Lipo Extended Semibold
Conglomeration Lipo Compressed Bold	Antiquarians Lipo Extra Condensed Bold	Coachwork Lipo Condensed Bold	Headache Lipo Semi Condensed Bold	Stripper Lipo Bold	Blames Lipo Semi Expanded Bold	Photo Lipo Expanded Bold	Glans Lipo Extra Expanded Bold	Post Lipo Extended Bold

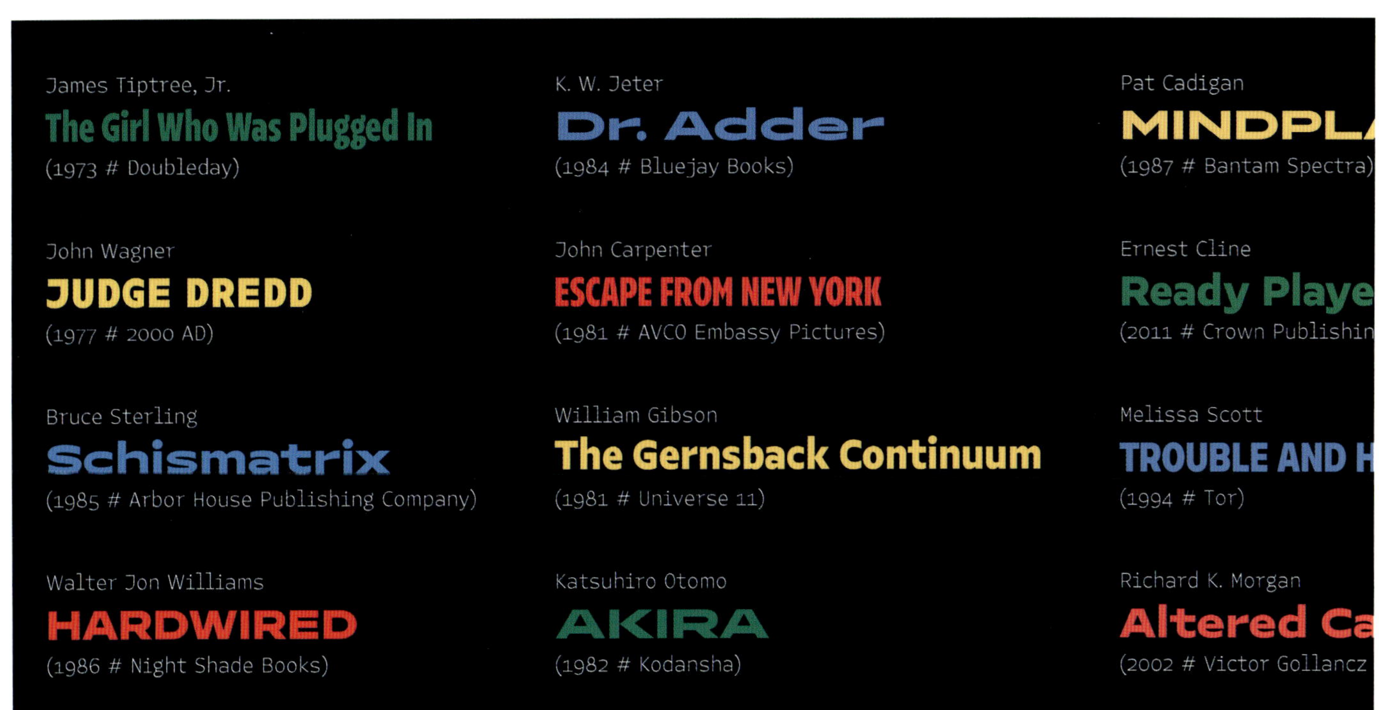

Lipo, the ultimate font for designers and typographers. With sixty-three styles available as separate OpenType fonts, Lipo spans two axes—nine width proportions from Compressed to Extended and seven weight proportions from Thin to Bold. This allows for unparalleled flexibility in design, allowing you to choose the perfect font for any project. Lipo also includes an Extended Latin set, Extended Cyrillic, and Greek, making it suitable for use in a variety of languages. Plus, with a number of stylistic sets included, you can diversify or enhance your type-setting to create truly unique designs. And if that wasn't enough, Lipo also includes Lipo Text—a proportional font with a monospaced character in seven weights with adequate italics.

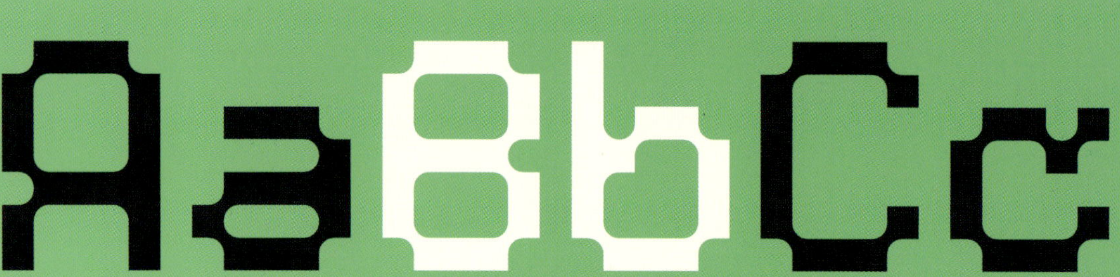

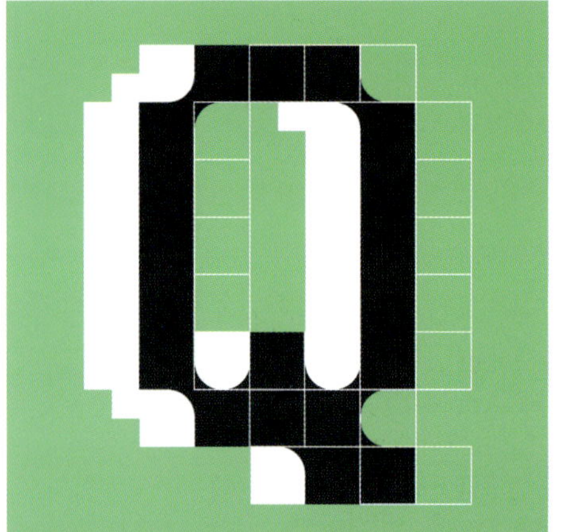

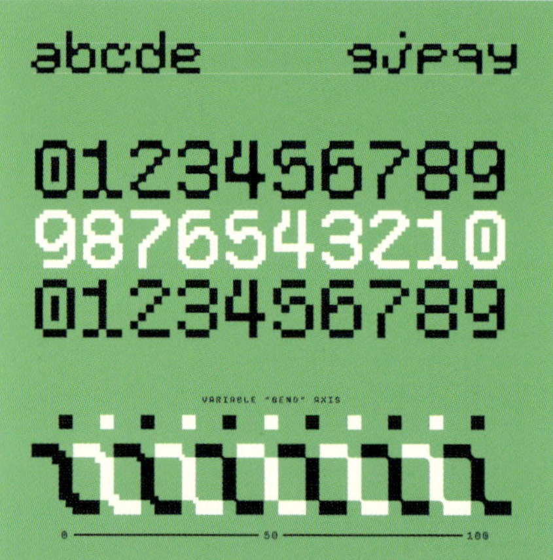

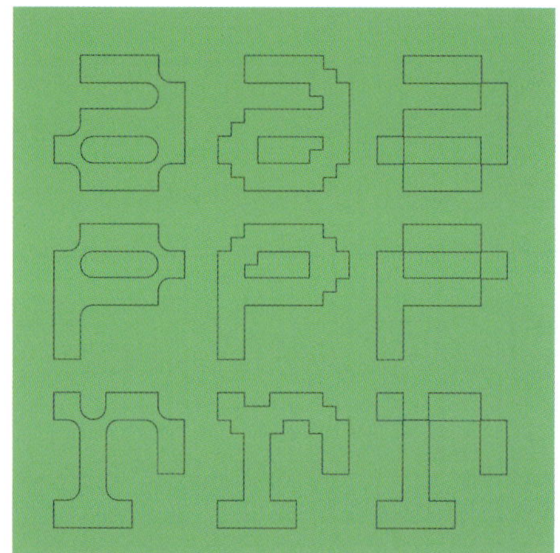

california waves guacamole mix
california waves guacamole mix
california waves guacamole mix
ithaca bar quiz flops when dog joke vexes many
ithaca bar quiz flops when dog joke vexes many
ithaca bar quiz flops when dog joke vexes many
Voting will begin after the queens unanimously pardon ex-convicts via jump kicking zebras
Voting will begin after the queens unanimously pardon ex-convicts via jump kicking zebras
Voting will begin after the queens unanimously pardon ex-convicts via jump kicking zebras

kale kale kale
ajar ajar ajar
lass lass lass
fads fads fads
jump jump jump
tuft tuft tuft
anti anti anti
tube tube tube

A wild and wacky monospace pixel(ish) font with no descenders! Three styles and a variable BEND *axis to control all corners and details.*

Quirque

etceteratype.co

Designed by *Ty Finck*
Published by *Etcetera Type Company*

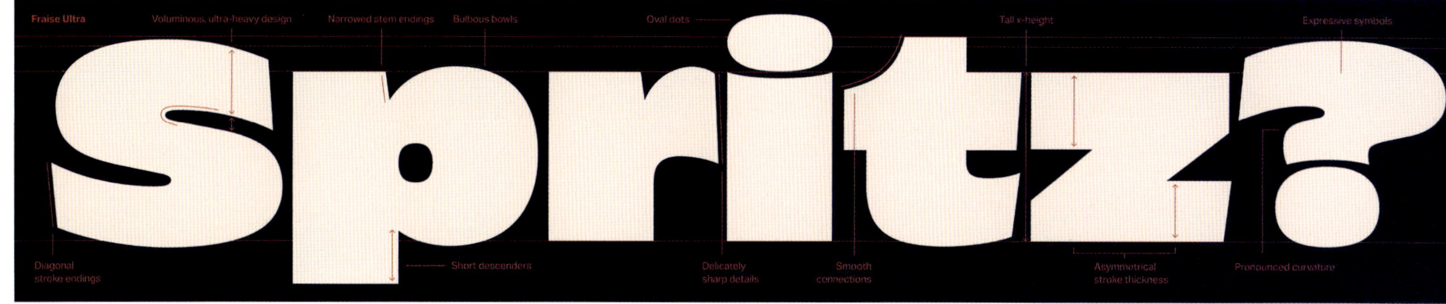

Miljøvernorganisasjoner
Energiförbrukningsnivå
Contemporaneamente
Rakentamispalveluista
Nejspecializovanějšími
Uneingeschränktheit
Telecommunication
Misinterpretation
Intercontinental
Entwicklungen

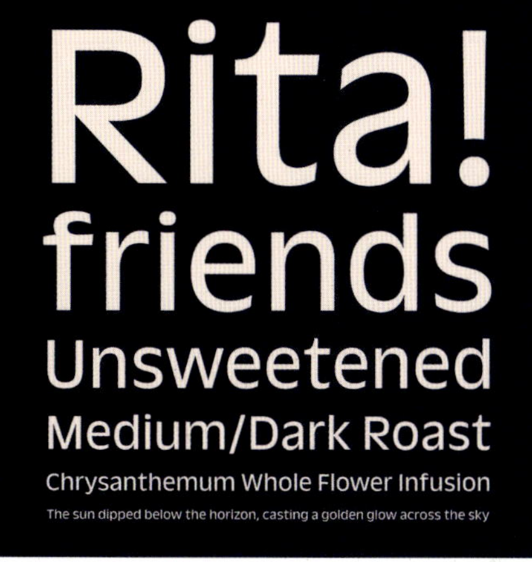

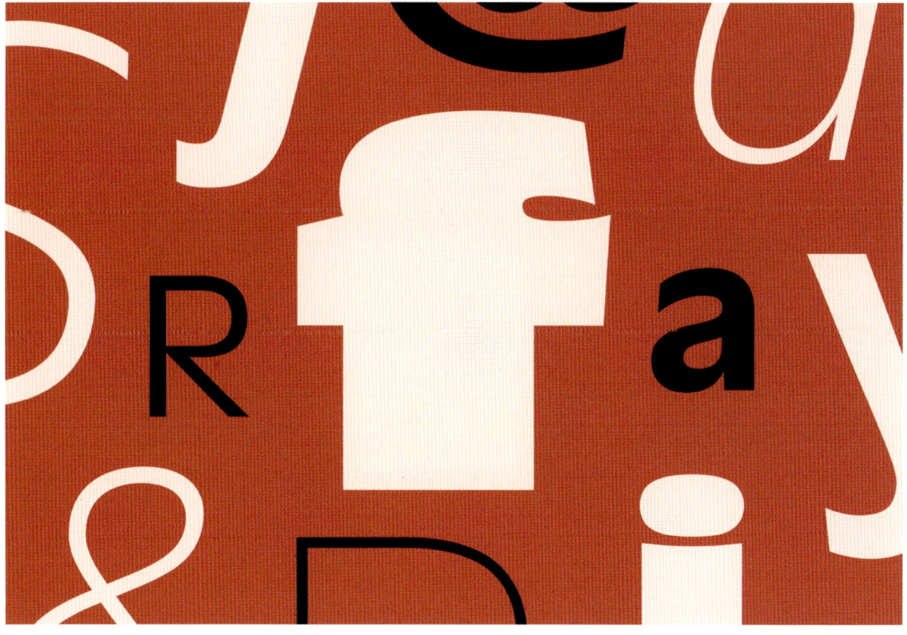

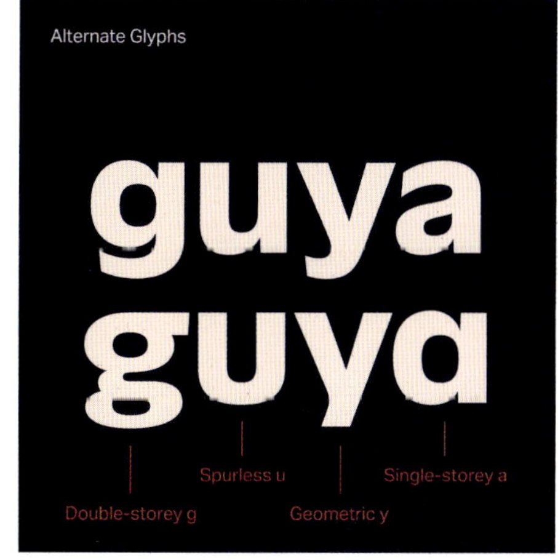

Fraise is a fresh and fruity humanist sans typeface with a tall x-height and distinctive round shapes, inspired by the work of Roger Excoffon. Its extensive Weight axis makes it suitable for a huge range of design and branding applications from body text to display.

daltonmaag.com

Fraise

Designed by *Pablo Bosch*
Published by *Dalton Maag*

VERBOSE-TABULAR FIGURES

0123456789
9876543210
0123456789

VERBOSE-VARIABLE

ABC ABC

75 "WDTH" 125

Verbose

etceteratype.co

Designed by *Ty Finck*
Published by *Etcetera Type Company*

FRANK

OCEAN OCEAN OCEAN OCEAN OCEAN

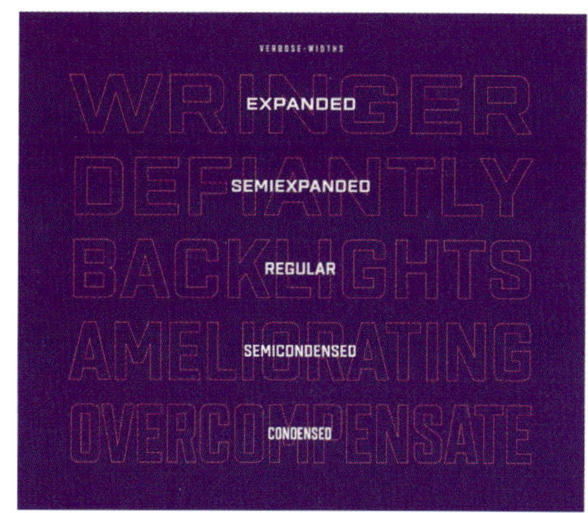

VERBOSE-UPPERCASE

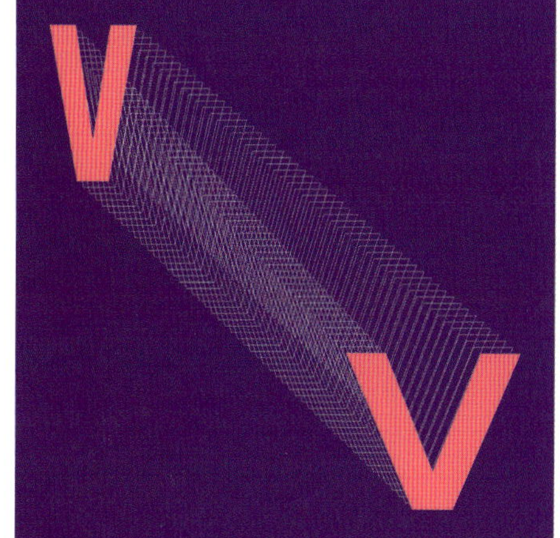

VERBOSE-LOWERCASE

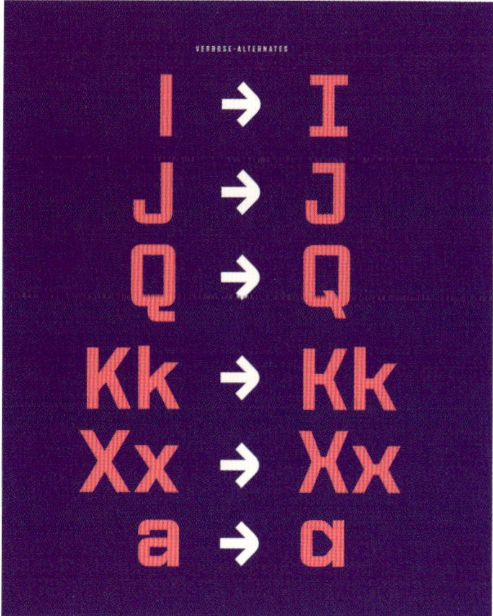

VERBOSE-SMALL CAPS

A sturdy, clean, mechanical-looking font in a variety of widths. While it contains very nice lowercase forms, the intended use was for ALL CAPS. *So there are some small caps, too. It's versatile, even in only one weight.*

Quousque Tandem Abutere, Catilina, Patientia Nostra?
An Essay by Erik Spiekermann

An earlier version of Erik's essay first appeared on the FontShop website and then again in the printed specimen book for his typeface neue Serie57 (page 88).

A hundred years ago, designing typeface specimens must have been a dream job for a commercial artist. It was about creating an image of printed matter where nothing was real except for the fonts used. Although the fonts offered were supposed to set the scene for advertisements, leaflets, letterheads, and business cards, and make them look good, text and all content could be freely invented and subjected entirely to the aesthetic concerns of the designed page. Miraculously, each sentence came together in perfect rhythmic lines and even the rarest letter combinations, special characters, vignettes, and lines were used to show how each new and unique typeface would give every printed matter, no matter how banal, an unmistakable expression.

The efforts those in-house printers went to were enormous. The compositor in charge was not only able to use the full repertory of the type foundry and imagine typeface mixtures unseen before, they were also allowed to intervene where manual typesetting revealed aesthetic shortcomings. For example, they could cut out annoying gaps such as the distance between *T* and *e* with a lead saw—no commercial client would have paid for this laborious work. Apart from the publishers of these typeface specimens, which were often more than eight hundred pages long, no one else would have put in the effort with which the in-house printers of the foundries produced their products in special colors on the finest paper, using the latest printing presses. The pages of the specimen books had as little to do with the reality of commercial printers as the illustrations in cookbooks by star chefs had anything to do with the products of everyday cooks. However, both fulfill their purpose: The hobby chef gets the desire to cook from the image of the dishes created under laboratory conditions, just as the typesetter gets the appetite for new typefaces from the sample book of the type foundry.

Mind you, buying a new typeface for hot metal typesetting was a much more expensive pleasure than shopping at the weekly market. Metal fonts were sold by weight and even the minimum set of a 9-point typeface came to 6 kg and cost many times the monthly wage of a typesetter at that time. According to the casting slip, this minimum contained —depending on the required language—about twenty lowercase *a*'s, thirty *e*'s, and five *x*'s, so it was never enough to typeset a page of a novel, but only a few business cards. Investments in commercial typefaces had to be carefully considered, especially since several sizes had to be purchased and, in addition to mechanical wear and tear, there was also wear and tear by fashion, which typographic products in particular were subject to. Type specimens had to reflect as closely as possible the commercial reality of the type buyer, and at the same time make the typefaces look so good that typographic salivation set in.

Beyond the culinary illustrations in the elaborately produced color section of the samples, as many characters as possible had to be shown in all deliverable grades in the actual listings for all available sizes. Not all characters, mind you, because repro technology had advanced to the point where new punches and dies could be made from negatives of alphabets shown, which were then used to produce qualitatively inferior but cheaper imitations. This was still a lot of work, but it involved less entrepreneurial risk than designing and making a face known in the market.

This approach may sound familiar. Unfortunately, today's digital copy does not show any

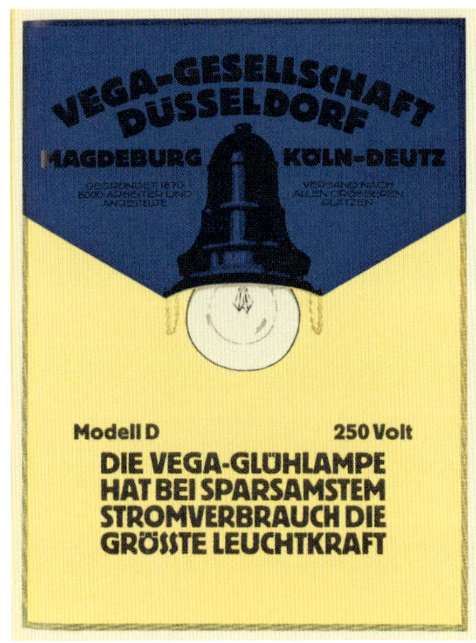

↑ *The designers of this specimen for Berthold's Block family invented their own brands, complete with logos and illustrations. Vega supposedly made light bulbs. The four lines at the bottom show how to achieve a justified block of type, using alternate characters: wide and narrow forms of E, H, R, and a sexy double-s ligature.*

↓ *Akzidenz Grotesk Serie 57 in 16 point has kerned characters as alternatives.The top line shows Ta, Ve, Wo und Yn not kerned. The line below are the kerned pairs. Next to them: additional ligatures for ch and ck.*

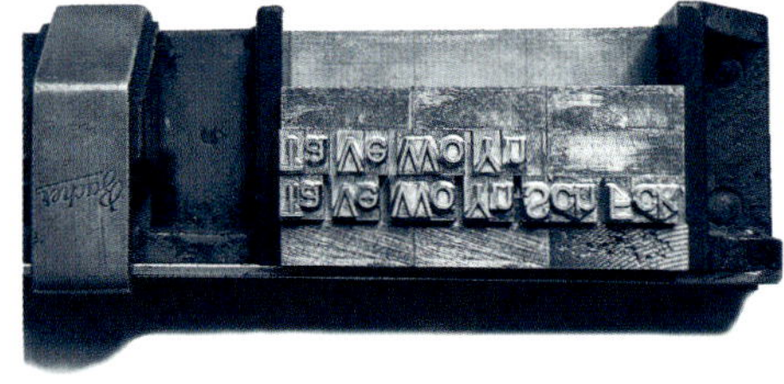

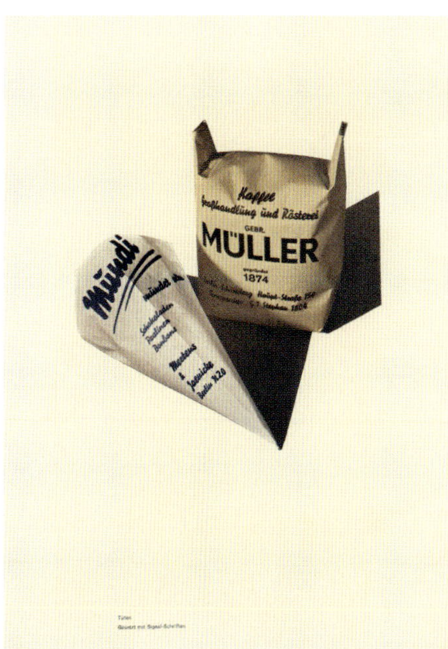

↑ *A long time before Photoshop, made-up packages as in this page from a 1934 specimen for Signal, had to be letterpress-printed on paper, arranged for the photograph, reproduced, and then printed again.*

↓ *To cover all practical applications, Akzidenz Grotesk Medium was cast in 4/5, 5/6, 8, 10 (small body), 10 (large body), 12, 14, 16, 20, 24, 28, 36, 48, and 60pt. The type is displayed in two languages to show an audience of German printers how internationally successful the face had become.*

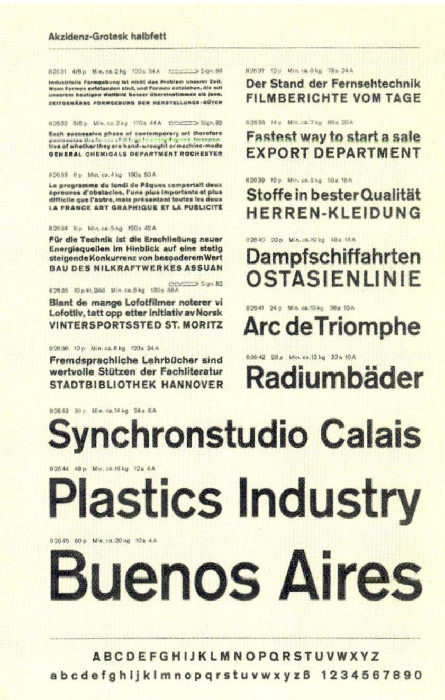

Akzidenz-Grotesk halbfett

82631 4/6 p Min. ca. 2 kg 170a 34A Sign. 86
Industrielle Formgebung ist nicht das Problem unserer Zeit. Wenn Formen entstanden sind, und Formen entstehen, die mit unserem heutigen Weltbild besser übereinstimmen als jene.
ZEITGEMÄSSE FORMGEBUNG DER HERSTELLUNGS-GÜTER

82632 5/6 p Min. ca. 3 kg 170a 44A Sign. 82
Each successive phase of contemporary art therefore [illegible] tive of whether they are hand-wrought or machine-made
GENERAL CHEMICALS DEPARTMENT ROCHESTER

82633 6 p Min. ca. 4 kg 190a 50A
Le programme du lundi de Pâques comportait deux épreuves d'obstacles, l'une plus importante et plus difficile que l'autre, mais présentent toutes les deux
LA FRANCE ART GRAPHIQUE ET LA PUBLICITÉ

82634 8 p Min. ca. 5 kg 150a 42A
Für die Technik ist die Erschließung neuer Energiequellen im Hinblick auf eine stetig steigende Konkurrenz von besonderem Wert
BAU DES NILKRAFTWERKES ASSUAN

82635 10 p kl. Bild Min. ca. 6 kg 130a 38A Sign. 82
Blant de mange Lofotfilmer noterer vi Lofotliv, tatt opp etter initiativ av Norsk
VINTERSPORTSSTED ST. MORITZ

82636 10 p Min. ca. 6 kg 120a 34A
Fremdsprachliche Lehrbücher sind wertvolle Stützen der Fachliteratur
STADTBIBLIOTHEK HANNOVER

82637 12 p Min. ca. 6 kg 78a 24A
Der Stand der Fernsehtechnik
FILMBERICHTE VOM TAGE

82638 14 p Min. ca. 7 kg 66a 20A
Fastest way to start a sale
EXPORT DEPARTMENT

82639 16 p Min. ca. 8 kg 56a 18A
Stoffe in bester Qualität
HERREN-KLEIDUNG

82640 20 p Min. ca. 10 kg 48a 14A
Dampfschiffahrten
OSTASIENLINIE

82641 24 p Min. ca. 10 kg 38a 10A
Arc de Triomphe

82642 28 p Min. ca. 12 kg 32a 10A
Radiumbäder

82643 36 p Min. ca. 14 kg 24a 8A
Synchronstudio Calais

82644 48 p Min. ca. 16 kg 12a 4A
Plastics Industry

82645 60 p Min. ca. 20 kg 10a 4A
Buenos Aires

ABCDEFGHIJKLMNOPQRSTUVWXYZ
abcdefghijklmnopqrstuvwxyzß 1234567890

physical loss of quality, hiding the intellectual theft much more cleverly than the technique of electroplating, which was also widespread at the time, where the thief still had to get hold of a set of original letters, which they then reproduced galvanically; for example, by covering a letter with a thin layer of copper, which would then provide the matrix for casting lead type.

While the designers of the colored, reality-imitating type specimens could and should pull out all the stops of their skills, the representation of black-and-white printed alphabets required cooperation between typesetter and author. Short fragments of sentences or—in the case of larger sizes—individual words had to be invented and arranged in such a way that they did not produce legible context and thus did not turn the viewer into a reader. A whole page of such words and phrases represented all available sizes of a typeface, brought to the same line width. In the example below left, a Berthold Akzidenz Grotesk Medium specimen, the sizes range from 4, 5, 6, 8, 10, 12, 14, 16, 20, 24, 28, 36, and 48 to 60 point.

Today, type families have up to nine weights and sometimes four widths, all plus italics. There are no longer any fixed sizes, but one original must suffice for everything, from tiny text in 4 point to page-filling headlines. In order to represent this range, the designers of today's digital type specimens also resort to reproducing each weight in a word, creating a fine rhythm between large and small, bold and fine, narrow and wide, roman and italic. Since every language has its own appearance, different character frequencies, and sometimes an accent on every other character, almost all languages can be found in a sample to be typeset with the Latin alphabet.

As nowadays everything that comes into the world digitally is copied anyway, a type specimen can now show all characters without fear of photographic reproduction. There are often more than seven hundred glyphs just for one set in the complete range with Cyrillic and Greek alphabets, ligatures, special characters, diacritics, ornaments, small caps, and at least four types of numerals. A complete overview of all glyphs in tabular form is thus mandatory, while pangrams (sets containing every letter of the alphabet) are popular for displaying the normal letters. For the sake of brevity, such pangrams are popular in which each letter occurs only once, if possible. For English, *the quick brown fox jumps over the lazy dog* is well known because all twenty-six letters occur in a sentence with only thirty-five characters. French, but still quite short is, *portez ce vieux whisky au juge blond qui fume,* albeit without accents, while the German sentence *Victor jagt zwölf Boxkämpfer quer über den Sylter Deich* contains all umlauts for that language. *Hamburgefonstiv,* a short test word that shows all the different shapes of letters, had become established among type foundries in the twentieth century. This word is sufficient for the designer to judge a new typeface, because not only are the round, oblique, and straight forms—as well as ascender, descender, and capital—represented, but also the most common and form-defining letters: *e, n, s,* and *a*. When I wanted a word for my own publications that had these properties—but was shorter and just as memorable—I invented the nonsense word *Handgloves,* a somewhat redundant word in English, but a nod to the German *Handschuhe,* which literally means "hand-shoes."

The shortcomings of these representations, which can never depict all languages with their letter frequencies, accents, and peculiarities—such as umlauts or special forms like our German ß (a double-s ligature)—to general satisfaction, were avoided by the king of letterpress printers and printer of kings, Giambattista Bodoni. He set his type specimens in Latin—still the language of science and the church in his day at the beginning of the nineteenth century. With its classical mixture of vowels and consonants without annoying accents or umlauts, but lots of short words, Latin looks above all good and elegant. Even though many typefaces are neither elegant nor classical, quite a few type specimens since then have quoted the text Bodoni chose for the fonts from his Officina (workshop). We know it from Latin classes as the incipit: the beginning of the first of the four speeches against Catilina that Cicero delivered in the Roman Senate. The most famous dummy text since then reads: *Quousque tandem abutere, Catilina, patientia nostra? (When, O Catiline, do you mean to cease abusing our patience?)*

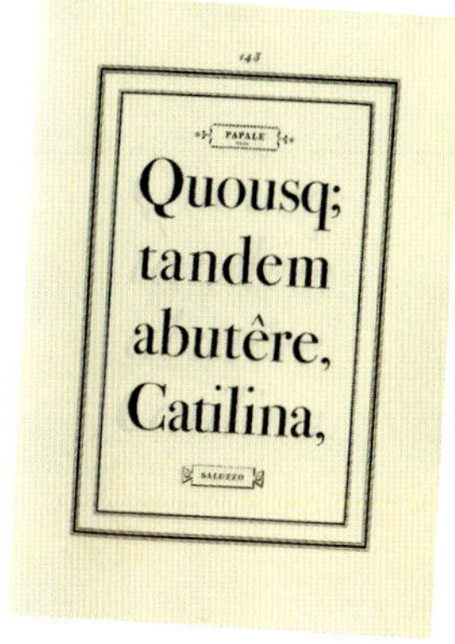

Quousq;
tandem
abutêre,
Catilina,

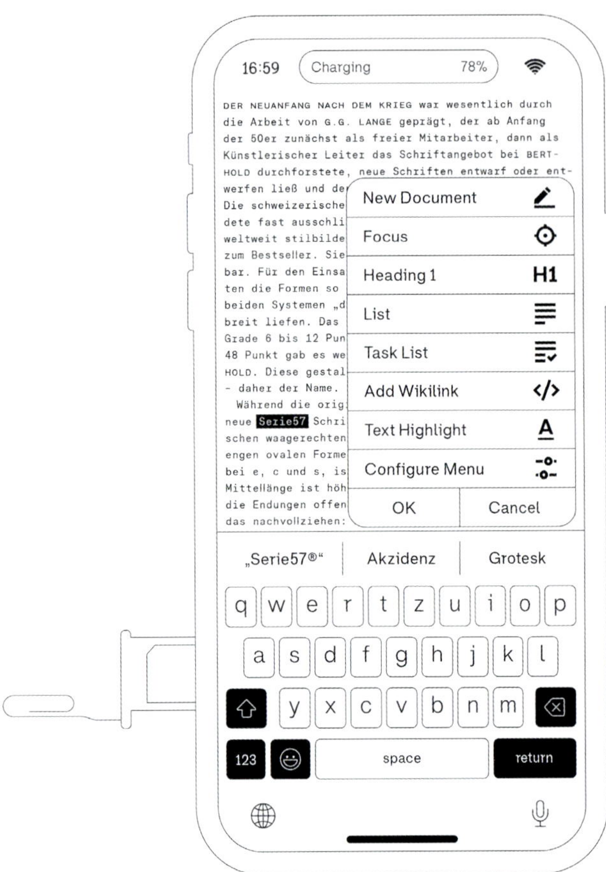

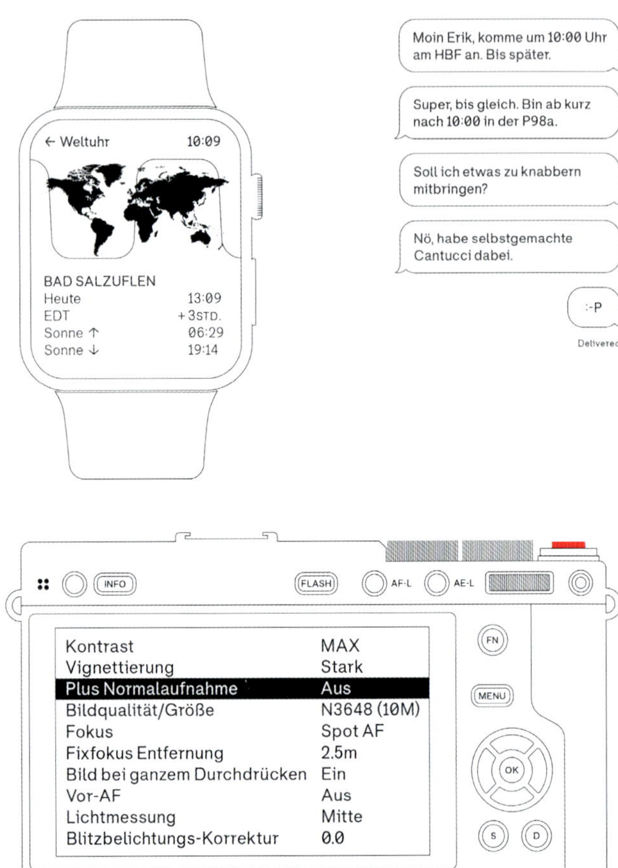

neue Serie57 is neither a revival, nor a reworking of an old type. It is a discovery—or rather a rediscovery. Designed by Günter Gerhard Lange in 1957, who had caught the spirit of the times and simplified the youngest child of the Akzidenz-Grotesk family. Unfortunately, it was never made into a family—until Erik Spiekermann discovered it in a mislabelled case. Prints from the original metal type were used by Alexander Roth to design the very first digital version of Akzidenz-Grotesk Serie 57.

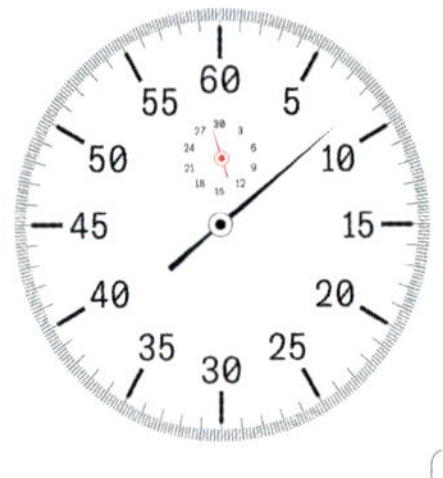

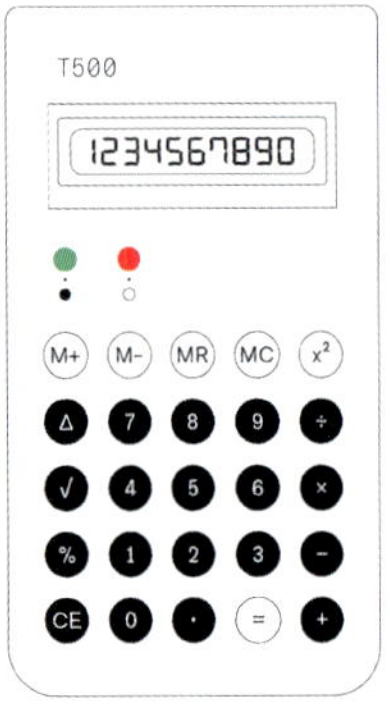

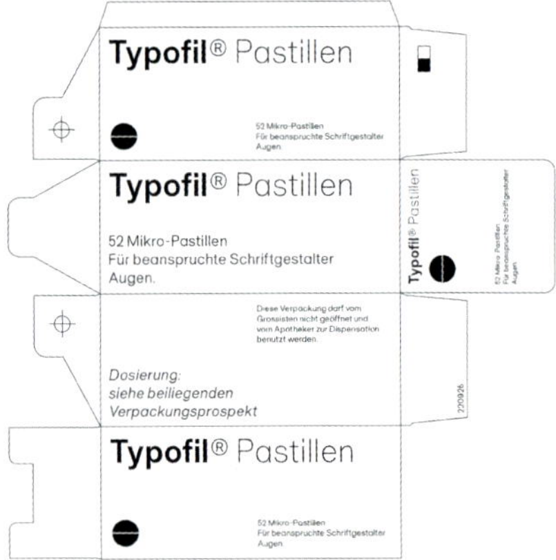

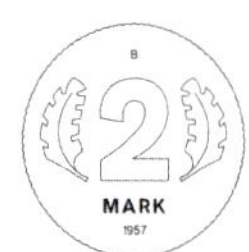

neue Serie57

neue.shop

Designed by *Erik Spiekermann, Alexander Roth*
Published by *Neue*

Empfänger: Name, Vorname / Firma (max. 27 Stellen)
Alexander Roth
Konto-Nr. des Empfängers
2305091030
Bankleitzahl
48250110
bei (Kreditinstitut)
SPARKASSE LEMGO
Währung
EUR
Betrag
19,57
Kunden-Referenznummer – noch Verwendungszweck, ggf. Name und Anschrift des Auftraggebers (nur für Empfänger)
neue Serie57® Monospaced
noch Verwendungszweck (insgesamt max. 2 Zeilen à 27 Stellen)
Schriftmuster
Kontoinhaber/Einzahler: Name (max 27 Stellen, keine Straßen- oder Postfachangaben)
Erik Spiekermann
Konto-Nr. des Kontoinhabers
30051947

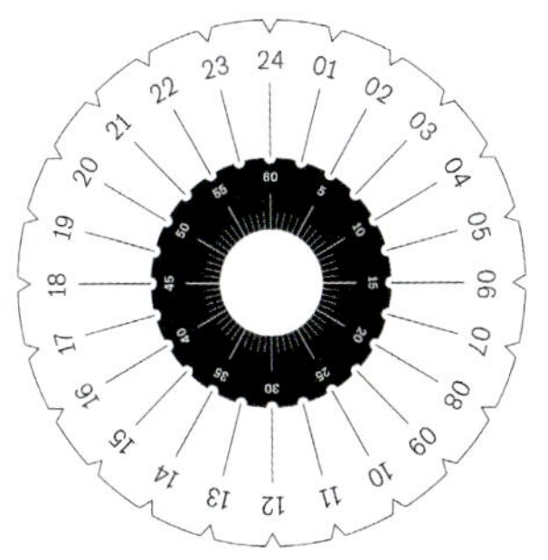

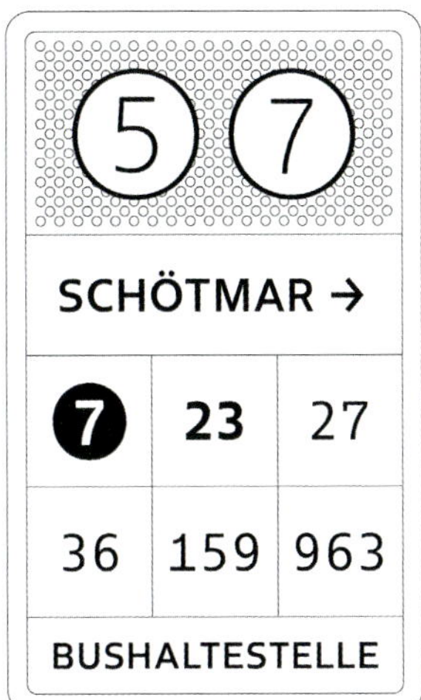

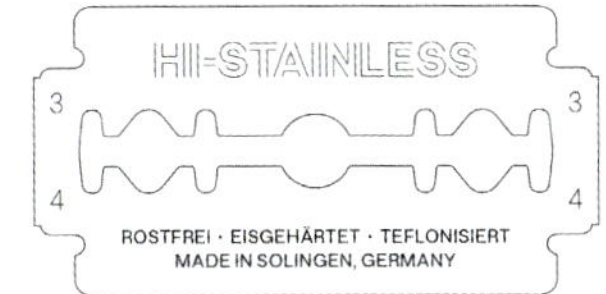

neue Serie57® Schablone 32 pt
1 in. 25,4 mm
Made in Germany

ABCDEFGHIJKLMNOPQRSTUVWXYZ .,!?[{(–+÷
aabcdefgghijklmnopqrstuvwxyzß 0123456789 ⊖

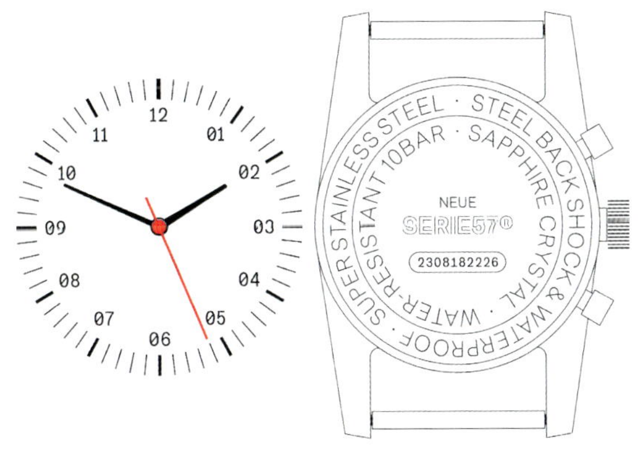

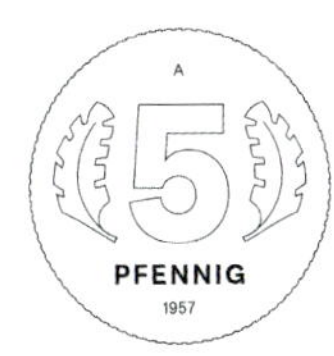

A109

Technischer Betrieb

BERLIN

Der Senat von Berlin

Fachbereich
Betriebswerkstätten
Planbüro
Dr. Prof. Florian Heinz

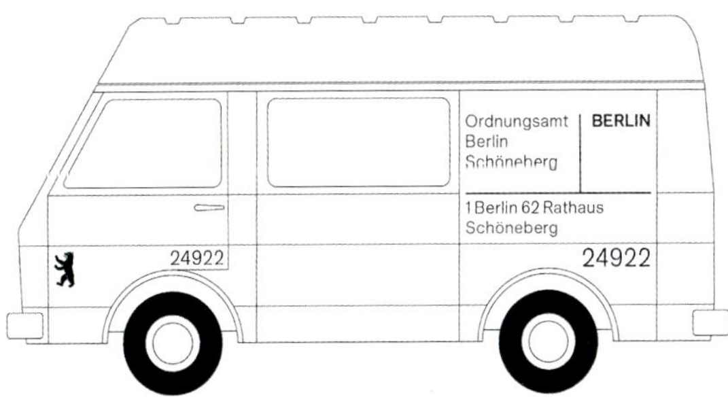

Deutsches Turnfest 1968

BERLIN

In Anerkennung der von Dir im Wettkampf erzielten Leistung

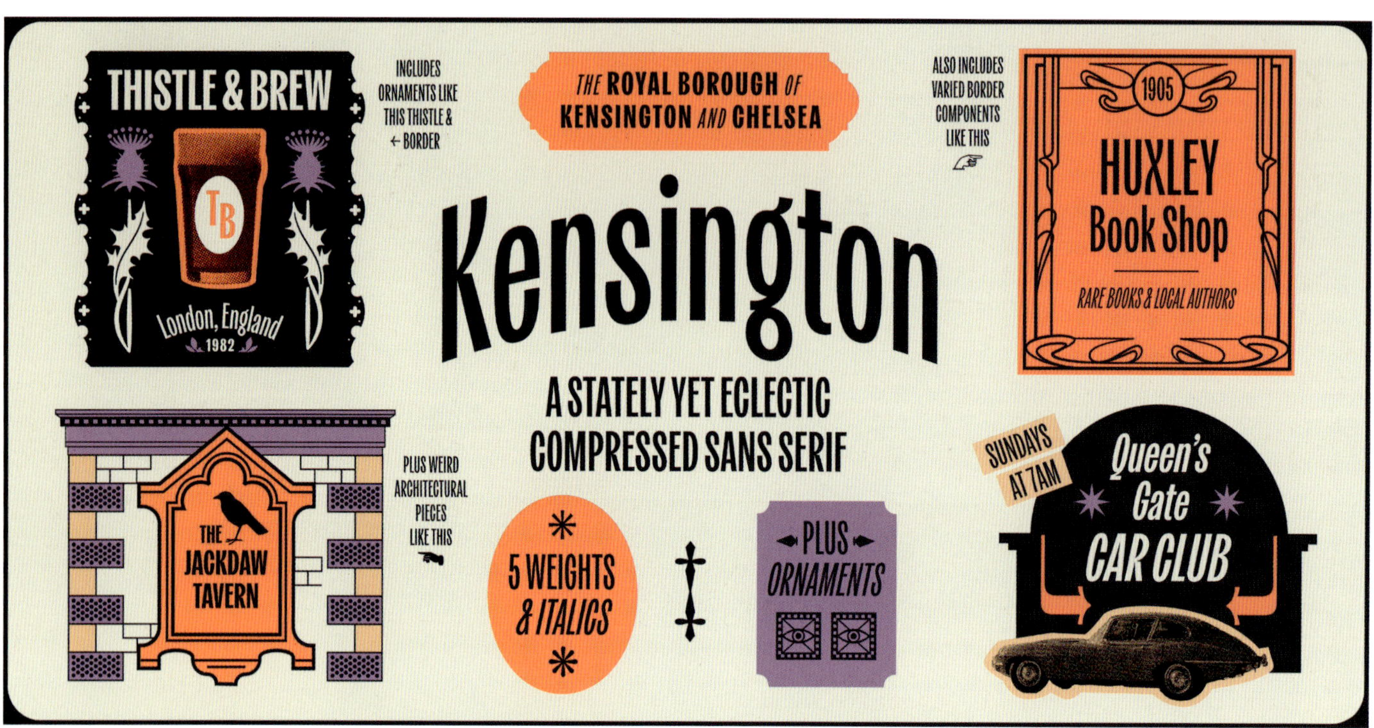

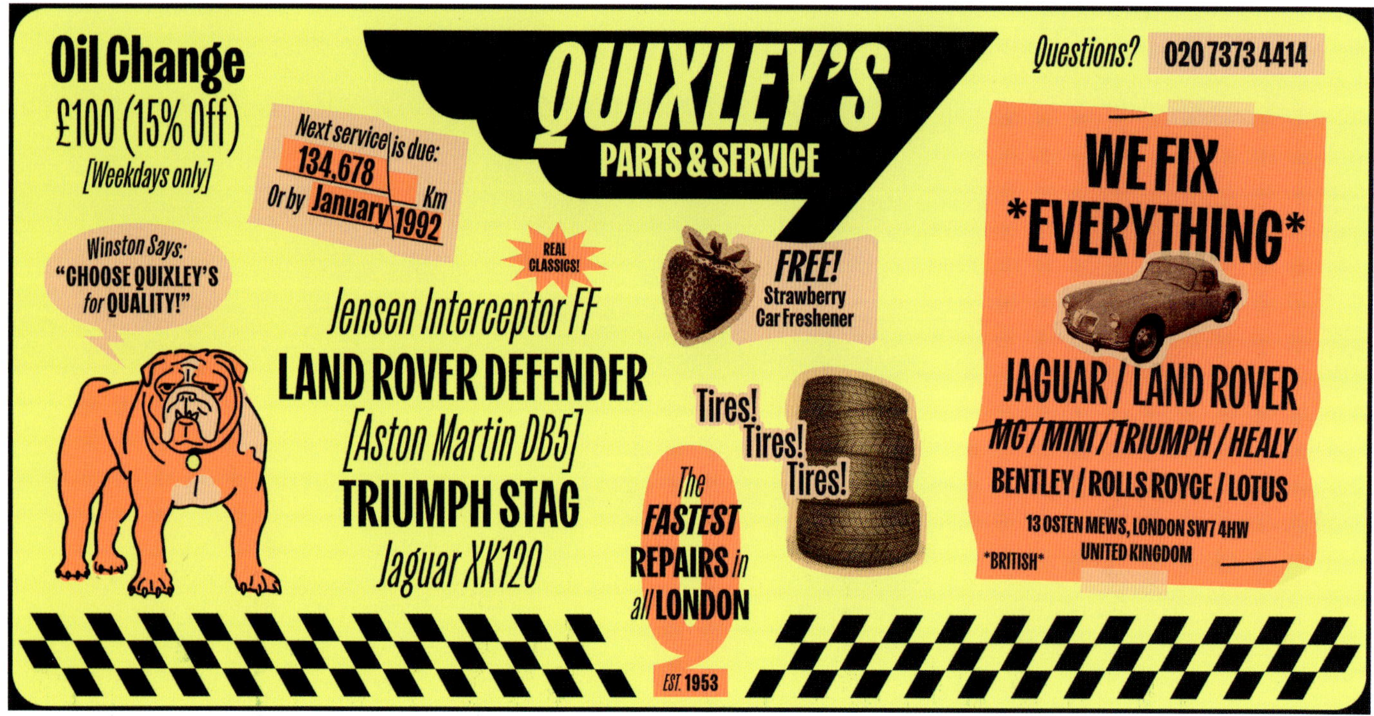

Kensington

fortfoundry.com

Designed by *Jennifer Hood*
Published by *Fort Foundry*

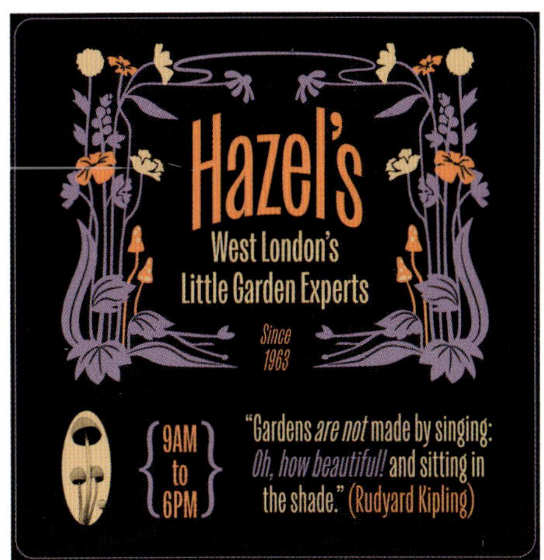

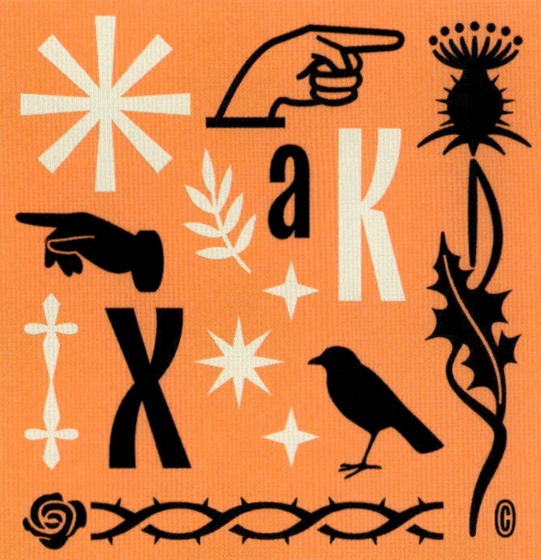

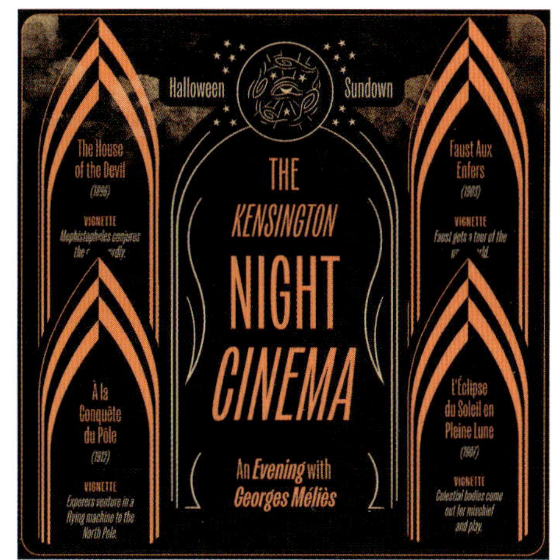

The lake Kensington Gardens *Fish & Chips* *Cask Ales* ← REGULAR

Exquisite narrow homes *iced with* *brick and stucco* MEDIUM

Located @15 Adam and Eve Mews, *London W8 6UG!* DEMI

Wandering the ✻ quaint ✻ cobblestone Mews BOLD

Brompton Cemetery *established 1840* BLACK

5 WEIGHTS + ITALICS, PLUS ORNAMENTS & ALTERNATES

a → a g → g x → x

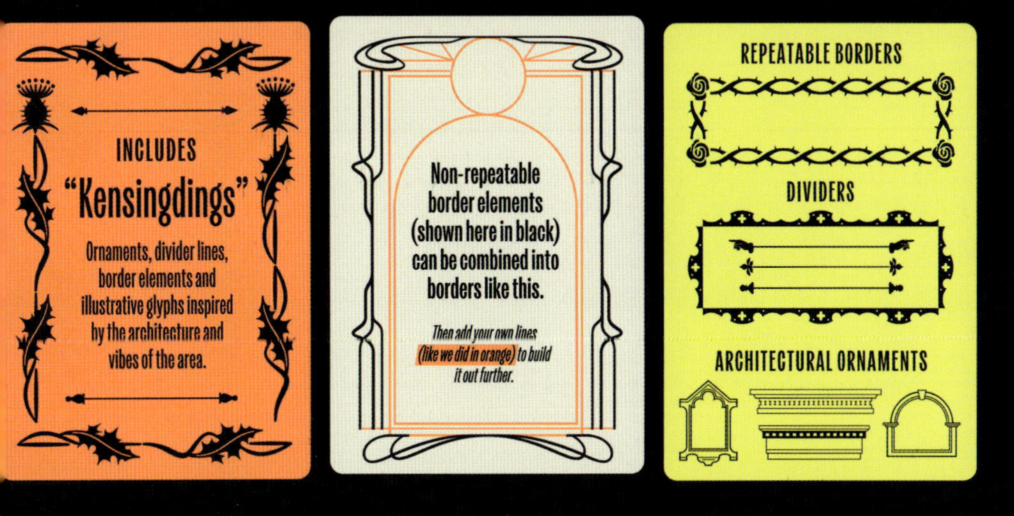

Kensington is a narrow, stately, and eclectic sans serif inspired by the exquisitely compact and charming area of West London. From the stately porticos of Victorian-style townhomes, to the quaint, cobblestoned mews, the ornate museums and embassies, the spires and steeples peeking through the chimney tops, and the whimsical gardens—Kensington's appeal is in its densely packed variety. This typeface offers the same: a compact charm that you can't quite tie to one style or time. Available in five weights plus italics, the typeface can sway from elegant to bold. Unexpected flourishes in letters like the x, g, and k, lend whimsicality to any text. Kensington features international language support, stylistic alternates, and ornamental dingbats that the designer affectionately calls Kensingdings.

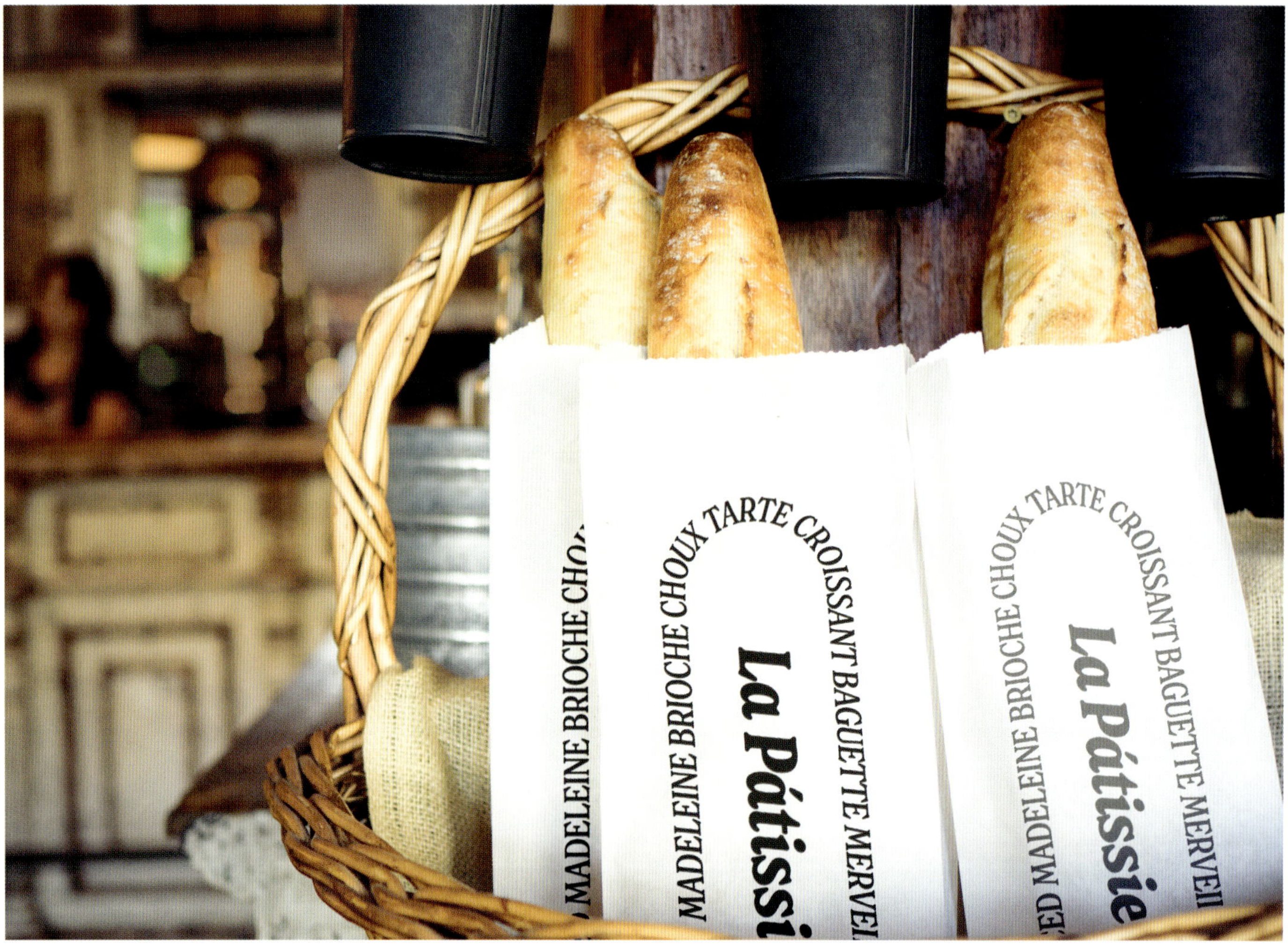

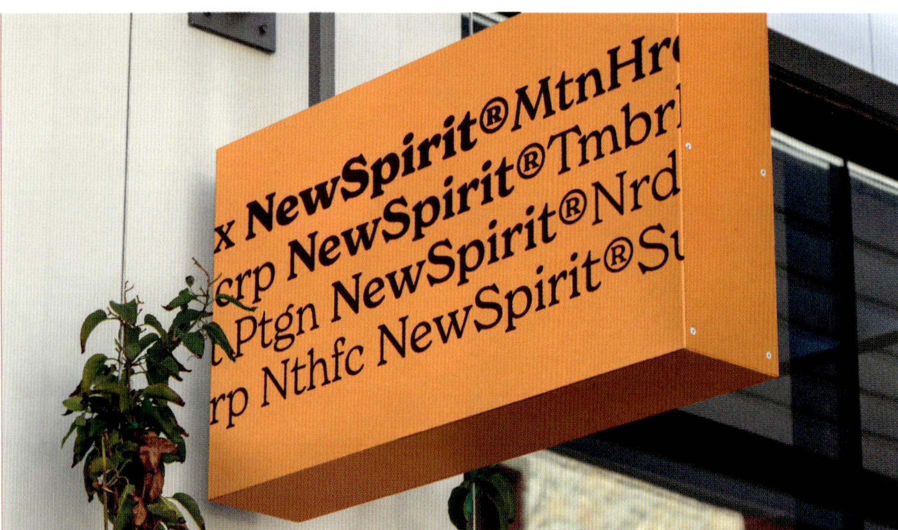

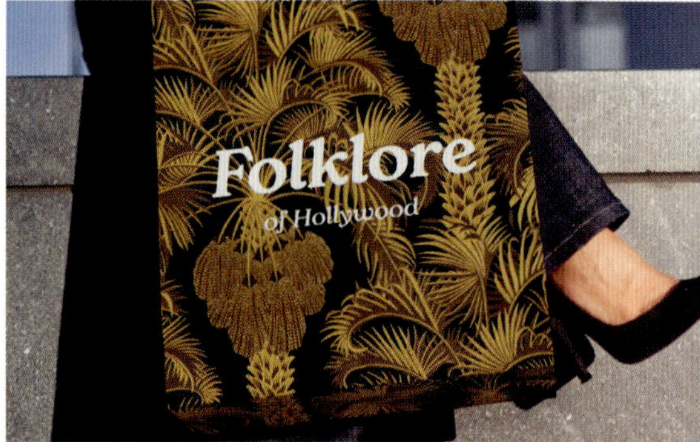

Like a half-remembered dream—entirely familiar, sort of comforting, but can't be pinpointed to a particular time or place—New Spirit is both nostalgic and entirely enigmatic.

New Spirit

newlyn.com

Designed by *Miles Newlyn*
Published by *Newlyn*

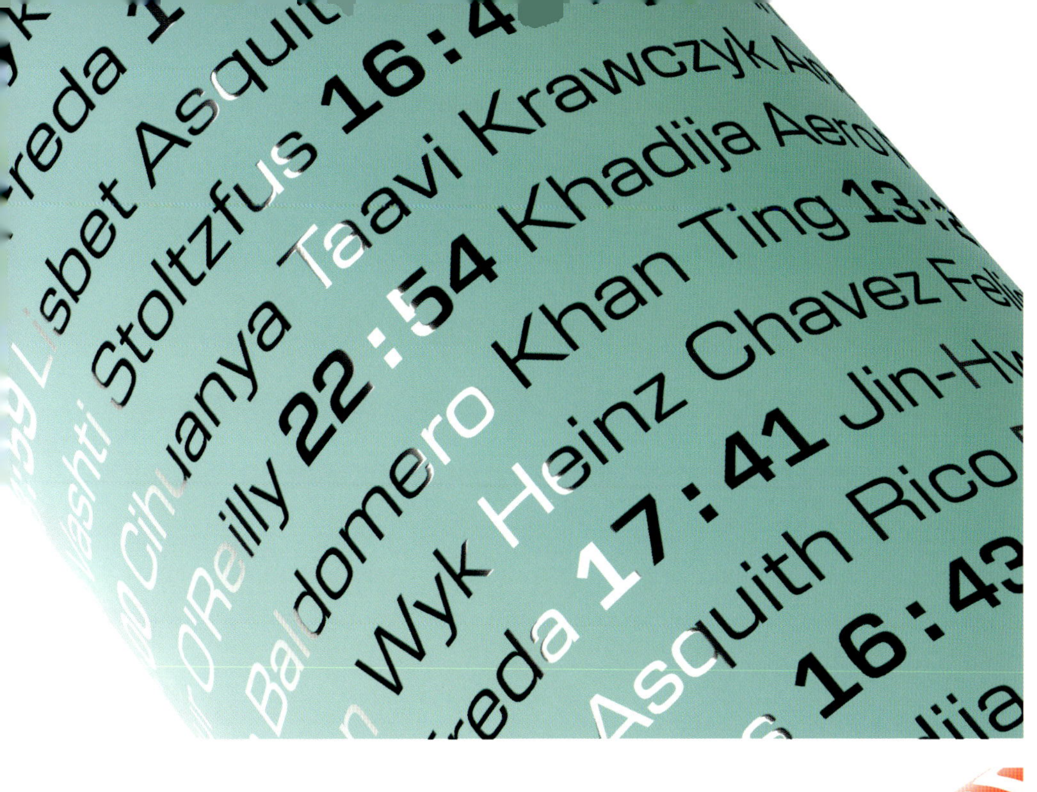

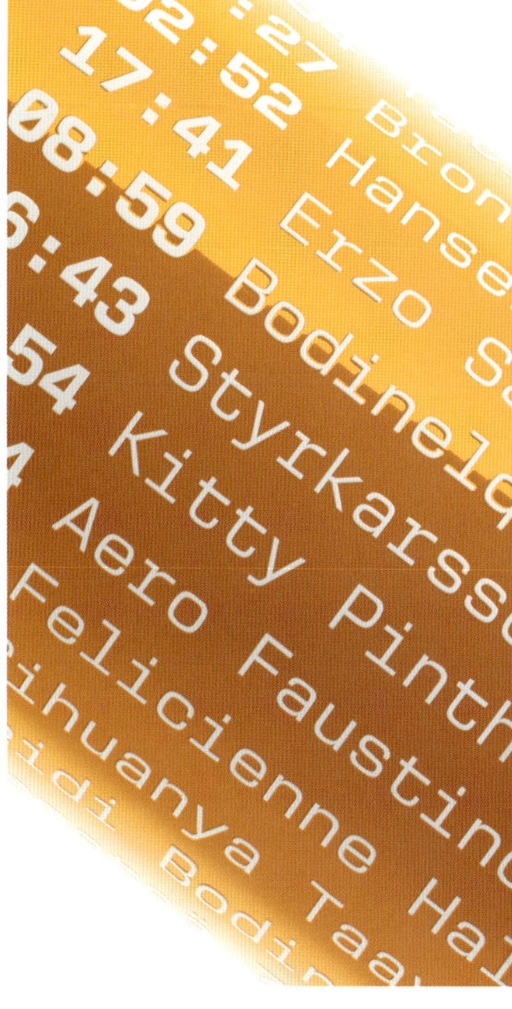

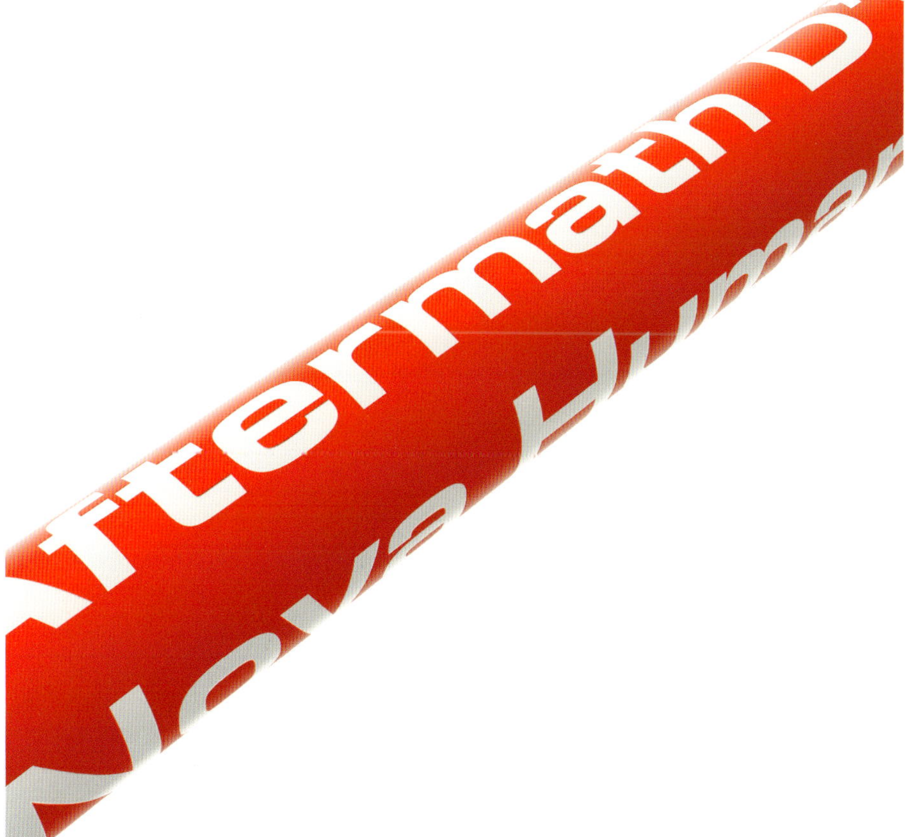

New Science is a typeface designed to embody a sense of precision, technological advancement, and stability. It's inspired by Eurostile, but refines its features to create a more contemporary look. The typeface explores the concept of square-shaped letterforms—a design approach that evokes a structured, high-tech feel, making it suitable for branding and identity work in industries associated with innovation.

---

newlyn.com

New Science

Designed by *Miles Newlyn*
Published by *Newlyn*

Brighten up your design

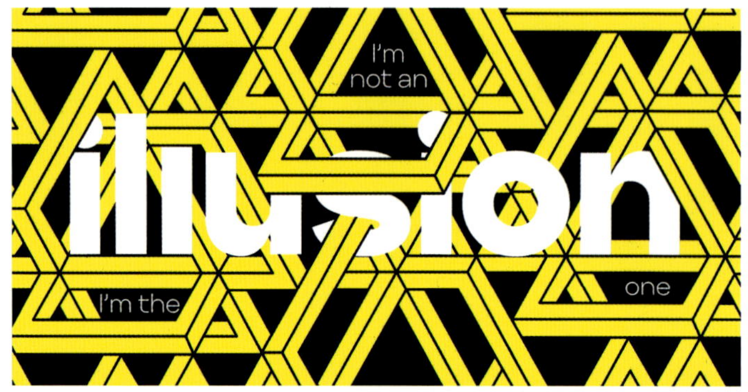

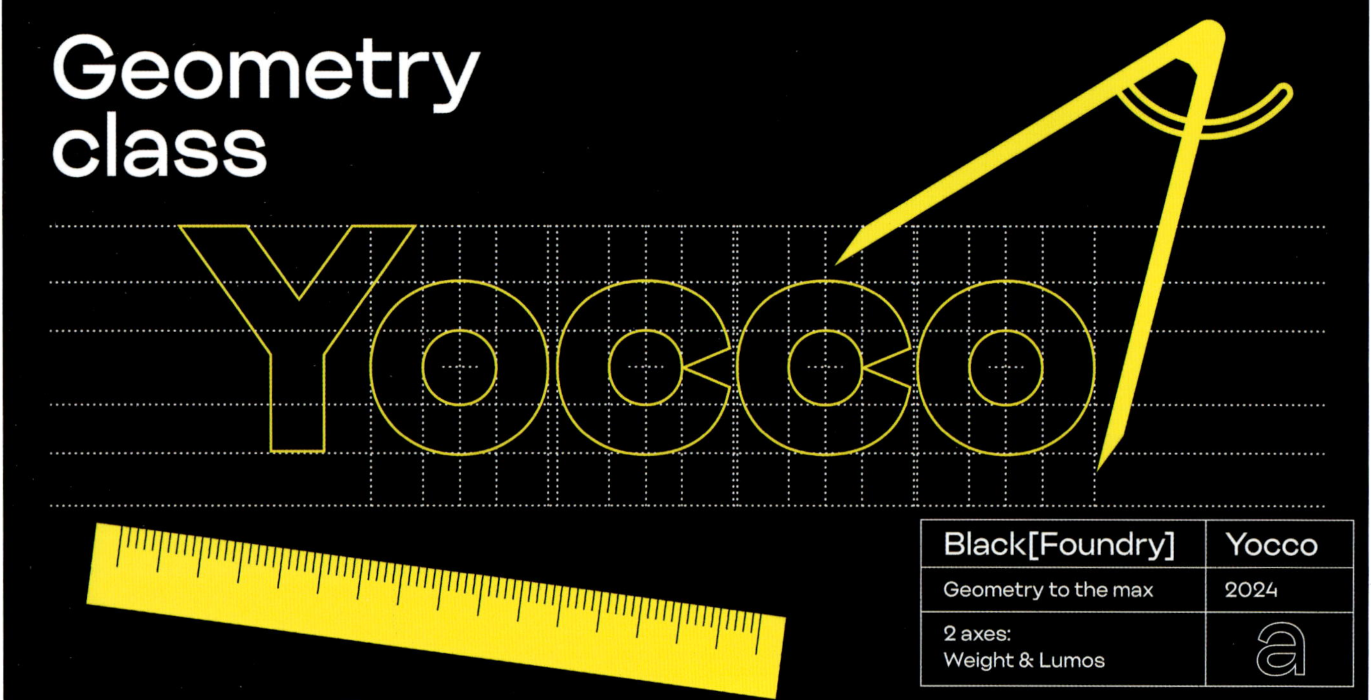

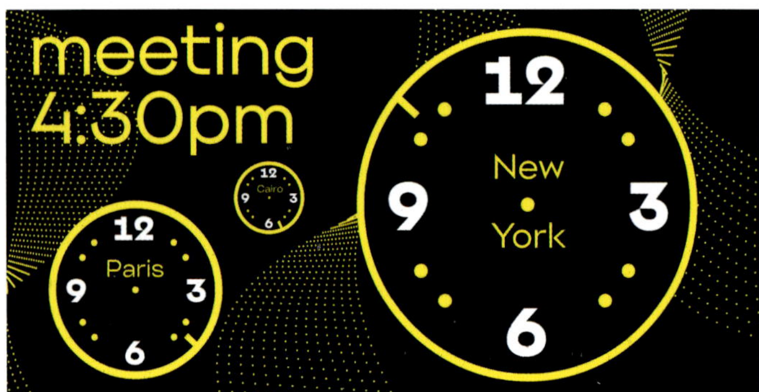

Yocco takes geometry to the max, with barely a hint of contrast. It offers a blend of geometric precision and functional design, striking a harmonious balance between form and readability. With closed terminals on characters like a, c, e, s, *and so on, Yocco achieves a distinctive aesthetic while maintaining legibility. It is available as a variable font, offering flexibility through two axes of variation (Weight and Lumos) as well as in ten static versions. The Lumos axis feature is aimed at enhancing readability, especially in smaller sizes. This innovative addition subtly refines details such as junctions and contrasts for optimal legibility without compromising on style. This diverse range caters to a wide array of typographic preferences and design requirements, allowing for both display and text usage.*

Yocco

black-foundry.com

Designed by *Gaëtan Baehr*
Published by *Black[Foundry]*

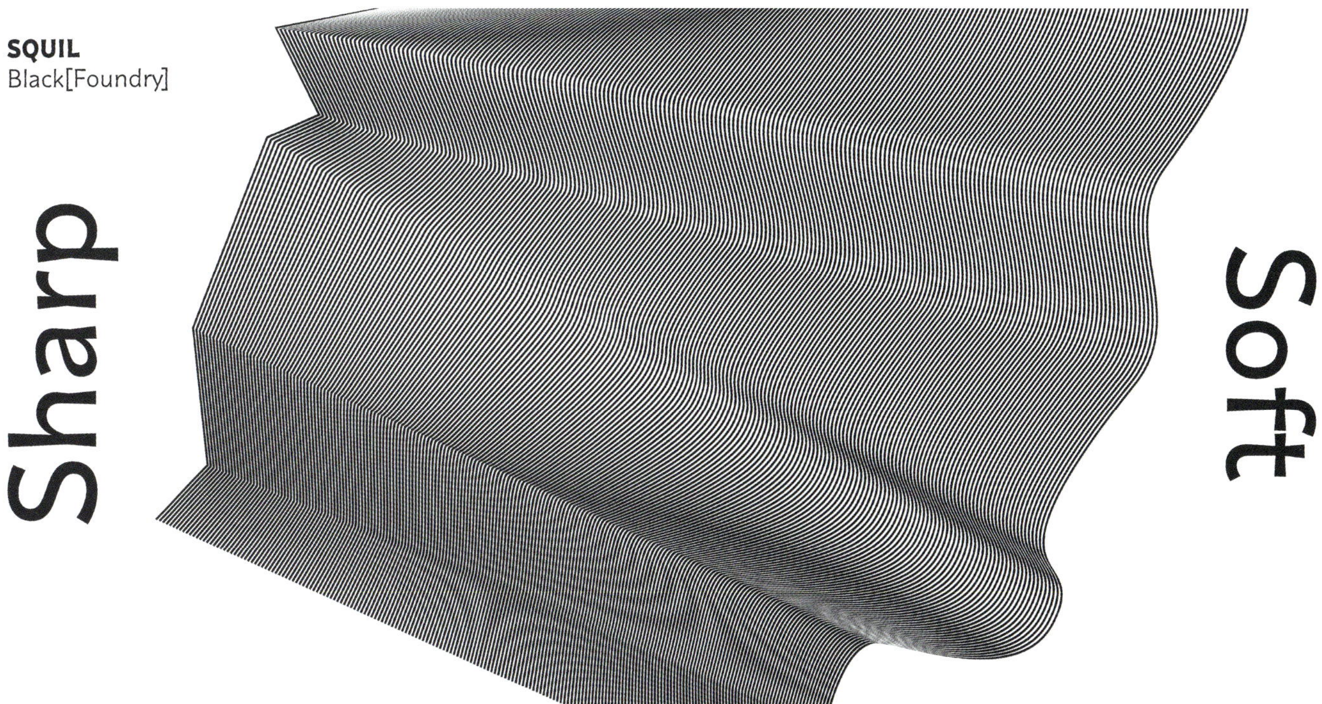

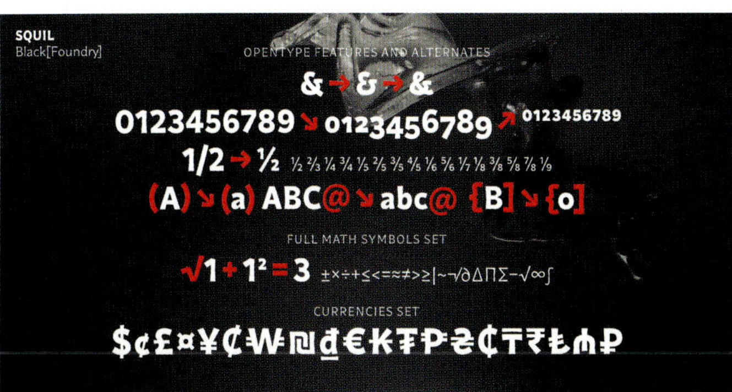

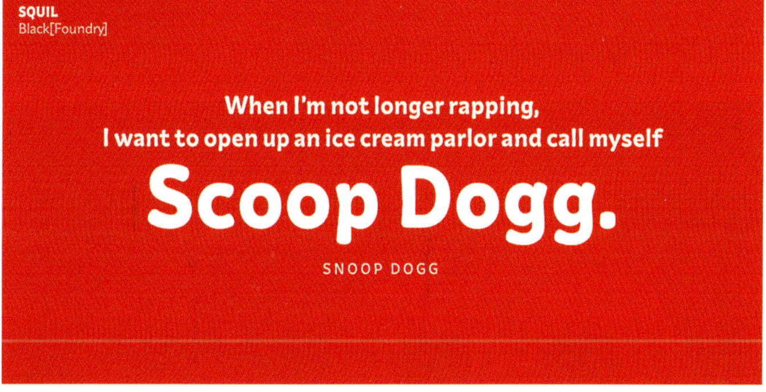

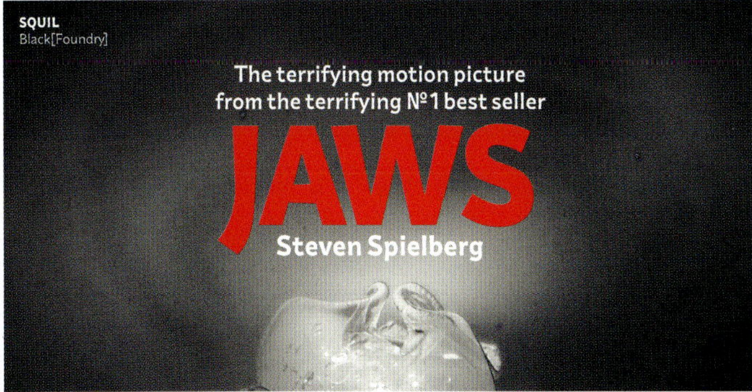

Squil is a warm and joyful sans serif, shaped by an imaginary tool that resembles handwriting, and has humanist qualities with a distinctive gentle flair. The subtle calligraphic influence is evident in the pinched stems while a slightly angled axis and gentle curves add coziness to the design. With weights spanning from Light to ExtraBold, Squil covers all the bases. Want to amp up the friendliness? Just crank up the Round axis for extra smooth, rounded terminals for a softer look. You can tweak the terminals from straight-edged to fully rounded, giving you the autonomy to fine-tune its personality.

black-foundry.com

Squil

Designed by *Jérémie Hornus, Pranavi Chopra*
Published by *Black[Foundry]*

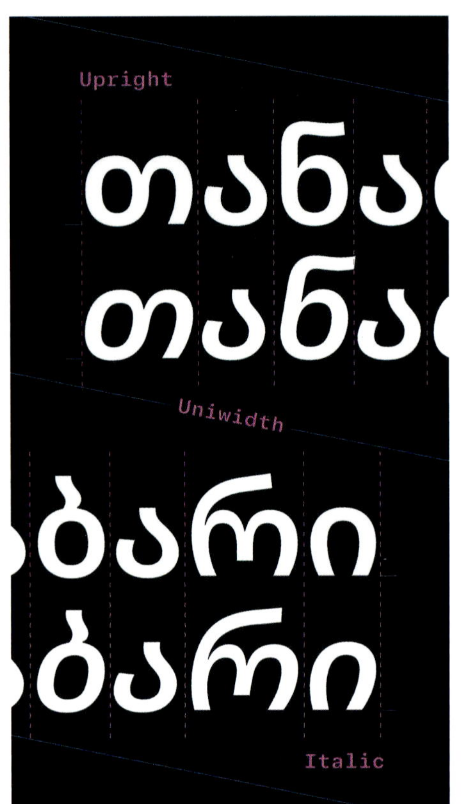

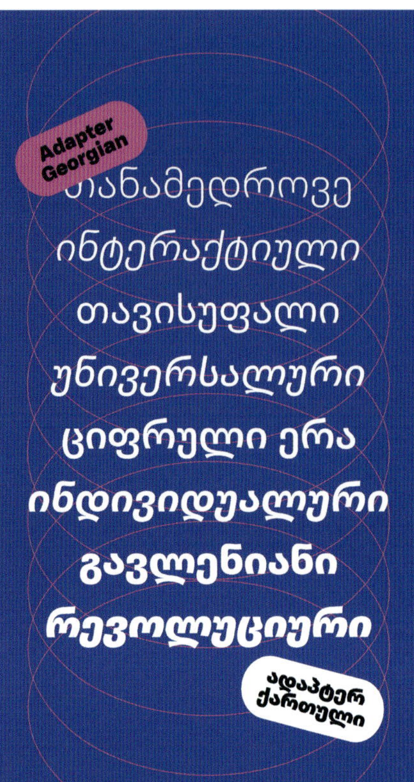

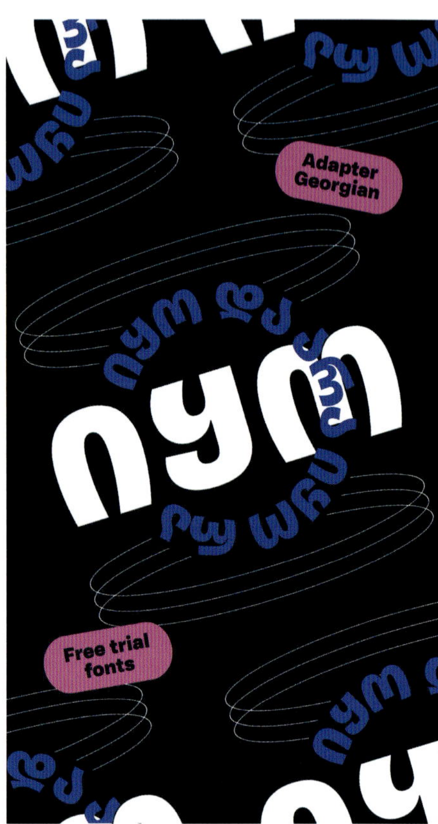

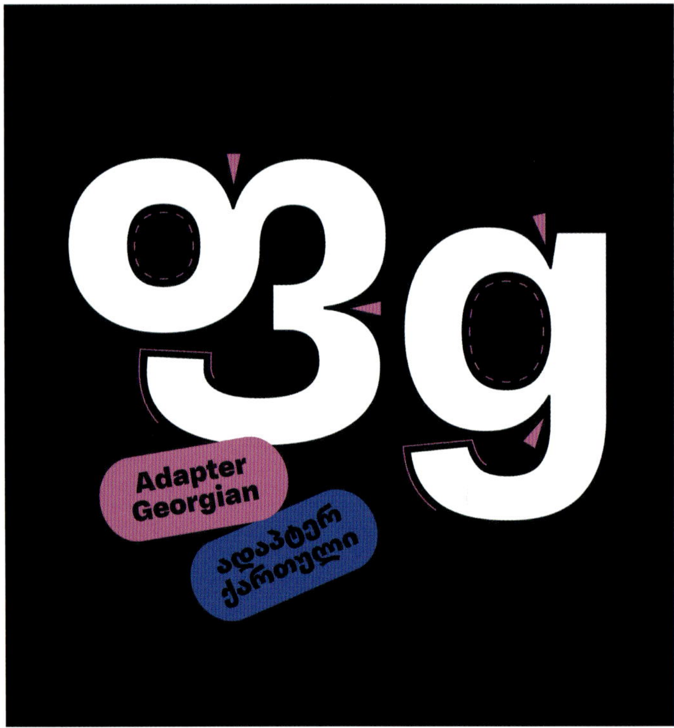

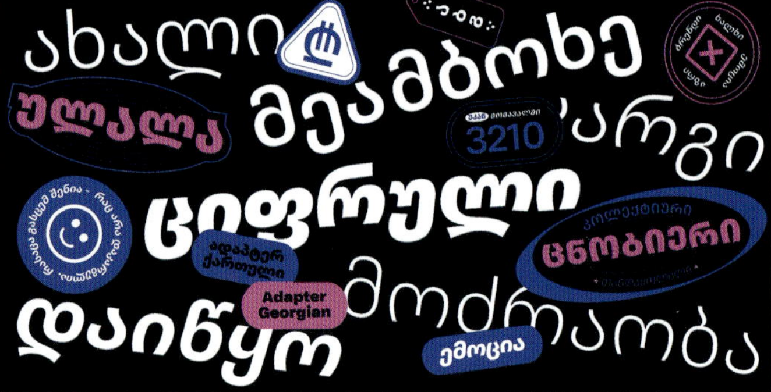

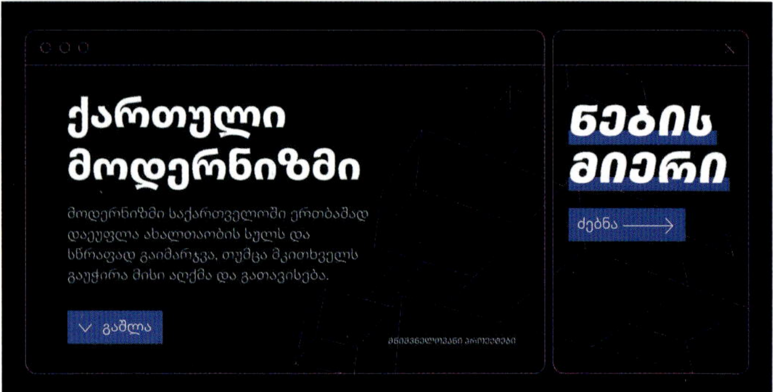

Adapter Georgian

rosettatype.com

Designed by *Ana Sanikidze*
Published by *Rosetta*

அடெப்ட்டர், உங்களின் வடிவமைப்பு தேவைகளுக்கு ஏற்றவாறு மாறுபட்ட எடை, சாய்வு மற்றும் அளவுகளை ஒரே எழுத்துரு கோப்பில் கொண்டுள்ளது.

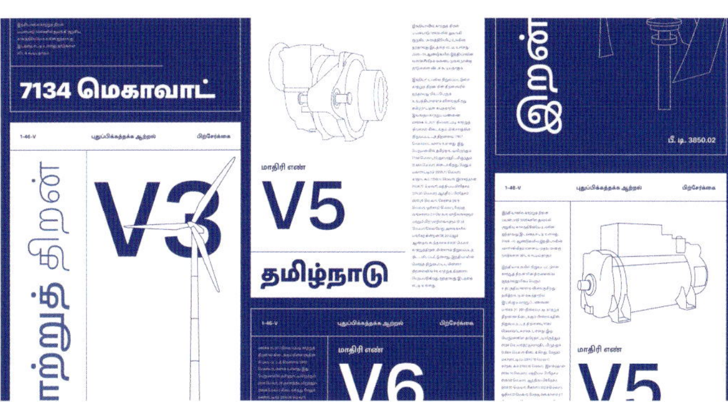

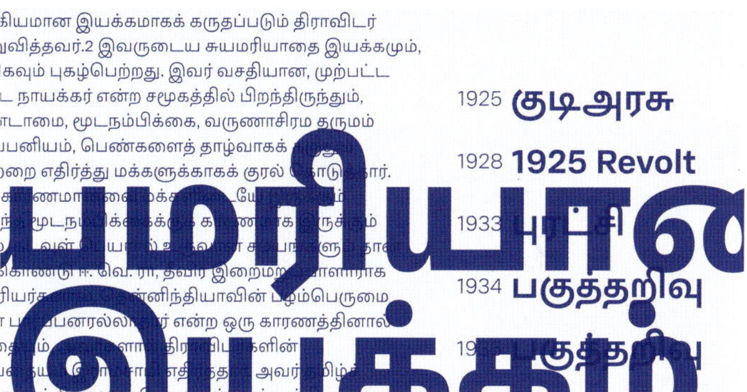

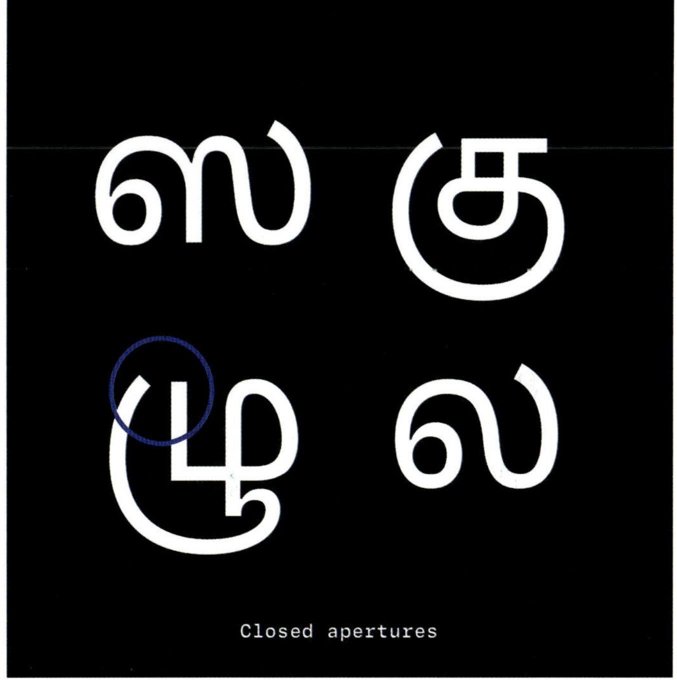

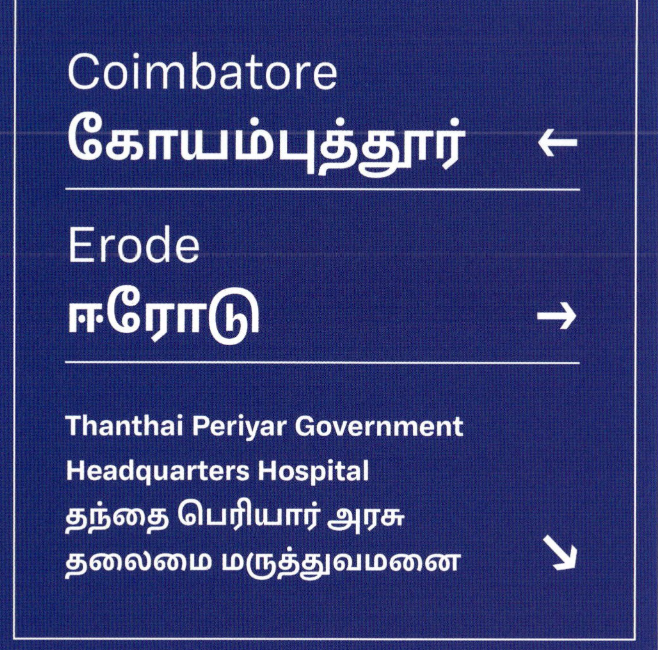

A universal monolinear typeface with contemporary aesthetics. The text-oriented styles with a wide range of weights are packed into a single variable font.

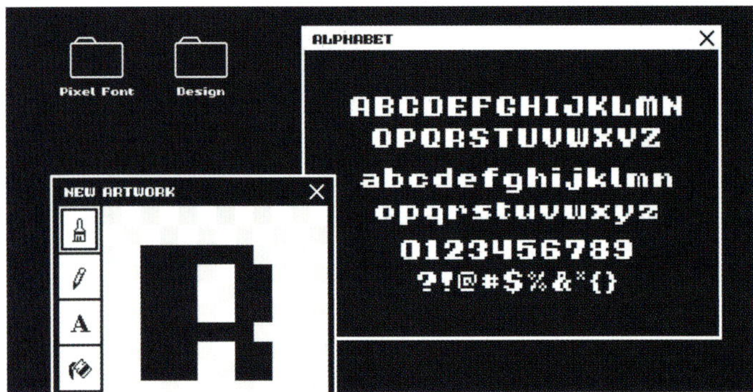

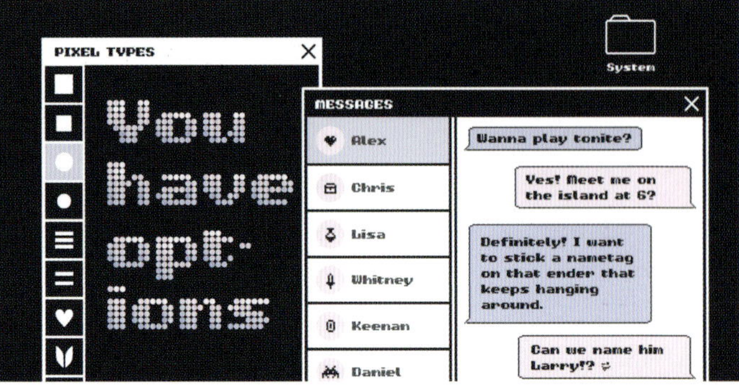

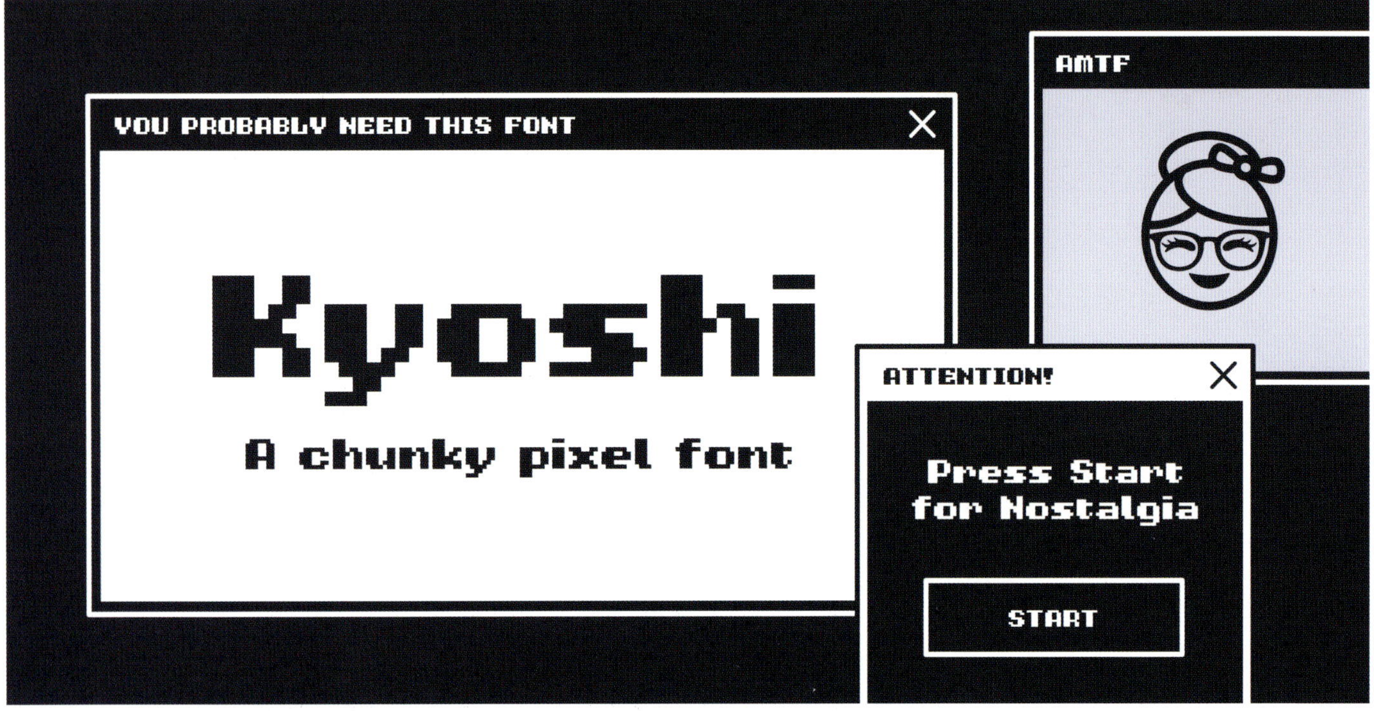

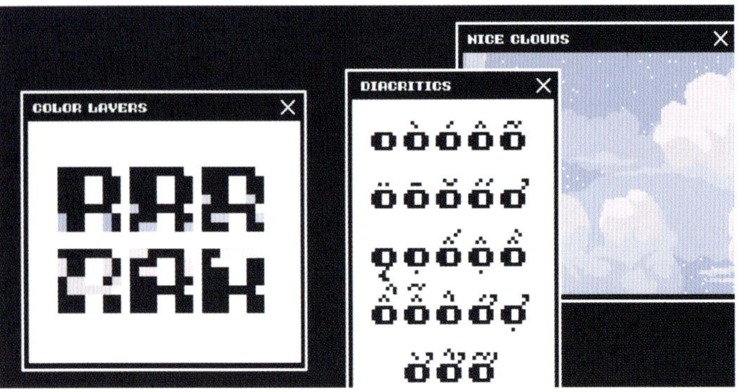

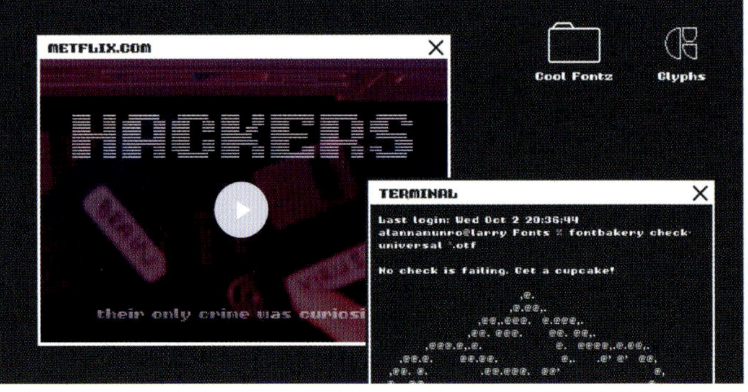

A typeface for 8-bit nostalgia nerds! This well-balanced pixel font features a heavy weight, eight pixel styles, and a full-color version of the family.

Kyoshi

arcanetype.com

Designed by *Alanna Munro*
Published by *Arcane Type Foundry*

ABCDEFGHIJKLMN
OPQRSTUVWXYZ
abcdefghijklmn
opqrstuvwxyz
0123456789
?!@#$%&*

European Origins But It Grew Up On The West Coast

RRRRRRR
RRRRRRRR
RRRRRRRRR
RRRRRRRRRR

74 STYLES

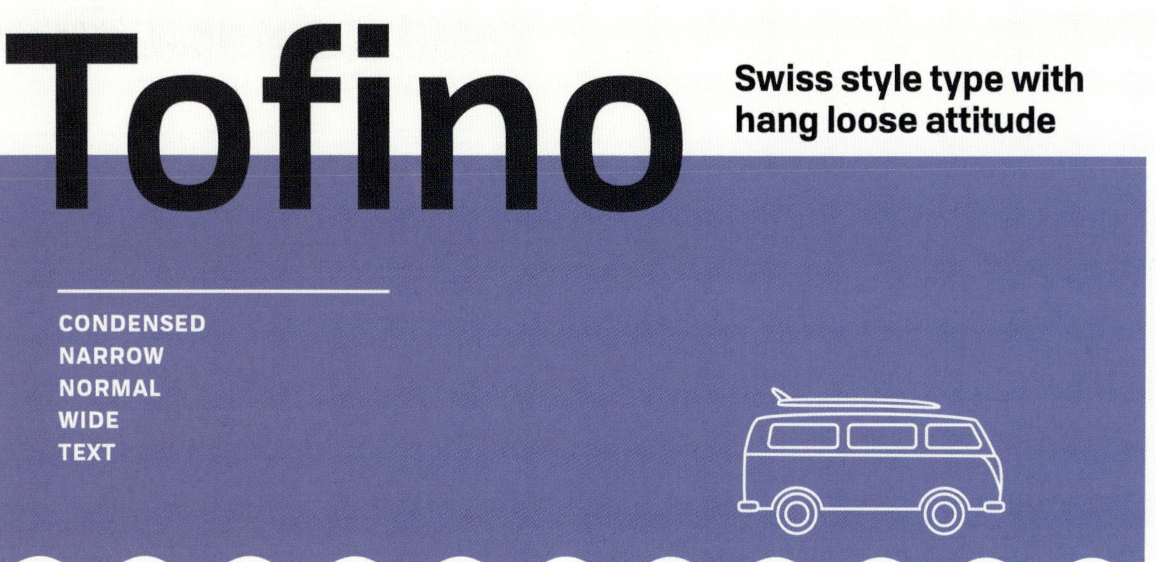

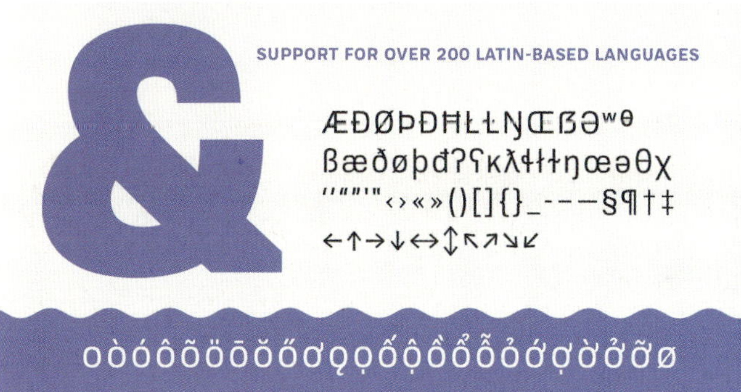

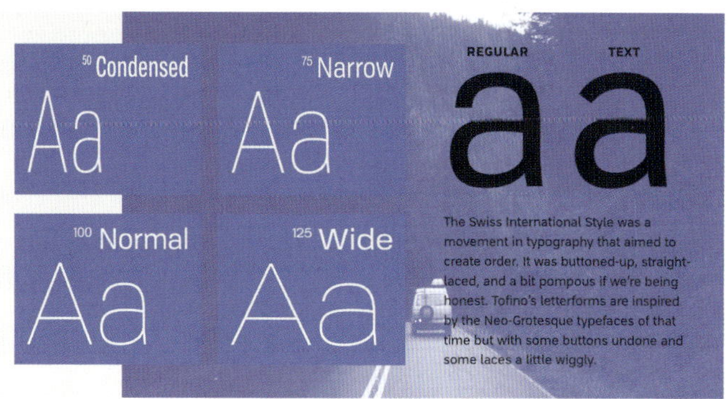

Swiss-style typography with a more "hang loose" attitude! Tofino is a large family of seventy-four styles—a true workhorse with a clean look and an edge of West Coast charm.

arcanetype.com

Tofino

Designed by *Alanna Munro*
Published by *Arcane Type Foundry*

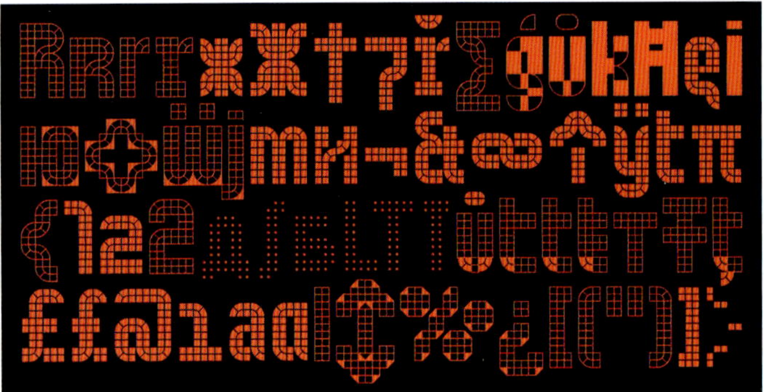

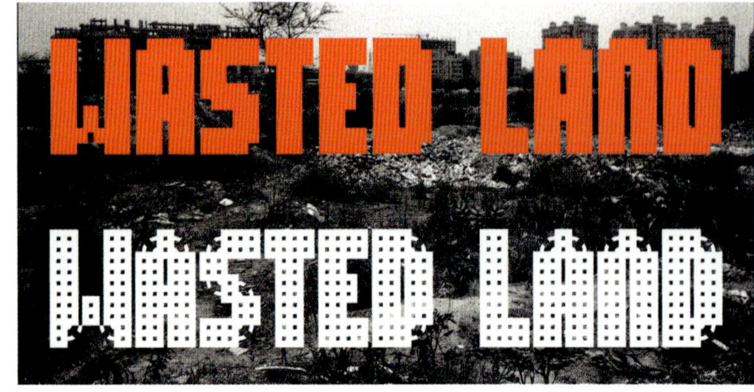

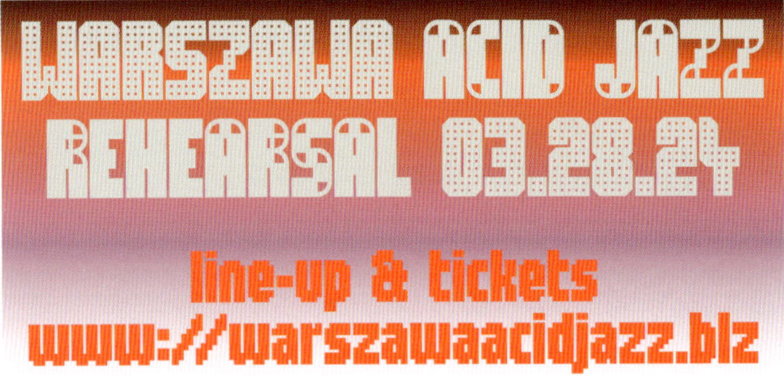

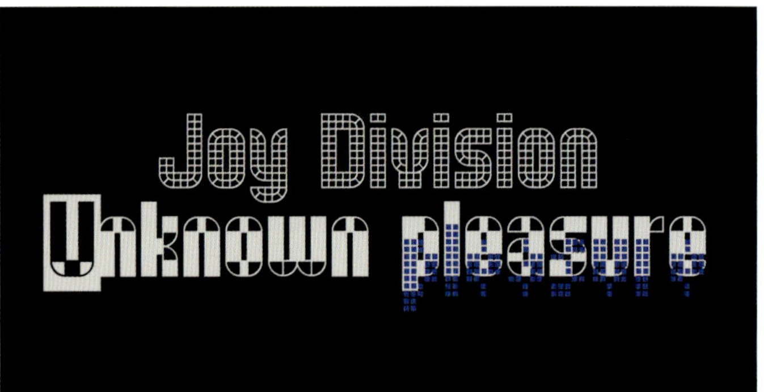

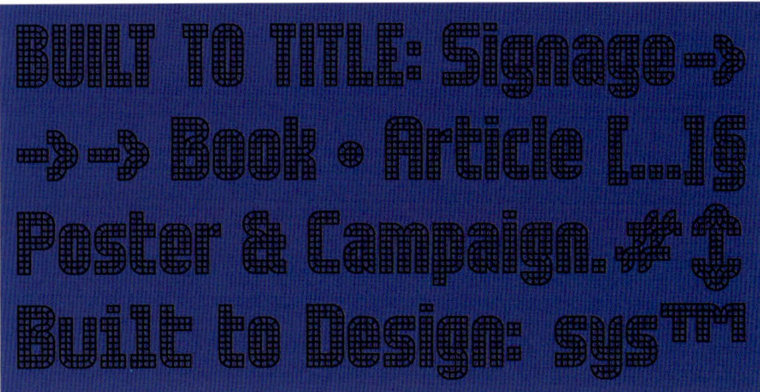

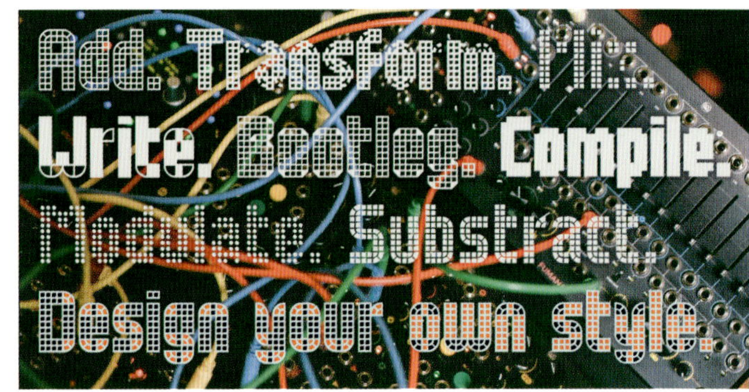

SYSTM is a modular and metric font family built by two components—a quadrant and a square—displayed on a grid. Its design has been made to satisfy any grid obsession while echoing brutalist architecture, early interface designs, and modular design in the broadest sense. Featuring one variable axis, applied to the outlines' thickness, SYSTM lets designers reach any kind of style, weight, and text grayness. Above all, SYSTM has been designed to provide an efficient and versatile visual identity tool—including over one thousand glyphs, multiple stylistic sets, and grids both for Latin and Cyrillic letters.

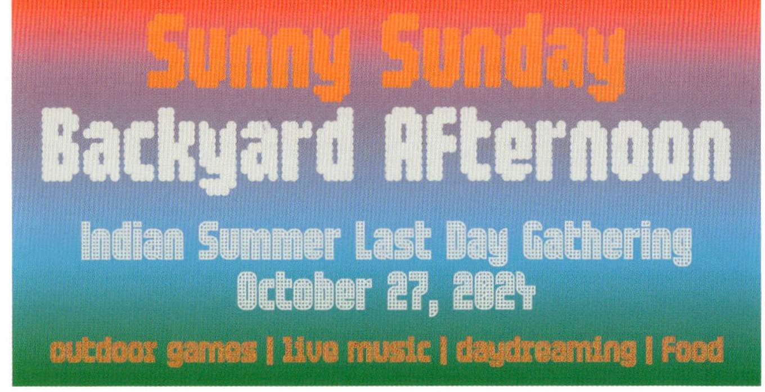

SYSTM

blazetype.eu

Designed by *Simon Helmstetter*
Published by *Blaze Type*

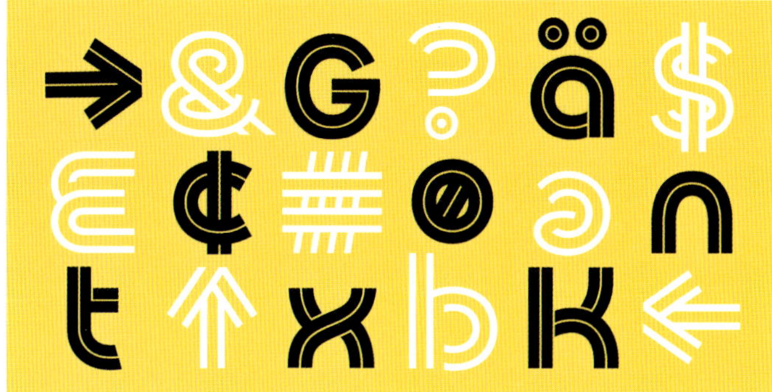

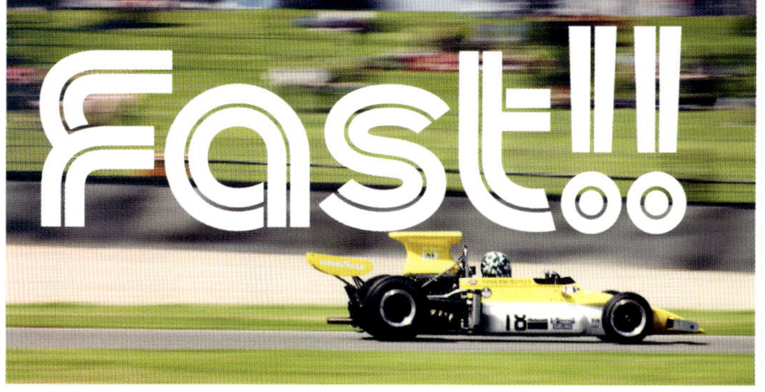

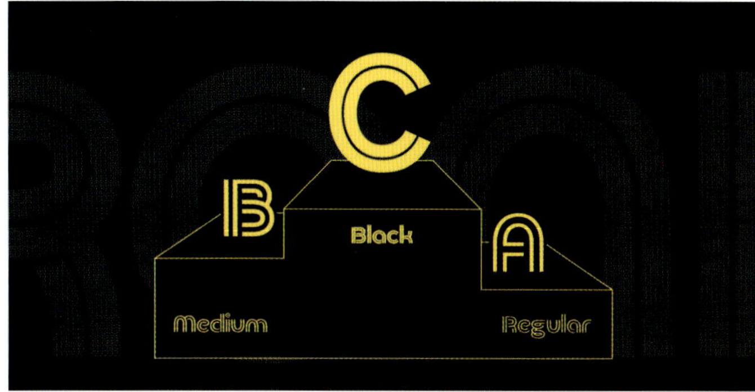

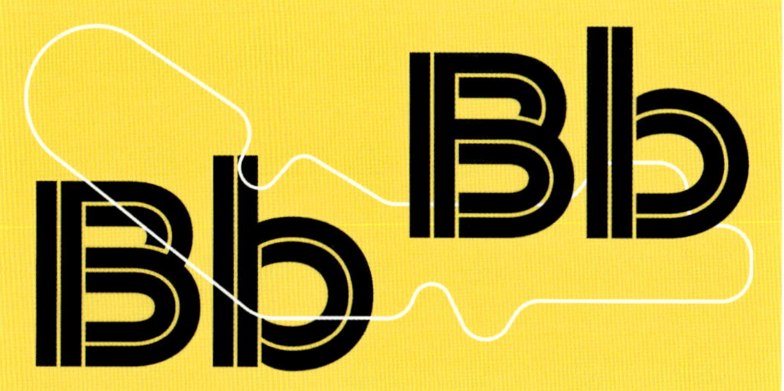

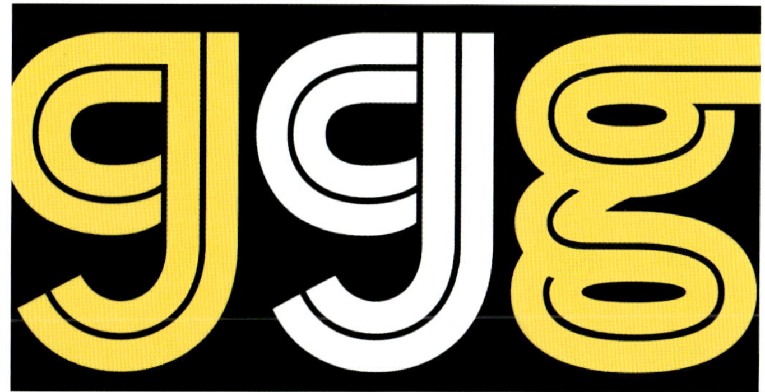

Rondette's design is steeped in historical references, bridging the timeless and the modern. Inspired by Joseph Churchward's iconic Churchward Design 70 (No-End version) and the striking work of Unimark International for Agip in the 1970s, it also pays homage to the bold, geometric style of Herbert Bayer's Universal alphabet and the clean, functional forms of 1930s sans serifs like Futura and Kabel. From these roots, Rondette extends into the contemporary sports world, capturing the energy and precision of modern athletic aesthetics. It's rich in stylistic alternatives—like the unique legs of the R *and* K, *the distinctively shaped bowls of* b, d, p, *and* q, *and both single- and double-storey g's—allowing for compositions that stand out with variety and flair. The typeface's sharp diagonal cuts on letters like* S, C, *and* G, *combined with rounded elements in* A, E, *and* F, *give it a vibrant, athletic quality.*

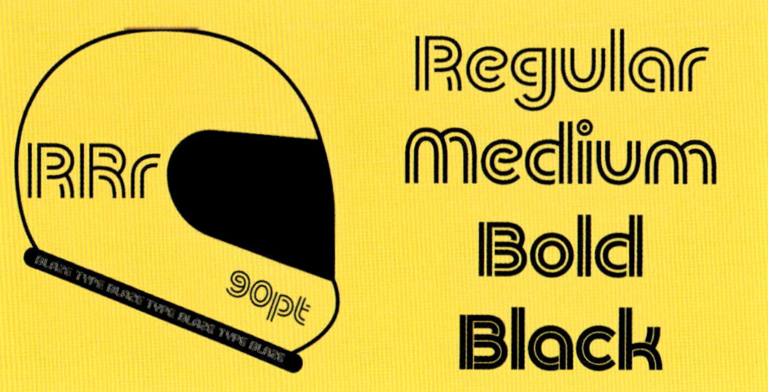

---

blazetype.eu

Rondette

Designed by *Fabrizio Falcone, Alex Bossi*
Published by *Blaze Type*

45rpm

De Nederlandse band Rigby werd opgericht in 2008, de naam is afgeleid van het hitliedje Eleanor Rigby van The Beatles. Labels: Universal Music en F.A.M. Records

NORTHERN SOUL

C # notuyla [Em ölçeğinde 6]

Terence Rigby (ur. 2 stycznia 1937 [1] r. w Birmingham w Wielkiej Brytanii [2], zm. 10 sierpnia 2008) – brytyjski [3] aktor filmowy i telewizyjny.

KOORDINÁTÁK 43° 40′ 26″ N ~ 111° 54′ 59″ W

A 97-year-old document that is containing clues to the identity of Eleanor Rigby, the subject of one of the Beatles' best-loved songs, sold for £115,000 ($177,000) at auction. 1966 The total fell well short of high estimates by the likes of £500,000 ($769,000) for the piece of Beatles memorabilia. https://billboard.com

UK Billboard Charts

Réjouissance

Nimi **Rigby** taas on poimittu **Bristolissa*** sijaitsevan liikkeen nimestä *"Rigby & Evens Ltd, Wine & Spirit Shippers".* Yksinäisyydestä kertovine ...

Melodia

1967 wurde Bob Marley durch *„Eleanor Rigby"* zu seinem Pop Titel *„Sun is shining"* inspiriert.

The top 10 best-selling Britpop singles of all time

No	BAND	TITLE	RELEASED	
01	Oasis	Wonderwall	October	1995
02	Oasis	Don't Look Back In Anger	February	1996
03	The Verve	Bitter Sweet Symphony	June	1997
04	Oasis	D'You Know What I Mean?	July	1997
05	Cornershop	Brimful of Asha	August	1997
06	The Verve	The Drugs Don't Work	September	1997
07	Oasis	Whatever	December	1994
08	Blur	Country House	August	1995
09	Oasis	Roll With It	August	1995
10	Oasis	Some Might Say	April	1995

ELEANOR RIGBY (7", SINGLE, RP) + €3.00 SHIPPING

John, Paul, George & Ringo

→ *Sir John Rigby, CP (8 janvier 1834 ~ 26 juillet 1903), est un juge britannique et homme politique libéral qui siège à la Chambre des communes entre 1885 et 1894.*

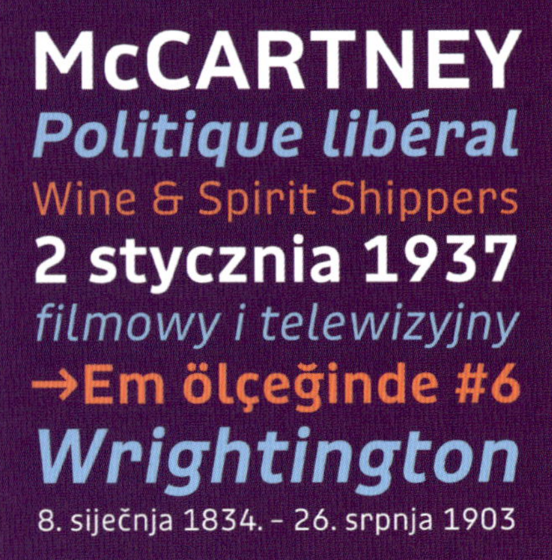

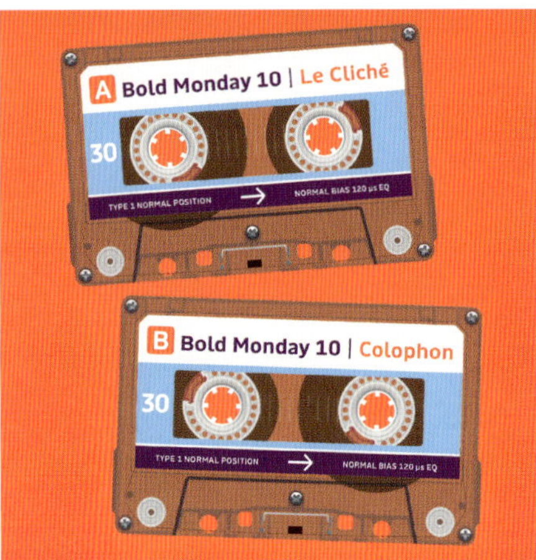

Rigby started as a retail version of a custom typeface developed for NTR, a Dutch public broadcaster specializing in information, education, and culture. While the NTR fonts were sharp and rounded at the same time, Rigby has all-sharp, angular terminals but still keeps personable letterforms like the unique lowercase g *and* e.

Rigby

boldmonday.com

Designed by *Pieter van Rosmalen*
Published by *Bold Monday*

Cake Stencil Light

Cake Stencil Light Applied

Cake Stencil Regular

Cake Stencil Regular Applied

Cake Stencil Bold

Cake Stencil Bold Applied

predetermine AVTREKKSRØR
ATTIECĪGAJĀS modeltreintje
bruksföremål CONSERVAÇÃO
MANÉIERLECH appreciations
comparability АКЦІОНЕРНОЇ

«Ǫ ₴ ǽ §»
ӹ % ẞ 8 ể

?98765
43210#

IRRESOLUTELY kehittymässä
kolmepäevast KOILARAKADA
MEKANIĞINDE neurosurgery
structureless CYNHYRCHIAD
IMPAKWINTER öreindafræði!

magnetohydrodynamic бед acrafóibe egyértelműsítési verhältnismäßigkeit adsbøl aktů міжконтинентального thermodynamiquement vos eimbaǒ vadītājsuzbrūkošais

Cake Stencil originated from uppercase letters drawn in 2006 for use in the logo of Bureau Jeugdzorg Noord-Holland. In 2023, the character set was completed, and Light and Normal weights were added.

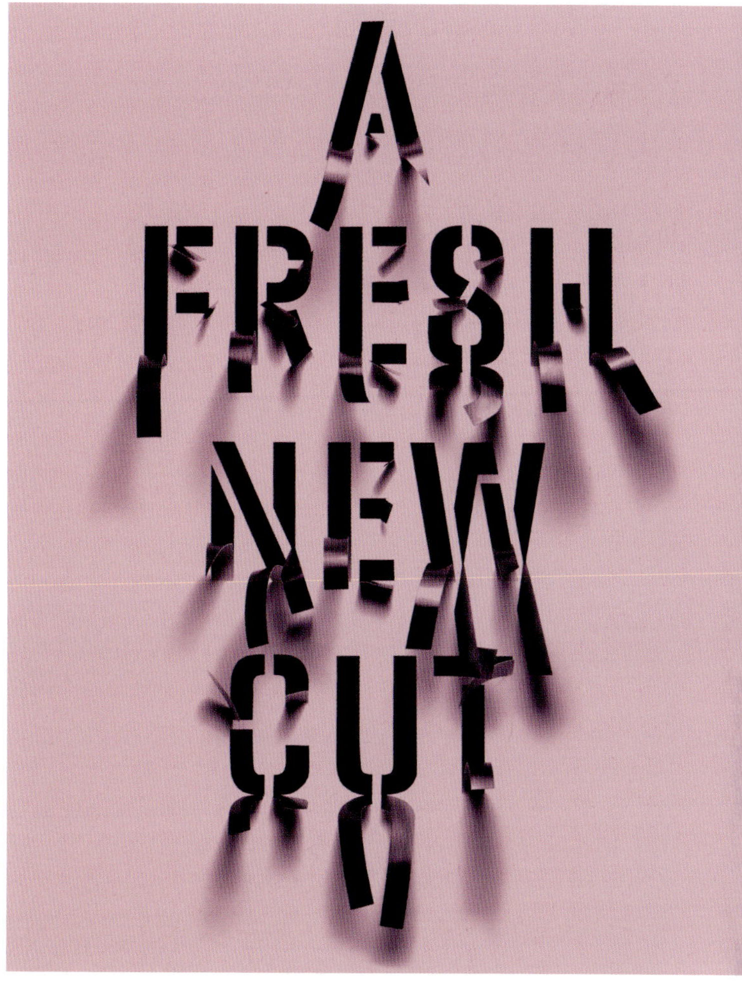

Cake Stencil type specimen — 22 / 30 — Cake Stencil all weights

Cake Stencil Light

Paleontological classifications or previously used Hydrochoeridae for all capibaras, while using their Hydrochoerinae for the living and genus and its closest fossil hegje relatives, such as Neochoerus, but more recently have adopted the classification of Hydrochoer within Caviidae and the taxonomy

Cake Stencil Regular

Paleontological classifications or previously used Hydrochoeridae for all capibaras, while using their Hydrochoerinae for the living and genus and its closest fossil hegje relatives, such as Neochoerus, but more recently have adopted the classification of Hydrochoer within Caviidae and

Cake Stencil Bold

Paleontological classifications or previously used Hydrochoeri-dae for all capibaras, while using their Hydrochoerinae for the living and genus and its closest fossil hegje relatives, such as Neochoerus, but more recently have adopted the classification of Hydrochoer within Caviidae

Cake Stencil Light Applied

Paleontological classifications or previously used Hydrochoeridae for all capibaras, while using their Hydrochoerinae for the living and genus and its closest fossil hegje relatives, such as Neochoerus, but more recently have adopted the classification of Hydrochoer within Caviidae and the taxonomy

Cake Stencil Regular Applied

Paleontological classifications or previously used Hydrochoeridae for all capibaras, while using their Hydrochoerinae for the living and genus and its closest fossil hegje relatives, such as Neochoerus, but more recently have adopted the classification of Hydrochoer within Caviidae and

Cake Stencil Bold Applied

Paleontological classifications or previously used Hydrochoeri-dae for all capibaras, while using their Hydrochoerinae for the living and genus and its closest fossil hegje relatives, such as Neochoerus, but more recently have adopted the classification of Hydrochoer within Caviidae

www.CAKETYPE.com

caketype.com

Cake Stencil

Designed by *Pieter van Rosmalen*
Published by *Cake Type*

ICELANDIC
Árásarmaðurinn
DANISH
Væddeløbshest
GERMAN
Rückwärtsgang
UKRAINIAN
Без обмежень
FINNISH
Herättämään
POLISH
Jeździczynią
FRENCH
Récupérer
BULGARIAN
Одисея

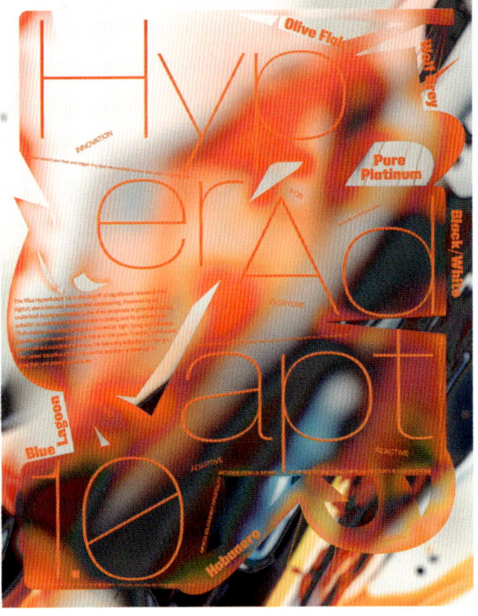

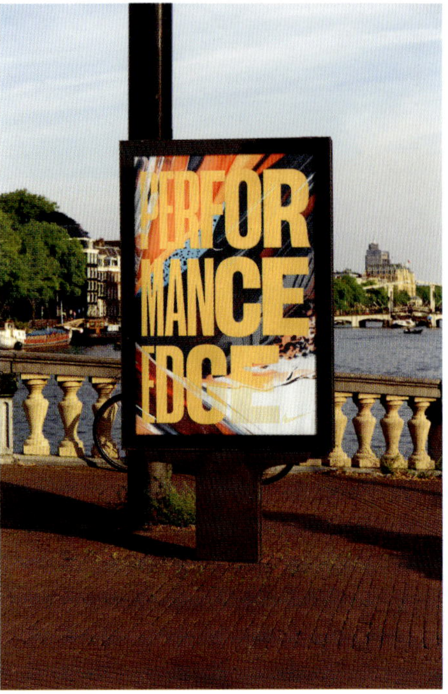

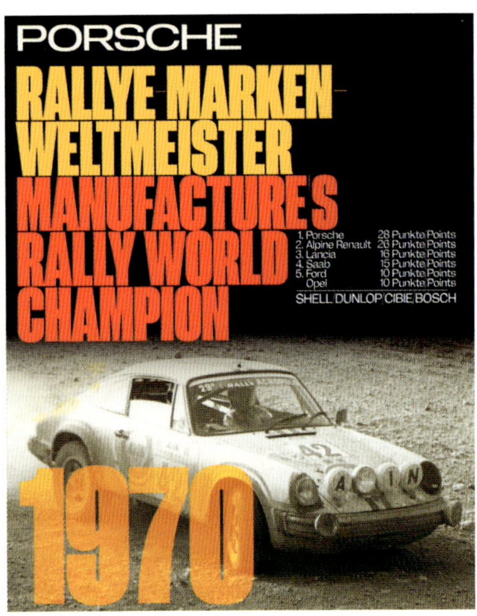

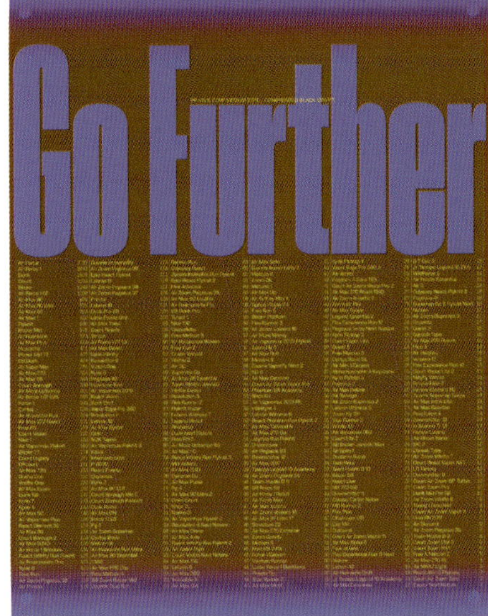

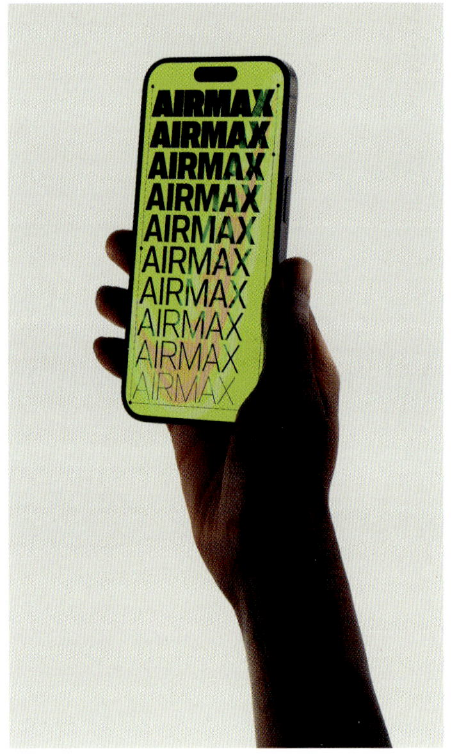

Neue Corp is a versatile typeface, crafted to be the ultimate creative tool for any advertising, marketing, or digital endeavor. Designed with a broad range of widths and weights, it empowers designers and studios to adapt it to any context, from bold headlines to refined body text. Balancing character with neutrality, it combines the eccentricity of old wood type with the precision of neo-grotesques. The Black and Condensed styles are inspired by classic Hamilton Manufacturing Co. typefaces, while the wide Bolds are influenced by Helvetica Extended. Regular styles draw from Univers, but with softened details for a friendlier tone. Alternate stylistic sets offer even more flexibility: One set makes the typeface more geometric and neutral, while the other brings out a bold, grotesque character with added spurs. With a design spectrum ranging from subtle Thin to powerful Black, and from narrow Compressed to bold Extended, this typeface is ready to elevate any project with style and precision.

Neue Corp

pangrampangram.com

Designed by *Maksym Kobuzan, Mat Desjardins, Francesca Bolognini*
Published by *Pangram Pangram*

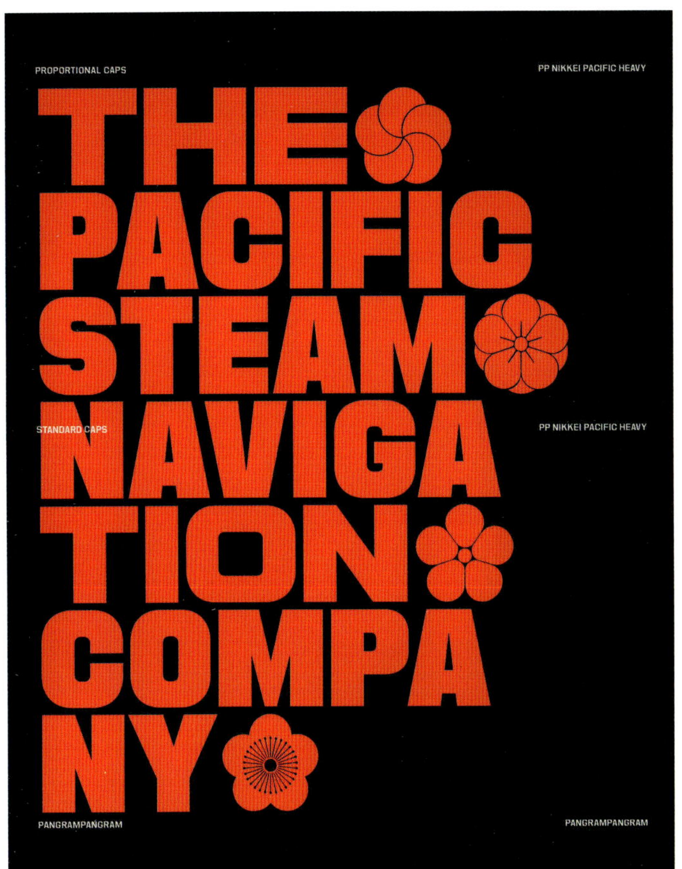

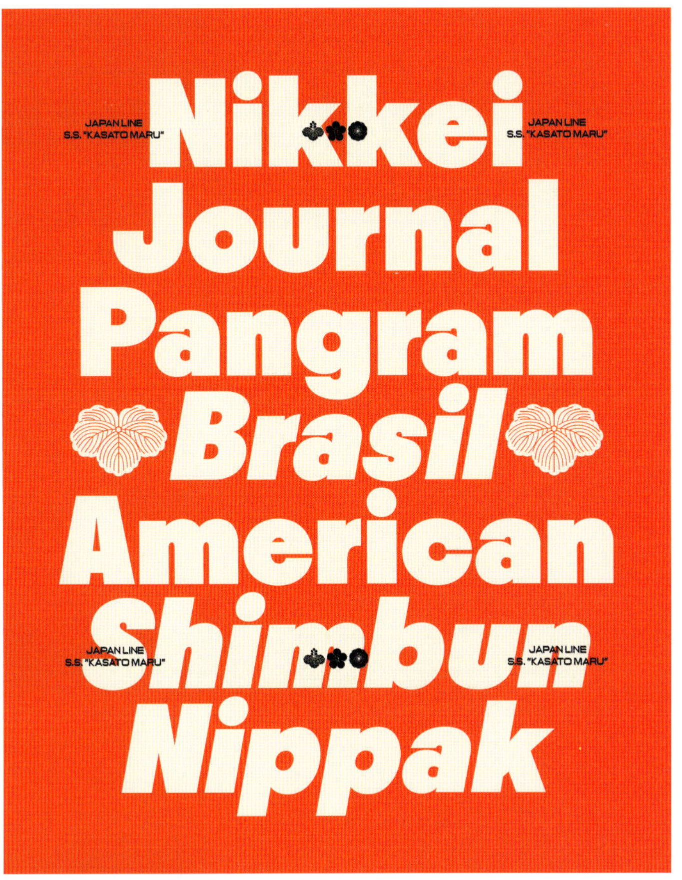

THIN	THIN	Thin	Thin
ULTRALIGHT	ULTRALIGHT	Ultralight	Ultralight
LIGHT	LIGHT	Light	Light
REGULAR	REGULAR	Regular	Regular
MEDIUM	MEDIUM	Medium	Medium
SEMIBOLD	SEMIBOLD	Semibold	Semibold
BOLD	BOLD	Bold	Bold
ULTRABOLD	ULTRABOLD	Ultrabold	Ultrabold
HEAVY	HEAVY	Heavy	Heavy
THIN	THIN	Thin	Thin
ULTRALIGHT	ULTRALIGHT	Ultralight	Ultralight
LIGHT	LIGHT	Light	Light
REGULAR	REGULAR	Regular	Regular
MEDIUM	MEDIUM	Medium	Medium
SEMIBOLD	SEMIBOLD	Semibold	Semibold
BOLD	BOLD	Bold	Bold
ULTRABOLD	ULTRABOLD	Ultrabold	Ultrabold
HEAVY	HEAVY	Heavy	Heavy
THIN	THIN	Thin	Thin
ULTRALIGHT	ULTRALIGHT	Ultralight	Ultralight
LIGHT	LIGHT	Light	Light
REGULAR	REGULAR	Regular	Regular
MEDIUM	MEDIUM	Medium	Medium
SEMIBOLD	SEMIBOLD	Semibold	Semibold
BOLD	BOLD	Bold	Bold
ULTRABOLD	ULTRABOLD	Ultrabold	Ultrabold
HEAVY	HEAVY	Heavy	Heavy
THIN	THIN	Thin	Thin
ULTRALIGHT	ULTRALIGHT	Ultralight	Ultralight
LIGHT	LIGHT	Light	Light
REGULAR	REGULAR	Regular	Regular
MEDIUM	MEDIUM	Medium	Medium
SEMIBOLD	SEMIBOLD	Semibold	Semibold
BOLD	BOLD	Bold	Bold
ULTRABOLD	ULTRABOLD	Ultrabold	Ultrabold
HEAVY	HEAVY	Heavy	Heavy

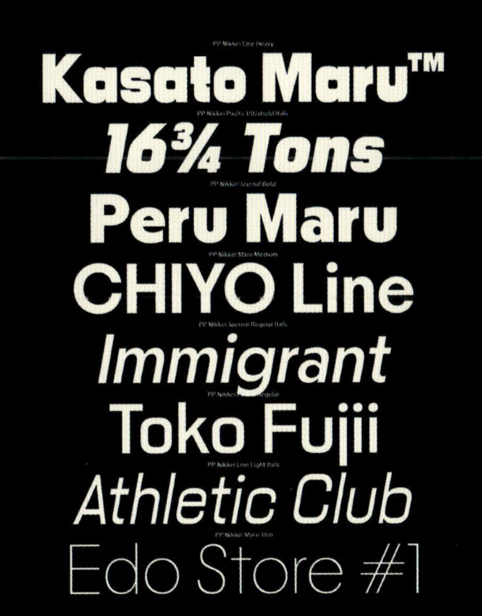

PP Nikkei is a tribute to Japanese immigration to America through typography, honoring the stories of Japanese immigrants and their descendants. "Nikkei" refers to Japanese individuals and their descendants who live outside Japan. Five typographic systems were made, each expressing unique concepts, yet all interlaced by a common historical narrative. The inspiration came from various sources, including hand lettering on ships, newspapers of the Nikkei communities, and Japanese family crests, offering versatile titling fonts whose proportions and stylistic alternatives allow for playful options for title compositions.

pangrampangram.com

PP Nikkei

Designed by *Caio Kondo, Francesca Bolognini, Mat Desjardins*
Published by *Pangram Pangram*

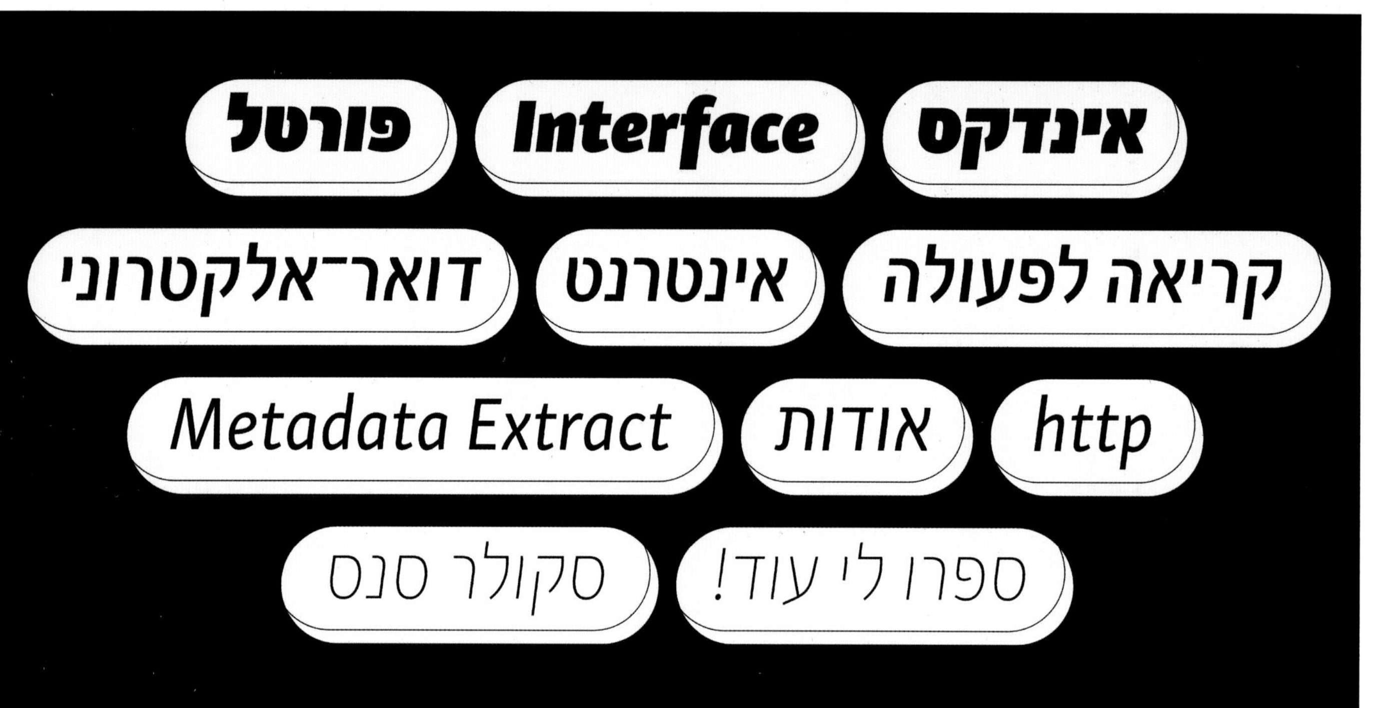

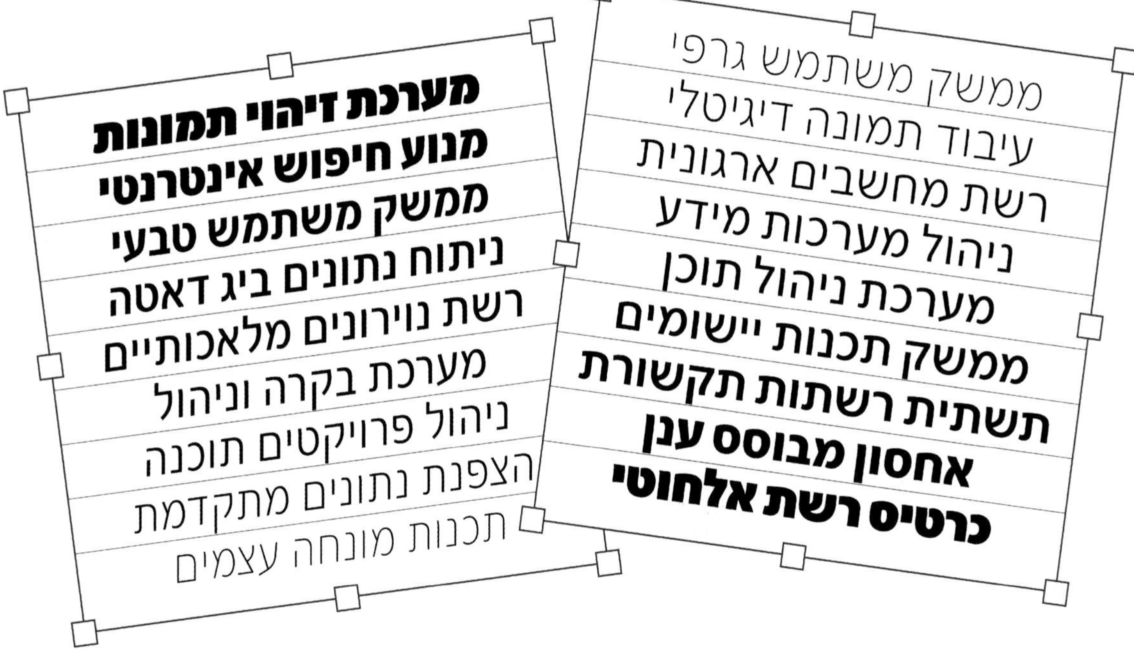

A comprehensive low-contrast type system with styles ranging from gently thin to black.

Skolar Sans Hebrew

rosettatype.com

Designed by *Eran Ben Barak*
Published by *Rosetta*

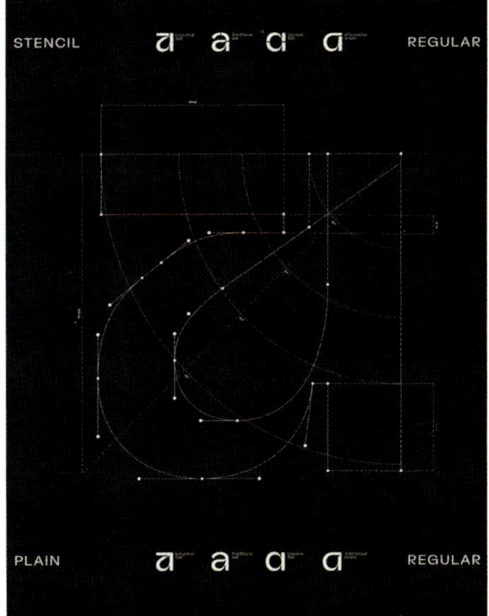

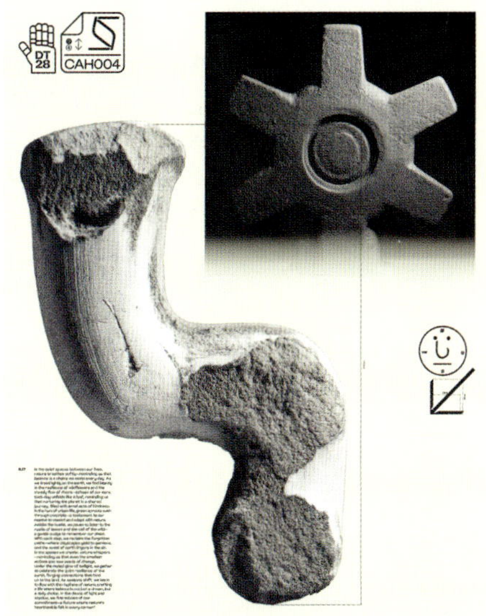

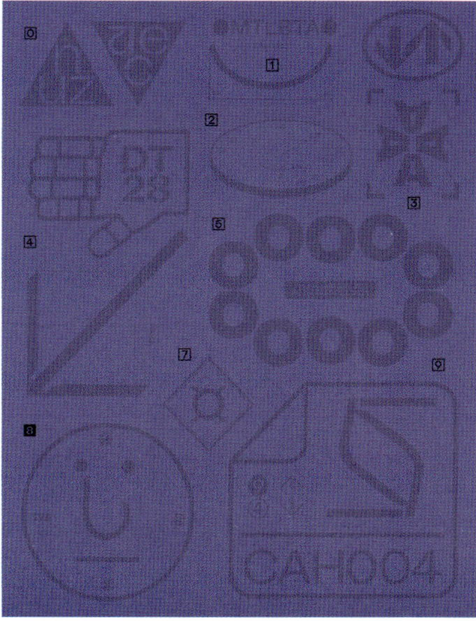

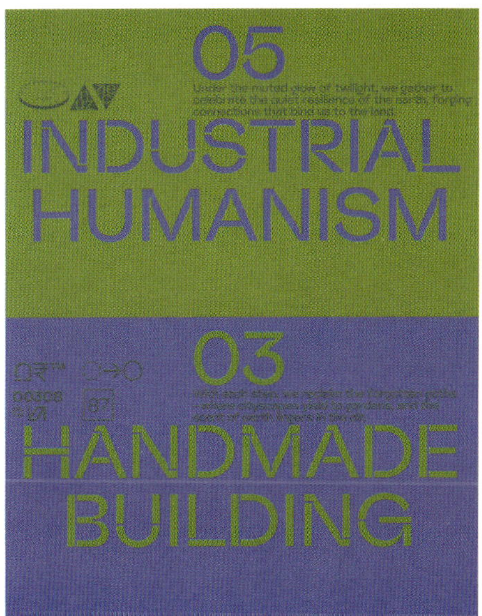

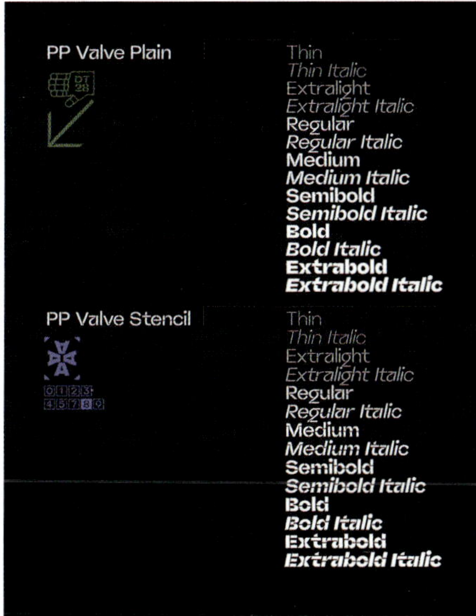

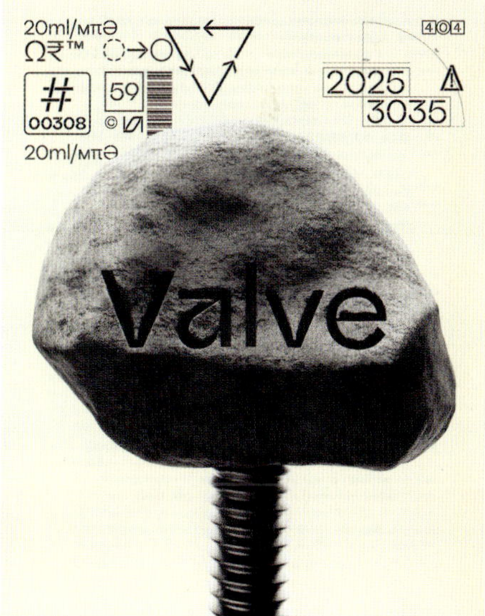

Valve is a versatile typeface collection that blends grotesque, geometric, gestural, industrial, monospaced, and cursive sans serif styles into a unified, cohesive ensemble. Defying conventional classifications, Valve provides a wide range of typesetting options through its two distinct families: an ink-trapped workhorse designed for excellent readability at small sizes, and a striking stencil companion that reveals the font's modular structure and underlying design connections. Valve features three main stylistic sets: a blocky semi-monospaced variant, a familiar humanist style, and a lively cursive option—each showcasing unique contextual ligatures that adapt to tracking for smooth text flow in any combination. With its adaptability and dynamic nature, Valve allows you to control and fine-tune the expressive qualities of your text, making it ideal for a variety of projects, from bold branding and impactful signage to refined editorial design.

pangrampangram.com

Valve

Designed by *Valerio Monopoli*
Published by *Pangram Pangram*

LOWERCASE LIGHT SERIF
ΑΘΛΗΤΙΚΟΣ ΟΜΙΛΟΣ
LOWERCASE SERIF
ΣΤΑΣΗ ΛΕΩΦΟΡΕΙΩΝ
LOWERCASE MEDIUM SANS
ΝΕΑ ΦΙΛΑΔΕΛΦΕΙΑ
LOWERCASE SEMIBOLD SANS
ΜΟΝΤΕΡΝΑ ΚΑΤΟΙΚΙΑ
LOWERCASE BOLD SERIF
ΑΡΙΣΤΟΤΕΛΟΥΣ 82
LOWERCASE BLACK SANS
ΠΕΙΡΑΪΚΗ ΕΝΩΣΗ
LOWERCASE EXTRA BLACK SERIF
ΛΕΩΦΟΡΟΣ ΝΑΤΟ

LOWERCASE LIGHT SERIF
ВАСИЛИЙ СМИРНОВ
LOWERCASE SERIF
СЕРПУХОВСКАЯ
LOWERCASE MEDIUM SERIF
ПАРК КУЛЬТУРЫ
LOWERCASE SEMIBOLD SANS
КАЗИМИР МАЛЕВИЧ
LOWERCASE BOLD SERIF
АЛЕКСЕЙ ДУШКИН
LOWERCASE BLACK SANS
ЛЕОНИД ПОЛЯКОВ
LOWERCASE EXTRA BLACK SERIF
ОКТЯБРЬСКАЯ

THE GREAT USE OF LIFE IS TO SPEND IT FOR SOMETHING THAT WILL OUTLAST IT

WILLIAM JAMES

PF Kleos is a dynamic variable typeface with a dual sans and serif personality, offering a rich texture and endless expressive possibilities. Balancing opulence with versatility and style with timelessness, Kleos stands out with its elevated aesthetics, distinctive character, and refined composure in a world of fleeting impressions.

PF Kleos

parachutefonts.com

Designed by *Panos Vassiliou*
Published by *Parachute*

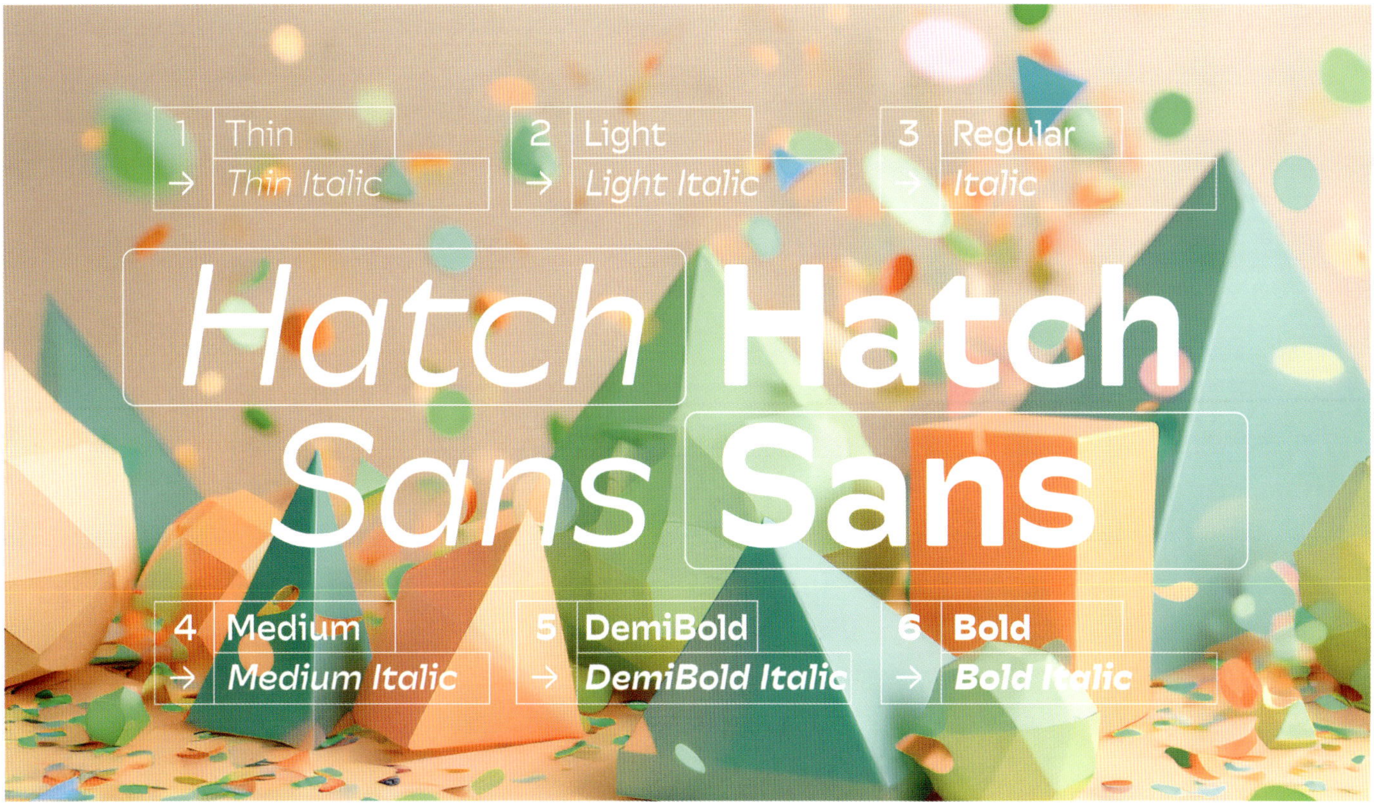

1 Thin → *Thin Italic*
2 Light → *Light Italic*
3 Regular → *Italic*

Hatch Sans **Hatch Sans**

4 Medium → *Medium Italic*
5 DemiBold → *DemiBold Italic*
6 Bold → *Bold Italic*

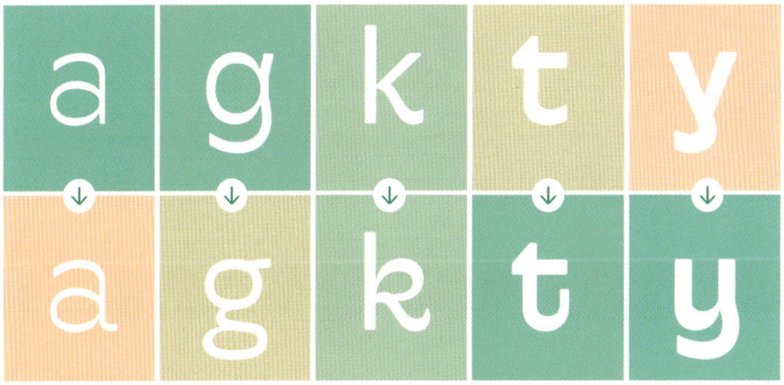

a g k t y
↓ ↓ ↓ ↓ ↓
a g k t y

Forestalled *Coronation* **Forestalled** ***Coronation***
Milkshakes *Swampiest* **Milkshakes** ***Swampiest***
Inclemency *Subtracted* **Inclemency** ***Subtracted***
Cellophane *Antibiotics* **Cellophane** ***Antibiotics***
Alliterative *Periphrasis* **Alliterative** ***Periphrasis***
Judiciously *Evaporates* **Judiciously** ***Evaporates***
Symbolists *Astronauts* **Symbolists** ***Astronauts***
Formulates *Bewitching* **Formulates** ***Bewitching***
Topsyturvy *Encourager* **Topsyturvy** ***Encourager***
Defilement *Footballers* **Defilement** ***Footballers***
Mechanical *Cliffhanger* **Mechanical** ***Cliffhanger***
Ricocheted *Throwaway* **Ricocheted** ***Throwaway***

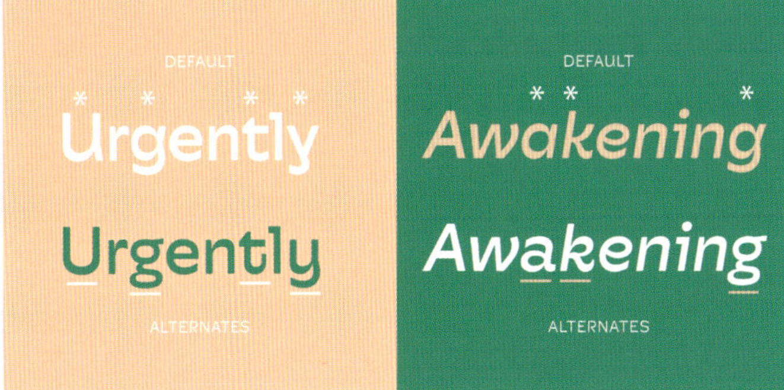

The East Coast companion to the West Coast slab. The sans retains the overall feeling, typographic quirks, and general vibe of the original Hatch family, but expands upon it with an increased weight spectrum and character set.

pstypelab.com

Hatch Sans

Designed by *Mark Caneso*
Published by PSTL

The exceedingly strange case of

DR JEKYLL

London's outwardly respectable master of medicine

who unleashes

his deepest cruelties & most murderous instincts when he is transformed into sinister

MR HYDE

Published as a 'shilling shocker' in 1886 by

R.L. STEVENSON

Gothic

a chilling exploration of humanity's basest capacity for evil

masterpiece

DARK PSYCHOLOGICAL FANTASY

VARIABLE!

aaaaaaaaaaaaa

Variable fonts bundled free in each family pack:

- *single font files, unlimited design options*
- *2 axes (weight + width), customise at will*
- *all base weights, style sets & alts included*

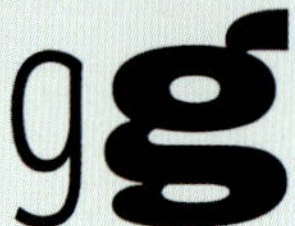

ARE YOU MORE JEKYLL OR HYDE?

great

Jekyll's letterforms are more contemporary & neo-humanist sans serif in nature.

Hyde's letterforms adopt a distinctly more grotesque sans look and feel.

great

STYLE SET 1 (grotesque)

grotesque

change the styling with the click of a button!

grotesque

easily switch to classic grotesque letterforms

abject failure » abject failure

STYLE SET 2 (alternate G & g)

grüß Gott!
grüß Gott!

STYLE SET 3 (alternate K k & R)

KkR » KkR
UKRAINE

STYLE SET 4 (infant a)

great **taste**

STYLE SET 5 (alternate y)

yın & **yang**

SMALL CAPS + STYLE SET 6 (straight K)

Dvořák » DVOŘÁK

Buvez de ce whisky que le patron juge fameux!

Buvez de ce whisky fameux!

Jekyll & Hyde is a crafty sans serif, given the J&H moniker because it's two typefaces in one: The default (Jekyll) appearance can be altered significantly by swapping to the font's Stylistic Set 1 (Hyde), which is more "Grotesque" in nature. G-Type founder Nick Cooke was also born in Hyde, near Manchester, so the name is quite apt. Three widths and multiple weights increase the versatility of this typeface, which also comes in variable format. Stand-alone fonts are also available, so if you're more Hyde (grotesque) than Jekyll (contemporary), you can choose to have your preferred styling on the default positions.

Jekyll & Hyde

g-type.com

Designed by *Nick Cooke*
Published by *G-Type*

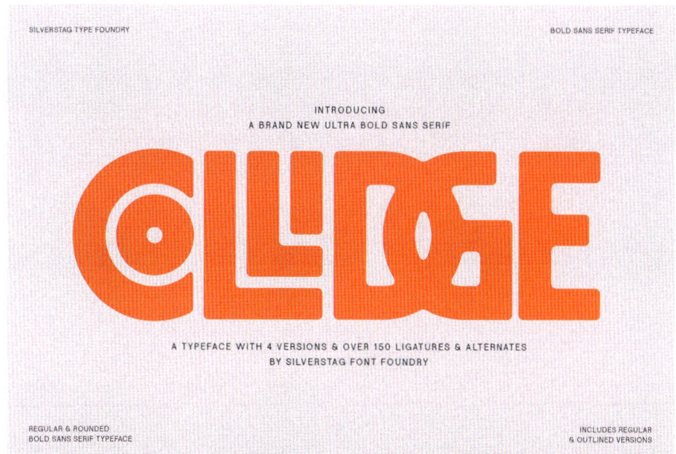

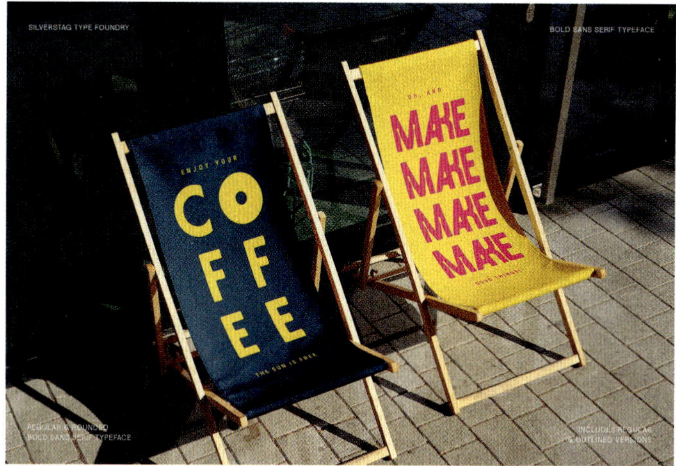

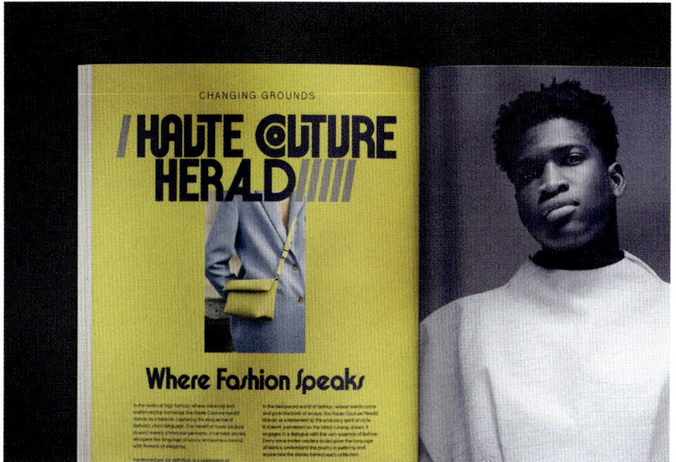

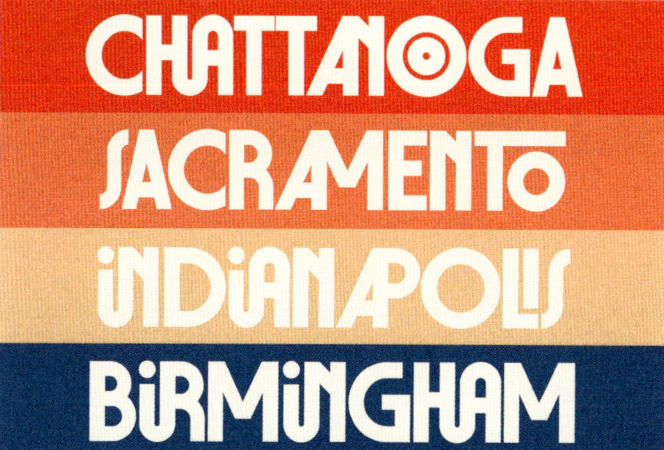

Collidge is a fearless sans serif font made for maximum impact. With chunky strokes, bold angles, and four versatile styles—Regular, Regular Outlined, Rounded, and Rounded Outlined—Collidge is built to own headlines, branding, and anything that needs unapologetic energy. Designed for visual punch, Collidge includes over 150 ligatures and alternates that let you create standout typography with personality and edge. From sharp and structured to smooth and rounded, each version offers a unique twist to match your creative vision.

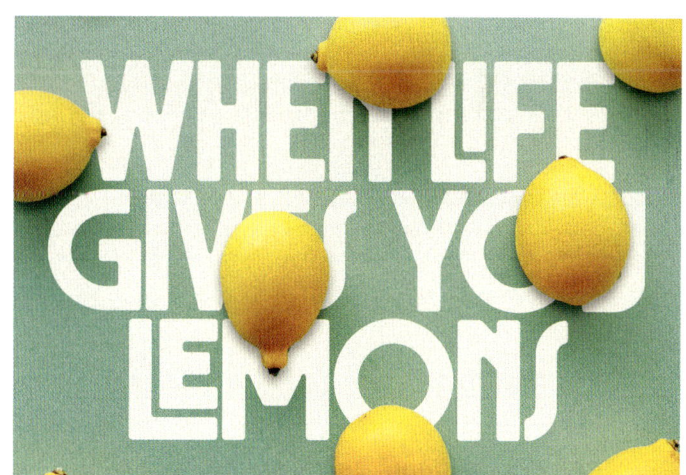

---

silverstagtype.com

Collidge

Designed by *Alen Kapetanovic*
Published by *SilverStag Type Foundry*

Icona™ is a fixed system of alphanumeric characters with specific characteristics to be used repetitively.

Latin

Jackna

Cyrillic

Убедит

Greek

Θέατρο

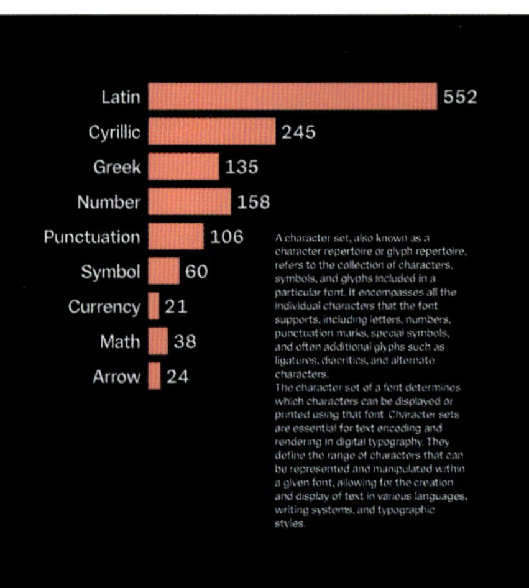

American Enlightening Readers.

Icona Sans is a neutral typeface with a high x-height, a wide range of weights with adequate italics, and an extensive character set covering Latin, Cyrillic, and Greek. Many alternative characters change personality, but stand out especially in display sizes, where they attract attention even in serious settings.

Country

Мансаптың да, қызметтің де, атақтың да, байлықтың да дәрігер үшін құны көктиын. Дәрігерге ең қажеті — адамның денсаулығы, оның тағдыры.

Mastermind

He performed his famous water bowl trick, in which he did a somersault at age 73 and ended up standing with a goldfish bowl in his left hand.

Garlic

The history of neutral sans-serif fonts dates back to the 19th century when the concept of sans-serif typefaces emerged as a departure from the more ornate and decorative serif fonts of the time. The development of neutral sans-serifs was influenced by various design movements and technological advancements: Early Sans-Serifs (19th Century): The first sans-serif typefaces appeared in the early 19th century, characterized by their lack of serifs and a relatively simple design. These early sans-serifs were often used for advertising and display purposes. Bauhaus and Modernism (Early to Mid-20th Century): The Bauhaus movement, with its focus on functional and minimalist design, played a significant role in shaping neutral sans-serif fonts. Designers like Herbert Bayer and Jan Tschichold contributed to the development of geometric and simplified sans-serif typefaces during this period. Swiss Style (Mid-20th Century): The Swiss design movement emphasized clarity, simplicity, and readability. Designers like Max Miedinger created fonts like Helvetica (1957), which epitomized the neutral sans-serif aesthetic. Helvetica's balanced proportions and clean lines made it highly versatile and widely adopted. Digital Typography (Late 20th Century): The advent of digital typography and desktop publishing allowed for greater experimentation and refinement of neutral sans-serif fonts. This era saw the creation of type families like Arial, which aimed

Джеймс Нейсміт назвав свою гру «Basket Ball» — від basket («кошик») і ball («м'яч»). Надалі назва трансформувалася у basketball — слово, яким в англійській мові називають як гру, так і баскетбольний м'яч.

It was an entirely new medium.

They drink alcohol and smoke traditional tobacco cigarettes less often, but are more likely to consume marijuana and electronic cigarettes.

Ολυμπιακοί θεωρούνταν

Strategic

Тројанската војна има свои корени

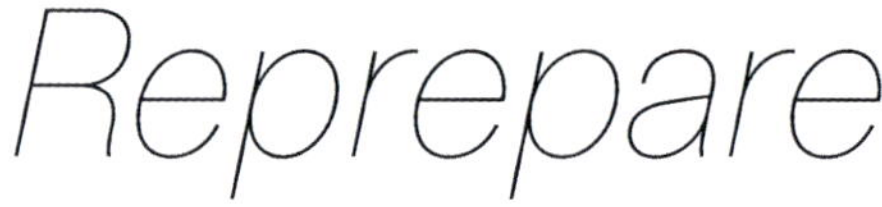

Η Λιθογραφία είναι μια τεχνική εκτύπωσης η οποία επινοήθηκε το 1798 περίπου από τον Α. Ζένεφελντερ (Alois Senefelder), στηριζόμενος στο γεγονός ότι το νερό και οι λιπαρές ουσίες δεν αναμιγνύονται ποτέ.

Black and gold later became the colours used by the Imperial House of Habsburg.

Καλλιεργήθηκε

camel-like shape and leopard-like colouration

Architecture

Icona Sans

suitcasetype.com

Designed by *Tomáš Brousil*
Published by *Suitcase Type*

ดัคส์ฮุนท์

ผู้ชนะไฮเปอร์ไฟต์ สกายฮาวด์ซ

คุณสามารถกำจัดขนกระจุกที่หลุดออกได้อย่างง่ายดายด้วยแปรงสำหรับสุนัข

บอสตันเทอร์เรียร์

คะแนนบุญด้านเทคนิคและศิลปะ

ประสาทสัมผัสของหมา[28] ได้แก่ การมองเห็น การได้ยิน การดมกลิ่น การรับรู้รสชาติ* การสัมผัสและการตอบสนองไวต่อสนามแม่เหล็กของโลก[4]

นักวิ่งที่รวดเร็ว

ความแตกต่างของตำแหน่งส้นเท้าในขณะที่ผู้ควบคุมเคลื่อนจากซ้ายไปขวาแล้วกลับมาอีกครั้ง

บุลล์แมสติฟฟ์

บิยานูโกเดลัสเองการ์ตาซิโอเนส

แจพานีสเทอร์เรียร์
โบฮีเมียนเชพเพิร์ด
๙ อิงลิช มาสทิฟฟ์
บูวิเยเดฟลองเดรอะ

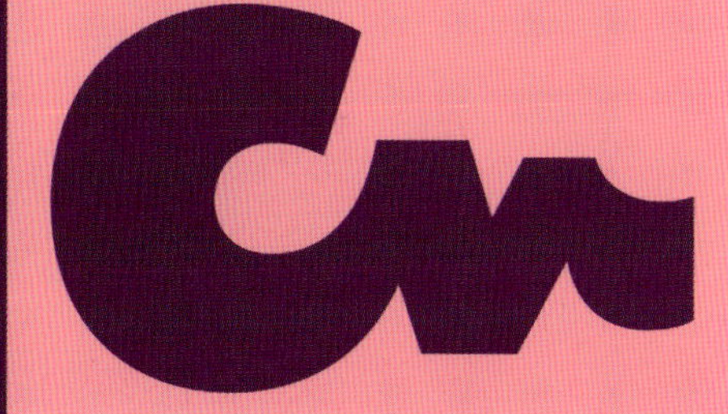

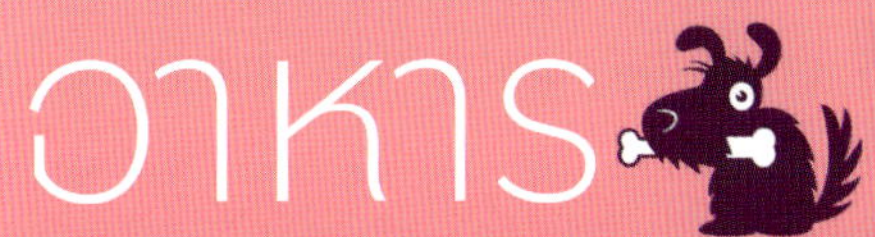

#1 โรลเลอร์เบลด

Bilo วิ่งได้เร็วถึง ๓๖ กม./ชม

๒๐๒๔ เวสต์ไฮแลนด์ ไวท์เทอร์เรีย

คว้าขนมทั้งหมด!

วัตถุเจือปนอาหาร วิตามินเอ 15.000 IU — วิตามินดี[93] 1.500 IU — วิตามินอี 150 มก. — ทองแดง (เช่น คอปเปอร์(II)ซัลเฟต, เพนทาไฮเดรต) 12.5 มก. — เหล็ก (เช่น เหล็ก(II)ซัลเฟต, โมโนไฮเดรต) 200 มก. — แมงกานีส (เป็นแมงกานีส (II) ออกไซด์) 40 มก. — สังกะสี[94](เป็นซิงค์ออกไซด์) 150 มก. — ไอโอดีน[95] (เป็นแคลเซียมไอโอเดต, แอนไฮดรัส*) 2.0 มก. — ซีลีเนียม[96] (ในรูปของโซเดียมซีลีไนต์) ~0.05 มก [ที่มา C] **สารเติมแต่งเทคโนโลยี** เลซิติน 1.600 มก. — สารสกัดจากธรรมชาติที่มีปริมาณโทโคฟีรอลสูง* (วิตามินอีธรรมชาติ) 48 มก — อาหารที่สำคัญ

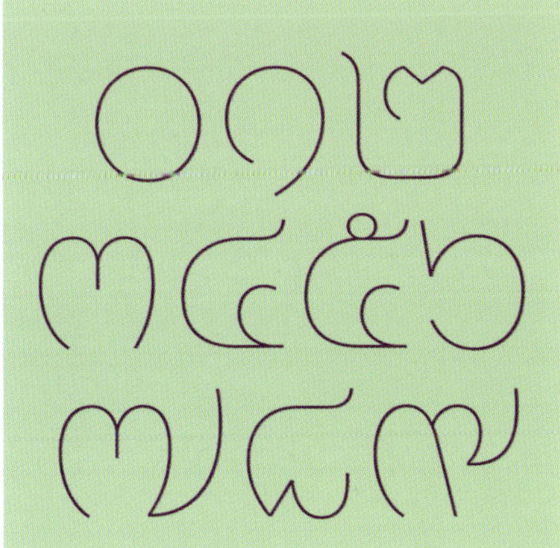

ฎ

Bilo Thai is a translation of Latin Bilo's occasional curious detail and unique flavor into loopless Thai letterforms. The moderate x-height of Latin Bilo made it easy to match the proportions of the Thai and its need for room for vowels and tone marks above and below the middle (consonant) height.

boldmonday.com

Bilo Thai

Designed by *Promphan "Boom" Suksumek, Pieter van Rosmalen*
Published by *Bold Monday*

POSTEA ARABIC

For brands and headlines

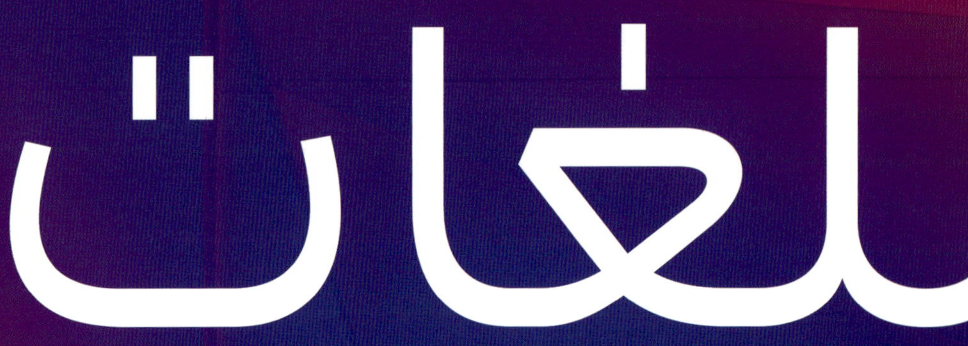

Postea پوستيا

Постеа Sans

Serif פוסטאה

Taking up space
and declaring
its presence

Ποστέα

Beginning with Bauhaus virtues, Postea is the rational response for pixel or paper text—a lyrical take on geometric sans serifs. Classic curves and purposeful details make it ideal for branding, signage, corporate typefaces, and magazines.

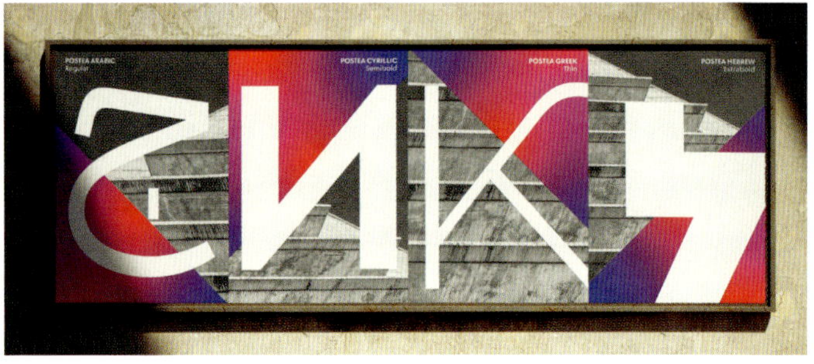

Postea

type-together.com

Designed by *Veronika Burian, José Scaglione, Azza Alameddine, Yorlmar Campos, Vera Evstafieva, Tom Grace*
Published by *TypeTogether*

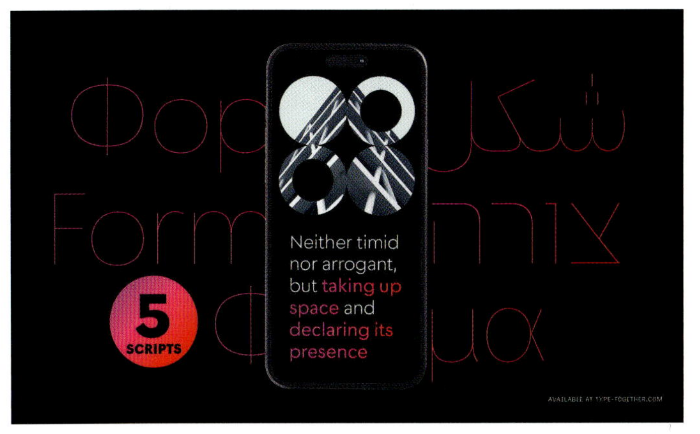

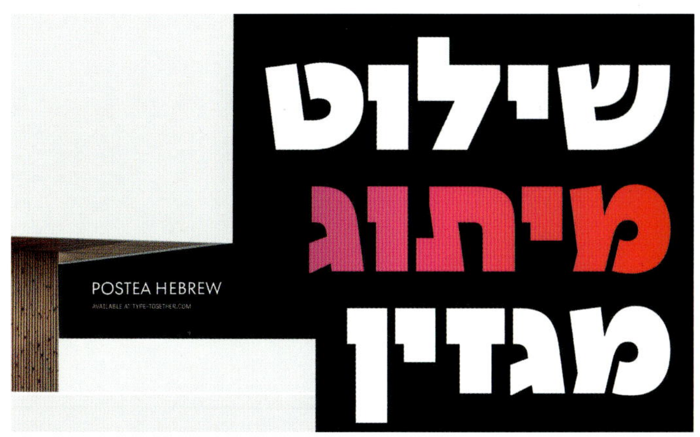

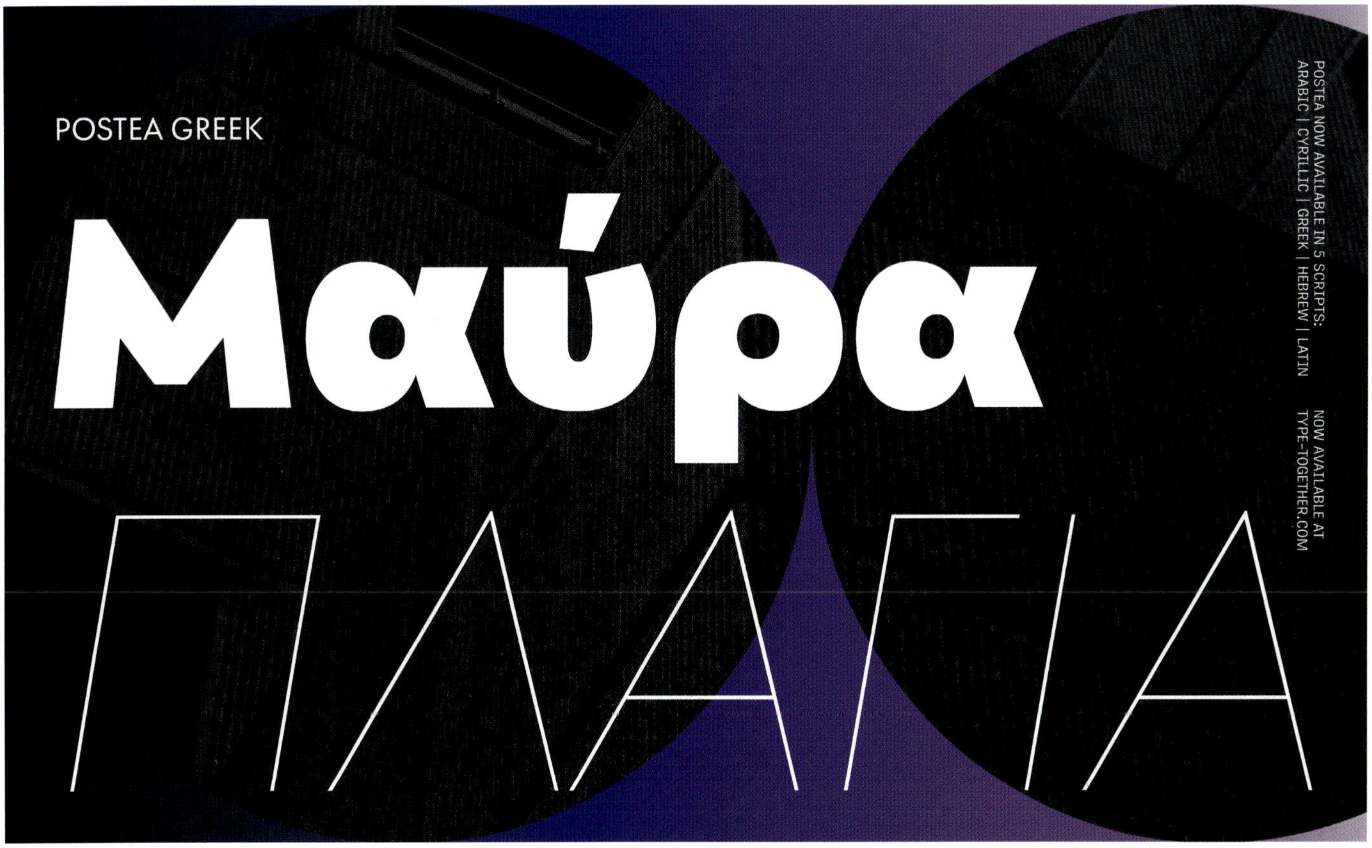

POSTEA GREEK

Μαύρα

ΠΛΑΓΙΑ

POSTEA NOW AVAILABLE IN 5 SCRIPTS:
ARABIC | CYRILLIC | GREEK | HEBREW | LATIN

NOW AVAILABLE AT
TYPE-TOGETHER.COM

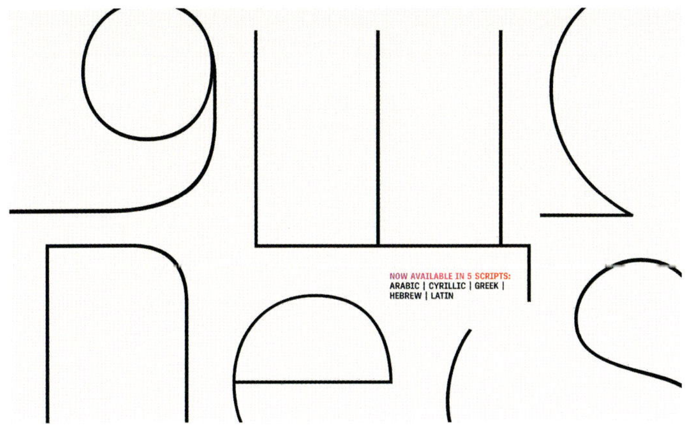

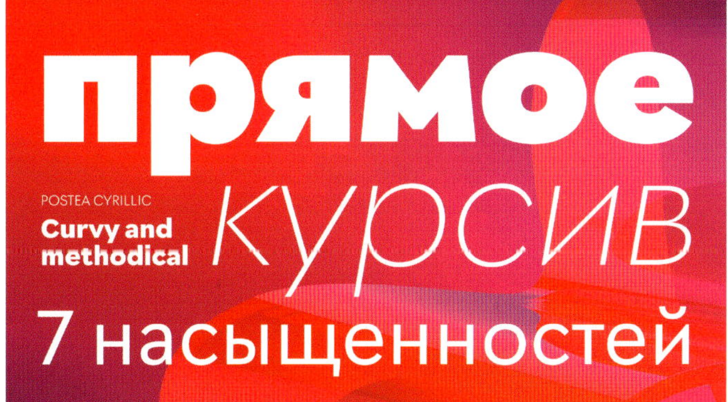

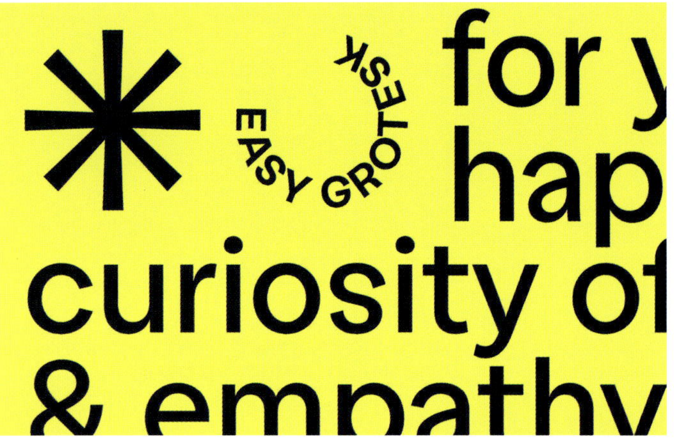

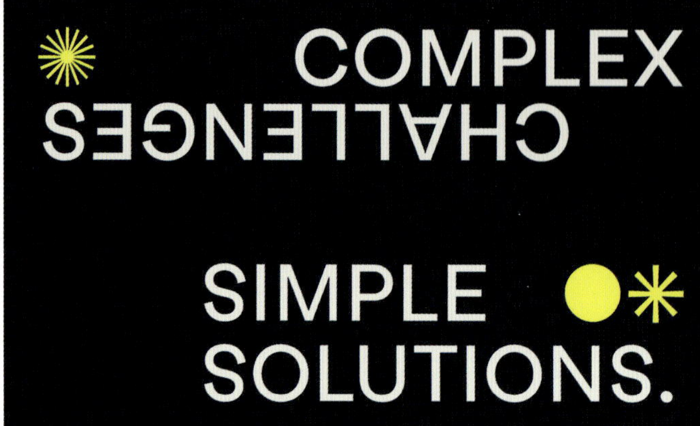

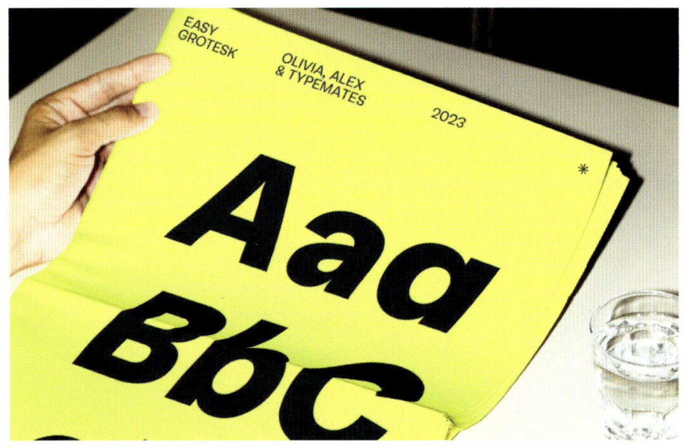

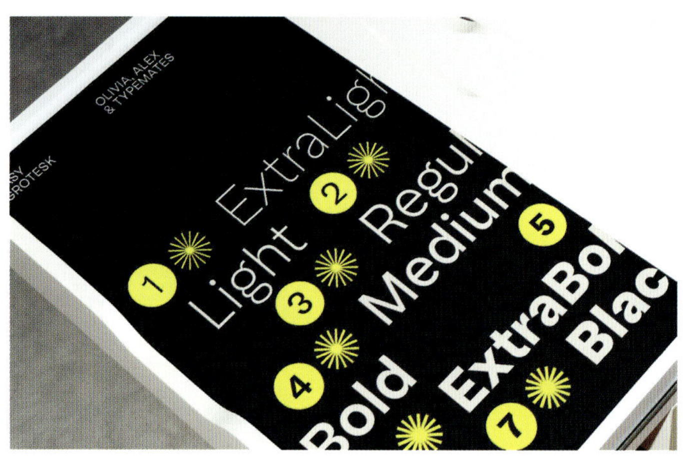

✱ EASY GROTESK 2023

navigate ↗
→ change
↳ ↔ ↖

4 Our growing awarene
that *sustainability* is not t
matter of preference; it's a
necessity.

SIZE AND GROWTH

SHARING ECONOMY

There is a conceptual and semantic confusion cau
by the many facets of Internet-based sharing lead
discussions regarding the boundaries and the sco
sharing economy and regarding the definition of
economy. Arun Sundararajan noted in 2016 that he is *"unaware of a
on a definition of the sharing economy"*. 27–28 As of 2015, according to
Center survey, only 27% of Americans had heard of the term *"sharing econ*
respondents who had heard of the term had divergent views on what it me
thinking it concerned *"sharing"* in the traditional sense of the term.
The term *"sharing economy"* is often used in an ambiguous way and can
characteristics. For example, the sharing economy is sometimes underst
as a peer-to-peer phenomenon while at times, it has been framed as a b
customer phenomenon. Additionally, the sharing economy can be unders

Easy Grotesk? It's confident and optimistic. It's fresh, friendly, and combines the conventional with the surprising; trust and familiarity with a visual twist. Easy Grotesk brings together two opposing aesthetics: There's the easygoing typographic texture on the one hand, and quirky character on the other. Useful and functional, this cheerful helper is carefree, but not careless. It's Easy, not lazy!

Easy Grotesk

typemates.com

Designed by *Alexander Rütten, Olivia Wood*
Published by *TypeMates*

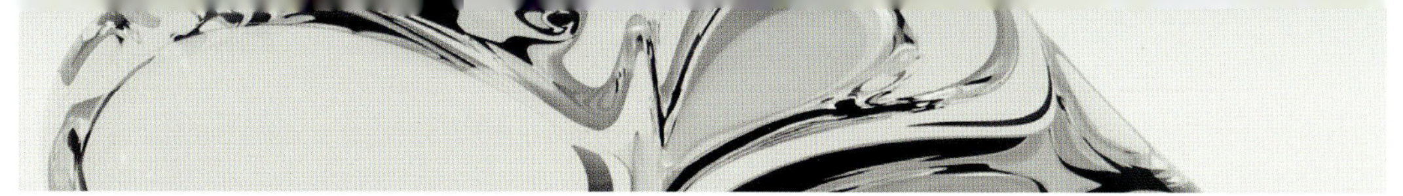

Q: Write two sentences. One about urban transportation and one about the anatomy of the human face.

**After a long , I rented a and dro
to the station, where I caught a
to the city center and then took a
my hotel. The , with its cartilage an
nostrils, the with its iris and pupils
and the with its lips and teeth are**

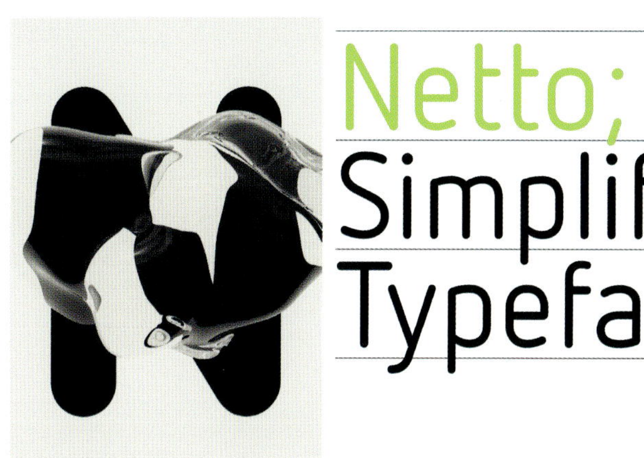

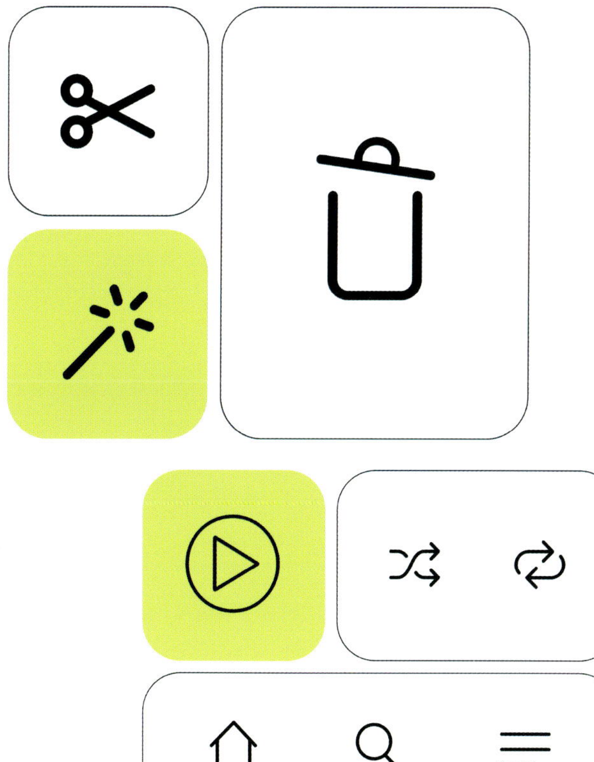

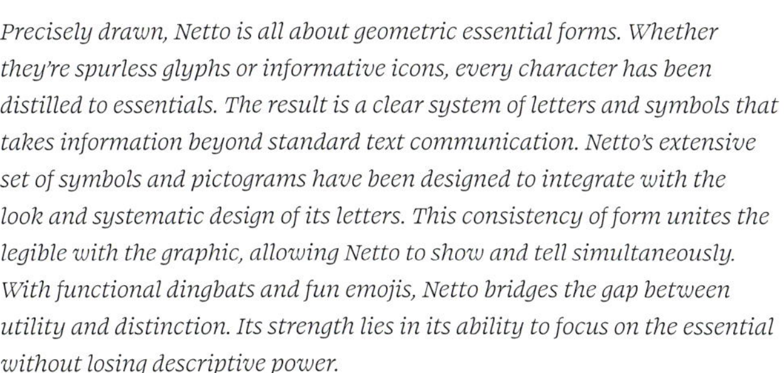

Precisely drawn, Netto is all about geometric essential forms. Whether they're spurless glyphs or informative icons, every character has been distilled to essentials. The result is a clear system of letters and symbols that takes information beyond standard text communication. Netto's extensive set of symbols and pictograms have been designed to integrate with the look and systematic design of its letters. This consistency of form unites the legible with the graphic, allowing Netto to show and tell simultaneously. With functional dingbats and fun emojis, Netto bridges the gap between utility and distinction. Its strength lies in its ability to focus on the essential without losing descriptive power.

typemates.com

Netto

Designed by *Daniel Utz*
Published by *TypeMates*

What Designers Talk About When They Talk About Typefaces

An Essay by Laura Meseguer

Whether it's a new typeface or an old favorite, it still needs to be shown—either to graphic designers or to a client. So how do you showcase it in a way that makes people actually want to use it? It's elegant, a little retro, a bit fancy, and looks great on Instagram, especially if it's animated and has some unexpected twist, like super sharp contrast in the serifs. Likes roll in. Comments say things like: "love the vibe," "great bold," "so clean." Or maybe the designer drops it into a mood board with some familiar visuals, shows it to the client, and boom—they're impressed.

It's a familiar scene—in studios, classrooms, and scrolls through social media. It's quick, emotional, instinctive. But as a type designer and educator, I keep wondering: Do we really know what we're seeing when we look at a typeface? Or, more to the point: How do designers talk about fonts,[1] and what does that say about how we / they use them?

Over the past twenty years, the way designers find and use fonts has changed a lot. Fonts are everywhere. They are accessible, downloadable, shareable... Platforms like Instagram, Behance, and Pinterest have turned typography into a visual loop—circulating more as a style trend than a design item or artifact. Fonts are picked for the "vibe" and the "like" of that moment, and often stripped of context. And when we *do* talk about them, we tend to use vague, overused words: clean, bold, quirky, nostalgic, modern, contemporary. They describe mood, but they don't really tell us much.

As someone who draws type for a living, I know how much gets lost in that simplification. Whether it's the innocent humanism of Rumba; the freshness of signpainting of Lalola; the warm geometry of Sisters; or the calligraphic details turned into a touch of brutalism in Ella, every typeface I design is full of intention.[2] Each one is built on specific references, gestures, rhythms, ideas, and even conversations. But when designers find these fonts in a pop-up menu or as a post on Instagram, all of that disappears. The work, the craft—even the authorship—gets reduced to a quick read.

I think part of the problem is how typography is taught. In many bachelor design programs, type education is split into compartments: a history course here, a layout class there, maybe a short intro to type design. But students rarely get a full picture of how type is made, and for what, how it communicates, and how to choose it with care. As a typography and type design teacher, when I ask my students about these issues, or about how they choose typefaces, they'll say things like "I like it," or "This one feels more serious," or "That one's more playful," but they often don't know how those feelings are actually built into the design, and they struggle when I ask them to go deeper.

Every typeface carries traces of the time, place, and purpose. Take Cooper Black: It's not just "retro"—it's warm, optimistic, and a little kitschy. That comes from its curves, its weight, and everything it's been associated with over the decades. When we flatten it to one word, we miss what makes it powerful. And let's be clear—there's nothing wrong with emotional responses to type. In fact, they're essential. Fonts speak before the words do. But we need to pair that emotion with literacy. Designers should be able to read a typeface the way musicians read music: seeing the structure, rhythm, contrast, and nuance. This shows that fonts aren't tools—they're cultural, emotional, and make language visible. You can also say that a typeface is a material, as it was exposed at the *Matter Matters* exhibition, at the DHUB in

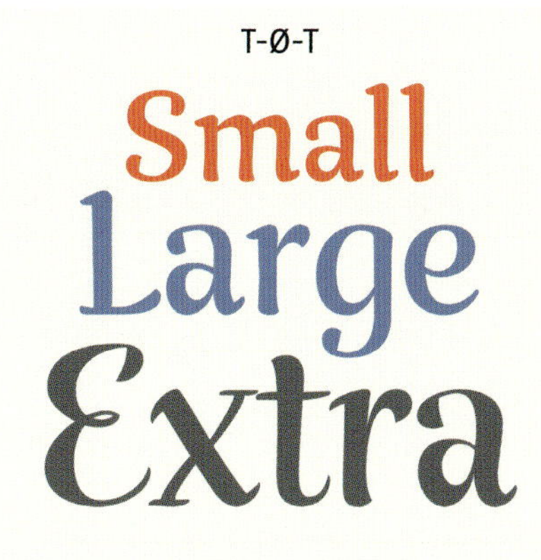

Rumba, designed by Laura Meseguer

T-Ø-T
Lalola
also in Cyrillic
Лалола

Lalola Cyrillic, designed by Laura Meseguer

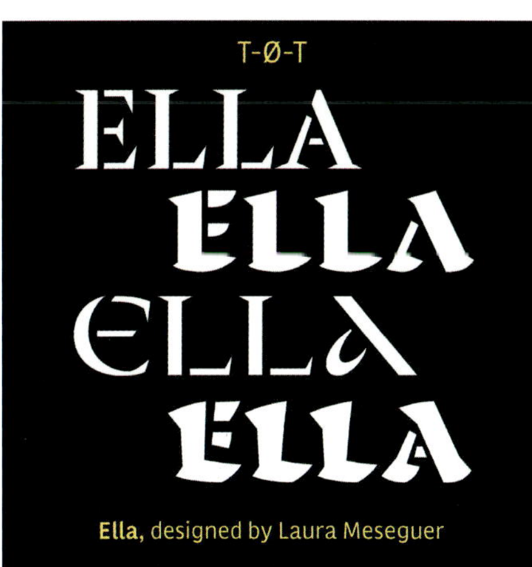

Ella, designed by Laura Meseguer

Barcelona,[3] and, as material, you can model, transform them and they can become the essence of any graphic piece.

Social media has added another layer. Typefaces today are marketed like fashion: seasonal releases, curated bundles, trending styles. It's easy to grab what looks good and move on. But in that process, even the most thoughtful, experimental fonts can become surface-level style picks. I've seen typefaces used in ways that beautifully honor its voice and purpose—and in others where it's clearly chosen just for flair.

There's also pressure—especially on younger designers—to not get it wrong. With endless choices and little shared language to talk about them (this is something I try to address in my classes, too), many end up copying what's trending or relying on safe brand fonts. Custom type is gaining traction, but it's still seen as something only big clients can afford (and this is not really true!).

Type Specimens

One encouraging shift I've seen lately is the rise of the type specimen—not just as a catalog, but as a creative tool. Specimens used to be functional documents, showing glyph sets and sizes. But now they've become something much more: experiments, stories, visual essays.

They show how a typeface moves, breathes, performs in real contexts. They don't just sell a font—they introduce it. And they let the typeface speak.

For independent designers like me, specimens are gold. They give us a way to connect with graphic designers—not with instructions, but with ideas. They show what a typeface can do emotionally, culturally, stylistically. And they're quietly educational too: revealing how a font behaves across languages, uses, and tones. In a world of font overload, specimens offer a chance to slow down and choose with intention. I think it is the perfect platform for typeface designers to show their design intentions and purposes.

That's also what we try to do at Tipo-g,[4] the school I codirect. We don't just teach how to design typefaces—we teach how to see and show them. We ask questions like: What is this letter trying to say? Where does it come from? What cultural references does it carry? What's the relationship between style and meaning? The ideas can take the shape of a book, a newspaper, an online publication…

In my experience, the most meaningful design choices happen when people pause. When they see printed typefaces and compare them side by side, when they stop and ask themselves, "What kind of voice does this project need?" or "What's the right font for this project right now?"

Design events help, too—especially the ones that go beyond show-and-tell. I think of gatherings like ATypI[5] or smaller conferences where people talk about authorship, context, and responsibility. Those conversations need to happen more often—and not just in the type world, but across the whole design field.

Type designers can talk about letter shapes and how to use them, but how these chats are delivered is another question. I'm not saying every designer needs to be a type historian or a teacher. But we do need more typographic literacy. Just like we teach color theory or layout principles, we should talk and teach type as a living language. A system of forms, yes—but also a set of voices. In the end, the way we speak about type reflects our design culture. If we reduce it to looks, we lose its meaning. But if we speak about it with care—with curiosity about where it comes from, how it works, and what it can say—we become better designers.

And better listeners.

So the next time a font walks into your moodboard, ask it: *Where are you from? What do you want to say? And am I really hearing you?*

1 *This title works as a wink to the book* What We Talk About When We Talk About Love, *suggesting layers of emotion and misunderstanding. It is a 1981 collection of short stories by American writer Raymond Carver, as well as the title of one of the stories in the collection.*

2 *See my typefaces at type-o-tones.com and at my site laurameseguer.com*

3 *dissenyhub.barcelona/en/exhibition/matter-matters-designing-world*

4 *tipo-g.com*

5 *atypi.org*

بدأ فن البوب في خمسينيات القرن العشرين لكنه لم يحصل على قوته العظمى في أميركا حتى ستينيات القرن ذاته. جاء مصطلح «فن البوب» بشكل رسمي في ديسمبر عام ١٩٦٢، وكان ذلك في مناسبة «ندوة عن فن البوب» التي نظمها متحف الفن الحديث (نيويورك). بحلول هذا الوقت، كان الإعلان الأميركي قد اعتمد العديد من العناصر والتطويرات في الفن الحديث وبدأ يعمل على مستوى رفيع للغاية. نتيجة لهذا الأمر، اضطر الفنانون الأمريكيون إلى البحث العميق عن

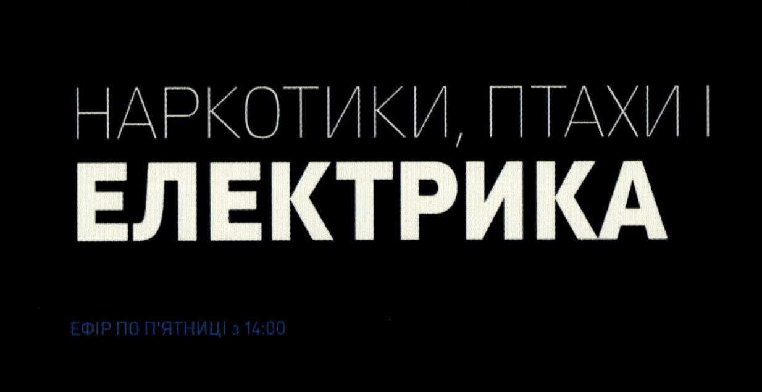

١. ارفع الورقة إلى الضوء
٢. فضح نفسك هناك لمدة دقيقة
٣. خذ إجازة قصيرة عندما تمر الأشعة
٤. المضي قدما وخلطها
٥. المضي قدما وربطه

Interdit de fumer
Курити Заборонено
Απαγορεύεται το κάπνισμα
ممنوع التدخين

DINosaur Sharp is a refined evolution of the original DINosaur. Its design captures the essence of an era when industrial labeling was hand-drawn, using tools like freehand techniques or stenciled alphabets, with its extreme roundness reflecting the mechanical effect of tracers or "rOtring" pens. DINosaur Sharp features reduced terminal rounding and redesigned characters for a sharper aesthetic. This version also expands its character set to include Arabic, Cyrillic, Greek, and Vietnamese.

DINosaur Sharp

type-o-tones.com

Designed by *José Manuel Urós*
Published by *Type-Ø-Tones*

joc de table

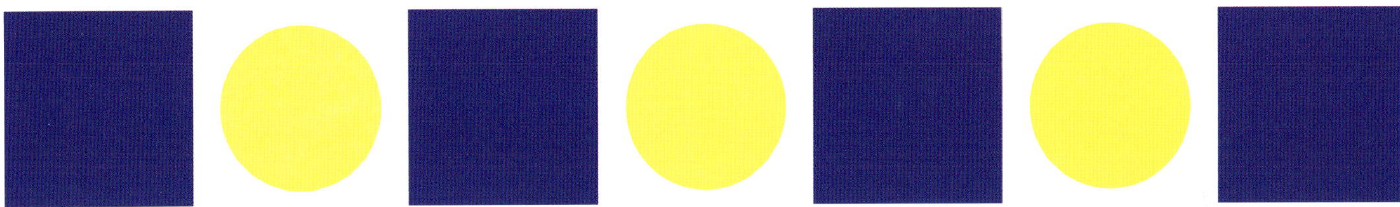

switches to recyclable packaging under pressure from child consumers
the Panama Canal to Panama Britney Spears releases “Baby One More Tim
ock 6, 1998 Microsoft gives the mouse an optical sensor Seattle Public Libra
r group has a revenue ($106 billion) comparable to India’s GDP ($139 billion)
arket for Eastern & Southern Africa Prada New York, 2000-2001 The “Matrix
me out – the best selling PC game of all time The Colombia Space Shuttle,
2003 Royal Dutch Shell’s revenues are greater than Venezuela’s gross dome
ternet worldwide Shanghai Study, 2003 Time names Albert Einstein the Pers
eries of Ricky Gervais’ “The Office” is aired on the BBC for the first time
ingapore sign Free Trade Agreement At G8 meeting the group G20 is formed
e move, 1999 Sierra Delta Concorde flew from Paris to New York Radiohead
e film, “Attack of the Clones”, produced entirely in digital format Barcelon

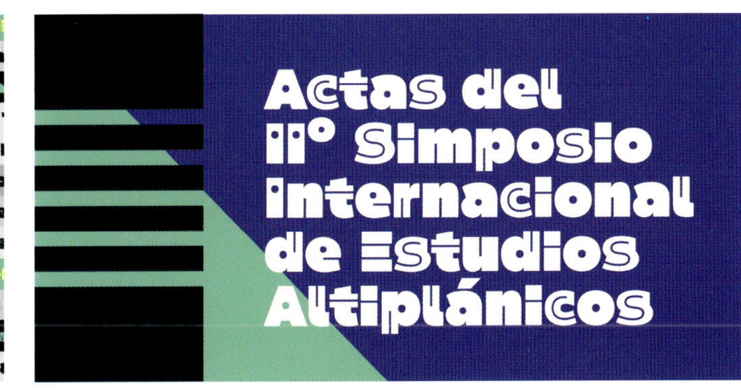

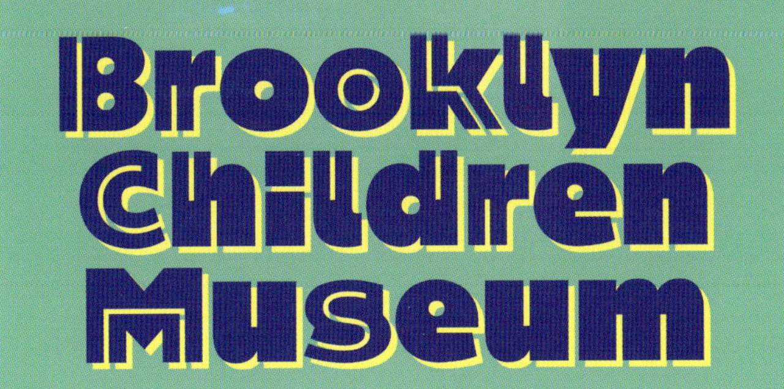

Joc Display was originally designed for Sara San Gregorio’s exhibition Juguetoría a l’altura del Joc *at La Panera Art Center in Lleida, Spain—a playful space where children aged five to nine create toys by combining shapes. The typeface draws inspiration from these shapes, translating them into its character set, while its name, “Joc” (Game), bridges Catalan and Romanian, reflecting both the exhibition’s spirit and designer Sabina’s roots.*

---

type-o-tones.com

Joc Display

Designed by *Sabina Chipară*
Published by *Type-Ø-Tones*

velocity improve
hammer glorious
kilowatt apricot

Zuume adam ladd design

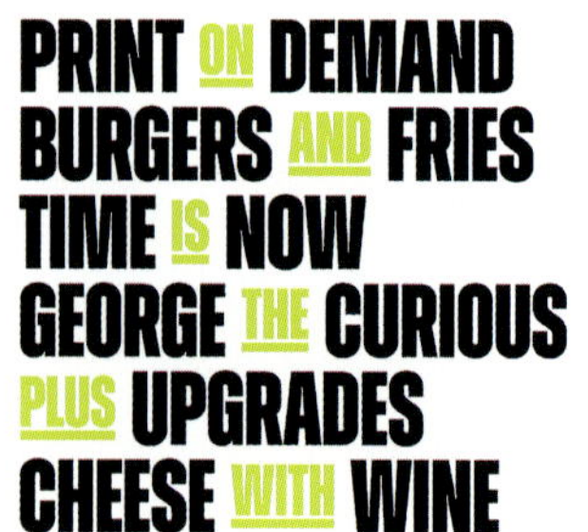

↓ CATCHWORDS
A AN AND AT BY DO
FOR FROM IN IS IT JUST
MORE NEW NOW OF ON
ONLY PLUS THE THIS TO
TOO WITH YOUR

Zuume adam ladd design

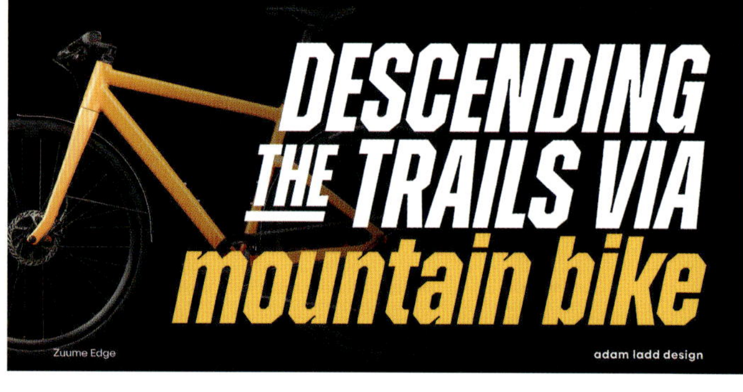

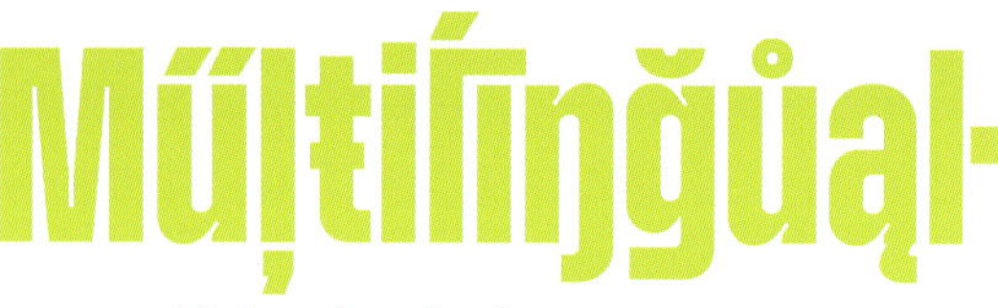

100+ Latin Languages

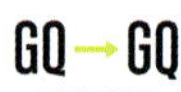
STYLISTIC ALTERNATES

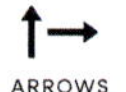
ARROWS

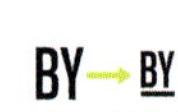
CATCHWORDS

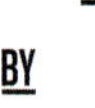
FRACTIONS

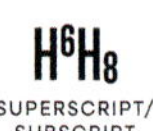
SUPERSCRIPT/ SUBSCRIPT

Zuume adam ladd design

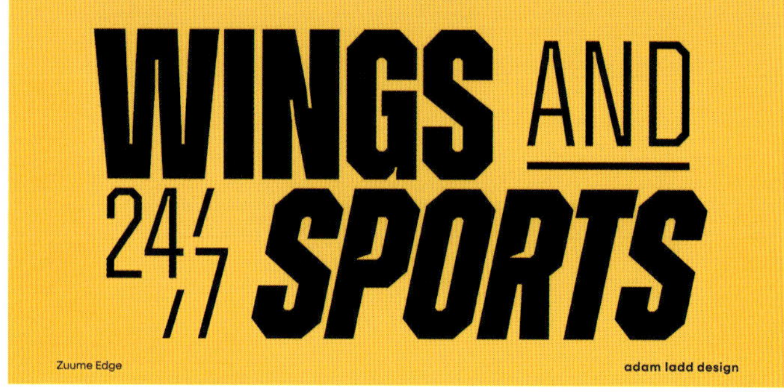

Zuume and Zuume Edge are certifiable look-at-me powerhouses. These typefaces are built to invigorate magazine headlines, media brands, fitness packaging, in-your-face entertainment, or anywhere else designers need maximum impact. The design has a sharp, technical feel that looks great, tightly spaced, and stacked for a visual punch. The sliced-out segments in Zuume Edge create more movement, aggression, and intentional speed.

Zuume & Zuume Edge

ladd-design.com

Designed by *Adam Ladd*
Published by *Adam Ladd Design*

OPEN HOUSE
INTERIOR DESIGN AND DECOR
ISSUE 72

Modern Scottish Charm

Interiors to keep you warm and cozy during a rainy autumn in the Scottish highlands.

SEPTEMBER 2024

HIGH & LOW CONTRAST	7 WEIGHTS	TRUE ITALICS

Styles

The high contrast styles are great for eye-catching display type and the low contrast styles pair well for paragraph text. The true italics create a special sparkle and 7 weights offer a huge range.

EX LIGHT	LIGHT	REGULAR	SEMIBOLD	BOLD	EX BOLD	CHONKY
a	a	a	a	a	a	a
EX LIGHT	LIGHT	REGULAR	SEMIBOLD	BOLD	EX BOLD	CHONKY
a	a	a	a	a	a	a

A high-contrast sans serif inspired by Scotch Roman style typefaces. The Stornoway family is designed to be versatile and communicate an elegant look without becoming too frail or delicate.

arcanetype.com

Stornoway

Designed by *Alanna Munro*
Published by *Arcane Type Foundry*

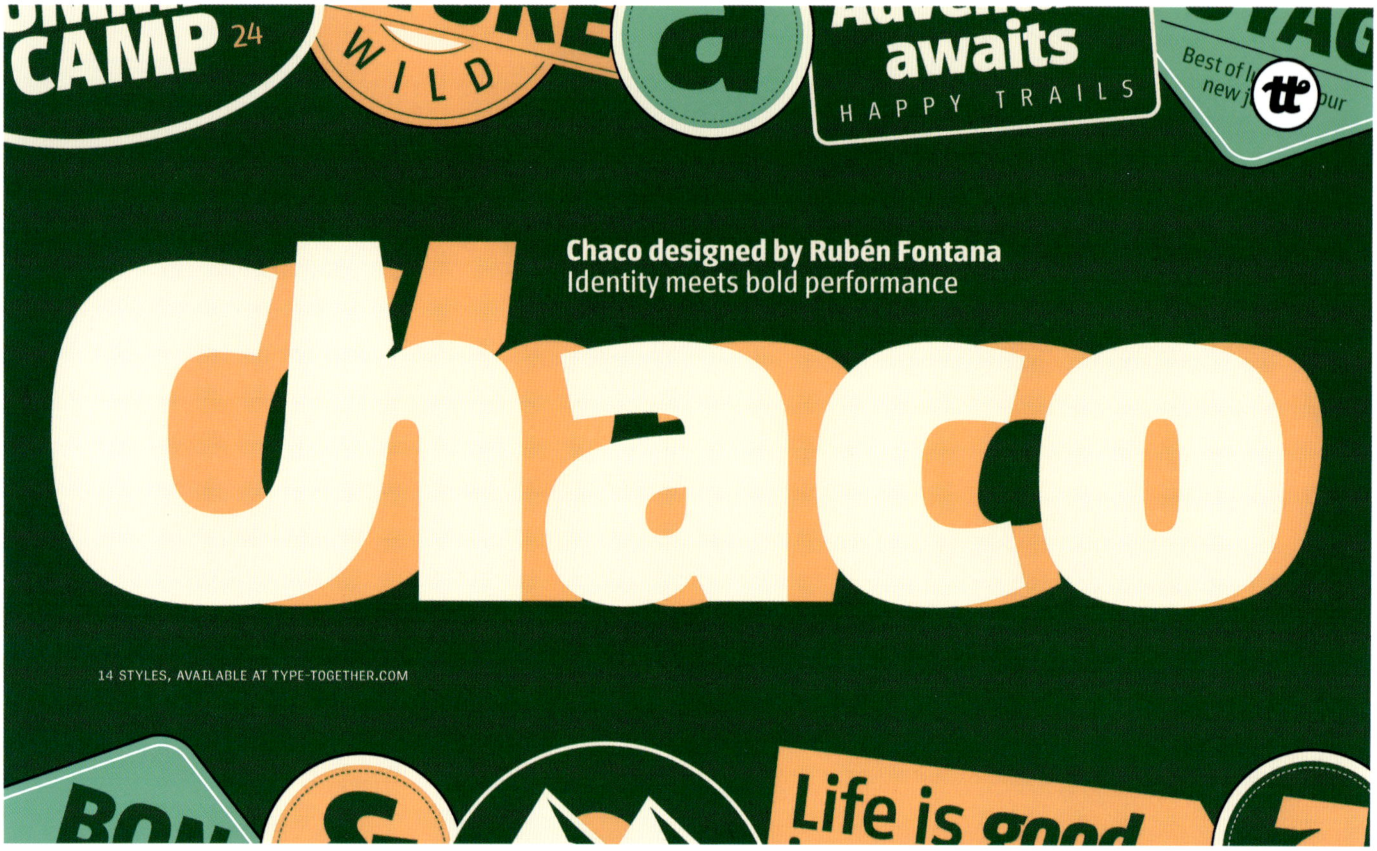

CAMP 24

WILD

awaits
HAPPY TRAILS

Best of
new
our

Chaco designed by Rubén Fontana
Identity meets bold performance

Chaco

14 STYLES, AVAILABLE AT TYPE-TOGETHER.COM

Life is good

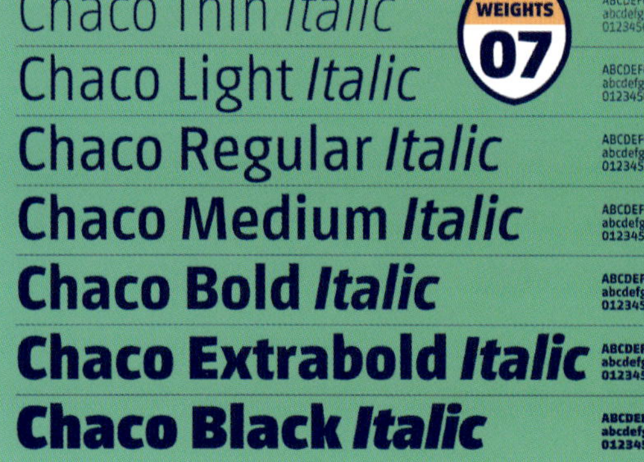

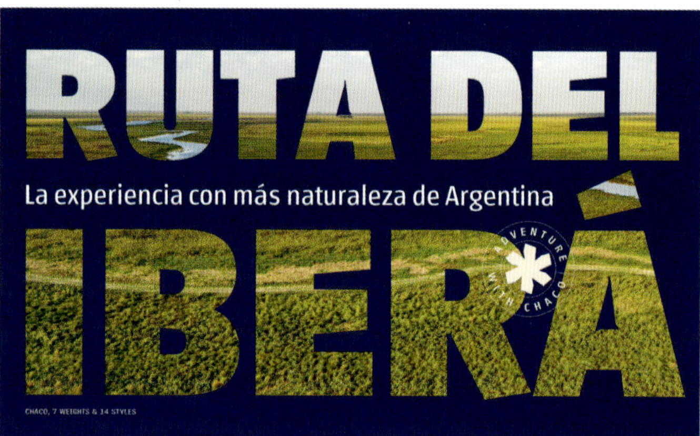

Combining aesthetic needs for identities, international wayfinding research, and the extreme details needed for small text, Rubén Fontana's Chaco font family is an outrageously contemporary offering from classic roots. His solution is the perfect typeface for identity and branding work, wayfinding, and composing immersive reading texts. Chaco began as a research project to solve specific wayfinding and roadway signage problems in Argentina, expanding to become a signage system based on the international standards of seven additional countries. Since differentiating between easily confused signs at a long distance or in small sizes is such a major concern, many of its solutions account for this issue. Chaco was designed with the rare ability to maintain internal space in word composition, offer better performance, and avoid word shortenings that are naturally illegible on a sign. In addition to the traditional ligatures, the "ch" digraph was specially designed, since it is a prominent sound in native South American languages. And with the intention of optimizing Chaco's distinction in the font world, some vertical strokes have their weight reversed.

Chaco

type-together.com

Designed by *Rubén Fontana*
Published by *TypeTogether*

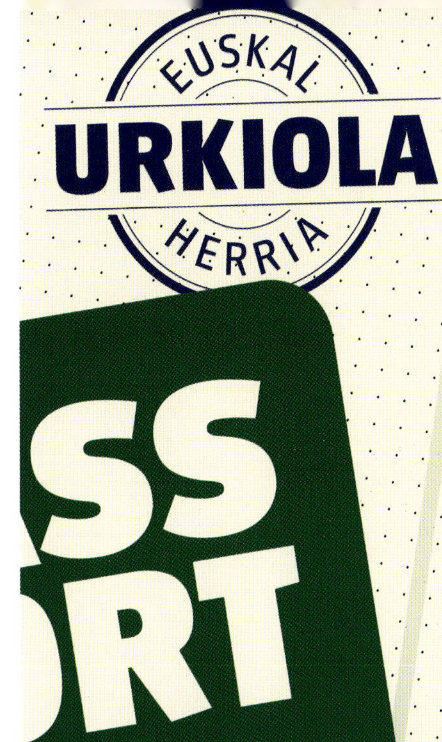
EUSKAL
URKIOLA
HERRIA

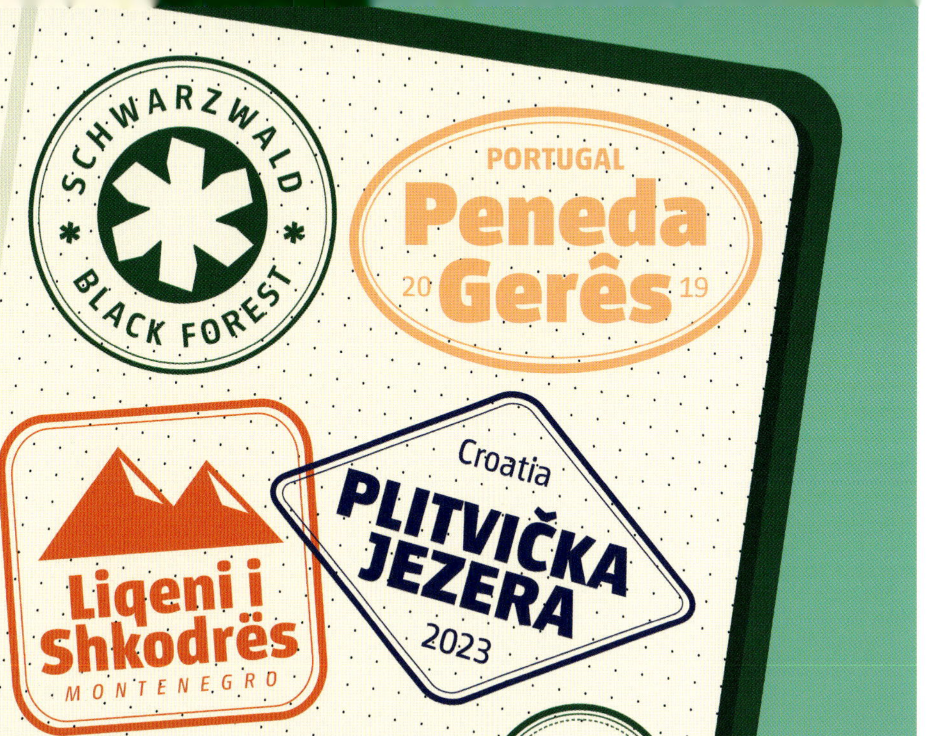
SCHWARZWALD
BLACK FOREST
PORTUGAL
Peneda Gerês
20 19
Liqeni i Shkodrës
MONTENEGRO
Croatia
PLITVIČKA JEZERA
2023

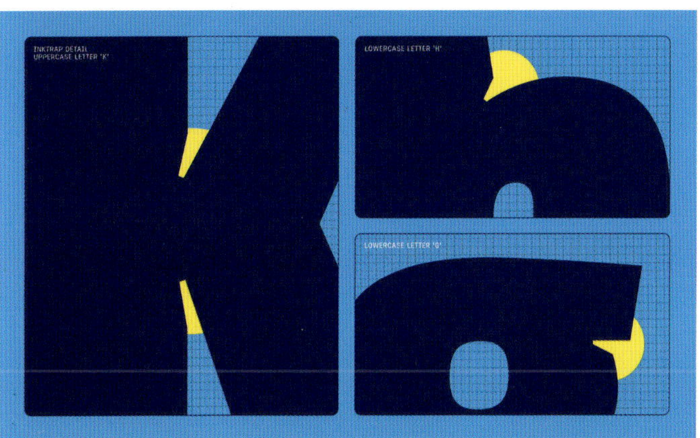
INKTRAP DETAIL
UPPERCASE LETTER "K"
LOWERCASE LETTER "H"
LOWERCASE LETTER "O"

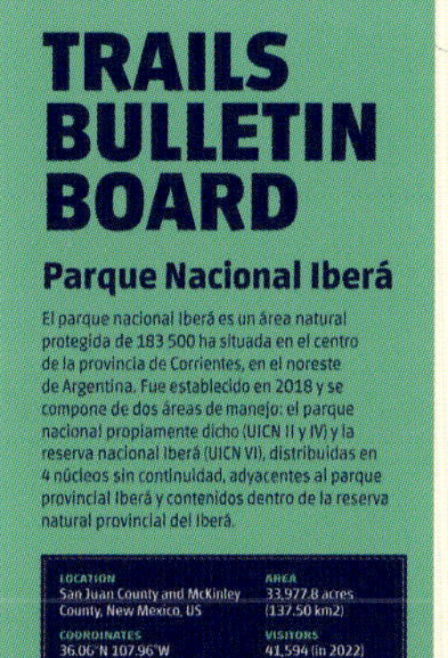
TRAILS BULLETIN BOARD
Parque Nacional Iberá
El parque nacional Iberá es un área natural protegida de 183 500 ha situada en el centro de la provincia de Corrientes, en el noreste de Argentina. Fue establecido en 2018 y se compone de dos áreas de manejo: el parque nacional propiamente dicho (UICN II y IV) y la reserva nacional Iberá (UICN VI), distribuidas en 4 núcleos sin continuidad, adyacentes al parque provincial Iberá y contenidos dentro de la reserva natural provincial del Iberá.
LOCATION
San Juan County and McKinley County, New Mexico, US
AREA
33,977.8 acres (137.50 km2)
COORDINATES
36.06°N 107.96°W
VISITORS
41,594 (in 2022)

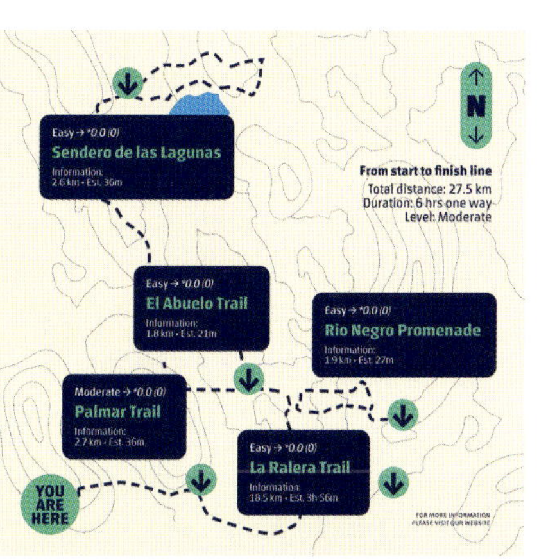
N
Easy → *0.0 (0)
Sendero de las Lagunas
Information:
2.6 km • Est. 36m
From start to finish line
Total distance: 27.5 km
Duration: 6 hrs one way
Level: Moderate
Easy → *0.0 (0)
El Abuelo Trail
Information:
1.8 km • Est. 21m
Easy → *0.0 (0)
Rio Negro Promenade
Information:
1.9 km • Est. 27m
Moderate → *0.0 (0)
Palmar Trail
Information:
2.7 km • Est. 36m
Easy → *0.0 (0)
La Ralera Trail
Information:
18.5 km • Est. 3h 56m
YOU ARE HERE
FOR MORE INFORMATION PLEASE VISIT OUR WEBSITE

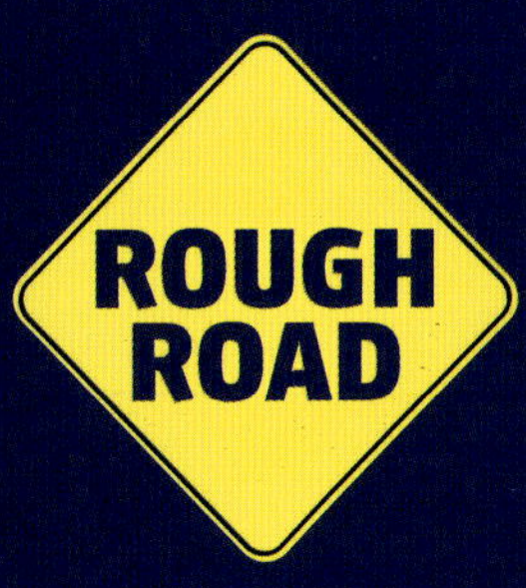
ROUGH ROAD

STOP

Islas de Santa Fe
km
45
Perito Moreno
km
80
Tourist Information
REDUCE SPEED AHEAD
EXIT
25
MPH
ROUTE
40
Monte León
NEXT INTERSECTION
Laguna Blanca

Astra is a sophisticated geometric sans serif typeface, offering nine weights that range from delicate Thin to robust Bold. It merges geometric precision with subtle humanist details, creating a clean yet inviting appearance. The result is a modern and elegant design that feels both fresh and refined.

Drawn With
The User
In Mind

ANTHROPOLOG
INSTRUMENTATI
CONVENTIONAL
INTERCHANGEAB

Sta

ASTRA BLACK

9 Weights
Matching Italics

Aa	Aa	Aa
THIN	EXTRALIGHT	LIGHT
THIN ITALIC	EXTRALIGHT ITALIC	LIGHT ITALIC
REGULAR	MEDIUM	SEMIBOLD
REGULAR ITALIC	MEDIUM ITALIC	SEMIBOLD ITALIC
BOLD	EXTRABOLD	BLACK
BOLD ITALIC	EXTRABOLD ITALIC	BLACK ITALIC

Nebul

ASTRA MEDIUM ITALIC

Astronomers Unveil New Co
Hidden Galaxies and Uncha
Systems Discovered in Vast
Survey, Expanding Our Und
of the Universe, Cosmos an

ASTRA REGULAR

Astra

positype.com

Designed by *Neil Summerour*
Published by *Positype*

NNNNN
NNNNN
NNNNN
NNNNN
NNNNN

AD
ASTRA
PER
ASPERA

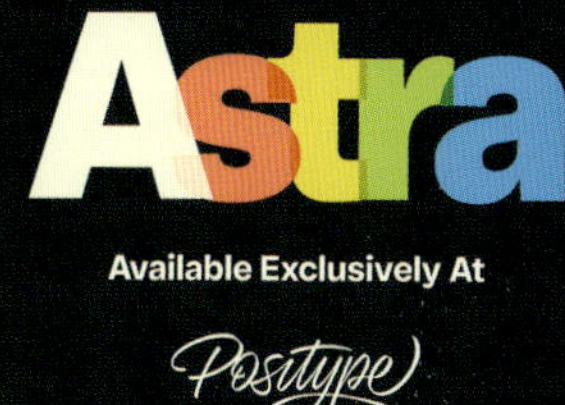

Available Exclusively At

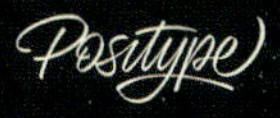

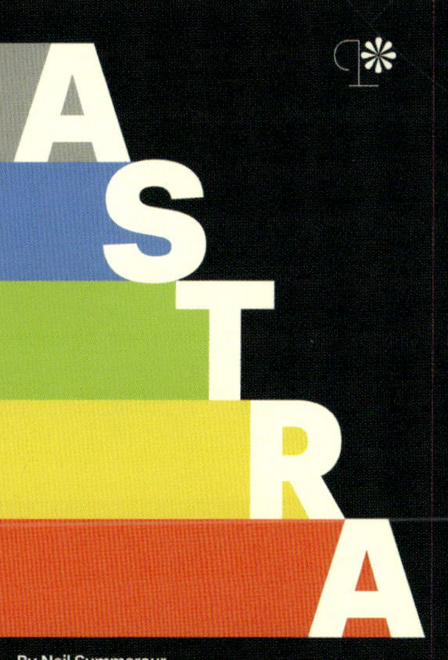

1 2 3
4 5 6
7 8 9
1 2 3
9 5 8
3 6 7

Ää Øø Əə
Ếế Çç Ẳẳ
Ğğ Şş Ợợ
Ứứ Ħħ Ỷỷ
Ññ Ậậ Üü
Ŗŗ Ẫẫ Ạạ

Extensive Language Support

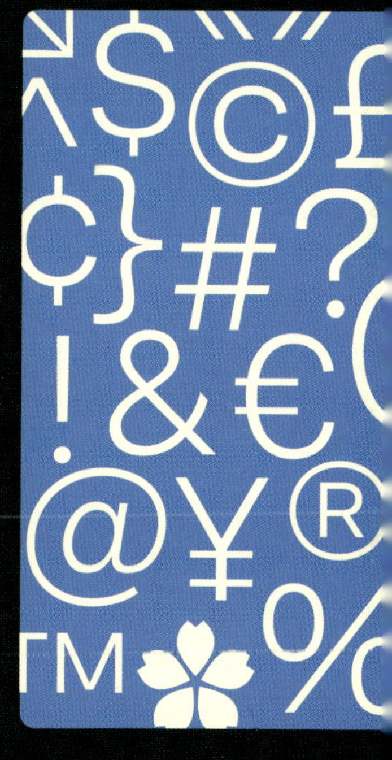

r

e

Map:
tar
ctic
ding
ond.

abcdefg
hijklmno
pqrstuv
wxyz

Optimized For Your Screens

Research related to "Astra" encompass
diverse array of disciplines, each explor
different facets of the cosmos and its
phenomena. Astronomical research, for
instance, delves into the study of celes
bodies such as stars, galaxies, and plan
unraveling their origins, behaviors, and
interactions. This research often involve
the use of telescopes, space probes, ar
other advanced instruments to observe
distant objects and phenomena. In addi
to observational astronomy, research in
astrophysics focuses on understanding
underlying physical principles governin
the universe. This includes studying top
such as stellar evolution, cosmology, ar
the nature of dark matter and dark ener
Astrophysical research often involves
theoretical modeling, computational
simulations, and experimental observat
to elucidate fundamental aspects of
the cosmos. Furthermore, astrobiology
explores the possibility of life beyond
Earth, investigating environments withi
our solar system and beyond that coulc
harbor microbial or even complex life fc
This interdisciplinary field draws upon
insights from astronomy, biology, chem
and geology to assess the habitability
of other worlds and search for signs of
extraterrestrial life. Space exploration
research, closely intertwined with "Astr
encompasses efforts to explore and
understand the cosmos through manne
and unmanned missions. This includes
studying the effects of space travel on

Research related to "Astra"
encompasses a diverse ar
of disciplines, each explori
different facets of the
cosmos and its phenomer
Astronomical research, for
instance, delves into the
study of celestial bodies s
as stars, galaxies, and plan
unraveling their origins,
behaviors, and interaction
This research often involve
the use of telescopes,
space probes, and other
advanced instruments to
observe distant objects ar
phenomena. In addition to
observational astronomy,
research in astrophysics
focuses on understanding
underlying physical princip
governing the universe. Th
includes studying topics
such as stellar evolution,

Research r
"Astra" enc
a diverse a
disciplines
exploring
facets of t
and its phe
Astronomi
for instanc
into the st
celestial b
as stars, g
planets, ur
their origir
and interac
This resea
involves th
telescopes

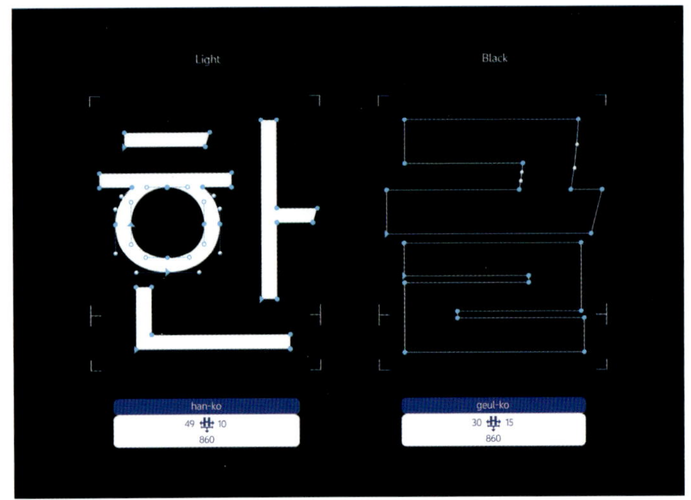

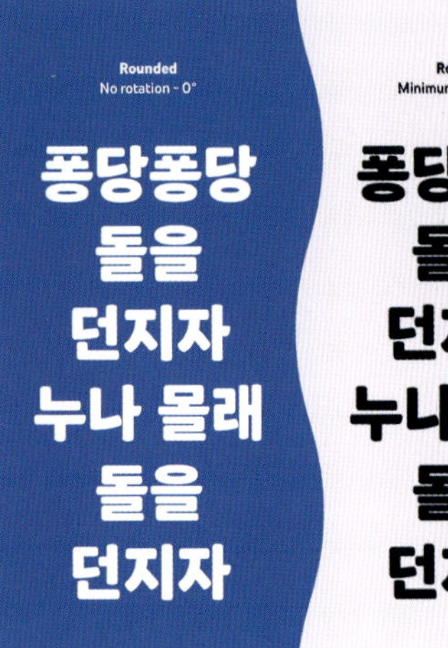

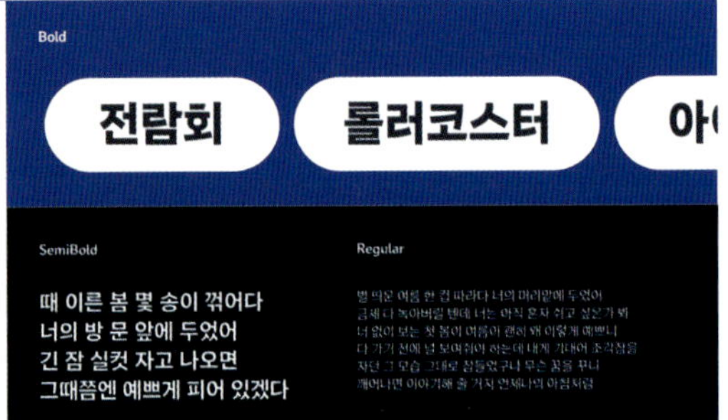

Family

Grades - Regular

Grades - Overlay

Grades - Dark

Rounded
Rmin. 0°

Rounded
Rmin. 1°

Rounded
Rmax. 3°

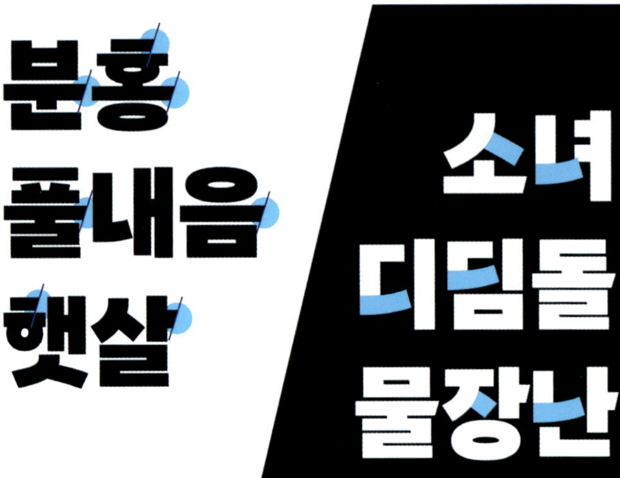

This Korean typeface is a member of the increasingly larger multi-script family of YouTube Sans. Designed as a low contrast typeface, intended for screens, at sizes 18 point and above. Drawing from the original Latin version, the design result is a font that reflects the brand attributes of warmth and inclusivity, while maintaining efficient legibility. This Korean script is inspired by the natural curves from handwritten strokes and the well-balanced structure of Hangeul Humanist sans serif. This typeface spans across seven weights in a variable axis, a full Hangeul character set of 11,172 characters, and includes a Sans, Rounded, and Grades version of the font.

YouTube Sans Korean

Designed by *Mingoo Yoon, Jieun Kim*
Custom designed for *YouTube*

A Hangeul sans serif typeface designed to accommodate a wide range of literary tones. It echoes the classical feel of newspaper typefaces from the 1980s and 1990s, while its balanced structure has been refined for modern digital use.

YMG 문체고딕—『중』 레귤러 Regular

YMG 문체고딕—『태』 미디움 Medium

YMG 문체고딕—『견출』 볼드 Bold

글을 쓴다는 것은 결국 하나의 형태를 만들어내는 일이다. 생각들이 흐르는 대로 두는 것이 아니라, 그것을 가두고 의미를 부여하는 것이다. 하지만 그 과정에서 많은 것이 사라진다. 처음 떠오른 문장은 너무 길거나, 직설적이거나, 혹은 흐릿했다. 나는 몇 번이고 다시 쓴다. 단어를 고쳐 적고, 문장을 다듬으며, 때로는 한 줄을 통째로 지운다. 결국 그렇게 수정하고 또 수정하며, 글을 완성해 간다.

나는 기억을 조금씩 변형시키고, 결국 처음 떠올린 것과는 전혀 다른 문장이 남는다. 종이 위에 연필을 올려둔다. 손끝이 가볍게 닿아 있는 연필은 아직 움직일 생각이 없다. 선을 긋기 시작하면 그것은 끝을 향해 나아가게 된다. 하지만 나는 끝을 정해놓지 않았다. 연필이 어디로 가야 할지 알지 못한 채, 나는 조용히 머문다. 멈춰 있는 동안에도 내 안에서는 계속해서 새로운 문장이 떠오른다.

나는 계속해서 글을 쓴다. 말은 사라지지만, 글은 남는다. 나는 언제나 말의 무상함을 느끼며 살아왔다. 순간의 감정을 담은 말들은 결국 사라지고 만다. 공기 중에 흩어져 다시는 돌아오지 않는다. 그러나 글은 다르다. 한 번 종이에 새겨지면, 시간이 흘러도 잊히지 않는다. 손끝을 떠난 글자들은 기억을 대신한다. 그리고 그 글들은 결국 나의 생각과 감정을 그대로 오랫동안 머물게 한다.

꽃	낮	몇	십	마	맑
옜	폄	챠	죠	샀	터
렸	넨	꾸	맛	를	빼

윤민구 타입 파운드리 YMG Type Foundry **www.yoonmingoo.tf**

yoonmingoo.tf

YMG Munche Gothic

Designed by *Mingoo Yoon*
Published by *YMG Type Foundry*

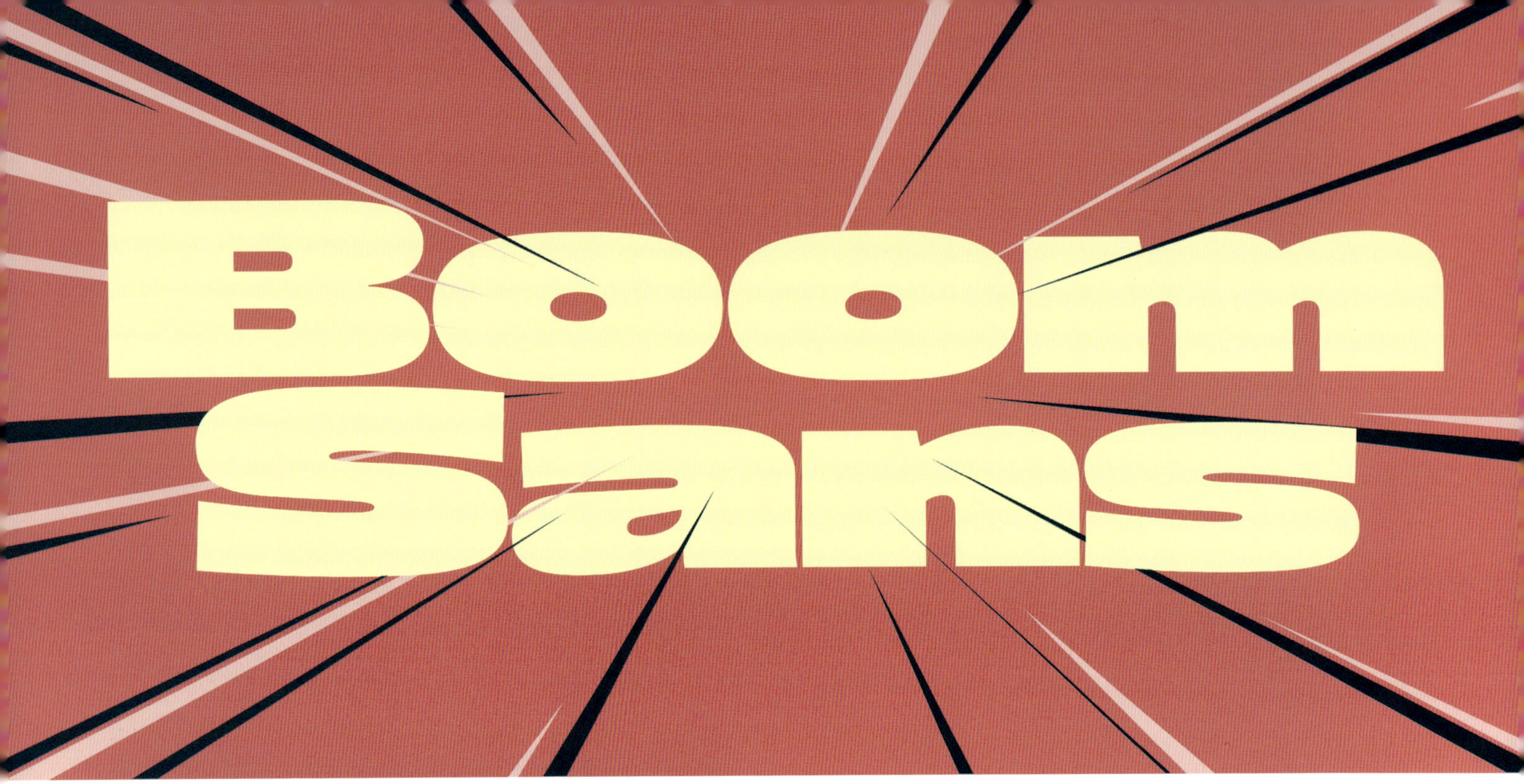

Boom Sans

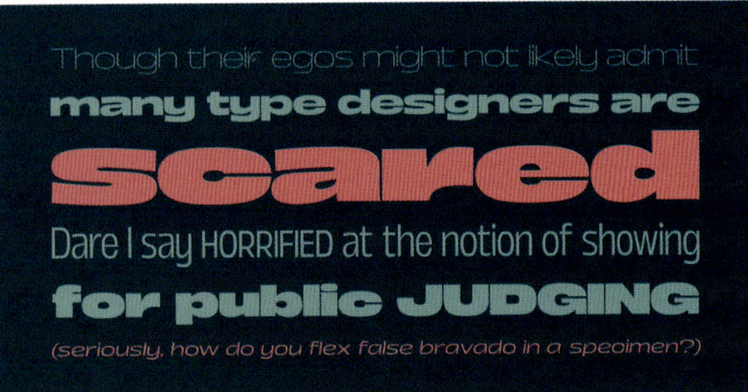

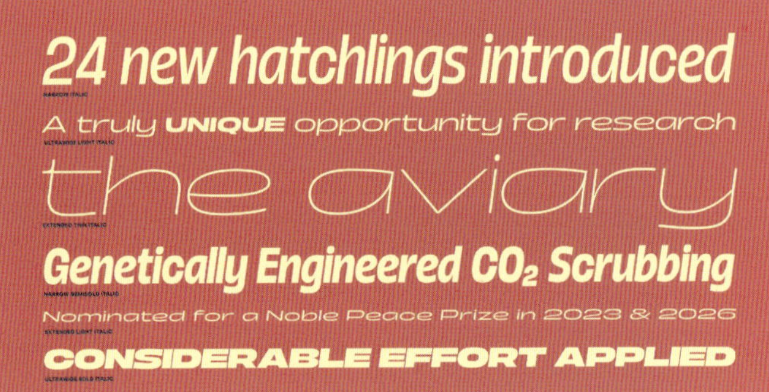

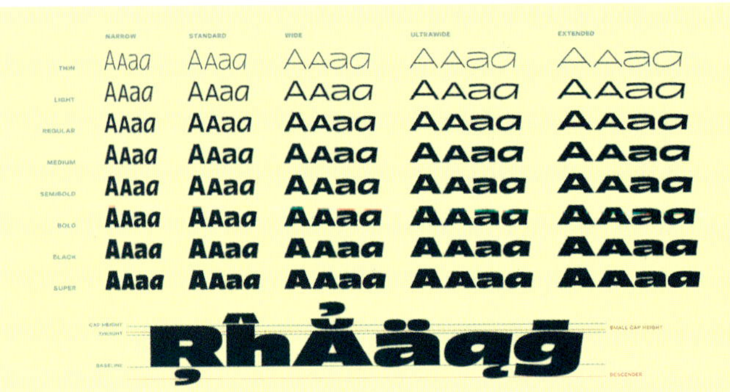

Boom Sans doesn't just make an impression—it makes a statement. With five widths, eight weights, and matching italics, it ensures your message stands out, with balanced curves, smooth transitions, and a stance that commands attention. Designed for impact and versatility, Boom Sans delivers a confident tone across everything from bold headlines to branding.

Boom Sans

positype.com

Designed by *Neil Summerour*
Published by *Positype*

Juno V is a type revival based on the chamfered block letters on the side of NASA's Saturn V launch vehicle. It's a single style display typeface perfect for space articles, large sci-fi uses, and big titles in more industrial contexts. It has a stylistic set that turns numerals into roman numerals—perfect for typesetting space mission names.

PARKER SOLAR PROBE
EVENT HORIZON
EPOCH OF REIONIZATION
ARTEMIS II
JAMES WEBB SPACE TELESCOPE
SUPERCLUSTER

IMAGE CREDITS: NASA & ESA

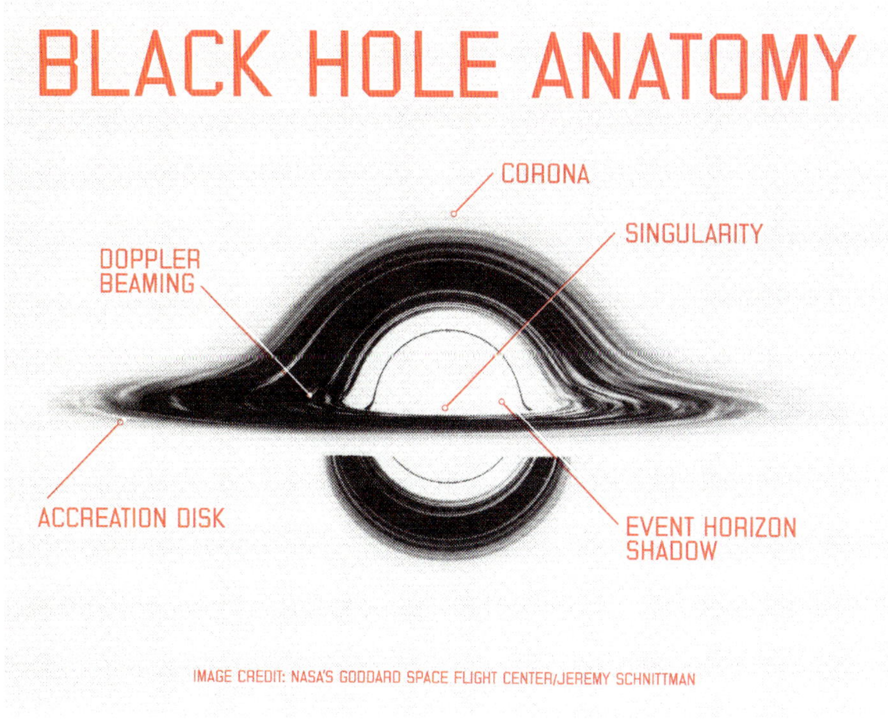

IMAGE CREDIT: NASA'S GODDARD SPACE FLIGHT CENTER/JEREMY SCHNITTMAN

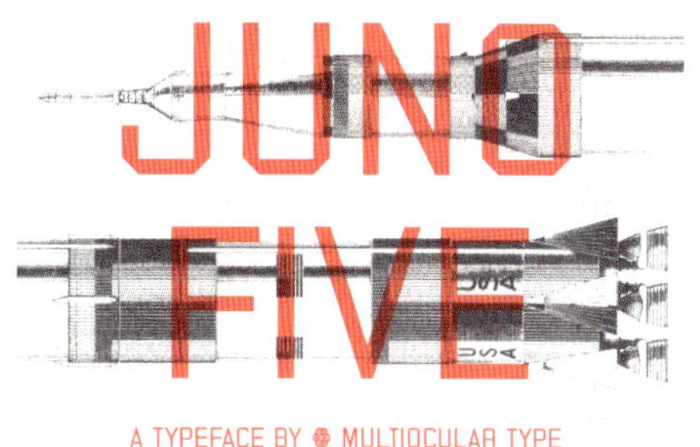

A TYPEFACE BY MULTIOCULAR TYPE

multioculartype.co

Juno V

Designed by *John Boran Jr.*
Published by *Multiocular Type*

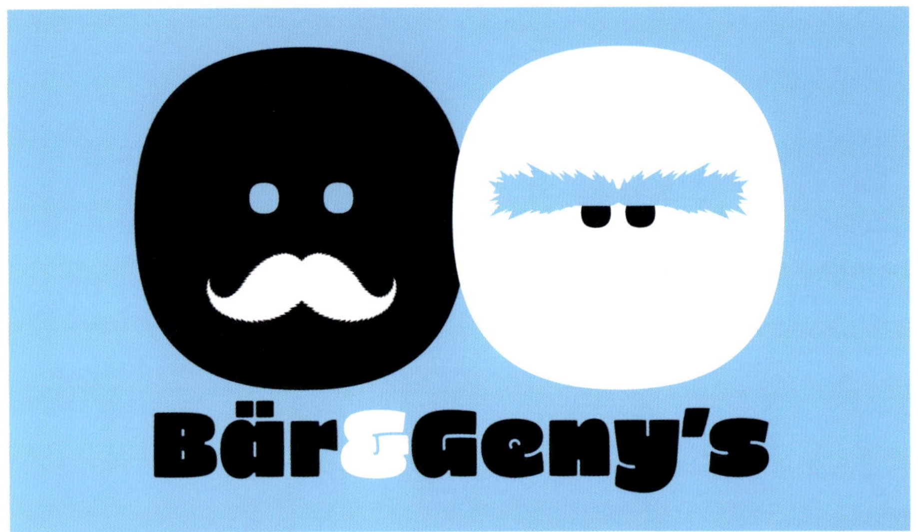

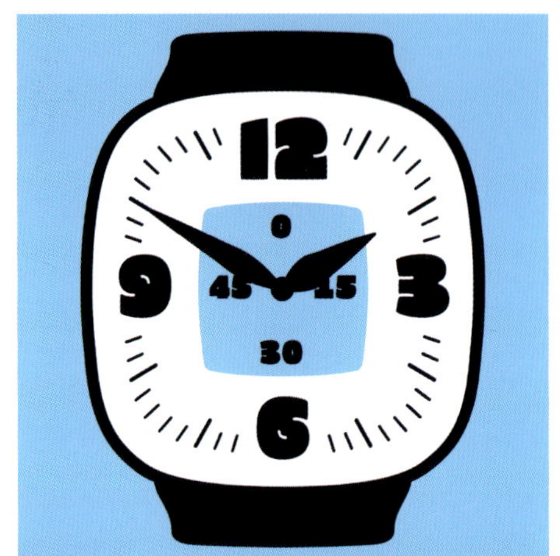

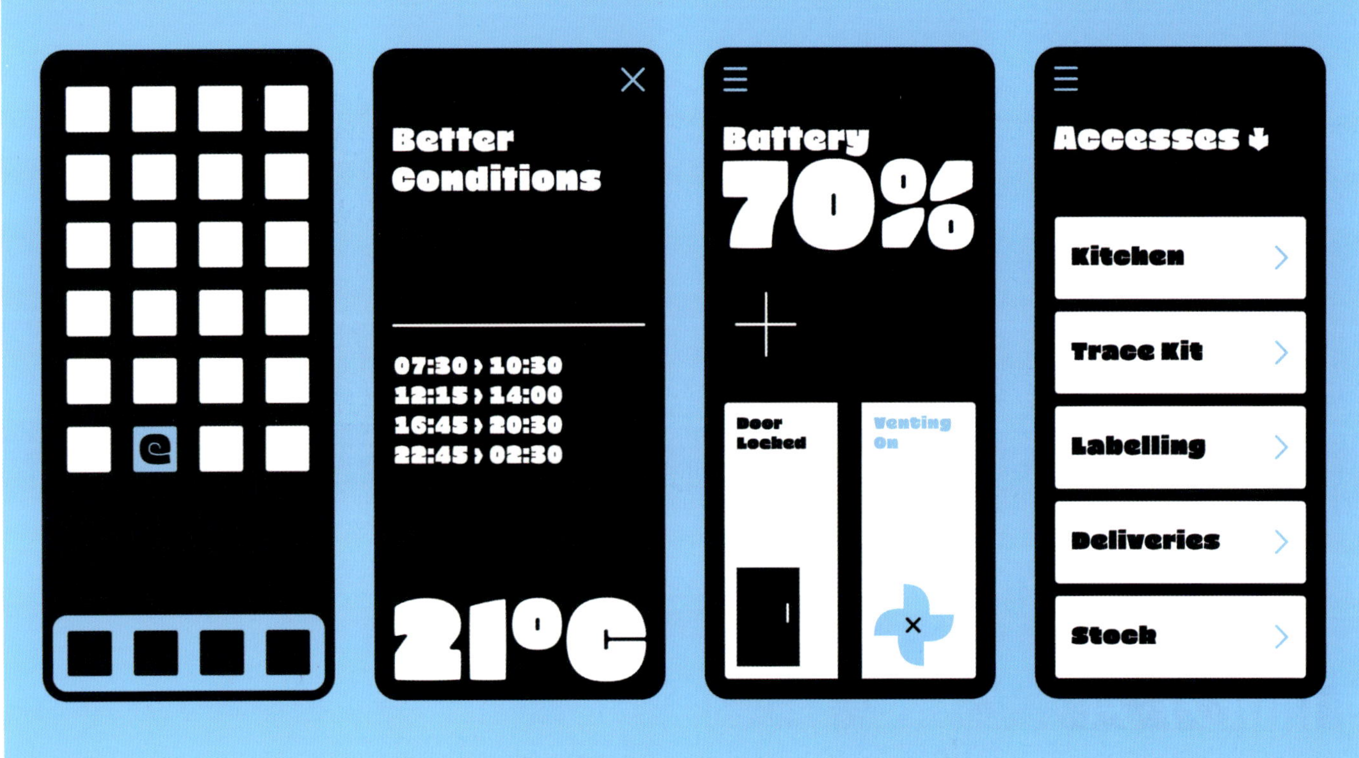

The Piggle family is a sweet and powerful display font. With its friendly roundness, it dresses text with warmth and strength. The shapes are generous and each glyph takes as much space as possible before we lose legibility—like a balloon right before the popping point.

Piggle

marmitedefontes.com

Designed by *Guillaume Berry*
Published by *Marmite Defontes*

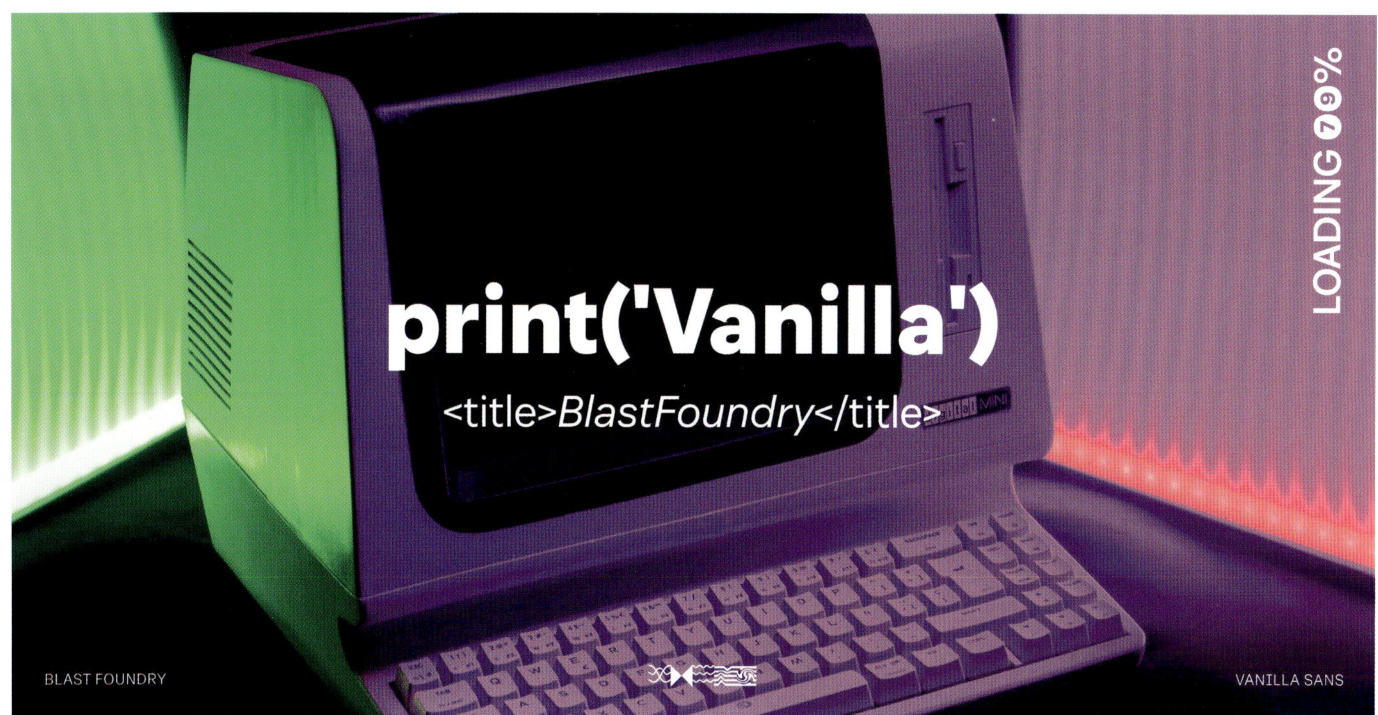

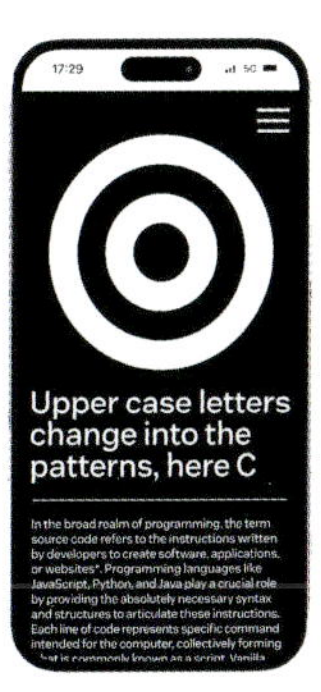

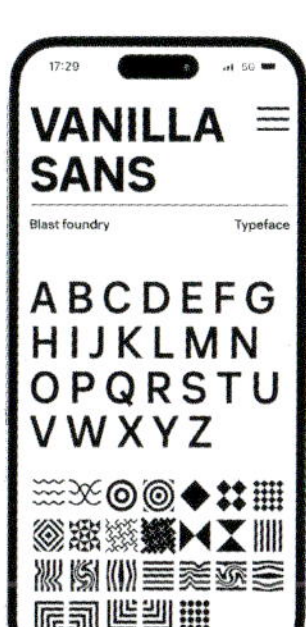

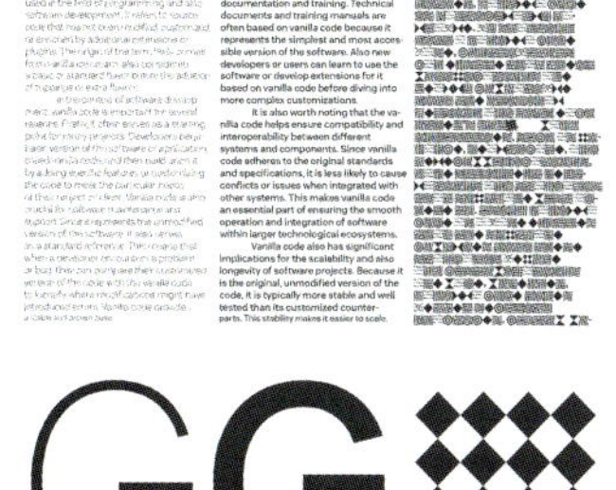

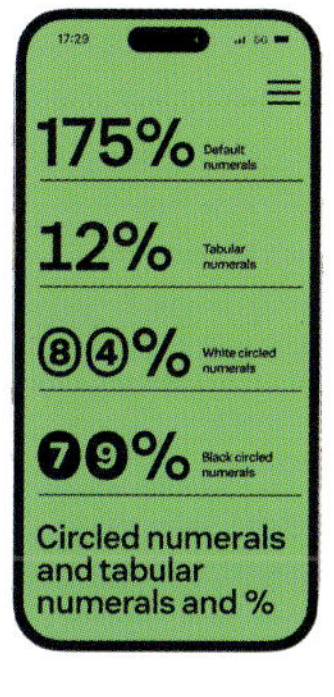

Function	Black	***Operator***	Black Italic
Variable	Bold	***Constant***	Bold Italic
Method	SemiBold	*Scopes*	SemiBold Italic
Execution	Medium	*Arrays*	Medium Italic
Debug	Regular	*Undefined*	Italic
Parameter	Light	*Boolean*	Light Italic
Objects	ExtraLight	*Integer*	ExtraLight Italic
Console	Thin	*Algorithm*	Thin Italic

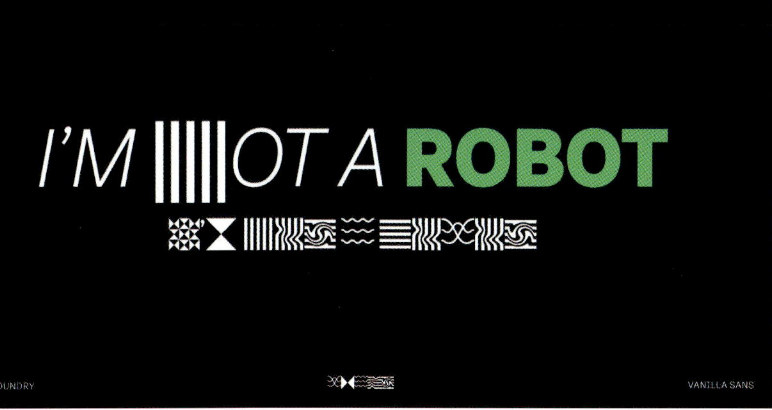

Vanilla Sans is the most normal sans Blast Foundry could draw—understated, timeless, and designed for maximum legibility and scalability. With low contrast and slightly open apertures, it offers a clean and adaptable look, making it perfect for a variety of design needs, from branding to editorial and logo design. Though it can comfortably blend into the background, Vanilla Sans gives you the flexibility to make a statement with its many alternates. What truly sets it apart are the twenty-six unique patterns for uppercase letters (A–Z via Stylistic Set 7), giving you a creative edge while maintaining a clean and modern aesthetic. It's a typeface that can be as simple or as unique as you need, ready to elevate any project with effortless sophistication.

blast-foundry.com

Vanilla Sans

Designed by *Barbara Bigosińska, Rafał Buchner*
Published by *Blast Foundry*

môj jazyk لغتي मेरी भाषा իմ լեզուն

ჩემი ენა என் மொழி моят

език 我的语言 η γλώσσα μου

ภาษาของฉัน ನನ್ನ ಭಾಷೆ ᐅᖃᐅᓯᖅ

મારી ભાષા මගේ භාෂාව ꯑꯩꯒꯤ ᱟᱹᱱ

എന്റെ ഭാഷ আমার ভাষা

Arabic

Armenian

Devanagari

Georgian

Japanese

Kannada

Odia

Ol Chiki

Bangla

Canadian Syllabics

Greek

Gujarati

Khmer

Korean

Sinhala

Tamil

Chinese

Cyrillic

Gurmukhi

Hebrew

Malayalam

Meetei

Telugu

Thai

Most twentieth-century sans serif typefaces are design compromises—they tend to be display typefaces that also have to work in text settings. Zed directly addresses this shortcoming, with radically different text and display versions developed using the latest research into which letterforms are found the easiest to read by the widest range of readers. Zed is designed to be inclusive; in particular, it identifies and addresses situations where people are excluded from using certain technologies. Typotheque tested the typefaces with help from visually impaired readers and worked with marginalized linguistic communities and native designers around the world. As a result, Zed is a highly accessible typeface for diverse populations.

Zed

typotheque.com

Designed by *various type designers (please see foundry website for full credits)*
Published by *Typotheque*

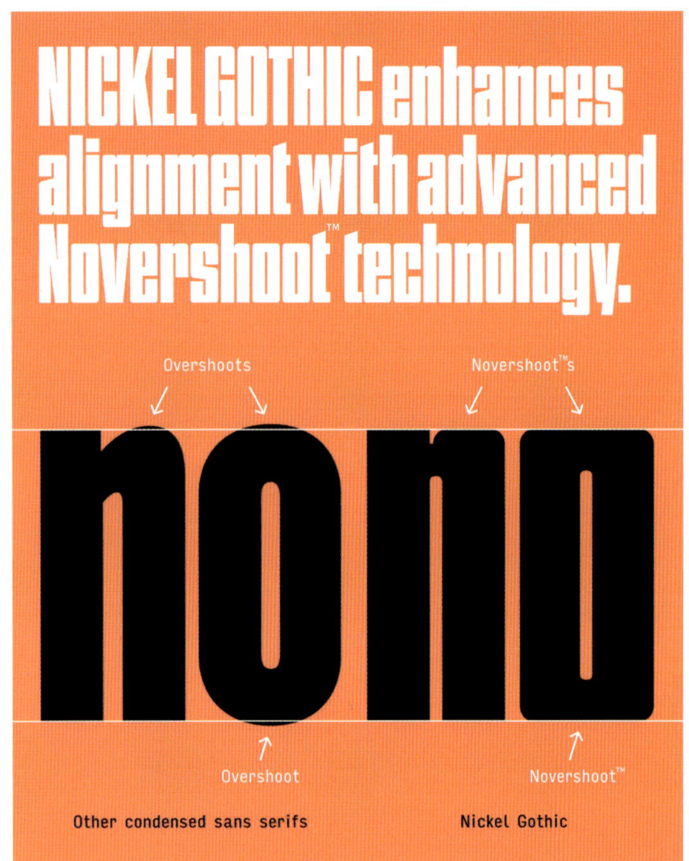

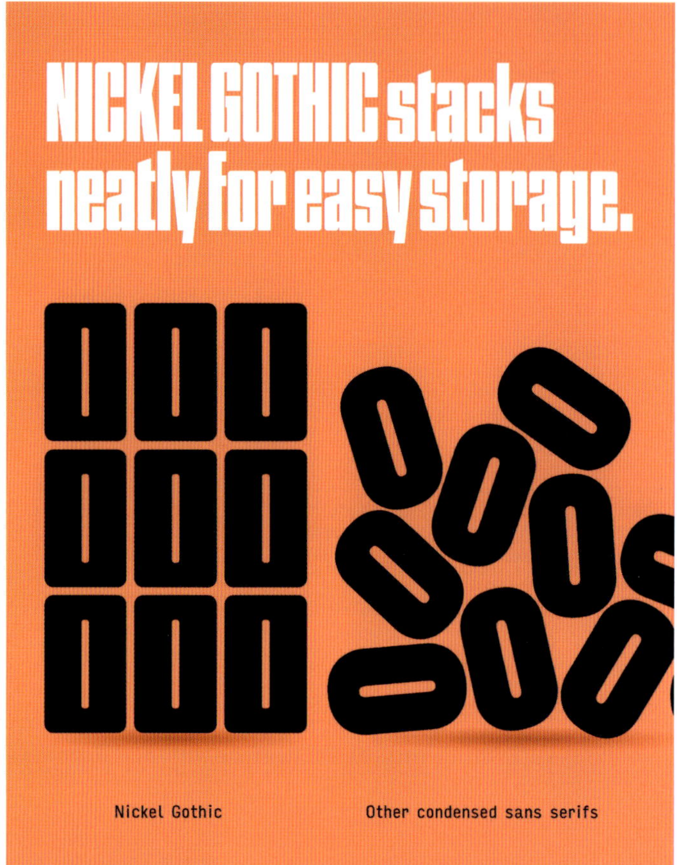

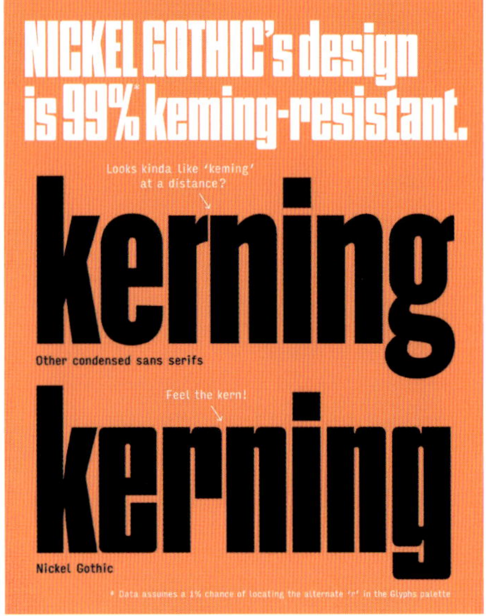

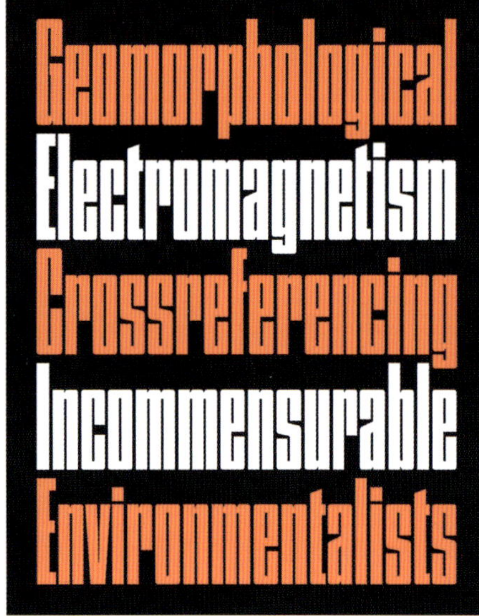

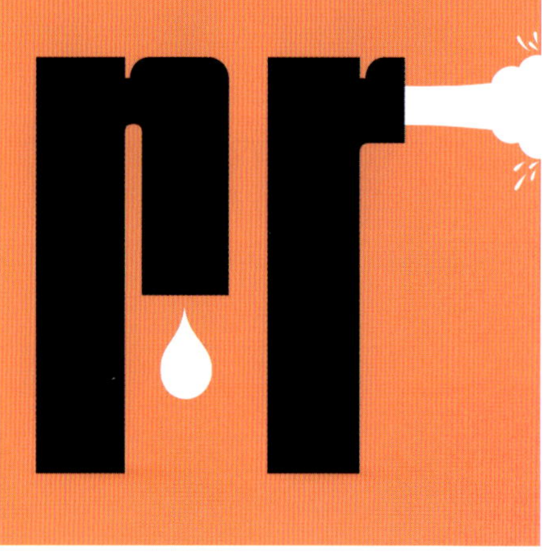

Nickel Gothic is a stocky, multiwidth grotesque based on lettering found on a 1918 Chinese banknote. It's constructed with durable straight sides, square shoulders, and hefty weights, ensuring that each word lands with a thud.

Nickel Gothic

djr.com

Designed by *David Jonathan Ross, Bea Korsh*
Published by *DJR Type*

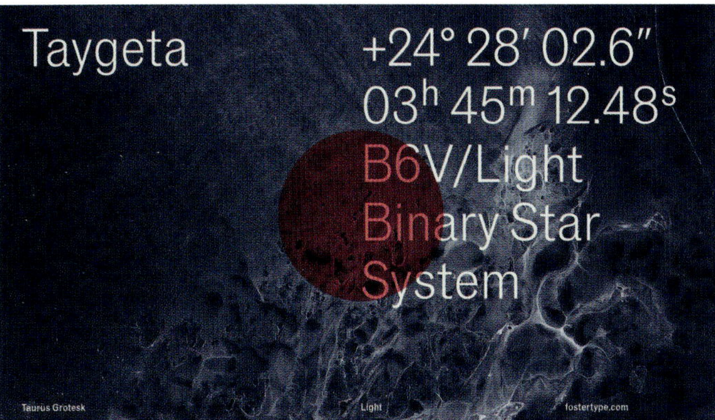

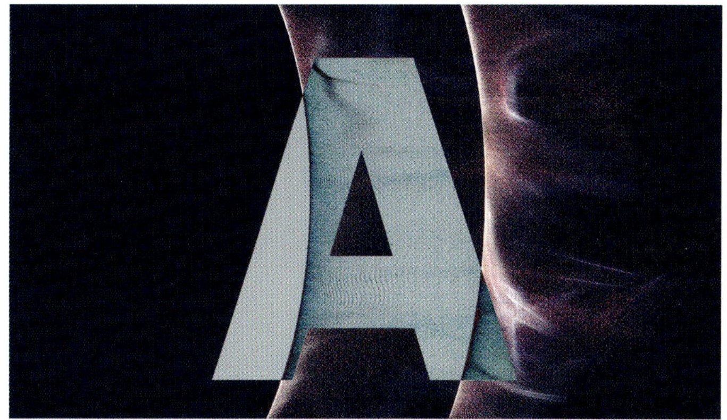

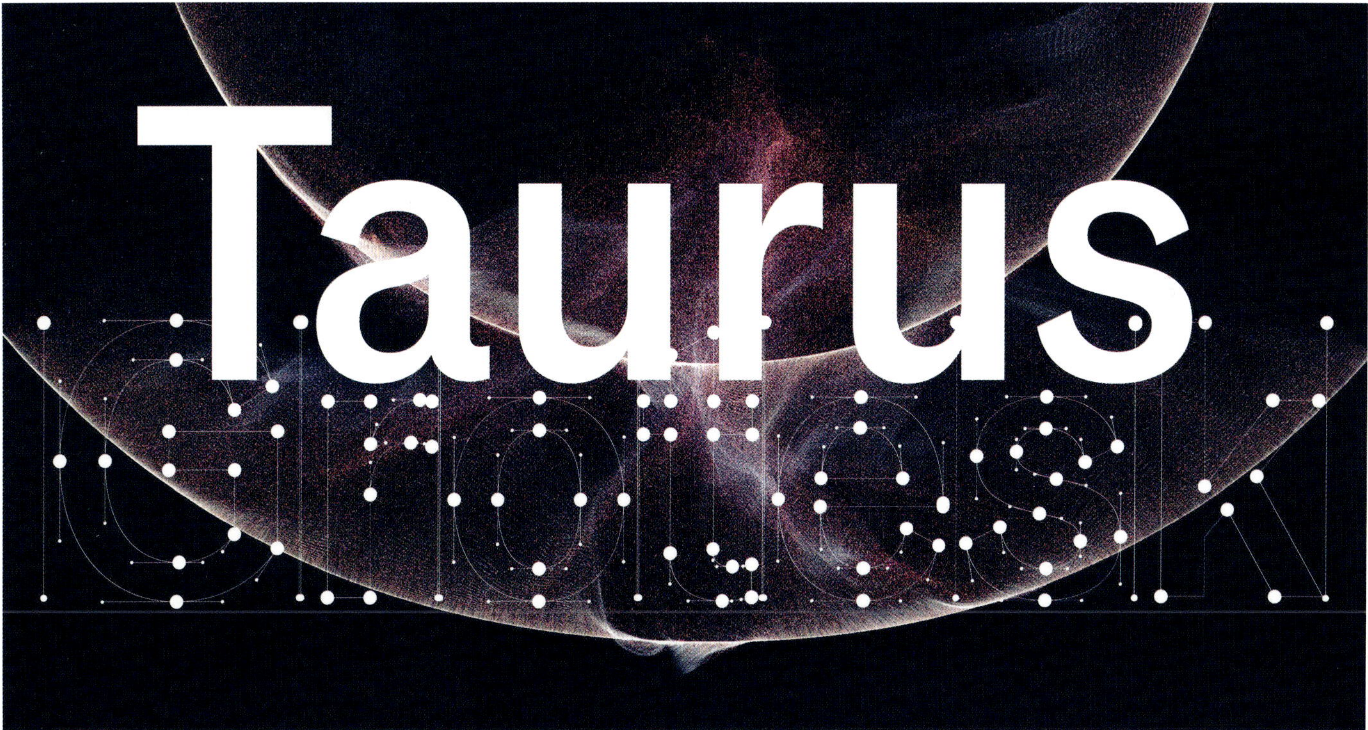

	Taurus Grotesk	Weight range	Roman
Th	Archaeoastronomical	EXTRATERRESTRIAL	
Li	Protons and neutrons	NUCLEOSYNTHESIS	
Re	Hertzsprung–Russell	ASTRAL RESEARCH	
Me	**Observable universe**	**FORMS OF MATTER**	
Bo	**Subatomic particles**	**PROTOPLANETARY**	
He	**Universal expansion**	**BEFORE TIME ZERO**	
Bl	**Quark-gluon plasma**	**MICROMETEOROID**	

Taurus Grotesk secures a position between the extremes of clinical rationality and impractical weirdness, which affords it character and utility. Its origins lie in the lively, early twentieth-century German Grotesk, Venus. Although it inherits features from Venus, it builds upon the legacy of the spirited design through interpretation rather than the mere duplication of outlines. The high-waisted capitals introduce a consistent flavor that is recognizable, and which charms across all seven weights. Flared terminals with a crisp bite provide texture and legibility to body copy and remain subtle in headlines. Heavily slanted italics offer a distinct emphasis in smaller sizes and enable energetic communications at larger sizes. The narrow horizontal proportions and discreet descenders allow economical typesetting, especially in digital environments.

fostertype.com

Taurus Grotesk

Designed by *Dave Foster*
Published by *Foster Type*

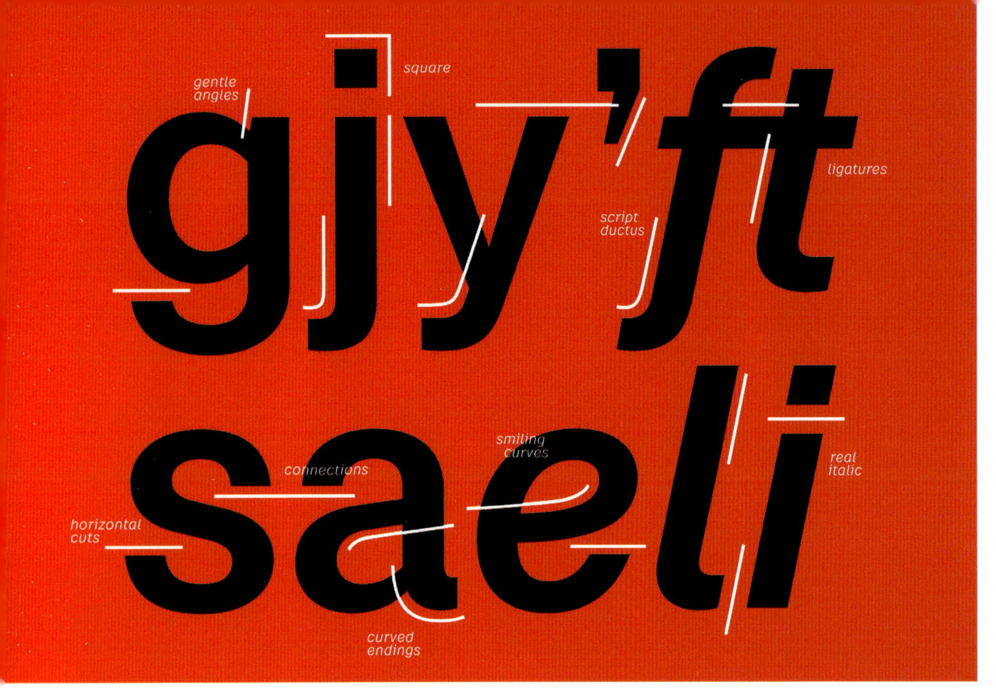

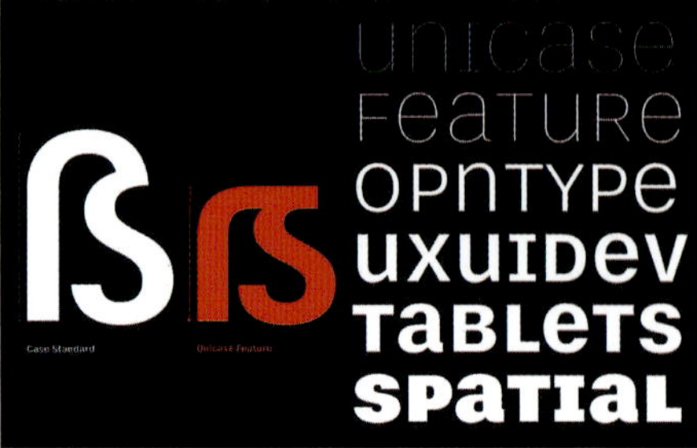

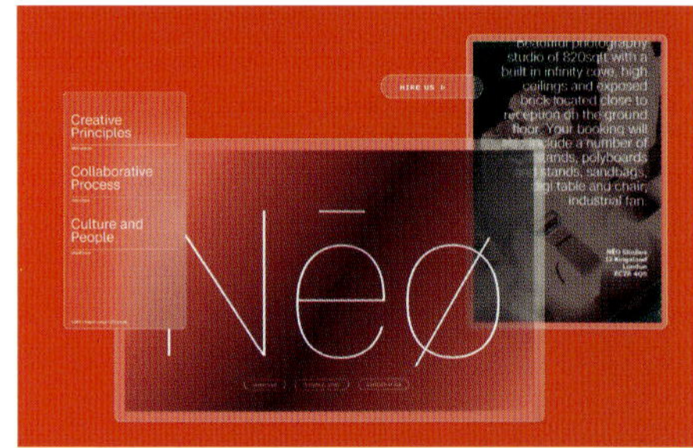

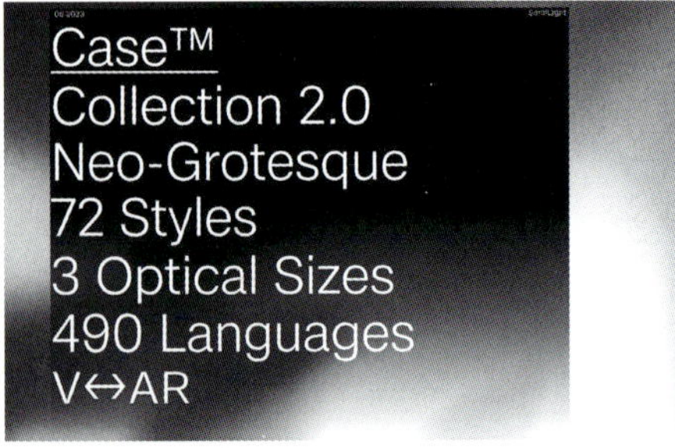

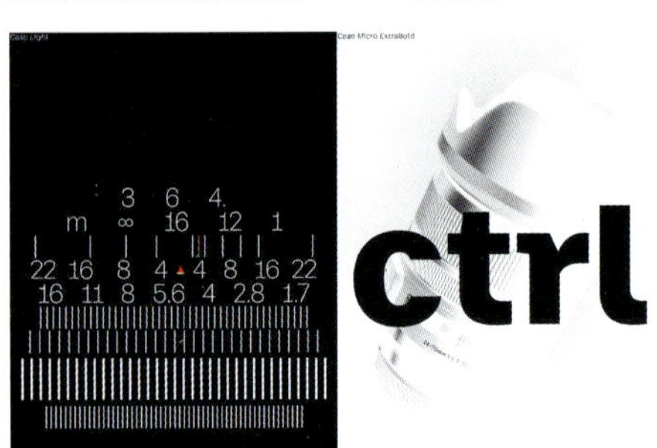

x-Height

Legibility
Leserlichkeit
Case

Legibility
Leserlichkeit
Case Text

Legibility
Leserlichkeit
Case Micro

Case, Case Text
Case Micro

A matter-of-fact Neo-Grotesque with surprising nuances—a refreshing alternative to the classics—revised from the ground up and with double the number of fonts and characters.

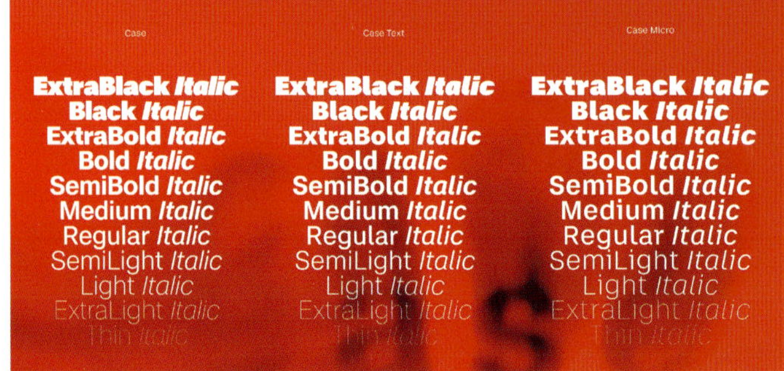

Case

fontwerk.com

Designed by *Erik Spiekermann, Anja Meiners, Ralph du Carrois*
Published by *Fontwerk*

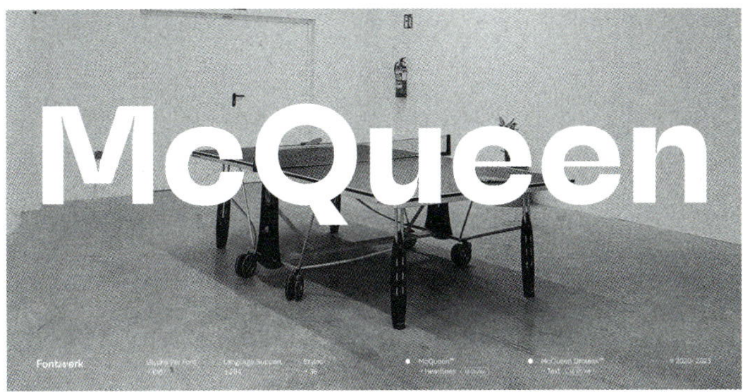

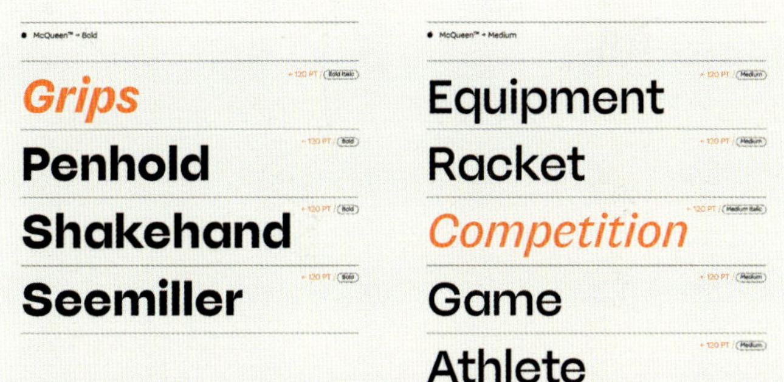

McQueen™ (18 Styles) +8 w/ Version 2.0

01 XLight 02 XLight Italic
03 Light 04 Light Italic
05 Regular 06 Italic
07 Medium 08 Medium Italic
09 SemiBold 10 SemiBold Italic
11 Bold 12 Bold Italic
13 XBold 14 XBold Italic
15 Black 16 Black Italic
17 XBlack 18 XBlack Italic

McQueen Grotesk™ (18 Styles) +6 w/ Version 2.0

01 XLight 02 XLight Italic
03 Light 04 Light Italic
05 Regular 06 Italic
07 Medium 08 Medium Italic
09 SemiBold 10 SemiBold Italic
11 Bold 12 Bold Italic
13 XBold 14 XBold Italic
15 Black 16 Black Italic
17 XBlack 18 XBlack Italic

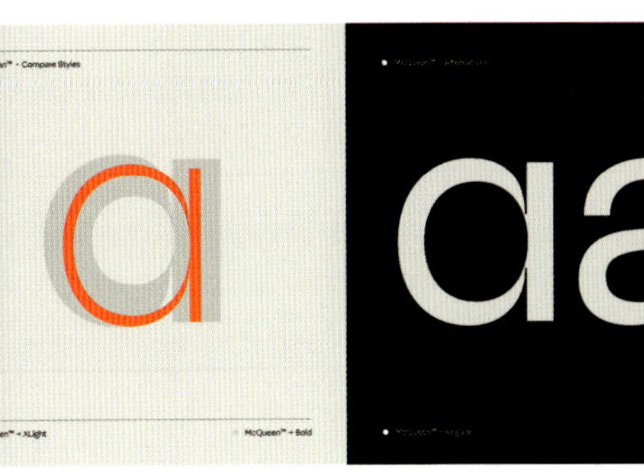

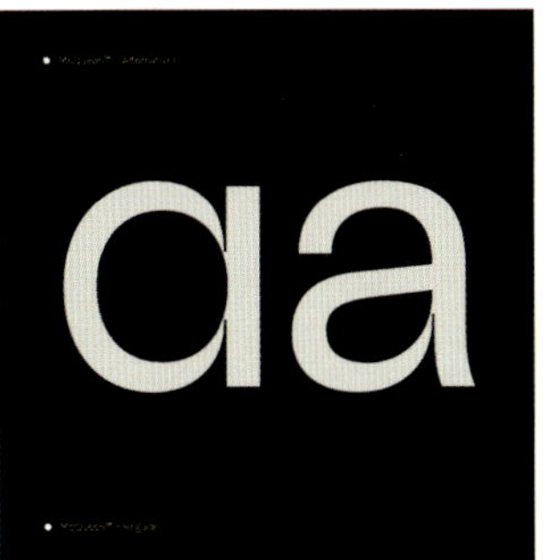

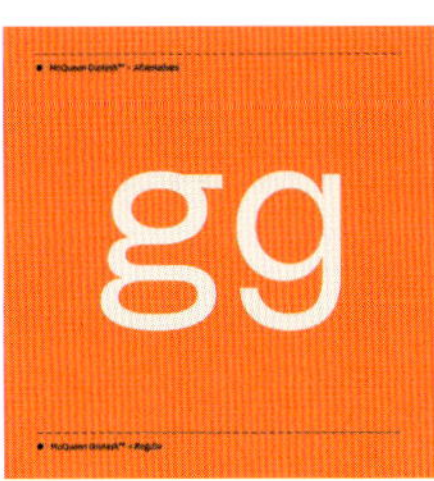

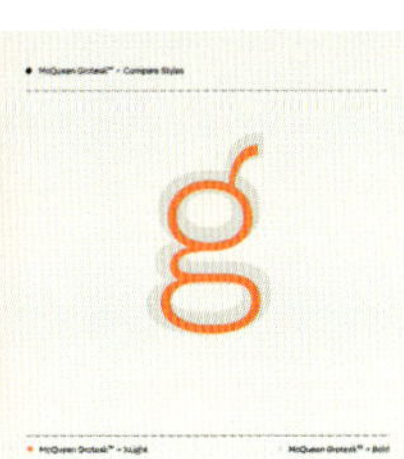

The McQueen collection is the popular anti-hero with two faces. One is the ambitious eccentric who loudly lives by his own rules; the other is the reserved individualist who questions conventions in a restrained but determined manner.

fontwerk.com

McQueen Collection

Designed by *Loris Olivier, Noheul Lee, Katja Schimmel, Olli Meier*
Published by *Fontwerk*

GRIT AND PATCHWORK: Designing Community Gothic

Elizabeth Goodspeed

In most typeface revivals, a type designer starts small. A single piece of reference, perhaps a name chiseled into stone or a line of type on an old train ticket, is studied in detail, and then extrapolated into a complete set of letters, weights and widths that follow the same consistent construction, free of contradiction. The operation is a precious one, where every curve of the original is carefully studied and meticulously ushered into the 21st Century—translated from ink on a page to a network of carefully placed points and handles on a set of vector drawings. These typical revivals could be thought of as a process of growth, wherein a unified set of styles expands outwards from a single origin point to create a group. A family.

But there are many ways that typefaces, and individuals, can come together to form a network. Whereas a family emerges out of a sense of continuity, other forms of grouping operate more like a chosen family: happenstance, sure, but formed with intention and decisiveness rather than a sheer sense of inevitability. If a family is a collection of individuals cut from the same cloth, a community is a quilt of different fabrics sewn together. Communities tend to emerge more organically out of the muck, a unification of components that share some traits and diverge on others. Personalities may clash, but a common purpose links them together to accomplish a goal.

The designers at Frere-Jones Type are no strangers to revival families. Tobias Frere-Jones' type catalog includes many, from Benton Modern, a revival of the Century type family, to Griffith Gothic, a take on Bell Gothic intended for display sizes. More recently, senior designer Nina Stössinger led a project to revive and translate a non-typographic source for Essex Market. The foundry has also traded in the revival-adjacent (that is to say, historically inspired, but with a little more reimagining required), as in the Trajan-influenced Empirica, designed by Frere-Jones and Stössinger. In the foundry's newest typeface, Community Gothic, all three of the foundry's designers—Tobias Frere-Jones, Fred Shallcrass, and Nina Stössinger—take on the revival via a completely new and all-together inverted approach. The result, a sans serif made up of 10 styles across five weights and two widths, is an homage to the mid-to-late 19th Century—an era when the idea of a type family was looser and not yet a standardized package to be sold. It also nods to the methods of typesetting of the period: a chucking together of unbranded "jobbing" typefaces by printers (the de facto designers of the time) to suit the spatial constraints or aesthetic needs of a given brief.

Superb Transatlantic Passenger Service
Printing from Movable Types Invented at Mentz
We Recommend This Beautiful Series of Gothic Condensed
The Metropolitan Express Question

Gothic Condensed Nos. 2, 5, 6, 8 by A. D. Farmer and Son, New York. (1897 specimen)

The forms of the glyphs within Community Gothic are unconventional as well, with subtly irregular curves that operate unexpectedly at different scales. They contain a peculiar irregularity that from afar, affords a warmth and patina, and from close up, shows a pleasantly notable wonkiness. Just like the everyday typographic detritus from the period they take inspiration from—the bus transfer card, the theater ticket, the city directory—the forms of Community Gothic are deeply tactile, but not via a fetishization of the analog, like a fake rubber stamp display font. Rather, they tap into the joyful, wabi-sabi imperfectness of human taste, and the zig-zagging history of letterforms themselves.

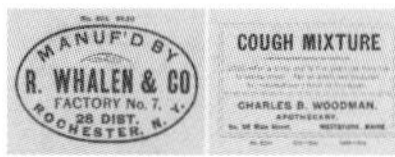

Left: Catalogue and Specimen Book of Rubber Hand Stamps, F. W. Maxson, Rochester circa 1886; Right: Catalogue, Randolph Paper Box Co, Richmond, circa 1900

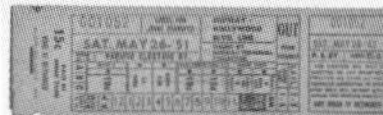

Fare transfer, Pacific Electric Railway, Los Angeles 1951

Like the myriad of metal type in a printer's shop, each weight and width of the Community Gothic family takes its inspiration from a different piece of typographic history. Some weights are revivals in the truest sense of the word, like the Bold, a classic and confident style with a pleasantly high-waisted lowercase 'g' and chunky, serpentine 'S', which references a German modification of an English face from the late 1900s and is adjusted modestly, only in respect to the needs of moving from paper to screen. Other styles are less rigid, more intentional departures from historic reference that use found type less as a map, and more as a compass—a jumping off point for exploration. The Regular weight is an example of this kind of semi-revival: while it originates with a single sample of "Breite Etienne", a German copy of a popular American design, Frere-Jones and Shallcrass have pruned the serifs and diminished the contrast between upper and lowercase weights (a higher contrast between the two being indicative of the source material's original time period) to create a jaunty contemporary style that stands apart from its source.

ABCDEFGHIJK
abcdefghijklmnc
ABCDEFGHIJKL
abcdefghijklmnopc

Above: Breite Etienne, Schelter & Giesecke, Leipzig (Specimen circa 1937) Below: Community Gothic Regular

More fascinating still are the styles that can't be pinned down to a specific reference at all, but rather, use hypothetical models of type history to create something akin to a typographic fan fiction; improvisational method acting in the manner of a time period without an actual script to follow. The Black, which in Frere-Jones' words is "from nowhere," is one of these speculations, the result of an imagined investigation into what a Black weight from this period might look like if drawn from the mind's eye—pulled from an extended slab serif, pruned, scaled and re-weighted, so that all that persists is that blunt crudeness. The resulting style has a charming roundness to it, with nearly enclosed counters punctuated by moments of squatness as in the arm of the lowercase 'r'.

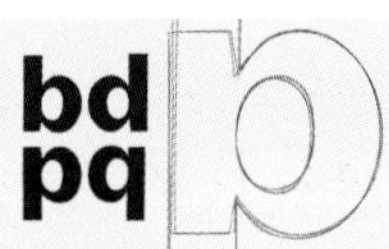

Above: unidentified typeface, shown in A Cheap Book of Alphabets Designed for the Use of Painters, Sign Writers, Draughtsmen, &c, pub. Jesse Haney ca1874 Below: Community Gothic Black

This unusual, mixed approach to reference inherently leads to a mixed model of construction as well. Frere-Jones notes that "in conventional families, features and themes are planned and negotiated, so they can be sustained across all, or most, styles. In Community Gothic, the view is entirely local." In other words, it doesn't matter if a construction from the Light is implausible in the Black, as long as they can play nicely together. Each adheres to its own framework. In this way, Community Gothic operates less like a conventional family, and more like a very specific kind of community: an orchestra. The different widths and weights of the typeface are like musicians, each with their own voice, clef, tonal range, and equipment, but unified as one body working in time for a common purpose. Notably, a similar dogleg relationship occurs within a family most readers are likely quite familiar with: Times. The roman is very much an old style, while the bold uses a Victorian modern frame for its lowercase.

aaaaa
aaaaa

Lowercase 'a' across Normal and Condensed styles of Community Gothic

Of course, no matter how different their individual qualia may be, musicians in an orchestra still have to be in tune with one another—and the same goes for type. In order to maintain some semblance of continuity between letterforms within a style as well as between styles themselves, the Frere-Jones team had to develop a standard metric and value system to assess how much each glyph and weight could deviate from the norm. "We needed to set an internal compass in a way that allowed for something lively, but that still assembled in a reliable way," Frere-Jones says. As such, individual styles were tweaked on a high level, with global adjustments to width, weight, proportion, and spacing made to help establish a clearer linear relationship from one face and glyph to the next, as well as a smooth overall cadence of use. The spectrum of traits the team devised to guide these adjustments ran from strict to lenient, with traits on the strict end being closer to the team's typical approach—relatively consistent across all letterforms and styles—and traits on the lenient end varying dramatically across the family. Or, going by another internal description, the endpoints were "by the ruler" and "from the hip." The resulting gamut places more value on design traits that allow for high functionality (like spacing) while rejecting too much precision in more aesthetically driven traits (like symmetry or alignment. In practice, this means that the lowercase 'a's of the Medium and the Bold weights share almost no similarities in terms of actual letter construction—the former has a bowl which connects to the stem in a sloping curve, while the latter connects at a blunt, nearly 90° angle. But both, when set in a full adjacent paragraph and viewed from afar, have a similar cadence and equal amount of greyness that renders them compatible and balanced.

bd
pq

Lenient repetition: Community Gothic Bold, lowercase b/p, and rotated d/q

This kind of system, where each style and each letter is considered with a particular independence, required the Frere-Jones team to develop a unique approach to glyph drawing, one more akin to the work of a punchcutter than a contemporary digital typeface designer. In all modern typefaces, the final format of a glyph is a vector drawing; an infinitely scalable form made from a series of points and lines that span the space between. Typically, these glyphs are constructed to contain as few points as possible, with the final glyph defined by points and handles that direct the interstitial curves like arrows. Community Gothic circumvented this conventional, economic construction in favor of something more instinctual—a manual process that feels like sculpting, where curves are constructed via a range of facets chipped out of a larger form. With this alternate drawing method, instead of moving one control point, whose influence is then evenly distributed across the shape, if anything moves, it's because it's been directly adjusted; weight can be shaved off or added locally in any area of the glyph without the overall shape being affected. "This requires you to work simultaneously fast and slow, with individual points shuffled quickly into approximate locations where their effect on the shapes accumulates slowly", says Shallcrass. Once the final faceted form is deemed complete, these contours are converted back into the typical bezier point-and-handle construction for use (a process the team referred to as resplining), though the irregularity of the curves is maintained. In addition to allowing for a much finer tuning of letterforms, this method also freed the designers from the tyranny of symmetry—the natural outcome of evenly spaced beziers—creating instead a constant tension between a certain type of exactness and a willful asymmetry. While this method was invented by the team to suit the needs of Community Gothic, Frere-Jones later discovered that a similar technique of chiseled vectors is used by the TypeMedia program at the Royal Academy of Art (KABK) in The Hague as a quick way to rough out shapes early in the type development process—though not necessarily with the same goals, as the wonkiness afforded by the approach there typically isn't preserved as closely in the transition to smooth curves.

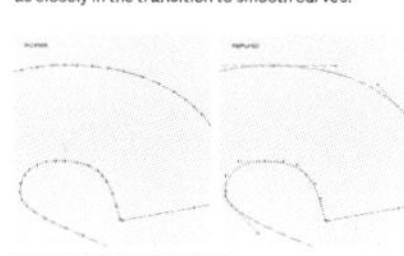

Stages of drawing and resplining

While this method of constructing letters is helpful for baking in idiosyncrasy, it unsurprisingly didn't allow for the team to use many typical time-saving techniques that require more glyph-to-glyph consistency, like interpolation (a method that creates intermediary weights between two extremes by matching the points and proportionally repositioning them). Instead, the team developed a range of new digital tools to make the process easier on themselves. Stössinger in particular led the charge, establishing a range of inventive shortcuts that supported the unique needs of Community Gothic.

One tool, the "Omeletterer" (a name inspired by the team's frequent deli visits), smashes and scrambles the points of a contour in a controlled manner, imbuing the letters with a warm randomness difficult to manually invent. Another tool, the "Point Broom," operated like a liquify brush, and allowed the designers to nudge points with more immediacy and intuition. In order to keep kerning, arguably the longest and most tedious part even of the normal type design process, from multiplying wildly across all of these more independent styles, Stössinger also developed tools to assist in kerning that helped synchronize the spacing and positioning of outlines in intermediate weights and propagate kerning across the designspace, thereby reducing the need for manual adjustments to a manageable level.

With these tools, the Frere-Jones team takes a new approach to how digital intervention can, and should, support type design. Their unconventional process can be seen as a meditation on the patina that the analog provides, and a reimagining of how digital tools can be used without resulting in sterility. What benefit is there to dissonance or willful inefficiency in a medium that, in its contemporary form, is often built on gratuitous precision? Instead of using digital tools to create exactitude, as in most revivals, which then need the manual addition of warmth, Community Gothic's digitally native methodologies imbue warmth throughout development, resulting in a family that privileges conceptual fidelity over surface fidelity.

Community Gothic's origins can be traced to the mid-90s, with an informal personal exploration by Frere-Jones into a typeface made from dissonant sources. Shortly after, in 2002, as part of a collaboration with Nike, Frere-Jones pitched their Jordan brand the concept of a warm, historically-inspired typeface made up of individual designs that worked less like a family, and more like a team—each retaining its own origin but uniting to play as one body. While the faces that were created and briefly used for the Jordan campaign—a Bold Italic and a Wide Regular—ultimately didn't make it into the final set of styles for Community Gothic, they served as a proof of concept for Frere-Jones; they reinforced the value of investigating a collection of independent designs that could work together despite visible difference, and that individually incorporated as much of the feeling and atmosphere of analog reality as possible.

Plowshares
SHELBURNE TRAIL
Elements
Deltoid Muscle

Jordan Gothic No. 1 and No. 2, 2002

For the next decade, Frere-Jones undertook a slow process of experimentation, in which he would make one-off translations of various historic sans serifs, strictly localized to single styles, and guided solely by what looked interesting to him at the time. Throughout this period, he was also trying new variations of the drawing technique that would eventually lead to Community Gothic's peculiar way of using the faceted approach to preserve grit.

ABCDEFGHIJKLMNOP RSTU W
abcdefghijklmnoprstuvw y 1234
ABCDEFGHIJKLMNOPQRSTUVWX
abcdefghi klmnop rstuvwxyz fi
ABCDEFGHIJKLMNOPQRSTUVW
abcdefghi klmnopqrstuvw y fifl
ABCDEFGHIJKLMNOPRSTUV Y

Gothic Condensed No. 241, Bruce Type Foundry, New York. Detail of concordance from multiple specimens, made by Tobias Frere-Jones and Julia Ma, 2018.

In the later part of the 2010s, this vast collection of sketches was moved into what Frere-Jones Type refers to as the "auditioning" phase, where they were stripped of their names and identified only by the date on which they were started. This intentional obscuring of origin eliminated attachments or bias and allowed each style's traits to be assessed neutrally, without its history getting in the way. A blind audition. It also allowed the rest of the team, who joined the project in 2019, to more organically assess which styles would make it into the final commercial set, and where they would be placed in the grid matrix of weight and width. Once candidates had been selected, the strict-lenient spectrum was applied between styles as well, with the team tweaking weights and widths until a clear linear progression emerged. Explaining the process, Frere-Jones says that he "imagined the width and weight names as a kind of interface to the family, and as such they needed to be intuitive—contemporary, really." What may have been labeled as "bold" within a set of styles in its original context might actually feel "regular" when seen next to a different set of peers (an issue anyone who has bought multiple pants in a size "medium" from different brands will likely find familiar). This auditioning phase, like all parts of the development of Community Gothic, required careful compromise: Too much streamlining to fit the traditional, expected metrics of a family would counteract the deliberate work already done to preserve individual idiosyncrasies, while too little would make the family difficult to use. Candidates often swapped places, and tweaks were occasionally reversed in order to ensure that adjacent weights or widths still squabbled, at least a bit. The resulting span of styles is instinctively arranged, with the traits across neighbors feeling both expected and surprising.

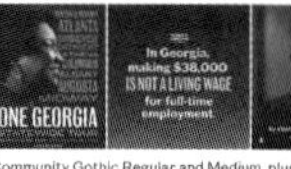

Community Gothic Regular and Medium, plus yet-unreleased Extra Condensed and Wide styles, in use by the Stacey Abrams campaign for Georgia's 2022 gubernatorial election (Wide Eye Creative, consultants)

So far Community Gothic has been soft-launched in one notable location: Stacey Abrams' campaign for Governor. Used mostly for headlines, alongside a logo set in Vocal Type's Marsha (another typeface rich in historic roots), it perfectly embodies the kind of grass-roots support of Abrams' mission; defined by a diverse body of supporters and many different reasons for support. Since acquiring a trial of the typeface from the Frere-Jones team myself, I've used it for a project with overlapping ideals—a new community platform that helps empower restaurant gig workers to find better jobs for better pay. Actually sitting down and typesetting text in Community Gothic inspires many echoes of its irregular and asymmetrical creation. I find myself jumping between weights organically, sometimes forgetting which style I'm using in real time. I'm less precious about consistency, choosing different styles for headlines and footers based on need. And, besides the obvious wow factor of being able to sell a client on a typeface with such a perfectly apt name for the project, I'll admit I found myself similarly inspired by lofty feelings of community and a connection to the past whenever I work with it.

There's an imperfect negotiation at every level of Community Gothic—between each style, between the letters within each style, and between the curves themselves. To create a typeface with this level of anti-modernist imperfection requires an almost philosophical mindset; a continued commitment to making a choice that often goes against years of training and reflex. Considering the multi-year development of the family, Frere-Jones remarks on how unexpectedly emotional the type design process became: "It didn't matter how many times I had spelled out the reasons to leave in the grit. I could still feel the impulse to find the One Right Answer, and had to then consciously restage the realization that sometimes there is no One Right Answer."

In design, as in life, it can feel as though perfection is only accomplished via the sanding away of rough edges. We're encouraged to remove the things in our work, or about ourselves, that feel messy or unresolved, leaving only the clean, tidy, and supposedly beautiful bits behind. Reduction as a means of revelation. But, in the course of making Community Gothic, Frere-Jones ultimately reflects that he's come to learn that this sort of editing isn't a given. "Sometimes the complexity, what we rush to scrape away like mud, is the real character."

a knot of toads

A Train of Camels

The story of Community Gothic begins with the sans serif "jobbing" typefaces of the nineteenth century. These typefaces were clear and durable, while often being coarse and even awkward. In many cases they were developed in isolation, without any deliberate relationship to each other. Community Gothic revives not only the gritty forms of this genre but also the patchwork sets assembled by typefounders and printers alike. Each style was conceived and drawn independently but integrated in a conventional progression of weights and widths for intuitive use. Designers Tobias Frere-Jones, Fred Shallcrass and Nina Stössinger referred to historical sources from American and European foundries in developing each style. With design tools they made specifically for this family, the designers pursued irregularity with asymmetric curves and buckled lines. Community Gothic consciously resists the usual smoothness of digital type, and the result is a powerful and emphatically human quality.

Community Gothic

frerejones.com

Designed by *Tobias Frere-Jones, Fred Shallcrass, Nina Stössinger, Julia Ma*
Published by *Frere-Jones Type*

SUPERM

SUPERMASSIVE III, 110PT

MAMMOTH

TELESCOPE DETECTS EARLIEST KNOWN BLACK HOLE MERGER, JUST 740 MILLION YEARS AFTER THE BIG BANG

SUPERMASSIVE III, 30PT

SUPERMASSIVE II, 110PT

COLOSSAL

ASTRONOMERS SPOT A MASSIVE 'SLEEPING GIANT' BLACK HOLE LESS THAN 2,000 LIGHT-YEARS FROM EARTH

SUPERMASSIVE II, 30PT

SUPERMASSIVE I, 110PT

GINORMOUS

CHURNING SPACETIME AND DESTROYED STARS HELP REVEAL HOW FAST SUPERMASSIVE BLACK HOLES SPIN

SUPERMASSIVE I, 30PT

ASSIVE

Hefty and idiosyncratic, Supermassive squeezes maximal weight and density out of the available space without sacrificing subtlety or soul. Responding to themes from 1960s handlettering styles, it presents long superelliptical curves and a teetering balance of vertical and horizontal weights. Minimal negative spaces push mass to a precarious extreme. In three cap-only styles drawn for headline sizes—and larger!—Supermassive is not quite stable, but always forceful.

---

frerejones.com

Supermassive

Designed by *Tobias Frere-Jones, Rosie Mai, Fred Shallcrass, Nina Stössinger*
Published by *Frere-Jones Type*

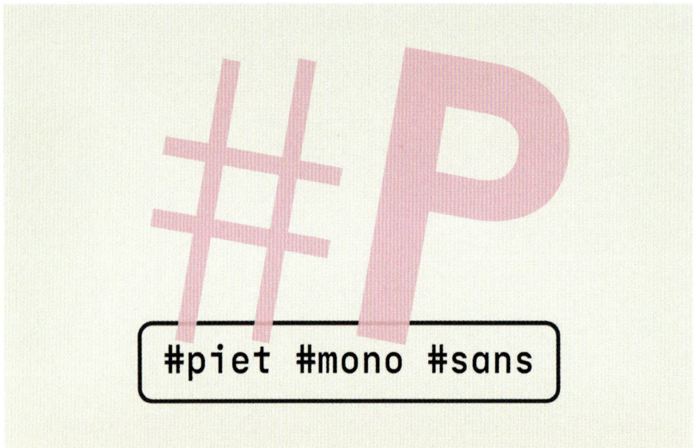

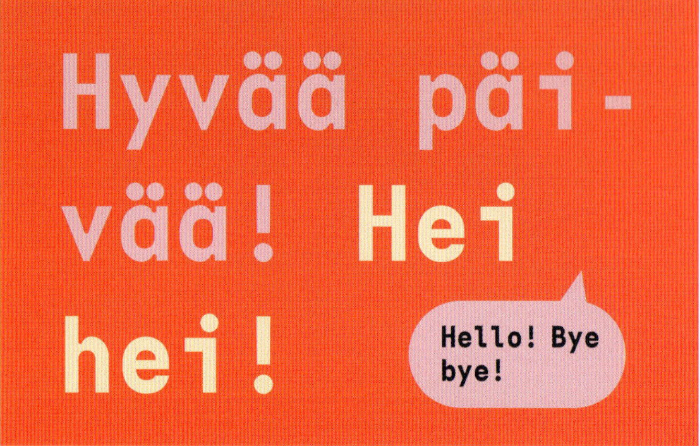

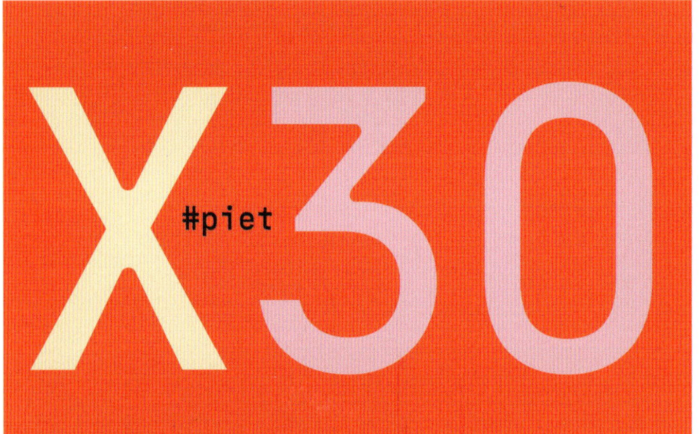

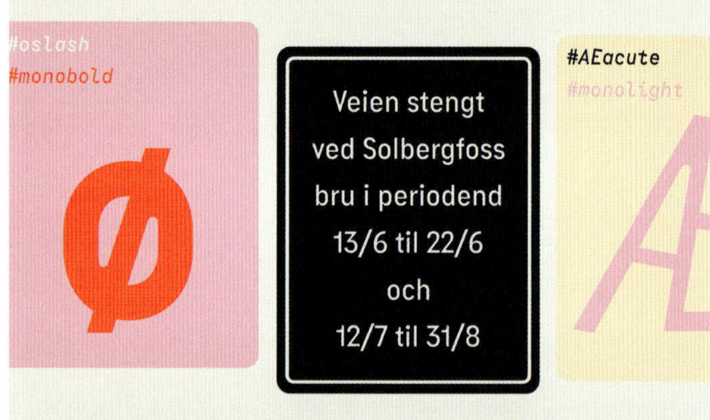

MONO **Blind vej**

A.013 En blind ve
der ikke er flere fr
Der kan dog sagtens
disse er så lukket
biltrafik. Stier kan
men mulighed for vi
er der ikke.

B.014 Ordet sti er
stige, som oprindel
gå". En sti er alts

SANS **Blind vej**

A.013 En blind vej, er en
der ikke er flere frakørsels
der. Der kan dog sagtens
veje, men disse er så lukk
nemgående biltrafik. Stier
til vejen, men mulighed fo
kørsel med bil er der ikke.

B.014 Ordet sti er beslæ
stige, som oprindeligt bar
gå". En sti er altså et sted,

↗ 103 GÄVLE
↑ 1 FORSBACKA
→ 80 BOLLNÄS

Inspired by Finnish licence plates, Piet is a playful pair of constructed typefaces defined by strange numbers and deep, rounded ink traps. Consisting of Mono and Sans, Piet is bureaucratic at first sight, but with a closer look you'll find the utilitarian hooked up to the weird, the stiff wired to the wonky, and the italics connected to the battery. Not pretty, nor refined, Piet is unmistakable. Its shapes are practical and almost unbreakable. With chunky forms and more and less than the expected optical corrections, it is functional, visually unbalanced, and narrow. With no cruise control on its ever-present idiosyncrasy, Piet turns its "limitations" into fuel.

Piet

typemates.com

Designed by *Nils Thomsen*
Published by Published by *TypeMates*

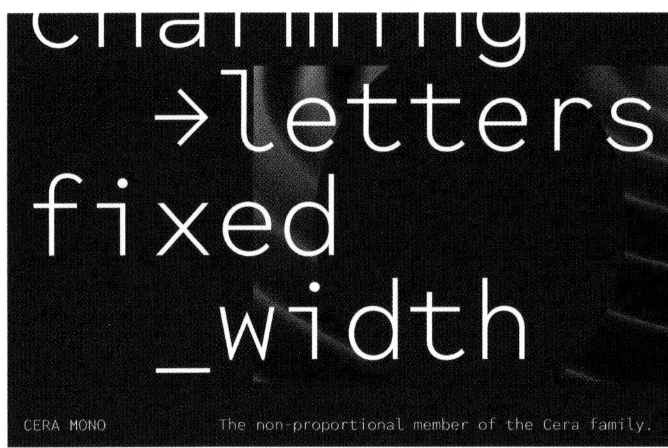

Monospace fonts combine practicality with aesthetics, offering visual consistency and versatility across a range of design and communication applications. Whether in technical documentation, coding environments, design projects, their advantages make them essential in typography.

2024

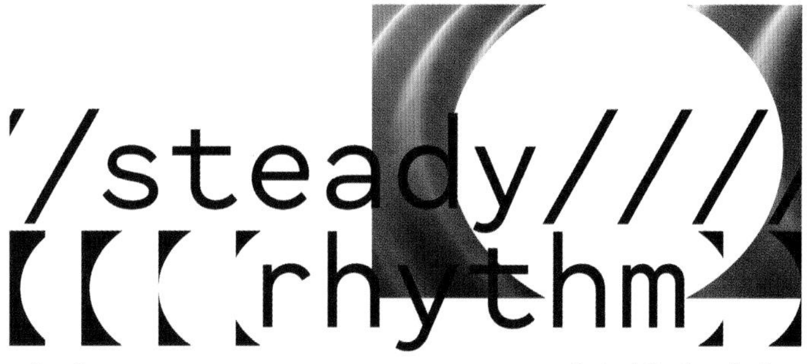

industrial_ &

[2024]

[CERA]

>>>code-inspired

aesthetics

[meets]

[MONO] geometric

& progressive → human

design

[PART OF CERA FAMILY]

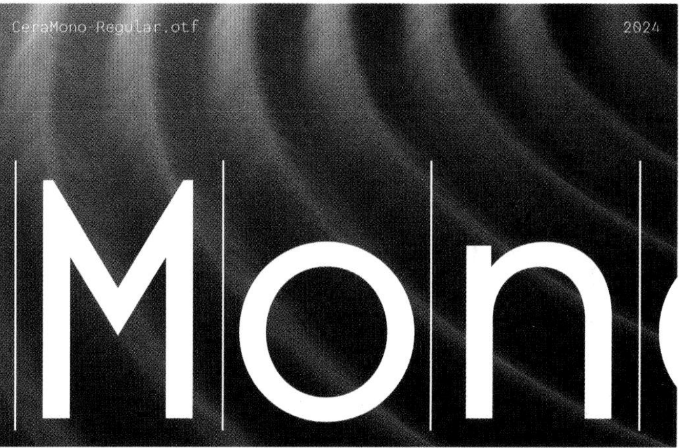

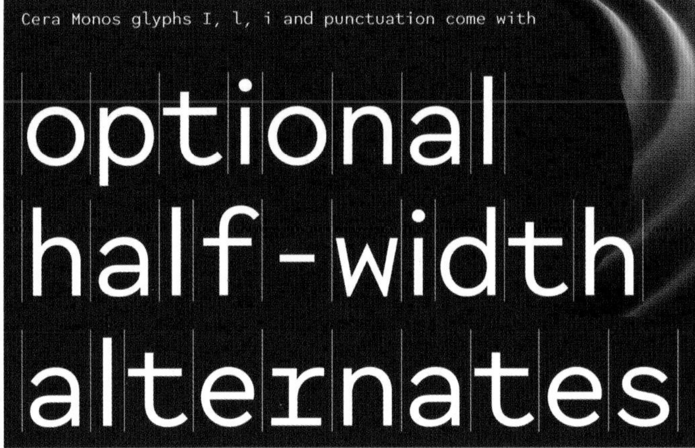

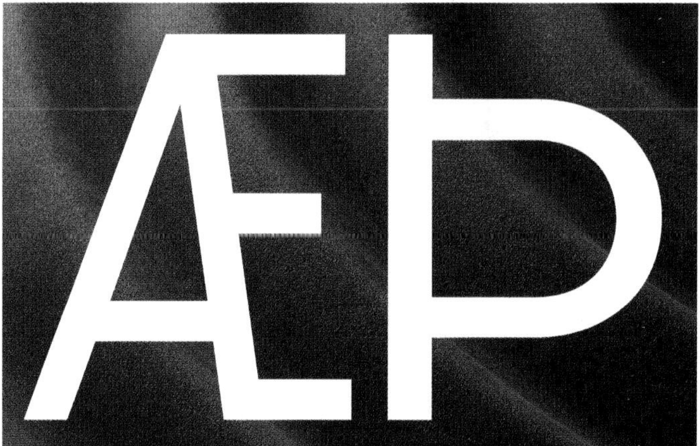

With a fixed width for all characters, Cera Mono is the nonproportional companion to the warm, geometric workhorse Cera Pro. Cera Mono brings a human voice to code-inspired aesthetics. With a technical texture, controlled dissonance, and inharmoniously balanced shapes, Cera Mono pairs the "undesigned" qualities of typewriter fonts with geometric focus. In artistic and cultural contexts, the resulting bureaucratic (and slightly glitchy) texture gives its light weights expressive power, while for those that generate value from code and data, its utilitarian design and carefully selected spectrum of six weights can refine the noisiest data into information.

---

typemates.com

Cera Mono

Designed by *Jakob Runge*
Published by *TypeMates*

Under the Same Roof

An Essay by Min-Young Kim

Type is everywhere. While typefaces' aesthetics often capture our attention first, they serve a much deeper purpose: to deliver messages, to document information, to guide wayfinding. As a fundamental tool of communication, type carries an immense amount of cultural significance within each writing system. Although some languages share the same script, it's uncommon for countries using the same script to have entirely unrelated cultural backgrounds, as the script itself inherently reflects its culture.

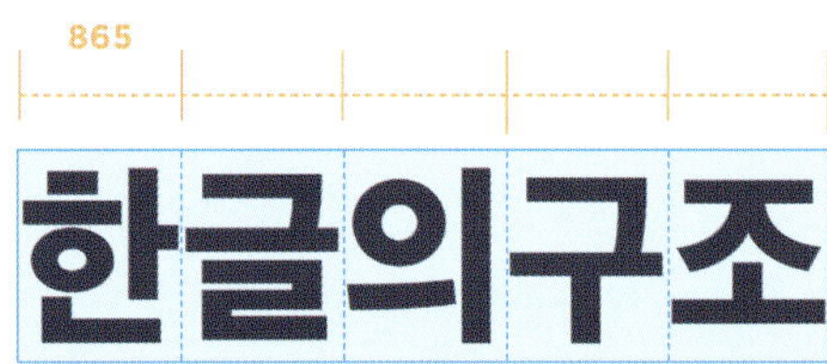

What happens when someone writes or speaks in multiple languages and scripts? Is there a seamless translation between each? As a trilingual myself, I can say this is rarely the case.

Each language and script conveys its unique cultural nuances, so multilingual individuals often engage in liberal translation to transcreate words and align them with the tone of each script. This process of transcreation also happens in the process of type design.

In multiscript type development, it's essential to balance common design elements—such as shape of serif, letterform proportions, curve dynamics, and so on—with the distinct attributes of each script that reflect its culture. For instance, when creating a Hangeul (Korean script) version of an existing Latin typeface, it's crucial to avoid an overly "Latinized" interpretation of the design. Such designs can feel artificial to native Korean readers and risk losing the intrinsic beauty of the script. Scripts should not be forced into the same box; instead, they should coexist under the same roof, each with its own space to express its unique charm. They are a family, after all.

Some scripts may share broader categorizations. For example, many are derived from the Latin alphabet, such as English, French, Spanish, and Vietnamese. Similarly, East Asian scripts are often grouped under the term "CJK"—short for Chinese, Japanese, and Korean. But does this categorization truly capture their individuality?

It's true that East Asian scripts share a historical connection to Chinese characters. Chinese characters are ideograms, meaning that each character conveys "meaning" in addition to its phonetic value. A distinctive feature of Chinese characters is that they are designed within a square box, including punctuation marks, aligning centrally within this framework, unlike the Latin alphabet, which follows a baseline and proportional designs. While other East Asian scripts share some of these traits, they also diverge in significant ways.

Korea, for instance, once used Chinese characters to write its language but later transitioned to Hangeul, the national script created in 1443. Hangeul is a phonographic script, with each letter forming syllabic blocks rather than independent ideograms. Unlike Chinese characters, its design is rooted in phonetics and the shapes of the vocal organs. Up until the early 1900s, Hanja (Chinese characters used in Korea) coexisted with Hangeul, but its usage has steadily declined since the 1990s. By the 2000s, Hanja education became optional, and today, its presence in official publications and media is minimal.

In addition, Korea adopted a Latin-style punctuation and word-spacing system, making Korean typesetting structurally closer to Latin than to other East Asian scripts. Punctuation marks are proportionally spaced, following Latin conventions, while Hangeul characters remain monospaced, similar to other East Asian scripts. A recent trend in Hangeul typography involves slightly narrowing the monospaced width—typically to around 850 to 950 units wide—to better accommodate the script's natural stacking structure, where components are arranged from top left to bottom right. As a result, Hangeul fonts become a blend of monospaced and proportional characteristics.

Japan, on the other hand, continues to use Kanji, a localized adaptation of Chinese characters, alongside two phonographic scripts—Hiragana and Katakana. This unique combination of ideograms and phonograms not only affects how Japanese is read but also has a significant impact on type design.

Hiragana, derived from simplified Kanji forms, and Katakana, developed from fragments of Kanji, carry no substantial meaning like the ideographic Chinese characters do. To enhance legibility and balance visual density, Kanji characters are typically designed slightly larger than Hiragana and Katakana. This ensures that complex Kanji remain legible, and phonetic characters remain distinguishable, within a line of text.

Even within Chinese characters, regional variations exist. Mainland China primarily uses Simplified Chinese, while Taiwan and Hong Kong retain Traditional Chinese, each with different localized letterforms. Punctuation usage also varies slightly between these regions. Similarly, Japan's Kanji and Korea's Hanja have regional forms as well, while some characters are shared here and there.

The differences among CJK scripts are as significant as their similarities, and when we conveniently group these scripts under the label "CJK," we risk overlooking their unique traits.

Are we boxing them together, or can we bring them under the same roof while respecting their distinctiveness? This question extends beyond East Asian scripts, including the Latin alphabet. Recognizing these nuances allows us to design typefaces that respect each script's individuality, while fostering harmonious coexistence in multiscript typography.

What happens when combining CJK typefaces and Latin? Let's consider some examples. In most Korean typography, because they use Latin-style punctuation and word-spacing system, many designers prefer using pure Latin typefaces for Latin, punctuation, and sometimes numerals as well—rather than using the Latin alphabet supported in the Hangeul font. Even though technically Korean and Latin share the same punctuation, the ideal position, size, and sometimes design of them differs, because the fundamental structure of the letterforms are different. The Latin alphabet is designed on a baseline, and most of the weight in the line is heavily focused on the x-height of lowercase letters. Hangeul is a block-based letter that consist of three different parts: first sound (consonant), second sound (vowel), and last sound (consonant again), forming a syllable in just one letter. Some letters are simpler and do not have the last sound, which is drawn in the bottom half of the box. So, naturally, all the letters are higher than the Latin alphabet, and the optical flow of the reading is set slightly higher than the strict center of the box. Thus, the ideal position and size of the punctuation changes from Latin. Recently, many Korean designers have started to draw several sets of the same punctuation, with each one designed to match more appropriately with Hangeul or with Latin, respecting the conventions of each script.

The Latin alphabet designed in Japanese typefaces is called Subordinate Latin. Because Japanese type is designed in a monospaced square box, the Latin doesn't have enough room for descenders and ascenders, and some letters need to have a smaller x-height to draw legible descenders. This is a unique design solution that you can only see in Japanese fonts.

The best design application can vary depending on its origin. Each script brings its own visual flow, structural rules, and cultural context, all of which shape the way the font functions across languages. Understanding these origins is not merely a technical detail; it's essential to achieving a cohesive and contextually respectful design. As design continues to cross typographic boundaries, this awareness becomes a crucial part of working responsibly and creatively with type.

12がつのあるあさのランニングのあと、こう
んでToGoしたCoffeeをのんでいるとマ
メンのLisaがLUUPでやってきて「Toda
のScheduleはFree?」としつもんしてき
した。LunchをするやくそくをAgreeして
12:30にしゅうごうすることになりました。

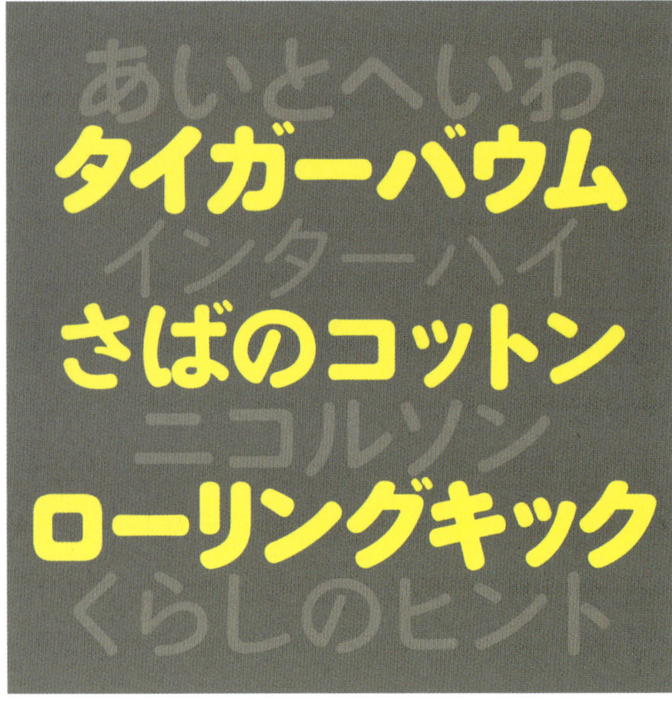

Yokohama
Seoul
Kinshasa
Goteborg
Kyiv
Cartagena
TOKYO
2345678

This typeface is a unique rounded gothic inspired by the forms of vintage metal type.

NPR Ena

nipponia.in

Designed by *Kazuhiro Yamada*
Published by *Nipponia*

TUES · WED · THURS
ONLY

PLUS ALL WEEK

JULY 25 · 30

FRI · SAT · SUN · ONLY

THE YARDBIRDS
JAMES COTTON BAND
RICHIE HAVENS
THE DOORS

BILL GRAHAM PRESENTS AT THE FILLMORE IN SAN FRANCISCO

Got Brain · I am The Walrus · Are you Experi
te Rabbit · Echoes · Guinnevere · Eight Miles
stal Spider · Magic Carpet Ride · Mr. Tambou
stic Fantastic Four · CRIMSON & CLOVER · Ove
ays Down · The End · Itchycoo Park · Oscill
stellar Overdrive · Mona · Paper Sun · Help, I
el Free · In-A-Gadda-Da-Vida · The Garden of E
ts · Tomorrow Never Knows · Lucy in the S

Unicaster is a grotesque Unicase typeface with a unified height for both uppercase and lowercase, ideal for display uses like titles, short texts, and packaging. Inspired by the lettering on the 1967 album Part One *by the West Coast Pop Art Experimental Band, its design reimagines the original's irresistible charm through a fresh, personal interpretation.*

type-o-tones.com

Unicaster

Designed by *José Manuel Urós*
Published by *Type-Ø-Tones*

탄소 융합 중력 은하계 탐험가

백색 왜성 빛 메아리 시간 왜곡

성운 카시오페아 별자리 폴라리스

은하계 연구 센터 큰곰자리 천체

베텔게우스
붉은 초거성

베텔게우스(Betelgeuse)는 밤하늘에서 여덟번째로 밝으면서 오리온 자리에서 첫 번째로 밝은 별이다. 베텔게우스는 뚜렷하게 붉은색으로 빛나며, 겉보기 밝기가 0.2등급에서 1.2등급까지 바뀌는 반규칙 변광성이고 1등급 별 중 밝기 변화가 가장 큰 별이기도 하다. 베텔게우스는 겨울의 대삼각형을 이루는 별 중 하나이며 겨울의 대육각형 중심부에 있는 별이기도 하다.

창조

안타까운 파괴의 순간이
새로운 창조를 꽃피우는
순간이 될 수도 있는
우주의 역설적인 운명

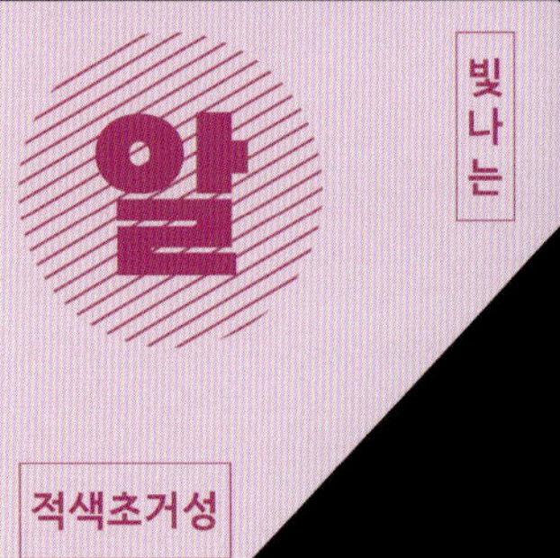

오리온자리
초신성
폭발*

파

㉠ 목적지 금성

새로운
별의 탄생

케플러(Kepler)
티코(Tycho)

㉡ 출발 화성

초신성*

Hangeul—the alphabet used for the Korean language—is structurally larger than Latin, requiring adjustments to visually align with the original and maintain the script's integrity. Also important is balancing grotesque and geometric details to capture the essence of Proxima Nova. Available in eight weights—Thin to Black—this growing family is ready to become even more popular worldwide.

Proxima Nova Hangeul

marksimonson.com

Designed by *Noheul Lee, Loris Olivier*
Published by *Mark Simonson Studio*

บรรยากาศ แคสสิโอเปีย

เนบิวลาของแอนโดรเมดา

ดาวโจร กล้องโทรทรรศน์

ดาว จักรวาล กาแลคซี

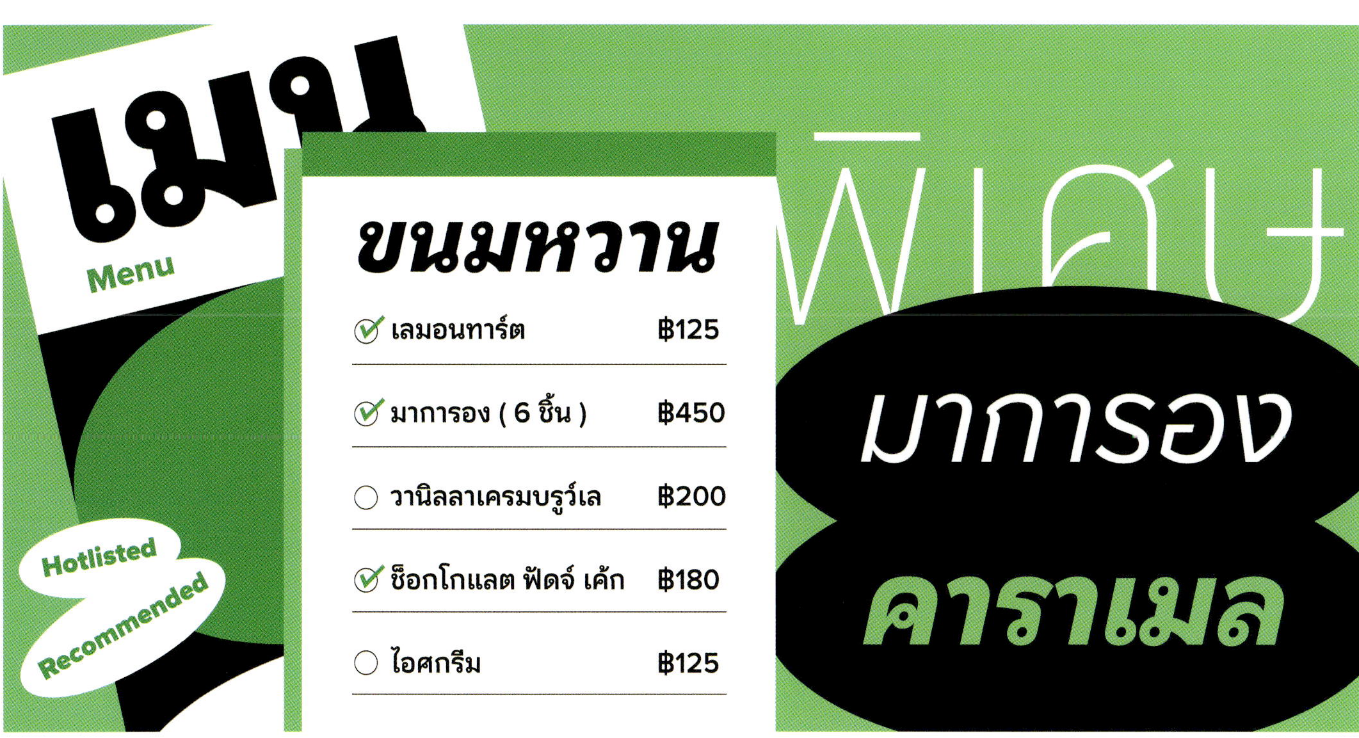

Available in a practical loopless style for display settings and a traditional looped for text and UI, each in eight weights and matching italics,

Proxima Nova Thai works seamlessly with the original Latin without losing the script's texture or cultural significance.

marksimonson.com

Proxima Nova Thai

Designed by *Smich Smanloh*
Published by *Mark Simonson Studio*

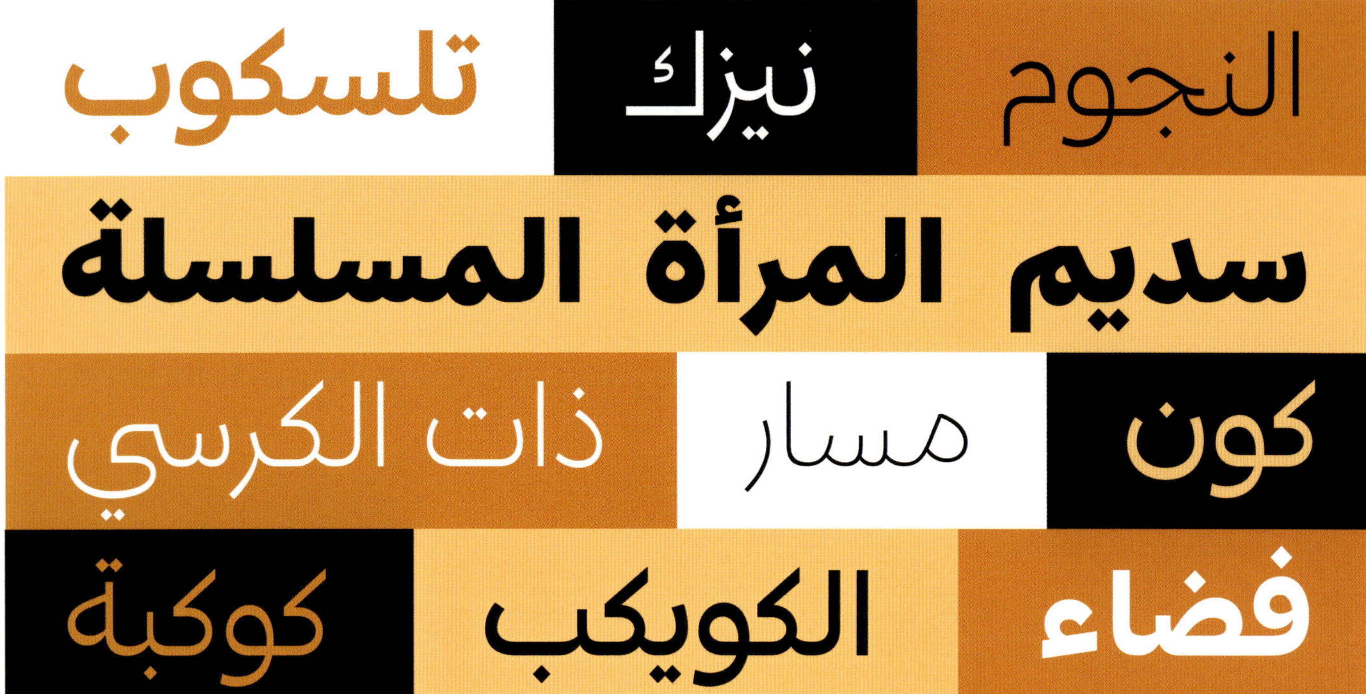

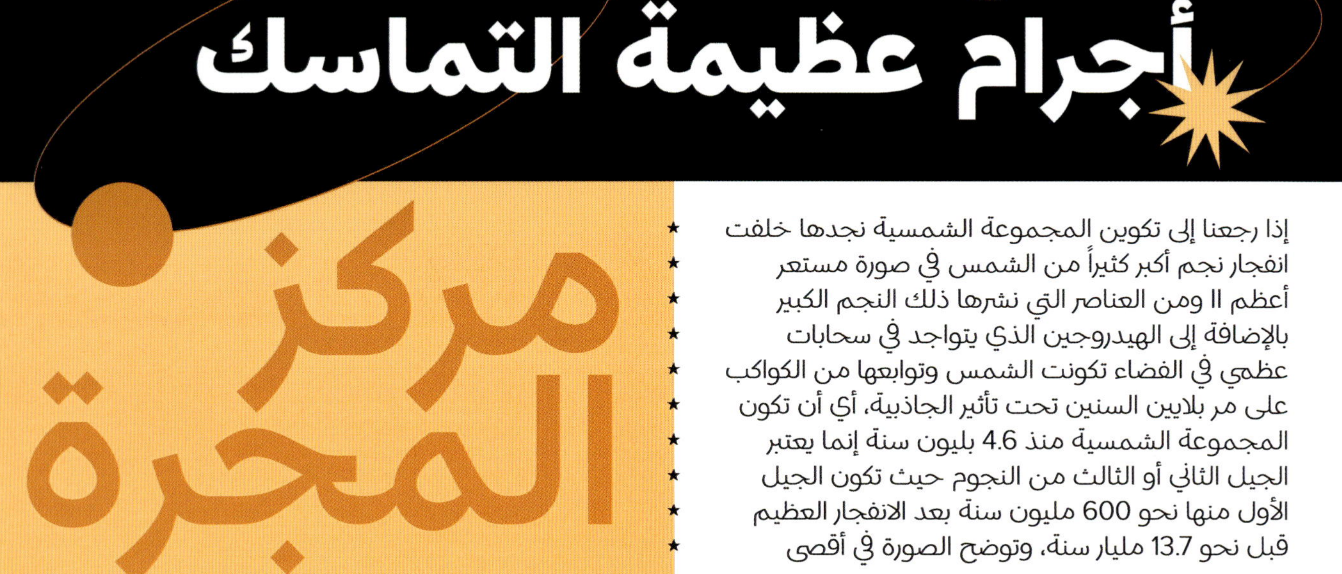

Using a sculptural approach, a balance was reached between the calligraphic and geometric, giving graphic designers and typographers an Arabic script with the look and utility of a modern sans serif for print and screen use.

Proximia Nova Arabic

marksimonson.com

Designed by *Khajag Apelian, Wael Morcos*
Published by *Mark Simonson Studio*

खगोलशास्त्र मार्गक्रमण

सौर यंत्रणा आकाशमन्डल

कक्षा संचार उप लघुग्रह

खगोलीय धूमकेतु संपण

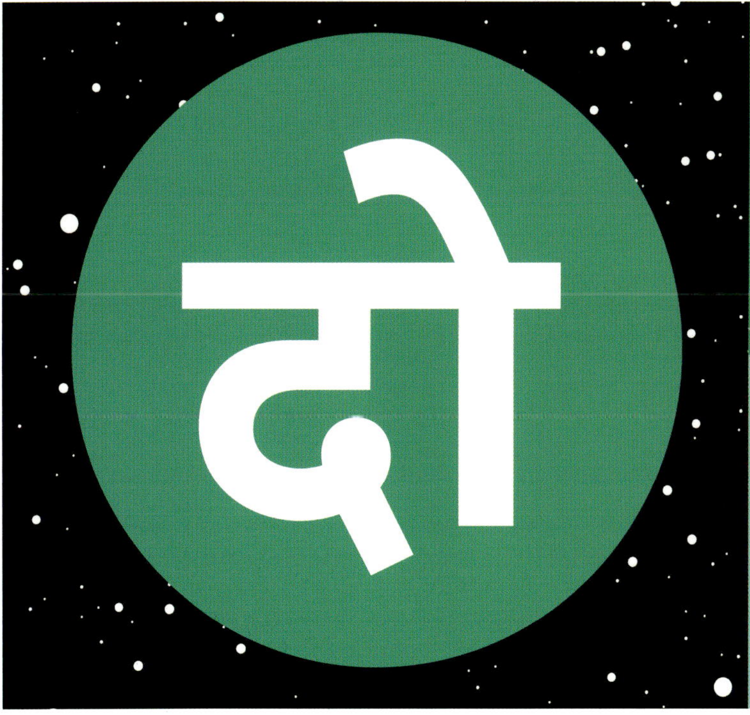

ब्रह्मांड

प्राथमिक जानकारी

यह नोटिस एक व्यक्ति द्वारा किसी दूसरे
सूचना है जो उन्हें सूचित करती है कि वे
औपचारिक संचार स्थापित करने की कई
यह नोटिस आम तौर पर तब भेजा जाता

The script was created with subtleties of flavor, making it distinctly its own without Latinization, as a partner for use with Proxima Nova that features an extended Latin and Devanagari character set with Marathi and Nepali stylistic sets in eight weights, from Thin to Black.

---

marksimonson.com

Proxima Nova Devanagari

Designed by *Vaibhav Singh, Alessia Mazzarella*
Published by *Mark Simonson Studio*

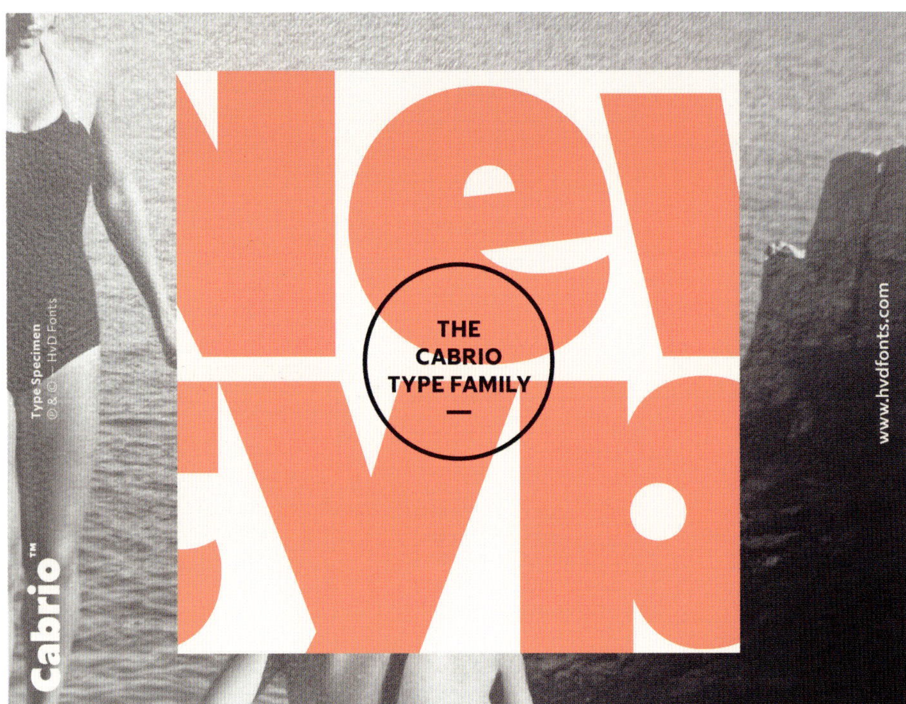

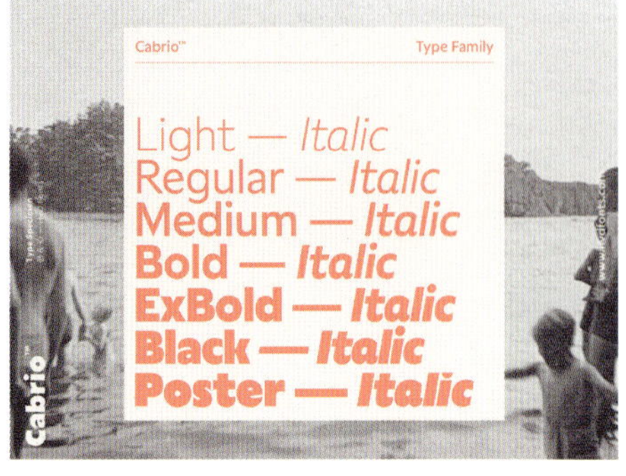

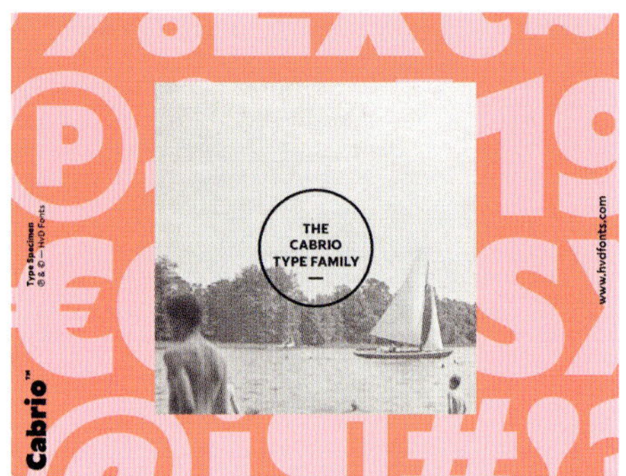

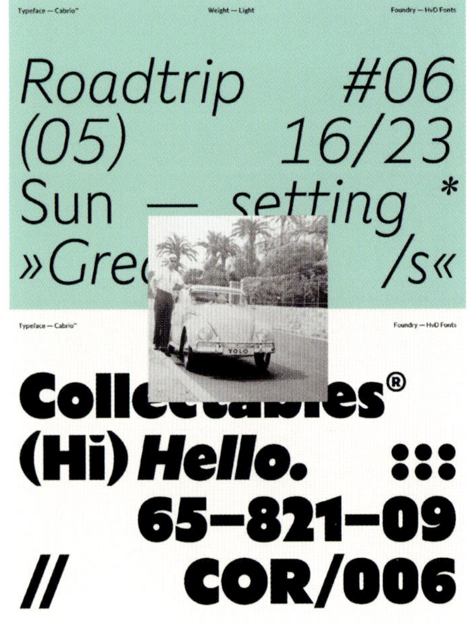

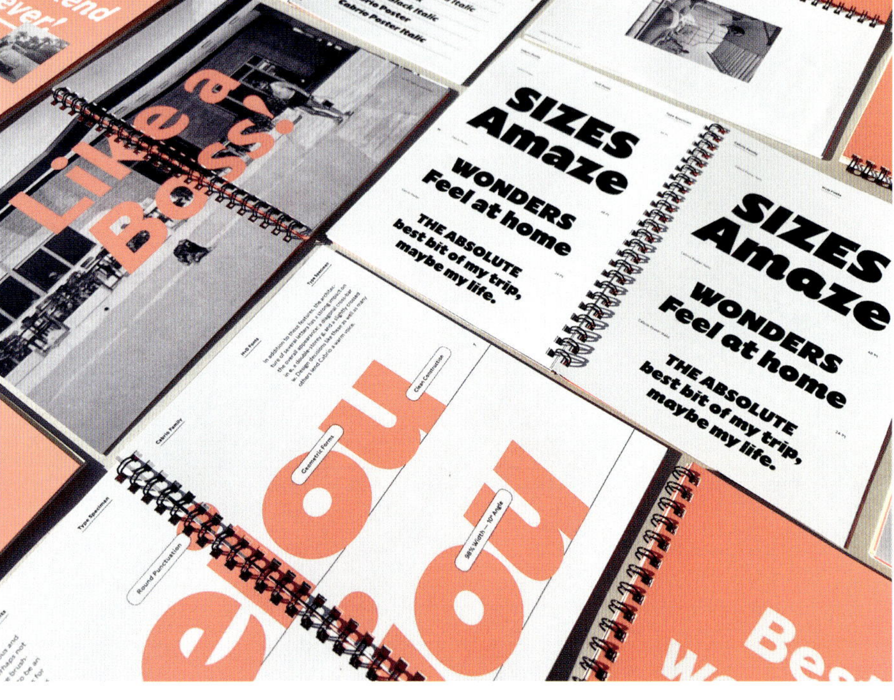

Cabrio is a humanist sans serif type family that combines geometric shapes with subtle but playful details of a script typeface.

Cabrio

hvdfonts.com

Designed by *Hannes von Döhren*
Published by *HvD Fonts*

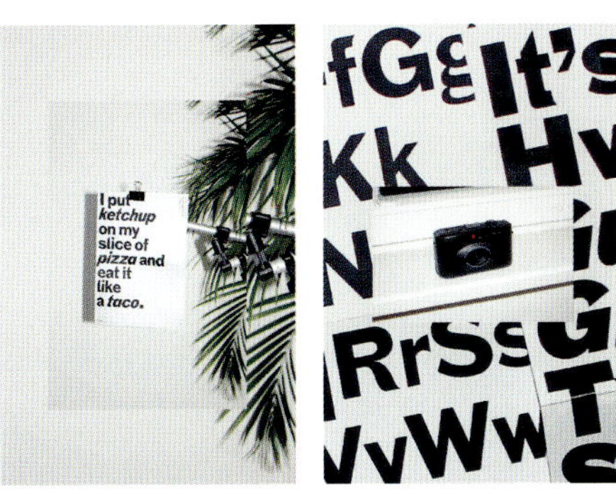

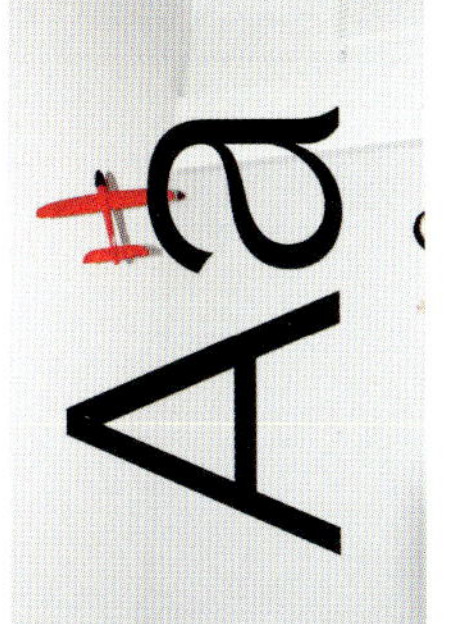

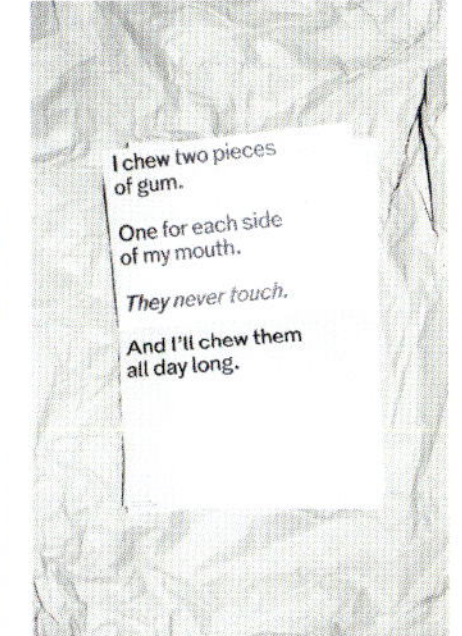

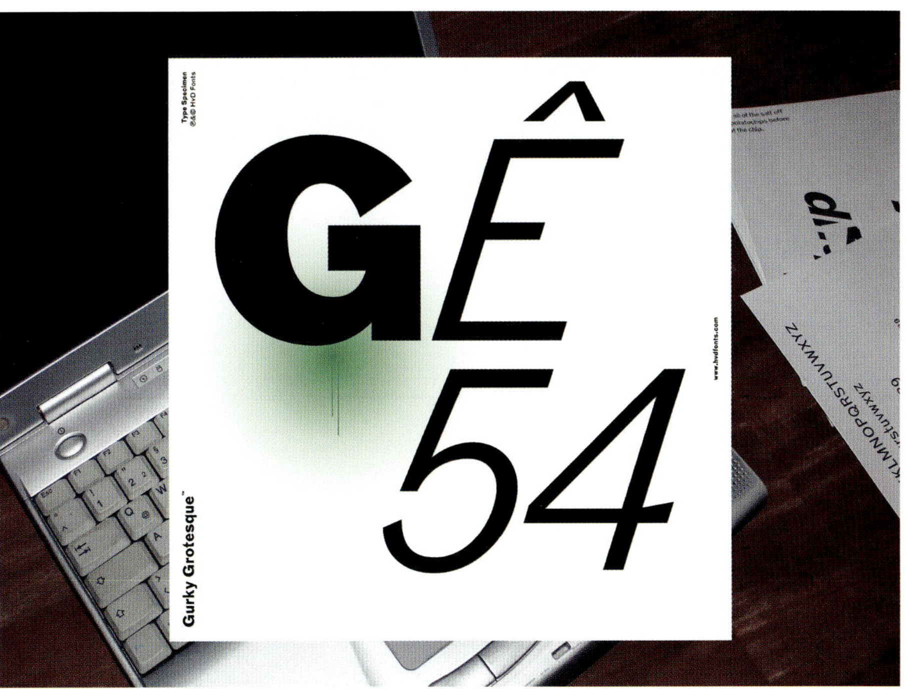

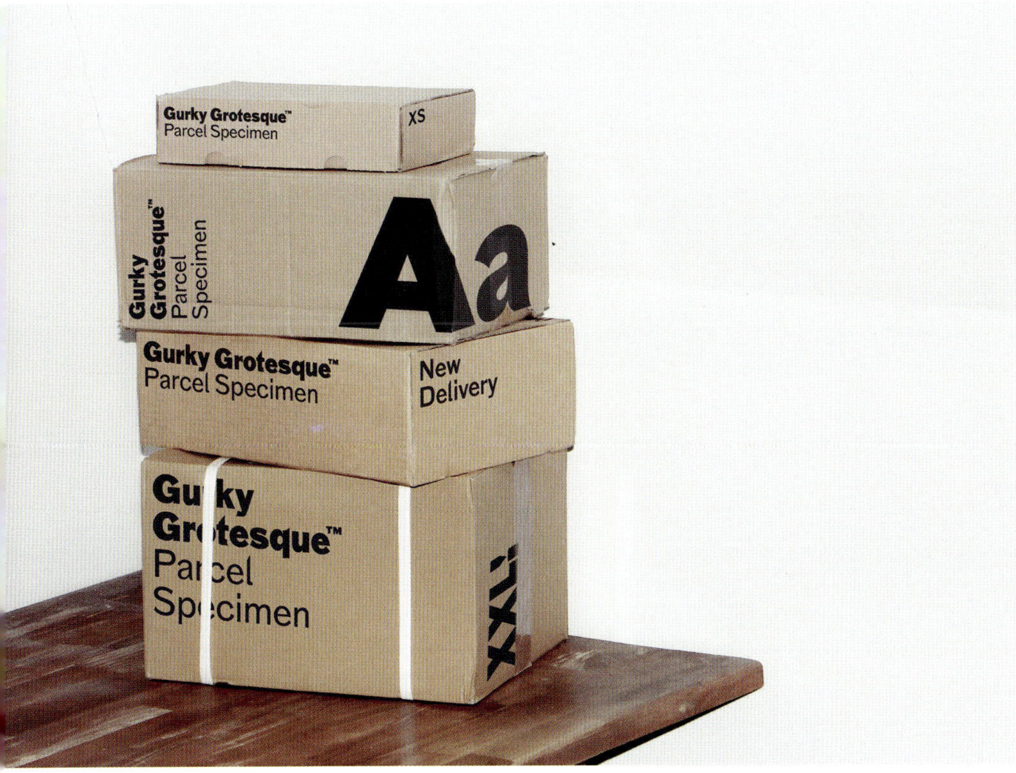

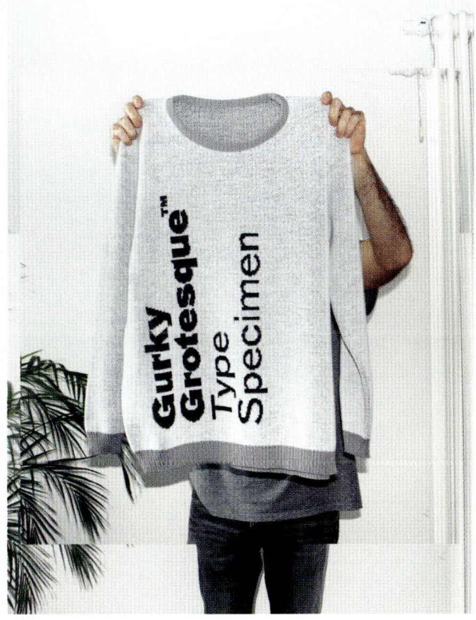

Gurky Grotesque is reminiscent of old metal type, favoring quirky imperfections over smooth curves. HvD Fonts went on a search for character and unique solutions to bring back the charm of vernacular type and the appeal of imperfection.

---

hvdfonts.com

Gurky Grotesque

Designed by *Hannes von Döhren*
Published by *HvD Fonts*

F37 Randy takes its inspiration from a somewhat unlikely quarter: some eccentric DIY England and Wales Cricket Board signage. F37 Randy went out to bat for the foundry after coming across a curious hand-crafted ECB sign that read "Official Non Turf Cricket Pitch System Supplier." The F37 team loved its naive, slightly clumsy sans serif letterforms and were reminded of "outsider" typographic art. It was decided to riff off the sign's DIY aesthetic, picking up on some of its odd quirks to create an entire font family. Deliberate idiosyncrasies are woven in across all weights, like letters that are wider at the top than the bottom, so they feel a little off-kilter along with strokes that curve back slightly in on themselves. The upright letters have wide, roomy spacing, while the italic is condensed, tight, and slanted at a steep sixteen degrees. The alternates are truly eccentric. F37 Randy comes in six weights, all with true italics, so twelve styles in all.

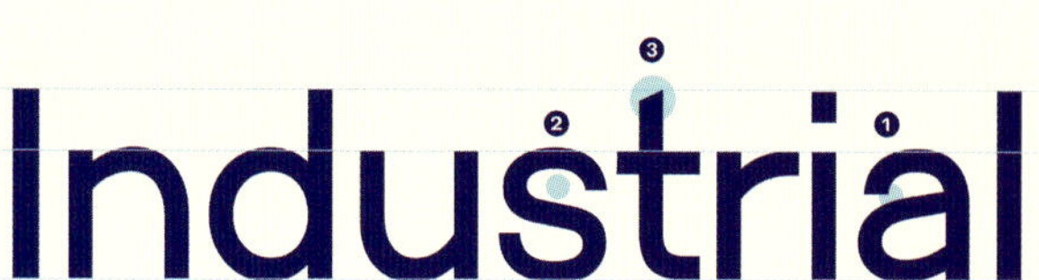

Randy embraces the naive, clumsy and occasionally, a little bonkers, sans serif lettering, commonly found in early industrial revolution advertising. Awkward 'a'❶ aperture, top heavy 's'❷ and uncomfortably tall lower case 't'❸.

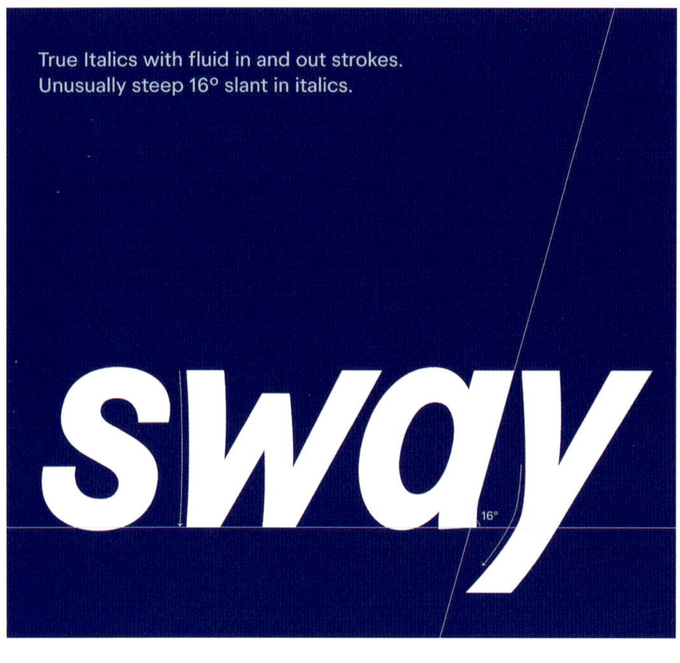

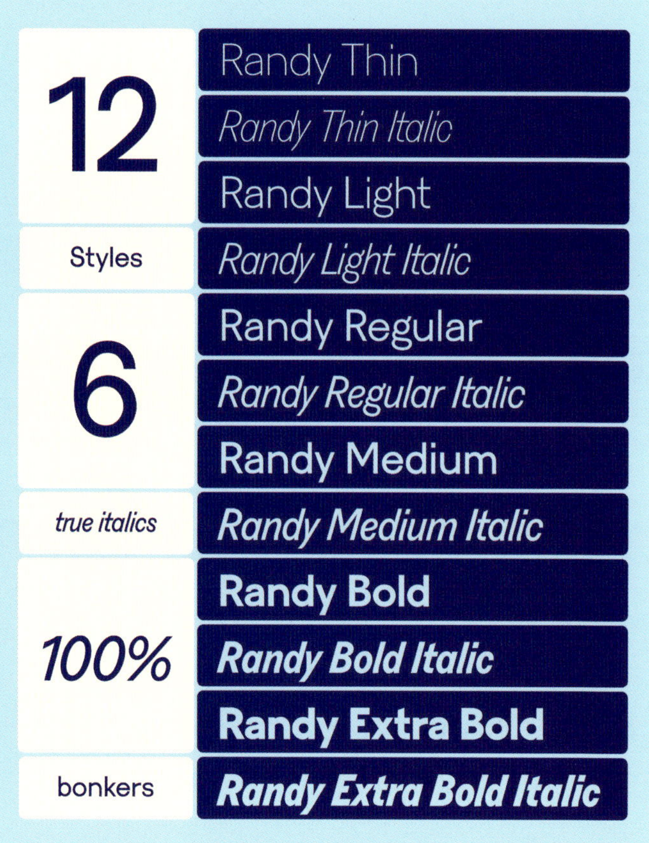

F37 Randy

f37foundry.com

Designed by *Ryan Williamson, Rick Banks*
Published by *F37 Foundry*

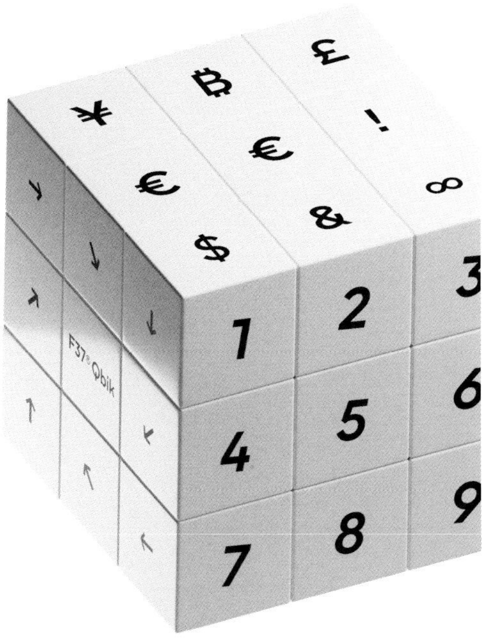

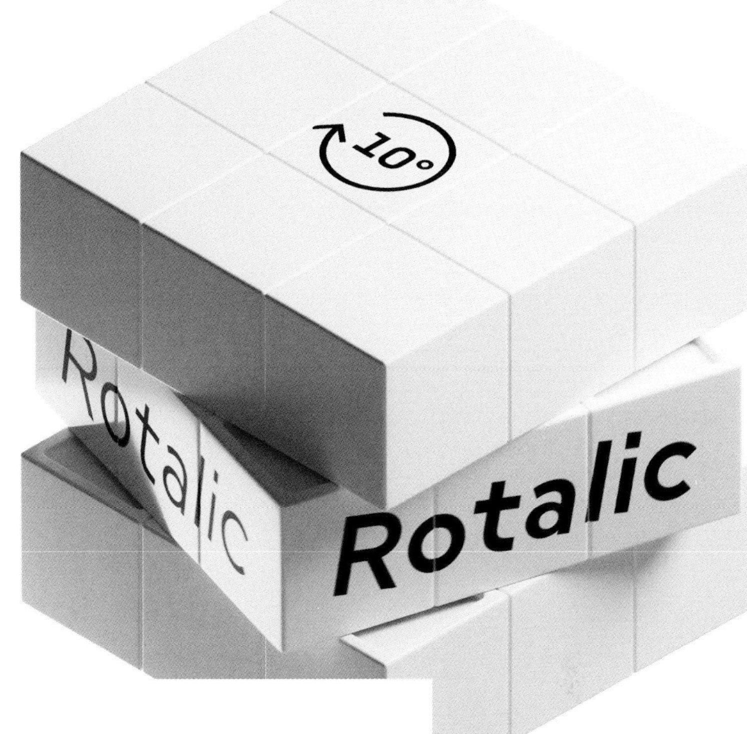

F37 Qbik puts a new slant on a hardcore geometric sans. It's bold, powerful and uncompromising… although not so much in its rotalic form. Qbik is born from a brutalist design aesthetic—most of its characters are created out of basic geometric forms and with minimal optical adjustments. It feels hard, pure, and confident—a font that knows exactly what it stands for and refuses to budge on principle. Apart from a couple of characterful quirks, like the cap Q, which resembles an upside-down yo-yo. Or the lowercase alternate g, which looks like it has tank tracks. This all starts to change in the companion variant version, which instead of the usual italics come as "rotalics." With italics, the letterforms are slanted, with their feet planted firmly on the baseline. Rotalics, however, are rotated to the right, so the characters kind of look like they're ice-skating, or at least off-balance and tottering forward. F37 Qbik is available across five weights, in both upright and rotalic, so ten styles in all. Medium and Regular work best for longer text, while Light, Bold, and Black are just the job for display and titling.

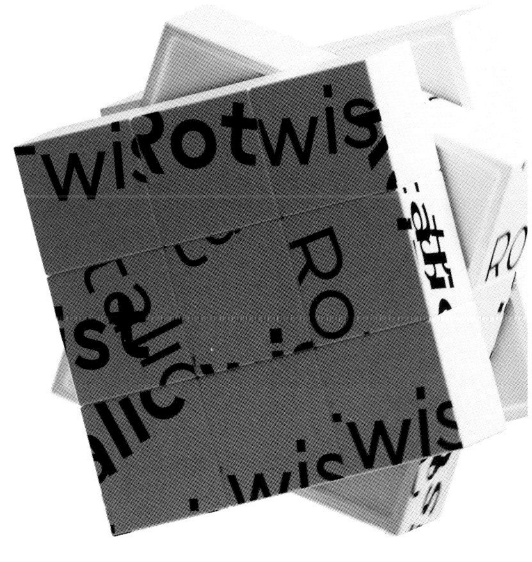

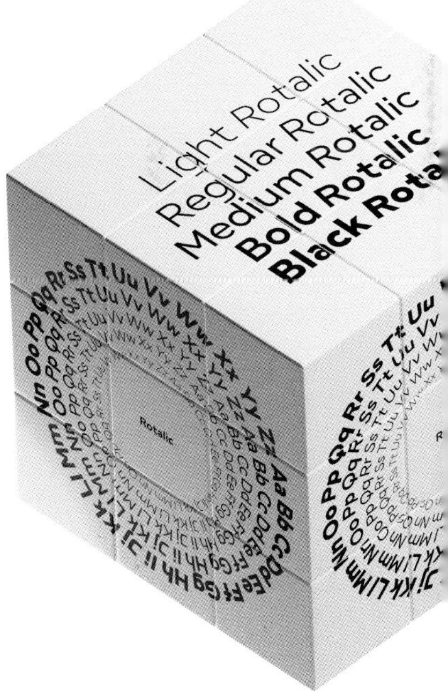

---

f37foundry.com

F37 Qbik

Designed by *Rick Banks, Rodrigo Fuenzalida*
Published by *F37 Foundry*

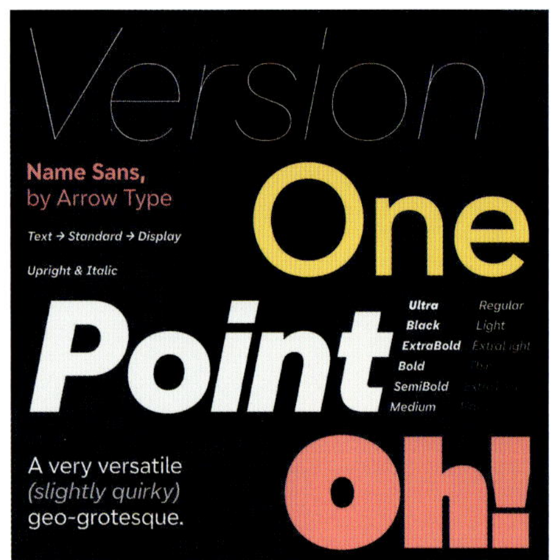

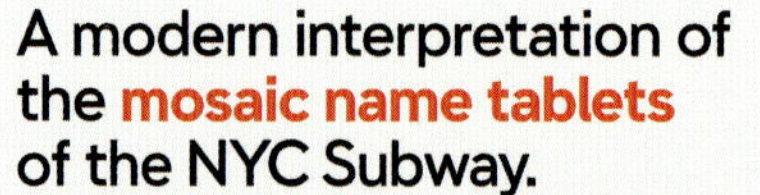

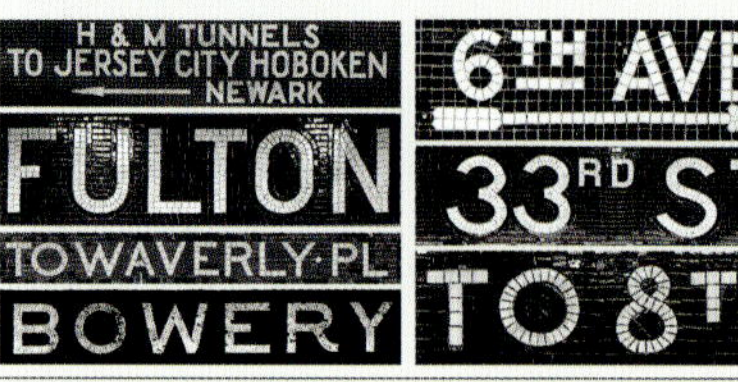

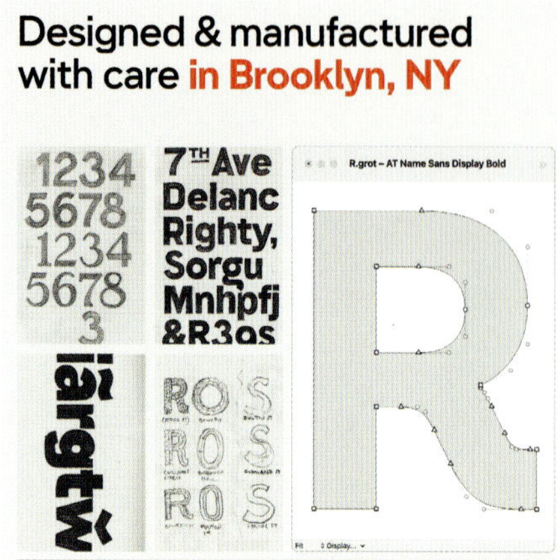

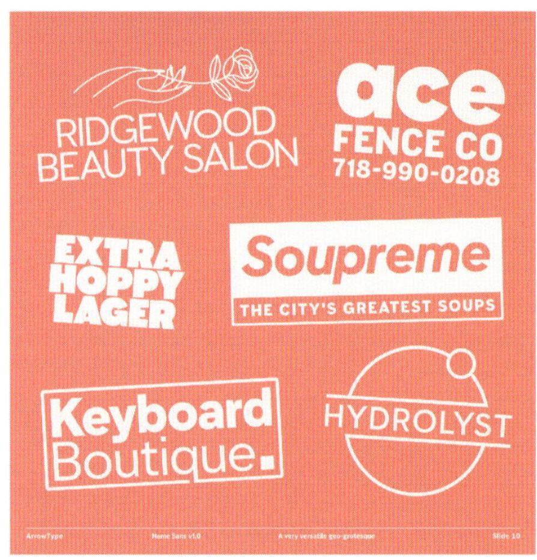

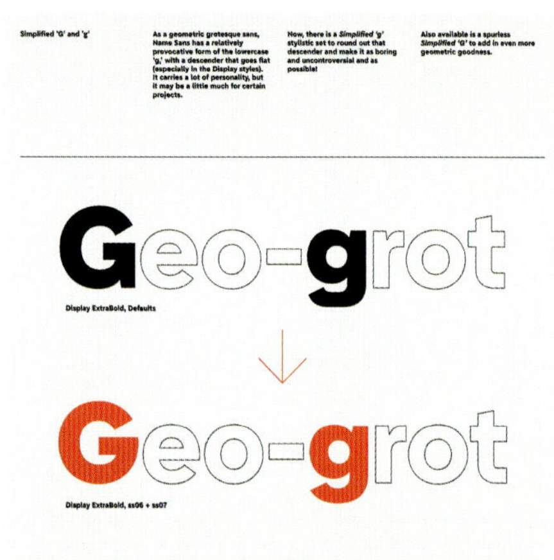

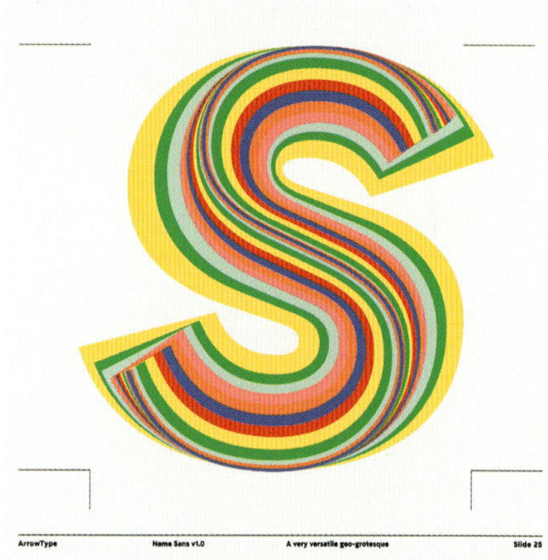

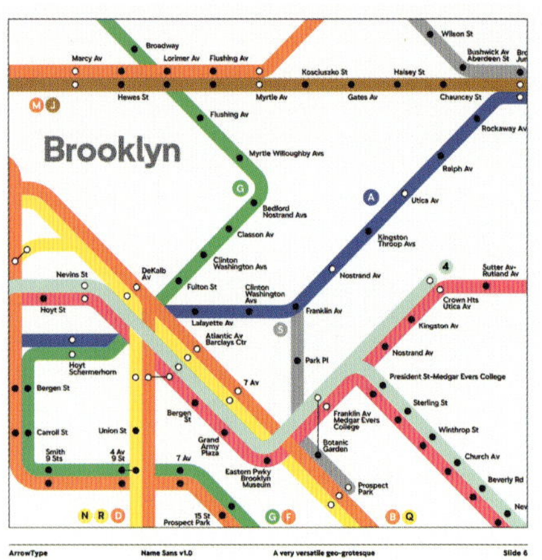

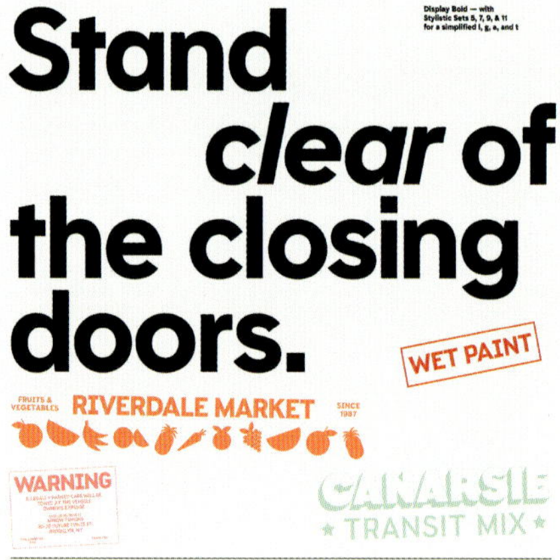

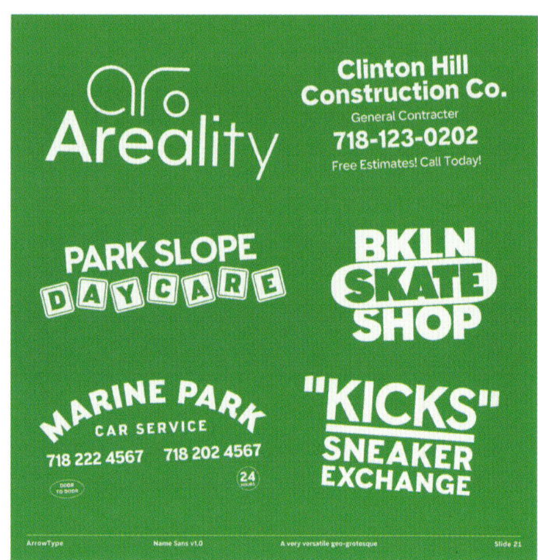

Name Sans

arrowtype.com

Designed by *Stephen Nixon*
Published by *ArrowType*

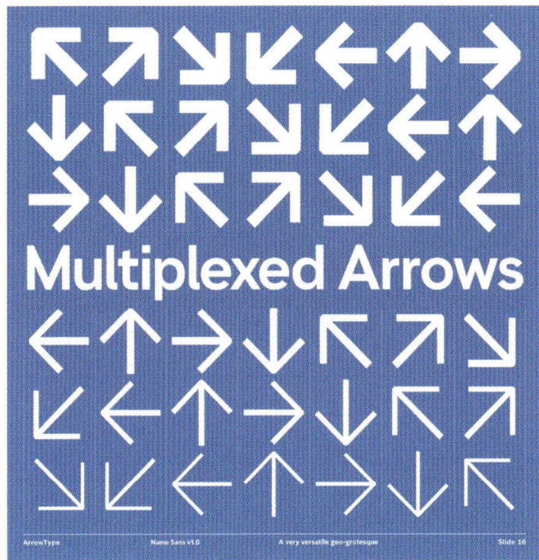

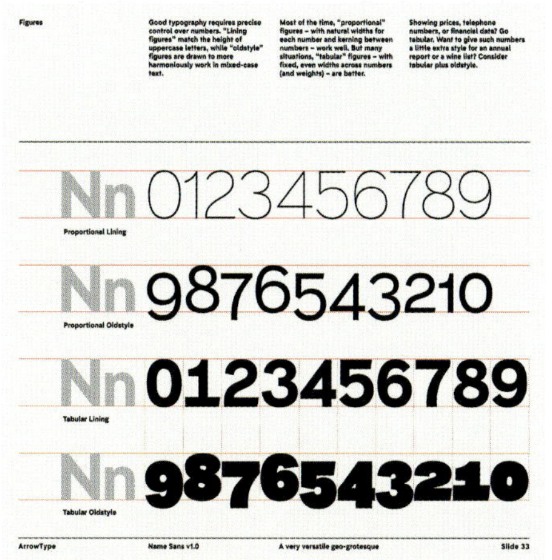

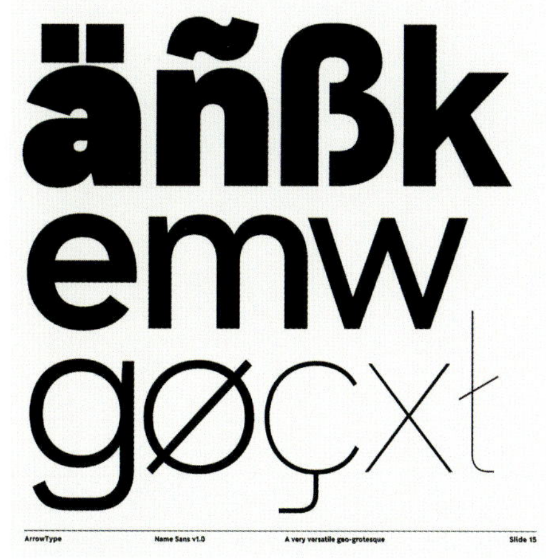

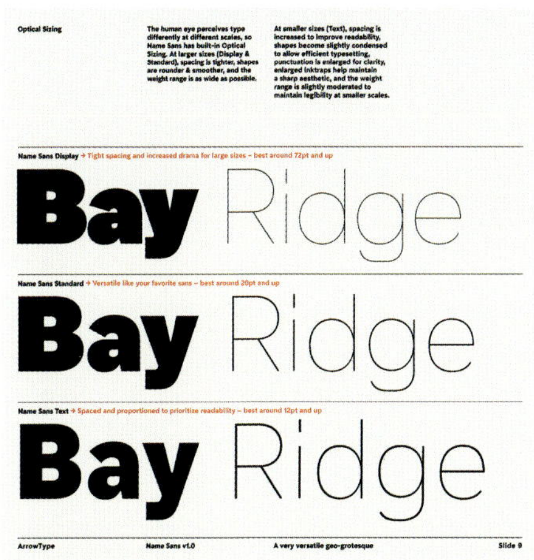

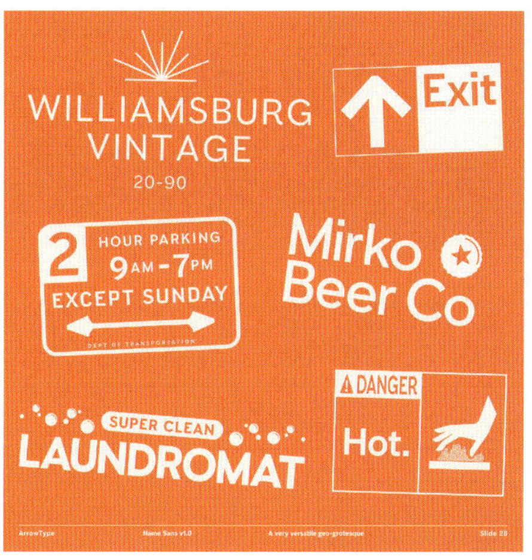

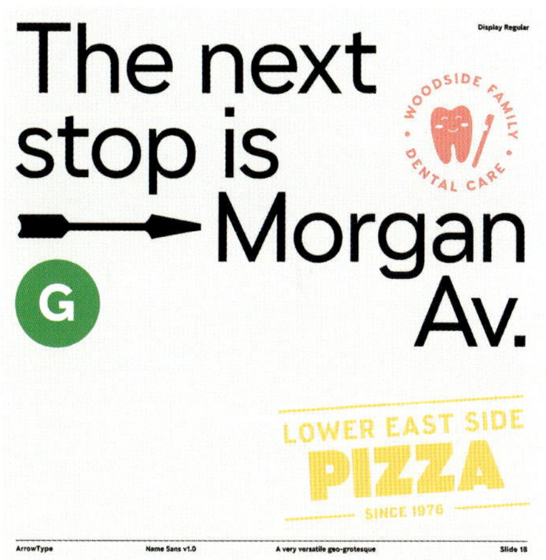

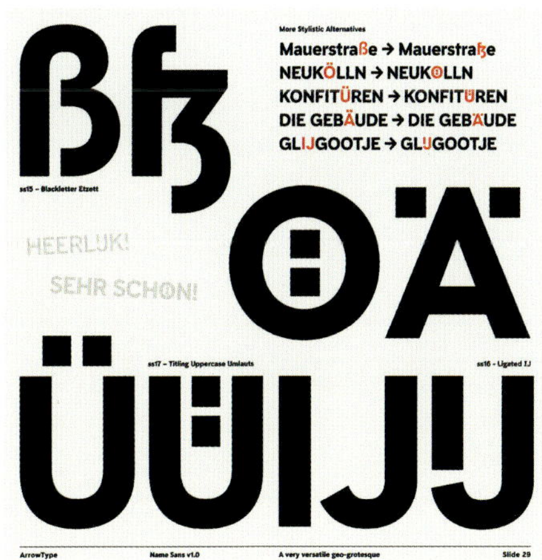

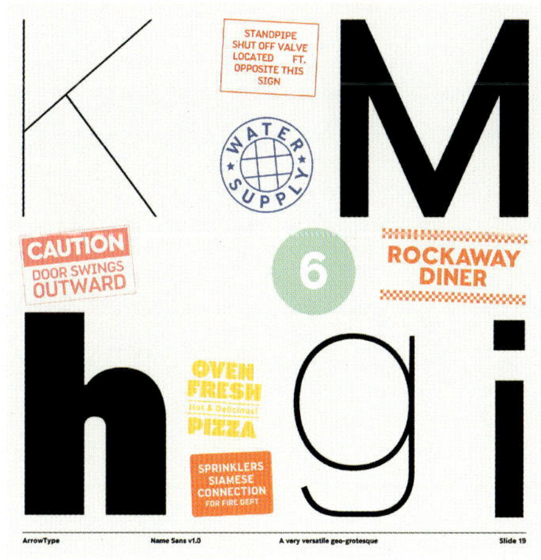

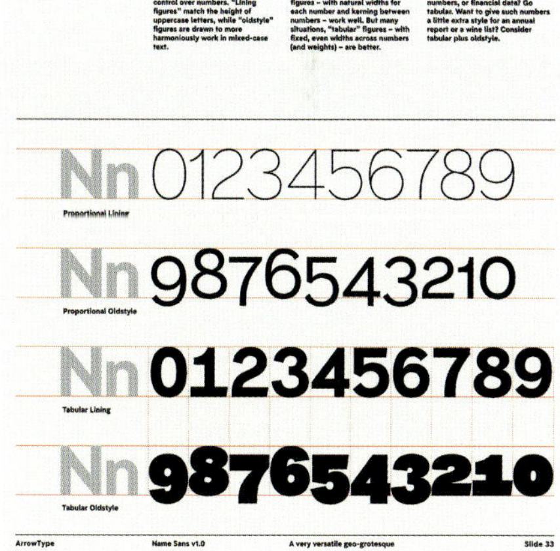

Name Sans is a modern interpretation of the tile mosaic name tablets of the New York City subway. The architects and craftworkers who designed and laid these tiles used a letter construction that was part geometric and part grotesque, with typographic optical corrections often either exaggerated or totally missing. Name Sans interprets these ideas into an extensive type system that is at once anonymous and full of personality, useful for everything from branding to wayfinding to digital interfaces. The project began as a series of sketches in notebooks, drawn during daily commutes in New York, and was subsequently formalized into a typeface over about four years. The original mosaic letterforms vary from station to station, but this project harmonizes the sometimes divergent ideas into a useful, extensive type system.

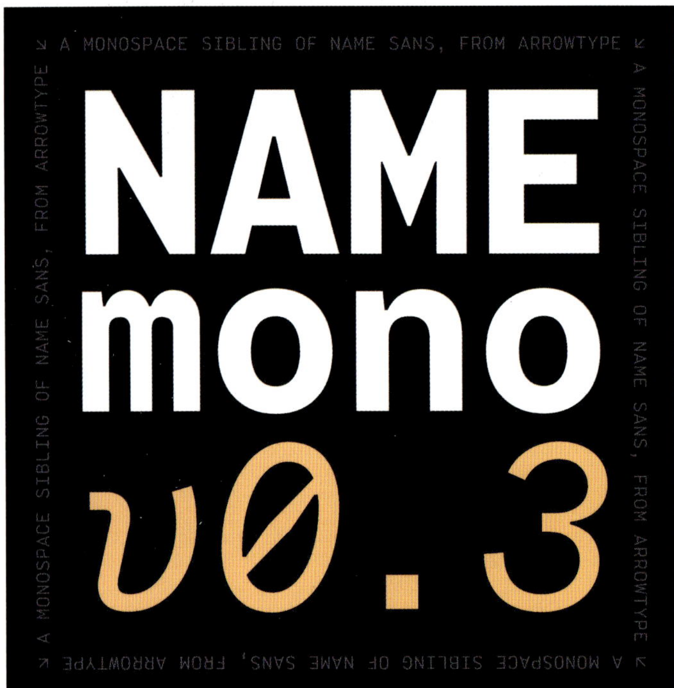

Font metrics *(x-height, etc)* are matched between Name Mono & Name Sans for natural pairing:

Hlg Hlg

Name Sans Text Bold
Optical Size = 12

Name Mono Bold

v0.3 characters

STYLES IN NAME MONO

Black	**& *Italic***	**# *v0.3***
ExtraBold	**& *Italic***	**# *v0.3***
Bold	**& *Italic***	**# *v0.3***
SemiBold	& *Italic*	# *v0.3*
Medium	& *Italic*	# *v0.3*
Regular	& *Italic*	# *v0.3*
Light	& *Italic*	# soon
ExtraLight	& *Italic*	# soon
Thin	& *Italic*	# soon

Name Mono

arrowtype.com

Designed by *Stephen Nixon*
Published by *ArrowType*

NAME MONO IS *A MONOSPACE SIBLING* OF NAME SANS, FROM ARROWTYPE.

Name Mono started as *Name Sans.* It is adapted into a fixed-width system *for code, data, captions, writing, art, fashion, and more.*

The *Italics* are a more *free and expressive* take on the concept, for *better ergonomics* in code.

v0.3 adds alts: a *classic uppercase, brutalist punctuation, oldstyle numerals,* and *high-legibility 6 & 9*

ABCDE ABCDE
FGHIJ FGHIJ
KLMNO KLMNO
PQRST PQRST
UVWXY UVWXY
Z”096 Z"096

```
    17: 'styleName'     # Style Name
}

# GET / SET NAME HELPER FUNCTIONS

def getFontNameID(font, ID, platformID=3, platEncID=1):
    name = str(font['name'].getName(ID, platformID, platEncID))
    return name

def setFontNameID(font, ID, newName):
    print(f"\n\t• name {ID}:")
    macIDs = {"platformID": 3, "platEncID": 1, "langID": 0x409}
    winIDs = {"platformID": 1, "platEncID": 0, "langID": 0x0}

    oldMacName = font['name'].getName(ID, *macIDs.values())
    oldWinName = font['name'].getName(ID, *winIDs.values())

    if oldMacName != newName:
        print(f"\n\t\t Mac name was '{oldMacName}'")
        font['name'].setName(newName, ID, *macIDs.values())
        print(f"\t\t Mac name now '{newName}'")

    if oldWinName != newName:
        print(f"\n\t\t Win name was '{oldWinName}'")
        font['name'].setName(newName, ID, *winIDs.values())
        print(f"\t\t Win name now '{newName}'")


def cleanName(name, particleToRemove):
    """
        Because these are being left in right now, and appearing in font
    """
```

Franklin St – Prospect Av

Saratoga Av – Delancey St

Bay 50th St – Nostrand Av

Atlantic Av – Winthrop St

Sterling St – Rockaway Av

Montrose Av – Chambers St

Chauncey St – New Lots Av

Kingston Av – Bleecker St

Crescent St – Parkside Av

Name Mono is a monospaced sibling to Name Sans, which is a modern interpretation of the tile mosaic name tablets of the New York City subway. Name Mono adapts the same conceptual framework into a fixed-width system for code, data, captions, writing, art, fashion, and more. Name Mono's italics are a more expressive take on the theme. In many contexts of monospace typography, this yields better ergonomics (and it also looks pretty cool).

~VERY IMPORTANT NOTICE~

START THE PARTY!

Monochromic.js

```
// Load up your new fav coding font!
function setup() {
  getThisFont(TRUE);}

function partyStart() {
  createCanvas(width, height);
  background('electricBlue');
  positiveEnergy(25000);

  for (let fun = 0; fun < 5; fun++) {
  // Runs 5 times, adding lots of joy!
  console.log("Join the party y'all!");
  generateFestivities(300);}
}
```

~*Choose Your Fav Style*~

ST Monochromic Thin
ST Monochromic Extralight
ST Monochromic Light
ST Monochromic Regular
ST Monochromic Medium
ST Monochromic Semibold
ST Monochromic Bold

Think of all the cool ASCII art U can make! :)

A

~3~

OwO

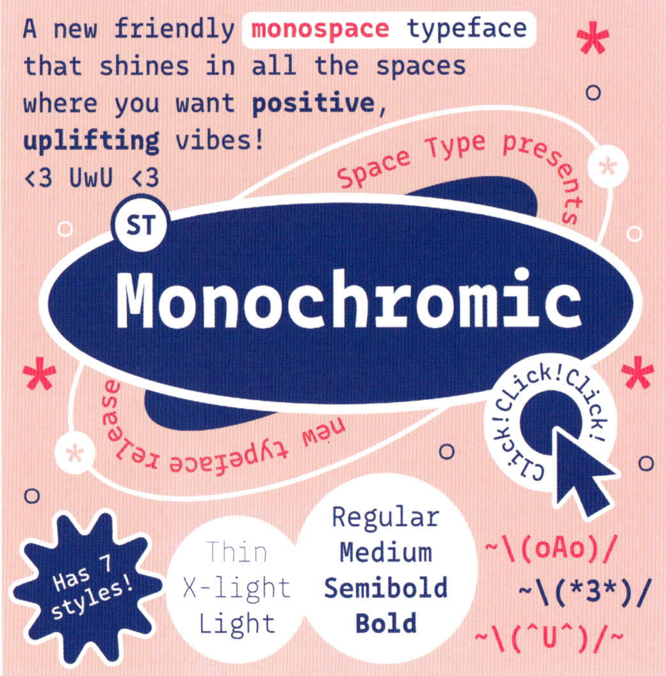

A friendly monospace typeface that shines in typographic spaces where you want a friendly interface. Best suited for a variety of information-dense applications such as user interfaces, programming environments, technical manuals, and exhibition tags, it softens the mood while maintaining cool tech vibes.

Monochromic

spacetypeco.com

Designed by *Lynne Yun, Kevin Yeh*
Published by *Space Type*

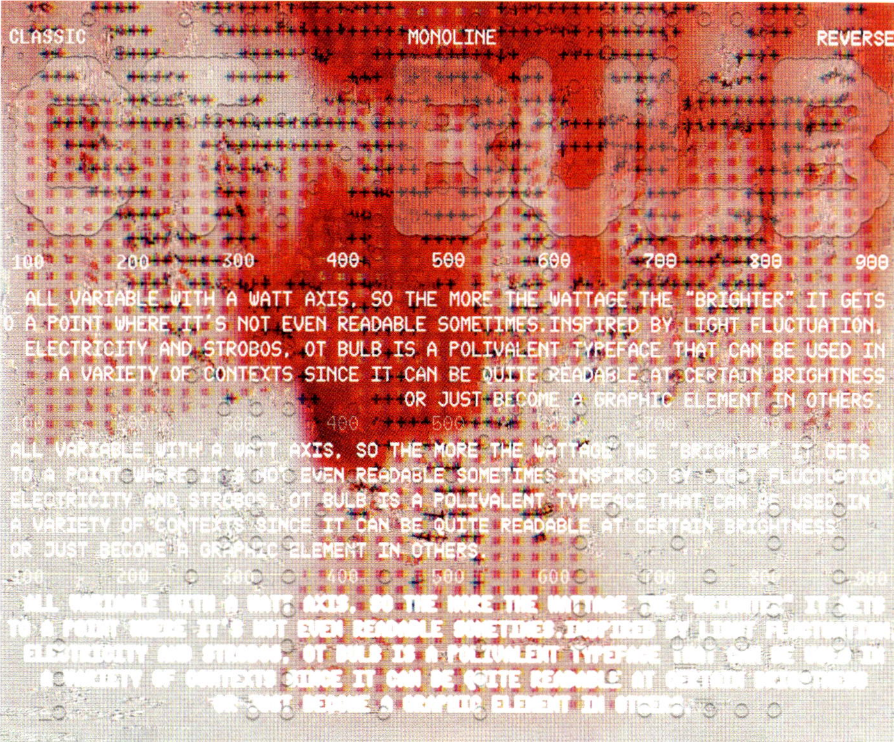

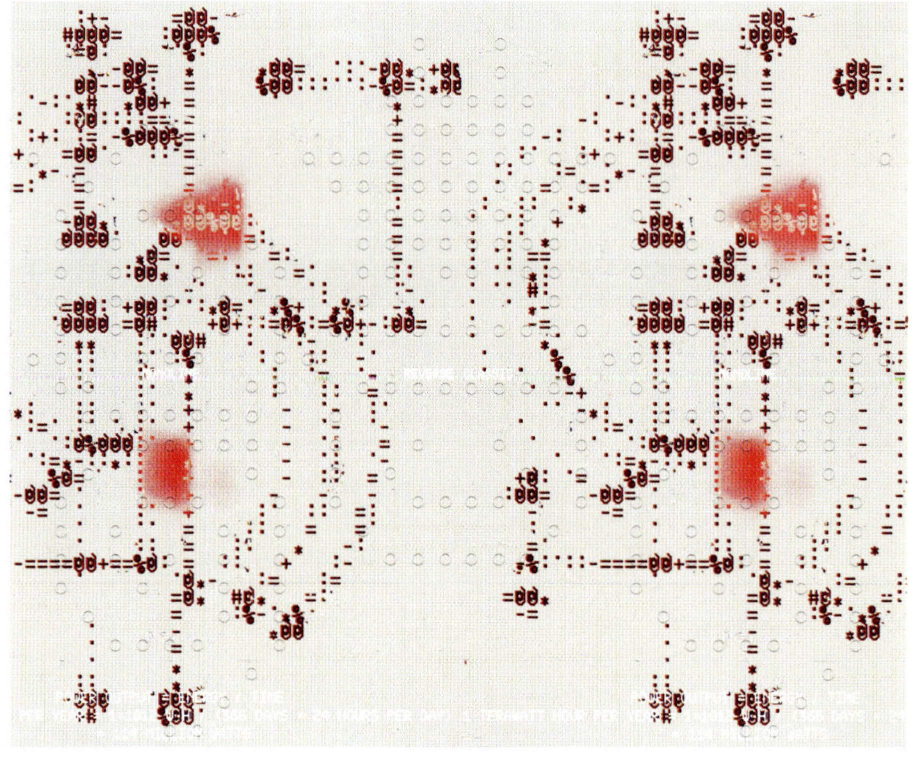

Let there be light! An enduring luminosity to the world of Off Type, OT Bulb infuses the timeless charm of old punch printers with the brilliance of light bulbs, embodying the captivating allure of light leaks—overlapping, growing, and colliding in constellations. In casting a spectacular glow that dances across the page, Bulb has an ineffable splendor, from its shimmering darker weights to its clarifying monoline cut. Unlike traditional weight axes, Bulb employs a unique Watt-based axis, ranging from 100—its dimmest glow—to 900, where it's at its most blurry and brilliant. Radiant in its versatility. Type in a new light. Bulb comprises three distinct sub-families: Bulb Classic with its classic contrast, Bulb Reverse with reverse contrast, and Bulb Monoline. Each family and style is also adorned with a delightful array of icons and glyphs, there to help shed some light on the situation, if necessary.

off-type.com

OT Bulb

Designed by *Mat Desjardins*
Published by *Off Type*

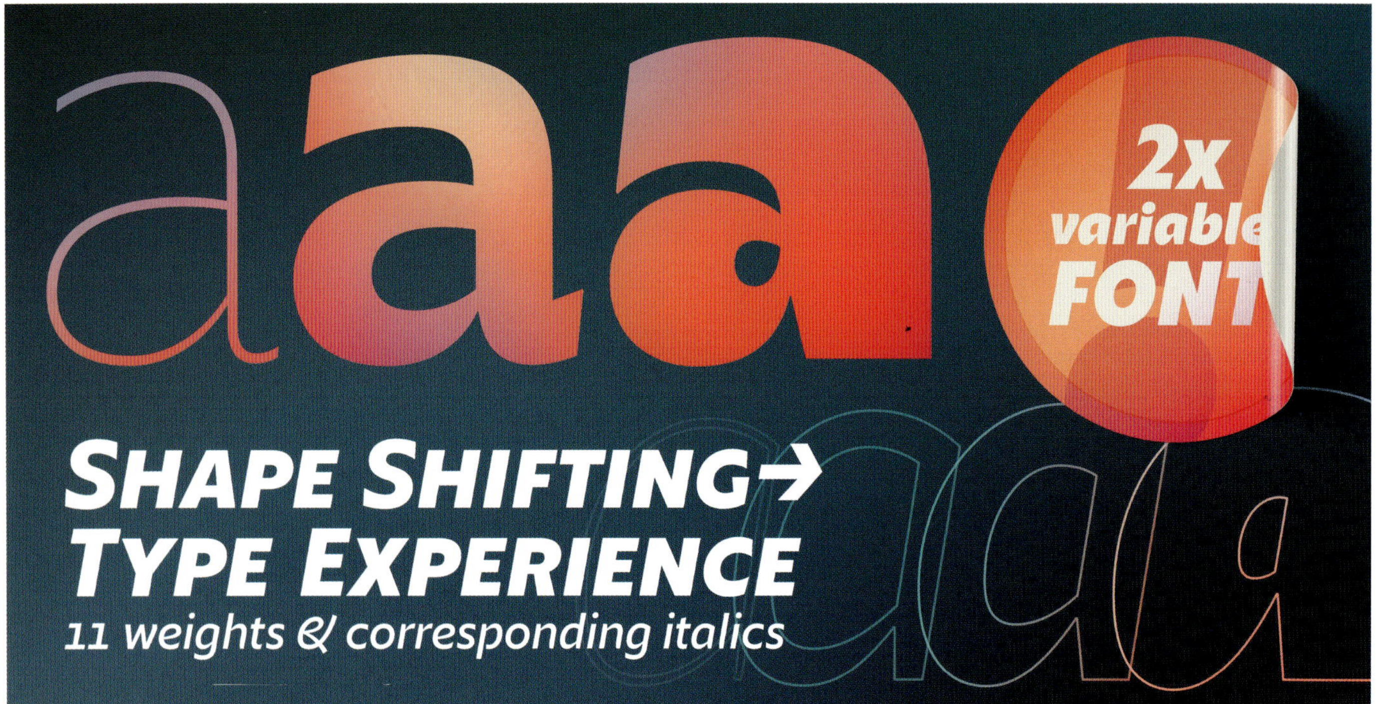

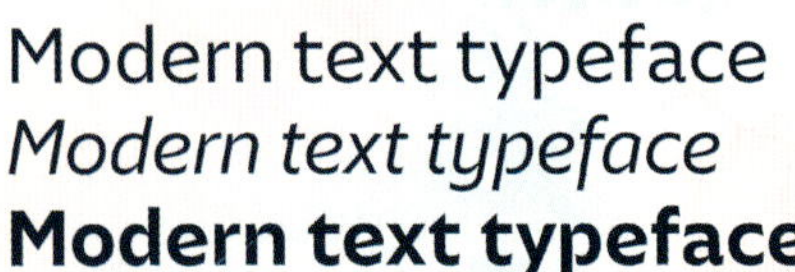

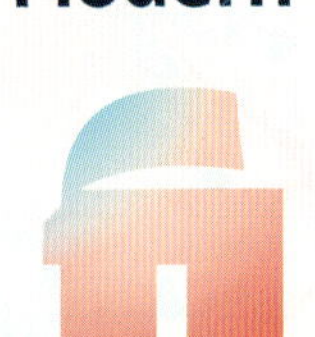

AS THE RANGE OF TYPEFACE DESIGNS INCREASED and requiren
publishers broadened over the centuries, fonts of *specific weig*
or lightness) and *stylistic variants* (most commonly regular or r
distinct to italic, as well as condensed) have led to font familie
of closely related typeface designs that can include hundreds
family is typically *a group of related fonts* which vary only in we

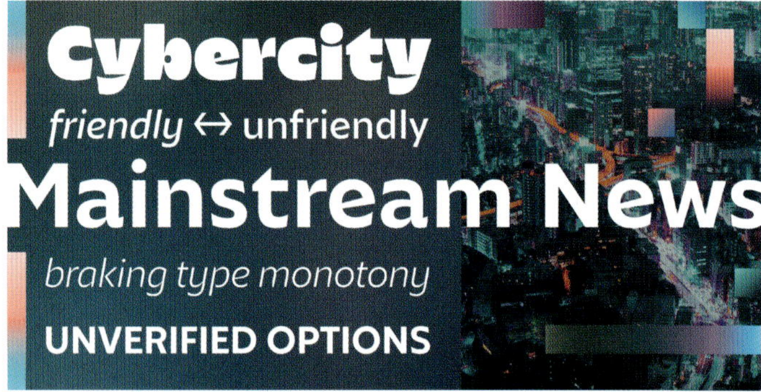

Aa Bb Cc Dd Ee Ff Gg
Hh Ii Jj Kk Ll Mm Nn
Oo Pp Qq Rr Ss Tt Uu

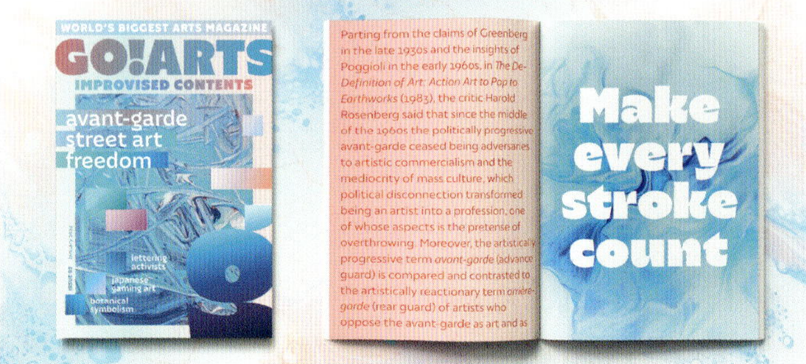

Glycerin is a contemporary geo-humanist sans with an unmistakable personality—clear, confident, and with a radiating style. It has the right mix of precision, elegance, and warmth—perfect for keeping things professional but never boring.

Glycerin

rohhtype.com

Designed by *Roch Modrzejewski*
Published by *ROHH Type Foundry*

Gigafly

contemporary display face

15 OpenType styles
1 variable fonts

funky symbols
daring & powerful design

ROHH

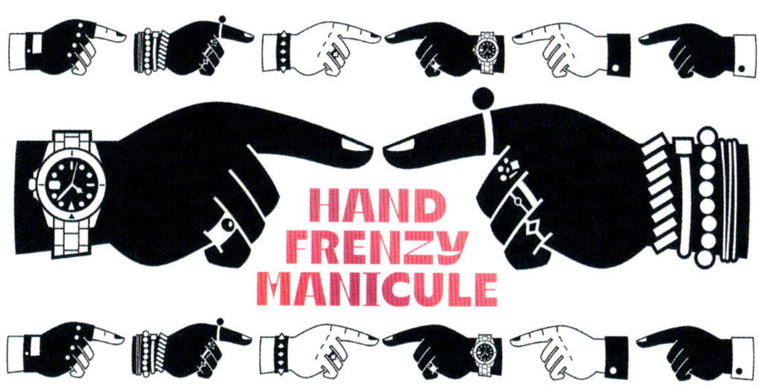

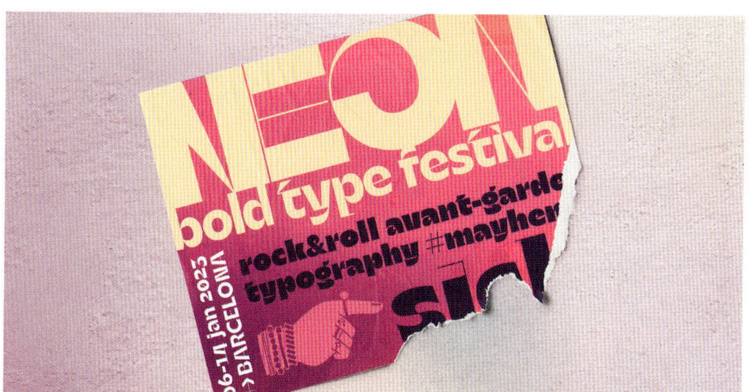

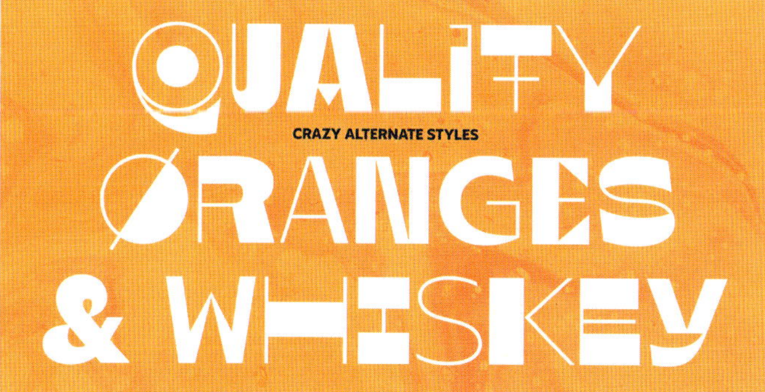

Are you ready for some daring fonts with a side of attitude? If your answer is anywhere around "YES, YES, PLEASE, YES!," then let's hope you're sitting down for this one, as Gigafly is here to ruffle feathers. It's bold, eccentric, and loud—designed for those who think blending in is overrated.

---

rohhtype.com

Gigafly

Designed by *Roch Modrzejewski*
Published by *ROHH Type Foundry*

Blackletter, Script, Calligraphic, Handwritten

Typefaces: Kyrios, designed by Stephen Nixon (page 167); Superscript, designed by Neil Summerour (page 178); Mancine, designed by Matthijs Herzberg (page 180); Playpen Sans, designed by Veronika Burian, Laura Meseguer, José Scaglione (page 188)

While it's certainly true that blackletter, script, calligraphic, and handwritten typefaces can be distinct categories of their own, there's also enough overlap between them—and a fair amount of gray area as the distinctions blend—that they've been grouped together here as a way of representing (very loosely) type that wears the influence of the human hand very much on its sleeve.

Sometimes these genres get bucketed within the somewhat arbitrary category of "decorative" type, but this book takes the opinion that it's the clear visual link to the hand that sets them apart from their serif and sans serif siblings (and keeps them grouped together here rather than in our *Classification-Defying* section).

As ever, this labeling is more a suggestion than a rule. I mean, maybe some of these blackletters are really a bit more *textura,* right?

EXTRA LIGHT	VALLEY MIST TRAIL
LIGHT	CATHEDRAL GROVE
REGULAR	MYSTIC HOLLOW
SEMIBOLD	EMERALD LOOP
BOLD	CASTLE GROVE

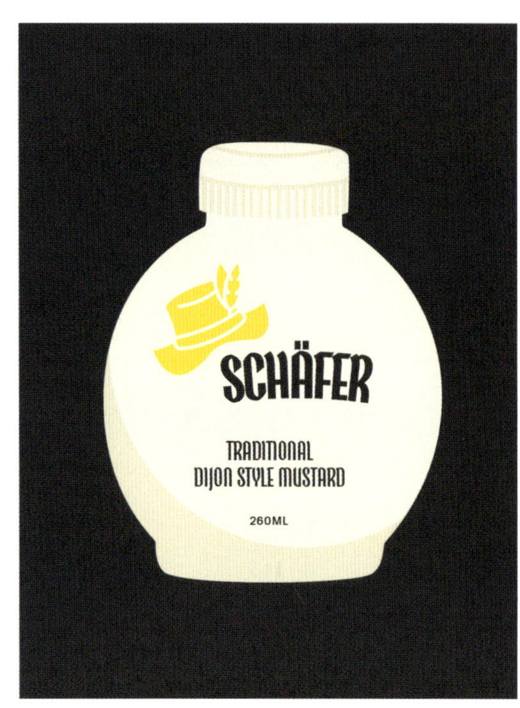

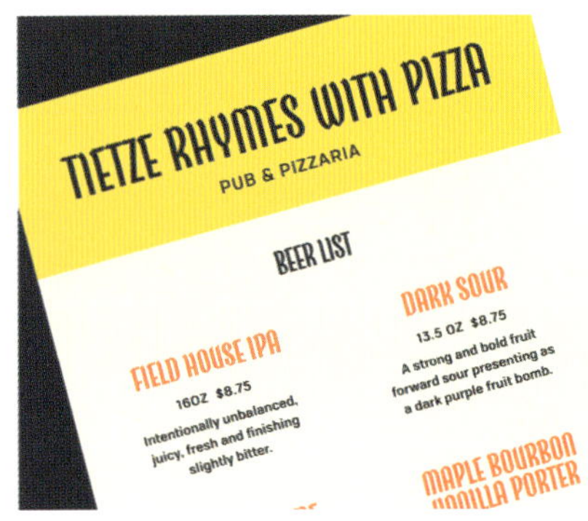

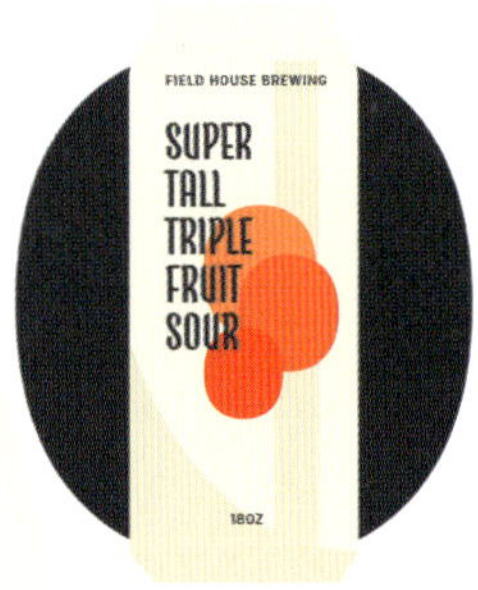

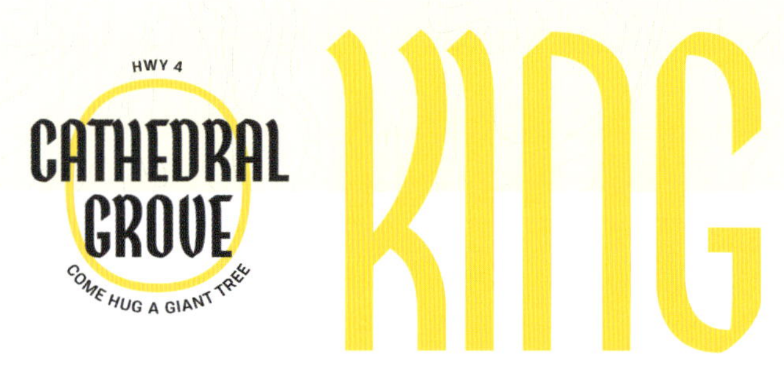

Amberwood is a merging of sans serif and blackletter-style letterforms. With a unique blend of deliberate curves and a solid stance on the baseline, it resembles tall trees in a dense wood.

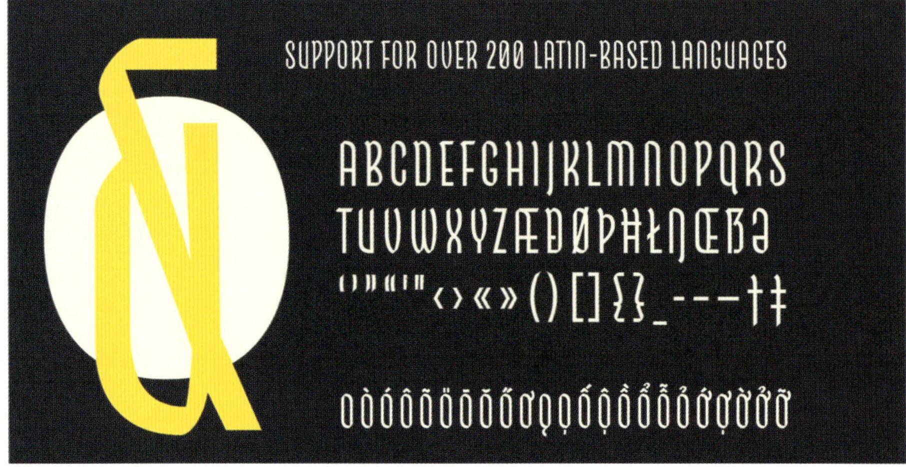

Amberwood

arcanetype.com

Designed by *Alanna Munro*
Published by *Arcane Type Foundry*

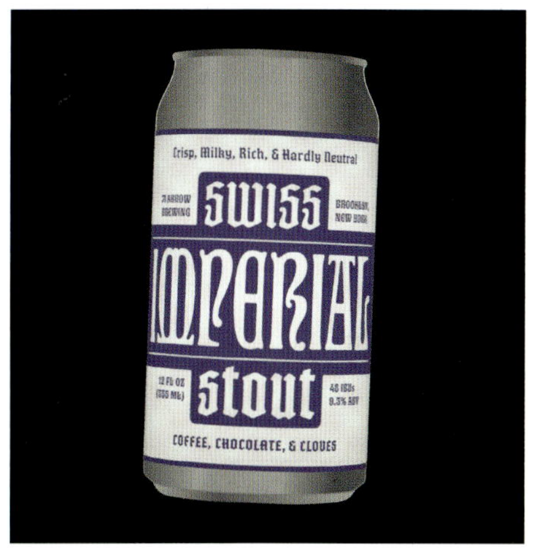

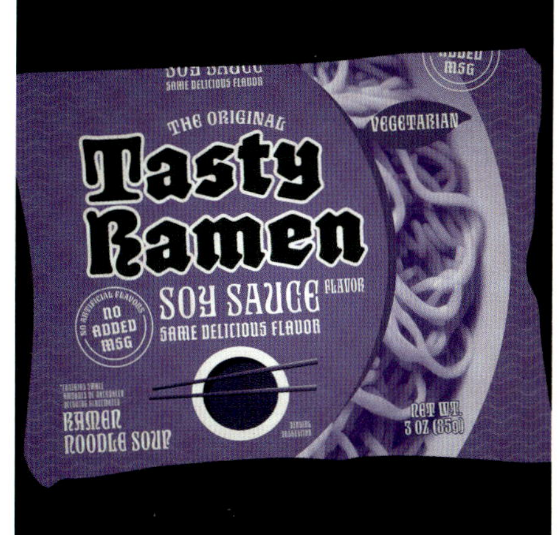

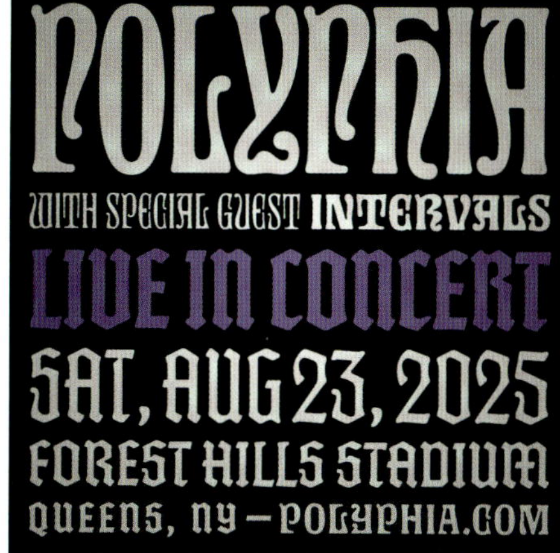

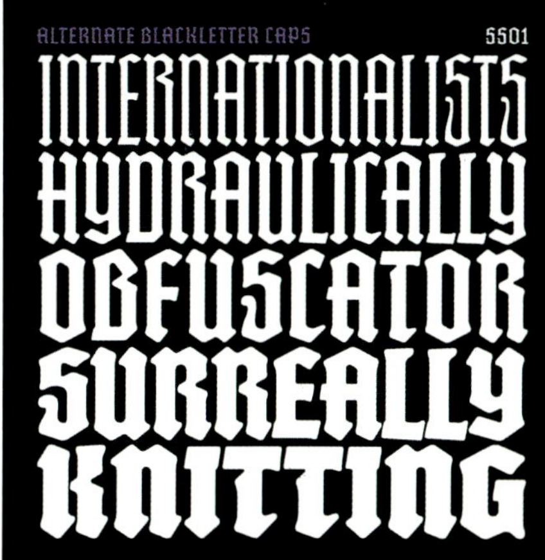

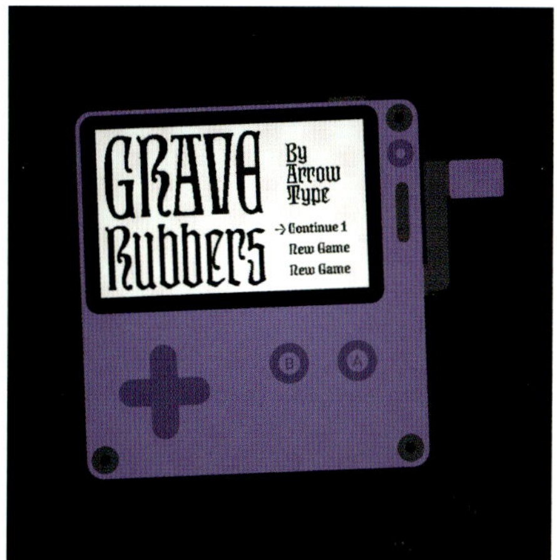

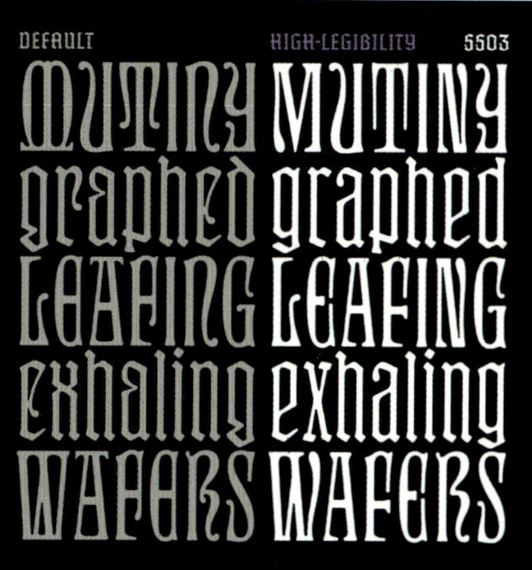

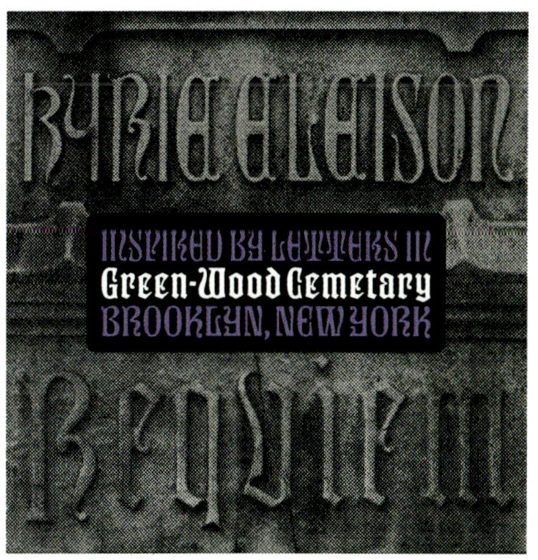

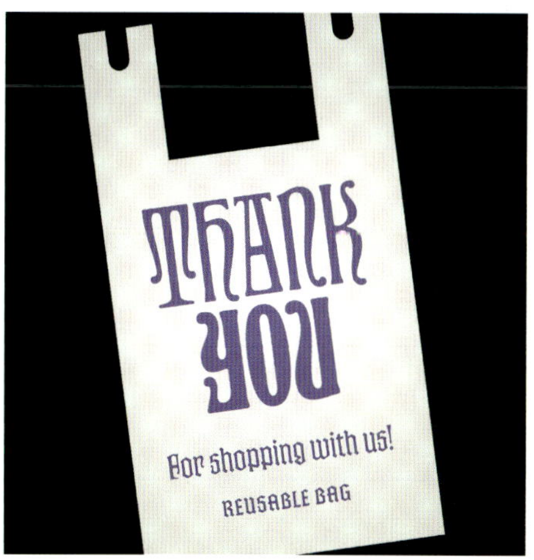

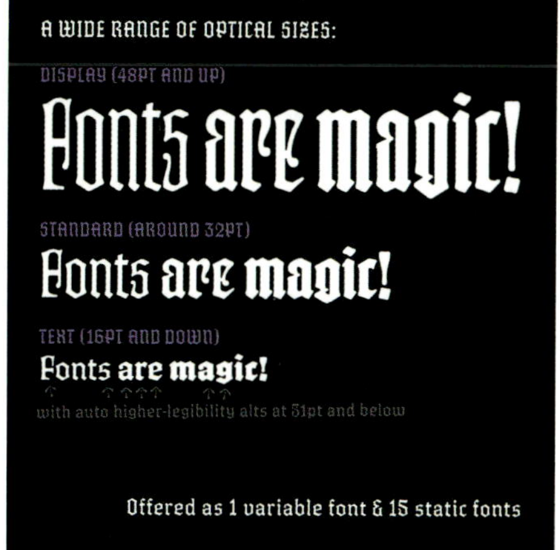

Kyrios is a curious, slightly psychedelic blackletter family. It is an interpretation of lettering from a grave monument carved in the late 1800s, found in the Green-Wood Cemetery in Brooklyn, New York, and is made for modern typographic fun.

arrowtype.com

Kyrios

Designed by *Stephen Nixon*
Published by *ArrowType*

30th ANNIVERSARY COLLECTION

ltimate Modernit

ACE TRACKIN

machine célibatair

ossumovi univerzální robot

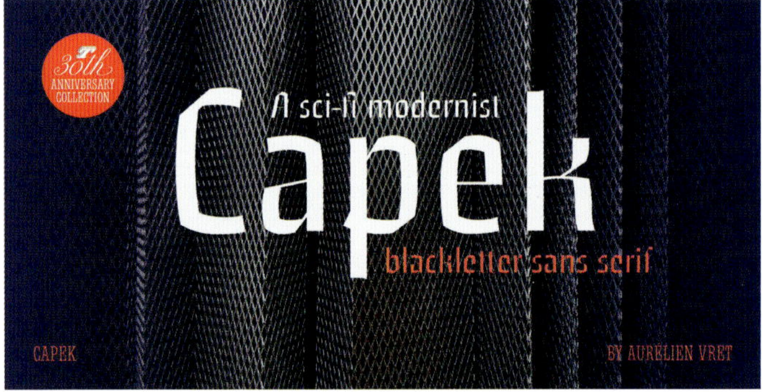

ONLYFANS
Space algorithms
METADATA
73 Triphenedioxazine
Vera Molnár
L'opérateur booléen

G

A NEW TYPEFACE had to be found with a desiGn that
ded to today's taste. Thus we have created it, a mod
typeface, both practical & robust. In recent years, a n
has become manifest in the decorative arts. While t
of the lines has been preserved, the straightness is
distinguished elegance is coming into its own again.
has not been neglected in these developments, whic
expressed by an obvious reversion to certain styles.
of the existing types were old-fashioned & not adapt

Capek is a blackletter sans serif, whose forms are inspired by the technophile universe and science fiction. With its expressionist and modular style, influenced by display faces created in Europe and the United States on the margins of the "New Typography," it's a design that plays with contrasts, intended for display and short texts.

Capek

typofonderie.com

Designed by *Aurélien Vret*
Published by *Typofonderie*

Der Froschkönig
Hänsel und Gretel
Die Bremer Stadtmusikanten

AaBbCcDdEeFf
GgHhIiJjKkLlMm
NnOoPpQqRrSsTt
UuVvWwXxYyZz
&!?1234567890

AaBbCcDdEeFf
GgHhIiJjKkLlMm
NnOoPpQqRrSsTt
UuVvWwXxYyZz
&!?1234567890

AaBbCcDdEeFf
GgHhIiJjKkLlMm
NnOoPpQqRrSsTt
UuVvWwXxYyZz
&!?1234567890

abcdefghijklmnopqrst
uvwxyz 1234567890 & .,:;“”
ABCDEFGHIJKLMNOPQ
RSTUVWXYZ !? []{}()

JAF Lapture is an unusual hybrid typeface combining blackletter and roman type. Updated in 2025, it now includes extra heavy weights and condensed styles.

justanotherfoundry.com

JAF Lapture

Designed by *Tim Ahrens*
Published by *Just Another Foundry*

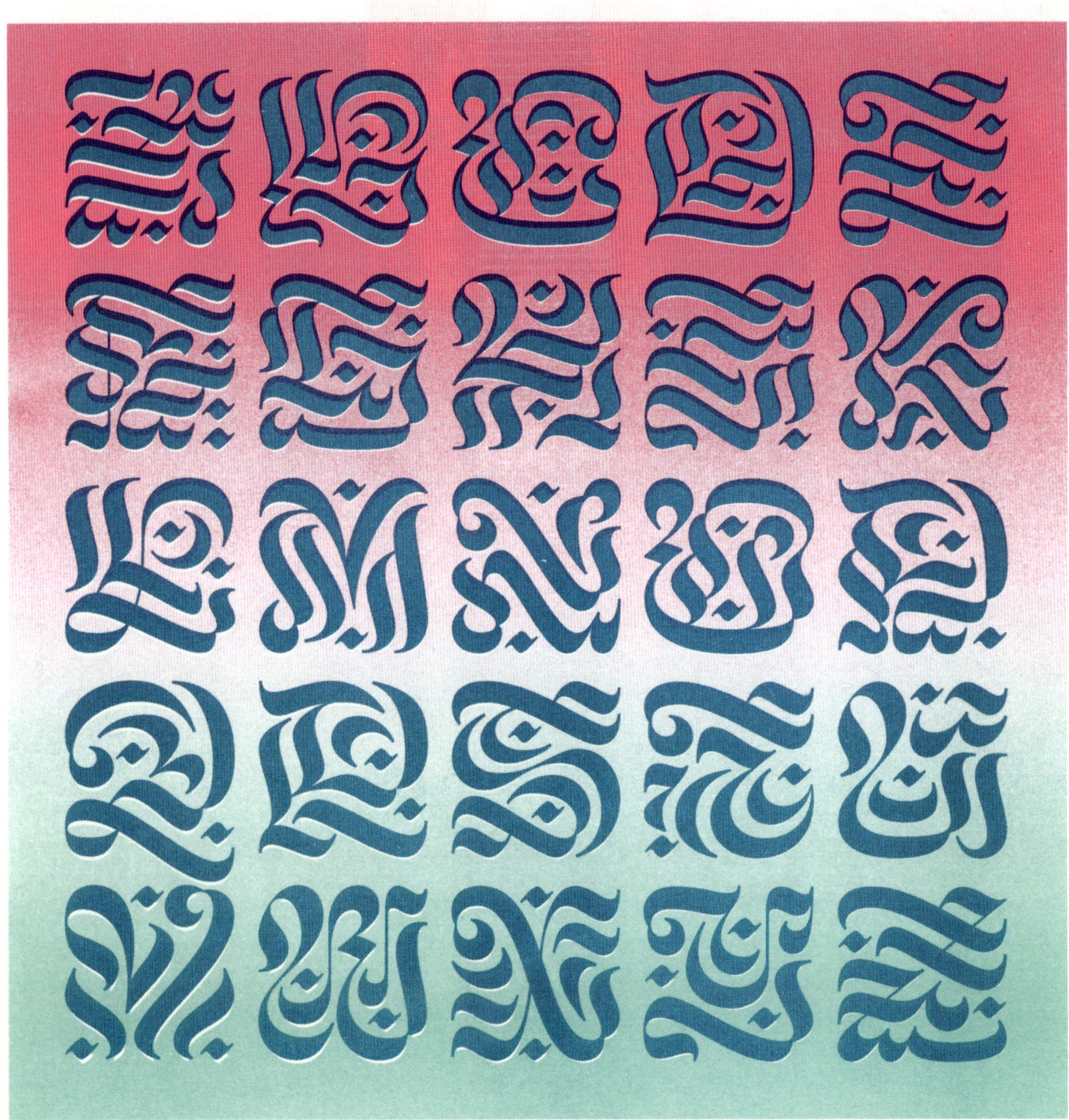

An experimental calligraphic typeface inspired by the vastness of the cosmos and the edges of possibility, capturing the fluidity and dynamism of celestial movement.

Nebulis

spacetypeco.com

Designed by *Lynne Yun, Kevin Yeh*
Published by *Space Type*

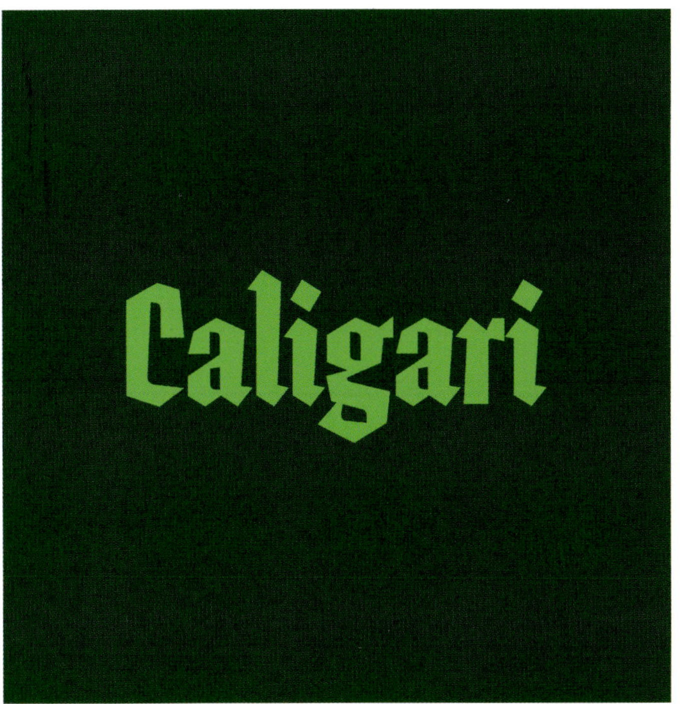

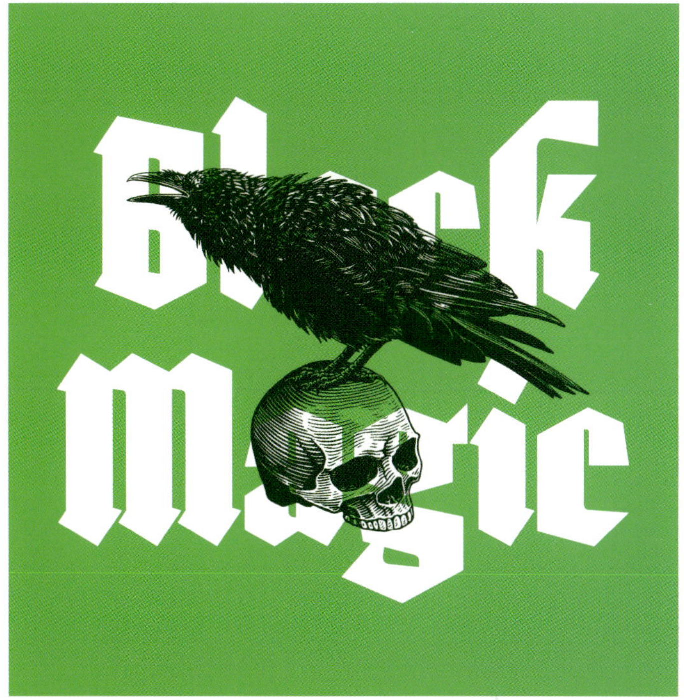

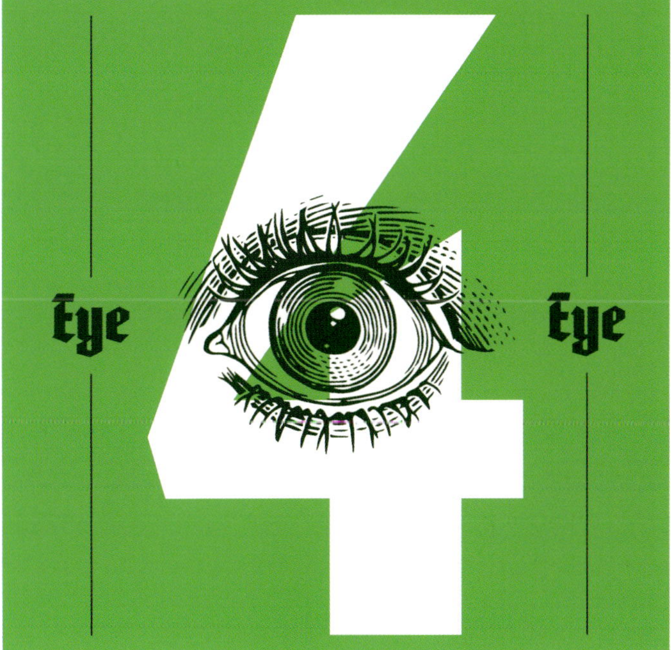

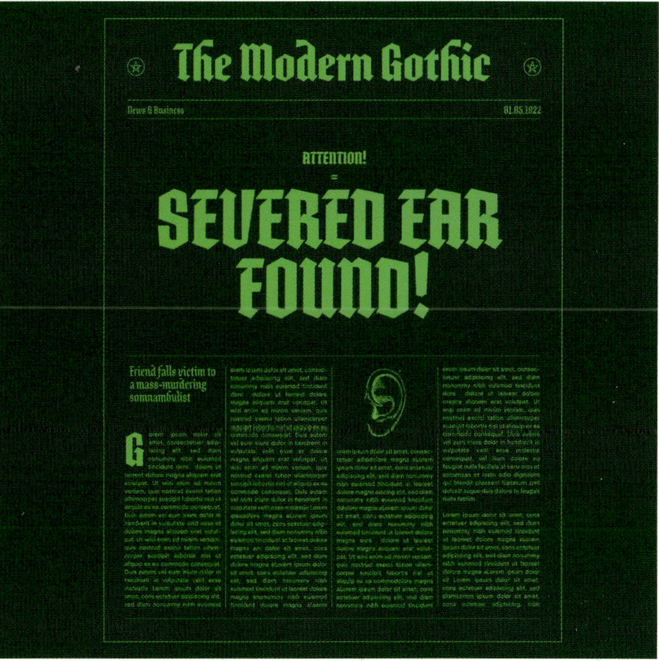

Blackletter is a genre steeped in history and ripe for modernization. Named after the titular character of the first true horror film, F37 Caligari is as vivid and expressive as its namesake. It embraces the limitations of a traditional Textura hand, but dials up the angularity and sharpness of the style for a modern audience, well past anything a medieval scribe would dare to do. F37 Caligari is available in six weights. Throughout the weights, the energy of the typeface changes. The lighter weights are made up of uniform and parallel strokes, while the heavier weights from flared and lively strokes. F37 Caligari also comes with swashed capitals, perfect for drop caps, logos, or your next illuminated manuscript.

---

f37foundry.com

F37 Caligari

Designed by *Rodrigo Fuenzalida*
Published by *F37 Foundry*

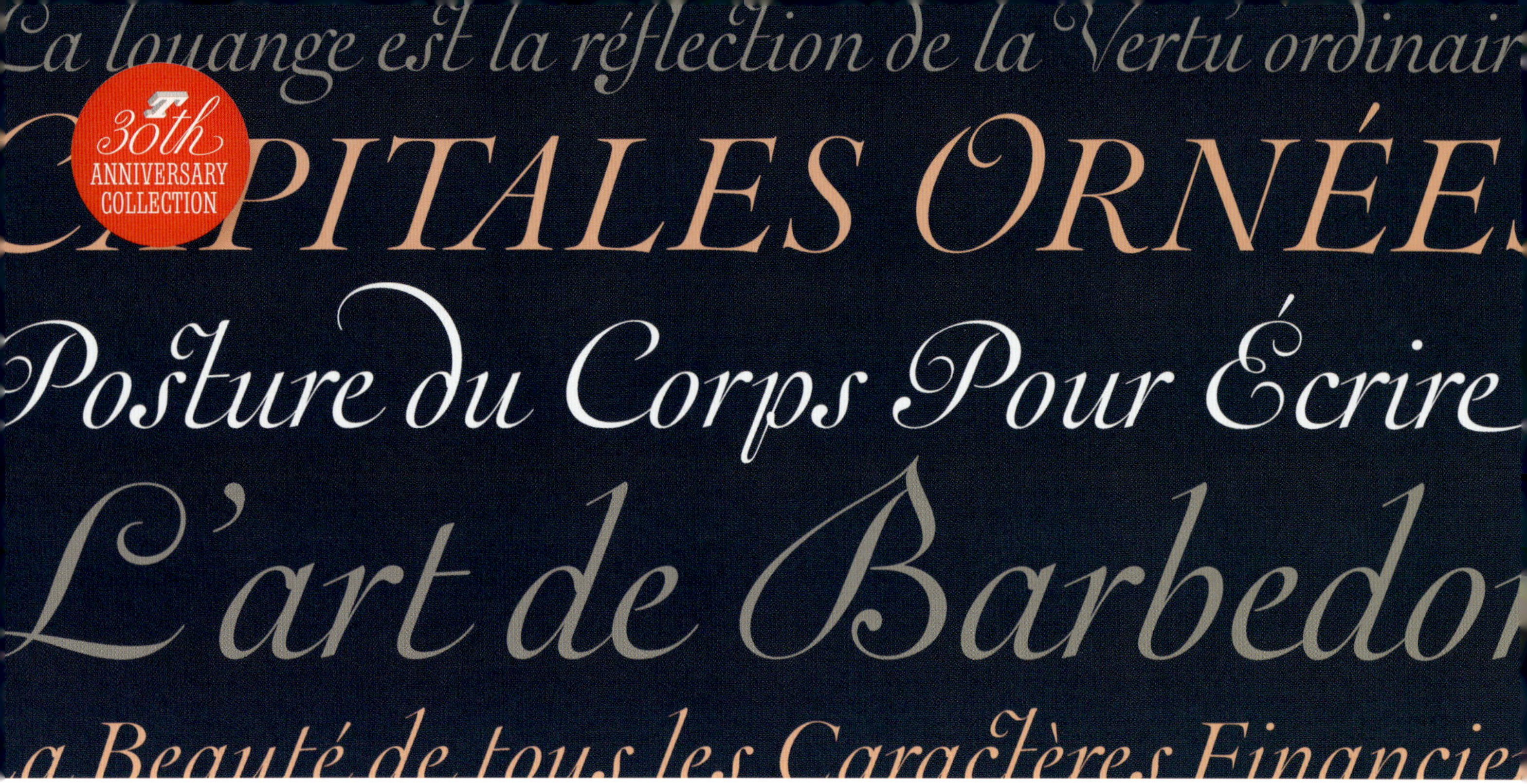

La louange est la réflection de la Vertu ordinair

30th ANNIVERSARY COLLECTION

CAPITALES ORNÉES

Posture du Corps Pour Écrire

L'art de Barbedor

La Beauté de tous les Caractères Financie

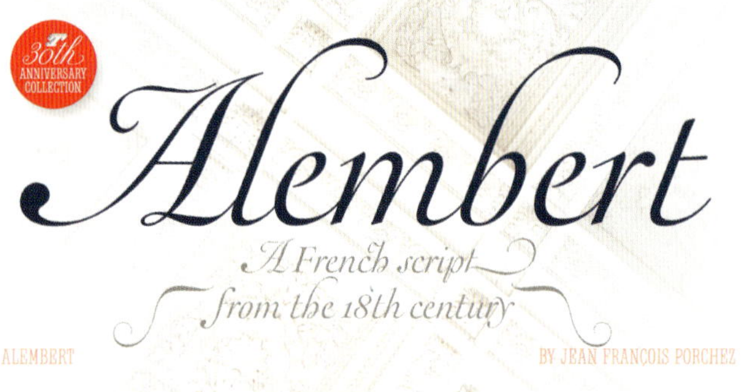

Alembert draws its influence from the work of the maitres écrivains *(master writers) of seventeenth- and eighteenth-century France, particularly the Bâtardes and Coulées script models. It can be seen to bridge the gap between typographic italics, roman type companions, and the Anglaise (copperplate) script that emerged in the nineteenth century. Offering a warmer, less rigid alternative to the Anglaise script, Alembert adds a refined touch to graphic projects.*

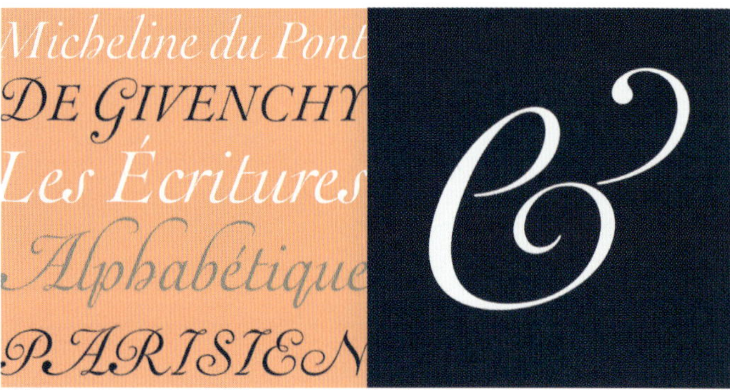

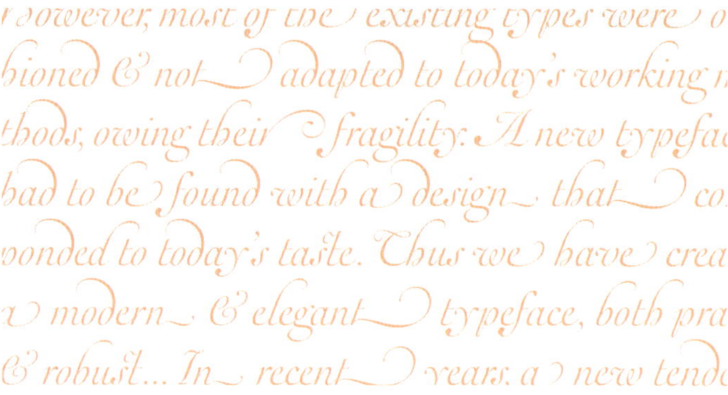

owever, most of the existing types were o
hioned & not adapted to today's working m
thods, owing their fragility. A new typefa
had to be found with a design that co
ponded to today's taste. Thus we have crea
a modern & elegant typeface, both pra
& robust... In recent years, a new tend

Alembert

typofonderie.com

Designed by *Jean François Porchez*
Published by *Typofonderie*

LDN BOW SCRIPT CHARACTER SET (INCLUDES MANY ALT LIGATURES)

LDN BOW SCRIPT THIN DESIGNED BY PAUL HARPIN

London Bow Script. Inspired by a dedication to John Milton
by John Dryden on a wall plaque at Saint Mary-le-Bow church.

Loads of
Lush, Loveable,
Letterforms And
Luxurious, Lovely,
Lavish Ligatures.
Lucky you!

Designed by Paul Harpin Esq in Blackheath, London SE3.
ANNO MMXXIII
The London Type Foundry

LDN BOW SCRIPT — THIN, LIGHT, REGULAR AND BOLD

London Bow Script Thin

London Bow Script Light

London Bow Script Regular

London Bow Script Bold

LDN Bow Script was inspired by a memorial plaque to the Republican poet John Milton, spotted high up on the wall of Saint Mary-le-Bow Church. Unusually, the weight of the lowercase strokes are at the top and bottom, but when they come together with the caps, and simpler small caps, they blend together harmoniously. LDN Bow Script is loaded with extra ligatures, swashes, and alternate characters.

londontype.co.uk

LDN Bow Script

Designed by *Paul Harpin*
Published by *The London Type Foundry*

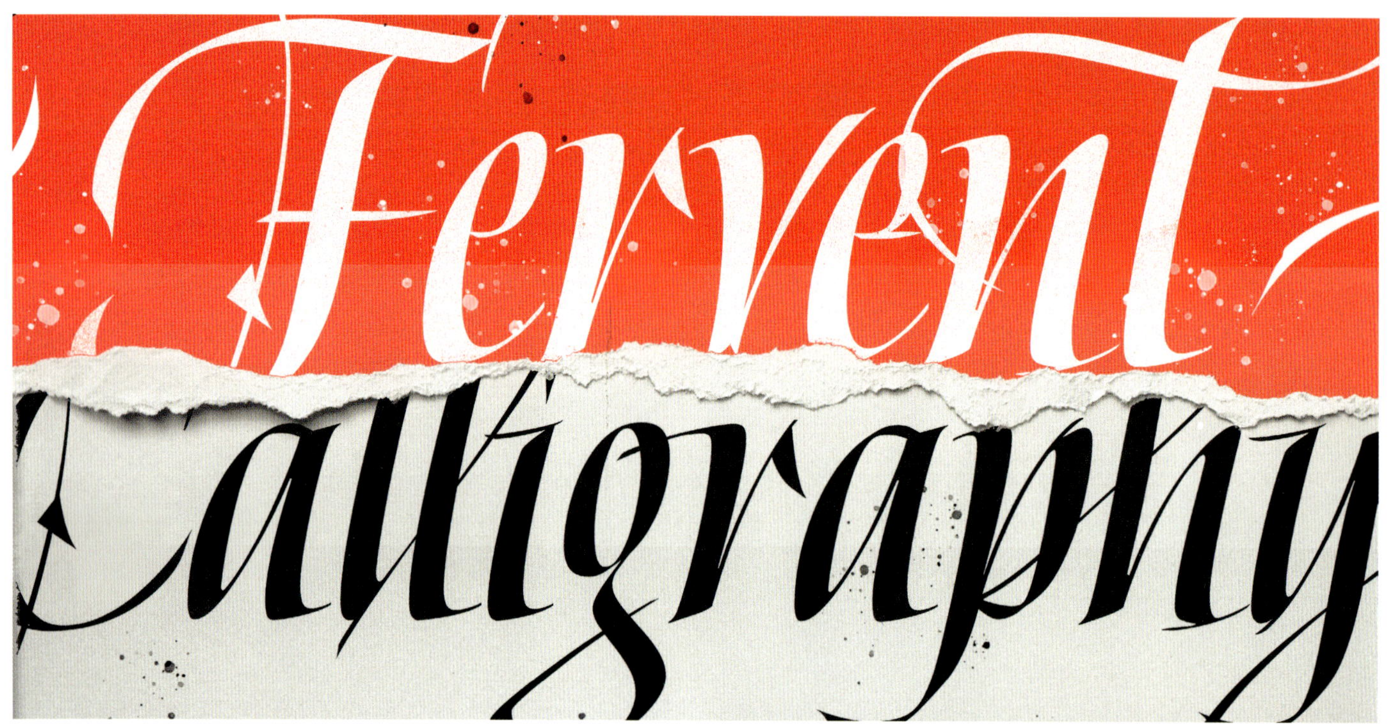

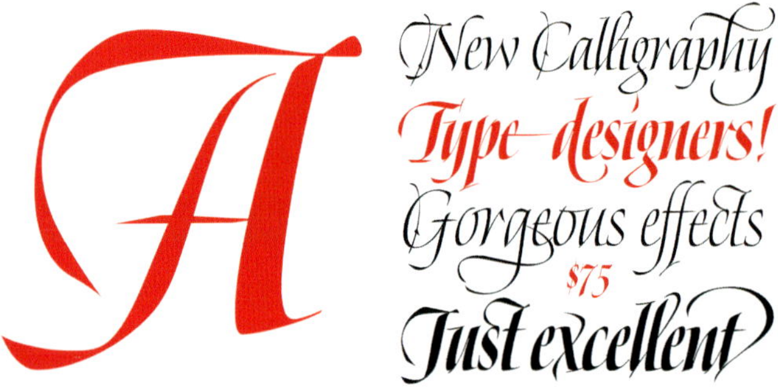

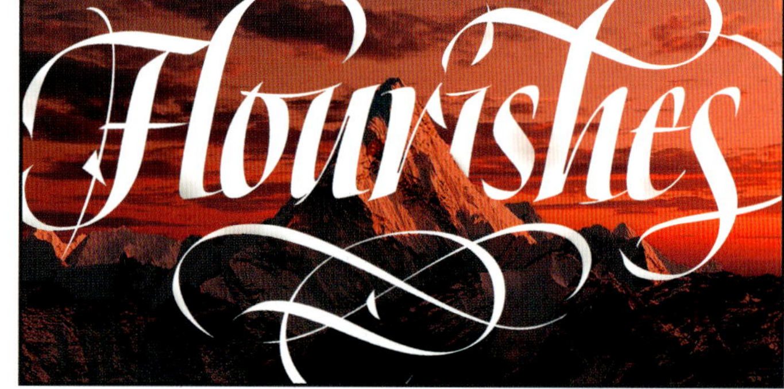

wi Type conference of
ish are about **letters** and
s. Must have a great th

Gratia is a mesmerizing blend of serenity and intensity in a script. With its angular curves, it takes cues from the timeless elegance of Cancelleresca calligraphy. The typeface is infused with Sproviero's unmistakable expressiveness and sense of movement as it embodies speed, sophistication, and versatility. Its extensive range of alternates provides ample opportunities for creative exploration. From fashion spreads to international brands, Gratia adds a touch of elegance to every project.

Gratia

sproviero-type.com

Designed by *Maximiliano Sproviero*
Published by *Sproviero Type*

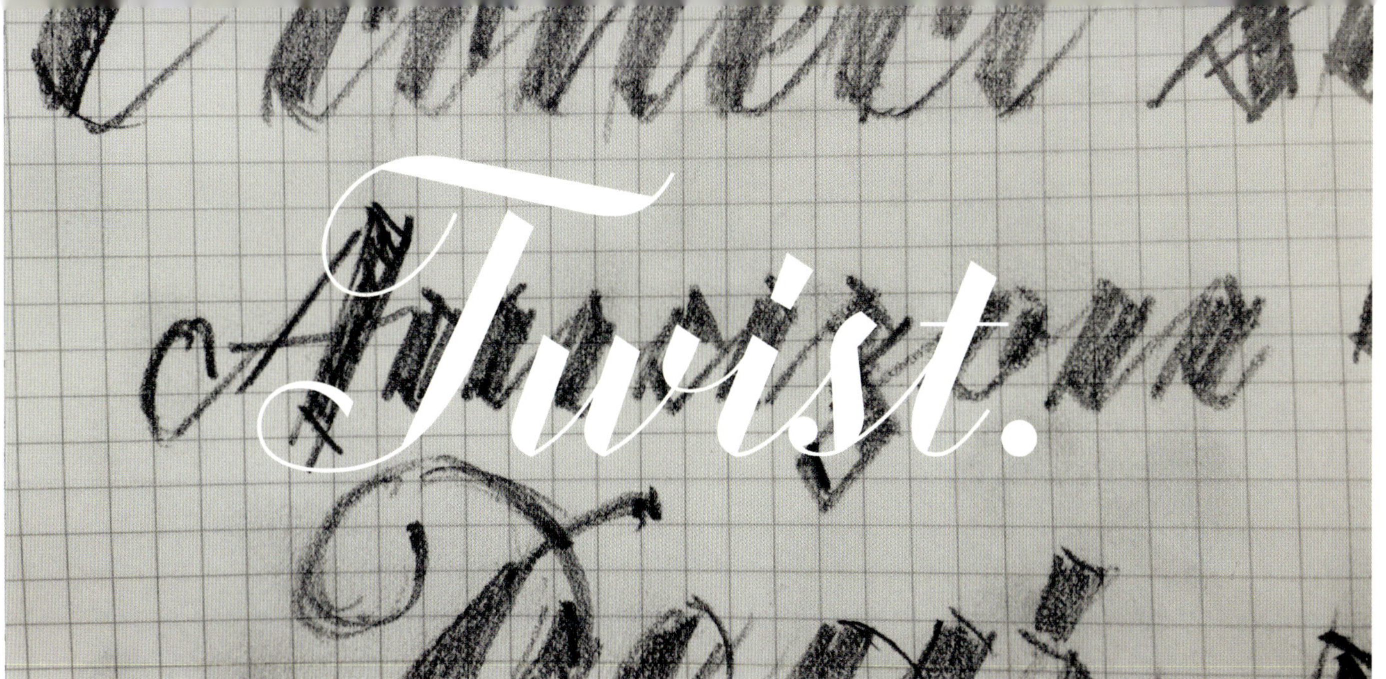

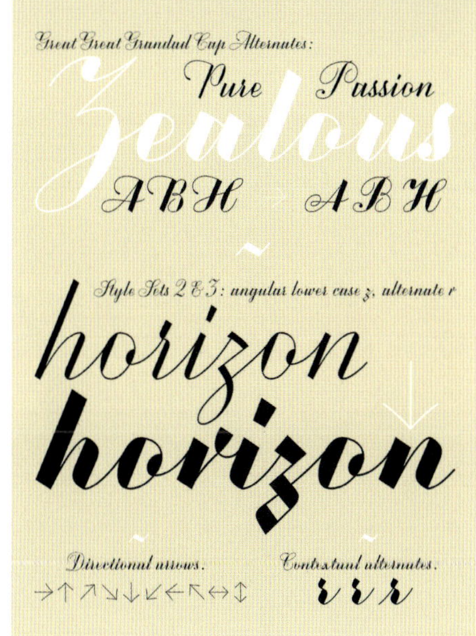

As the name suggests, this typeface is a constructed Copperplate script, an archaic style given a modern typographic twist. Copperscript comes with six base weights ranging from ExtraLight to ExtraBold, but there are infinite options available along the weight axis in the variable version of the font. The typeface contains a series of lead-in and end characters, which kick in automatically when the contextual alternates feature is active. Copperscript reads beautifully at all sizes and includes directional arrows, an alternate set of caps, and lowercase r and z stylistic set variations.

The Joy of Six:

contrasted
connected
contoured
contextual
constructed
copperscript

Copperscript comes with six base weights ranging from ExtraLight to ExtraBold but of course there are infinite options available along the weight axis in the variable version of the font which is bundled with the family pack. The typeface contains a series of lead-in and end characters which kick in automatically when the contextual alternates feature is active. Copperscript reads beautifully at all sizes.

g-type.com

Copperscript

Designed by *Nick Cooke*
Published by *G-Type*

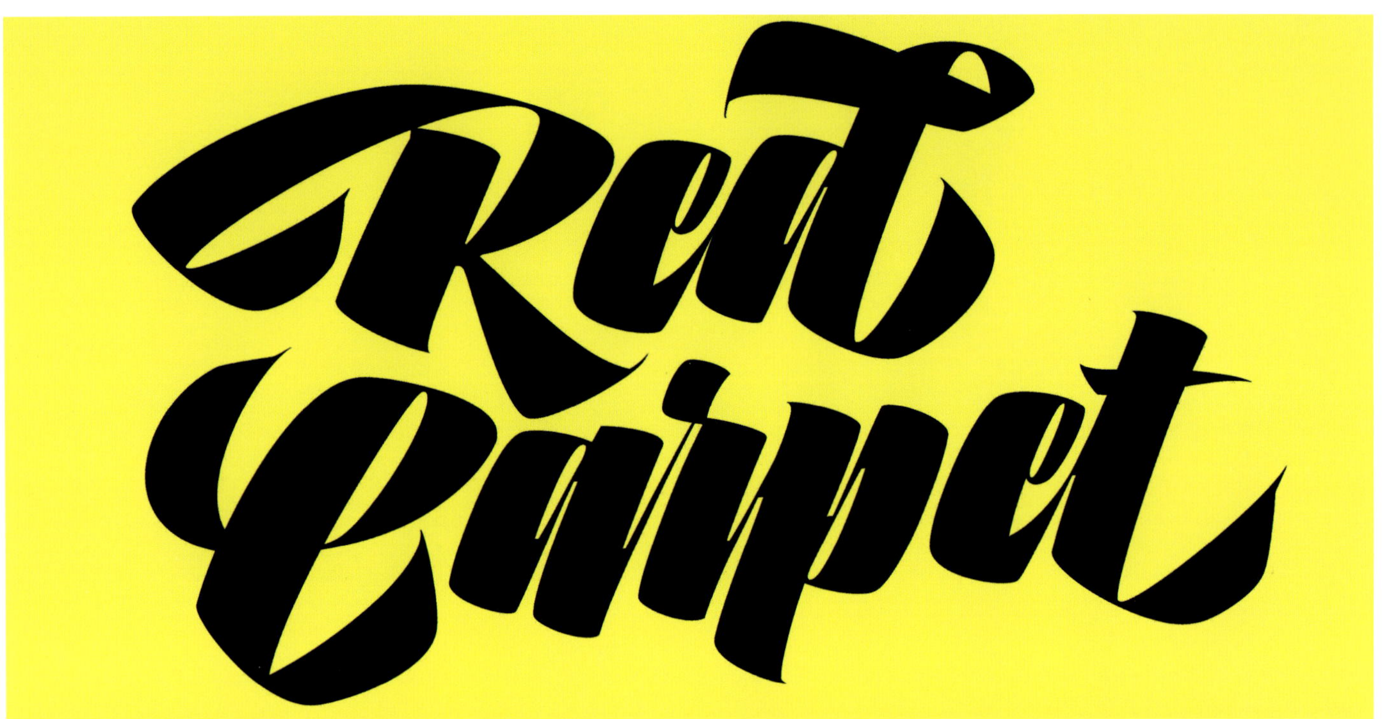

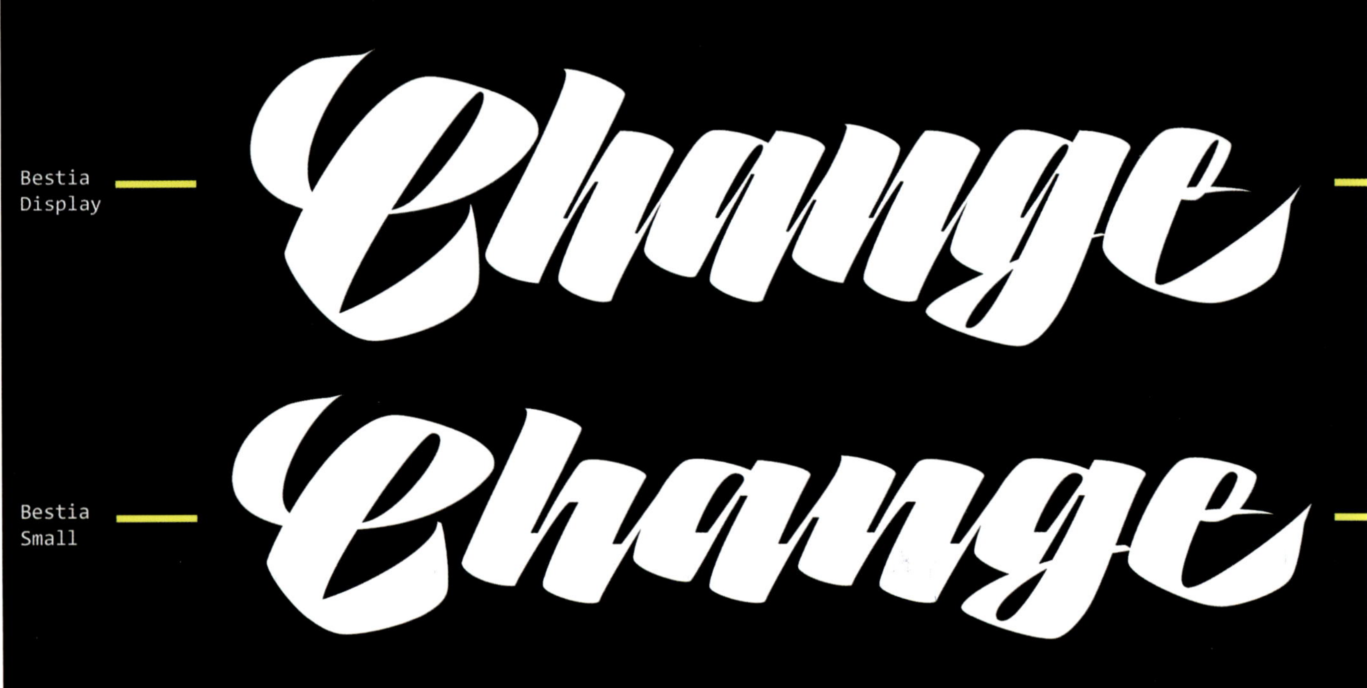

Bestia is a high-contrast brush script that commands attention with bold sweeping strokes inspired by Max's pointed brush calligraphy practice. Conveying raw energy, the gestural forms are perfect for high-end brands and glossy magazines. Subtle shifts in contrast provide dramatic emphasis for large type and improved readability at smaller sizes. Available as a variable font or in four styles: Display, Heading, Subhead, and Small.

Bestia

sproviero-type.com

Designed by *Maximiliano Sproviero*
Published by *Sproviero Type*

هرتل و هرتسفلد، گشتاسپ، شاه حامی زرتشت
همان گشتاسپ، پدر داریوش هخامنشی بدانند
اما از آنجا که در اوستا هیچ اشاره‌ای به شاهان
هخامنشی نیست و جغرافیای آن در مناطق دورد
شرقی ایران است، عده‌ای از دانشمندان را برآن
داشته که درباره این تاریخ تجدید نظر کنند.

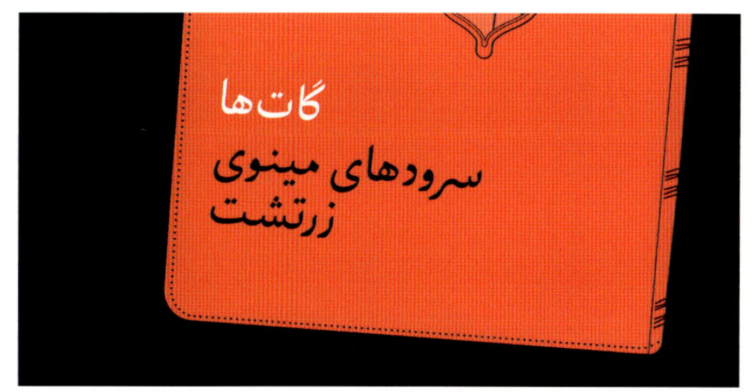

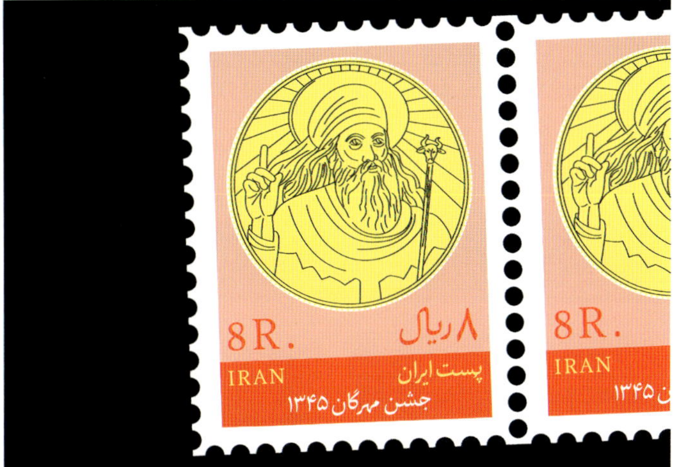

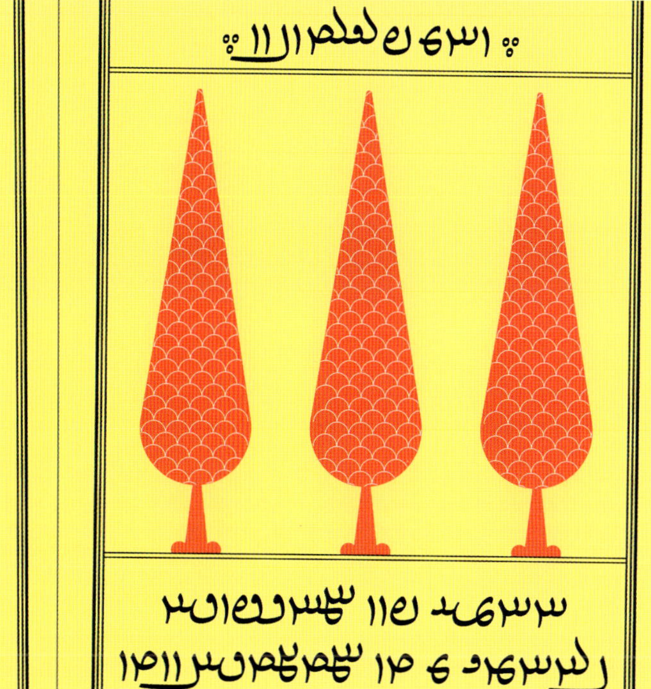

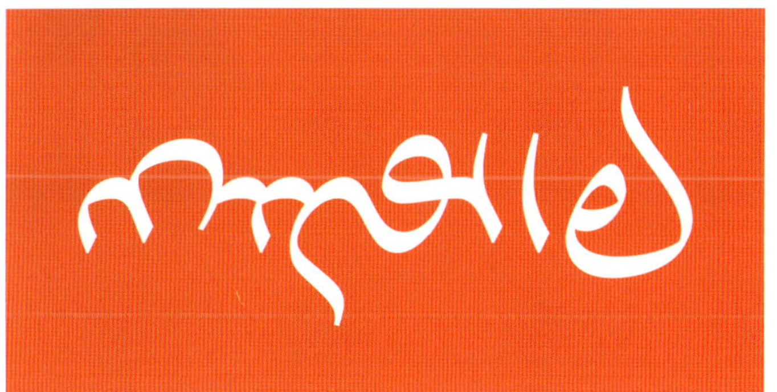

الفبای دین دبیره

Mehraban Avestan is a typeface designed for texts in the Avestan script used in Middle Persian studies and in Zoroastrian communities. Mehraban Book Pahlavi is the first typeface designed for the Book Pahlavi script of ancient Persia. Developed from a careful study of manuscript specimens, adapted for contemporary typesetting projects.

rosettatype.com

Mehraban Avestan

Designed by *Amir Mahdi Moslehi*
Published by *Rosetta*

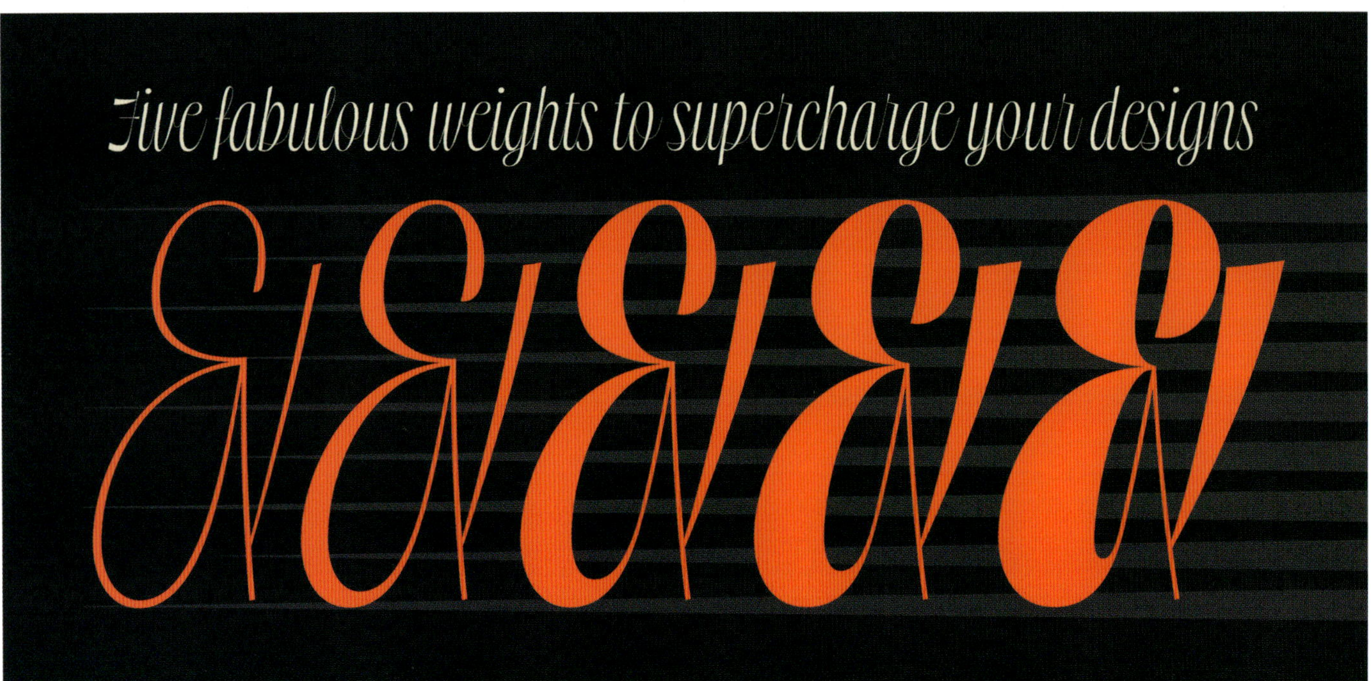

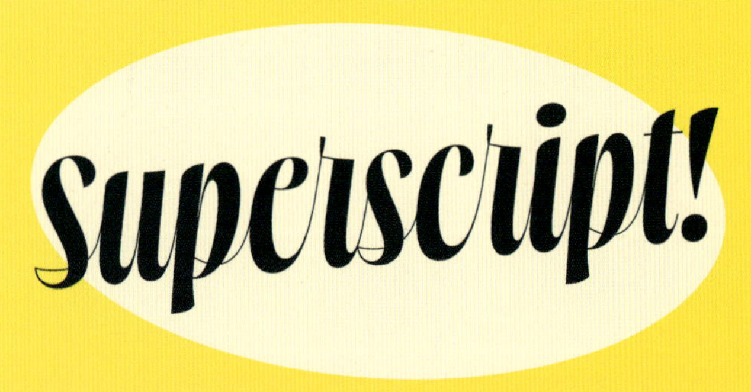

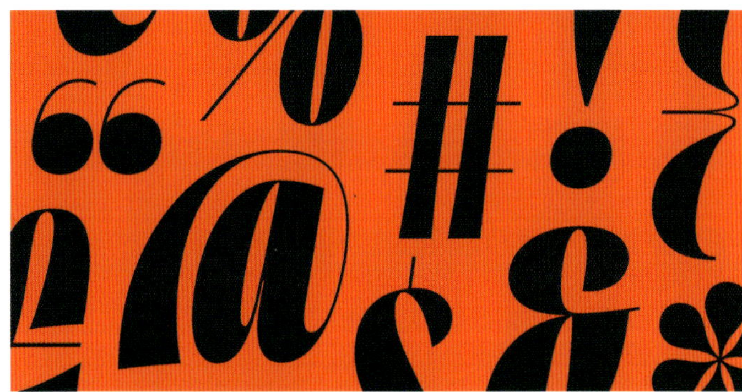

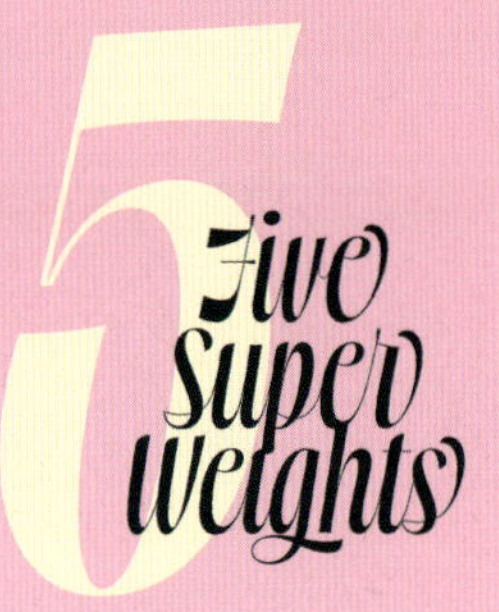

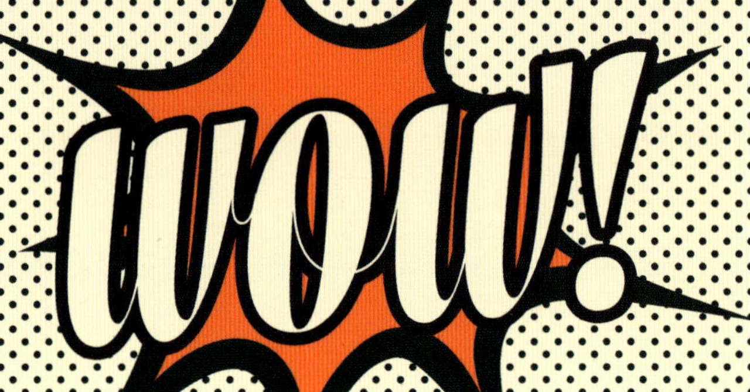

Superscript started as a personal challenge: sumi brush doodles of compressed, high-contrast, connected script letterforms. It eventually expanded into a multi-weight typeface thanks to Potch Auacherdkul, who insisted it needed a Thin weight. He was right—and the result speaks for itself.

Superscript

positype.com

Designed by *Neil Summerour*
Published by *Positype*

Magnetohydrodynamics
Hypercholesterolaemia
Compartmentalisation
Sphygmomanometer
Uncomprehendingly

Localized Expression
trải nghiệm sâu sắc
with Language Support

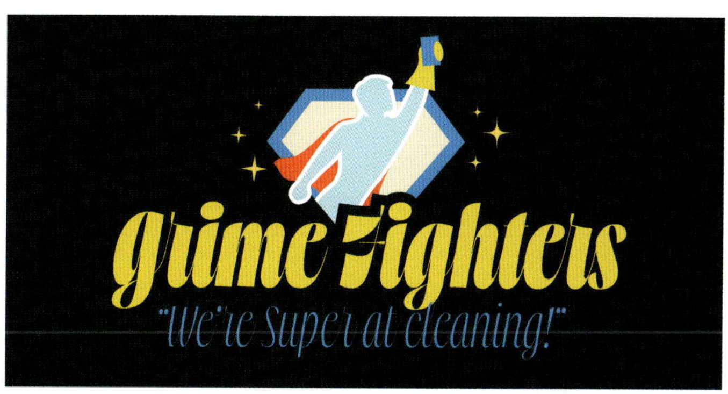

who lives in Gotham City.
e witnesses the murder of his parents, Thomas and
Wayne, in a mugging gone wrong when he is just
This traumatic event shapes his future and motivate
seek justice. Determined to rid Gotham City of crim
Wayne dedicates his life to becoming the vigilante
ighter known as Batman. He trains himself physical
entally to the peak of human capability and adopts
me bat-inspired costume to strike fear into the hea
alter ego is known for using his int

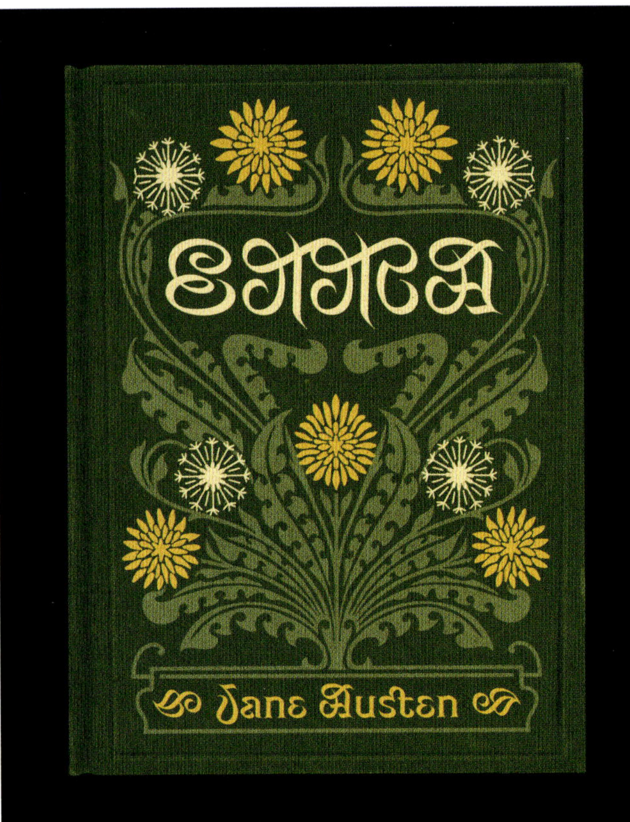

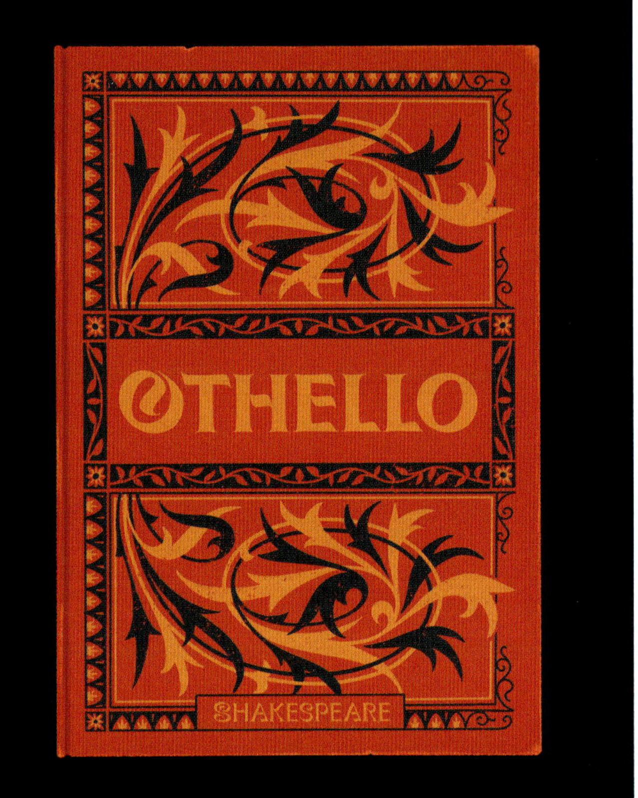

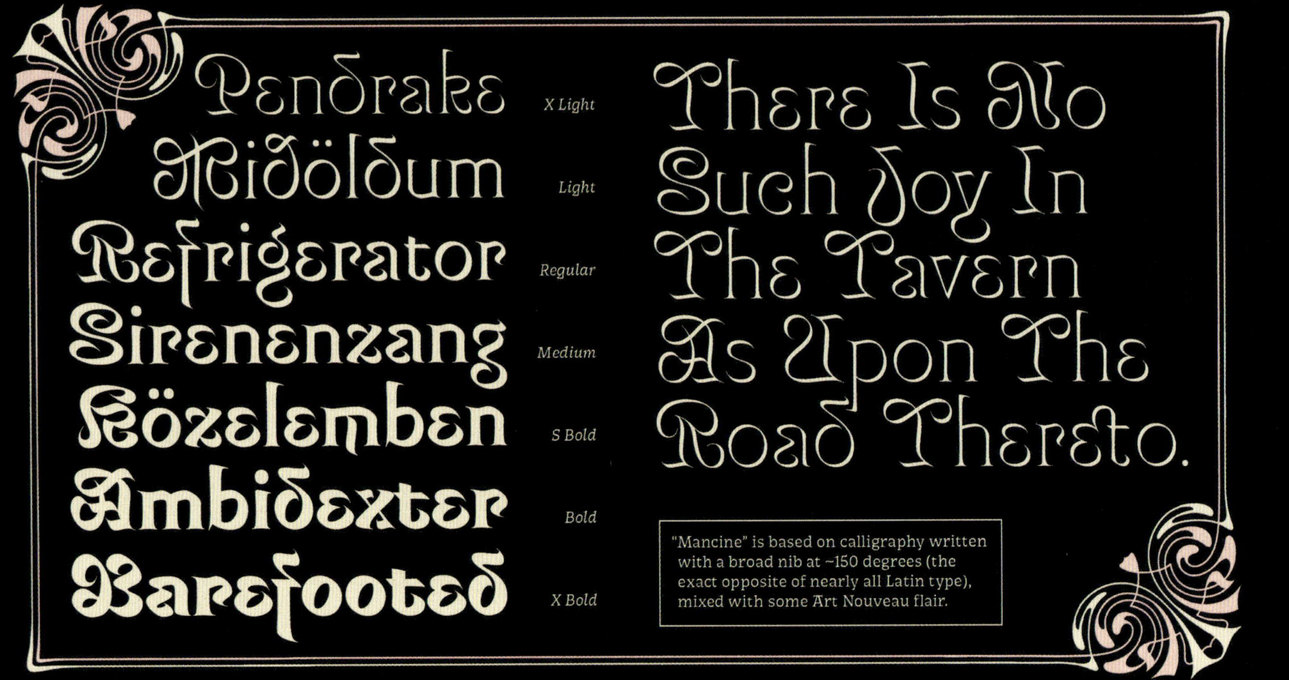

Mancine

herzbergdesign.com

Designed by *Matthijs Herzberg*
Published by *Herzberg Design Co*

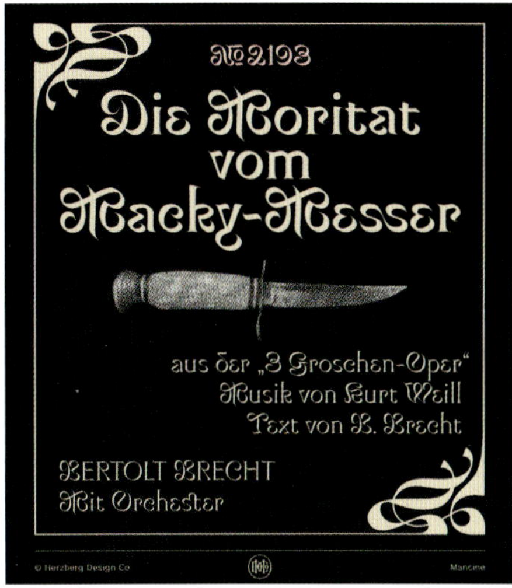

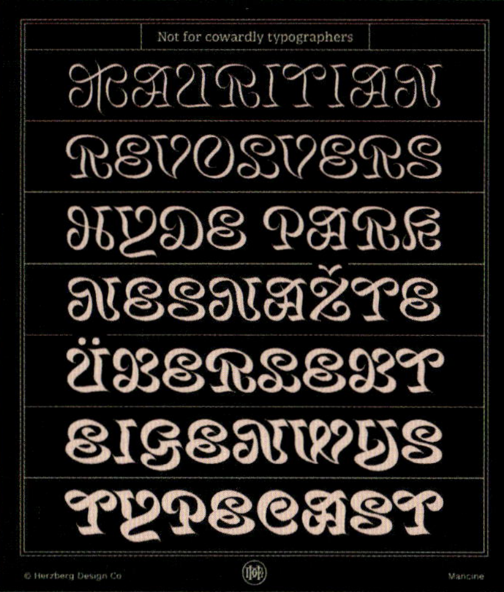

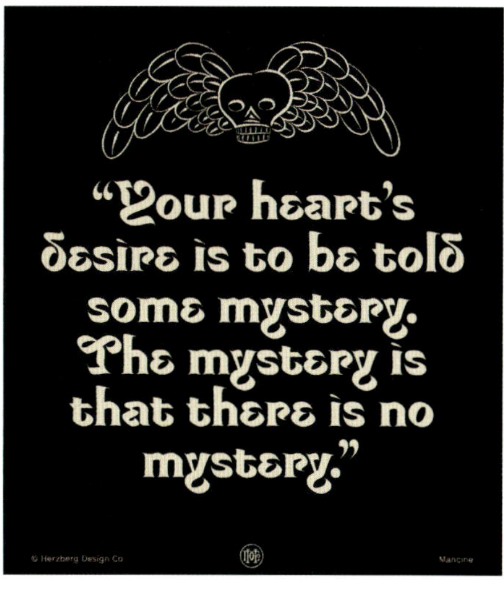

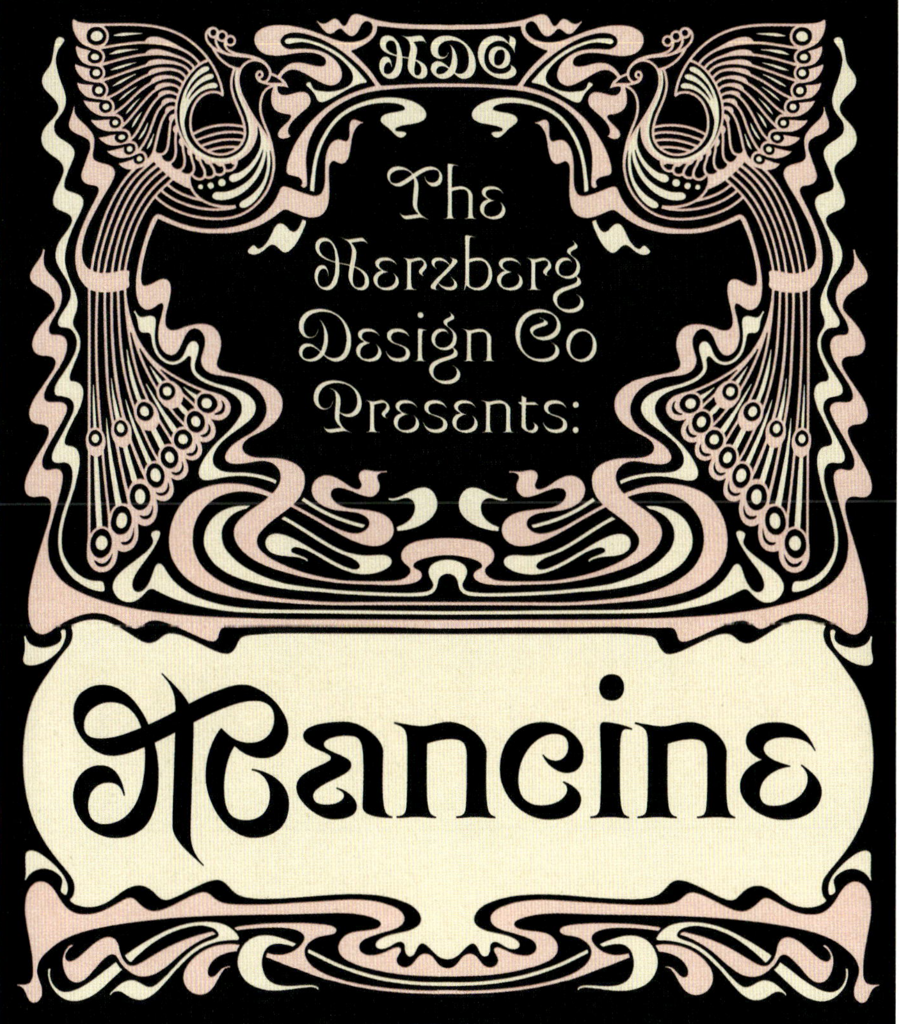

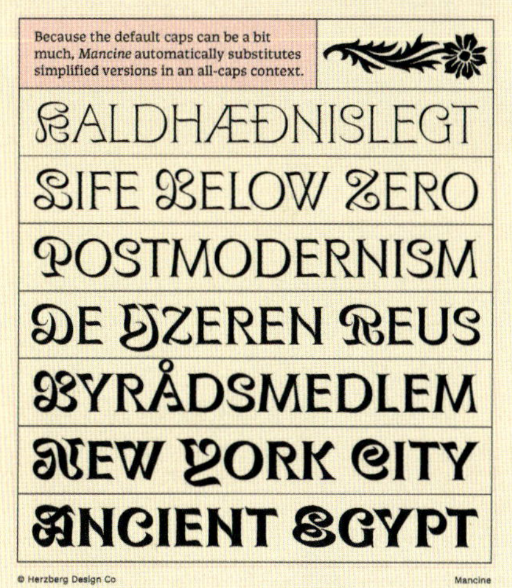

Mancine is based on calligraphy written with a broad nib at about 150 degrees (the exact opposite of nearly all Latin type), mixed with some Art Nouveau flair.

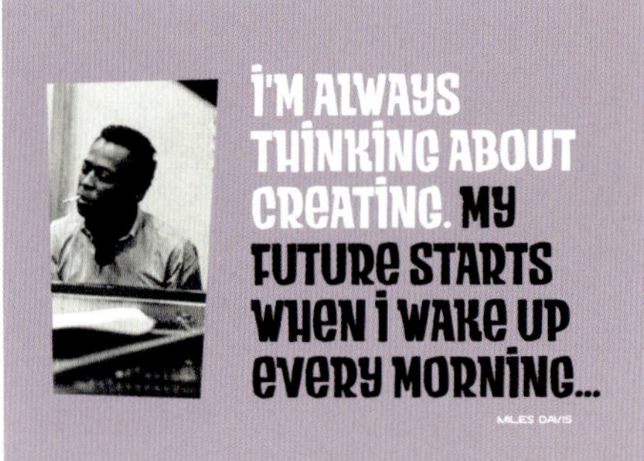

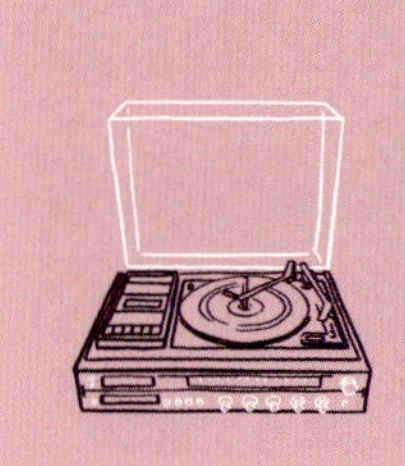

SOMEBODY WAS TRYING TO TELL ME THAT CDS ARE BETTER THAN VINYL BECAUSE THEY DON'T HAVE ANY SURFACE NOISE. I SAID, "LISTEN, MATE, LIFE HAS SURFACE NOISE."

JAZZMAN DISPLAY FONT

THE PERFECT RETRO FONT FOR YOUR JAZZ OR MID CENTURY MODERN DESIGNS

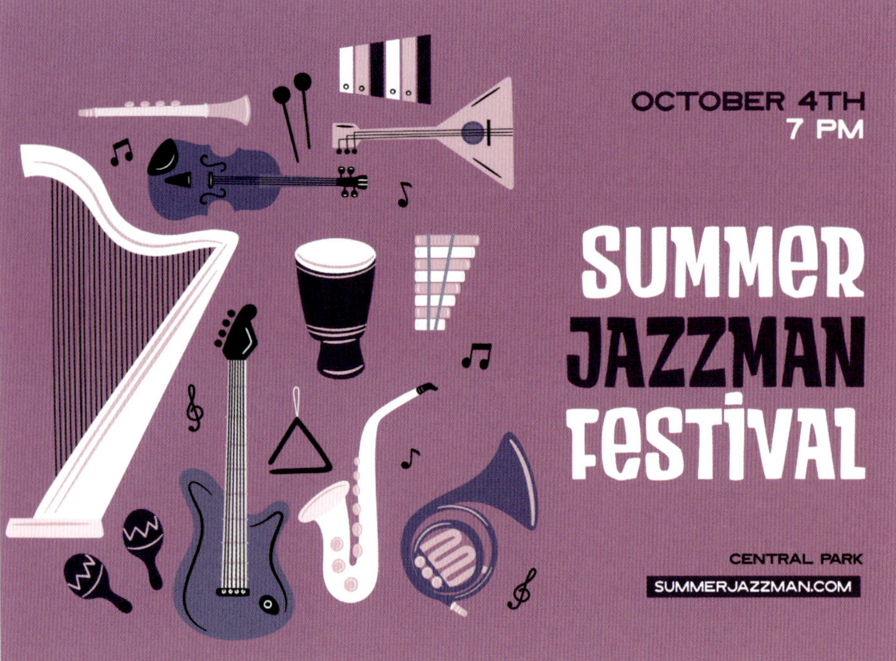

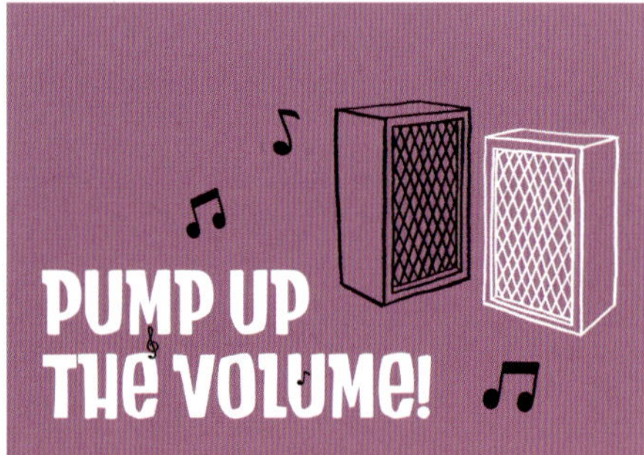

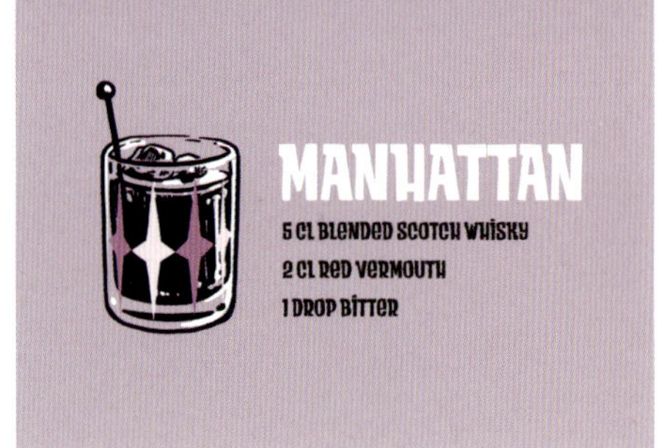

A big fan of jazz and of mid-century modern design, Francis Chouquet had created a few fonts in the style, but in Jazzman, he wanted to create something more functional with many uses. Inspiration comes from old 1950s/1960s lettering, mostly from the US, with a hand-drawn style. This was something important to the designer: that you can see this is handmade. It's not perfect—it's human.

Jazzman

francischouquet.com

Designed by *Francis Chouquet*
Published by *Francis Chouquet*

IVIENNE WESTWOOD ECCENTRICITY

30th ANNIVERSARY COLLECTION

ed your spirit, not your fear

arming Clove Tea With Hints of Cinnamon & Nutme

ogue Singapore fashion

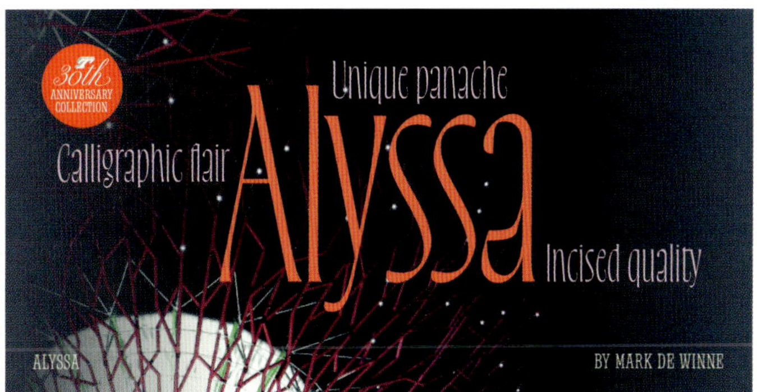

ohn Galliano
VANDA MISS JOACHIM ORCHID
Bon Chic Bon Genre
Ogg, Salden and Baker genius
Asymmetrical Mystic Energy

65S

modern & elegant typeface, both practical & robust. In recent years, a new tendency has
the decorative arts. While the simplicity of the lines has been preserved, the straightness
shed elegance is coming into its own again. Typography has not been neglected in thes
have been expressed by an obvious reversion to certain styles. However, most of the exist
hioned & not adapted to today's working methods, owing their fragility. A new typeface
design that corresponded to today's taste. Therefore we have created it, a modern & ele
tical & robust... In recent years, a new tendency has become manifest in the decorative

However, most of the existing types were old-fashio
& not adapted to today's working methods, owin
their fragility. A new typeface had to be found wit
design that corresponded to today's téstbHe. Thu
have created it, a modern & elegant typeface, both

Alyssa is a dynamic single-weight display typeface that brings flair and sophistication to any project, whether it's a striking logotype, a vibrant magazine spread, or refined branding. Balancing calligraphic flair with an incised quality gives it a unique panache, ideal for designers seeking to balance expressiveness with authority. Alyssa thrives in large sizes, where its vivid details can fully unfold, creating distinctive word shapes.

typofonderie.com

Alyssa

Designed by *Mark De Winne*
Published by *Typofonderie*

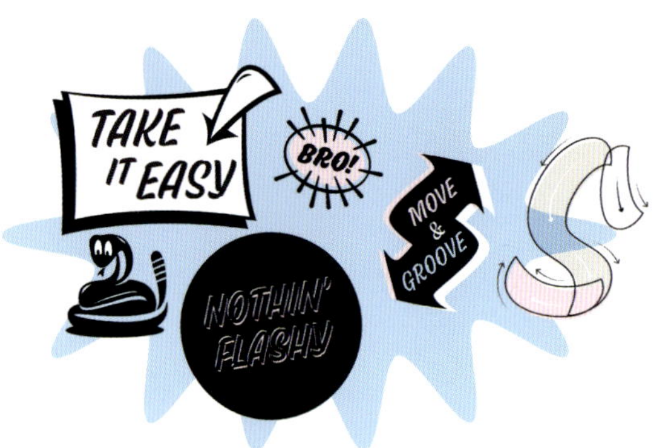

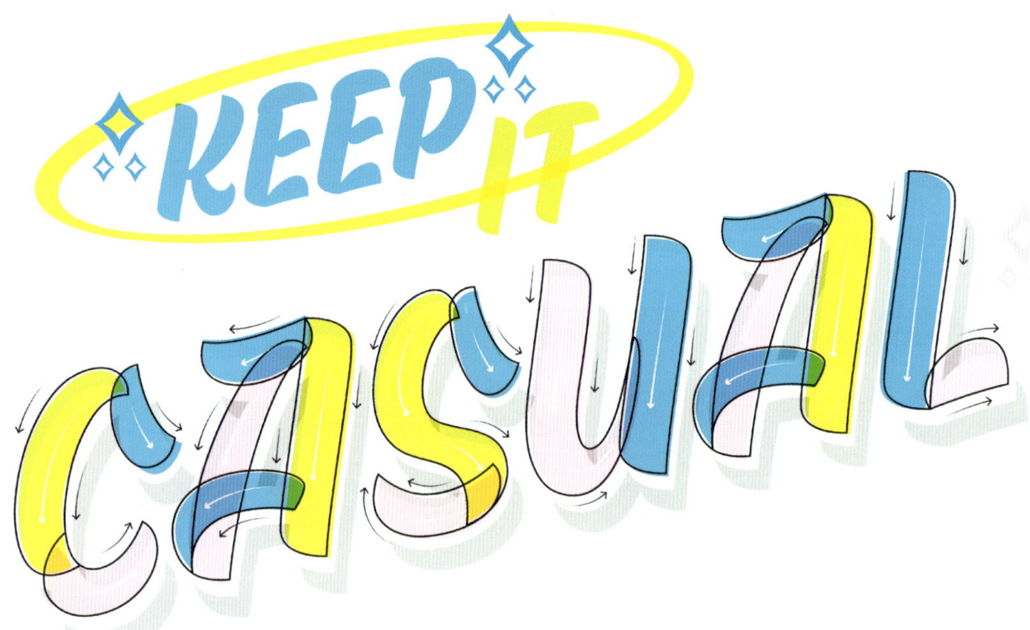

Skew is a brush-inspired display face that doesn't shy away from the individual strokes that construct the forms.

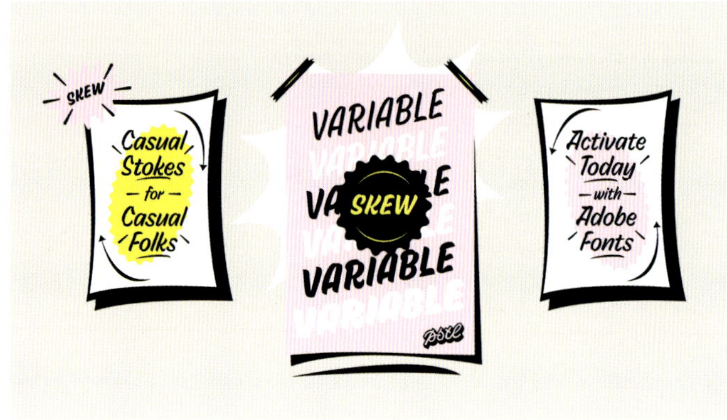

Skew

pstypelab.com

Designed by *Mark Caneso*
Published by *PSTL*

atmosphere of enchantme

Celebrate the Rebirth of the Sun

the season. Midwinter's dr

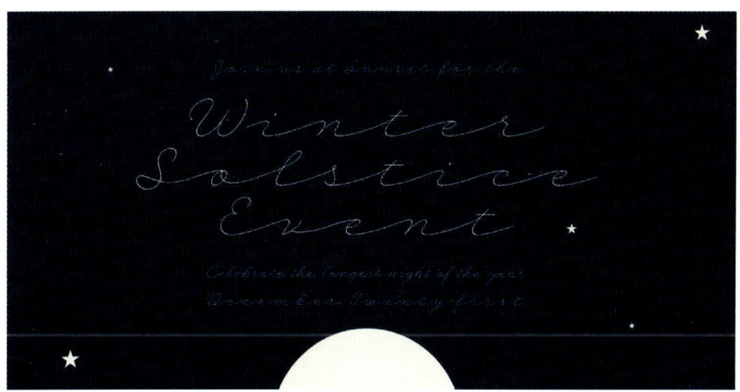

The great tide ebbs and leaves
the strand
So bare and bleak and brown.
How quickly the sea runs out
from land
And the waves drop, one by one.

Amy Lowell
An American Poet

Theodosia is an ethereal roundhand-style script with a feeling of the coming and going of the tide. Inspired by the long, languid, clean lines of calligraphy, it is light as air and able to add a distinguishing pattern and texture to invitations, packaging, brand design, magazine spreads, and book jackets. Laura Worthington intentionally designed it to expand and contract without manipulation or distortion. Theodosia is available in Regular, Condensed, and Expanded, or as a variable font.

Theodosia
Laura Worthington

lauraworthingtondesign.com

Theodosia

Designed by *Laura Worthington*
Published by *Laura Worthington Design*

Selling a Voice
An Essay by Veronika Burian

The term "specimen" is derived from the Latin root "specere," which means "to look" or "to see" and going even further back, from the Sanskrit "spasati," which means "sees." Historically, it was commonly used in scientific, academic, and artistic settings to refer to a sample or representative example of something being studied or exhibited.

The concept of a specimen in typography today remains true to its original meaning: It provides a representative example that allows viewers to assess and appreciate the broader design system or purpose behind a typeface. In the days of metal type, specimens were crucial, when printers needed physical examples to choose typefaces for their projects. These were often distributed as printed booklets or posters by type foundries, featuring elaborate and creative layouts to demonstrate the capabilities of a typeface. Since then, there has been a huge shift from the physical / analog to the digital realm in all parts of society, and typefaces are no exception.

The physicality of printed matter has its own fascination. It is a tactile encounter that in some people can provoke sighs of profound satisfaction when browsing through books and pamphlets hot off the press. The experience of a *digital* specimen, on the other hand, is rather taste- and scentless, but does have other favorable advantages. There is the potential playfulness and experimentation, limited only by one's own imagination and technology. The readiness to change, adapt, and expand at a reasonable pace and cost. And the ability to customize content according to its application. As Paula Scher commented: "A type specimen isn't just about selling letters—it's about selling a voice, a tone, and a function." Similarly, Jessica Hische emphasizes this idea, stating: "Good type specimens don't just show you a font—they make you want to design something immediately." Ultimately, a specimen's task is to create an almost visceral connection with the reader.

Over the past twenty years, the design of digital specimens has radically evolved from a layout prepared for printing, with visual ties to classic specimen books, to something more organic and flexible, competing for attention in a saturated media landscape. It can be said that digital specimens serve three distinct functions, each with its own unique appearance:

First, the technical approach focuses on presenting comprehensive details about the typeface family, including its character set, OpenType features, font styles, sample words, sentences, and paragraphs, as well as background information such as the designer, release date, and a detailed font description. Its goal is to quickly inform about the context of the typeface, to help the user understand the design intention that the creator had in mind, and enable them to easily compare with other typefaces. Over the years, type specimens have evolved into highly interactive tools, allowing users to engage with them in dynamic and intuitive ways. Features like toggling buttons, moving sliders, and adjusting settings enable users to explore the finer details and functions of a typeface in real time. Type testers, once quite rudimentary, now have also advanced to more complex specimens with goodies such as glyph viewers, font combinations, and paragraph builders.

Secondly, foundries began creating more visually engaging and enticing graphics to showcase typefaces. This is achieved by highlighting design details, incorporating additional graphic elements, and presenting real or simulated type-in-use scenarios. The function of such material is to encourage the viewer to become excited about the font, imagine it in their own work, wanting to know more about it, and ultimately to convince them to buy a license. They are promotional graphics used in social media, distributors' platforms, newsletters, and any other channel prepped to advertise font releases. Within this group, there is a broad variety of expressions, ranging from simple lines of words set against a pleasant color background to elaborate design mock-ups showcasing the typeface in action, or even 3D renderings of shapes. To complement these creative presentations, many foundries strive to develop a recognizable and consistent visual style for their type families, reinforcing their brand value and identity.

The third and most recent development is motion design—in the best case, playfully showing the essence of the typeface by cleverly combining motion, type, and music. They have basically the same function as their static counterparts, but adhere more to the rules of social media trends and modern marketing strategies. However, creating such type animations is quite challenging and resource-intensive, both in financial terms as well as in human power. As a result, this process has raised the potential font buyers' expectations, while foundries struggle to keep up.

It can be said that digital specimens have become an important staple in a foundry's toolbox, propelled by the strong shift of reading habits from paper to on-screen and the overall media environment and its related font usage. In this kind of context, though, all the material produced by the plethora of foundries and type designers has a very fleeting existence. The pace of social media feeds is relentless and even the biggest typophiles lose track of it all. From a type historian's perspective, the rapid pace of change in the typographic world presents a significant challenge. It leaves little time to process, document, or even fully appreciate the creative output of today's type designers.

So what is the remedy, if there is one at all? One potential solution lies in returning to a physical medium, such as this printed book. Such a compendium can serve as a tangible, lasting artifact that captures and preserves contemporary typographic culture, acting as both a witness and a snapshot of a specific design aesthetic of its time. By doing so, it not only provides a clearer lens to observe and understand emerging trends but also creates a permanent record that ensures this creative legacy remains accessible for future generations of type users and creators. And, of course, type historians will rejoice!

CONTEXTUAL ALTERNATES | CHARACTER SET | NUMBERS | EMOJIS

CONTEXTUAL ALTERNATES OFF

Freddy frog fancied
feasting on fresh flies

CONTEXTUAL ALTERNATES ON

Freddy frog fancied
feasting on fresh flies

PLAYPEN SANS NOW AVAILABLE AT TYPE-TOGETHER.COM

AVAILABLE IN 8 WEIGHTS

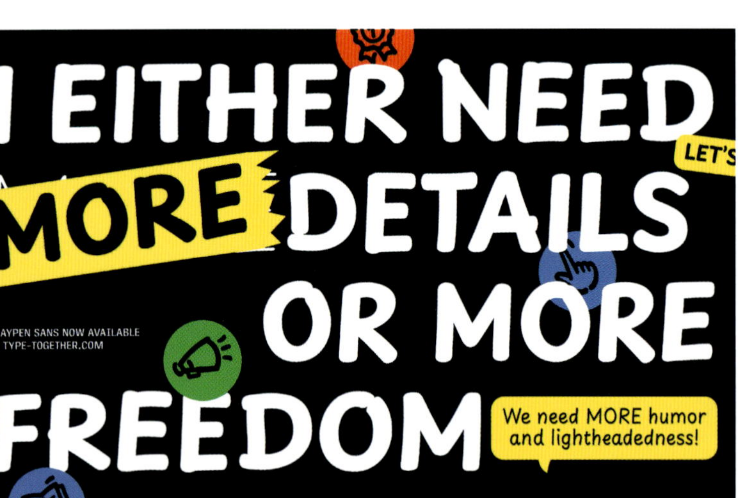

Casual handwriting
Casual handwriting
Casual handwriting
Casual handwriting
Casual handwriting
Casual handwriting
Casual handwriting
Casual handwriting

+EMOJIS IN 8 WEIGHTS

8 WEIGHTS

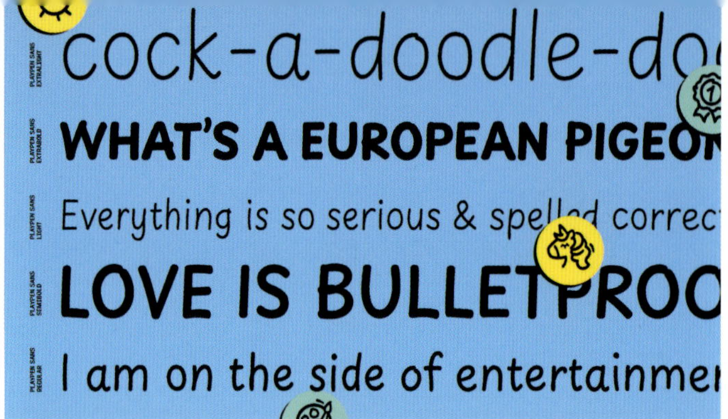

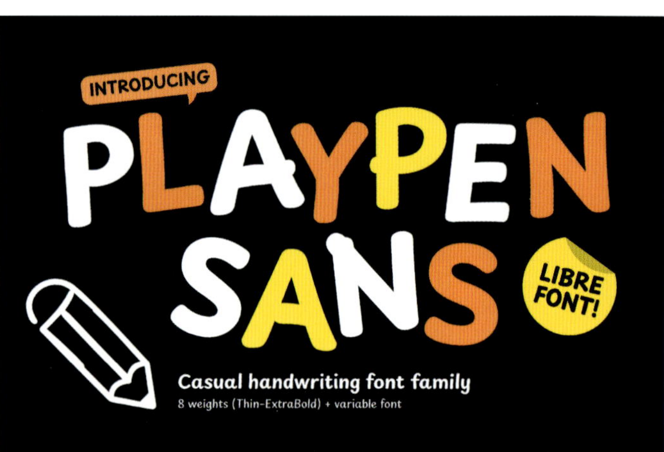

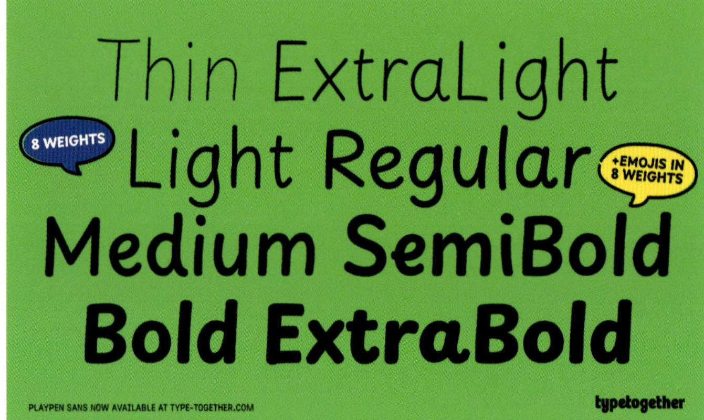

The Playpen Sans font family excels at imitating casual handwriting with a completely natural look—the aesthetic form of something made by hand and the digital function of a professional typeface. A typeface with a set of characters that are "the same but different" has the authenticity everyone craves. The main problem with casual fonts is not having enough alternate characters to look real. And when a family has more than one alternate, another problem arises in controlling how and when a character gets replaced. To solve these problems, Playpen Sans was designed with seven versions of each character, along with a built-in shuffler so no single shape is repeated in close proximity. The result is text with spontaneous inconsistencies that feel fun and organic—all the benefits of a modern, pro typeface that looks natural.

Playpen Sans

type-together.com

Designed by *Veronika Burian, Laura Meseguer, José Scaglione*
Published by *TypeTogether*

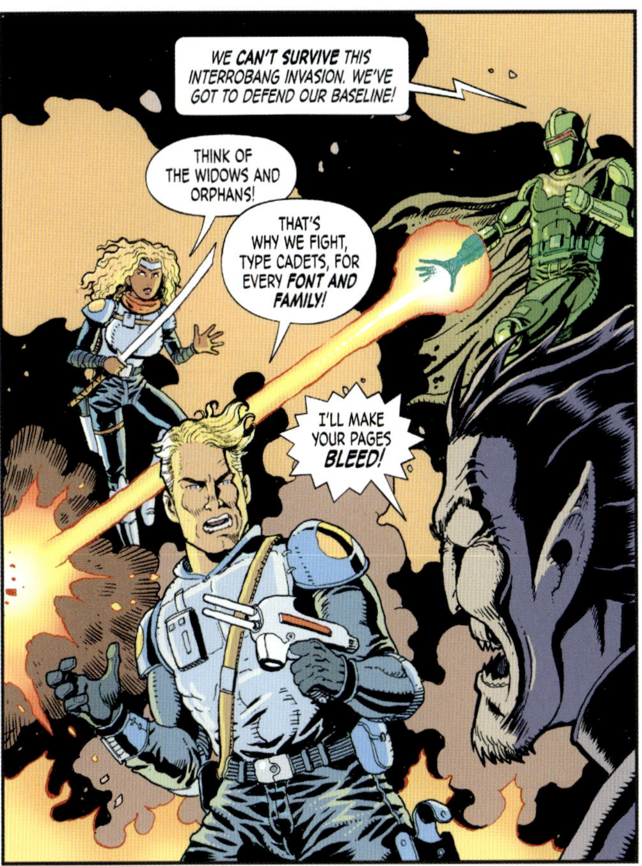

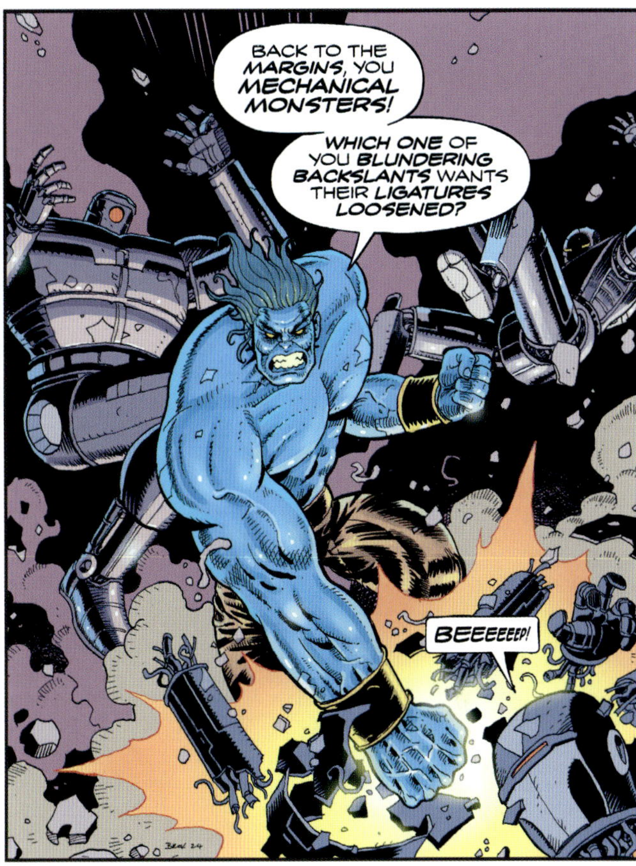

COMIC BOOK COLLECTORS OFTEN EX
LIFELONG PASSION FOR THE DRAM
WITHIN COMICS, OFTEN FOCUSING ON

TEXT IS FREQUENTLY INCORPORATED INTO
SOUND EFFECTS. ***SPEECH BALLOONS*** INC
OF THOUGHT BALLOONS), WITH TAILS POINT

WHILE COMICS ARE OFTEN THE WORK OF A SINGL
BETWEEN A ***NUMBER OF SPECIALISTS***. THERE M
SPECIALIZE IN PARTS OF THE ARTWORK SUCH AS

OVER THE COURSE OF THE FIRST FEW BATMAN STRIPS EL
THE ***ARTISTIC DEPICTION*** OF BATMAN EVOLVED. KANE
CHARACTER'S JAWLINE MORE PRONOUNCED, AND LENGTH

ONE SUPERPOWERED CHARACTER WAS PORTRAYED AS AN ANTIHEROI
ITS TIME: ***THE BLACK WIDOW***, A COSTUMED EMISSARY OF SATAN WH
EVILDOERS IN ORDER TO SEND THEM TO HELL. HER SURPRISING DEBU

UNDERGROUND COMICS WERE ALMOST NEVER SOLD AT NEWSSTANDS, BUT RATHER IN S
HEAD SHOPS AND RECORD STORES, AS WELL AS BY MAIL ORDER. THE UNDERGROUND CO
PUBLISH THEIR WORK INDEPENDENTLY SO THAT THEY WOULD HAVE FULL OWNERSHIP RIG

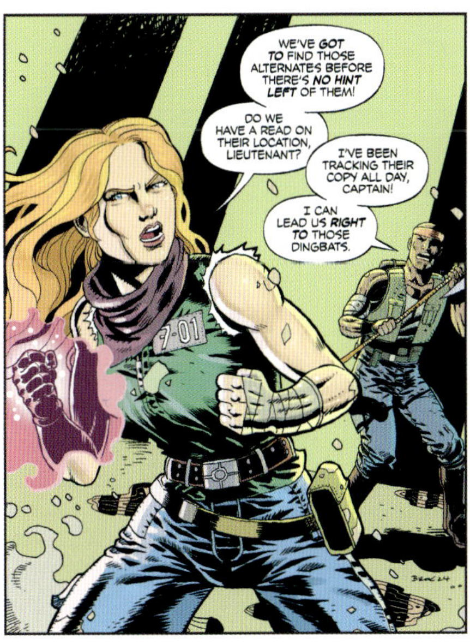

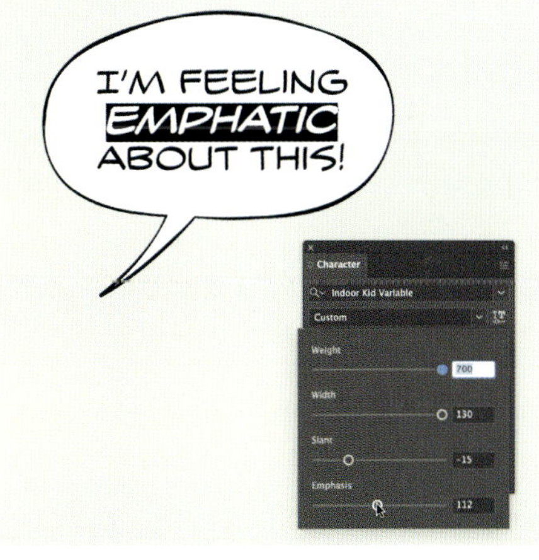

Indoor Kid is a variable-first comic book superfamily designed by DJR Type and comics writer/editor/publisher Ellis Bojar. It has all the weights, widths, and accoutrements you might expect from a workhorse sans, but is designed specifically for a wide range of comics dialogue and caption styles.

---

djr.com

Indoor Kid

Designed by *David Jonathan Ross, Ellis Bojar*
Published by *DJR Type*

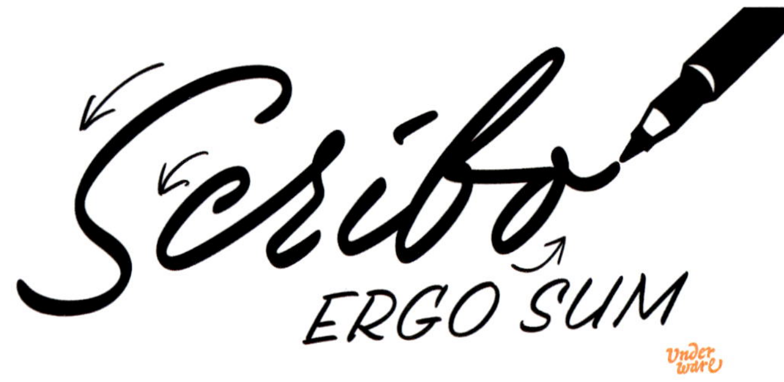

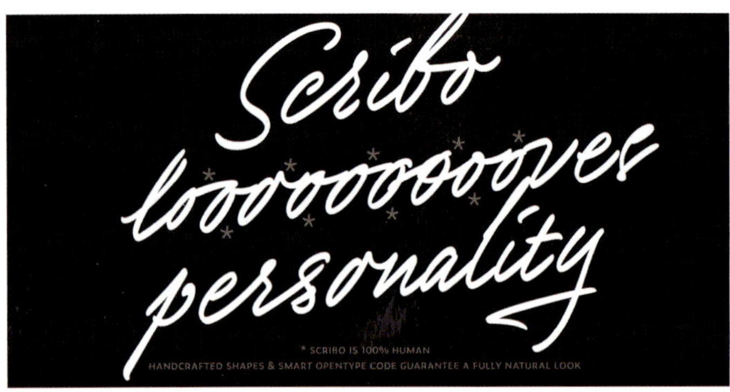

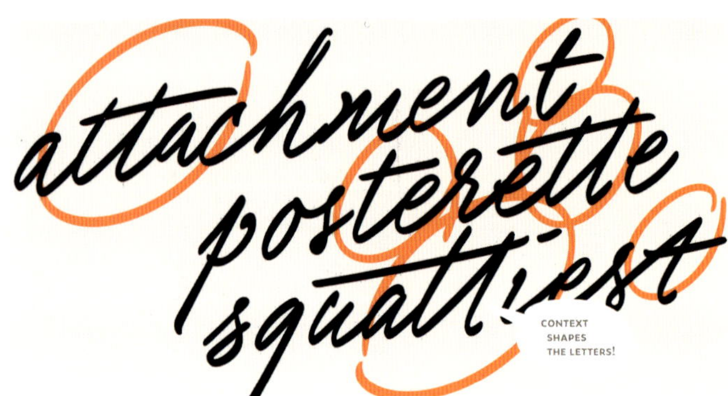

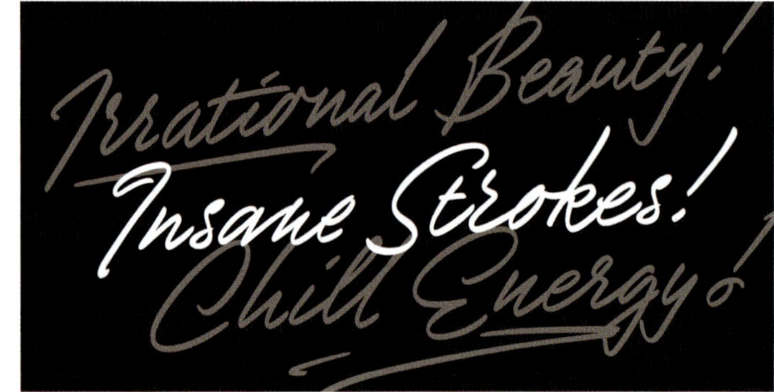

With Scribo, what started as a desire to capture the act of writing ended up as a set of dynamic and static fonts that forced Underware to push their own boundaries. The dynamic fonts (Scribo Write) allow texts to be really written, as all the writing dynamics (stroke order, speed variations) are included in the digital font file. The static fonts (Scribo Pro) offer a wide range of handwriting styles, created with five different writing tools: marker, pencil, and three different brushes. In a technological age that offers far more possibilities than twenty years ago, most of our software—as well as our habits of working with computers—are based on existing conventions and don't take advantage of these new possibilities. So it's time to rethink our existing practices. It's possible to include time as a dimension in a digital font file, but what does that mean? In Scribo's case, it means that we can finally capture the action of writing in a font file. For example, ink bleed can be neatly controlled, and the visual impact of writing extended as a result. The dynamic font Scribo Write brings together the two worlds of analog handwriting and technolgical digital typography, opening up new, previously unknown possibilities.

Scribo

underware.nl

Designed by *Akiem Helmling, Sami Kortemäki, Bas Jacobs*
Published by *Underware*

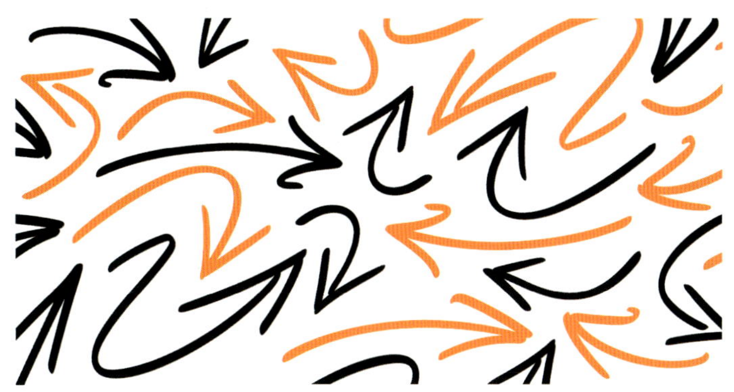

Nobody loves the ABC more than René Descartes.

COMBINE SCRIBO & SCRIBO CAPS

Nobody loves the ABC more than René Descartes.

Every letter in Scribo is animated faithfully, following the natural rhyt of gentle handwriting.

Scribo

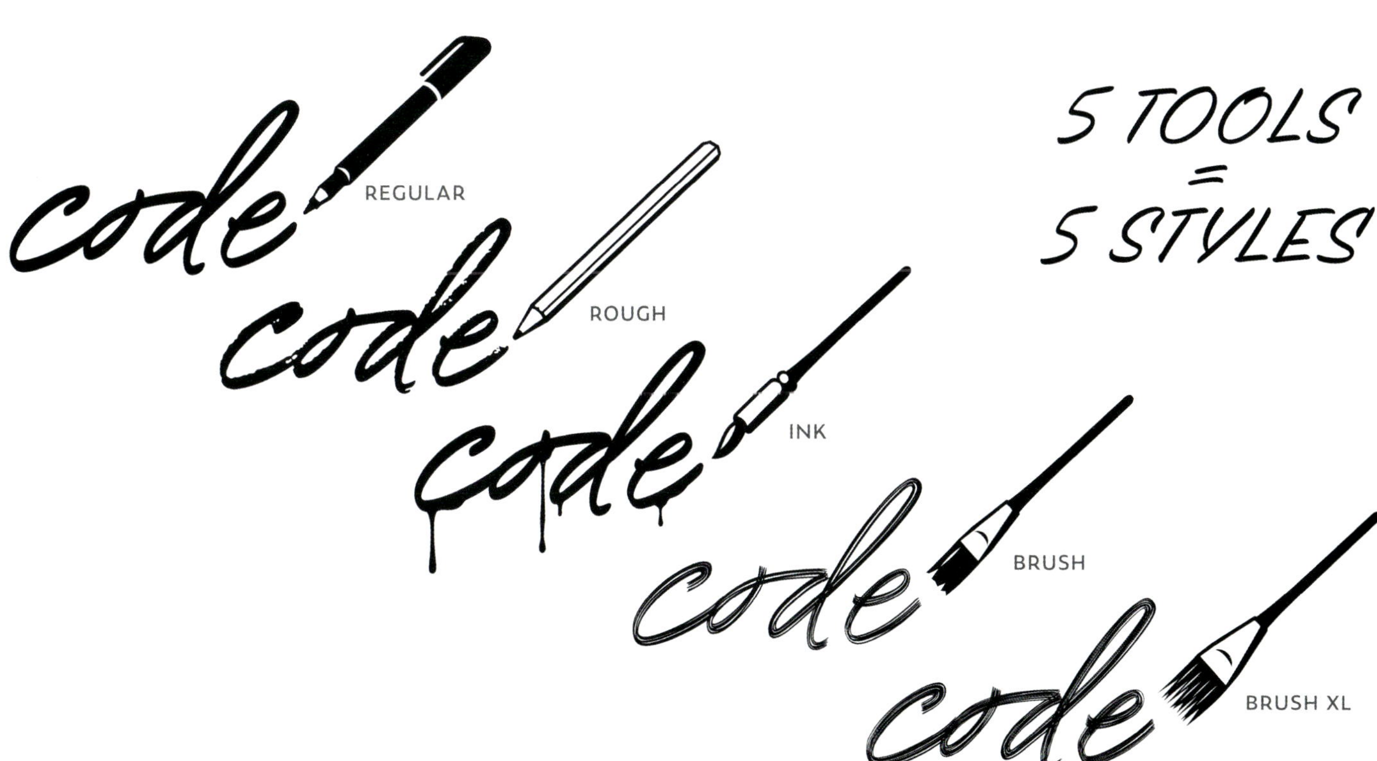

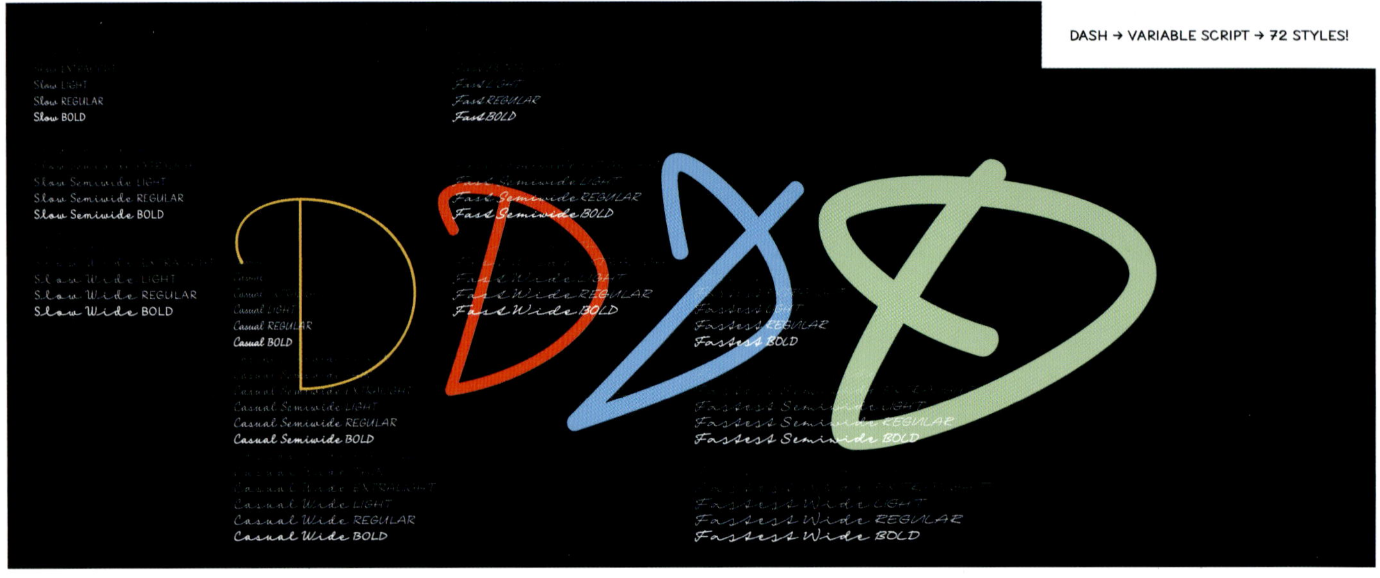

German — Stephan

Czech — Štefan

English — Joaquin

Spanish — Joaquín

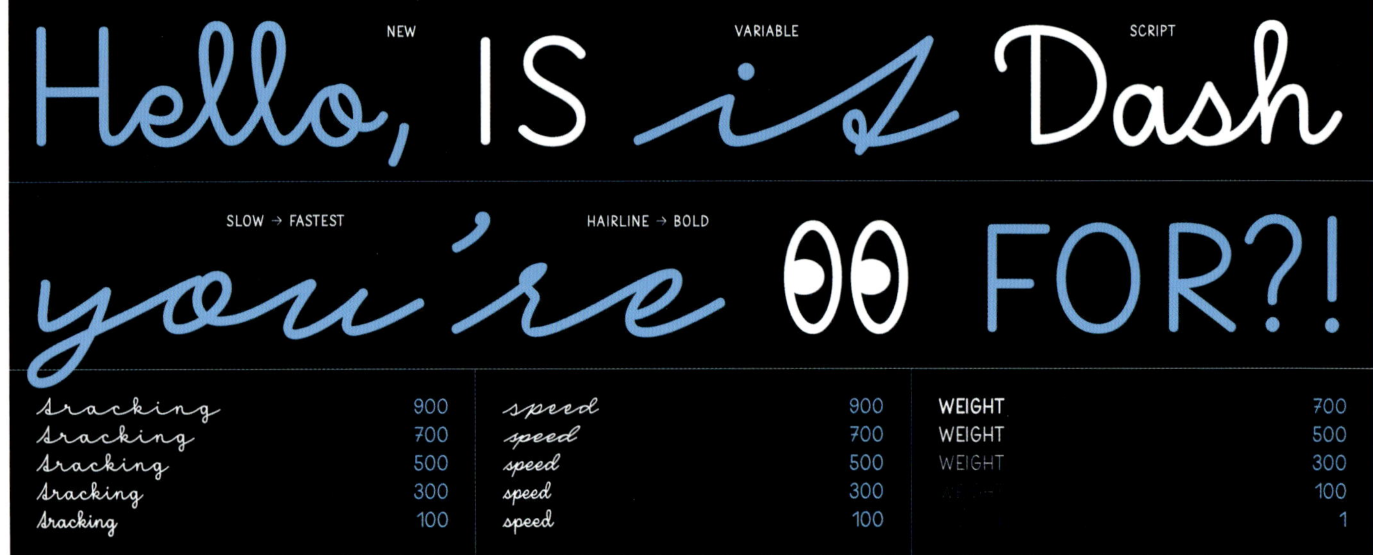

Dash is a connected script typeface that comes in four writing "speeds." This casual and natural style is based on a young adult's handwriting. Dash switches automatically to the preferred forms of letters based on the language being used.

Dash

typotheque.com

Designed by *Petra Dočekalová, Peter Biľak, Héctor Mangas Afonso, Sébastien Morlighem*
Published by *Typotheque*

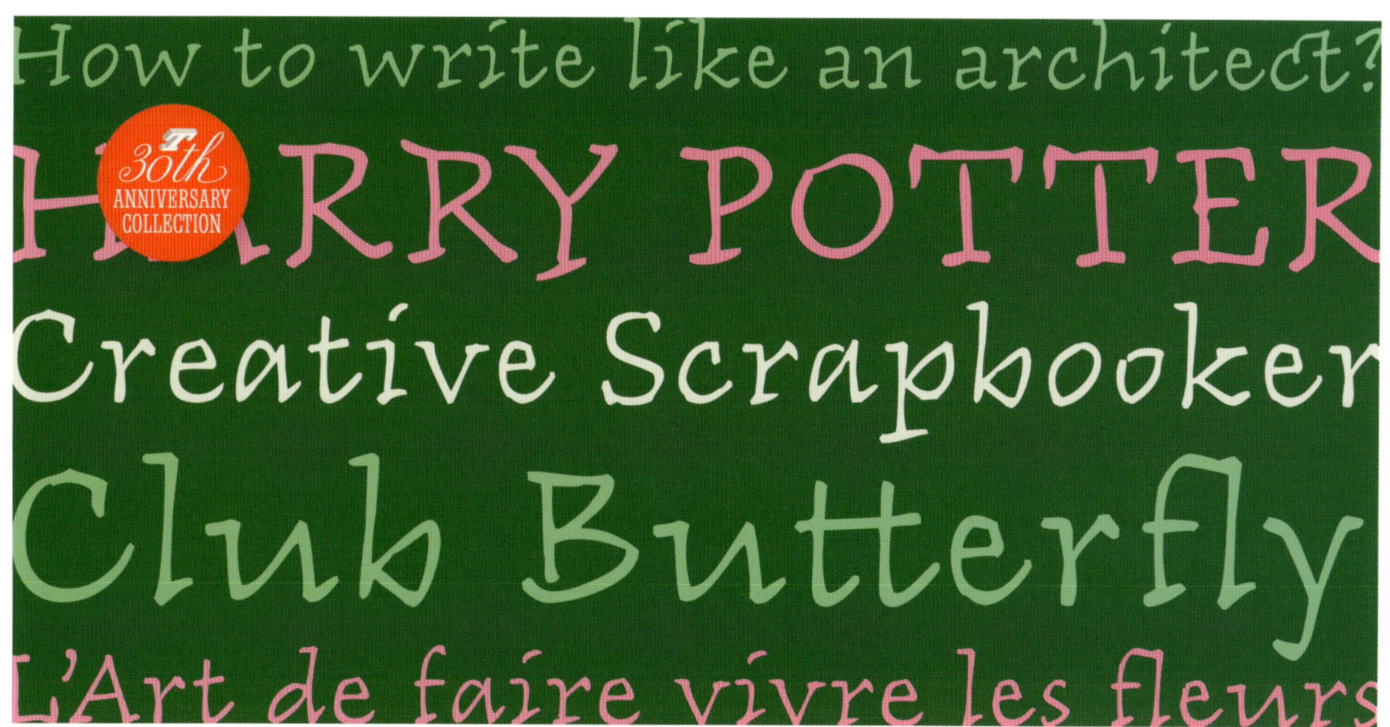

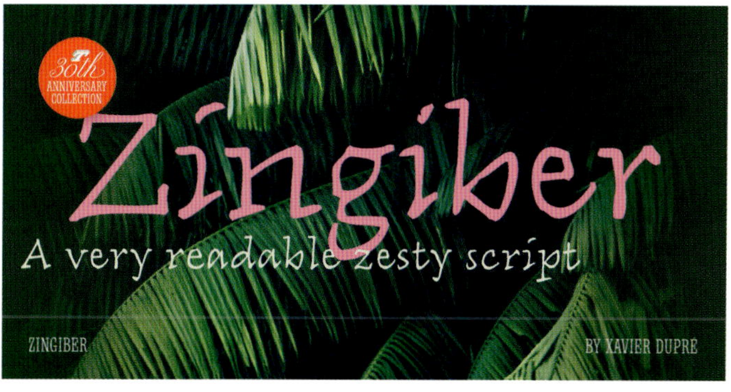

herbarium
MICROCOSMOS
Spring
Fairy tales
IKEBANA

ee
ee

that corresponded to today's taste. Thus we
created it, a modern & elegant typeface, both
tical & robust. In recent years, a new tenden
become manifest in the decorative arts. Whi
simplicity of the lines has been preserved, th
straightness is yielding & a distinguished ele
is coming into its own again. Typography ha

were old-fashioned & not adapt
today's working methods, owin
their fragility. Thus we have c
ted it, a modern & elegant type
both practical & robust... In re

Zingiber is an elegant yet relaxed script typeface, showcasing the skilled touch of a handcrafted design. Its serifs ensure excellent readability, making it perfect for headlines and short texts in a variety of contexts—children's books, historical publications, or even cookbooks. Its artisanal style lends itself beautifully to visual identities, packaging, and social media communication with its subtle elegance and charm—much like fine foods in a delicatessen.

typofonderie.com

Zingiber

Designed by *Xavier Dupré*
Published by *Typofonderie*

CLASSIFICATION-DEFYING

Typeface: Casserole (Lombardic), designed by James Edmondson (page 198)

Our final (and admittedly rather short) part of the book is a collection of typefaces that don't fit neatly into the usual buckets. Here, we have classification-defying type that either blends between distinct genres or simply does its own thing entirely. And I'll be honest: I really wrung my hands for quite some time about what should or shouldn't go here and whether or not it was even okay to make a part of the book for type that... well... just didn't fit anywhere else.

Ultimately, my (potentially controversial) opinion is this: Classification is somewhat meaningless. It can be a useful way of setting up some parameters to help us choose our type, but ultimately the specific factors that influence the suitability of the type to the job have very little to do with what arbitrary, probably outdated, and most certainly limiting classification they've been given. Treat these groupings as nothing more than ways to group seemingly related content—and embrace the chaos.

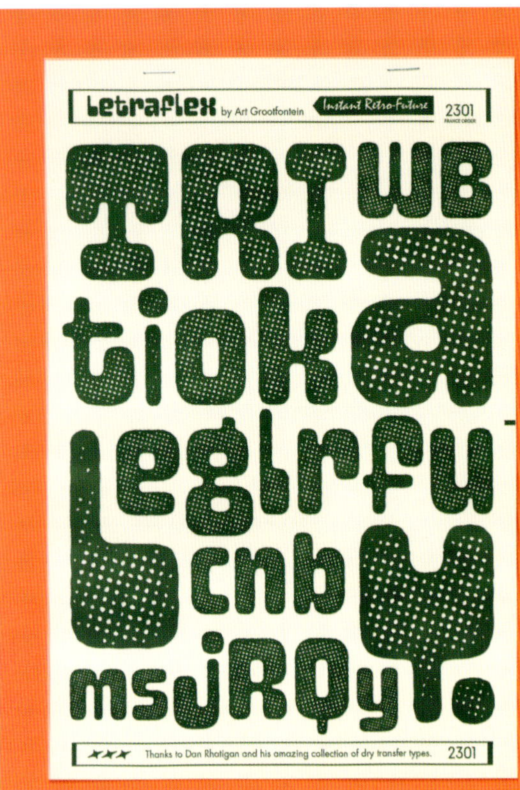

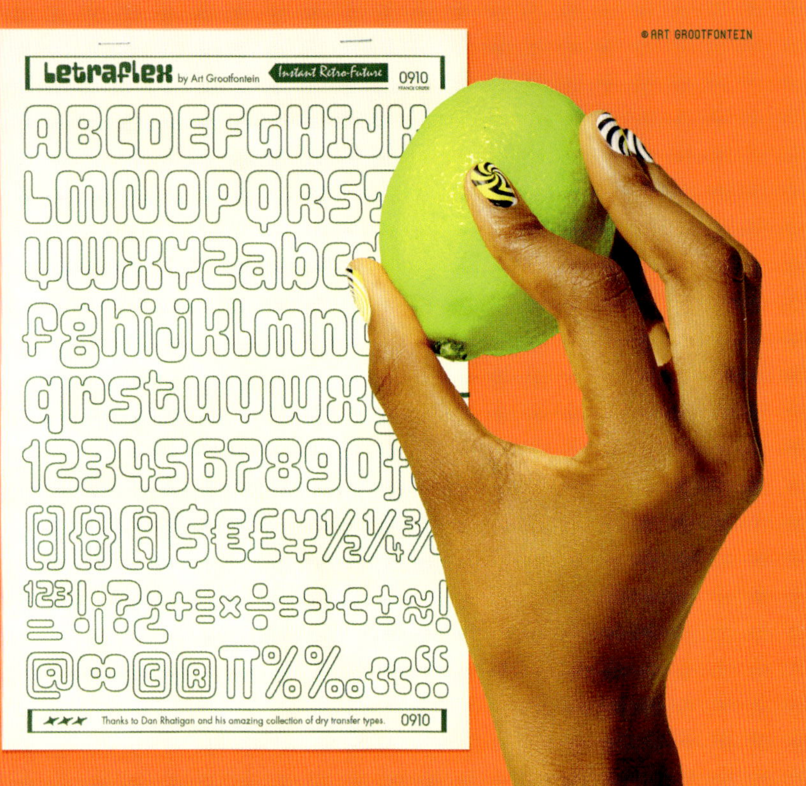

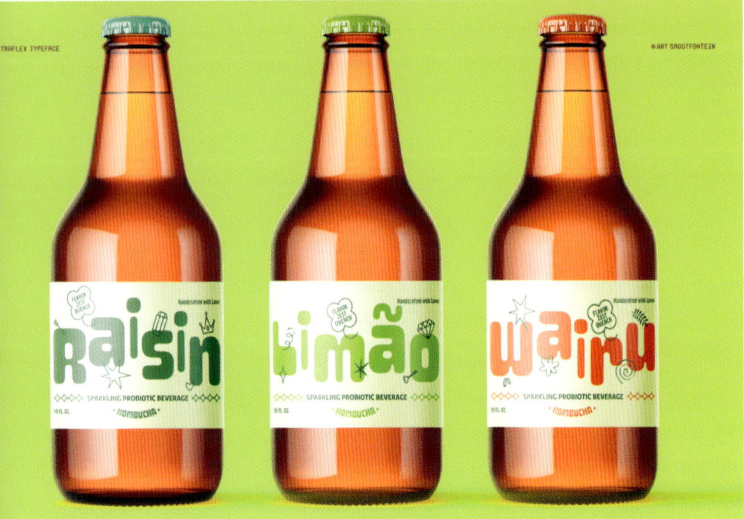

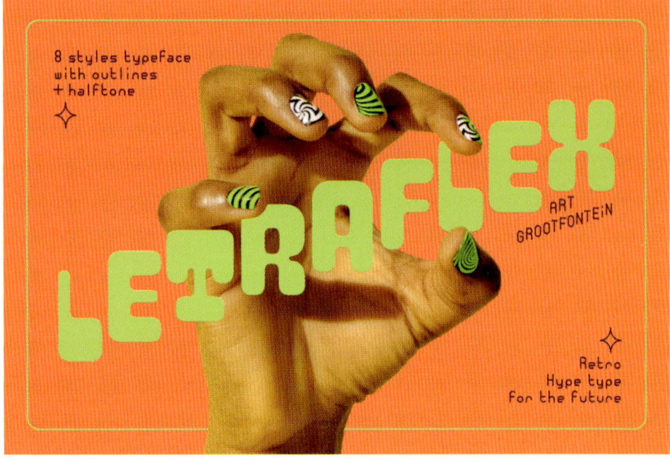

A retro hype type for the future, Letraflex is a bold, retro-inspired typeface with a slightly futuristic style. The family is based on old computer lettering and Magnetic Ink Character Recognition (MICR), with a little contemporary twist, including nice ink traps.

Letraflex

grootfontein.net

Designed by *Stéphane Mattern*
Published by *Art Grootfontein*

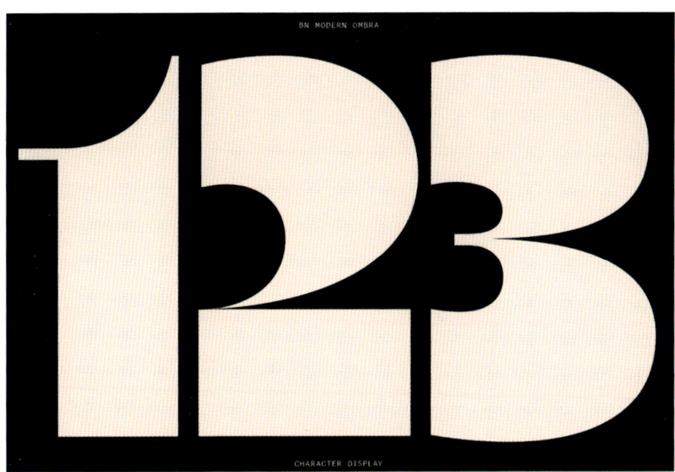

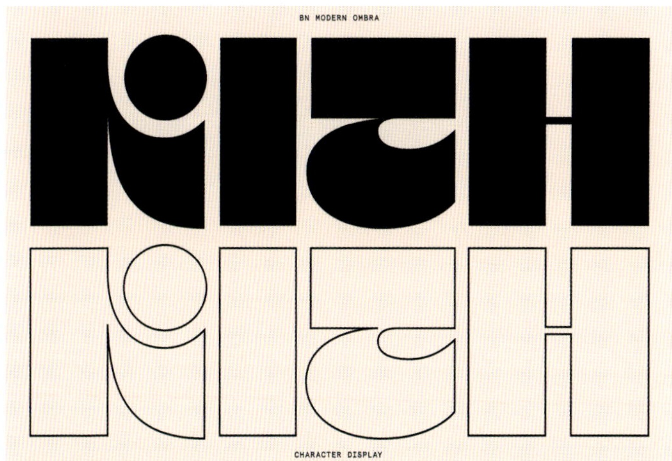

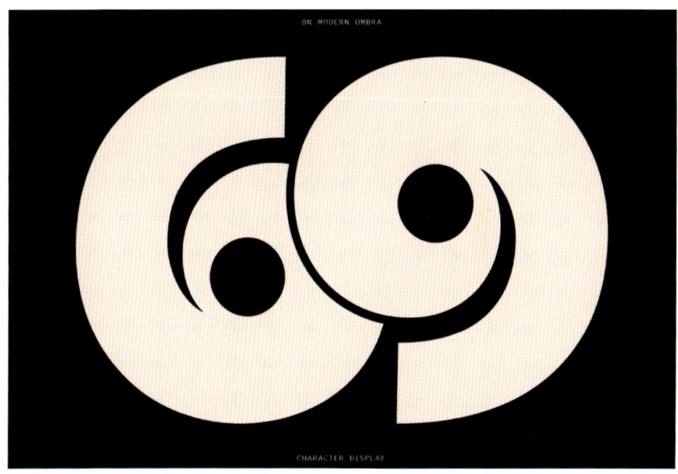

A modern take on the classic "Motter Ombra" originally designed by Othmar Motter in 1973 and digitized by Linotype. The typeface came to be while creating a logotype for a client. The simplified result of the custom lettering sparked the idea to recreate the entire font. Using geometric circles versus teardrop shapes and completely remodeling certain letters, BN Modern Ombra was born.

bnicks.com

BN Modern Ombra

Designed by *Brandon Nickerson*
Published by *Brandon Nickerson*

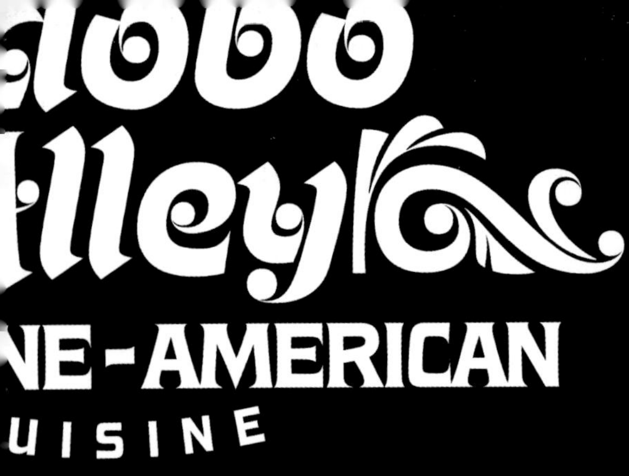

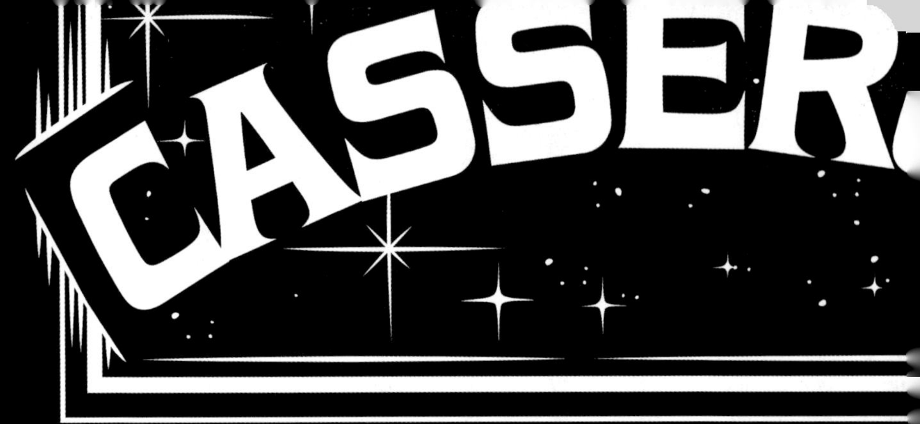

NE NIGHT ONLY

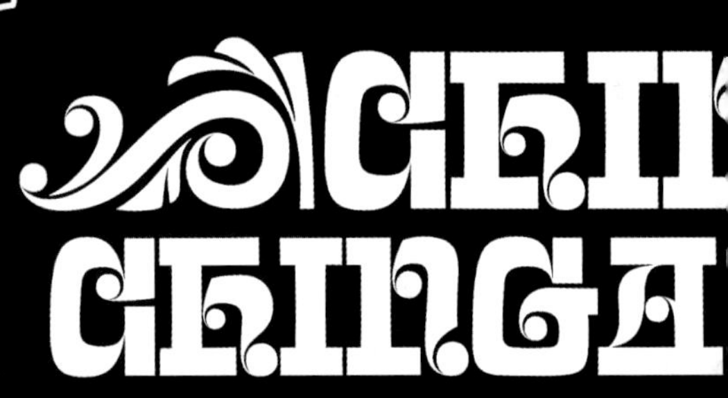

23456789
23456789
23456789
23456789
23456789

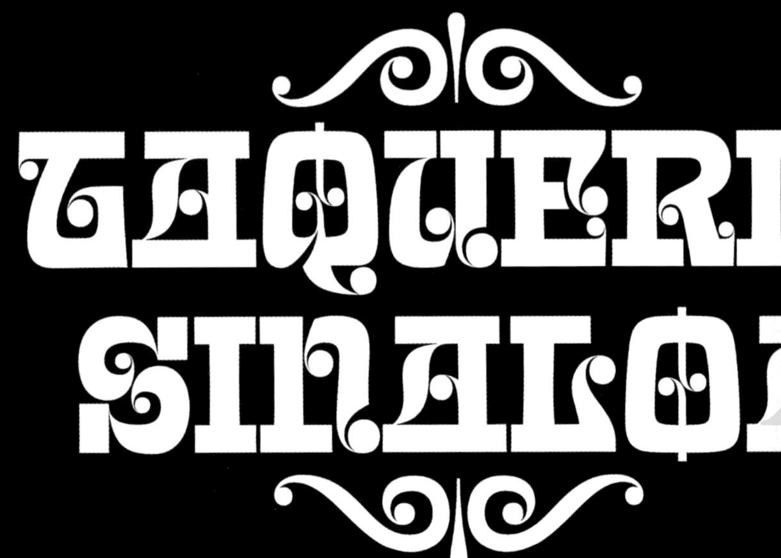

Casserole

ohnotype.co

Designed by *James Edmondson*
Published by *OH no Type Co*

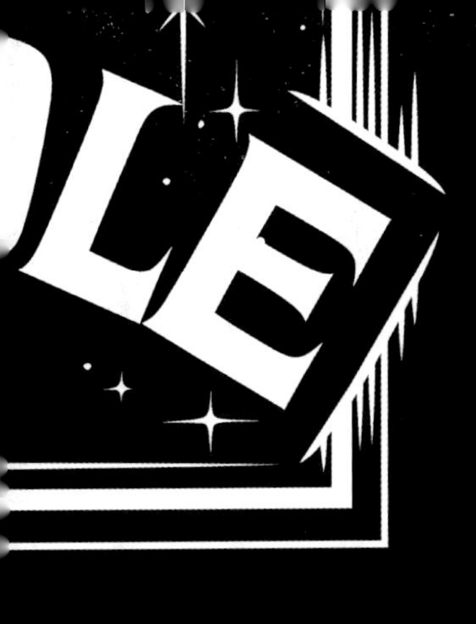

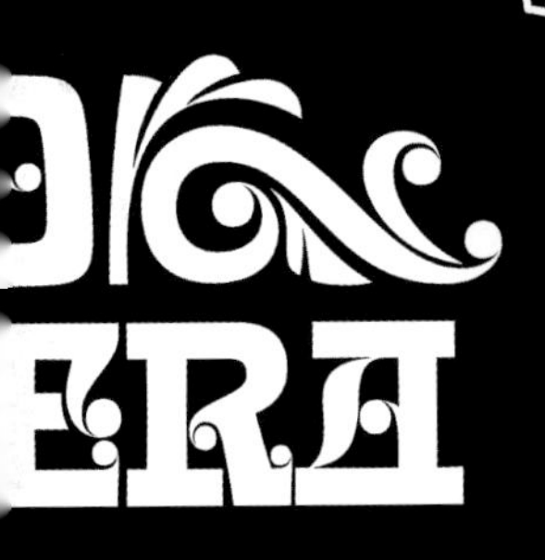

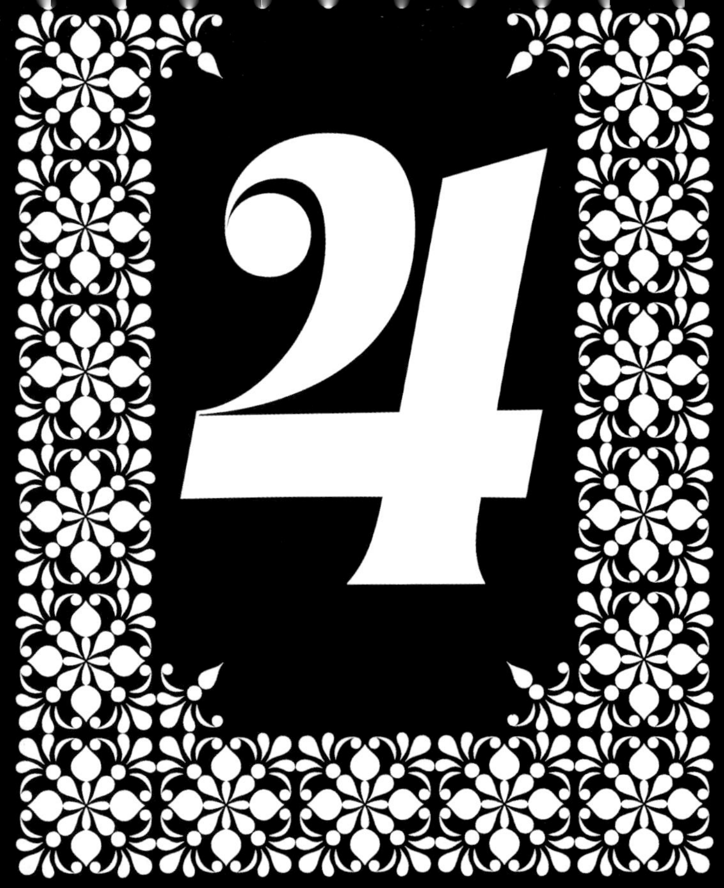

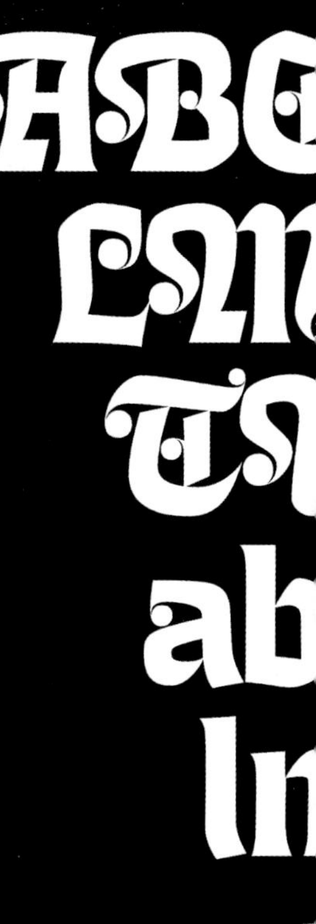

An exhaustive resusitation of Davida, the 1966 certified banger from Louis Minott.

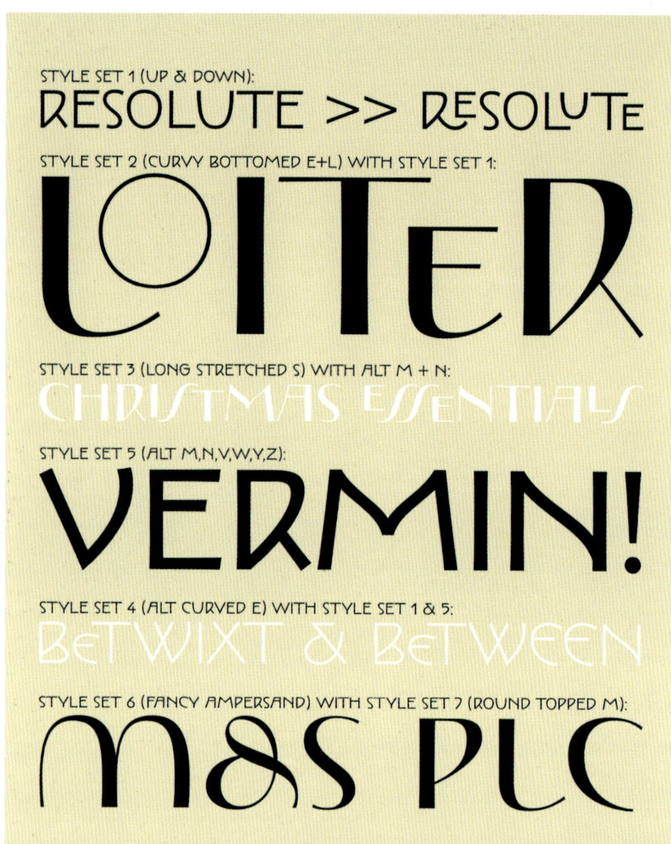

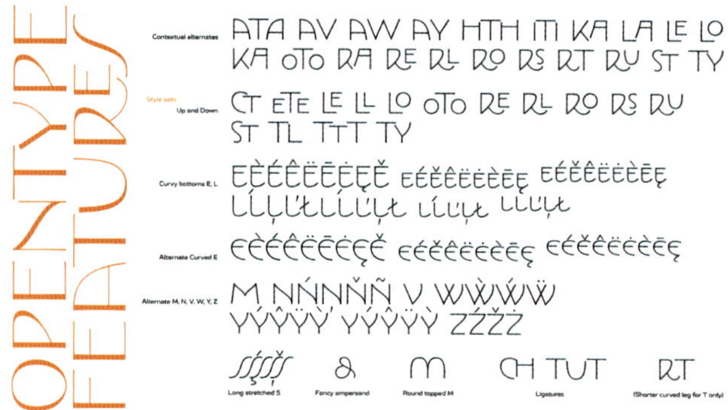

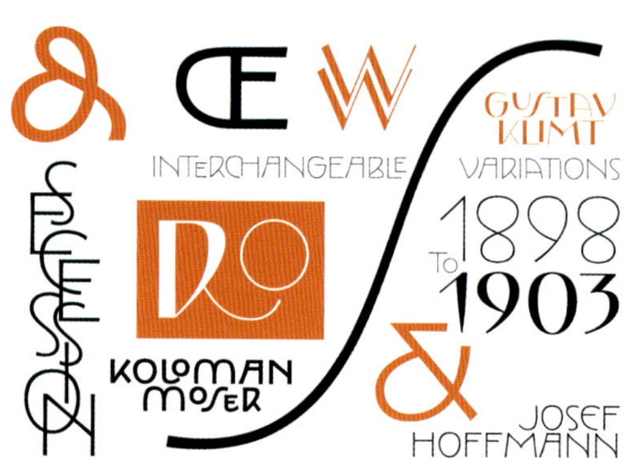

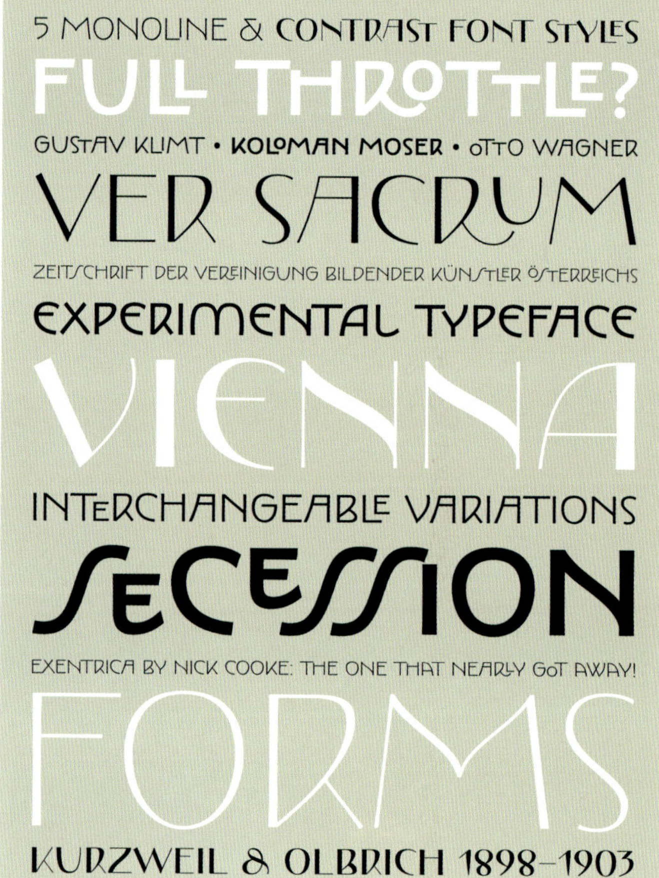

During a visit to the Museum of Applied Arts in Vienna, G-Type founder Nick Cooke couldn't help being impressed by the work of the Secession artists and their distinctive typographic styling. Exentrica is the result of that Viennese inspiration, merging the various design strands into one striking type family, with myriad extra stylistic variations for increased variety. Further versatility is achieved with both Monoline and Contrast versions of each weight, from Thin to Medium.

Exentrica

g-type.com

Designed by *Nick Cooke*
Published by *G-Type*

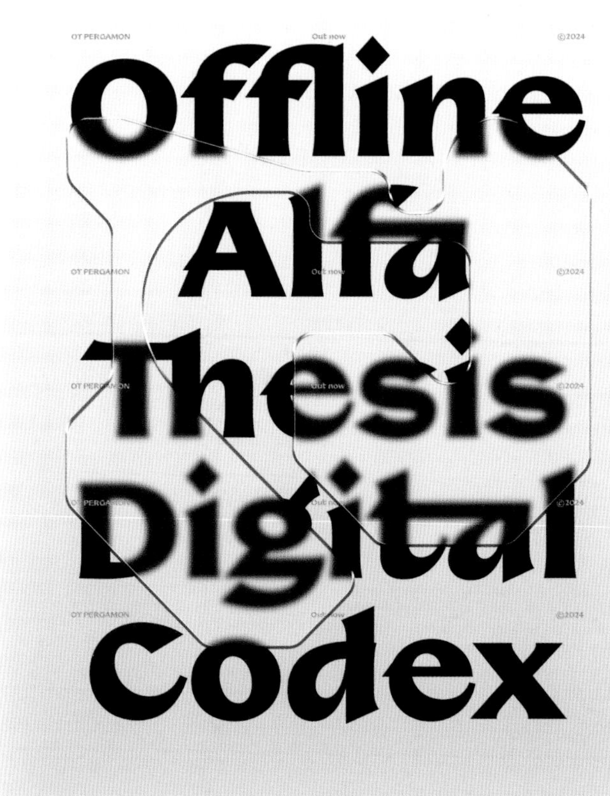

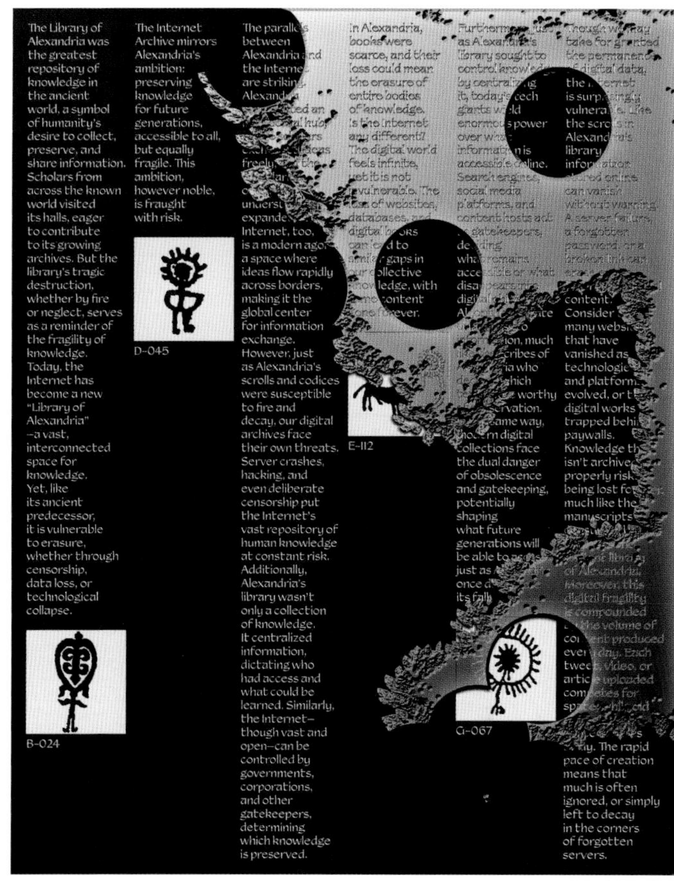

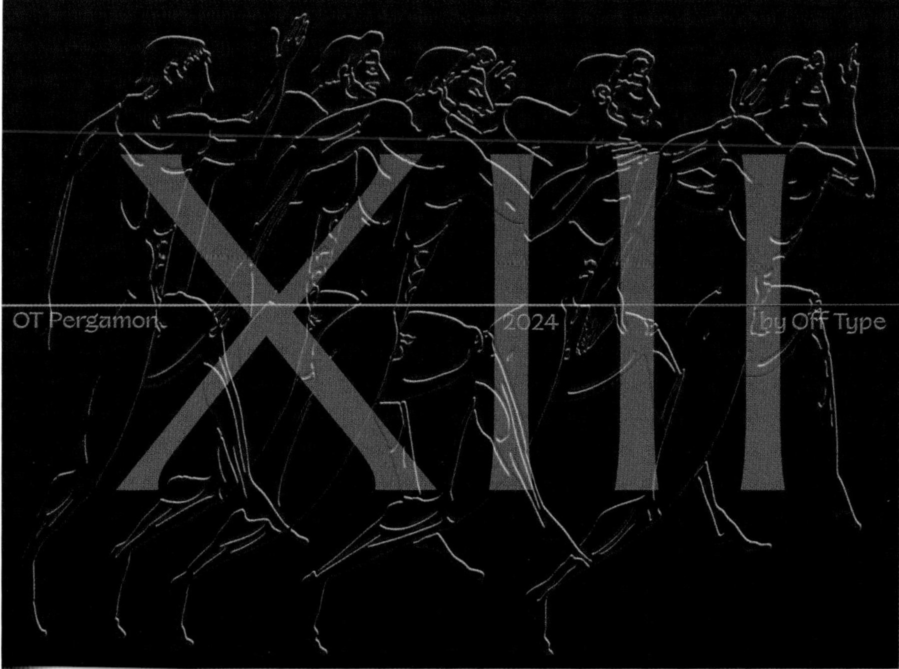

Meet OT Pergamon, the spiritual heir to one of the most recognizable—and polarizing—digital calligraphic fonts. Named after the city where parchment (the successor to papyrus) was invented, Pergamon brings the nuances of parchment nib contrast into a structured and versatile typeface, achieving a harmonious balance between the organic flow of gestural strokes and the precision of digital design. Designed with digital editorial projects in mind, Pergamon stays sharp and legible at any size, ensuring every text block feels refined and readable. Whether in print or on-screen, it transforms the endless scroll into a seamless reading experience. In a nod to its historical roots, Pergamon is also the first typeface on Off Type or Pangram Pangram to feature monotonic Greek compatibility. More than just an Easter egg, the Greek script integrates naturally into the typeface's aesthetic, enhancing its connection to its ancient origins.

off-type.com

OT Pergamon

Designed by *Valerio Monopoli*
Published by *Off Type*

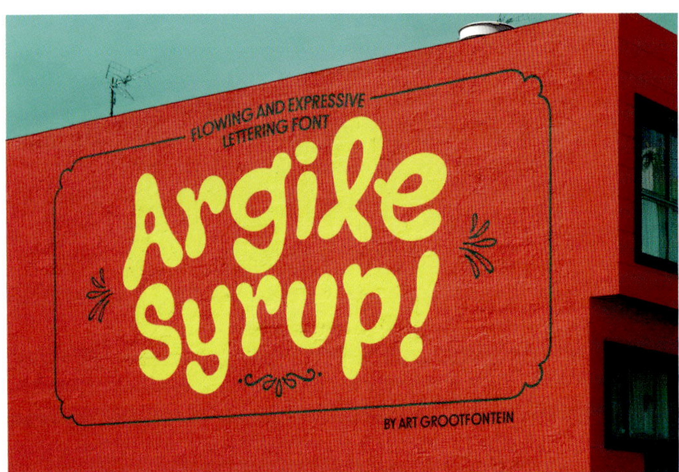

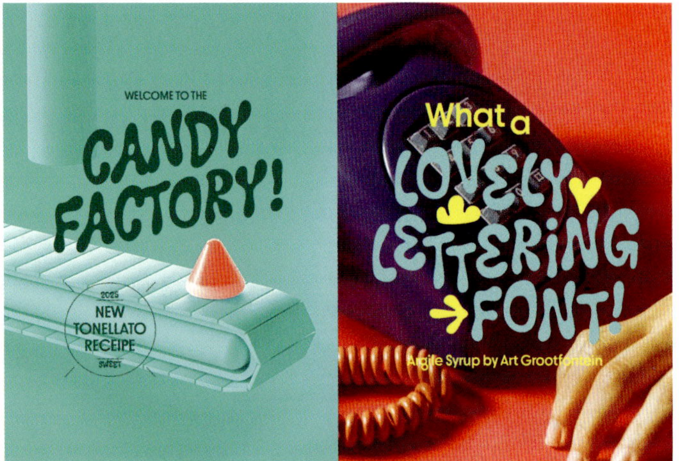

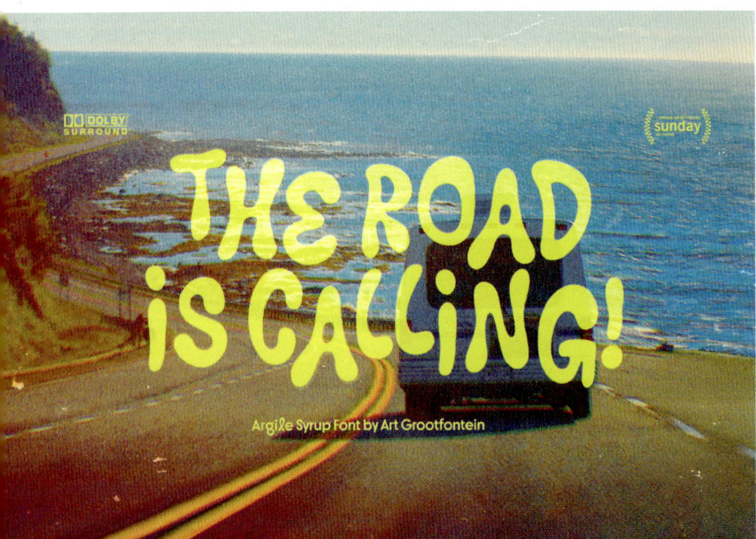

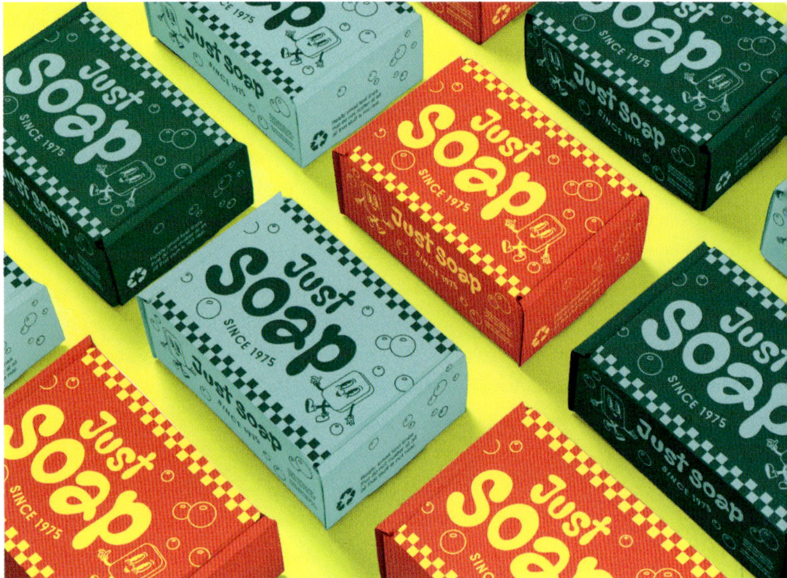

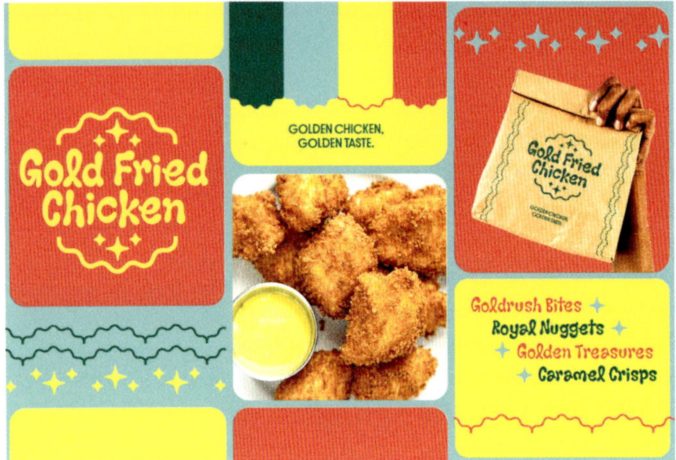

Argile Syrup is a flowing and expressive typeface. Its unique liquid design and numerous dynamic letter combinations give it the hand-drawn look of a lettering designer.

Argile Syrup

grootfontein.net

Designed by *Stéphane Mattern*
Published by *Art Grootfontein*

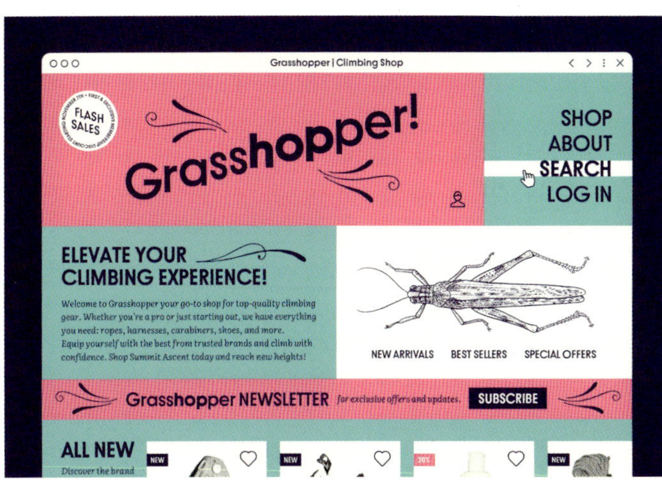

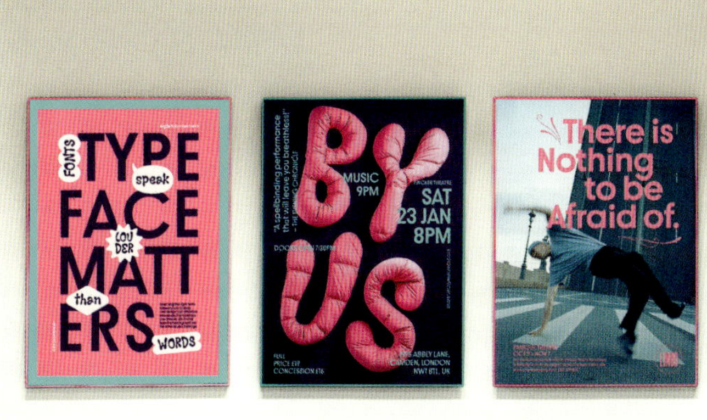

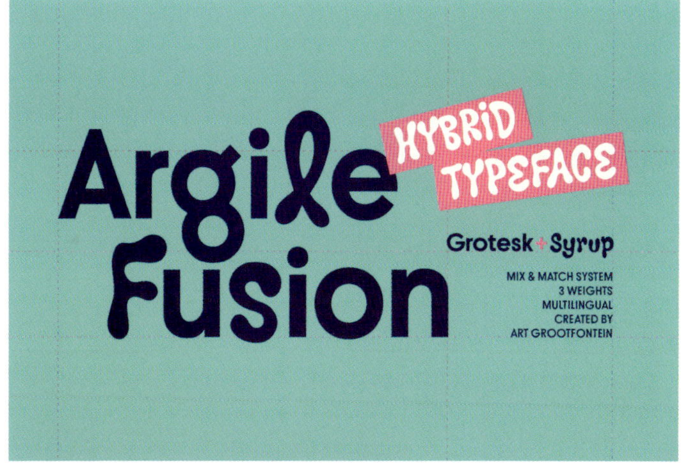

SOUND SHOPS · Red Wine
ATLANTICA · Boogie Night · 4 Ricefish
CANTALOUPE ISLAND · 1975
William
STRATOSPHERIC · Oblique Fjörds
8 · Casino Royale · TROPICAL VIBES
TWIRLERS · ARRIVALS
Cupcakes · Two Alphabets · 5

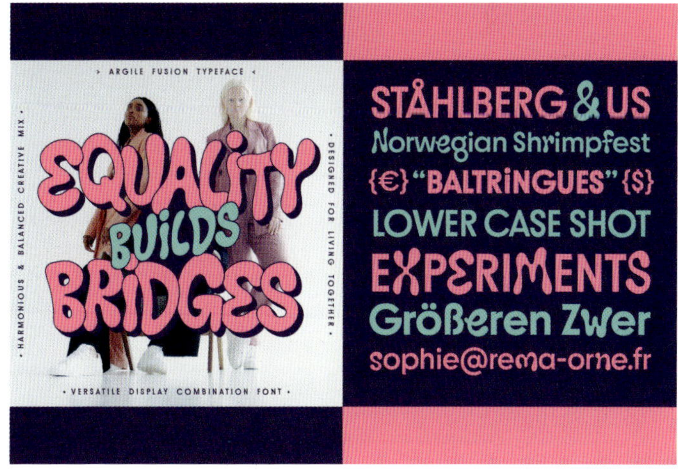

Explore innovative typography with Argile Fusion—a combination of sleek geometric sans and expressive hand-drawn lettering. Seamlessly mix and match fonts for stunning designs that balance precision and personality.

grootfontein.net

Argile Fusion

Designed by *Stéphane Mattern*
Published by *Art Grootfontein*

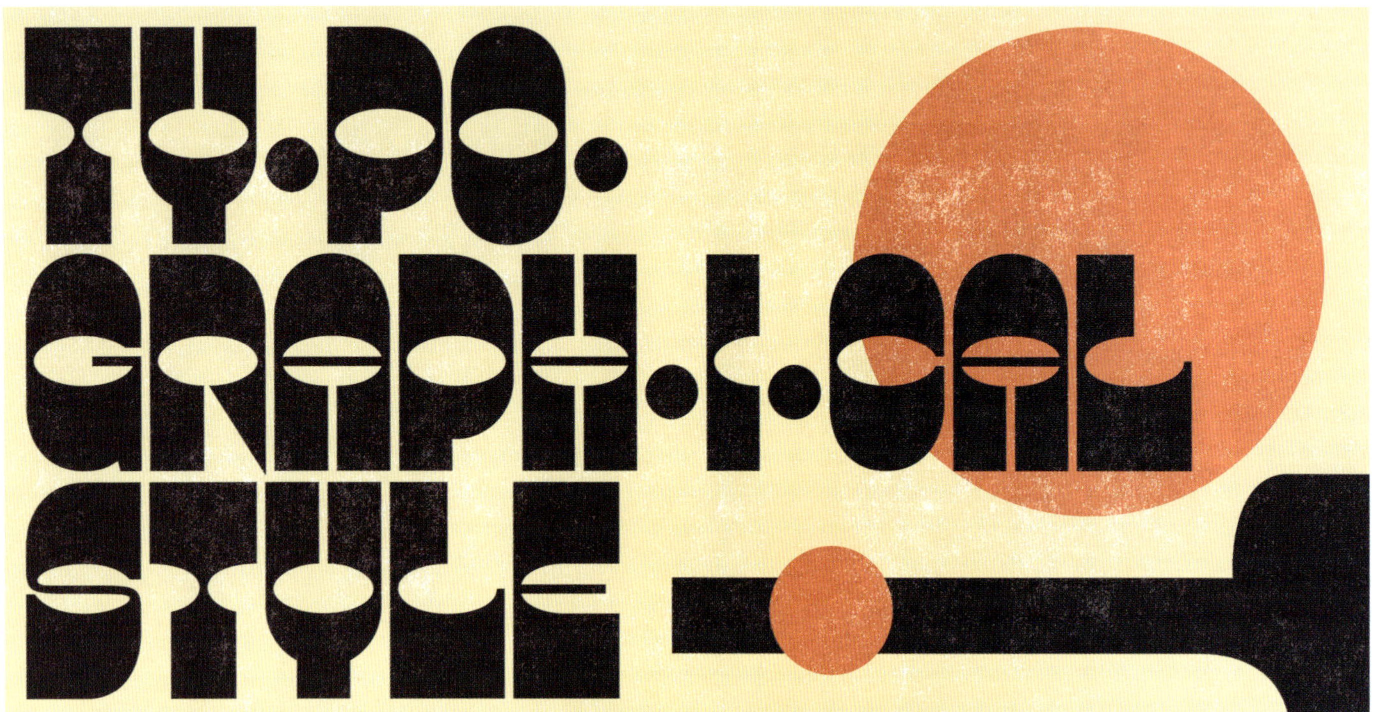

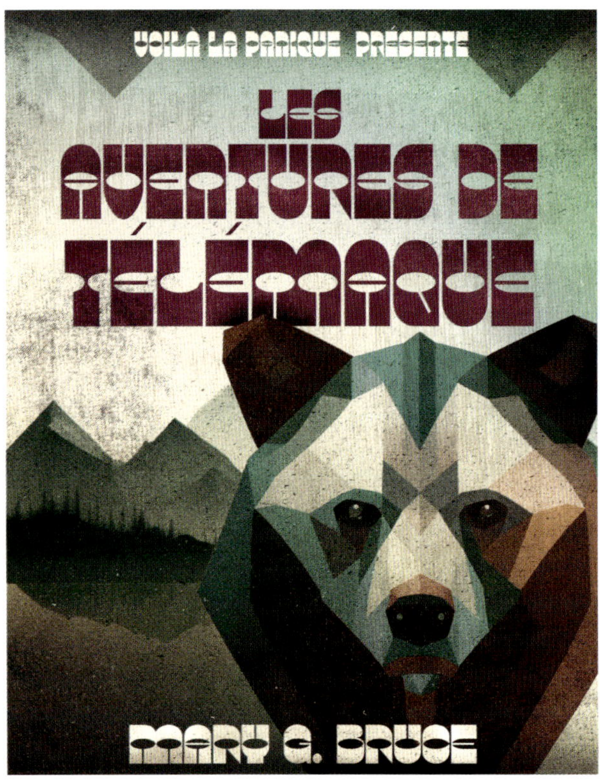

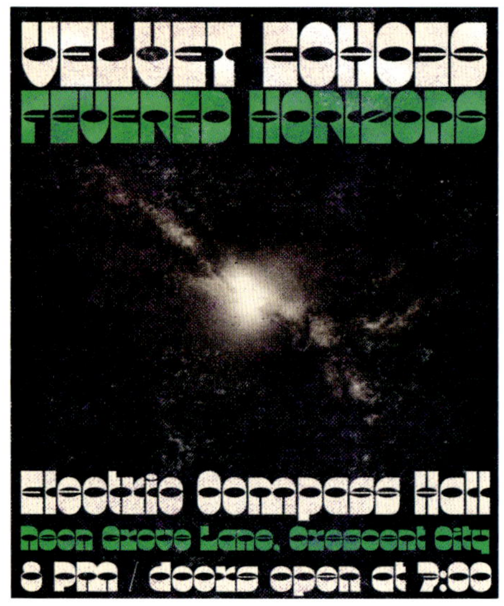

Lunatique Variable is a highly decorative font with a 1970s spirit. It draws inspiration from the Lucky typeface, designed in 1972 by André Pless for the Mecanorma Permanent Type contest. The font has a variable width and extended language support, as well as alternates for some glyphs.

Lunatique Variable

pintassilgoprints.com

Designed by *Erica Jung, Ricardo Marcin*
Published by *PintassilgoPrints*

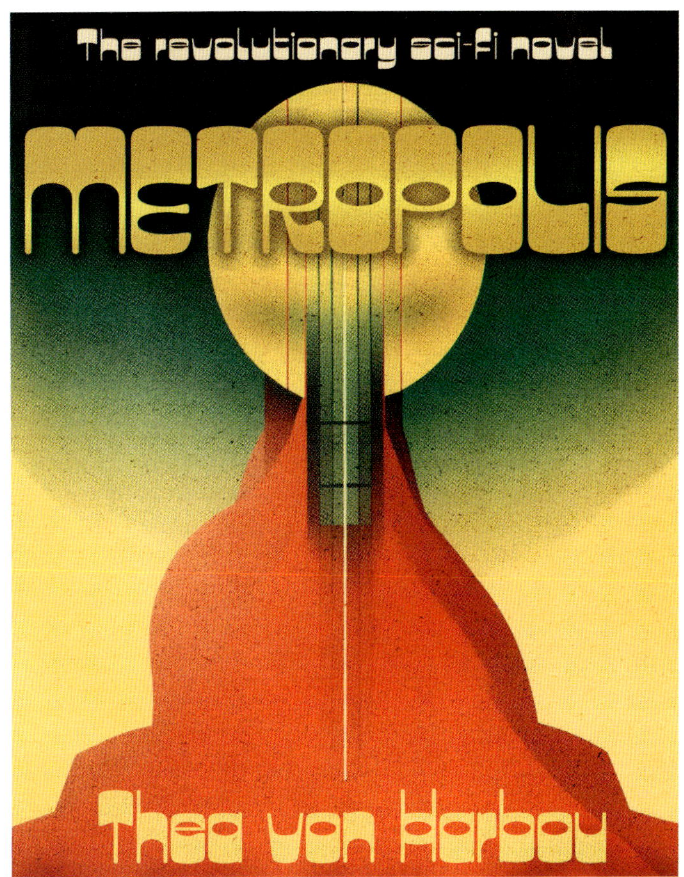

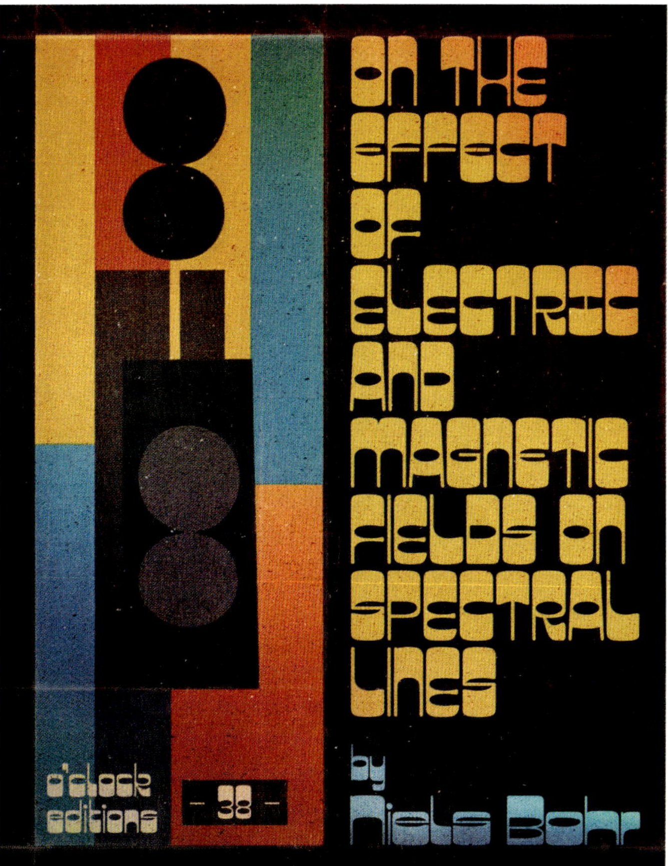

Aquatronik Variable is a decorative display face with a somewhat retro-futuristic flair. It has alternate glyphs for some letters and numerals, a variable width, and an extended character set, speaking more than two hundred languages.

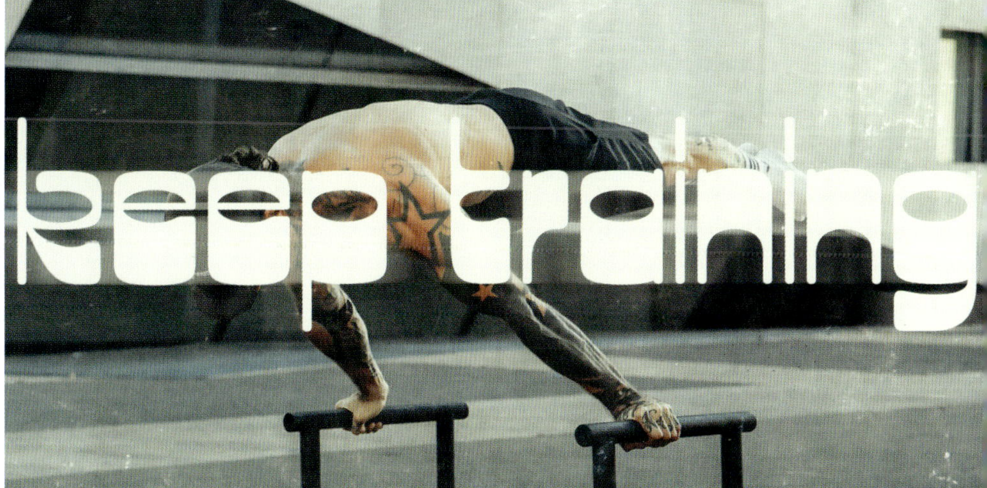

pintassilgoprints.com

Aquatronik Variable

Designed by *Erica Jung, Ricardo Marcin*
Published by *PintassilgoPrints*

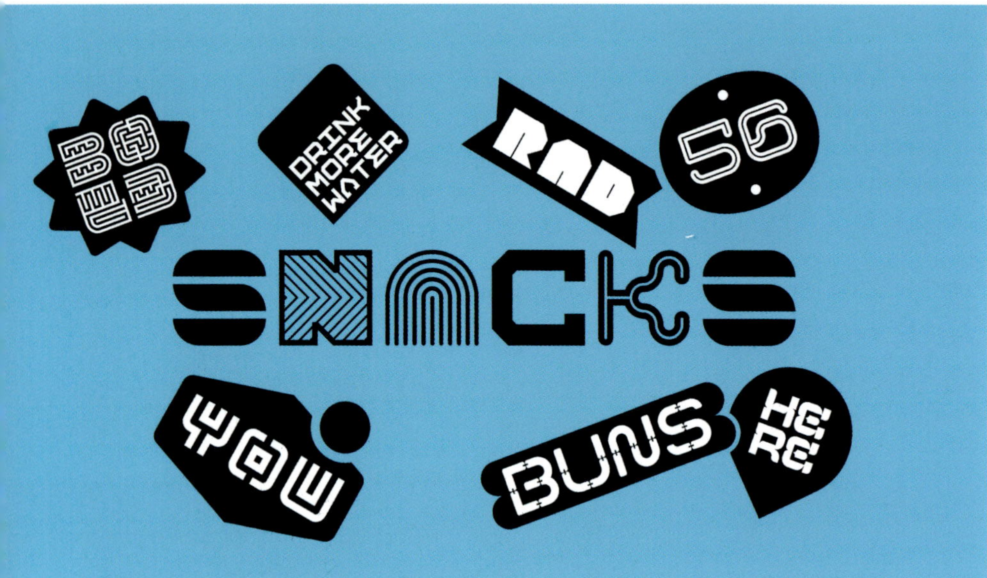

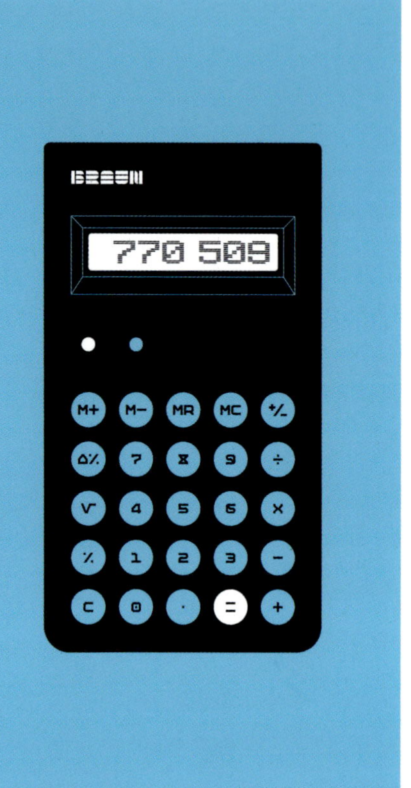

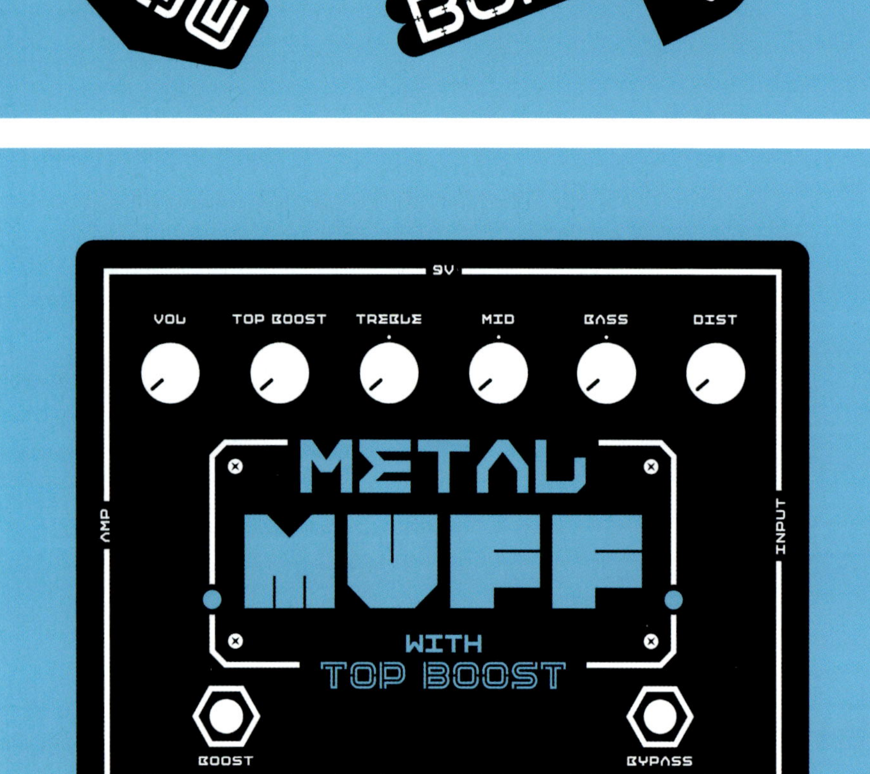

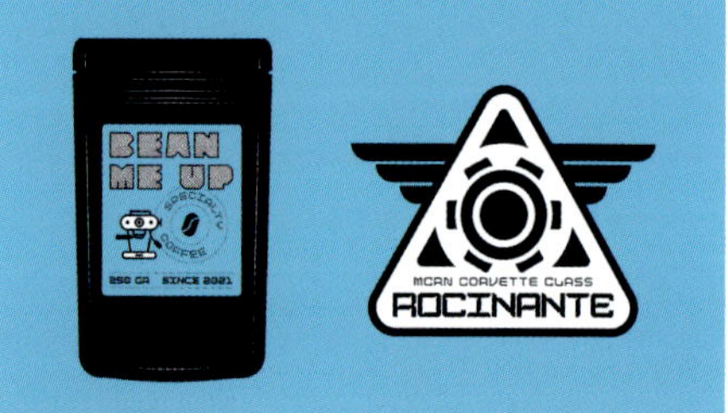

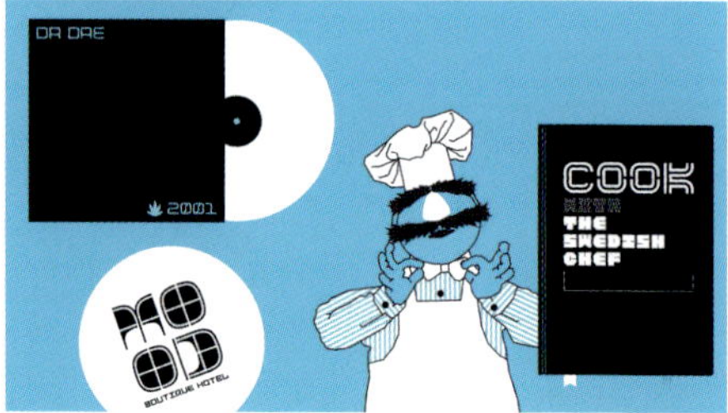

Snacks is a collection of twenty monospaced fonts in twenty very different styles. Very useful to draft a visual identity, or prepare mockups and props in a movie or TV show, or textures and decals in a video game.

Snacks

marmitedefontes.com

Designed by *Guillaume Berry*
Published by *Marmite Defontes*

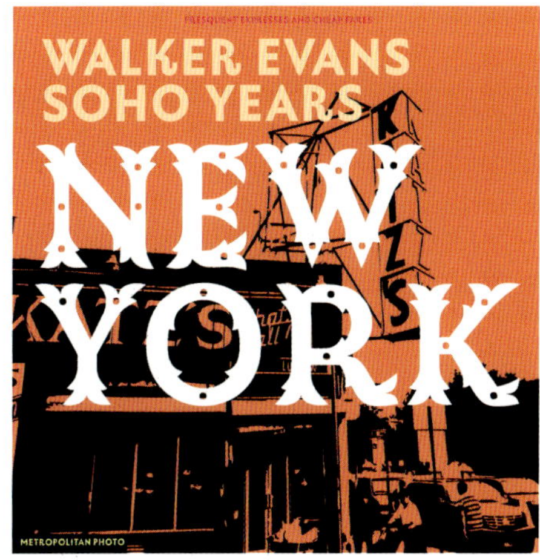

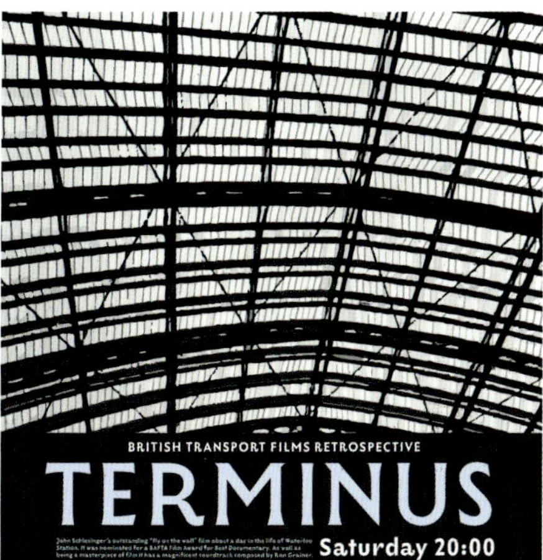

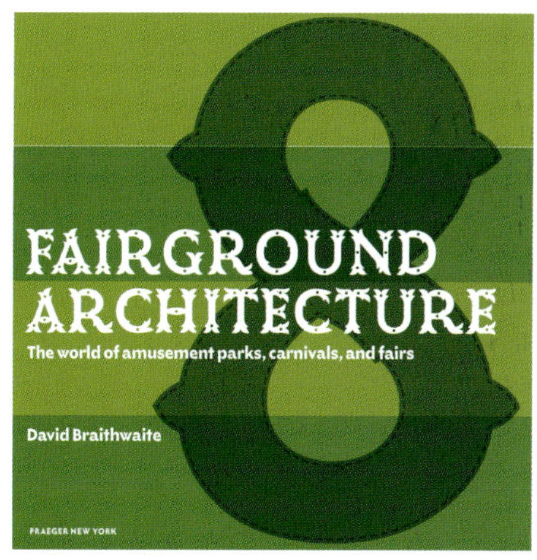

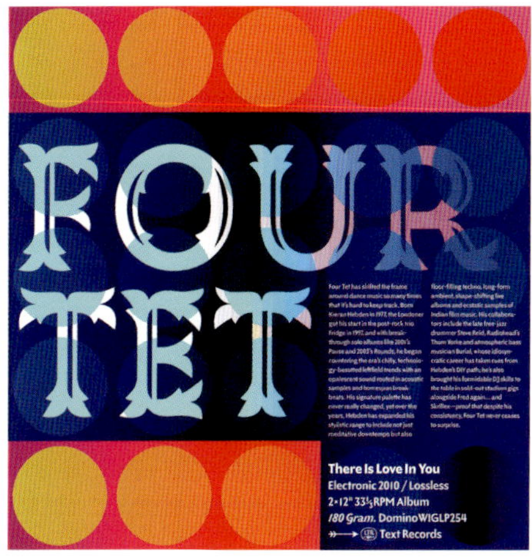

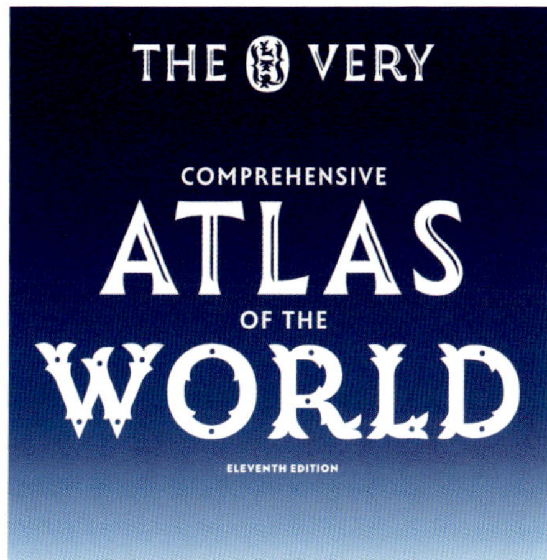

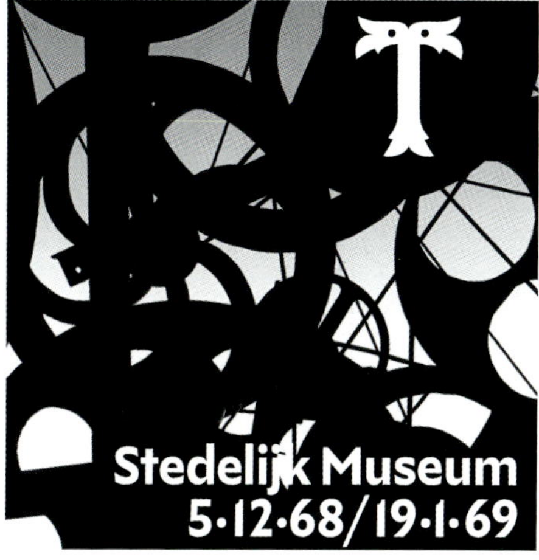

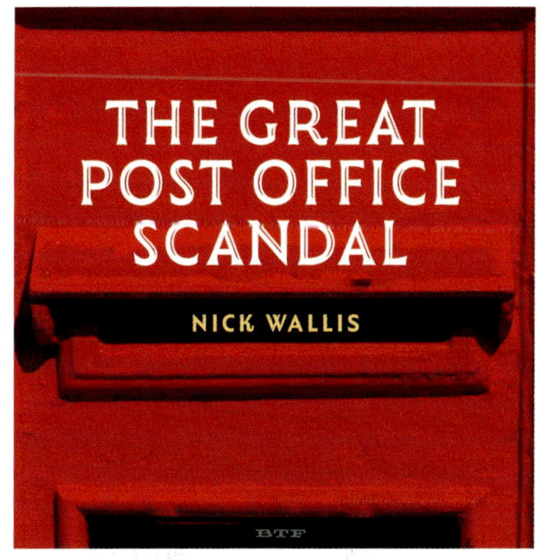

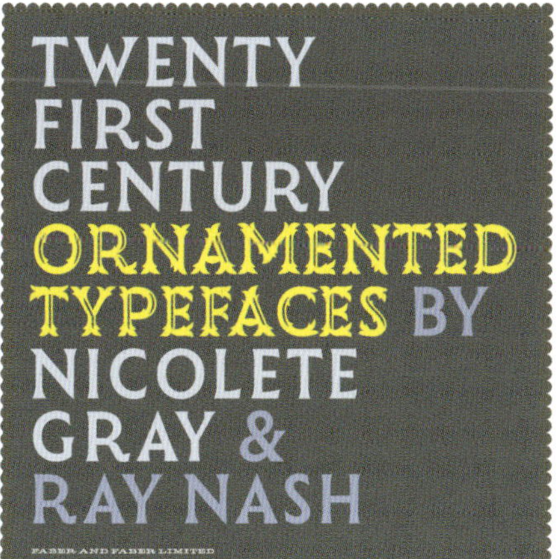

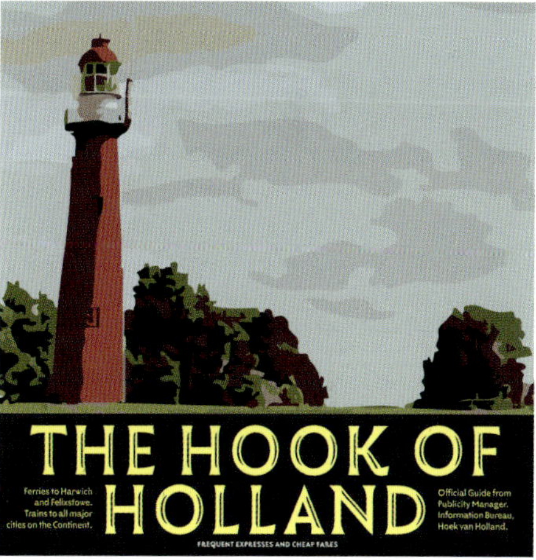

LTR Very Bauble shows its pretty Tuscan terminals in a series of imagined typographic teasers.

---

letterror.com

LTR Very Bauble

Designed by *Erik van Blokland*
Published by *LettError*

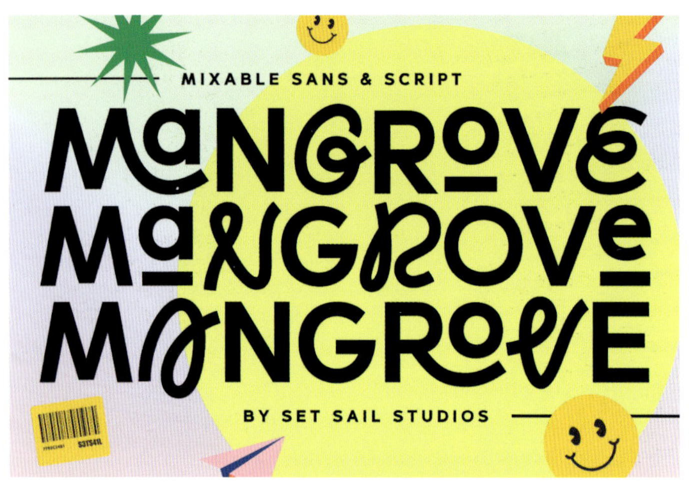

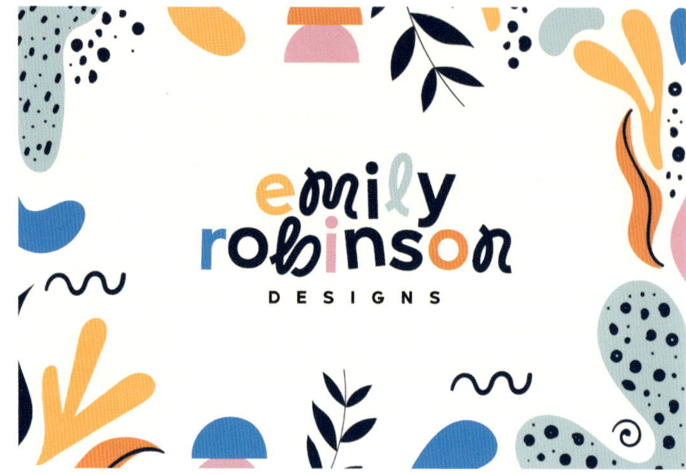

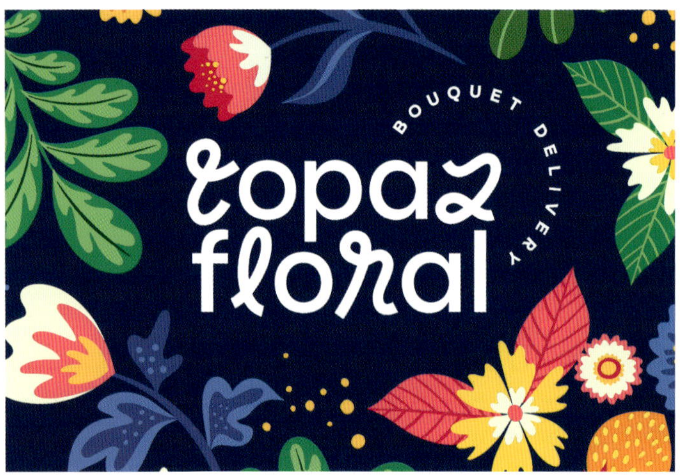

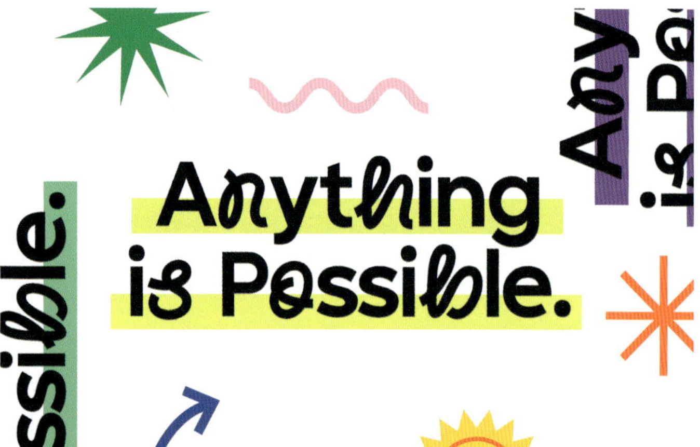

Mangrove Font Duo is a family of three sans and three monoline script fonts, and guarantees to bring your letters to life. A delightfully playful combination, these perfectly balanced typefaces have been carefully designed not only to work as stand-alone fonts but also to pair together effortlessly—delivering undeniably eye-catching typography bursting with character. Throw a script letter in the middle of the sans font, try the swooping sans ligatures or its uplifting small caps. You can also combine letters in lowercase or uppercase, giving you so many options to have fun and let your creativity run wild.

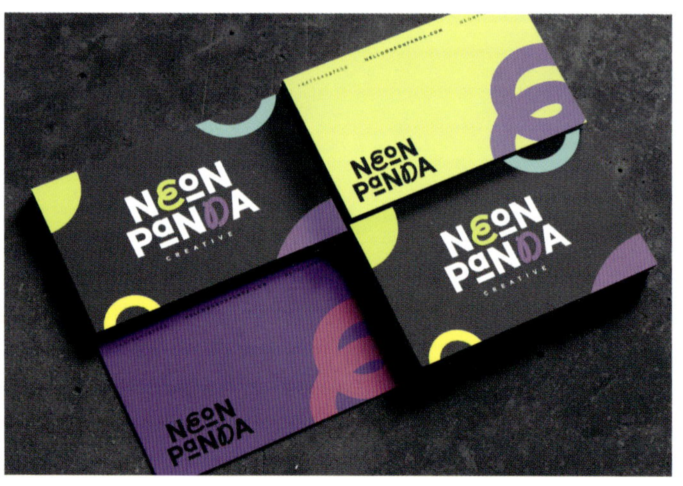

Mangrove Font Duo

setsailstudios.com

Designed by *Sam Parrett*
Published by *Set Sail Studios*

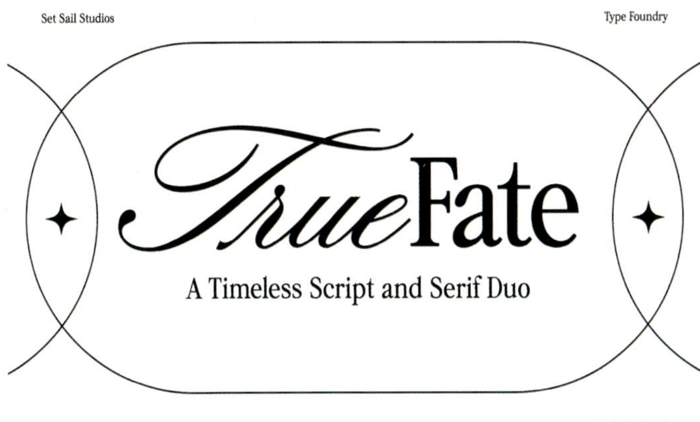

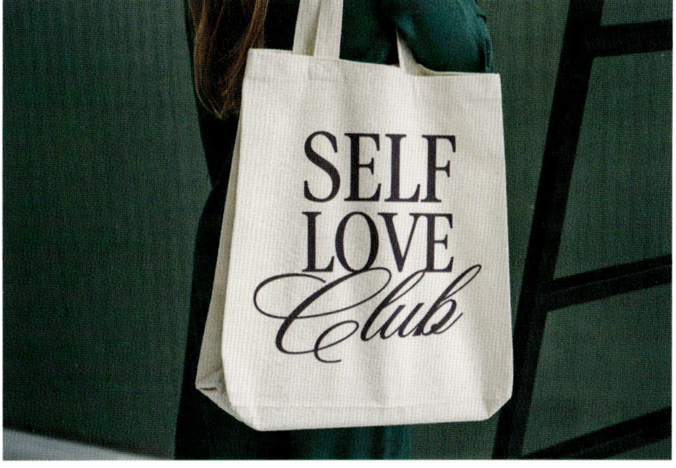

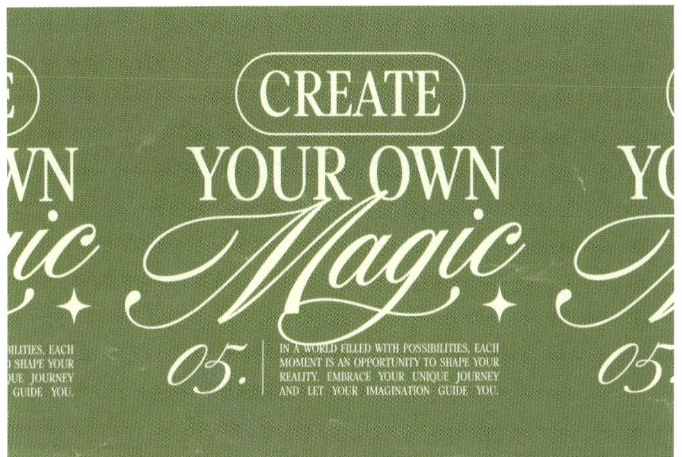

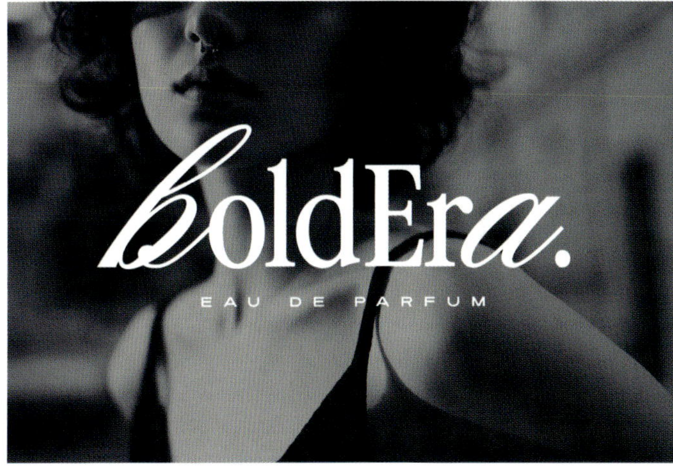

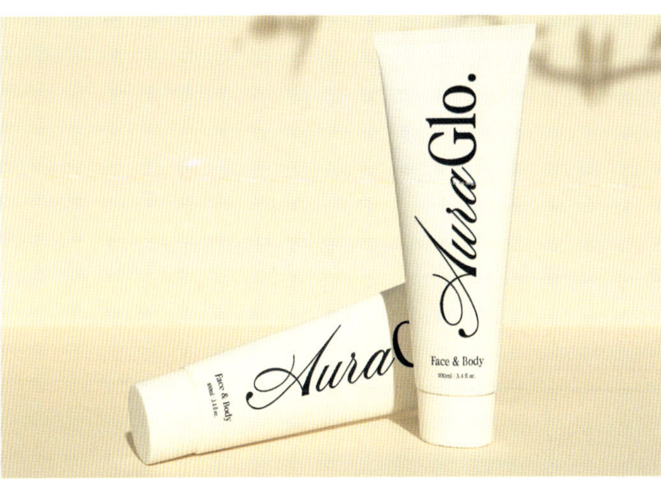

True Fate Font Duo is a perfect pairing of a timeless script and a classic serif, designed from the ground up to work in harmony, saving you the work of finding that ideal font pairing for your branding or print projects. True Fate Script is a clean, cursive calligraphy font based on traditional roundhand script, with a little extra flair added for a strikingly elegant and stylish modern aesthetic. True Fate Serif takes inspiration from nostalgic headlines, refined to give you a hugely versatile and classic serif that can be used in a wide range of projects. These fonts can be used as strong stand-alone fonts or combined with ease for more creative display uses.

setsailstudios.com

True Fate Font Duo

Designed by *Sam Parrett*
Published by *Set Sail Studios*

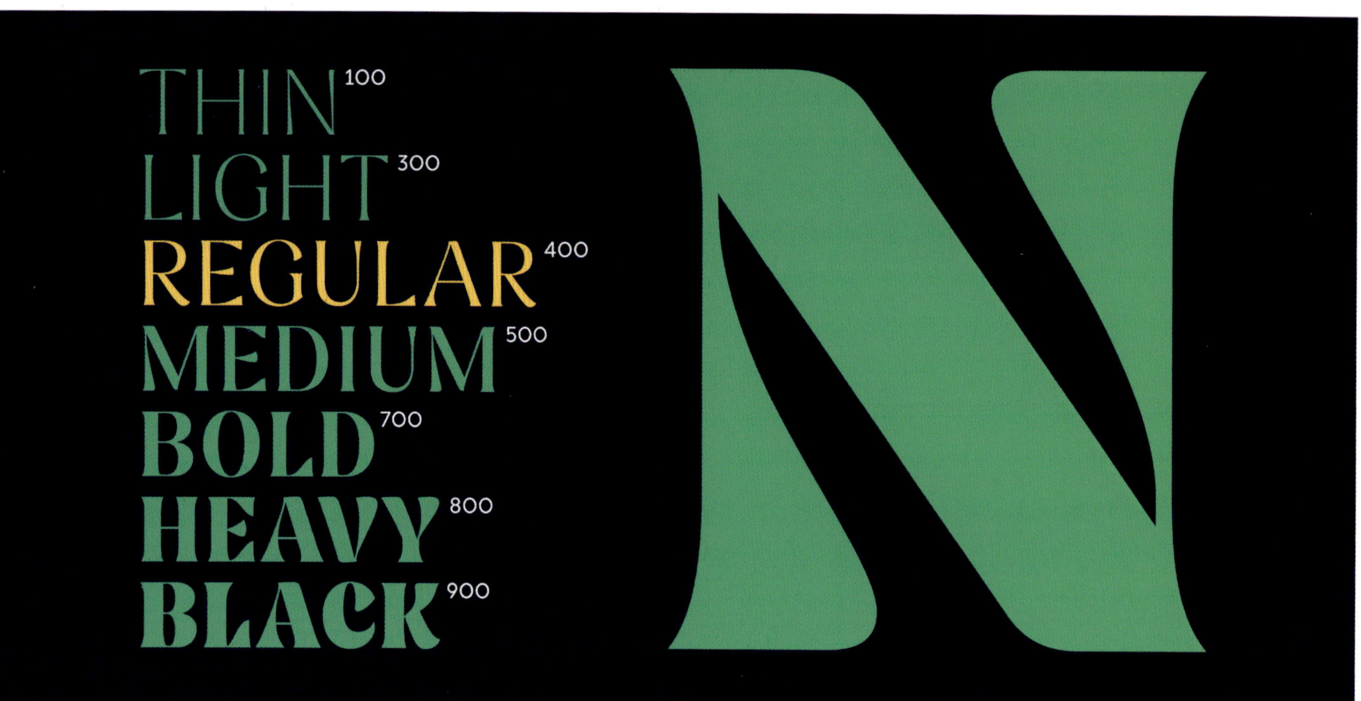

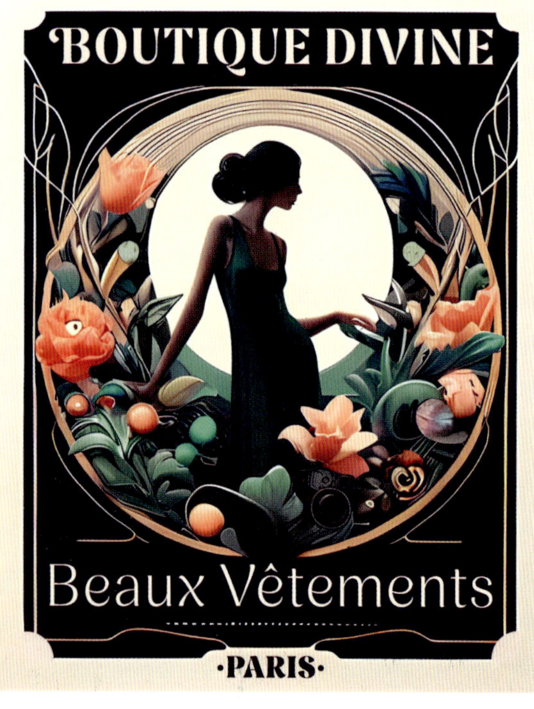

TRADITIONAL

Yet adventurous

An unexpected twist

A flowing, sensuous inner form

CAPTIVATING

Contrasting Qualities

Nave

jamieclarketype.com

Designed by *Jamie Clarke*
Published by *Jamie Clarke Type*

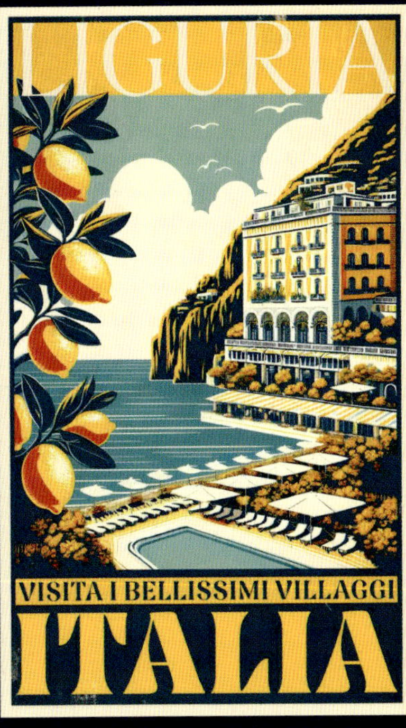

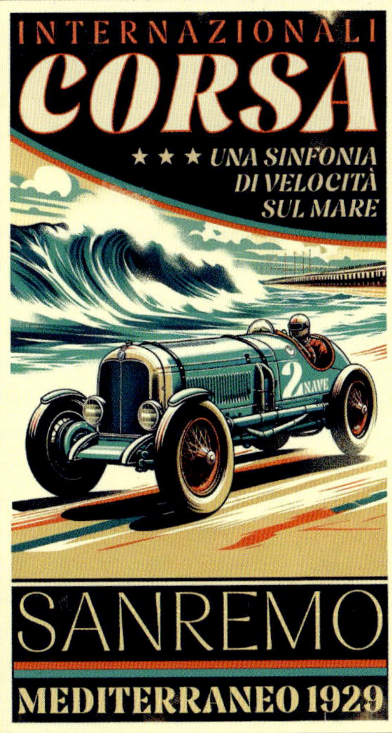

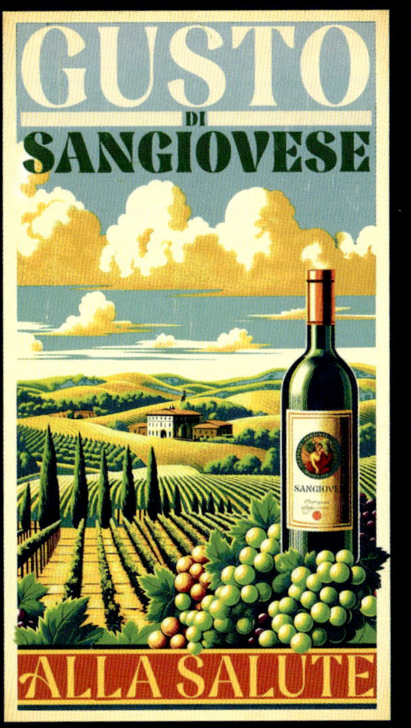

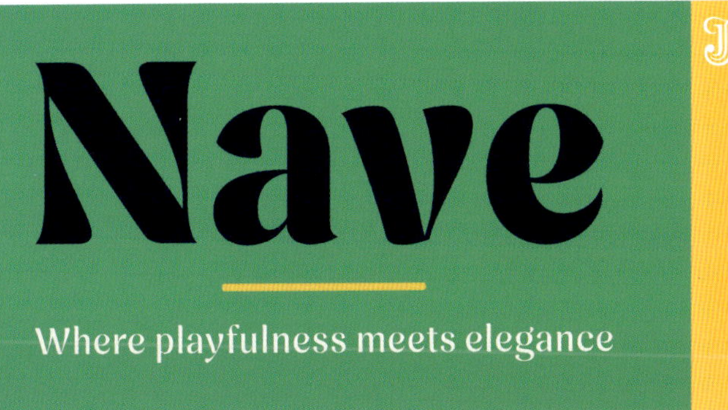

TRADITIONAL

Yet adventurous

An unexpected twist

Contrasting Qualities

BLACK	Here's looking at you, kid. Rick Blain
HEAVY	Eighty percent of success is showing
BOLD	Three can keep a secret, if two of the
MEDIUM	Life is like riding a bicycle. To keep yo
REGULAR	All the world's a stage, and all the men
LIGHT	He travels the fastest who travels alon
THIN	If you want something done right, do i

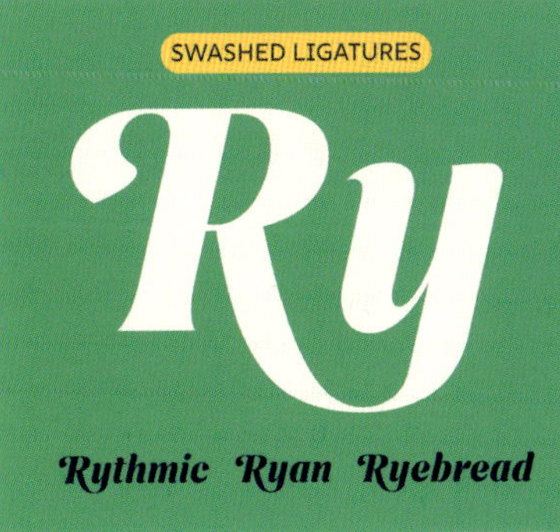

fk

fb fh fi

fj fl ft

MORE LIGATURES

Nave blends tradition with creativity. Its characters feature a formal, structured outer shape, balanced by flowing, sensuous inner forms, adding elegance to any project. Designed for forward-thinking creatives, Nave combines classic design with personality and warmth. Its contrasting qualities breathe life into words, making it as versatile as it is distinctive.

About the Contributors

John Boardley is a historian, author, booklover, and avid reader. Born in England, he now calls Ho Chi Minh City, Vietnam, home. His books include the award-winning *Typographic Firsts* (2019) and *Remarkable Renaissance Books* (2025), both published by Bodleian Library at the University of Oxford.

Ellen Lupton teaches in the graduate program at Maryland Institute College of Art in Baltimore and is the author of numerous books about design, including *Thinking with Type,* which is now in its third edition.

Erik Spiekermann is an art historian, printer, type designer, information architect, and author. Founder of MetaDesign (1979), FontShop (1989). Honorary Royal Designer for Industry (2007). Type Directors Club Medal and German National Design Award for Lifetime Achievement (2011), etc. Runs the typographic workshop Hacking Gutenberg in Berlin.

Laura Meseguer is an award-winning type and brand designer specializing in custom fonts, wordmarks, and expert consultancy in typography. She is also a founder of Type-Ø-Tones, offers classes and workshops, and combines traditional craftsmanship with experimental innovation.

Min-Young Kim is a trilingual typography consultant and researcher, with expertise in CJK-Latin. She leads multiscript type development projects for major corporations and type foundries and teaches typography at Musashino Art University. She is currently pursuing a PhD at the University of Reading.

Veronika Burian is a product and type designer, and cofounder of TypeTogether. She is one of the founding members of Alphabettes, cochairwoman of the GRANSHAN project, and cocurator / organizer of TypeTech MeetUp. She gives lectures and leads workshops at conferences and universities around the world.

Elliot Jay Stocks is a designer, author, speaker, and musician who has long been obsessed with type and has become known for his typographically themed side projects—including the magazine (and later book) *8 Faces,*[1] the podcast *Hello, type friends!,*[2] and the newsletter *Typographic & Sporadic*[3]—as well as his roles at Adobe Fonts and Google Fonts. He is the author / editor of several books, including *Universal Principles of Typography,* published by Rockport Publishers in 2024.

Elliot was an early adopter of and vocal advocate for web fonts and captured this newfound enthusiasm for typography in 2010 by founding *8 Faces,* which sold out of its first issue in under two hours and later became a book that raised over £50,000 in Kickstarter funding.

While running *8 Faces,* Elliot became the creative director of Adobe Typekit and helped evolve the service from its web font origins into a fully integrated part of the Creative Cloud, now known as Adobe Fonts.[4] After his first stint at Adobe, Elliot cofounded the lifestyle magazine *Lagom*[5] with his wife, which was published until the end of 2019. From 2020 to 2023, Elliot collaborated with Google to create the online typography resource known as Google Fonts Knowledge,[6] and in 2025, he returned to the design team at Adobe Fonts.

A familiar face at design and tech conferences around the world since 2007, Elliot has also taught a variety of workshops for several years—almost entirely on the subject of typography. He has served as a judge for the D&AD Awards, and his work has been profiled in publications such as *Communication Arts, Creative Review, Page, The Independent,* and *Design Week.*

Elliot lives in Somerset, UK, with his wife, their two daughters, and their dog. He also records electronic music under the name Other Form[7] and can be found online as @elliotjaystocks.

1 *8faces.com*

2 *hellotypefriends.com*

3 *elliotjaystocks.com/newsletter*

4 *fonts.adobe.com*

5 *readlagom.com*

6 *fonts.google.com/knowledge*

7 *otherform.uk*

Acknowledgments

Elliot would like to thank: My wife Samantha, and our daughters Thea and Gwen, for their patience while I devoted so many hours to this project, and for being a constant source of happiness and inspiration. Plus, it's such an honor to make books that you apparently (astonishingly!) want to put on your bookshelves.

All of the type foundries and type designers who contributed their work to this book. Without your designs—the typefaces themselves, the promotional graphics, their descriptions, everything—these pages would be quite literally empty. I'm so grateful for the trust you placed in me, and I sincerely hope this book helps bring some new fans your way. John, Ellen, Erik, Laura, Min-Young, and Veronika, who contributed such wise words and elevated this book beyond a simple collection of graphics. Thank you so much for lending these pages your passion and expertise.

Jonathan Simcosky, Kelly Desabrais, Elizabeth Weeks, and the wider Quarto team for the invitation to create this book and for all of your help in bringing the whole thing to life.

The Kickstarter backers who pledged their support to the original incarnation of *Fine Specimens*. The project didn't hit its funding goal, but your commitment demonstrated how many people wanted this book to exist in the world, and therefore led to the invitation from Quarto to revisit the idea and publish the book you now (finally) hold in your hands.

Jamie Clarke, for listening to me whine over pints, and Ty Finck, for listening to me whine over audio messages. Erik Spiekermann, again, for the accidental mentorship. My parents for always encouraging creativity and never pushing me towards a sensible career. My colleagues at Adobe Fonts for letting me pretend to have a somewhat sensible career (for the second time now).

Lastly, everyone who continues to follow my antics via my newsletter *Typographic & Sporadic*. Thank you so much for your ongoing support and for encouraging such ridiculous levels of nerdery.

Index

quarto.com

First published in 2026 by Rockport Publishers, an imprint of The Quarto Group,
100 Cummings Center, Suite 265-D, Beverly, MA 01915, USA.
T (978) 282-9590 F (978) 283-2742

EEA Representation, WTS Tax d.o.o.,
Žanova ulica 3, 4000 Kranj, Slovenia.
www.wts-tax.si

Rockport Publishers titles are also available at discount for retail, wholesale, promotional, and bulk purchase. For details, contact the Special Sales Manager by email at specialsales@quarto.com or by mail at The Quarto Group, Attn: Special Sales Manager, 100 Cummings Center, Suite 265-D, Beverly, MA 01915, USA.

10 9 8 7 6 5 4 3 2 1

ISBN: 978-0-7603-9891-3

Digital edition published in 2026
eISBN: 978-0-7603-9892-0

All specimen graphics and descriptions provided courtesy of the respective type foundry.

Library of Congress Cataloging-in-Publication Data available

Designed by Elliot Jay Stocks
Typeset in Degular and Swear from OH no Type Co, except where noted.

Printed in Pontian, Johor, Malaysia PC 102025